C# 24-HOUR TRAINER

C# 24-Hour Trainer

C# 24-Hour Trainer

Second Edition

Rod Stephens

wrox™
A Wiley Brand

C# 24-Hour Trainer, Second Edition

Published by
John Wiley & Sons, Inc.
10475 Crosspoint Boulevard
Indianapolis, IN 46256
www.wiley.com

Copyright © 2016 by John Wiley & Sons, Inc., Indianapolis, Indiana

Published simultaneously in Canada

ISBN: 978-1-119-06566-1
ISBN: 978-1-119-06564-4 (ebk)
ISBN: 978-1-119-06569-2 (ebk)

Manufactured in the United States of America

10 9 8 7 6 5 4 3 2 1

For general information on our other products and services please contact our Customer Care Department within the United States at (877) 762-2974, outside the United States at (317) 572-3993 or fax (317) 572-4002.

Wiley publishes in a variety of print and electronic formats and by print-on-demand. Some material included with standard print versions of this book may not be included in e-books or in print-on-demand. If this book refers to media such as a CD or DVD that is not included in the version you purchased, you may download this material at http://booksupport.wiley.com. For more information about Wiley products, visit www.wiley.com.

Library of Congress Control Number: 2015953613

ABOUT THE AUTHOR

ROD STEPHENS started out as a mathematician, but while studying at MIT, he discovered the joys of programming and has been programming professionally ever since. During his career, he has worked on an eclectic assortment of applications in such fields as telephone switching, billing, repair dispatching, tax processing, wastewater treatment, concert ticket sales, cartography, optometry, and training for professional football players.

Rod has been a Microsoft Visual Basic Most Valuable Professional (MVP) for more than 10 years. He has written 30 books that have been translated into languages from all over the world and more than 250 magazine articles covering C#, Visual Basic, Visual Basic for Applications, Delphi, and Java he has helped create. He's even published a couple of video training courses in addition to the videos that go along with this book.

Rod's popular *C# Helper* website www.csharphelper.com contains thousands of example programs that demonstrate tips, tricks, and useful techniques for C# programmers. His *VB Helper* website www.vb-helper.com provides similar material for Visual Basic developers.

ABOUT THE TECHNICAL EDITOR

JOHN MUELLER is a freelance author and technical editor. He has writing in his blood, having produced 98 books and more than 600 articles to date. The topics range from networking to home security and from database management to heads-down programming. Some of his current books include a book on Python for beginners, Python for data scientists, and MATLAB. He has also written a variety of books on both C# and C++. His technical editing skills have helped more than 65 authors refine the content of their manuscripts. John has provided technical editing services to both *Data Based Advisor* and *Coast Compute* magazines. Be sure to read John's blog at http://blog.johnmuellerbooks.com/.

CREDITS

PROJECT EDITOR
Adaobi Obi Tulton

TECHNICAL EDITOR
John Mueller

PRODUCTION EDITOR
Joel Jones

COPY EDITOR
Kimberly A. Cofer

MANAGER OF CONTENT DEVELOPMENT & ASSEMBLY
Mary Beth Wakefield

PRODUCTION MANAGER
Kathleen Wisor

MARKETING DIRECTOR
David Mayhew

MARKETING MANAGER
Carrie Sherrill

PROFESSIONAL TECHNOLOGY & STRATEGY DIRECTOR
Barry Pruett

BUSINESS MANAGER
Amy Knies

ASSOCIATE PUBLISHER
Jim Minatel

PROJECT COORDINATOR, COVER
Brent Savage

PROOFREADER
Nicole Hirschman

INDEXER
Nancy Guenther

COVER DESIGNER
Wiley

COVER IMAGE
© Antonio Guillem/Shutterstock

ACKNOWLEDGMENTS

THANKS TO KENYON BROWN, Bob Elliott, Adaobi Obi Tulton, Kim Cofer, Joel Jones, and all of the others who worked so hard to make this book possible.

Thanks also to John Mueller for giving me the benefit of his advice and extensive technical expertise.

CONTENTS

INTRODUCTION

SO YOU WANT TO learn C# programming? Excellent choice!

C# is a powerful, general-purpose programming language that lets you build desktop, Windows Store, Windows Phone, and web apps. C# provides all of the tools that you need to build a huge variety of applications such as:

➤ Database applications

➤ Point of sales systems

➤ Two- and three-dimensional graphics programs

➤ Image-processing and photo-manipulation systems

➤ Computer-aided design (CAD) systems

➤ Document layout and printing systems

➤ Hardware control systems

➤ High-performance games

➤ Much, much more

> **NOTE** *In case you ever need to mention it at parties, C# is pronounced "see sharp." It's written C# because the number sign (#) is the closest most keyboards can get to the musical sharp symbol (♯).*

Of course, you won't be able to solve every problem with C#. If you want a program that picks the winning number on a roulette wheel or that can predict stock prices, you may have better luck using tarot cards (or a degree in economics), but for tractable problems C# is a great choice.

This book is a self-paced guide to C# programming in the Visual Studio environment. It uses easy-to-follow lessons, reinforced by step-by-step instructions, screencasts, and supplemental exercises, to help you master C# programming quickly and painlessly. It explains how to write C# programs that interact with the user to read inputs, calculate results, and display outputs. It shows how to read and write files, make printouts, and use databases. It shows how to build programs that run on the Windows desktop, on tablet computers, and on Windows Phones.

This book won't make you an expert, but it will give you a solid understanding of how to write C# programs. When you've finished reading this book and working through the Try It sections and exercises, you'll be able to write non-trivial programs of your own. You may not be able to accurately pick winning lottery numbers (if you do, please let me know!), but you will be able to build some useful programs and you'll be ready to learn more about more specialized topics that interest you such as database programming, file processing, and graphics.

WHAT'S NEW IN THE SECOND EDITION

This second edition has been modified and expanded to provide more material than the first edition, but it's not intended to be the second in a series. If you read the first edition, don't get the second edition because there's a lot of overlap.

The main differences between this edition and the first are:

- ➤ More exercises (almost 400!)
- ➤ More screencast videos (more than 12 hours!)
- ➤ Windows Store apps
- ➤ Windows Phone apps
- ➤ A lot more material about Windows Presentation Foundation (WPF) and eXtensible Markup Language (XAML) (which you can use to build Windows Store and Windows Phone style apps)

To make room for the new material, some of the old material had to go. This edition doesn't cover:

- ➤ The clipboard and drag-and-drop
- ➤ Bitmap manipulation
- ➤ Parallel programming
- ➤ Console applications

I'd love to include those topics and many others, but there just isn't room in a book of this size.

WHO THIS BOOK IS FOR

This book is for anyone who wants to learn how to write programs using C#. Whether you want to move into a lucrative career as a software developer, add a few new skills to your résumé, or pick up a fascinating new hobby, this book can get you started.

This book does *not* assume you have any previous programming experience. It assumes you're uninformed rather than an idiot or a dummy. It assumes you can turn your computer on and surf the web but that's about it for previous qualifications. It is suitable as a first programming book for high school or college students, but its self-paced hands-on approach also makes it ideal if you're trying to learn to program on your own.

(I don't want to receive a bunch of flaming e-mails complaining that the material in this book is too basic, so I'm warning you right now. If you've been programming in C++ or Visual Basic for 16 years, don't blame me if a lot of this material seems pretty simple to you. Instead of wasting your time complaining, go find a more advanced book.)

WHAT THIS BOOK COVERS (AND WHAT IT DOESN'T)

This book explains C# programming. It explains how to write, debug, and run applications that interact with the user and the computer. It shows how to understand object-oriented concepts, perform calculations, manipulate files and strings, produce printouts, and interact with simple databases. It explains how to run programs on your desktop, from the Windows Start menu, with a Windows tablet-style interface, and on a Windows Phone.

Programming in any language is an enormous topic, however, so this book doesn't cover everything. It doesn't explain how to design databases, build cryptographically secure web applications, create multithreaded programs that run on multiple CPUs, or build Xbox games, all tasks that are possible using C#. When you're finished reading this book, however, you'll be ready to move on to more advanced books that cover those topics.

THE WROX 24-HOUR TRAINER APPROACH

Educators have known for many years that different people use different learning styles most effectively. Different students may learn best by:

➤ Reading a textbook

➤ Looking at nonwritten material such as pictures and graphs

➤ Listening to an instructor lecture

➤ Watching someone demonstrate techniques

➤ Doing exercises and examples

(Personally, I learn best by watching and doing.)

Good instructors try to incorporate material that helps students with all of these learning styles. Combining text, lecture, demonstration, discussion, and exercises lets every student pick up as much as possible using whichever methods work best.

Like a good instructor, this book uses materials that address each learning style. It uses text and figures to help visual learners, screencasts that provide visual demonstrations and auditory instruction, step-by-step instructions to help you do it yourself, and exercises for further study.

The book is divided into small, bite-sized lessons that begin with a discussion of a particular concept or technique, complete with figures, notes, tips, and other standard fare for instructional books. The lessons are short and tightly focused on a single task so you can finish each one in a single sitting. You shouldn't need to stop in the middle of a lesson and leave concepts half-learned (at least if you turn off your phone).

> **NOTE** *The "24-Hour" in the title means the book is available to train you 24 hours per day, not that you should be able to read then entire book in 24 hours. Unless you just skim the text and skip all of the Try Its and exercises, I'd be surprised if anyone could work through the whole thing in 24 hours.*

After describing the main concept, the lesson includes a Try It section that invites you to perform a programming exercise to solidify the lesson's ideas.

The Try It has several subsections. *Lesson Requirements* describes the exercise so you know what should happen. *Hints* gives pointers about possible confusing aspects of the problem, if they're needed. *Step-by-Step* provides a numbered series of steps that show how to solve the problem.

A screencast on the accompanying DVD shows me working through the Try It problem. Additional commentary at the end of the screencast highlights extensions of the lesson's main concepts.

After the Try It's Step-by-Step section, the lesson concludes with extra exercises that you can solve for further practice and to expand the lesson's main ideas. Some of the exercises extend the material in the main lesson, so I recommend that you at least skim the exercises and ask yourself if you think you could do them. Solutions to the Try Its and all of the exercises are available for download on the book's website. Additional screencasts show how to work through many of the exercises.

> **WEBSITES**
>
> To find the book's web page, go to www.wrox.com/go /csharp24hourtrainer2e. There you can find solutions to all of the Try Its and exercises, plus some additional resources. You can view the screencasts at www.wrox.com/go/csharp24hourtrainer2evideos.

The one thing that a good classroom experience has that this book doesn't is direct interaction. You can't shout questions at the instructor, work in a team with fellow students, and discuss exercises with other students in the campus coffee house.

Although the book itself can't help here, you can do at least three things to get this kind of interaction. First, join the Wrox P2P (peer-to-peer) discussion forum for this book. As the section "P2P.WROX.COM" later in this lesson says, you can join the discussion forum to post questions, provide answers, see what other readers are doing with the book's material, and generally keep tabs on book-related topics.

You can also sign up for other discussion groups on the Internet, too. You can post questions on those discussions, but it's also very interesting to see what other people are asking. Book discussion groups often don't have as much traffic, so the topics tend to be more limited than those in these other groups. (Although I watch my P2P groups closely, so go there if you want me to answer.)

Finally, if you get stuck on an exercise or some other program you're working on, e-mail me at RodStephens@CSharpHelper.com. I won't solve the exercises for you but I'll try to clarify problems or give you the hints you need to solve them yourself.

GETTING THE MOST OUT OF THE BOOK

This book provides a lot of tools that you can use to best match your learning style, but you have to use them. If you learn best by reading text, spend more time on the text. If you like step-by-step instructions, focus on the Try Its and their step-by-step instructions. If you learn best by watching and listening, focus on the screencasts.

Then, after you've finished a lesson, use the exercises to verify that you've mastered the material. Most of the lessons are fairly easy to just read through quickly. Unless you practice what you've learned, you can't be sure it's sticking, so plan to spend some time on the exercises. It would not be strange to spend half an hour reading the lesson and then several hours working through the Try It and exercises.

And don't be afraid to invent programs of your own. Just because an idea isn't in the book doesn't mean it wouldn't make good practice. Modify the programs you build for the exercises to find out what you can accomplish.

HOW THIS BOOK IS STRUCTURED

This book is divided into seven sections, each containing a series of short lessons. The lessons are generally arranged in order, with later lessons depending on earlier ones, so you should study the lessons more or less in order, at least through the first four sections. The lessons in sections V, VI, and VII cover slightly more specialized topics and you can study them in any order.

Many of the exercises are tagged with a topic as in [Games] or [WPF]. Those indicate a theme that you may find interesting. For example, the [Games] exercises involve techniques that you may find useful if you want to build game programs. The topics include:

➤   [WPF]—These ask you to use WPF. They are often harder than corresponding Windows Forms programs, but they sometimes produce better-looking results. (You also need to use WPF to build tablet-style and Windows Phone apps.)

➤   [Games]—These are generally amusing or demonstrate techniques that may be useful in building game programs.

➤   [SimpleEdit]—This is a simple word processing application that is built and enhanced over a sequence of exercises in several lessons.

➤ [Drawing]—These exercises make a program that draws lines and shapes.

➤ [Hard]—Exercises with this tag are generally harder than most of the other exercises so they may take some extra time. (I bet you guessed that!)

➤ [Advanced]—These exercises use more advanced techniques and may be harder.

➤ [Bonus]—These exercises extend the topic covered in the lesson and include extra instructions for performing a technique not covered in the main lesson.

PERSISTENT PROGRAMS

Many of the exercises ask you to edit an earlier version of a program. Just copy the previous version into a new directory and modify it there. (The section "Copying Projects" in Lesson 1 explains how to do that.)

If you skip an exercise, you may later not have a version that you need to copy. In that case just download the version you need from the book's website.

For example, the instructions for Exercise 24-1 ask you to copy the program you built for Exercise 23-1. If you skipped that exercise, you can download the Lesson 23 material from the book's website and use the version that it contains.

The book's sections are:

➤ **I: The Visual Studio IDE and Controls**—These lessons explain how to use the Visual Studio integrated development environment (IDE) and how to use the controls that make up a user interface. You need to study these lessons to get started.

➤ **II: Variables and Calculations**—These lessons deal with variables and calculations. They explain what variables are and how a program can use them to calculate results. They also explain how to debug programs.

➤ **III: Program Statements**—These lessons describe program statements and syntax. They explain how to control the program's flow, make decisions, and repeat operations.

➤ **IV: Classes**—These lessons deal with classes. They explain how to create and use classes and how to use more advanced class features such as generics and operator overloading.

➤ **V: System Interactions**—These lessons explain ways in which a program can interact with the operating system by reading and writing files and by generating printouts.

➤ **VI: Windows Apps**—These sections explain how you can build Windows Store and Windows Phone apps.

➤ **VII: Specialized Topics**—These lessons introduce topics that don't fit well in the other sections. They explain how to localize programs for different parts of the world, how to build simple database programs, and how to use Language Integrated Query (LINQ) to manipulate data in objects and databases.

WHAT YOU NEED TO USE THIS BOOK

To get the most out of this book, you need to install Visual Studio and C#. You don't need any fancy version of Visual Studio or C# Professional Edition. In fact, Visual Studio Professional and the other full-featured versions don't really add all that much that you're likely to want to use for a long time. Mostly they add support for performing unit tests, managing test cases, profiling code, building code libraries, and performing other tasks that are more useful for programming teams than they are for individuals.

To work through this book, the Community Edition should be good enough. (And it's free!)

> **NOTE** *In previous versions of Visual Studio, the free "starter" version was called Visual Studio Express Edition. Microsoft seems to be changing the name to Visual Studio Community Edition. It hasn't changed the name everywhere and some small differences exist between the earlier editions and the latest one, but you should be able to work with either version.*

The following list describes some links that you may find useful for learning about and installing different Visual Studio products:

➤ Compare Visual Studio 2015 Offerings: `www.visualstudio.com/products/compare-visual-studio-2015-products-vs.aspx`

➤ Visual Studio homepage: `msdn.microsoft.com/vstudio`

➤ Visual C# resources: `msdn.microsoft.com/vstudio/hh341490.aspx`

➤ Visual Studio free products page: `www.visualstudio.com/products/free-developer-offers-vs`

➤ Visual Studio Express: `www.visualstudio.com/products/visual-studio-express-vs.aspx`

➤ Visual Studio Downloads: `www.visualstudio.com/downloads/download-visual-studio-vs.aspx`

➤ C# Express Edition homepage: `www.microsoft.com/express/vcsharp`

At a minimum, visit the Visual Studio Express Edition page (`www.visualstudio.com/products/visual-studio-express-vs`) and download and install Visual Studio Community Edition.

Running any version of Visual Studio will require that you have a reasonably fast, modern computer with a large hard disk and lots of memory. For example, I'm fairly happy running my Intel Core 2 system at 1.60 GHz with 8 GB of memory and a huge 1 TB hard drive. (That's a lot more disk space than necessary but disk is relatively cheap.)

CONVENTIONS

To help you get the most from the text and keep track of what's happening, we've used several conventions throughout the book.

> **SPLENDID SIDEBARS**
>
> Sidebars such as this one contain additional information and side topics.

> **WARNING** *Boxes like this one hold important, not-to-be-missed information that is directly relevant to the surrounding text.*

> **NOTE** *Notes such as this contain tips, hints, tricks, and asides to the current discussion. They are offset and placed in italics like this.*

As for styles in the text:

➤ New terms and important words are *highlighted* when they are introduced.

➤ Keyboard strokes look like this: Ctrl+A.

➤ Code, URLs, and e-mail addresses within the text are shown in monofont type as in `x = 10`, `www.vb-helper.com`, and `RodStephens@CSharpHelper.com`.

➤ `Code snippets are shown in a monofont type like this.`

The code editor in Visual Studio provides a rich color scheme to indicate various parts of code syntax such as variables, comments, and C# keywords. That's a great tool to help you learn language features in the editor and to help prevent mistakes as you code, but the colors don't show up in the book.

SOURCE CODE

As you work through the examples in this book, you may choose either to type in all the code manually or to use the source code files that accompany the book. (I like to type in the code because it helps me focus on it so I get a better understanding.)

Many of the examples show only the code that is relevant to the current topic and may be missing some of the extra details that you need to make the example work properly. If you get stuck, e-mail me or download the solution from the book's web page.

All of the source code used in this book is available for download on the book's website. Any updates to the code will be posted there.

ERRATA

The Wrox editors and I make every effort to ensure that there are no errors in the text or in the code. However, no one is perfect, and mistakes do occur. If you find an error in one of our books, like a spelling mistake or faulty piece of code, we would be very grateful for your feedback. By sending in errata you may save another reader hours of frustration and at the same time you will be helping us provide even higher quality information.

To find the errata page for this book, go to www.wrox.com and locate the title using the Search box or one of the title lists. Then, on the book details page, click on the Errata link. On this page you can view all errata that have been submitted for this book and posted by Wrox editors. A complete book list including links to each book's errata is also available at www.wrox.com/misc-pages/booklist.shtml.

If you don't spot "your" error on the Book Errata page, go to www.wrox.com/contact/techsupport.shtml and complete the form there to send us the error you have found. We'll check the information and, if appropriate, post a message to the book's errata page and fix the problem in subsequent editions of the book.

P2P.WROX.COM

For author and peer discussion, join the P2P forums at p2p.wrox.com. The forums are a web-based system for you to post messages relating to Wrox books and related technologies and interact with other readers and technology users. The forums offer a subscription feature to e-mail you topics of interest of your choosing when new posts are made to the forums. Wrox authors, editors, other industry experts, and your fellow readers are present on these forums.

At http://p2p.wrox.com you will find a number of different forums that will help you not only as you read this book but also as you develop your own applications. To join the forums, just follow these steps:

1. Go to p2p.wrox.com and click on the Register link.
2. Read the terms of use and click Agree.
3. Complete the required information to join, as well as any optional information you wish to provide, and click Submit.
4. You will receive an e-mail with information describing how to verify your account and complete the joining process.

> **NOTE** *You can read messages in the forums without joining P2P, but to post your own messages, you must join.*

Once you join, you can post new messages and respond to messages other users post. You can read messages at any time on the web. If you would like to have new messages from a particular forum e-mailed to you, click on the "Subscribe to this Forum" icon by the forum name in the forum listing.

For more information about how to use Wrox P2P, be sure to read the P2P FAQs for answers to questions about how the forum software works, as well as many common questions specific to P2P and Wrox books. To read the FAQs, click on the FAQ link on any P2P page.

Using the P2P forums allows other readers to benefit from your questions and any answers they generate. I monitor my book's forums and respond whenever I can help.

If you have other comments, suggestions, or questions that you don't want to post in the forums, feel free to e-mail me at RodStephens@CSharpHelper.com. I can't promise to solve every problem but I'll try to help you out if I can.

C# 24-Hour Trainer

SECTION I
The Visual Studio IDE and Controls

The lessons in this section of the book explain how to use the *Visual Studio integrated development environment (IDE)*. They explain how to use the IDE to create forms, place controls on the forms, and set control properties. These lessons describe some of C#'s most useful controls and give you practice using them.

You can do practically all of this in the IDE without writing a single line of code! That makes C# a great environment for rapid prototyping. You can build a form, add controls, and run the program to see what it looks like without ever creating a variable, declaring a method, or getting stuck in an infinite loop.

The lessons in this section explain how to get that far. A few of these lessons show how to add a line or two of code to make a form more interesting, but for now the focus is on using the IDE to build forms and controls. Writing code (and fixing the inevitable bugs) comes later.

▶ **LESSON 1:** Getting Started with the Visual Studio IDE

▶ **LESSON 2:** Creating Controls

▶ **LESSON 3:** Making Controls Arrange Themselves

▶ **LESSON 4:** Handling Events

▶ **LESSON 5:** Making Menus

▶ **LESSON 6:** Making Tool Strips and Status Strips

▶ **LESSON 7:** Using RichTextBoxes

▶ **LESSON 8:** Using Standard Dialogs

▶ **LESSON 9:** Creating and Displaying New Forms

▶ **LESSON 10:** Building Custom Dialogs

1

Getting Started with the Visual Studio IDE

The Visual Studio integrated development environment (IDE) plays a central role in C# development. In this lesson you explore the IDE. You learn how to configure it for C# development, and you learn about some of the more useful of the IDE's windows and what they do. When you finish this lesson, you'll know how to create a new project. It may not do much, but it will run and will prepare you for the lessons that follow.

VISUAL C#

Visual Studio is a development environment that you can use with several programming languages including Visual C#, Visual Basic, Visual C++, and F#. All of those are high-level programming languages that you can use to perform complex calculations, organize your Pokémon cards, draw pretty fractals (see en.wikipedia.org/wiki/Fractal and mathworld.wolfram.com/Fractal .html), play games, download cat pictures from the Internet, and do everything else you would expect from a program.

They can also contain bugs that delete files accidentally, discard an hour's worth of typing without warning, balance your checkbook incorrectly, and cause all sorts of other problems. Programming languages can help you do things, but they can't force you to do the *right* things. That's up to you.

Visual C# combines C# with the Visual Studio development environment. You can use a text editor to write C# programs without Visual Studio, but it's a lot of work. You don't get all of the nice features that Visual Studio provides, such as special code editing features, drag-and-drop control creation, and a debugger. In short, it's a lot less fun, so I won't cover that kind of programming in this book.

continues

(continued)

Visual C# and C# go together like hockey and fistfights: if you mention one, most people assume you're also talking about the other. Most people simply say C#, so this book does, too, unless there's a reason to distinguish between C# and Visual C#.

The *.NET Framework* also plays an important role in C# programs. It includes classes that make performing certain tasks easier, runtime tools that make it possible to execute C# programs, and other plumbing necessary to build and run C# programs.

Normally you don't need to worry about whether a feature is provided by Visual Studio, the C# language, or the .NET Framework. They all go together, so for the purposes of this book at least you can ignore the difference.

INSTALLING C#

Before you can use C# to write the next blockbuster first-person Xbox game, you need to install it. So if you haven't done so already, install C#.

You can install one of the free Express Editions at `www.microsoft.com/express/Windows`. As I write this, that page lists versions of Visual Studio 2015, but when you visit that page it should let you install the latest version. (I'm using a preview build of Visual Studio 2015 to write the programs that go with this book.)

Several versions are available on that page, so be sure you pick the right one. Here's a quick summary of some of the versions that may be available:

➤ **Community**—This version lets you build web, Windows Store (including tablet and phone apps), Windows Desktop, Android, and iOS applications. This is probably the best version for you to download.

➤ **Express for Web**—This version focuses on building websites.

➤ **Express for Windows**—This version focuses on building Windows Phone and Windows Store apps.

➤ **Express for Windows Desktop**—This version focuses on desktop applications. You run these from the Windows desktop, not the start screen.

➤ **Team Foundation Server Express**—This edition is for people working in teams. This includes tools that you don't need right now and that can provide extra opportunities for confusion, so skip this version. (If you don't think things are confusing enough, e-mail me and I'll suggest some more confusing topics for you to study.)

The Community Edition includes tools to get started building any of these kinds of applications, so it's a good choice. You may never use it to build websites or iOS applications, but having those abilities installed won't hurt you.

The Express Editions are only intended to get you started, but they're seriously powerful so you probably won't need anything else for quite a while. I've been happily using Express Editions for about two decades.

If you think you need some other version of Visual Studio (for example, you're working on a big project and you need test management, source code control, and other team programming tools), go to msdn.microsoft.com/vcsharp and install the version that's right for you.

All of these are big installations (5 or 6 GB), so they could take a while. While a constant supply of cookies, caffeine, and conversation will help you pass the time more quickly, the other customers won't thank you if you hammer the Starbucks Wi-Fi for 12 straight hours. Be sure you have a reasonably fast connection before you start.

TALKIN' 'BOUT MY GENERATION

Developers talk about different generations of programming languages ranging from the very primitive to the remarkably advanced. In a nutshell, the different generations of languages are:

➤ **1GL**—Machine language. This is a series of 0s and 1s that the machine can understand directly. Here's a sample: `01001010 11010100 10101011 10001000`. Pretty hard to read, isn't it?

➤ **2GL**—Assembly language. This is a collection of mnemonic codes that represent machine language instructions. It is slightly more readable but provides no higher-level structure for performing complex tasks. Here's a sample: `brfalse.s IL_0028 leave.s IL_007a ldloc.0 ldloc.1`. This may be easier to read than binary, but it still looks like gibberish to me.

➤ **3GL**—A higher-level language such as FORTRAN or BASIC. These provide additional structure (such as looping and subroutines) that makes building complex programs easier. Here's a sample: `num_players = num_players + 1`. Finally something I can read and almost understand!

➤ **4GL**—An even higher-level language or a development environment that helps build programs, typically in a specific problem domain.

➤ **5GL**—A language where you specify goals and constraints and the language figures out how to satisfy them. For example, the database Structured Query Language (SQL) allows you to use statements like `SELECT FirstName FROM Employees`. You don't need to tell the database how to get the names; it figures that out for you.

Visual Studio provides code snippets that let you copy standard chunks of code into your program, IntelliSense that helps you select and use functions and other pieces of code, refactoring tools that help you rearrange and restructure your code, and much more. That makes Visual C# a 4GL. (Or perhaps a 3.5GL depending on how high your standards are.)

CONFIGURING THE IDE

When you first run Visual Studio, the dialog shown in Figure 1-1 appears to let you configure the IDE. (You may also see a few other dialogs before that point asking you to log in to your Microsoft profile. You can create one if you don't already have one.)

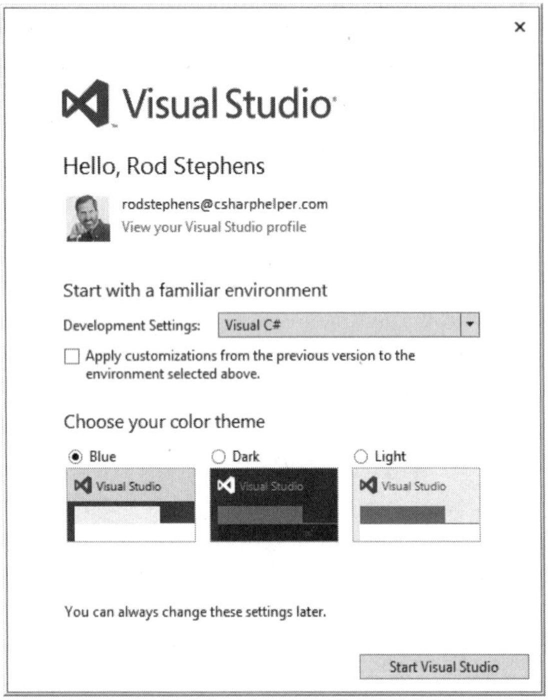

FIGURE 1-1

The dialog lets you pick settings for general development, Visual Basic, Visual C#, and so forth. Because you're going to be focusing on C# development, select that option.

> **NOTE** *These settings determine such things as what keystrokes activate certain development features. You can certainly write C# programs with the Visual C++ settings, but we may as well use the same playbook, so when I say, "Press F5," the IDE starts your program instead of displays a code window or whatever Visual C++ thinks F5 should do.*

The dialog also lets you pick a color scheme. Pick the one you think you'll like best (admittedly without getting to try them out) and click Start Visual Studio. (Then be ready to wait again because the initial configuration can take a while.)

If you ever want to switch to different settings (for example, if you initially picked the Dark colors but then discovered that they give you a headache), you can always change them later.

To change the settings, open the Tools menu and select Import and Export Settings to display the Import and Export Settings Wizard. You can use this tool to save your current settings, reload previously saved settings, or restore the settings to their default values.

To reset the settings, select the Reset All Settings option on the wizard's first page and click Next.

On the next page, indicate whether you want to save your current settings. When you've made your choice, click Next to display the page shown in Figure 1-2. Select the Visual C# choice and click Finish.

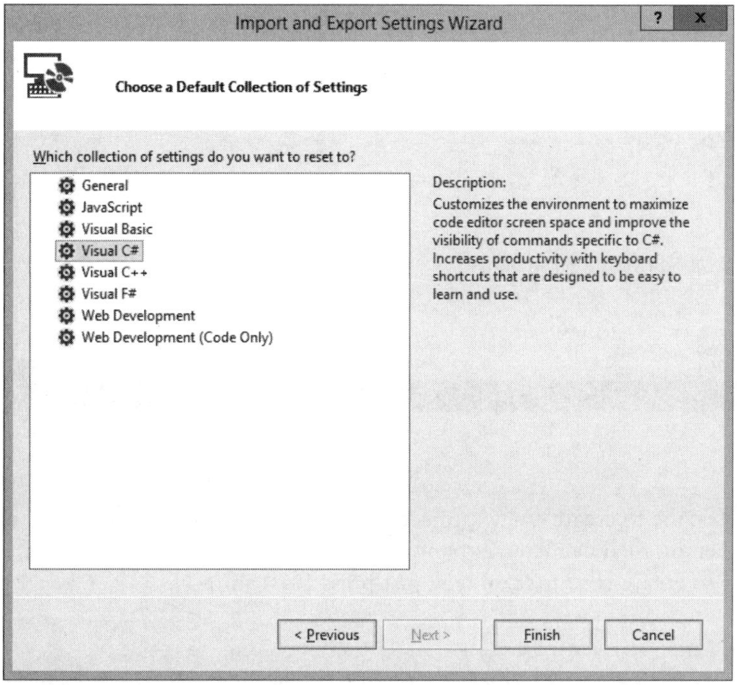

FIGURE 1-2

Then sit back and wait. Or better still, go get something to drink because this could take a while. Visual Studio has a *lot* of settings to reset, and it could take several minutes depending on how fast your computer is. (And how busy your computer is playing YouTube videos.)

BUILDING YOUR FIRST PROGRAM

Now that you've installed C#, you're ready to build your first program. Launch Visual Studio by double-clicking its desktop icon, selecting it from the system's Start menu, finding it with the Windows Search tool, or doing whatever you do to run programs on your version of Windows.

When it starts, Visual Studio should look more or less like Figure 1-3. You can use the links in the center pane to get more information about Visual Studio, .NET, Azure, and whatever else Microsoft thinks is important today.

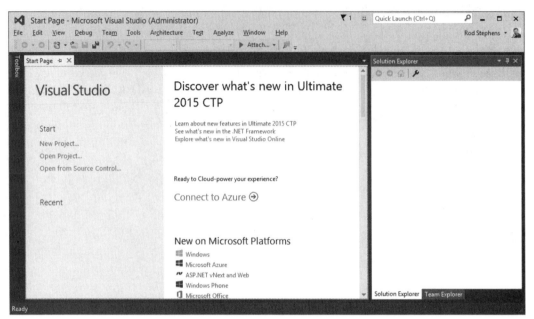

FIGURE 1-3

You can use the links in the left pane to create a new project or open an existing project. You can also create a new project by opening the File menu, expanding the New submenu, and selecting Project. Or if you're in a hurry to create your first project, just press Ctrl+Shift+N.

> **NOTE** *Often you have several ways to do something in Visual Studio. You may be able to use a menu command, keyboard shortcut, or toolbar button to do the same thing. Usually I'll just mention one or two ways to do something, such as creating a new project, but you'll probably discover other ways, too.*

All of those methods display the New Project dialog shown in Figure 1-4. Expand the Visual C# project types folder on the left and select the template for the type of project that you want to build on the right. For most of this book, that will be a Visual C# Windows Forms Application.

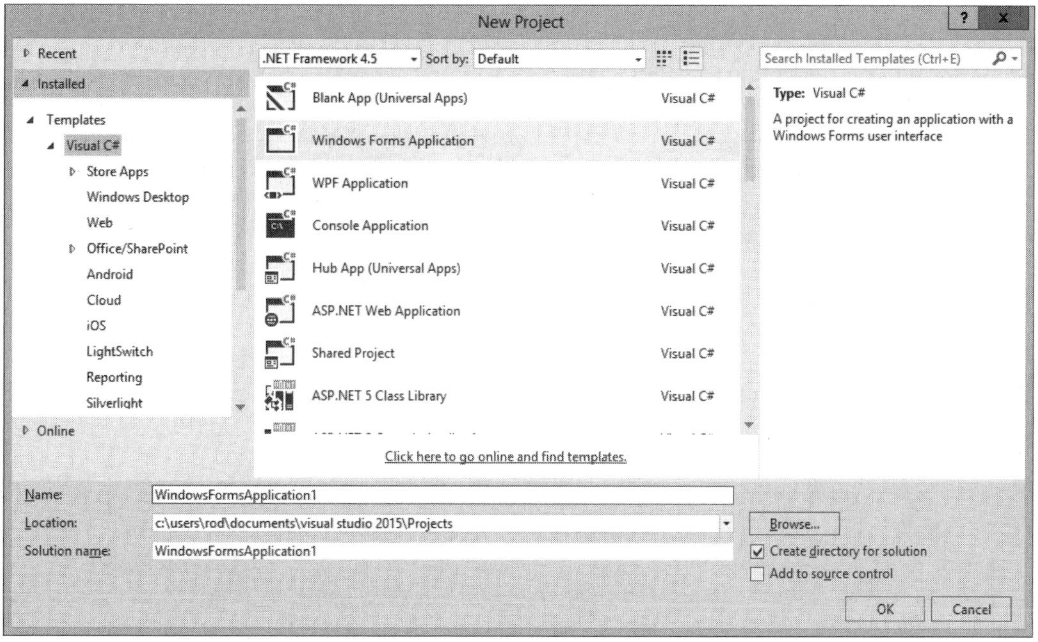

FIGURE 1-4

After you select a project type, you need to enter several pieces of information:

➤ **Name**—This is the application's name. Visual Studio creates a folder with this name to hold the program's files. It also uses this name for some key values in the project.

➤ **Location**—This is where you want Visual Studio to put the project's folder.

➤ **Solution Name**—If the Create Directory for Solution box is checked (which it is by default), Visual Studio creates a folder with this name at the location you entered. It then places the application's folder inside the solution's folder.

So if the Create Directory for Solution box is checked, you get a filesystem layout that looks like this:

SolutionFolder

   SolutionFiles

   ApplicationFolder

     ApplicationFiles

If the Create Directory for Solution box is not checked, you get a filesystem layout that looks like this:

ApplicationFolder

   ApplicationFiles

> **NOTE** *A project typically includes the files that make up a single application. A solution can contain several projects. A solution is useful when you want to build applications that go closely together. For example, a project could contain one program that builds three-dimensional data sets, another that displays them, and a third that lets you print them from different points of view.*
>
> *Solutions are particularly useful if you want to build a library of routines plus an executable program to test the library.*

The applications you build in this book are single programs so they don't really need to be inside a separate solution folder. Most of the time, I uncheck the Create Directory for Solution box to keep my filesystem simpler.

> **NOTE** *By default, Visual Studio places new projects in your Projects folder at some obscure location such as* C:\Users\MyUserName\Documents\Visual Studio 2016\Projects. *Later it can be hard to find these projects in File Explorer (for example, to make a copy).*
>
> *To make finding projects easier, set the location to something more intuitive such as the desktop or a folder on the desktop. In fact, you might want to make a folder to hold projects for this book and then give each lesson a subfolder.*
>
> *The next time you create a new project, Visual Studio will remember your last choice, so from now on it'll be easy to find your projects.*

If you open the New Project dialog while you have another project open, you'll see an additional dropdown that lists the choices Create New Solution and Add to Solution. The first choice closes the current solution and creates a new one. The second choice adds the new application to the solution you currently have open. Normally you'll want to create a new solution.

After you display the New Project dialog and enter a Name, Location, and Solution Name, click OK. The result should look like Figure 1-5.

> **NOTE** *If you have previously edited a project, you can quickly reload it from the File menu's Recent Projects and Solutions submenu. You can also load a solution into the IDE by using File Explorer to double-click the solution's* .sln *file.*

The rest of this lesson deals with the features available in Visual Studio, some of which are displayed in Figure 1-5. Before you launch into an inventory of useful features, however, open the Debug menu and select Start Debugging. Or if you're in a hurry, just press F5.

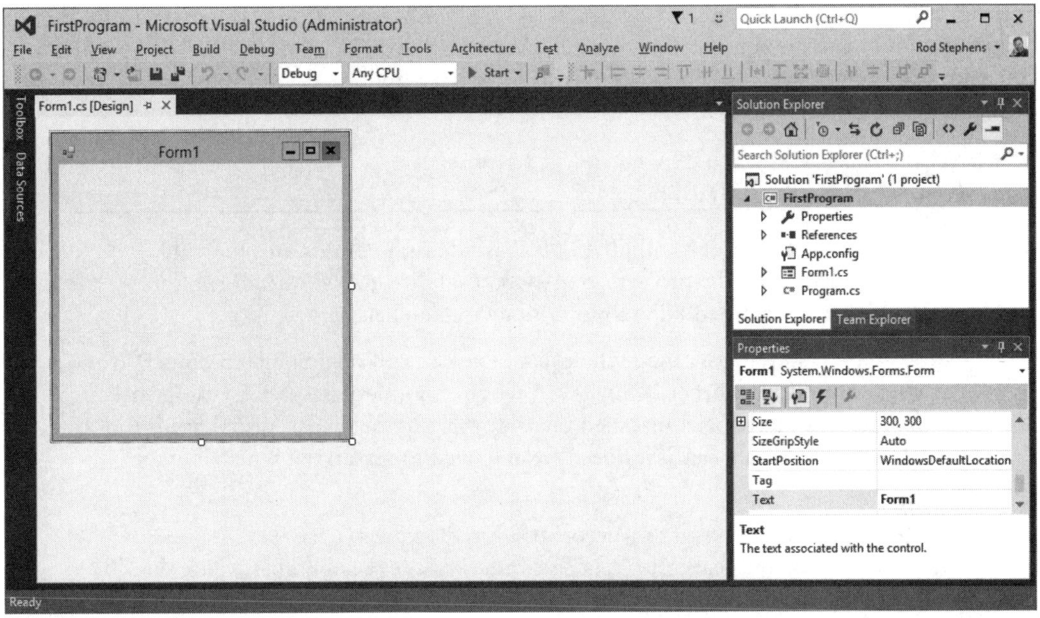

FIGURE 1-5

Your first program should look like Figure 1-6. Admittedly this first program isn't very fancy, but by the same token you didn't need to do much to build it. All you did was press Ctrl+Shift+N and then F5!

This first program may not seem terribly impressive, but there's a lot going on behind the scenes. C# has built a form with a bunch of useful features, including:

➤ A resizable border and a draggable title bar.

➤ Working minimize, maximize, and close buttons in the upper-right corner.

➤ A system menu in the upper-left corner that contains working Restore, Move, Size, Minimize, Maximize, and Close commands.

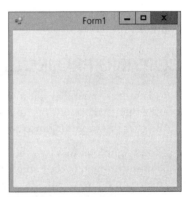

FIGURE 1-6

➤ An icon in the system taskbar that lets you minimize, restore, and close the program.

➤ The ability to use Alt+Tab and Flip3D (Win+Tab) to move between the application and others.

➤ Other standard window behaviors. For example, if you double-click the form's title bar it maximizes (or restores if it is already maximized), and if you press Alt+F4, the form closes.

Unless you're an absolute beginner to Windows, you probably take all of these features for granted, but providing them is actually a huge amount of work. Not too long ago you would have had to write around 100 lines of code to provide a subset of those features. Now Visual Studio automatically builds a form that handles most of the details for you.

You can still get in and change the way things work if you want to (for example, you can set a form's minimum and maximum allowed sizes), but usually you can ignore all of those issues and concentrate on your particular application instead of the Windows decorations.

A SUITABLE EXECUTABLE

Whenever you run a program in the IDE, Visual Studio builds an executable program, normally in the project's `bin\Debug` subdirectory. You can run the executable by finding it in File Explorer and double-clicking it.

Unfortunately that doesn't mean the executable can run on any old computer! If you copy that file to another computer, it won't run unless the .NET Framework runtime libraries have been installed there. If that computer has Visual Studio installed, you're all set, but if it doesn't you'll need to install the redistributable yourself.

To install these libraries, go to Microsoft's download web page `www.microsoft .com/downloads` and search for ".NET Framework redistributable." Pick the version that matches the one you're using (probably the most recent version if you just installed Visual Studio) and install it on the target computer.

Now you can copy C# executables onto the other computer and run them.

COPYING PROJECTS

Sometimes you may want to copy a project. For example, you might want to save the current version and then make a new one to try things out. Or you may want to give a copy of the project to a friend or your programming instructor so he or she can tell you why its New button makes the program exit.

You might look in Visual Studio's File menu and see the Copy As commands. Don't be tempted! Those commands copy single files, not the entire project. Later when you try to open one of those files, you'll discover that Visual Studio cannot find all of the other pieces that it needs and you'll be left with nothing usable.

To correctly copy a project, copy the *entire* solution or application folder and its directory hierarchy. Alternatively, you can compress the project directory and then copy the compressed file. Just be sure that whatever copying method you use brings along *all* of the project's files.

Note that you can delete the `bin` and `obj` subdirectories if you like to save space. Those directories contain files that Visual Studio creates when it loads and builds a program, and it will re-create them whenever it needs them later.

You can also delete the `.vs` directory, which contains user settings. Unfortunately that directory is hidden by default so it may be hard to find. To make File Explorer show you hidden files, open the Control Panel, click Appearance and Personalization, and select Folder Options. On the View tab, select Show Hidden Files and Folders, and then click OK. Now you can see the `.vs` directory to delete it.

> **NOTE** *Compressing a project is very useful because it keeps all of its files together in a package. In particular, if you ever need to e-mail a project to someone (for example, if you e-mail me at* RodStephens@CSharpHelper.com *for help), you can remove the* bin, obj, *and* .vs *directories, compress the project folder, and e-mail the package as a single file.*
>
> *If you're sending the project to your instructor as part of an assignment, rename the compressed file so it contains your name and the name of the assignment; for example,* RodStephens6-1.zip.

EXPLORING THE IDE

The Visual Studio IDE contains a huge number of menus, toolbars, windows, wizards, editors, and other components to help you build applications. Some of these, such as the Solution Explorer and the Properties window, you will use every time you work on a program. Others, such as the Breakpoints window and the Connect to Device dialog, are so specialized that it may be years before you need them.

Figure 1-7 shows the IDE with a simple project loaded and some of the IDE's most important pieces marked. The following list describes those pieces.

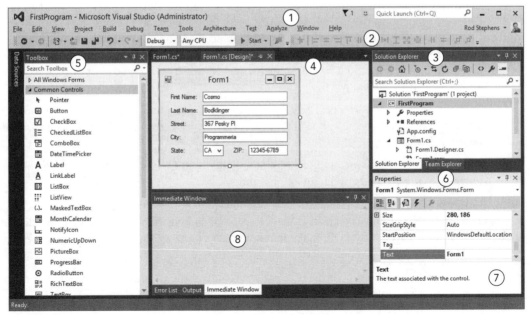

FIGURE 1-7

1. **Menus**—The menus provide all sorts of useful commands. Exactly which commands are available, which are enabled, and even which menus are visible depends on what kind of editor is open in the editing area (#4). Some particularly useful menus include File (opening old projects and creating new ones), View (finding windows), Project (adding new forms and other items to a project), Debug (build, run, and debug the project), and Format (arrange controls on a form).

2. **Toolbars**—The toolbars provide shortcuts for executing commands similar to those in the menus. Use the Tools menu's Customize command to determine which toolbars are visible.

3. **Solution Explorer**—The Solution Explorer lists the files in the project. One of the most important is `Form1.cs`, which defines the controls and code for the form named Form1. If you double-click a file in the Solution Explorer, the IDE opens it in the editing area.

4. **Editing Area**—The editing area displays files in appropriate editors. Most often you will use this area to design forms (place controls on them and set control properties) and write code for forms, but you can also use this area to edit other files such as text files, bitmaps, and icons.

5. **Toolbox**—The Toolbox contains controls and components that you can place on a form. Select a tool and then click and drag to put a copy of the tool on the form. Notice that the Toolbox groups controls in tabs (All Windows Forms, Common Controls, Containers, Menus & Toolbars, and so on) to make finding the controls you need easier.

6. **Properties Window**—The Properties window lets you set control properties. Click a control on the Form Designer (shown in the editing area in Figure 1-7) to select it, or click and drag to select multiple controls. Then use the Properties window to set the control(s) properties. Notice that the top of the Properties window shows the name (`label1`) and type (`System .Windows.Forms.Label`) of the currently selected control. The currently selected property in Figure 1-7 is `Text`, and it has the value `First Name:`. You'll spend a lot of time working with the Properties window.

7. **Property Description**—The property description gives you a reminder about the current property's purpose. In Figure 1-7, it says that the `Text` property gives the text associated with the control. (Duh!)

8. **Other Windows**—This area typically contains other useful windows. The tabs at the bottom let you quickly switch between different windows.

Figure 1-7 shows a fairly typical arrangement of windows, but Visual Studio is extremely flexible so you can rearrange the windows if you like. You can hide or show windows, make windows floating or docked to various parts of the IDE, make windows part of a tab group, and make windows automatically hide themselves if you don't need them constantly.

If you look closely at the right side of the title bar above one of the windows in Figure 1-7 (for example, the Properties window), you'll see three icons: a dropdown arrow (▾), a thumbtack (📌), and an X (✖).

If you click the dropdown arrow (or right-click the window's title bar), a menu appears with the following choices:

➤ **Float**—The window breaks free of wherever it's docked and floats above the IDE. You can drag it around and it will not re-dock. To make it dockable again, open the menu again and select Dock.

➤ **Dock**—The window can dock to various parts of the IDE. (This is kind of fun and I'll say more about it shortly.)

➤ **Dock as Tabbed Document**—The window becomes a tab in a tabbed area similar to #8 in Figure 1-7. Unfortunately, it's not always obvious which area will end up holding the window. To make the window a tab in a specific tabbed area, make it dockable and drag it onto a tab (described shortly).

➤ **Auto Hide**—The window shrinks itself to a small label stuck to one of the IDE's edges and its thumbtack icon turns sideways (⊟) to indicate that the window is auto-hiding. If you float the mouse over the label, the window reappears. As long as the mouse remains over the expanded window, it stays put, but if you move the mouse off the window, it auto-hides itself again (like a cockroach when you turn on the lights). Select Auto Hide again or click the sideways thumbtack to turn off auto-hiding. Auto-hiding gets windows out of the way so you can work in a bigger editing area.

➤ **Hide**—The window disappears completely. To get the window back, you'll need to find it somewhere in the bewildering assortment of menus. You can find many of the most useful windows in the View menu, the View menu's Other Windows submenu, and the Debug menu's Windows submenu.

The thumbtack in a window's title bar works just like the dropdown menu's Auto Hide command does. Click the thumbtack to turn on auto-hiding. Expand the window and click the sideways thumbtack to turn off auto-hiding. (Turning off auto-hiding is sometimes called *pinning* the window.)

The ✕ symbol in the window's title bar hides the window just like the dropdown menu's Hide command does.

In addition to using a window's title bar menu and icons, you can drag windows into new positions. As long as a window is dockable or part of a tabbed window, you can grab its title bar and drag it to a new position.

As you drag the window, the IDE displays little drop targets to let you dock the window in various positions. If you move the window so the mouse is over a drop target, the IDE displays a translucent blue area to show where the window will land if you drop it. If you drop when the mouse is not over a drop target, the window becomes floating.

Figure 1-8 shows the Properties window being dragged in the IDE. The mouse is over the right drop target above the editing area so, as the translucent blue area shows, dropping it there would dock the window to the right side of the editing area. The picture is kind of messy, but it's not too hard to see what's going on if you give it a try.

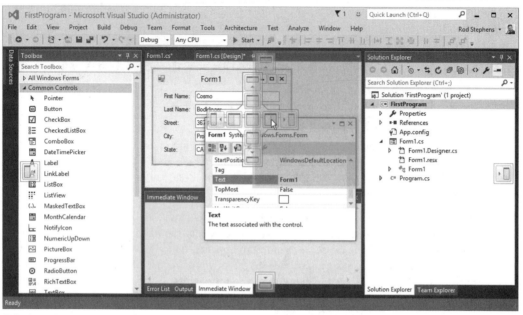

FIGURE 1-8

The drop area just to the left of the mouse represents a tabbed area. If you drop on this kind of target, the window becomes a tab in that area.

> **CUSTOMIZATION MODERATION**
>
> Visual Studio lets you move, dock, float, hide, auto-hide, and tabify windows. If you have multiple monitors, you can float a window and move it to another monitor, giving you a larger editing area. It's so flexible that it can present as many different faces as a politician during an election year.
>
> Feel free to customize the IDE to suit your needs, but if you do, keep in mind that your version of Visual Studio may look nothing like the pictures in this book. To minimize confusion, you may want to keep the IDE looking more or less like Figure 1-7, at least until you get a better sense of which tools will be most useful to you.

TRY IT

In this Try It, you prepare for later work throughout the book. You locate web resources that you can use when you have questions or run into trouble. You create and run a program, explore the project's folder hierarchy, and make a copy of the project. You also get a chance to experiment a bit with the IDE, displaying new toolbars, moving windows around, and generally taking the IDE for a test drive and kicking the tires.

> **NOTE** *Note that the solutions for this lesson's Try It and exercises are not all available on the book's website. The Try It and some of the exercises ask you to experiment with the IDE rather than produce a finished program, so there's really nothing to download. In later lessons, example solutions to the Try It and exercises are available on the book's website.*

Lesson Requirements

In this lesson, you:

➤ Find and bookmark useful web resources.

➤ Launch Visual Studio and start a new Visual C# project.

➤ Experiment with the IDE's layout by displaying the Debug toolbar, pinning the Toolbox, and displaying the Output window.

➤ Run the program.

➤ Find the program's executable, copy it to the desktop, and run it there.

➤ Copy the project folder to a new location and make changes to the copy.

➤ Compress the project folder to make a backup.

> **NOTE** *You can download the code and resources for this lesson from the website at* www.wrox.com/go/csharp24hourtrainer2e.

Hints

➤ When you create a new project, be sure to specify a good location so you can find it later.

➤ Before you compress the project, remove the `bin`, `obj`, and `.vs` directories to save space.

Step-by-Step

➤ Find and bookmark useful web resources.

1. Open your favorite web browser.

2. Create a new bookmark folder named C#. (See the browser's documentation if you don't know how to make a bookmark folder.)

3. Go to the following websites and bookmark the ones you like (feel free to search for others, too):

   ➤ My C# Helper website (www.CSharpHelper.com)

   ➤ This book's web page (www.CSharpHelper.com/24hour.html)

➤ This book's Wrox web page (go to www.wrox.com and search for *C# 24-Hour Trainer, Second Edition*)

➤ Visual C# Express Edition MSDN forum (social.msdn.microsoft.com/Forums/en-US/Vsexpressvcs/threads)

➤ Visual C# IDE MSDN forum (social.msdn.microsoft.com/Forums/en-US/csharpide/threads)

➤ Visual C# Language MSDN forum (social.msdn.microsoft.com/Forums/en-US/csharplanguage/threads)

➤ Visual C# General MSDN forum (social.msdn.microsoft.com/Forums/en-US/csharpgeneral/threads)

➤ MSDN (msdn.microsoft.com)

➤ Stack Overflow (www.stackoverflow.com)

➤ Code Project (www.codeproject.com)

➤ Launch Visual Studio and start a new Visual C# project.

1. If you don't have a desktop or taskbar icon for Visual Studio, create one. For example, in Windows 8, follow these steps:

   a. Open the Charms area, click Search, and type **VS Express** (or part of the name of the version you installed). If Visual Studio isn't in the result list, make sure the search box's dropdown list has Everywhere selected.

   b. In the search results, right-click the program and select Pin to Start or Pin to Taskbar.

2. Launch Visual Studio by clicking the tile you just pinned to the start screen or the icon you just pinned to the taskbar.

3. Create a new project.

   a. Press Ctrl+Shift+N or open the IDE's File menu, expand the New submenu, and select Project.

   b. Expand the Visual C# project types folder and select the Windows Forms Application template.

   c. Enter a project name and a good, easy-to-find location like the desktop or a folder named C# Projects on the desktop.

   d. Uncheck the Create Directory for Solution box.

   e. Click OK.

➤ Experiment with the IDE's layout by displaying the Debug toolbar, pinning the Toolbox, and displaying the Output window.

1. Open the Tools menu and select Customize. On the Customize dialog, select the Toolbars tab and check the box next to the Debug toolbar. Experiment with the other toolbars if you like. Close the dialog when you're done.

2. If the Toolbox is auto-hiding (it should be after you first install Visual Studio), float the mouse over it until it expands. Click the thumbtack to pin it.

3. To display the Output window, open the View menu and select Output. Grab the Output window's title bar and drag it around. Move it over some drop targets to see where it lands. When you're finished, drop it at the bottom of the IDE as shown in Figure 1-7.

➤ Run the program.

1. Press F5 or open the Debug menu and select Start Debugging.

2. Try out the form's minimize, maximize, and close buttons and the commands in the form's system menu. Move the form around and resize it. Marvel at the fact that you didn't need to write any code!

➤ Find the program's executable, copy it to the desktop, and run it there.

1. Start File Explorer and navigate to the location that you specified when you created the new program.

2. There you should find a folder named after the program. Open that folder and examine the files inside. Notice the .sln file that you can double-click to reopen the solution in Visual Studio. Notice also the bin, obj, and .vs directories.

3. Enter the bin directory and move into its Debug subdirectory. It contains several files including the executable, named after the program but with the .exe extension. Right-click the executable and select Copy.

4. Right-click the desktop and select Paste to copy the executable to the desktop.

5. Double-click the copy of the executable on the desktop.

➤ Copy the project folder to a new location and make changes to the copy.

1. In File Explorer, go to the directory that contains the project folder.

2. Right-click the project's folder and select Copy.

3. Right-click the desktop and select Paste to copy the project folder.

4. Open the copied project folder and double-click the .sln file to open the copied project in Visual Studio. If the form doesn't open in the Form Designer (#4 in Figure 1-7), look in Solution Explorer and double-click the file Form1.cs.

5. In the Form Designer, grab the handle on the form's lower-right corner and resize the form to make it tall and skinny.

6. Run the modified program. Then go back to the original project (which should still be running in another instance of Visual Studio) and run it. Notice that the two versions display forms of different sizes.

➤ Compress the project folder to make a backup.

1. In Visual Studio, close the project. (Or close Visual Studio.)

2. In File Explorer, return to the project's folder and delete the bin, obj, and .vs directories. (Note that you can't delete the bin directory if Visual Studio has the project open.)

3. Move up one level to the directory that contains the project folder. Right-click the folder, expand the Send To submenu, and select Compressed (Zipped) Folder.

4. E-mail copies of your first project to all of your friends and relatives. I'm sure they'll thank you!

EXERCISES

1. Build a solution that contains two projects. (Create a project named Project1. Check the Create Directory for Solution box and name the solution TwoProjects. Then open the File menu, expand the Add submenu, and select New Project to add a new project named Project2.)

2. This lesson explains only a tiny fraction of the ways you can customize Visual Studio. Try another one by making your own toolbar. Select the Tools menu's Customize command. On the Toolbars tab, click the New button, and name the new toolbar MyTools. On the Commands tab, select the Toolbar radio button and then select the new toolbar from the dropdown list. Now use the Add Commands button to add some commands to the toolbar.

3. This lesson also describes only a few of the windows Visual Studio offers. Use the menus to find and display the Output, Immediate, Error List, and Task List windows. Put them all in tabs at the bottom of Visual Studio (#8 in Figure 1-7).

4. Some tools are available only when Visual Studio is in a certain state. Look in the Debug menu's Windows submenu. Then start the program and look there again. Most of those windows are useful only when the program is running and you are debugging it. (I talk about some of them in later lessons.)

5. [WPF] Create a new WPF application. Run it side by side with a Windows Forms application. What are the differences? (Hint: There shouldn't be many and they should be cosmetic. You learn about more important but less obvious differences in later lessons.)

> **NOTE** *Please select the videos for Lesson 1 online at* www.wrox.com/go/ csharp24hourtrainer2evideos.

Creating Controls

Way back in the computer stone ages, when programmers worked by candlelight on treadle-powered computers and hand-carved wooden monitors, input and output were very simple. The computer wrote text in toxic green on the bottom of a monitor and the text scrolled up as the monitor became full. The user typed on a keyboard to enter text at a single input prompt, and that was about it. Multiple windows performing useful work simultaneously, mice, and forms displaying many labels and textboxes, buttons, scrollbars, and full-color images existed only in the fevered dreams of science-fiction writers.

Today these things are so commonplace that we take them completely for granted. They appear in desktop software, web pages, laptops, handheld computers, and even cell phones.

Building these sorts of objects in the old days would have been extremely difficult, but today it's practically trivial to add them to your application.

You already saw in Lesson 1 how easy it is to make an application (albeit a trivial one) that displays a form that runs independently of the others on the computer. It's almost as easy to use labels, textboxes, buttons, scrollbars, images, menus, popups, and everything else that makes up a modern application.

C# makes all of these objects and more available as controls.

In this lesson, you learn how to add controls to a form. You learn how to size, position, and arrange controls. You also learn how to use a control's properties to change its appearance and behavior at design time and at run time. When you're done with this lesson, you'll be able to build a professional-looking form.

UNDERSTANDING CONTROLS

A *control* is a programming entity that combines a visible appearance on the screen and code to manage it. The code defines the control's appearance and behavior.

For example, a `TextBox` control displays a blank area on the screen where the user can type information. The code inside the control determines how the control draws itself and provides normal textbox features such as multiline or single-line behavior; scrolling and scrollbars displayed as needed; copy, cut, and paste; a context menu displayed when you right-click the control; the ability to navigate when the user presses the Tab key; and much more.

> ### WHAT'S IN A NAME?
>
> By convention, in C# the names of control types (and other types) use *Pascal casing* where multiple words are strung together with the first letter of each word capitalized; for example, `TextBox`, `ProgressBar`, `Button`, and `PictureBox`.

In addition to controls, C# provides components. A *component* is similar to a control except it has no visible piece on the form. For example, the `Timer` component acts as a clock to let the program do something at regular intervals. The `Timer` interacts with the program but doesn't display anything visible to the user. (Some components such as `ErrorProvider` and `ToolTip` may display visible effects on the screen, but the components themselves are not visible on the form.)

The features of controls (and components) fall into three categories: properties, methods, and events.

Properties

A *property* determines the appearance and state of a control. If a `Car` were a control, its properties would be things like `Color`, `TransmissionType`, `CurrentSpeed`, and `NumberOfCupHolders`. Your program could set a `Car`'s `Color` to `HotPink` (to attract the attention of other drivers) or set its `CurrentSpeed` to `110` (to attract the attention of the police).

For a programming example, the `TextBox` control has a `Font` property that determines the font it uses and a `ForeColor` property that determines the color of its text.

Methods

A *method* is a feature of a control that makes the control perform some action. Your code can *call* a method to make the control do something. For example, the `Car` control might have methods such as `Start`, `Stop`, `EjectPassenger`, and `OilSlick`. Your program could call the `OilSlick` method to make the car spray oil out the back so you can escape from spies.

For a programming example, the `TextBox` has a `Clear` method that blanks the control's text and an `AppendText` method that adds text to the end of whatever the control is currently displaying.

Events

An *event* occurs when something interesting happens to the control. The control *raises* or *fires* the event to tell the program that something happened. For example, a `Car` might have `RanOutOfGas` and `Crashed` events. The `Car` control would raise the `Crashed` event to tell the program that the user had driven it into a tree. The program could then take action such as calling an ambulance and a tree surgeon.

For a programming example, the TextBox has a TextChanged event that tells the program that its text has changed. When the event occurs, the program could examine the text to see if the user had entered a valid input. For example, if the TextBox should hold a number and the user entered "One," the program could beep and change the TextBox's BackColor property to Yellow to indicate an error.

Later lessons discuss events and the code that handles them in greater detail. This lesson focuses on adding controls to a form, arranging them, and setting their properties.

CREATING CONTROLS

Adding controls to a form is easy. In fact, it's so easy and there are so many different ways to add controls to a form that it takes a while to describe them all.

Start by creating a new project as described in Lesson 1. Open the form in the Form Designer. (If the form isn't already open, double-click it in Solution Explorer.)

The following list describes some of the ways you can put controls on the form:

➤ Click a tool in the Toolbox to select it. Then click and drag on the form. When you release the mouse, Visual Studio creates the control in the area you selected and then selects the pointer in the Toolbox.

➤ Click a tool in the Toolbox to select it. Then hold down the Ctrl key while you click and drag on the form to place a copy of the control on the form. When you release the mouse, Visual Studio creates the control in the area you selected and keeps the control's tool selected in the Toolbox so you can make another control of that type.

➤ Double-click a tool in the Toolbox to create an instance of the control on the form at a default size and position. (You'll then probably want to resize and reposition it.)

➤ Select one or more controls that are already on the form, press Ctrl+C to copy them, and then press Ctrl+V to paste them onto the form. You can even copy and paste from one instance of Visual Studio to another.

➤ Select one or more controls on the form. While holding down the Ctrl key, drag the controls to a new location. Visual Studio makes a copy of the controls, leaving the originals where they started.

> **NOTE** *You have several ways to select controls on the Form Designer. Click a control to select only it. Click and drag to select multiple controls.*
>
> *Hold down the Shift or Ctrl key while clicking or clicking and dragging to toggle whether controls are in the current selection.*
>
> *And, if you want to deselect all controls, simply click an empty part of the form or press Esc.*

The first method (select a tool and then click and drag to create a control) is probably used most often, but some of the other methods are particularly useful for creating groups of similar controls.

For example, the form in Figure 2-1 displays five rows, each of which holds a `Label` and a `TextBox`. You could easily build all of these controls individually, but you can build them even faster by using copy and paste. First place one `Label` and `TextBox` on the form, arrange them next to each other, and give them any property values that you want all of the `Label`s or `TextBox`es to share. (For example, you may want to set their fonts or colors.) Now click and drag to select both controls, copy and paste, and drag the new controls into position. Repeat this three more times and you'll have all of the controls in position. You'll still need to change the `Label`s' text but the basic arrangement will be done without going back and forth to the Toolbox.

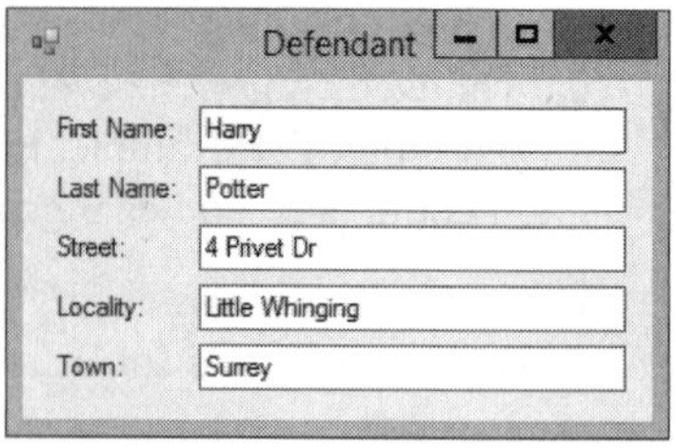

FIGURE 2-1

SETTING CONTROL PROPERTIES

After you've added controls to a form, you can use the Properties window to view and change their property values. If you have more than one control selected, the Properties window shows only the properties that the controls have in common.

For example, if you select a `TextBox` and a `Label`, the Properties window shows the `Text` property because both `Label`s and `TextBox`es have a `Text` property. However, it won't display the `Multiline` property because the `TextBox` control has that property but the `Label` control does not.

The Properties window provides special support for many control properties. For example, Figure 2-2 shows the Properties window when a `TextBox` is selected.

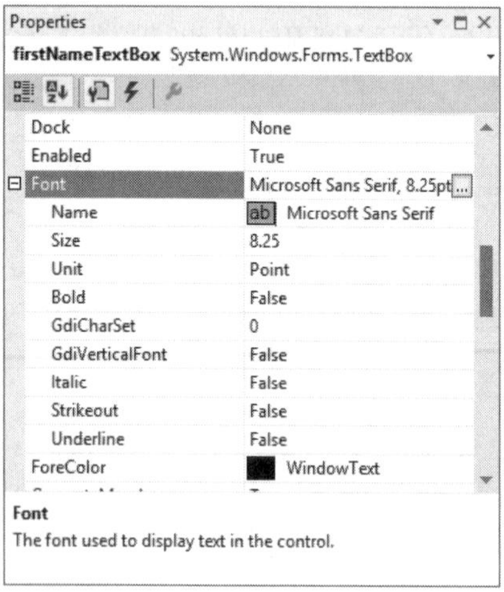

FIGURE 2-2

Notice that the `Font` property contains its own sub-properties: `Name`, `Size`, `Unit`, `Bold`, and so forth. Click the plus or minus sign next to a property to expand or collapse it and show or hide its sub-properties.

Also notice in Figure 2-2 the ellipsis to the right of the Font property. If you click that ellipsis, the dialog shown in Figure 2-3 appears. You can use this dialog to edit the font sub-properties and see a sample of the font.

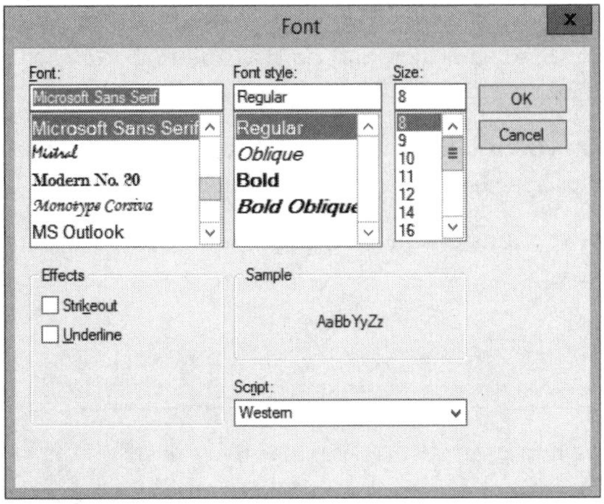

FIGURE 2-3

The Properties window provides appropriate support when it can for other properties. Many properties can hold only certain values. For example, the Font's Italic, Bold, Strikeout, and Underline sub-properties can only take the values True or False. The Font's Unit sub-property can only take the values World, Pixel, Point, Inch, Document, and Millimeter. In these cases, the Properties window provides a dropdown listing the allowed choices.

Figure 2-4 shows the editor that the Properties window displays when you click the dropdown arrow to the right of a TextBox's BackColor property. The Custom tab lets you pick a color from a palette, the Web tab lets you pick standard web page colors, and the System tab lets you pick system colors such as the normal control background color or the menu highlight color.

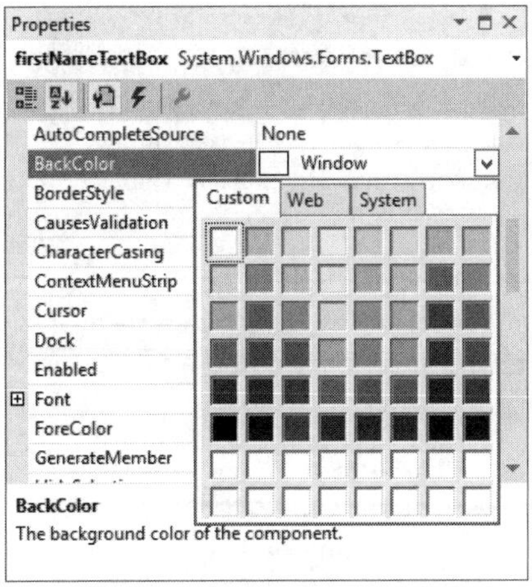

FIGURE 2-4

By using the Properties window's editors and typing in values when there is no editor, you can change a control's appearance and behavior.

Control Names

Whenever you create a control, Visual Studio gives it a rather nondescript name such as `label2`, `textBox5`, or `pictureBox1`. Although these names tell you what kind of object the control is, they don't tell you what it is for and that's much more important when you later need to use the control in your code. Names like `firstNameTextBox`, `hatSizeTrackBar`, and `mediaTypeComboBox` are much more meaningful than `textBox3` and `textBox7`.

Note that you don't need to give good names to *every* control, just the ones that you will need to use later in the code. You often don't need to name `Labels`, `GroupBoxes`, and other purely decorative controls.

You can learn more about Microsoft's naming conventions on the web page "Guidelines for Names" at `msdn.microsoft.com/library/ms229002.aspx`.

WHAT'S IN A NAME, REDUX

Earlier in this lesson I said that control *type* names use Pascal casing. By convention, the names of specific *instances* of controls use *camel casing*, where multiple words are strung together with the first letter of each word capitalized, except for the first word. For example, the control type `TextBox` uses Pascal casing and the specific control name `firstNameTextBox` uses camel casing.

It's called camel casing because it sort of looks like a camel lying down: low at the ends with one or more humps in the middle. I guess `stateLabel` would be a dromedary (one-humped) camel, `priceTextBox` would be a Bactrian (two-humped) camel, and `numberOfEmployeesCoveredByInsurancePlanTrackBar` would be some sort of camel created by Dr. Seuss.

WHAT'S IN A NAME, PART 3

Most C# developers add a control's type as a suffix to its name as in `first NameTextBox` or `resultLabel`, but it's becoming more common for developers to use a more generic word such as `value` or `field`. The idea is that if you decide to change the type of control that handles the value, you won't need to change the code that refers to the control.

For example, suppose your program uses a `TrackBar` to let the user select the number of UFO detectors to purchase. If you name this control `numUfoDetectorsValue`, then you won't need to change the code if you later decide to let the user select the value from a `NumericUpDown` control instead of a `TrackBar`.

Some developers even omit the suffix completely as in `numUfoDetectors`, although that can be confusing if you need more than one control to represent a similar concept or if you want a variable inside the code that holds the numeric value represented by the control.

For now, I recommend that you stick with the control's full type name as a suffix.

Popular Properties

You'll learn about key control properties as you go along, but for now Table 2-1 summarizes some of the most useful properties. Note that not all controls have every property. For example, a `Button` cannot display a border (or it always displays a border, depending on your point of view) so it has no `BorderStyle` property.

TABLE 2-1

PROPERTY	PURPOSE
Anchor	Determines how the control sizes itself to use the available space. This property is described further in Lesson 3.
AutoSize	Determines whether the control automatically resizes itself to fit its contents. This can be `True` or `False`. By default, `Labels` are born with `AutoSize = True`.
BackColor	Determines the control's background color.
BackgroundImage	Determines the image that the control displays.
BorderStyle	Determines whether the control displays a border. This can be `None`, `FixedSingle`, or `Fixed3D`.
Dock	Determines how the control sizes itself to use the available space. This property is described further in Lesson 3.
Enabled	Determines whether the control will interact with the user. Many controls display a special appearance when disabled such as being grayed out. This can be `True` or `False`.
Font	Determines the font that the control uses to display text.
ForeColor	Determines the control's foreground color. For controls that display text, this is usually the text's color.
Image	Determines the image that the control displays. (Some controls have `Image`, others have `BackgroundImage`, a few have both, and many cannot display any image. No one said this was completely consistent!)
Items	For controls such as `ListBox` and `ComboBox`, this is the list of items that the user can select.
Location	Gives the control's location in pixels from the upper-left corner of whatever it is in (for now, assume it's in the form). `Location` includes `X` and `Y` sub-properties. For example, the value `(10, 20)` means the control is 10 pixels from the form's left edge and 20 pixels from its top edge.
Name	Gives the control a name that your code can use to refer to it later. You should always give a *good* name to any control that you will refer to in code.

continues

TABLE 2-1 *(continued)*

PROPERTY	PURPOSE
Size	Gives the control's width and height in pixels. For example, the value (75, 30) means the control is 75 pixels wide and 30 pixels tall.
Tag	This property can hold any value that you want to store with the control. For example, you might put text or a number in the Tag properties of some Buttons so the code can easily tell the Buttons apart.
Text	Many controls have a Text property that determines what the control displays. For Labels and TextBoxes, Text determines the text they show (pretty obvious). For controls such as ComboBoxes and ListBoxes, Text determines the control's current selection. For a Form, which in a real sense is just another kind of control, Text determines what's displayed in the title bar.
TextAlign	Determines how text is aligned within the control.
Visible	Determines whether the control is visible. This can be True or False. Set it to False to hide a control from the user.

If you want some practice with these properties, create a new project and give them a try. Create a Button and set its Text property. Also click the form and set *its* Text property. Change the form's Font property and see what happens to the form and the button it contains. Experiment with some of the other properties such as Image and ForeColor if you like.

Modifying Properties in Code

This lesson doesn't really go into handling control events very much (that's the subject of Lesson 4), but I do want to explain how to set properties in code and you need event handlers to do that. Besides, it's easy and sort of fun, and it'll let you make a program that does something more than just sitting there looking pretty.

To make a simple event handler for a control, double-click the control in the Form Designer. That opens the Code Editor and creates an empty event handler for the control's default event. For Button controls, that's the Click event. Whenever the user clicks the control at run time, it raises its Click event and this code executes.

To change a property in code, type the control's name, a dot (or period), the name of the property, an equals sign, and finally the value that you want to give the property. Finish the line of code with a semicolon. For example, the following statement sets the Left property of the label named greetingLabel to 100. That moves the label so it's 100 pixels from the left edge of its container:

```
greetingLabel.Left = 100;
```

The following code shows a complete event handler:

```
// Move the Label.
private void moveLabelButton_Click(object sender, EventArgs e)
```

```
    {
        greetingLabel.Left = 100;
    }
```

In this code, I typed the first line that starts with two slashes. That line is a *comment,* a piece of text that is contained in the code but that is not executed by the program. Any text that comes after the // characters is ignored until the end of the current line. You can (and should) use comments to make your code easier to understand. They don't make the executable program bigger or slower, so don't be stingy with your comments!

I also typed the line that sets the Label's Left property.

Visual Studio typed the rest when I double-clicked the moveLabelButton control. You don't need to worry about the details of this code right now, but briefly the sender parameter is the object that raised the event (the Button in this example) and the e parameter gives extra information about the event. The extra information can be useful for some events (for example, in the MouseClick event it tells where the mouse was clicked), but it's not very interesting for a Button's Click event.

Simple numeric values such as the 100 used in this example are easy to set in code, but some properties aren't numbers. In that case, you must set them to values that have the proper data type.

For example, a Label's Text property is a string so you must give it a string value. The following code sets the greetingLabel control's Text property to the string Hello:

```
    greetingLabel.Text = "Hello";
```

> **NOTE** *Notice that you must include the string* Hello *in double quotes to tell C# that this is a literal string and not some sort of C# command. If you leave the quotes off, C# gets confused and gives you the error "The name 'Hello' does not exist in the current context."*
>
> *Over time, you'll get used to messages like this and they'll make sense. In this case, the message just means, "I don't know what the word 'Hello' means."*

Other property values have more exotic data types such as Date, AnchorStyles, Point, and BindingContext. When you set these properties, you must make sure that the values you give them have the correct data types. I'm going to ignore most of these for now, but one data type that is relatively simple and useful is Color.

A control's ForeColor and BackColor properties have the data type Color so you cannot simply set them equal to strings such as Red or Blue. Instead you must set them equal to something that also has the type Color. The easiest way to do that is to use the colors predefined by the Color class. This may seem a bit confusing, but in practice it's actually quite easy.

For example, the following two statements set a Label's BackColor and ForeColor properties to HotPink and Blue, respectively:

```
    greetingLabel.BackColor = Color.HotPink;
    greetingLabel.ForeColor = Color.Blue;
```

The following code shows how the MoveButton example program, which is available as part of this lesson's code download on the book's website, changes several `Label` properties when you click a `Button`:

```
// Change a Label's properties.
private void moveLabelButton_Click(object sender, EventArgs e)
{
    greetingLabel.Left = 100;
    greetingLabel.Text = "Hello";
    greetingLabel.BackColor = Color.HotPink;
    greetingLabel.ForeColor = Color.Blue;
}
```

ARRANGING CONTROLS

The Form Designer provides several tools to help you arrange controls at design time. The following sections describe some of the most useful: snap lines, arrow keys, the Format menu, and the Layout toolbar.

Snap Lines

When you drag a control around on the form, the Form Designer displays *snap lines* that show how the control lines up with the form and with other controls. Figure 2-5 shows the Form Designer displaying light blue snap lines indicating that the control is standard distances away from the form's top and left edges.

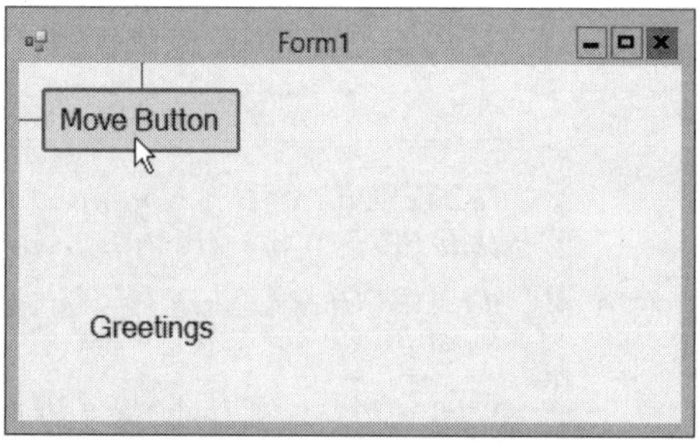

You can drag the control away from this position and, if you do so, the snap lines disappear. When you drag the control close to one of the form's edges, the control jumps to the standard distance and the Form Designer displays the snap lines again.

FIGURE 2-5

The Form Designer also displays snap lines to show how controls align. In Figure 2-6, I dragged a second `Button` below the first. Different snap lines show that:

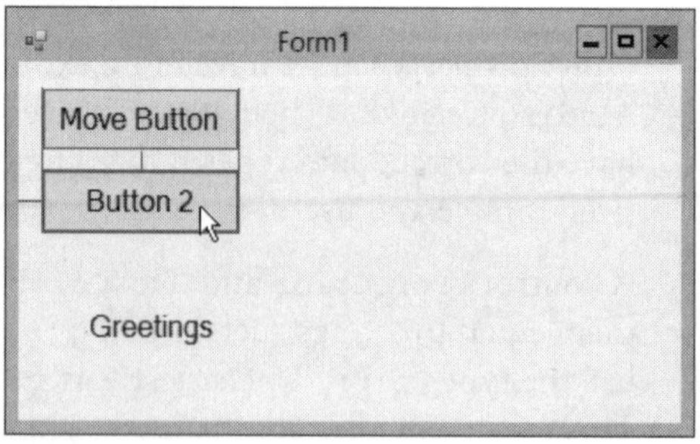

➤ The second `Button` is the standard distance from the form's left edge.

➤ The second `Button`'s left and right edges line up with the first `Button`'s edges.

➤ The second `Button` is a standard distance below the first `Button`.

FIGURE 2-6

Other snap lines show how the control contents line up. In Figure 2-7 snap lines show that the `Label` is the standard distance from the second `Button` and that the `Label`'s text baseline lines up with the baseline of the second `Button`.

For a more realistic example, consider Figure 2-8. In this figure I was laying out a small data entry form, and I wanted all of the Labels and TextBoxes to line up nicely. In this figure, snap lines show that the Street TextBox is lined up on the left and right with the other TextBoxes, is a standard distance from the TextBoxes above and below, is a standard distance from the form's right edge, and has its baseline lined up with the Street Label.

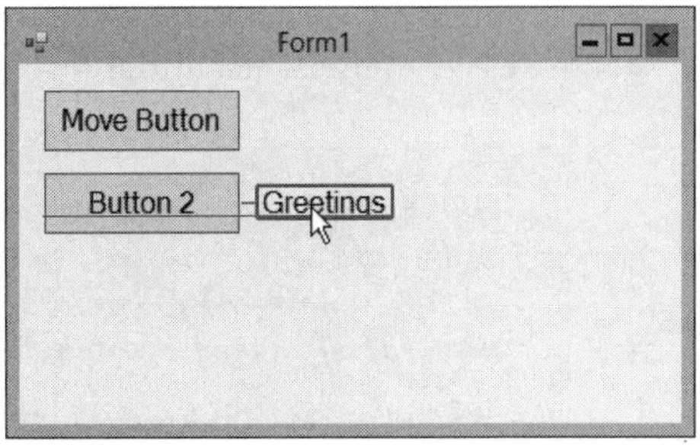

FIGURE 2-7

Arrow Keys

In addition to dragging controls with the mouse, you can move controls by pressing the arrow keys. Select one or more controls and then use the left, right, up, and down arrow keys to move the control(s) one pixel at a time. This method is slower than using the mouse but gives you finer control.

When you move controls with the arrow keys, the Form Designer doesn't display snap lines so you may want to keep an eye on the control's Location property in the Properties window to see where it is.

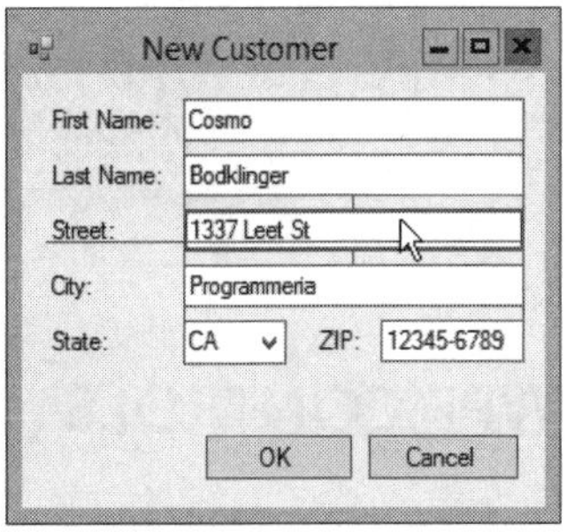

FIGURE 2-8

The Format Menu and Layout Toolbar

The Format menu contains many commands that arrange one or more controls. Table 2-2 summarizes the Format menu's submenus.

TABLE 2-2

SUBMENU	COMMANDS
Align	Aligns groups of controls on their lefts, middles, rights, tops, bottoms, or centers.
Make Same Size	Makes controls have the same width, height, or both.
Horizontal Spacing	Adjusts the horizontal spacing between controls. It can make the space between controls equal, smaller, larger, or zero.
Vertical Spacing	Works like the Horizontal Spacing submenu except it adjusts the vertical spacing between controls.
Center in Form	Centers the controls vertically or horizontally in their container. If the controls are inside a container like a Panel or GroupBox, these commands center the controls within the container, not the form.
Order	These commands send a control to the front or back of the stacking order. This is useful if you have controls that overlap so some are behind others.

The Layout toolbar contains the same commands as the Format menu but in a handy toolbar so they're easier to use. The buttons display little pictures that show how they align controls.

> **NOTE** *How these tools arrange controls depends on how you select the controls. One of the selected controls, normally the first one you select, is the group's dominant control. The dominant control is marked with white boxes at its corners, whereas the other controls are marked with black boxes.*
>
> *When you use an arranging tool, the dominant control determines how the others are arranged. For example, if you select the Format ➪ Align ➪ Lefts command, the other controls are moved so their left edges line up with the dominant control's left edge.*
>
> *To change the dominant control in a selected group, click the one you want to be dominant (without holding down the Ctrl or Shift keys).*

WPF CONTROLS

WPF applications use their own set of controls, some of which are similar to controls used by Windows Forms applications. Visual Studio for Windows lets you create WPF applications in roughly the same way Visual Studio for Windows Desktop lets you make Windows Forms applications. Both provide an editor where you can click and drag to create controls and a Properties window where you can set control properties.

One big difference is that Visual Studio also displays a XAML code editor for WPF applications. *XAML*, which stands for "eXtensible Application Markup Language" and which is usually pronounced "zammel," is a language that Visual Studio uses to define user interfaces for WPF applications.

Sometimes it's easier to edit the XAML code directly than it is to use the Window editor. In particular, it's often easier to make copies of controls by copying and pasting XAML code (and changing the new controls' names) than it is to copy controls in the Window editor.

For now, you should probably start with the Window editor, but you may also want to look at the XAML code and experiment with it a bit to see how it works.

TRY IT

In this Try It, you get some practice building a user interface. You place controls on a form and arrange them so they line up nicely. You also get some practice setting control properties at design time and changing them at run time.

Lesson Requirements

In this lesson, you:

➤ Add controls to a form and arrange them as shown in Figure 2-9. (Note the form's title and the fact that the form has a non-resizable border.)

➤ Give the key controls names.

➤ Set properties at design time on the result label (at the bottom in Figure 2-9) to make the label:

   ➤ Display its text centered.

   ➤ Show a border.

   ➤ Use a 16-point font.

   ➤ Remain invisible until the user clicks one of the buttons.

FIGURE 2-9

➤ Make the OK button be the form's default button so it fires when the user presses Enter. Make the Cancel button be the form's cancel button so it fires when the user presses Esc.

➤ Add code behind the OK button to display the result label with a green background as shown in Figure 2-9.

➤ Add code behind the Cancel button to display the result label with a hot pink background and the text "Operation Canceled."

> **NOTE** *You can download the code and resources for this lesson from the website at* www.wrox.com/go/csharp24hourtrainer2e.

Hints

➤ Create the First Name `Label` and `TextBox` first and arrange them. Then copy and paste them to make more `Labels` and `TextBoxes`.

➤ Use the Format menu or Layout toolbar to center the buttons and the result label.

Step-by-Step

➤ Add controls to a form and arrange them as shown in Figure 2-9. (Note the form's title and the fact that the form has a nonresizable border.)

1. Start a new project named NewCustomer. Remember to put it somewhere easy to find.

2. Use the Properties window to set the form's `Text` property to **New Customer**.

3. Use the Properties window to set the form's `FormBorderStyle` property to `FixedDialog`. (Feel free to experiment with the other values.)

4. Create the First Name `TextBox`.

    a. Click the Toolbox's `TextBox` tool and then click and drag to place a `TextBox` on the form.

    b. Drag the `TextBox` into the form's upper-right corner until the snap lines show that it is a standard distance from the top and right edges of the form.

5. Create the First Name `Label`.

    a. Click the Toolbox's `Label` tool and then click and drag to create the `Label`.

    b. Drag the `Label` to the form's upper-left corner so the snap lines show that the `Label` is a standard distance from the form's left edge and that its baseline aligns with the `TextBox`'s baseline.

    c. To determine the `Label`'s width, you need to set its text. Use the Properties window to set the `Label`'s Text property to **First Name**.

    d. Click the `TextBox`. Click the drag handle on the `TextBox`'s left edge and drag it until it is a standard distance from the `Label`.

6. Make copies of the `Label` and `TextBox`.

    a. Click and drag to select both the `Label` and the `TextBox`.

    b. Press Ctrl+C to copy the controls. Then press Ctrl+V to paste new copies of the controls.

    c. With the new controls still selected, click and drag the `TextBox` until the snap lines show it is standard distances away from the `TextBox` above and from the form's right edge.

    d. Use the Properties window to set the new `Label`'s Text property to **Last Name**.

    e. Repeat this four more times (using appropriate Text values) until you have five rows of `Label`s and `TextBox`es.

7. Make the ZIP `Label`.

    a. Set the bottom `TextBox`'s Text property to **12345-6789**. Then use the `TextBox`'s left drag handle to resize it so it's a bit bigger than its Text value (see Figure 2-9).

    b. Create a `Label` for the ZIP code and set its Text property to **ZIP**. Drag it so the snap lines show its baseline aligns with the baseline for the `Label` and `TextBox` on that same line, and it is the standard distance to the left of the `TextBox`.

    c. Use the Properties window to set the `TextBox`'s TextAlign property to `Right`.

8. Make the State ComboBox.

    a. Use the Toolbox to make a ComboBox. Set its Text property to **WW** and resize it so the text fits reasonably well.

    b. Drag the ComboBox so the snap lines show its baseline aligns with the Labels on that row and its left edge aligns with the left edges of the TextBoxes above.

    c. With the ComboBox selected, look in the Properties window and click the Items property. Then click the ellipsis (...) button on the right to open the String Collection Editor. Enter **CO, AZ, WY, UT,** and any other state abbreviations that you want to use and click OK. (If you want to enter **Confusion** and **Denial,** you'll need to make the ComboBox wider.)

    d. Use the Properties window to set the DropDownStyle property to DropDownList.

> **NOTE** *The* DropDownStyle *value* Simple *makes the* ComboBox *display a* TextBox *where the user can type and a list below it where the user can make selections.*
>
> *The value* DropDown *makes the* ComboBox *display a* TextBox *where the user can type and a dropdown arrow that makes a dropdown list appear.*
>
> *The value* DropDownList *is similar to* DropDown *except the user can only select from the dropdown list and cannot type new values.* DropDownList *is often the best choice because it prevents the user from typing invalid values.*

9. Make the Buttons.

    a. Double-click the Toolbox's Button tool twice to make two Buttons with standard sizes.

    b. Drag one Button so it is a nice distance below the TextBoxes. Drag the other Button so it's aligned vertically with the first, positioning it some reasonable distance to the side (the exact distances don't matter here).

    c. Click and drag to select both Buttons. Select Format ⇨ Center in Form ⇨ Horizontally.

    d. Use the Properties window to give the Buttons the Text values **OK** and **Cancel.**

10. Use the Toolbox to make the result Label. (Don't worry too much about its size and position right now. Just drop it somewhere close to where it is shown in Figure 2-9.)

➤ Give the key controls names.

1. Give the key controls the names shown in Table 2-3. You don't need to give names to the other controls because the program won't need to refer to them. (Actually this example doesn't refer to the TextBoxes or ComboBox either, but a real program certainly would. A form wouldn't contain TextBoxes and ComboBoxes that it won't use.)

TABLE 2-3

CONTROL	NAME
First Name TextBox	firstNameTextBox
Last Name TextBox	lastNameTextBox
Street TextBox	streetTextBox
City TextBox	cityTextBox
State ComboBox	stateComboBox
ZIP TextBox	zipTextBox
OK Button	okButton
Cancel Button	cancelButton
Result Label	resultLabel

➤ Set properties at design time on the result label (at the bottom in Figure 2-9) to make the label:

   ➤ Display its text centered.

      1. Set the Label's TextAlign property to MiddleCenter. (Use the Properties window's TextAlign editor to select the middle position.)

      2. Set the Label's AutoSize property to False.

      3. Set the Label's Size property to 218, 37. (Or expand the Size property and set the Width and Height sub-properties separately.)

      4. Use the Format menu or Layout toolbar to center the Label on the form.

   ➤ Show a border.

      1. Set the Label's BorderStyle property to Fixed3D.

   ➤ Use a 16-point font.

      1. Expand the Properties window's Font entry. Set the Size sub-property to 16.

   ➤ Remain invisible until the user clicks one of the buttons.

      1. Set the Label's Visible property to False.

➤ Make the OK button be the form's default button so it fires when the user presses Enter. Make the Cancel button be the form's cancel button so it fires when the user presses Esc.

   1. Click the form and use the Properties window to set the form's AcceptButton property to okButton.

   2. Similarly, set the form's CancelButton property to cancelButton.

➤ Add code behind the OK button to display the result label with a green background as shown in Figure 2-9.

1. Double-click the OK button to create an event handler for its Click event.

2. Type the bold text in the following code so the event handler looks like this:

```
// Create the new customer.
private void okButton_Click(object sender, EventArgs e)
{
    resultLabel.Text = "New Customer Created";
    resultLabel.BackColor = Color.LightGreen;
    resultLabel.Visible = true;
}
```

➤ Add code behind the Cancel button to display the result label with a hot pink background and the text "Operation Canceled."

1. Double-click the Cancel button to create an event handler for its Click event.

2. Type the bold text in the following code so the event handler looks like this:

```
// Don't create the new customer.
private void cancelButton_Click(object sender, EventArgs e)
{
    resultLabel.Text = "Operation Canceled";
    resultLabel.BackColor = Color.HotPink;
    resultLabel.Visible = true;
}
```

Now run the program and experiment with it. Notice what happens when you press the Enter and Esc keys while focus is in a TextBox. See what happens if focus is on one of the Buttons.

EXERCISES

1. [Games] Build a checkerboard similar to the one shown in Figure 2-10. (Hints: The squares are PictureBoxes with different background colors. Give the form a bluish background. Finally, use the Format menu or Layout toolbar to align the controls.)

2. [Games, WPF] Repeat Exercise 1 with a WPF application. (Hints: Place colored Rectangles inside a WrapPanel with a width that makes the Rectangles wrap in eight columns.)

3. [Games] Make a tic-tac-toe (or naughts-and-crosses) board similar to the one shown in Figure 2-11. (Hints: Make three Labels for each square, named after the rows and columns. For the upper-left square, name them x00Label for the

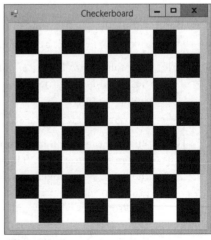

FIGURE 2-10

little X `Label`, `oOLabel` for the little O `Label`, and `takenOOLabel` for the big `Label`. Give the smaller `Labels` `Click` event handlers that set the `Text` property of the corresponding big `Label`. Don't worry about the rules such as not allowing someone to take a square that is already taken.)

4. [Games, WPF] Repeat Exercise 3 with a WPF application. (Hints: For each square, use a `Border` with `Margin` values set to 5. A `Border` can hold only one content control, so put a `Canvas` in each `Border`. Then put the three `Labels` inside the `Canvas`. Put the nine `Borders` inside a `WrapPanel` sized so they form three columns. See the video *Making Event Handlers* for instructions on how to make the small `Labels` act like buttons. Add interesting backgrounds if you like.)

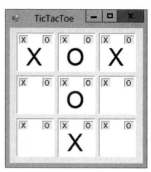

FIGURE 2-11

5. [Games] Modify the tic-tac-toe program from Exercise 3 so instead of displaying X or O in each square, it displays pictures. Use your favorite football team logos, a cat and a dog, your picture and your boss's, or whatever. (Hints: Use `PictureBoxes` instead of the large `Labels`. Add two hidden `PictureBoxes` to the form. To set their `Image` properties, click the ellipsis next to the `Image` property in the Properties window, click the Import button, and browse for the image files. Finally, instead of setting a `Label`'s `Text` property, the `Click` event handlers should set the appropriate `PictureBox`'s `Image` property equal to one of the hidden `PictureBox`'s `Image` properties. Set all `SizeMode` properties of the `PictureBoxes` to `Zoom`.)

6. [WPF] Repeat Exercise 5 with a WPF application. (Hints: Use `Image` controls instead of the large `Labels`. Use two `Images` with `Visiblity` = `Hidden` to store the X and O images. In an event handler, use code similar to `taken21Image.Source = oImage.Source`.)

7. Make a program with a `Label` that says "Move Me" and four `Buttons` with text (0, 0), (200, 200), (200, 0), and (0, 200). Make each `Button` move the `Label` to the corresponding position by setting its `Left` and `Top` properties.

8. [WPF] Repeat Exercise 7 with a WPF application. (Hints: Set the `Label`'s position with code similar to `moveMeLabel.Margin = new Thickness(0, 200, 0, 0)`.)

9. The solution to Exercise 7 moves its `Label` in two steps by setting its `Left` and `Top` properties. Modify the program so it sets the `Label`'s `Location` property in a single step using code similar to this:

```
moveMeLabel.Location = new Point(0, 0);
```

10. Build a hotel menu form similar to the one shown in Figure 2-12. (Hints: Copy and paste the `Labels` and `TextBoxes` from the Try It program. To set the `PictureBox`'s image, look in the Properties window and click the ellipsis next to the `Image` property. In the Select Resource dialog, click Import and browse to select a picture. Finally, set the `PictureBox`'s `SizeMode` property to `AutoSize`.)

FIGURE 2-12

11. [WPF] Repeat Exercise 10 with a WPF application.

12. Build a form similar to the one shown in Figure 2-13. (Don't worry about making the program perform any calculations. You'll learn how to do that later.)

13. [WPF] Repeat Exercise 12 with a WPF application.

14. Build a form similar to the one shown in Figure 2-14. (Search the Internet for "labeled diagram" and pick an interesting image. Use MS Paint or some other image editing program to remove the labels. Then add TextBoxes where the labels were so the user can fill them in.)

FIGURE 2-13

FIGURE 2-14

15. [WPF] Repeat exercise 14 with a WPF application.

16. Build a bar chart similar to the one shown in Figure 2-15. (Hints: Use a PictureBox for the chart's background and Labels for the bars.)

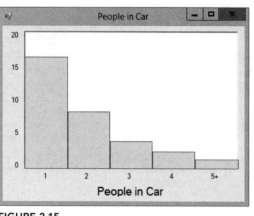

FIGURE 2-15

17. [WPF] Repeat Exercise 16 with a WPF application. Give the chart background a color gradient and label the Y axis with a sideways label that says "Occurrences."

18. Build a bar chart similar to the one shown in Figure 2-16. (Hints: Use `PictureBoxes` for the bars.)

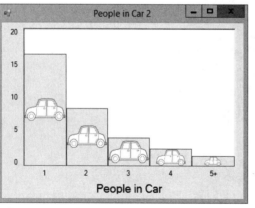

FIGURE 2-16

19. [WPF hard] Repeat Exercise 18 with a WPF application but fill the bar `Image` controls with a tile brush that uses a small picture of a car. Set the brush's `TileMode = Tile` and `Stretch = None`. Use the XAML editor to add the code `Viewport="0,0,55,27"` `ViewportUnits="Absolute"` inside the brush's definition. The result should be bars that are tiled with little pictures of cars.

20. Modify the program you made for Exercise 18 to add tooltips for the bars. (Add a `ToolTip` control named `peopleToolTip` to the form. Then use the Properties window to set the "ToolTip on peopleToolTip" property for the bar labels. For example, make the second bar's tooltip say "2 people.")

21. [WPF] Repeat Exercise 20 with a WPF application. (Hint: In WPF you don't need to use a `ToolTip` control. Just set the bars' `ToolTip` properties.)

22. [WPF hard] Build a WPF program similar to the one shown in Figure 2-17. (Hints: For the reflected text, use a `Label`. Make its `Foreground` brush shade from medium gray to light gray. In the Transform property category, set the scale in the Y direction to –1 and set the skew in the X direction to 30.)

FIGURE 2-17

23. [Games] Make a program named MovingButton. Make a `Button` named `clickMeButton` that says "Click Me." Add a `Timer` named `moveButtonTimer` to the form and set its `Interval` property to 500.

    Next double-click the `Timer` to open the code for its `Tick` event and add the bold text so the event handler looks like the following:

    ```
    Random Rand = new Random();
    private void moveButtonTimer_Tick(object sender, EventArgs e)
    {
        clickMeButton.Left = Rand.Next(0, 250);
        clickMeButton.Top = Rand.Next(0, 250);
    }
    ```

    Now double-click the `Button` and add the bold text in the following code to create its event handler:

    ```
    private void clickMeButton_Click(object sender, EventArgs e)
    {
        moveButtonTimer.Enabled = !moveButtonTimer.Enabled;
    }
    ```

    Run the program and have fun! Experiment with different values for the `Timer`'s `Interval` property such as 2000 and 10.

> **NOTE** *Please select the videos for Lesson 2 online at* www.wrox.com/go/
> csharp24hourtrainer2evideos.

Making Controls Arrange Themselves

Lesson 2 explained how to add controls to a form and arrange them nicely. Using those techniques, you can create forms like the one shown in Figure 3-1. (Although we haven't covered the code behind that program's form yet.)

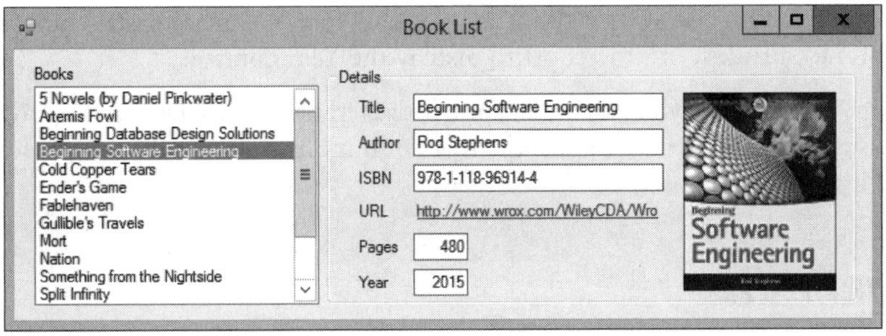

FIGURE 3-1

That form looks okay in Figure 3-1, but what if the user enlarges the form as shown in Figure 3-2? Pretty lame, huh? Although the form is bigger, the areas that contain data are not.

FIGURE 3-2

The URL for the book selected in Figure 3-2 is too long to fit within the GroupBox, so it is truncated even though the form has extra wasted space on the right. The ListBox isn't big enough to display all of its items even though there's wasted space at the bottom. It would be nice if the controls rearranged themselves to use the available space and display the entire URL and more list items.

Figure 3-3 shows another problem with this form. If the user shrinks the form, the TextBoxes and URL LinkLabel are chopped off, the Year Label and TextBox are chopped in half vertically, the ListBox doesn't fit, and the cover picture is completely missing.

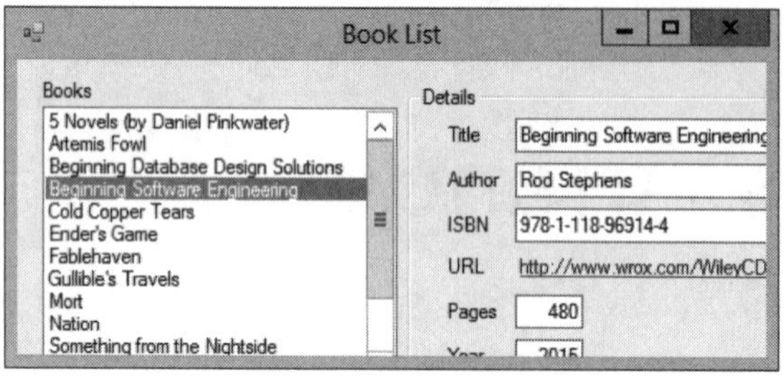

FIGURE 3-3

The program would look nicer if the controls were shrunk so you could at least see their edges. Some of the values still wouldn't fit, but at least the form wouldn't look so amateurish. You could even make the form refuse to shrink so it's too short to display the Year controls.

This lesson explains some simple ways you can make controls rearrange themselves to take advantage of whatever space is available, and how to give the form minimum and maximum sizes so the user can't resize it until it's completely useless.

RESTRICTING FORM SIZE

Forms (and in fact all controls) have MinimumSize and MaximumSize properties that you can use to restrict the form's size. Simply set these properties to a width and height (or set their Width and Height sub-properties) and the form does the rest.

For example, to prevent the user from making the form shown in Figure 3-3 too small, you can set the form's MinimumSize property to 663, 233.

USING ANCHOR PROPERTIES

The MinimumSize property prevents the user from making a form too small but it doesn't solve the problem shown in Figure 3-2. When the user resizes a form, it would be nice if the controls changed their sizes to match.

The Anchor property lets a Windows Forms control resize itself when its container resizes. This property can take one or more of the values Top, Bottom, Left, and Right, in any combination. These values indicate that the control's edge should remain the same distance from the corresponding edge of its container.

For example, initially a control's Anchor property is set to Top, Left so it remains the same distance from its container's top and left edges. If you resize the form, the control doesn't move.

For a more interesting example, suppose you place a TextBox on a form, set its Multiline property to True, arrange it so its edges are 12 pixels from the edges of the form, and set its Anchor property to Top, Bottom, Left, Right. Then when you resize the form, the TextBox resizes itself so all of its edges remain 12 pixels from the form's corresponding edges.

> **NOTE** *If an* Anchor's *values don't include either* Left/Right *or* Top/Bottom, *the control moves to keep itself the same distance from the middle of the form. For example, if a* Button's Anchor *property is* Bottom, *it moves so it remains the same distance from the horizontal middle of the form.*
>
> *This fact lets you keep one or more controls centered. For example, place several* Buttons *near the bottom of a form and choose Format ➪ Center in Form ➪ Horizontally to center them horizontally. Now if you set their* Anchor *properties to* Bottom, *the group of* Buttons *remains centered when the form resizes.*

> **NOTE** *The* Anchor *property cannot resize a control such as a* Label *or* LinkLabel *if that control has* AutoSize *set to* True. *In that case, the control has its own ideas about how big it should be.*

To set the Anchor property at design time, you can type a value like Top, Left, Right into the Properties window or you can use the Properties window's Anchor editor.

To use the editor, click the Anchor property in the Properties window. Then click the dropdown arrow to the right to make the editor shown in Figure 3-4 appear. Click the skinny rectangles to select or deselect the anchors that you want to use. (In Figure 3-4 the top, bottom, and right anchors are selected.) When you're finished, press Enter to accept your changes or Esc to cancel them.

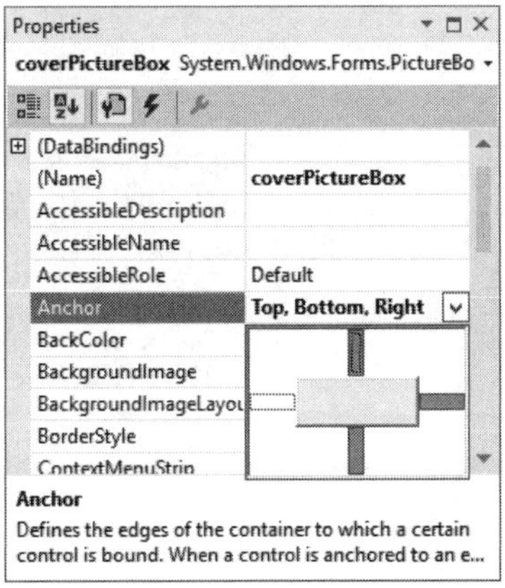

FIGURE 3-4

Using the `Anchor` property, you can solve the problem shown in Figure 3-2. Table 3-1 gives the `Anchor` property values used by the controls to let them take advantage of the form's available space.

TABLE 3-1

CONTROL	ANCHOR PROPERTY
`booksListBox`	`Top, Bottom, Left`
`detailsGroupBox`	`Top, Bottom, Left, Right`
`titleTextBox`	`Top, Left, Right`
`authorTextBox`	`Top, Left, Right`
`isbnTextBox`	`Top, Left, Right`
`urlLinkLabel`	`Top, Left, Right`
`coverPictureBox`	`Top, Bottom, Right`

Now when the form resizes:

➤ The `ListBox` stretches vertically to match the form's height.

➤ The `GroupBox` stretches vertically and horizontally to use as much of the form's width and height as possible.

➤ The `TextBoxes` and `LinkLabel` stretch horizontally to be as wide as possible while still fitting inside the `GroupBox`.

➤ The `PictureBox` moves with the `GroupBox`'s right edge so it leaves as much room as possible to the left for the `TextBoxes` and `LinkLabel`. It also stretches vertically as much as possible while fitting inside the `GroupBox`.

Figure 3-5 shows the result. Now the `ListBox` is big enough to show all of its items and the `LinkLabel` is big enough to show the entire URL.

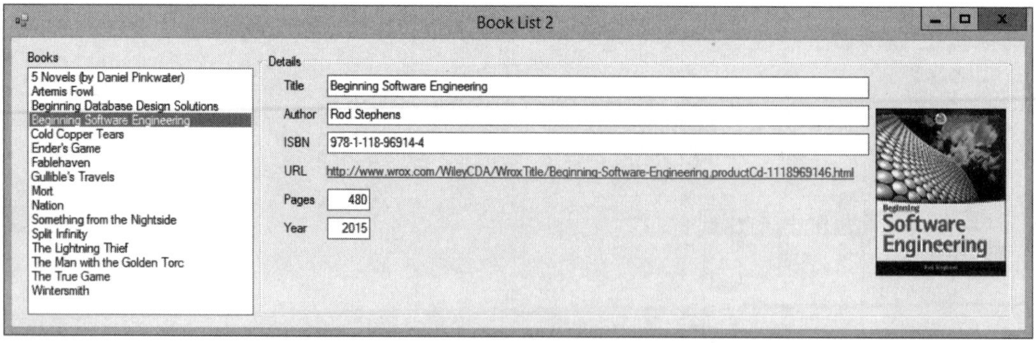

FIGURE 3-5

Note that the `TextBoxes` and `LinkLabel` do *not* stretch horizontally when the form resizes; they stretch when the `GroupBox` that contains them resizes. In this example, when the form stretches, the `GroupBox` stretches, and when the `GroupBox` stretches, the `TextBoxes` and `LinkLabel` stretch, so the result is the same.

USING DOCK PROPERTIES

The `Anchor` property can handle most of your arranging needs, but some combinations of `Anchor` values are so common that C# provides another property to let you handle these situations more easily: `Dock`. The `Dock` property lets you tell a control to attach itself to one of the edges of its container.

For example, a menu typically stretches across the top of a form. You could provide that behavior by setting the menu's `Anchor` property to `Top, Left, Right`, but setting `Dock` to `Top` is even easier.

The `Dock` property can take one of six values. `Left`, `Right`, `Top`, and `Bottom` attach the control to the corresponding edge of its container. `Fill` makes the control take up any space left over after any other controls' `Dock` properties have had their way. `None` detaches the control so its `Anchor` property can take over.

> **NOTE** *The `Dock` property cannot resize a control such as a `Label` or `LinkLabel` if that control has `AutoSize` set to `True`.*

The `Dock` property processes positioning requests in a first-come-first-served order based on the controls' stacking order on the form. In other words, it positions the first control that it draws first. The second control positions itself in whatever space is left over. Then the third control positions itself in the remaining space, and so on.

Normally the stacking order is determined by the order in which you add controls to the form, but you can change the order by right-clicking a control and selecting Bring to Front or Send to Back. However, if you're working with a complicated set of `Dock` properties and the stacking order gets messed up, it's often easier to delete all of the controls and start over from scratch.

Figure 3-6 shows a form holding five docked `Labels` (with `AutoSize = False`). The numbers in the controls' `Text` properties give the order in which they were created, which is also their stacking order.

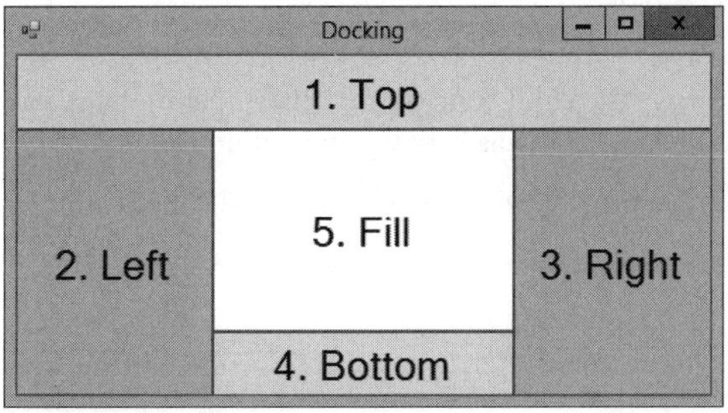

FIGURE 3-6

The following list explains how the form's space was divvied up among the Labels:

1. The first Label has Dock = Top, so it took the full width of the top part of the form.

2. The second Label has Dock = Left, so it took the left edge of the remaining area (after the first Label was positioned).

3. The third Label has Dock = Right, so it took the right edge of the remaining area.

4. The fourth Label has Dock = Bottom, so it took the bottom edge of the remaining area.

5. The final Label has Dock = Fill, so it filled all of the remaining area.

DOCKED MENUS

In one typical docking scenario, a form contains a MenuStrip with Dock = Top and a container such as a Panel with Dock = Fill so it takes up the rest of the form. All of the other controls are placed inside the Panel.

You can also add ToolStrips, ToolStripContainers, and StatusBars with the appropriate Dock properties to put those controls in their correct places. Figure 3-7 shows a form holding a MenuStrip (Dock = Top), a ToolStripContainer (Dock = Top) containing two ToolStrips, a StatusStrip (Dock = Bottom), and a Panel (Dock = Fill). I made the Panel slightly darker so it's easy to see where it is.

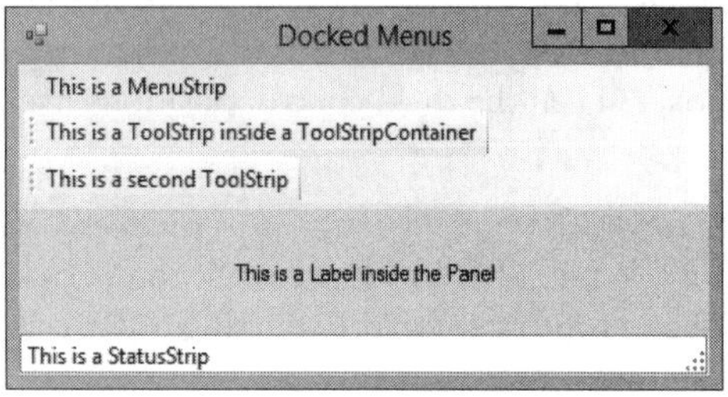

FIGURE 3-7

LAYOUT CONTAINERS

Visual Studio provides several controls that arrange the child controls that they contain in different ways. For example, the WPF Grid control can arrange controls in rows and columns.

The following sections summarize layout containers for Windows Forms and WPF applications.

Windows Forms Controls

Windows Forms applications use only a few layout controls. Often most of a form's controls are placed directly on the form.

The following list summarizes the most useful Windows Forms layout controls.

➤ Form—The form itself is a layout container that lets you arrange controls by setting their Top, Left, Width, Height, Anchor, and Dock properties.

➤ FlowLayoutPanel—Arranges controls left to right, right to left, top to bottom, or bottom to top, wrapping to new rows or columns if necessary.

➤ Panel—Lets you arrange controls much as a form does by setting their Top, Left, Width, Height, Anchor, and Dock properties.

➤ TableLayoutPanel—Lets you arrange controls in rows and columns. Set a control's RowSpan and ColumnSpan properties to let it span multiple rows or columns.

Those few controls let you arrange controls very flexibly.

WPF Controls

> **NOTE** *If you're focusing on Windows Forms applications for now, skip this section and come back to it later.*

WPF applications use a different control arrangement philosophy than the one used by Windows Forms applications. In a Windows Forms application, a control's Anchor and Dock properties arrange that control as needed. In contrast, a WPF application typically uses containers to arrange controls.

For example, in a Windows Forms application, you might make a collection of Labels and TextBoxes and line them up neatly in two columns and five rows. In contrast, in a WPF application you might create a Grid control with two columns and five rows. You would then place Labels and TextBoxes inside the Grid's rows and columns. When the Grid's rows and columns resize, the controls they contain resize.

The following list summarizes some of the most useful WPF container controls:

➤ Canvas—A simple control that lets you specify a control's X and Y positions.

➤ DockPanel—Lets you dock child controls to the left, right, top, and bottom edges. If the LastChildFill property is True, the last child fills the remaining area.

➤ Grid—Lets you arrange controls in rows and columns.

➤ StackPanel—Arranges child controls vertically in a column or horizontally in a row.

➤ WrapPanel—Arranges child controls vertically or horizontally much as a StackPanel does except it wraps to a new column or row if necessary.

For example, to make a layout similar to the one shown in Figure 3-5, you might use a Grid that defines two columns. The left column could hold a vertical StackPanel containing a Label and the ListBox. The right column could hold a GroupBox containing a second Grid that uses rows and columns to arrange the Labels, TextBoxes, and Image.

> **NOTE** *You can click a* Grid*'s borders to define rows and columns, but it's sometimes easier to edit them in the XAML Code Editor. For example, that lets you easily make rows have exactly the same size.*
>
> *Set a row or column's size to* * *to make it use any space not claimed by other rows or columns. If multiple rows/columns have* * *sizes, they split the available space. For example, if one row has a height of* * *and another has a height of* 2**, then the first gets a third of the available space and the second gets two thirds of the available space.*

After you define the StackPanels, Grids, and other containers, you can add Labels, TextBoxes, and other content controls to them.

Set a control's Margin property to make it resize with its container. For example, Margin="10,7,10,0" keeps a control's left, top, right, and bottom distances 10, 7, 10, and 0 pixels from its container's corresponding edges.

Set a control's Width and Height properties to give it a fixed size.

When you resize controls in the Window editor, you can click the symbols by the edges of a control's container to lock the sides of the control to the container's sides.

Arranging controls in this way can take a lot of work. Sometimes it's easier to just type XAML code in the Code Editor instead of using the interactive Window editor. However, the result is usually quite flexible and allows the controls to resize when the window resizes.

TRY IT

In this Try It, you get to practice using the Anchor and Dock properties by building the application shown in Figure 3-8.

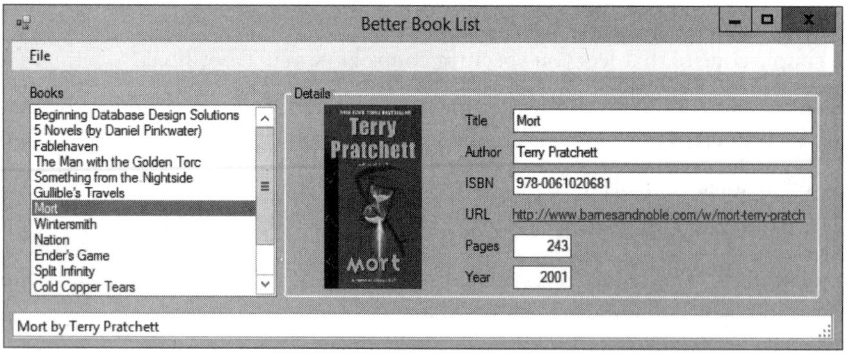

FIGURE 3-8

When the window resizes, the `TextBoxes` and `LinkLabel` stretch horizontally, and the `PictureBox` stretches vertically. Notice in Figure 3-8 that the cover image is rather tall and thin. When the `PictureBox` grows taller, it can display a larger version of the cover image. The control displays the image as large as possible without distorting it.

Note that the program you build won't actually do anything except sit there looking pretty and resizing controls when the form resizes. The techniques you need to make it respond to list selections are covered in later lessons.

Lesson Requirements

In this lesson, you:

➤ Create the program's three main controls: a `MenuStrip`, a `StatusStrip`, and a `Panel`. Use `Dock` properties to make these three controls stay in their proper positions.

➤ Add controls to the `Panel`.

➤ Use the `Anchor` property to make the `ListBox` stretch vertically when the form resizes.

➤ Use `Anchor` properties to make the `TextBoxes` and `LinkLabel` stretch horizontally when the form resizes.

➤ Use `Anchor` properties to make the `PictureBox` resize vertically when the form resizes.

> **NOTE** *You can download the code and resources for this lesson from the website at* www.wrox.com/go/csharp24hourtrainer2e.

Hints

➤ Remember that the `TextBoxes` and `LinkLabel` stretch with the `GroupBox` that contains them, not with the form itself. If you don't make the `GroupBox` stretch, the controls it contains won't either.

➤ To make the File menu, add a `MenuStrip` to the form, select it, click the Type Here box that appears, and type **&File**. (The ampersand makes the "F" underlined.) Making the menu do something useful is covered in Lesson 5, so don't worry about that right now.

➤ To make the status strip label, add a `StatusStrip` to the form and select it. Click the little dropdown arrow on the `StatusStrip` and select `StatusLabel`. Click the new `StatusLabel` and use the Properties window to set its `Text` to **This is a StatusStrip**.

➤ Add some items to the `ListBox`, add a picture to the `PictureBox`, and add text to the other controls, but don't worry about making the program take any actions.

Step-by-Step

➤ Create the program's three main controls: a MenuStrip, a StatusStrip, and a Panel. Use Dock properties to make these three controls stay in their proper positions.

    1.   Start a new project named Better Book List. Set the form's Size and MinimumSize properties to 726, 286.

    2.   Add a MenuStrip to the form. (Notice that by default the MenuStrip has Dock = Top.) Use the MenuStrip hint from the "Hints" section of this lesson to create the empty File menu.

    3.   Add a StatusStrip to the form. (Notice that by default the StatusStrip has Dock = Bottom.) Use the StatusStrip hint from the "Hints" section of this lesson to create the **This is a StatusStrip** label.

    4.   Add a Panel to the form. Set its Dock property to Fill. Set its BackColor property to light green.

➤ Add controls to the Panel.

    1.   Add controls to the form in roughly the positions shown in Figure 3-8.

    2.   Set the LinkLabel's AutoSize property to False and make it the same size as the TextBoxes.

    3.   Enter some Text values in the TextBoxes and LinkLabel so you have something to look at. Enter enough items in the ListBox so they won't all fit when the form has its initial size.

    4.   Set the PictureBox's SizeMode property to Zoom. Place a relatively tall, thin image in its Image property.

➤ Use the Anchor property to make the ListBox stretch vertically when the form resizes.

    1.   Set the ListBox's Anchor property to Top, Bottom, Left.

➤ Use Anchor properties to make the TextBoxes and LinkLabel stretch horizontally when the form resizes.

    1.   Set the GroupBox's Anchor property to Top, Bottom, Left, Right.

    2.   Set the TextBoxes' and the LinkLabel's Anchor properties to Top, Left, Right.

➤ Use Anchor properties to make the PictureBox resize vertically when the form resizes.

    1.   Set the PictureBox's Anchor property to Top, Bottom, Left.

Run the program and see what happens when you resize the form.

EXERCISES

    1.   [WPF] Repeat the Try It with a WPF application.

2. Make a New Customer dialog similar to the one shown in Figure 3-9. Make the First Name, Last Name, Street, City, and Email TextBoxes resize horizontally when the form resizes. Use the OK and Cancel buttons as the form's accept and cancel buttons, and attach them to the form's lower-right corner.

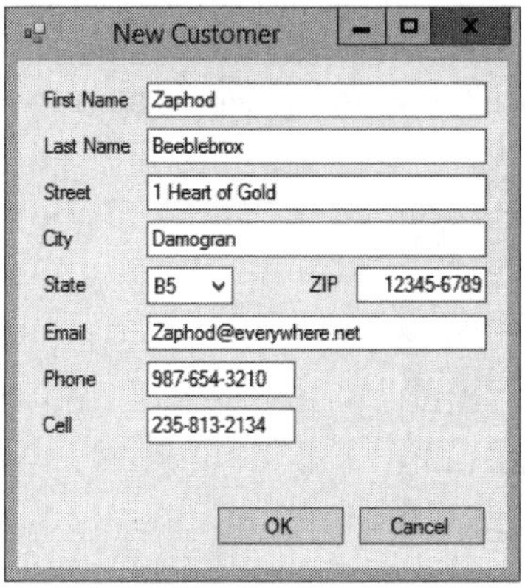

FIGURE 3-9

3. [WPF, Hard] Repeat Exercise 2 with a WPF application. Hints:

    ➤ Replace the window's initial Grid with a DockPanel. Add a Menu (docked to the top), a StatusBar (docked to the bottom), and a Grid (filling the rest of the DockPanel).

    ➤ Use the XAML editor to add a StatusBarItem inside the StatusBar. Inside the StatusBarItem add a Label.

    ➤ Give the Grid two columns. In the left column, place a Label and a ListBox. Set the ListBox's Height = Auto and use its Items property editor to add several ListBoxItems. Then use the XAML editor to add Labels to the ListBoxItems. For example, one of the ListBoxItems might look like this:

    ```
    <ListBoxItem>
        <Label Content="Beginning Database Design Solutions"/>
    </ListBoxItem>
    ```

    ➤ Add a GroupBox to the Grid's right column. A GroupBox can have only a single child control. Make it a Grid and give it the rows and columns you need to display the Image, Labels, and TextBoxes.

    A final tip: often it's easier to make one control just the way you want it and then copy and paste it in the XAML Code Editor. Don't forget to change the new control's name so you don't have two controls with the same name.

4. [SimpleEdit] Create a new project named SimpleEdit. Give it a MenuStrip and StatusStrip with appropriate (default) Dock values. Add a RichTextBox control and set its Dock property to Fill. (That's all for now. In later lessons you'll add features to this program.)

5. [WPF, SimpleEdit] Repeat Exercise 4 with a WPF application.

6. The `SplitContainer` control displays two areas separated by a splitter. The user can drag the splitter to divide the available space between the two areas. Make a program similar to the one shown in Figure 3-10. Feel free to use a different picture and information. Make the `PictureBox` display its image as large as possible without distortion. Set the bottom `TextBox`'s `MultiLine` property to `True` and make it stretch vertically and horizontally as the form resizes. Make the other `TextBox`es stretch horizontally. Set the `SplitContainer`'s `Panel1MinSize` and `Panel2MinSize` properties to `100`.

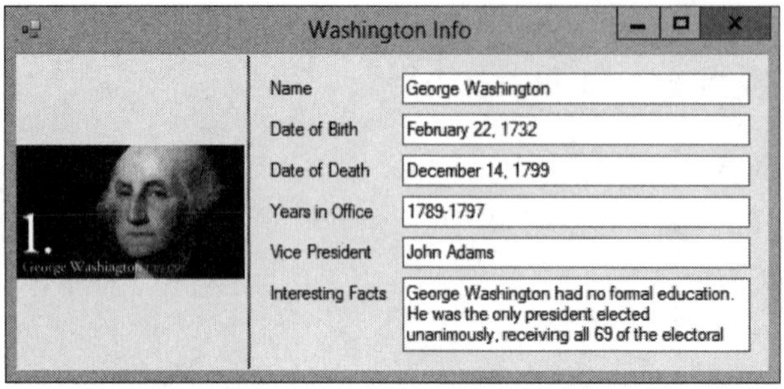

FIGURE 3-10

7. [WPF] Repeat Exercise 6 with a WPF application. Hints: To make a splitter in WPF, create a `Grid` control. Then add a `GridSplitter` to one of its rows or columns. The user can drag the `GridSplitter` to resize the rows or columns on either side of it.

    For this program, make a `Grid` with three columns that have widths 1*, 5, and 2*. Place an `Image` in the left column, a `GridSplitter` in the middle column, and another `Grid` in the right column.

    Then make the `GridSplitter`'s XAML code look like this:

    ```
    <GridSplitter Grid.Column="1" Margin="0,0,0,0"
        HorizontalAlignment="Stretch" VerticalAlignment="Stretch"/>
    ```

    Place the appropriate `Label`s and `TextBox`es in the `Grid` on the right. Use the "Interesting Facts" `Label`'s `Margin` and `VerticalContentAlignment` properties to make its text stay centered in its area when you resize the form.

8. Make a form similar to the one shown in Figure 3-11. When the form resizes, the three `ListBox`es should be as large as possible and the three columns should divide the form evenly. (Hint: Use a `TableLayoutPanel`.)

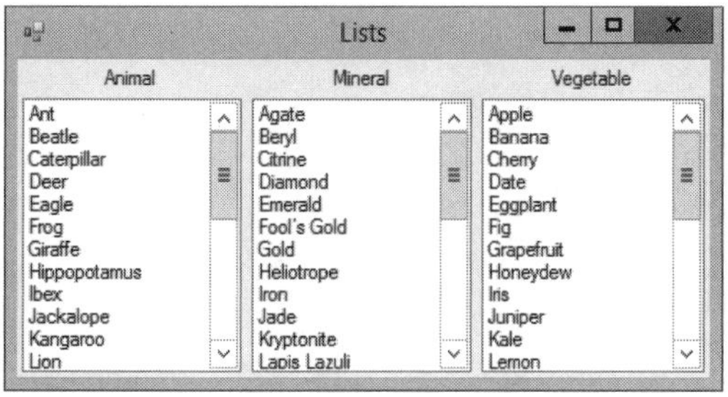

FIGURE 3-11

9. [WPF] Repeat Exercise 8 with a WPF application.

10. [WPF] One of the cooler new controls in WPF is the `Expander`. It displays a header and an expander arrow. When the user clicks the arrow, the `Expander` expands to display a child control, which is normally a `Grid`.

    Make a WPF program similar to the one shown in Figure 3-12. In that figure, the `Expander` for Jupiter is expanded and the `Expanders` for the other planets are collapsed. (Hints: The `Window` in Figure 3-12 contains a `StackPanel` that contains `Expanders` holding `Grids`. First create the `StackPanel`. Next make the `Expander` and child controls for Mercury. Then copy and paste that `Expander` in the XAML editor to make the `Expanders` for the other planets.)

FIGURE 3-12

NOTE *Please select the videos for Lesson 3 online at* `www.wrox.com/go/csharp24hourtrainer2evideos`.

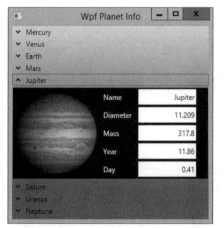

4

Handling Events

An *event* is something that a control raises to tell the program that something significant has happened. Events are extremely important because they are the main way the user controls the program. When the user clicks buttons, drags sliders, and selects menu items, events tell the program that something has happened so it can take action.

An *event handler* is a piece of code that *catches* the event and executes when an event occurs. The event handler might display a message, perform a calculation, or download the latest *Dilbert* comic from the web.

Lesson 2 briefly explained how you can catch a `Button`'s `Click` event, but that event is only one of hundreds (if not thousands) of events that your programs can catch.

This lesson explains how you can catch events other than `Click`. It describes some of the most useful events provided by common controls and, as a bonus, explains how you can display messages to the user when events occur.

MAKING EVENT HANDLERS

The easiest way to build an event handler is to double-click a control in the Form Designer. This creates an empty event handler for the control's default event and opens the event handler in the Code Editor. You can then type C# code to take whatever action is appropriate.

The following code shows the empty `Click` event handler created for a `Button`:

```
private void crashSystemButton_Click(object sender, EventArgs e)
{

}
```

Probably the most commonly used events are the `Click` events raised by `Buttons`, `ToolStripMenuItems` (which represent menu items), and `ToolStripButtons` (which represent toolbar buttons). For these controls and many others, you almost always want to use the default event handler, so double-clicking them is the easiest way to go.

> **NOTE** *If you're not ready to write the real event handler code, you can write a placeholder event handler. One easy way to do that is to use* `MessageBox.Show` *to display a message. For example, the following code displays a placeholder message for the File menu's Save command:*
>
> ```
> private void fileSaveMenuItem_Click(object sender, EventArgs e)
> {
>     MessageBox.Show("File > Save not yet implemented");
> }
> ```
>
> *Lesson 8 describes message boxes in greater detail.*

Most controls provide dozens of other events that you can catch. To create an event handler for one of these non-default events, select the control in the Form Designer. Then click the lightning bolt icon near the top of the Properties window to make the window list the control's events. Figure 4-1 shows the Properties window displaying some of the events that a `Button` can raise.

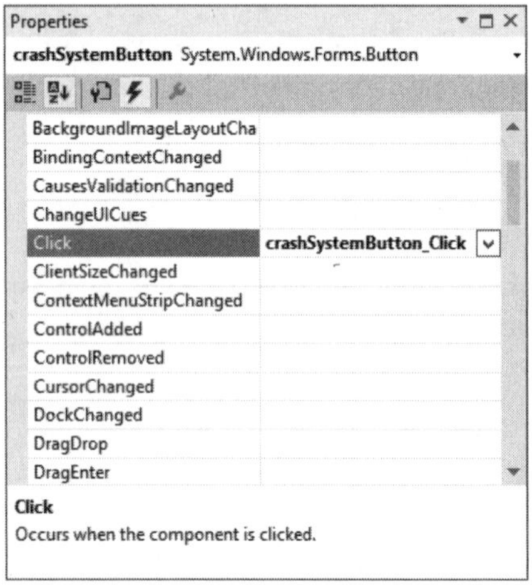

FIGURE 4-1

To create an empty event handler for an event, simply double-click the event's name in the Properties window's event list.

You can also type the name that you want to give the event handler. When you press Enter, Visual Studio creates the event handler and opens it in the Code Editor.

If your code already contains event handlers that could handle the event, you can click the event and then click the dropdown arrow to the right to select one of those event handlers.

USING EVENT PARAMETERS

All event handlers include parameters that give additional information about the event. Later lessons say more about parameters and how you can use them, but for now you should know that sometimes they can tell you more about the event.

For example, the following code shows a Button's Click event handler. The parameters sender and e give extra information about the event.

```
private void crashSystemButton_Click(object sender, EventArgs e)
{

}
```

In all event handlers, the sender parameter tells you what control raised the event. In this example, that's the Button control that the user clicked.

The e parameter has the EventArgs data type, which doesn't give you a lot of additional information. Fortunately, you usually don't need any additional information for a Button. Just knowing it was clicked is enough.

Some event handlers, however, provide really useful information in their e parameter. For example, the e parameter provided by the mouse events MouseClick, MouseMove, MouseDown, and MouseUp include the X and Y coordinates of the mouse over the control raising the event. Those values are crucial if you're trying to build a drawing application or need to track the mouse's position for some other reason.

The FollowMouse example program shown in Figure 4-2 uses a MouseMove event handler to make two scrollbars follow the mouse's position. When you click the area in the center of the form, the program moves the picture of the mouse to that position.

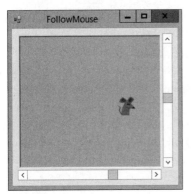

FIGURE 4-2

The program's form contains a green Panel control that holds a PictureBox holding the mouse image. The form also contains VScrollBar and HScrollBar controls. The program uses event handlers to do three things: set scrollbar properties, track mouse movement, and move the mouse picture.

Setting Scrollbar Properties

When you create a new scrollbar, it has Minimum = 0 and Maximum = 100 so it can take values between 0 and 100. However, this program sets its scrollbars to locations on the Panel control. For example, if the Panel is 200 pixels wide, the program might need to give the horizontal scrollbar a value between 0 and 199. Unfortunately if the scroll's Maximum property is 100 and the program sets its value to 199, the program will crash.

To prevent that, the program sets the scrollbars' Maximum properties to the width and height of the Panel. The Panel might resize at two different times, so the program needs to set the Maximum properties in two places.

First, when the program's form is initially displayed, the program needs to set the scrollbar Maximum properties. To detect when the form is displayed, you can catch the form's Load event.

> **NOTE** Load *is the default event for a form, so you can double-click the form to create a* Load *event handler.*

The following code shows the program's Load event handler:

```
// Set the scrollbar maximums to fit the Panel.
private void Form1_Load(object sender, EventArgs e)
{
    mouseHScrollBar.Maximum = fieldPanel.Width;
    mouseVScrollBar.Maximum = fieldPanel.Height;
}
```

This code sets the mouseHScrollBar control's Maximum property to the width of the Panel. It then sets the mouseVScrollBar control's Maximum property to the height of the Panel.

Now the program won't crash when you move the mouse around over the Panel control, unless you resize the form. The Panel control's Anchor property makes it resize with the form, so if you make the form bigger, the Panel gets bigger, too. In that case, the program needs to reset the scrollbars' Maximum properties to match.

You can do that in the form's Resize event. This isn't the default event for a form (Load is), so you can't just double-click the form to create a Resize event handler. Instead you need to select the form, go to the Properties window, click the Events button (the little lightning bolt), and double-click the Resize event.

The following code shows this program's Resize event handler:

```
private void Form1_Resize(object sender, EventArgs e)
{
    mouseHScrollBar.Maximum = fieldPanel.Width;
    mouseVScrollBar.Maximum = fieldPanel.Height;
}
```

This code does the same thing as the form's Load event handler.

Now even if you resize the form, the scrollbars can hold the coordinates of any point inside the Panel.

Tracking Mouse Movement

When you move the mouse over the Panel, the Panel control raises a MouseMoved event. For this program, I used the Properties window to create the following MouseMove event handler:

```
// Move the scrollbars to track the mouse.
private void fieldPanel_MouseMove(object sender, MouseEventArgs e)
{
    mouseHScrollBar.Value = e.X;
    mouseVScrollBar.Value = e.Y;
}
```

This code sets the horizontal scrollbar's value equal to the mouse's X position as reported by the event handler's e.X parameter. It then sets the vertical scrollbar's value equal to the mouse's Y position as reported by the event handler's e.Y parameter.

> **NOTE** *In C#, coordinates are measured with (0, 0) in the upper-left corner, X increasing to the right, and Y increasing downward.*

> **WARNING** *As the program is currently written, if you click and drag the mouse off of the* Panel, *the* Panel *receives* MouseMove *events with coordinates that are outside of the values allowed by the* ScrollBars *so the program crashes. For now, don't do that. In Lesson 18 you'll learn how to use tests to protect the program from that problem.*

The form's Load and Resize event handlers guarantee that the scrollbars' Maximum properties are big enough to hold any coordinates on the Panel.

Moving the Mouse Picture

When you click the Panel, the Panel raises a MouseClick event. For this program, I used the Properties window to create the following MouseClick event handler:

```
// Move the mouse PictureBox to the point clicked.
private void fieldPanel_MouseClick(object sender, MouseEventArgs e)
{
    mousePictureBox.Left = e.X;
    mousePictureBox.Top = e.Y;
}
```

This code simply sets the mouse PictureBox's Left and Top properties to the coordinates of the point that was clicked.

That's all there is to the program. If you like, you can download it and experiment with it.

REMOVING EVENT HANDLERS

Getting rid of an event handler isn't as simple as you might like. If you just delete the event handler's code, the program still includes automatically generated code that attaches the event handler to the control that raises it. When you try to move to the Form Designer, you'll get an error similar to:

> The designer cannot process unknown name 'fieldPanel_MouseClick' at line 51. The code within the method 'InitializeComponent' is generated by the designer and should not be manually modified. Please remove any changes and try opening the designer again.

All this really means is that C# is confused.

The Properties window gives you an easy way to safely remove event handlers. *Before* you delete the event handler's code, find the event handler in the Properties window. Right-click the event handler's name and select Reset to break the link between the event handler and the control. Now you can safely remove the event handler's code.

Alternatively, you can double-click the error in the Error window to see the automatically generated code that's making C# throw its temper tantrum. The line should look something like this:

```
this.fieldPanel.MouseClick +=
    new System.Windows.Forms.MouseEventHandler(this.fieldPanel_MouseClick);
```

Delete that line and you should be ready to run again.

> **WARNING** *Don't fool around inside the automatically generated code! If you accidentally mess up that code, you may remove controls from the form, change properties, or even make the form unloadable so you have to throw it away. Get in, delete that single line, and get out before you do any serious damage.*

WPF programs attach event handlers a bit differently. In a WPF application, the XAML code includes a property that defines the name of the event handler in C# code. For example, the following XAML code defines a button with a `Click` event handler:

```
<Button x:Name="clickMeButton" Content="Click Me"
    Width="75" Height="20" Click="clickMeButton_Click"/>
```

If you remove the event handler's C# code, you should also remove `Click="clickMeButton_Click"` from the XAML code.

ADDING AND REMOVING EVENT HANDLERS IN CODE

At design time, you can use the Properties window to attach and detach event handlers. Occasionally you may want to add or remove an event handler by using code at run time.

The following code shows a simple `Button Click` event handler. When this event handler executes, it displays a message to the user:

```
// Display a message box.
private void clickMeButton_Click(object sender, EventArgs e)
{
    MessageBox.Show("You clicked me!");
}
```

Suppose you have written this event handler but have not attached it to any control at design time. The following code attaches the event handler to the `clickMeButton` control's `Click` event:

```
clickMeButton.Click += clickMeButton_Click;
```

The `+=` operator means "add to," so this code adds the event handler to the `clickMeButton.Click` event.

After running this code, if the user clicks the `clickMeButton`, the event handler executes.

The following code removes the event handler from the button's `Click` event:

```
clickMeButton.Click -= clickMeButton_Click;
```

The `-=` operator means "subtract from," so this code removes the event handler from the `clickMeButton.Click` event.

The DynamicEvents example program shown in Figure 4-3 lets you add and remove event handlers at run time. Initially the Click Me button does nothing. Click the Attach button to attach an event handler to the Click Me button. Click the Detach button to remove the event handler.

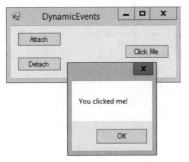

FIGURE 4-3

USEFUL EVENTS

Table 4-1 lists some of the more useful events raised by various controls.

TABLE 4-1

EVENT	MEANING
CheckedChanged	A `CheckBox`'s or `RadioButton`'s checked state has changed.
Click	The user has clicked the control.
FormClosing	The form is about to close. Set the `e.Cancel` parameter to `true` to cancel the closing and force the form to remain open.
KeyDown	The user pressed a key down while this control had focus.
KeyPress	The user pressed and released a key while this control had focus.
KeyUp	The user released a key while this control had focus.
Load	The form is loaded but not yet visible. This is the last place you can change the form's appearance before the user sees it.
MouseClick	The user pressed and released a mouse button over the control. Unlike the `Click` event, this event has parameters that give the click's location.
MouseDown	The user pressed a mouse button down over the control.
MouseEnter	The mouse entered the control.
MouseHover	The mouse hovered over the control.
MouseLeave	The mouse left the control.
MouseMove	The mouse moved while over the control.
MouseUp	The user released a mouse button over the control.
Move	The control has moved.
Paint	The control needs to be redrawn. (This is useful for drawing graphics.)
Resize	The control has resized.
Scroll	The slider on a `TrackBar` or scrollbar was moved by the user.
SelectedIndexChanged	A `ComboBox`'s or `ListBox`'s selection has changed.
TextChanged	The control's `Text` property has changed. (This is particularly useful for `TextBoxes`.)
Tick	A `Timer` control's `Interval` has elapsed.
ValueChanged	The value of a `TrackBar` or scrollbar has changed (whether by the user or by code).

TRY IT

In this Try It, you use event handlers to display color samples as the user adjusts red, green, and blue scrollbars.

Figure 4-4 shows the finished program in action. When you change a scrollbar's value, the label to the right shows the color component's new numeric value, and the large label on the far right shows a sample of the color with the selected red, green, and blue color components.

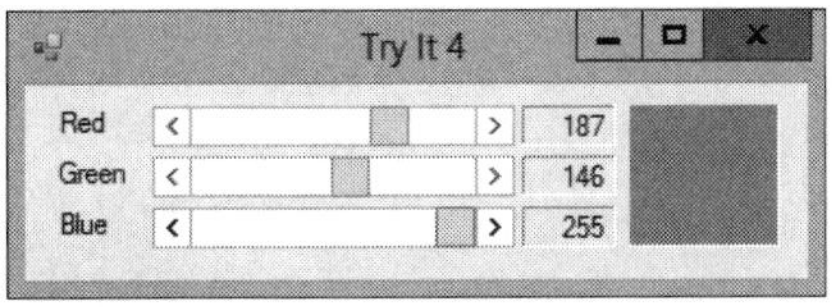

FIGURE 4-4

Lesson Requirements

In this lesson, you:

➤ Create the form shown in Figure 4-4. Arrange the controls and set their `Anchor` properties.

➤ Make an event handler for the red scrollbar that displays all three color values and the color sample.

➤ Attach the event handler to the green and blue scrollbars, as well as the red one.

> **NOTE** *You can download the code and resources for this lesson from the website at* `www.wrox.com/go/csharp24hourtrainer2e`.

Hints

This Try It requires a few techniques that haven't been covered yet, but it's not too hard to build with a couple of hints.

➤ A scrollbar's `Value` property is an integer. To convert it into a string so you can display it in a label, call its `ToString` method. For example, the following code makes the `redLabel` control display the `redHScrollBar`'s `Value` property:

```
redLabel.Text = redHScrollBar.Value.ToString();
```

➤ The `Color` class's `FromArgb` method returns a color with given red, green, and blue color components between 0 and 255. For example, `Color.FromArgb(255, 128, 0)` returns the color orange (red = 255, green = 128, and blue = 0). Pass this method the values selected by the scrollbars (returned by their `Value` properties) and assign the result to the sample label's `BackColor` property.

Step-by-Step

➤ Create the form shown in Figure 4-4. Arrange the controls and set their Anchor properties.

   1. Create the controls as shown in Figure 4-4. For the scrollbars, set Minimum = 0, Maximum = 264, SmallChange = 1, LargeChange = 10, and Anchor = Top, Left, Right.

> **NOTE** *For some bizarre reason, the largest value that a user can select with a scrollbar is* Maximum - LargeChange + 1. *If* Maximum = 264 *and* LargeChange = 10, *the largest selectable value is 264 – 10 + 1 = 255, so these properties let the user select values between 0 and 255.*

➤ Make an event handler for the red scrollbar that displays all three color values and the color sample.

   1. Double-click the red scrollbar to create an empty event handler for the control's Scroll event. Type the bold lines in the following code so the event handler looks like this:

```
// Display a color sample.
private void redHScrollBar_Scroll(object sender, ScrollEventArgs e)
{
    redLabel.Text = redHScrollBar.Value.ToString();
    greenLabel.Text = greenHScrollBar.Value.ToString();
    blueLabel.Text = blueHScrollBar.Value.ToString();
    sampleLabel.BackColor = Color.FromArgb(
        redHScrollBar.Value,
        greenHScrollBar.Value,
        blueHScrollBar.Value);
}
```

The first three lines of code make the Labels display the corresponding scrollbar values. The final statement, which is split across four lines of code, sets the sample Label's BackColor property to a color defined by the scrollbars' values.

➤ Attach the event handler to the green and blue scrollbars, as well as the red one.

   1. In the Form Designer, click the green scrollbar. In the Properties window, click the event button (the lightning bolt). Then click the control's Scroll event, click the drop-down arrow to the right, and select the event handler you already created.

   2. Repeat the previous steps for the blue scrollbar.

Run the program and experiment with it. Note how the largest value you can select in the scrollbars is 255.

EXERCISES

   1. Build the FollowMouse example program shown in Figure 4-2.

   2. [WPF, Hard] Repeat Exercise 1 with a WPF application. WPF does several things differently (such as finding the mouse's position), so this exercise is kind of hard. Here are some hints:

➤ Use two `ScrollBar` controls, one with `Orientation = Horizontal`.

➤ Use a `Canvas` instead of a `Panel` and an `Image` instead of a `PictureBox`.

➤ Instead of catching the form's `Load` and `Resize` events, catch the `Canvas` control's `SizeChanged` event and give it the following event handler:

```
// Set the scrollbar maximums to fit the Canvas.
private void fieldCanvas_SizeChanged(object sender, SizeChangedEventArgs e)
{
    mouseHScrollBar.Maximum = e.NewSize.Width;
    mouseVScrollBar.Maximum = e.NewSize.Height;
}
```

➤ Use the following code for the `Canvas`'s `MouseMove` event handler:

```
// Move the scrollbars to track the mouse.
private void Canvas_MouseMove(object sender, MouseEventArgs e)
{
    Point location = Mouse.GetPosition(fieldCanvas);
    mouseHScrollBar.Value = location.X;
    mouseVScrollBar.Value = location.Y;
}
```

➤ Initially position the `Image` control in the `Canvas` control's upper-left corner. Then use the following `MouseDown` event handler:

```
// Move the mouse Image to the point clicked.
private void fieldCanvas_MouseDown(object sender, MouseButtonEventArgs e)
{
    Point location = Mouse.GetPosition(fieldCanvas);
    mouseImage.Margin = new Thickness(location.X, location.Y, 0, 0);
}
```

3. Build the DynamicEvents example program shown in Figure 4-3. What happens if you click Attach twice? Three times? What happens if you then click Detach once? Five times?

4. [WPF] Repeat Exercise 3 with a WPF application.

5. Create a form with one `Button` labeled "Stop" and two `Timers` named `leftTimer` and `rightTimer`. Set the `Timers`' `Interval` properties to 1000. At design time, set `leftTimer`'s `Enabled` property to True.

➤ In each `Timer`'s `Tick` event handler, disable that `Timer` and enable the other one.

➤ Make one `Timer`'s `Tick` event handler also move the `Button` to (10, 10) by setting its `Left` and `Top` properties.

➤ Make the other `Timer`'s `Tick` event handler move the `Button` to (200, 200).

➤ In the `Button`'s `Click` event handler, set `Enabled = false` for both `Timers`.

Run the program. Experiment with different values for the `Timers`' `Interval` properties. What happens if `Interval = 10`?

6. Copy the FollowMouse program you built for Exercise 1. Modify the copy so the user can adjust the scrollbars to move the `PictureBox`.

7. [WPF] Copy the program you build for Exercise 2. Modify the copy so the user can adjust the scrollbars to move the Image. (Hints: To save code, use the same event handler for both scrollbars. To prevent the mouse image from appearing on top of the scrollbars and in the small area on the window's lower-right corner, set the Canvas control's ClipToBounds property to True.)

8. Make a program similar to the one shown in Figure 4-5. When the user unchecks the Breakfast, Lunch, or Dinner checkbox, the program should disable the corresponding GroupBox.

FIGURE 4-5

Hints:

➤ Make the OK button be the form's accept button. Make the Cancel button be the form's cancel button.

➤ Blank the GroupBoxes' Text properties. Then place the CheckBoxes over the GroupBoxes where their text would go. (Be sure not to place the CheckBoxes *inside* the GroupBoxes. Try it to see why it won't work. You may need to position the CheckBoxes first and then move the GroupBoxes into position.)

➤ To enable or disable a GroupBox, set its Enabled property equal to the corresponding CheckBox's Enabled property as in the following code:

```
// Enable or disable the corresponding GroupBox.
private void breakfastCheckBox_CheckedChanged(object sender, EventArgs e)
{
    breakfastGroupBox.Enabled = breakfastCheckBox.Checked;
}
```

9. [WPF] Repeat Exercise 8 with a WPF application. Hints:

➤ A WPF CheckBox doesn't display a background so the checkboxes in this program won't cover the GroupBox borders below them. To work around that problem, place each CheckBox inside a Canvas and make the Canvas use a white background.

➤ A GroupBox can have only a single child. Give each GroupBox a StackPanel holding RadioButtons. Use the RadioButtons' Margin properties to add some spacing between the choices.

➤ The WPF `CheckBox` control doesn't have a `CheckChanged` event. Use the `Click` event instead.

➤ To enable or disable a `GroupBox`, set its `IsEnabled` property equal to the corresponding `CheckBox`'s `IsChecked.Value` property as in the following code:

```
// Enable or disable the appropriate GroupBox.
private void breakfastCheckBox_Click(object sender, RoutedEventArgs e)
{
    breakfastGroupBox.IsEnabled = breakfastCheckBox.IsChecked.Value;
}
```

➤ To set a WPF window's accept button, set the `Button`'s `IsDefault` property to `True`.

➤ To set a WPF window's cancel button, set the `Button`'s `IsCancel` property to `True`.

10. Make a program similar to the one shown in Figure 4-6.

FIGURE 4-6

➤ Create a `PictureBox` and load an image into it. Set its size to match the picture's size and set its `ScaleMode` property to `StretchImage`. (Also see what happens if you set this to `Normal`.)

➤ Position the scrollbars next to the `PictureBox`. Set their `Maximum` properties so the user can select values between 0 and the picture's width/height.

➤ Initially set the scrollbars' `Value` properties equal to the image's width/height.

➤ Make the scrollbars' `Scroll` event handlers set the `PictureBox`'s width/height equal to the scrollbars' values.

11. [WPF] Repeat Exercise 10 with a WPF application. Hints:

➤ Set the `Image` control's `Stretch` property to `Fill`. (Also see what happens if you set this to `None`.)

➤ In a WPF program, the user can set a `ScrollBar` to its `Maximum` value.

12. [WPF, Games, Hard] One thing that's hard to do in a Windows Forms application that's easy in a WPF application (at least if you set it up properly) is transforming objects. For example, it's relatively easy to scale, rotate, and skew controls. For this exercise, make a program similar to the one shown in Figure 4-7. When the user adjusts the scrollbar at the bottom, the program should rotate the image and display the angle of rotation in the `Label` in the lower right.

FIGURE 4-7

Hints:

➤ Lay out the window and its controls. Put a picture in the `Image` control. Name the label control **degreesLabel**.

➤ Use the Properties window's Transform section to rotate the `Image` by 360 degrees.

➤ Edit the XAML code to give the `rotateTransform` a property called `x:Name` with value `rotateTransform`. The `Image` control's code should look something like this:

```
<Image x:Name="image" HorizontalAlignment="Left"
    VerticalAlignment="Top" Source="ScienceGirl.png"
    Stretch="None" Grid.ColumnSpan="2"
    Margin="10,10,0,0" RenderTransformOrigin="0.5,0.5">
    <Image.RenderTransform>
        <TransformGroup>
            <ScaleTransform/>
            <SkewTransform/>
            <RotateTransform x:Name="rotateTransform" Angle="360"/>
            <TranslateTransform/>
        </TransformGroup>
    </Image.RenderTransform>
</Image>
```

➤ Make the `ScrollBar`'s `ValueChanged` event handler look like this:

```
// Rotate the Image.
private void degreesScrollBar_ValueChanged(object sender,
```

```
                    RoutedPropertyChangedEventArgs<double> e)
        {
            rotateTransform.Angle = degreesScrollBar.Value;
            degreesLabel.Content = degreesScrollBar.Value.ToString("0");
        }
```

13. [WPF] Build a WPF application with a `Grid` that contains an `Image`. Give the `Grid` a `MouseMove` event handler that moves the `Image` to the mouse's location. (Hint: By default, the window's main `Grid` has a transparent background so it won't receive mouse events correctly. To fix that, set its `Background` brush. You can use any brush as long as it's not transparent.)

14. Build a Windows Forms program that displays a `TrackBar` and an `HScrollBar`. Set their `Maximum` properties to 10, and set the scrollbar's `LargeChange` property to 1. When the controls' values change at run time, display the new values in `Labels`.

15. [WPF] Make a WPF application that displays two `Sliders` and a `ScrollBar` all with `Maximum` set to 10. Set `IsSnapToTickEnabled` to `True` for one of the `Sliders`. When the controls' values change at run time, display the new values in `Labels`.

16. Make a bar chart similar to the one shown in Figure 4-8. When you click the button, it should assign random values to the bars.

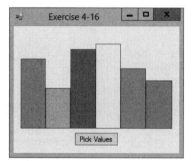

FIGURE 4-8

Hints:

➤ For the bars, use `Labels` inside a multi-column `TableLayoutPanel`.

➤ To make the `Labels` appear at the bottom of the `TableLayoutPanel`, set their `Anchor` properties to `Bottom`, `Left`, `Right`.

➤ To make the `Labels` touch, set their `Margin` properties to 0, 0, 0, 0.

➤ Use code similar to the following to give random heights to the `Labels`. Note that the statements in bold are outside of the event handler.

```
// Make a random number generator.
private Random Rand = new Random();

// Pick random values for the Labels.
private void pickValuesButton_Click(object sender, EventArgs e)
```

```
    {
        label1.Height = Rand.Next(10, 150);
        label2.Height = Rand.Next(10, 150);
        label3.Height = Rand.Next(10, 150);
        label4.Height = Rand.Next(10, 150);
        label5.Height = Rand.Next(10, 150);
        label6.Height = Rand.Next(10, 150);
    }
```

17. [WPF] Repeat Exercise 16 with a WPF application.

18. Modify the program you wrote for Exercise 16 so it uses a `Timer` to pick random `Label` heights instead of using a `Button`. Set the `Timer`'s properties `Enabled = True` and `Interval = 500`.

> **NOTE** *Please select the videos for Lesson 4 online at* www.wrox.com/go/
> csharp24hourtrainer2evideos.

5

Making Menus

In addition to buttons, labels, and textboxes, menus are one of the most common user interface elements in interactive programs. This lesson explains how to add menus and context menus to forms. It also explains how to catch their events so your program can take action when the user selects menu items.

CREATING MENUS

To create a menu, simply drop a MenuStrip control on a form. By default, the MenuStrip is docked to the top of the form so you don't really need to position it carefully. Just double-click the Toolbox's MenuStrip tool and you're set.

Unlike most controls, the MenuStrip appears in the *Component Tray* below the form in addition to appearing on the form itself. Figure 5-1 shows the SimpleEdit program in the Form Designer. Below the form you can see the Component Tray containing a MenuStrip and a StatusStrip.

When you select a MenuStrip in the Form Designer, either on the form's surface or in the Component Tray, the menu bar at the top of the form displays a Type Here box. Click that box and type the menu's caption to create a main menu.

If you create a main menu entry and then click it to select it, the Form Designer displays a new Type Here box to let you create menu items. Figure 5-2 shows the top of the Form Designer after I created the top-level File menu.

You can continue clicking menu items to add submenus as deeply as you like. Continue entering text in the Type Here boxes to build the whole menu structure. Figure 5-3 shows the Edit menu for a new version of the SimpleEdit program. Notice that the menu contains several cascading submenus. The Offset submenu is expanded in Figure 5-3.

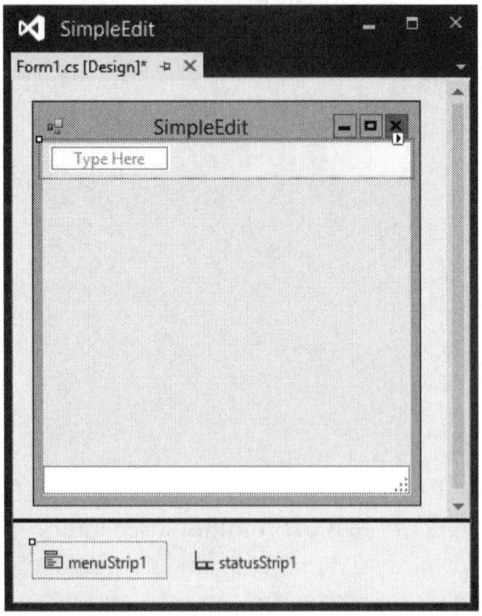

FIGURE 5-1

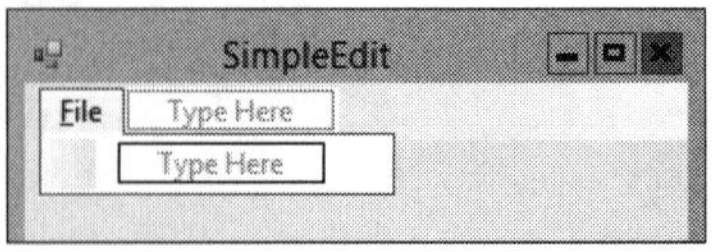

FIGURE 5-2

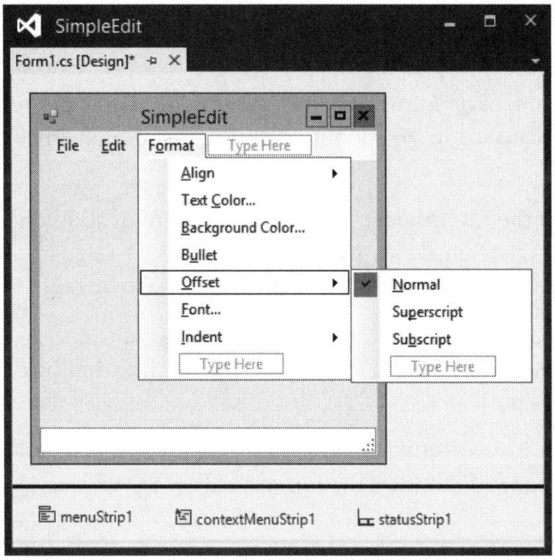

FIGURE 5-3

You can use the Type Here boxes to create submenus to any depth, although in practice three levels (as in Edit ⇨ Offset ⇨ Subscript) are about all the user can stomach.

In addition to menu items, you can place Separators, TextBoxes, and ComboBoxes in menus. TextBoxes and ComboBoxes are unusual in menus, so I won't cover them here. Separators, however, are quite useful for grouping related menu items.

To create a Separator, right-click an item, open the Insert submenu, and select Separator. Alternatively, you can create a normal menu item and set its Text to a single dash (-).

SETTING MENU PROPERTIES

The items in a menu are `ToolStripMenuItems`, and like other controls, they have properties that determine their appearance and behavior. Table 5-1 summarizes the most useful `ToolStripMenuItem` properties.

TABLE 5-1

PROPERTY	PURPOSE
Checked	Determines whether the item is checked. In Figure 5-3, the Normal item is checked. (See also `CheckOnClick`.)
CheckOnClick	If you set this to `True`, the item automatically toggles its checked state when the user selects it.
Enabled	Indicates whether the item is enabled.
Name	The `ToolStripMenuItem`'s name. Normally you should give a good name to any menu item that makes the program do something at run time so your code can refer to it.
ShortcutKeys	Indicates the item's shortcut key combination (if any). Either type a value such as **Ctrl+N** or click the dropdown arrow to the right to display the shortcut editor shown in Figure 5-4.
Text	The text that the item displays. Place an ampersand before the character that you want to use as the item's accelerator (if any). For example, if you set an item's `Text` to &Open, the item appears as <u>O</u>pen in its menu and the user can activate it by pressing Alt+O while the menu is open.

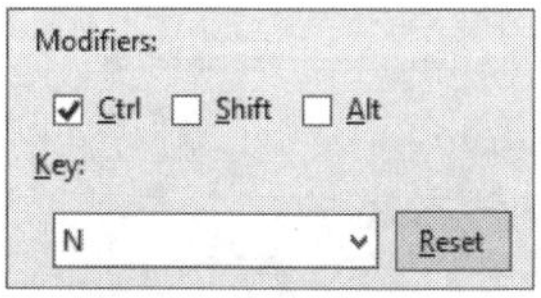

FIGURE 5-4

ESSENTIAL ELLIPSES

By convention, if a menu item opens a dialog or requires some other input from the user before proceeding, its `Text` should end with an ellipsis (...). If the menu item starts an action immediately, it should not include an ellipsis.

For example, the <u>O</u>pen... menu item displays a file open dialog, so its caption ends with an ellipsis. In contrast, the Edit menu's <u>C</u>opy item immediately copies the selected text so it doesn't need an ellipsis.

Accelerators allow the user to navigate menus with the keyboard instead of the mouse. When the user presses Alt, the menu's items display underlines below their accelerator keys. For example, if the File menu appears as File, the user can press Alt+F to open that menu and then use other accelerators to select the menu's items.

> **NOTE** *Recent versions of the Windows operating system typically don't underline menu accelerators until you press the Alt key.*

You should give accelerators to most if not all of your program's menus, submenus, and menu items. Experienced users can often navigate a menu system faster by using accelerators than they can by using the mouse.

> **WARNING** *Be sure not to give the same accelerator character to two items in the same menu. For example, in the File menu, don't have Save and Save As menu items.*

Shortcuts allow the user to instantly activate a menu item. For example, in many programs Ctrl+O opens a file and Ctrl+S saves the current file. (You can remember the difference between accelerators and shortcuts by realizing that "accelerator" and the Alt key both begin with the letter "a.")

> **WARNING** *Be extra sure not to give two menu items the same shortcut!*

> **TIP** *Use standard accelerators and shortcuts to help users learn how to use your application more quickly and with fewer mistakes. The web pages* support
> .microsoft.com/kb/126449 *and* windows.microsoft.com/en-us/windows/
> keyboard-shortcuts *list some shortcuts that Microsoft uses. I haven't seen a good list of standard accelerators, but you can try to make yours match those used by other common applications such as Visual Studio and Word.*

HANDLING MENU EVENTS

When the user clicks a menu item, its control raises a Click event exactly as a clicked Button does, and you can handle it in the same way. You can even create default event handlers in the same way: by double-clicking the control.

CREATING CONTEXT MENUS

A context menu appears when you right-click a particular control. In a Windows Forms application, using a context menu is almost as easy as using a main menu. Figure 5-5 shows an application displaying a context menu.

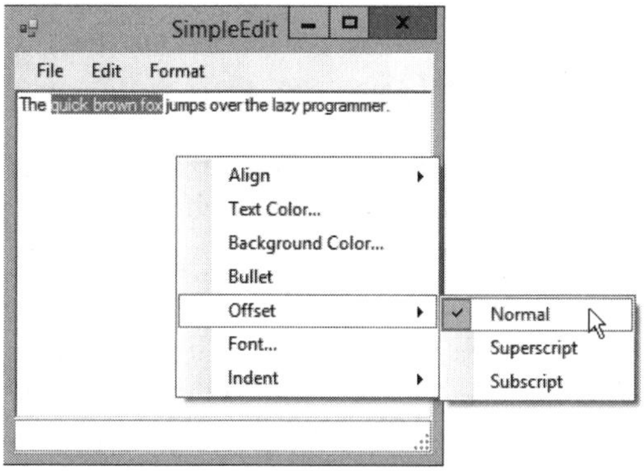

Start by dropping a `ContextMenuStrip` on the form. Like a `MenuStrip`, a `ContextMenuStrip` appears below the form in the Component Tray so you can just double-click the Toolbox's `ContextMenuStrip` tool and not worry about positioning it.

Unlike a `MenuStrip`, a `ContextMenuStrip` does not appear at the top of the form. In the Form

FIGURE 5-5

Designer, you can click a `MenuStrip` either on the form or in the Component Tray to select it. To select a `ContextMenuStrip`, you must click it in the Component Tray.

After you select the `ContextMenuStrip`, you can edit it much as you can a `MenuStrip`. The big difference is that a `ContextMenuStrip` does not have top-level menus, just submenu items.

Figure 5-6 shows the Form Designer with a `ContextMenuStrip` selected. By now the menu editor should look familiar.

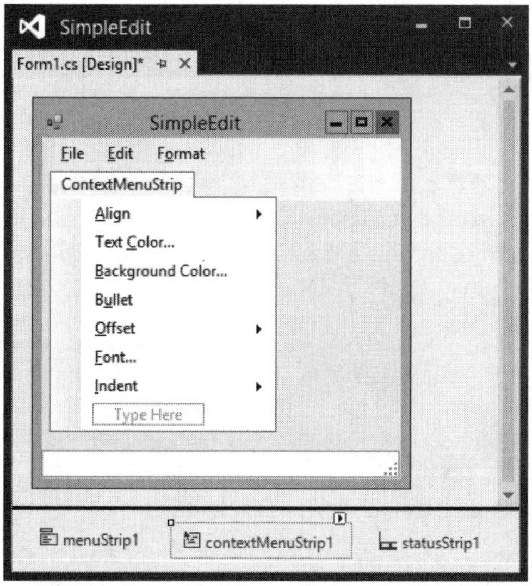

FIGURE 5-6

After you create a `ContextMenuStrip`, you need to associate it with the control that should display it. To do that, simply set the control's `ContextMenuStrip` property to the `ContextMenuStrip`. To do that, select the control's `ContextMenuStrip` property in the Properties window, click the dropdown arrow on the right, and select the `ContextMenuStrip`. The rest is automatic. When the user right-clicks the control, it automatically displays the `ContextMenuStrip`.

WPF MENUS

To create a menu in a WPF application, add a `Menu` control to the window and use your preferred method to make it attach itself to the top. For example, if the window contains a `Grid`, you can make the `Menu` fill the `Grid`'s top row. Alternatively, if the window contains a `DockPanel`, you can dock the `Menu` to the top.

After you create the `Menu`, you can add items to it in two ways. First, you can use the Properties window's menu editor. Select the `Menu`, find the `Menu`'s `Items` property in the Properties window, and click the ellipsis to the right to open the editor shown in Figure 5-7.

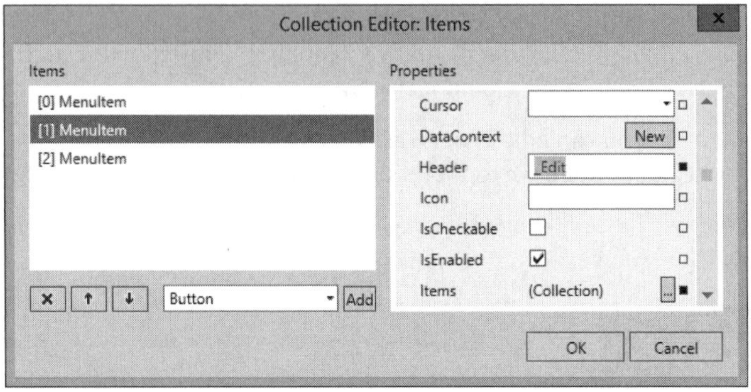

FIGURE 5-7

Use the editor to add and modify the items in the menu. Set a menu item's `Header` property to the text that you want it to display. Place an underscore in front of the character that you want the item to use as an accelerator key. For example, the menu item in Figure 5-5 has `Header` set to _Edit so when you press Alt at run time, it will appear as <u>E</u>dit.

To make a submenu, click the ellipsis to the right of the `Items` property in the menu item editor (in the bottom right in Figure 5-5).

> **NOTE** *You can put practically anything inside a WPF menu. A menu could hold* `CheckBoxes`, `RadioButtons`, `ComboBoxes`, `Sliders`, *even a* `Grid` *containing a whole slew of other controls.*
>
> *However, that's not what users expect to see in a menu, so adding too many unusual items can make a menu confusing. Normally menus should contain only* `MenuItems` *and* `Separators`.

The second way you can create a menu hierarchy is to edit the XAML code manually. That may seem intimidating, but it's actually not too hard, particularly if you make a few menu items and then copy and paste their code.

The following code shows the XAML code for a menu structure that contains File and Format menus. Notice that the Format menu has two submenus, Align and Offset:

```xaml
<Menu x:Name="menu" VerticalAlignment="Top" DockPanel.Dock="Top">
    <MenuItem Header="_File">
        <MenuItem Header="_New"/>
        <MenuItem Header="_Open..."/>
        <MenuItem Header="_Save"/>
    </MenuItem>
    <MenuItem Header="_Format">
        <MenuItem Header="_Align">
            <MenuItem Header="_Left" IsChecked="True"/>
            <MenuItem Header="_Right"/>
            <MenuItem Header="_Center"/>
        </MenuItem>
        <MenuItem Header="_Offset">
            <MenuItem Header="_Normal" IsChecked="True"/>
            <MenuItem Header="Su_perscript"/>
            <MenuItem Header="Su_bscript"/>
        </MenuItem>
    </MenuItem>
</Menu>
```

If you click a menu item in the XAML editor, the Window Designer opens to show that item. You can then double-click the item to give it a `Click` event handler.

WPF CONTEXT MENUS

Like Windows Forms applications, WPF applications let you associate a context menu with a control. When the user right-clicks the control at run time, the context menu appears.

To add a context menu to a control, first select the control. Then in the Properties window, find the `ContextMenu` property (in the Miscellaneous section), and click the New button to its right.

After you create a `ContextMenu`, you can edit it much as you can edit a main menu. The items inside a `ContextMenu` are `MenuItems` just as they are inside a `Menu`. In the Properties window, you can click the ellipsis next to its `Items` property to open the menu item editor. Alternatively, you can edit the `ContextMenu`'s XAML code.

WPF COMMANDING

WPF has a whole system for handling standard *commands* such as Open, New, and Copy. You can even define your own commands.

The idea is that you might want to allow several different methods for invoking the same command. For example, you might allow the user to click a `Button`, select a `MenuItem`, or check a `CheckBox` to invoke the Save command. The commands provide a central location for invoking the appropriate behaviors.

You can define code to execute when a command is invoked. Then you can assign a `MenuItem` (or `Button` or `CheckBox` or whatever) to a command so when the user clicks the control, it invokes the command. You can even assign *gestures* to a command. For example, you could make the Ctrl+L gesture invoke a custom `LeftAlign` command.

Gestures are quite powerful, but they're also fairly complicated so I'm not going to cover them in this book. You can learn more about them in the article "Commanding Overview" at `msdn` `.microsoft.com/en-us/library/ms752308`.

Meanwhile, you can just create `Click` event handlers for menu items.

TRY IT

In this Try It, you create a main menu and a context menu. The main menu includes an Exit command that closes the form. Both menus contain commands that let you change the appearance of a `TextBox` on the form. Figure 5-8 shows the finished program displaying its context menu.

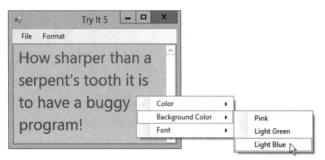

FIGURE 5-8

Lesson Requirements

In this lesson, you:

➤ Create the form shown in Figure 5-8.

➤ Create the following main menu structure (note the accelerator keys and shortcuts):

File
    Exit
Format
    Color
        Red   Ctrl+R
        Green   Ctrl+G
        Blue   Ctrl+B
    Background Color
        Pink
        Light Green
        Light Blue

<u>F</u>ont

    <u>S</u>mall   Ctrl+S

    <u>N</u>ormal   Ctrl+N

    <u>L</u>arge   Ctrl+L

➤ Add code behind the main menu items.

➤ Make the context menu duplicate the main menu's Format submenu.

➤ Attach the context menu items to the same event handlers used by the main menu.

➤ Attach the context menu to the `TextBox`.

> **NOTE** *You can download the code and resources for this lesson from the website at* `www.wrox.com/go/csharp24hourtrainer2e`.

Hints

➤ The E<u>x</u>it menu item can close the program's form by calling `this.Close()`.

➤ Creating a font isn't trivial (and I haven't covered that yet). It's much easier to keep a sample of a font in a control somewhere on the form and then set the `TextBox`'s `Font` property equal to that control's `Font` property. And what better control to store the font than the menu item itself?

Step-by-Step

➤ Create the form shown in Figure 5-8.

  1. Create the main menu by double-clicking the Toolbox's `MenuStrip` tool.

  2. Add a `TextBox` to the form. Type some text into its `Text` property and set its properties: `Name = contentsTextBox`, `MultiLine = True`, `Dock = Fill`, `ScrollBars = Both`.

  3. Create the context menu by double-clicking the Toolbox's `ContextMenuStrip` tool.

➤ Create the main menu structure.

  1. Select the `MenuStrip`. Click the Type Here box and type **&File**.

  2. In the Type Here box below the <u>F</u>ile menu, type **E&xit**.

> **NOTE** *By convention, the E<u>x</u>it command uses X as its accelerator. It never has a shortcut because it would be too easy to accidentally close the program while banging your head on the keyboard (or if you fat-finger the keys, the keyboard is hit by a flying tennis ball, or your cat walks across the keyboard).*

3. Click the File item again. In the Type Here box to the right, type **F&ormat**. (You can't use the F character as this menu's accelerator because it's already used by the File menu.)

4. Use the Type Here boxes below the Format menu to create the format menu items and their submenus.

5. Use the Properties window to set the font sizes for the Font menu's Small, Normal, and Large items to 6, 9, and 20, respectively.

6. Give the Color and Font submenu items appropriate shortcuts.

7. Give the menu items that take action appropriate names. For example, name the Font menu's Small item `formatFontSmallMenuItem`.

➤ Add code behind the main menu items.

1. Double-click the Exit menu item and type the bold line in the following code so the event handler looks like this:

```
private void fileExitMenuItem_Click(object sender, EventArgs e)
{
    this.Close();
}
```

The keyword `this` means "the object currently executing this code," which in this case means the current form, so this line of code tells the current form to close itself.

2. Double-click the Format ⇨ Color ⇨ Red menu item and type the bold line in the following code so the event handler looks like this:

```
private void formatColorRedMenuItem_Click(object sender, EventArgs e)
{
    contentsTextBox.ForeColor = Color.Red;
}
```

3. Repeat step 2 for the Green and Blue menu items.

4. Repeat step 2 for the Format ⇨ Background Color menu items.

5. Double-click the Format ⇨ Font ⇨ Small menu item and type the bold line in the following code so the event handler looks like this:

```
private void formatFontSmallMenuItem_Click(object sender, EventArgs e)
{
    contentsTextBox.Font = formatFontSmallMenuItem.Font;
}
```

6. Repeat step 5 for the Normal and Large menu items.

➤ Make the context menu duplicate the main menu's Format submenu.

Do either 1 or 2:

1. Build the structure from scratch. (This is straightforward but slow.)

    a. Click the `ContextMenuStrip` in the Component Tray to open it for editing.

    b. Use steps similar to the ones you used to build the main menu's structure to build the context menu's structure. End context menu item names with `ContextMenuItem`, as in `colorRedContextMenuItem`.

2. Copy the Format menu's structure. (This is sneakier and faster, and therefore much cooler!)

    a. Click the `MenuStrip` in the Component Tray to open it for editing. Expand the Format menu. Click the Color item and then shift-click the Font item to select all of the menu's items. Press Ctrl+C to copy the menu items into the clipboard.

    b. Click the `ContextMenuStrip` in the Component Tray to open it for editing. Press Ctrl+V to paste the menu items into the context menu.

    c. Give appropriate names to the new menu items.

➤ Attach the context menu items to the event handlers used by the main menu.

1. Open the `ContextMenuStrip` for editing. Expand the Color submenu and click the Red item. In the events page of the Properties window, select the `Click` event. Open the dropdown on the right and select `formatColorRedMenuItem_Click`.

2. Repeat step 1 for the `ContextMenuStrip`'s other items, attaching them to the correct event handlers.

➤ Attach the context menu to the `TextBox`.

1. Click the `TextBox`. In the Properties window, set its `ContextMenuStrip` property to `formatContextMenu`.

EXERCISES

1. [WPF] Repeat the Try It with a WPF application Hints:.

    ➤ You might save time by building some menus and then copying and pasting them in the XAML Code Editor.

    ➤ Set the `TextBox`'s colors as in `contentsTextBox.Foreground = Brushes.Red`.

    ➤ Set the `TextBox`'s font size as in `contentsTextBox.FontSize = formatFontSmallMenuItem.FontSize`.

2. [SimpleEdit] Copy the SimpleEdit program you started in Lesson 3, Exercise 4 (or download Lesson 3's version from the book's website at `www.wrox.com`) and add the following menu structure. Set the `Checked` property of the bold items to `True`.

File

    New   Ctrl+N

    Open...   Ctrl+O

    Save   Ctrl+S

    Save As...

    -

    Print Preview...

    Print...   Ctrl+P

    -

E<u>x</u>it

<u>E</u>dit

    <u>U</u>ndo   Ctrl+Z

    <u>R</u>edo   Ctrl+Y

    -

    <u>C</u>opy   Ctrl+C

    Cu<u>t</u>   Ctrl+X

    <u>P</u>aste   Ctrl+V

    <u>D</u>elete   Del

    -

    Select <u>A</u>ll   Ctrl+A

F<u>o</u>rmat

    <u>A</u>lign

        <u>L</u>eft

        <u>R</u>ight

        <u>C</u>enter

    Text <u>C</u>olor...

    <u>B</u>ackground Color...

    B<u>u</u>llet

    <u>O</u>ffset

        <u>N</u>ormal

        Su<u>b</u>script

        Su<u>p</u>erscript

    <u>F</u>ont...

    <u>I</u>ndent

        <u>N</u>one

        <u>H</u>anging

        <u>L</u>eft

        <u>R</u>ight

        <u>B</u>oth

Add the code behind the E<u>x</u>it item, but don't worry about the other items yet.

Eventually the user will be able to use the Bullet menu item to toggle whether a piece of text is bulleted. To allow C# to toggle this item for you, set the menu item's `CheckOnClick` property to `True`.

Add a `ContextMenuStrip` that duplicates the Format menu and use it for the `TextBox`'s `ContextMenuStrip` property.

3. [WPF, SimpleEdit] Repeat Exercise 2 with a WPF application. Hint: To check a menu item, set its `IsChecked` property to `True`.

4. [SimpleEdit] Copy the SimpleEdit program you built for Exercise 1 and add images to its menu and context menu items. (You can find suitable image files in the `PngFiles` directory of the Lesson 5 downloads available on the book's website.) Figure 5-9 shows what the menus should look like when you're finished.

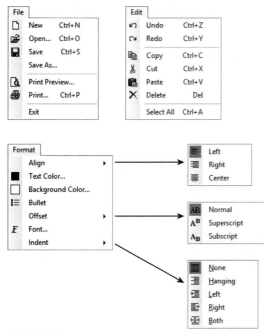

FIGURE 5-9

5. [WPF, SimpleEdit] Repeat Exercise 4 with the WPF application you built for Exercise 3. The Properties window in the version of Visual Studio I'm using doesn't seem to allow you to set a menu item's `Icon` property, but this isn't too hard to do in the XAML editor. First use the Project menu's Add Existing Item command to add the image files to the project. Then use XAML code similar to the following to add icons to the appropriate menu items:

```
<MenuItem Header="_New" Name="fileNewMenuItem">
    <MenuItem.Icon>
        <Image Source="New.png" />
    </MenuItem.Icon>
</MenuItem>
```

6. [SimpleEdit] Copy the SimpleEdit program you built for Exercise 4 and add placeholder routines for the menu items' event handlers. The routines should display simple message boxes indicating what they should really do. For example, the following code shows the File menu's `Save` event handler:

```
private void fileSaveMenuItem_Click(object sender, EventArgs e)
{
    MessageBox.Show("Save");
}
```

Add placeholders for all menu items (except separators) that do not contain items. For example, add a placeholder for the Format ⇨ Align ⇨ Left item but not for Format ⇨ Align because it contains items.

Attach the context menu's items to the same event handlers except give the context menu's Bullet item its own event handler. (If you make these two share the same event handler, they will interfere with each other because of their toggling behavior.)

7. [WPF, SimpleEdit] Repeat Exercise 6 with the WPF application you built for Exercise 5. Hints:

   ➤ If you click a menu item's XAML code to select it, then you can double-click it in the Window Designer to create an event handler for it.

   ➤ You may need to edit the XAML code directly to define its event handler, as in `Click="alignLeftContextMenuItem_Click"`. Then you can right-click the event handler's name and select Go To Definition to create the event handler.

8. [SimpleEdit] Copy the SimpleEdit program you built for Exercise 7 and add code to manage exclusive selections in the Format menu's Align, Offset, and Indent submenus. For example, the user can select only one of the Align submenu's choices at a time.

   Modify the items' placeholder code so when the user selects a choice, the code:

   a. Checks the selected submenu item

   b. Unchecks the other submenu items

   c. Checks the corresponding context menu item

   d. Unchecks the other context menu items

   For example, the following code executes when the user selects the Align submenu's Left choice:

```
private void formatIndentLeftMenuItem_Click(object sender, EventArgs e)
{
    formatIndentNoneMenuItem.Checked = false;
    formatIndentHangingMenuItem.Checked = false;
    formatIndentLeftMenuItem.Checked = true;
    formatIndentRightMenuItem.Checked = false;
    formatIndentBothMenuItem.Checked = false;
    indentNoneContextMenuItem.Checked = false;
    indentHangingContextMenuItem.Checked = false;
    indentLeftContextMenuItem.Checked = true;
    indentRightContextMenuItem.Checked = false;
    indentBothContextMenuItem.Checked = false;
    MessageBox.Show("Indent Left");
}
```

9. [WPF, SimpleEdit] Repeat Exercise 8 with the WPF application you built for Exercise 7. (Hint: In WPF you need to set the `IsChecked` property instead of the `Checked` property.)

10. [SimpleEdit] Copy the SimpleEdit program you built for Exercise 8 and add code to make the Format ⇨ Bullet menu item and the bullet context menu item check and uncheck each other. (Hint: Set one item's `Checked` property equal to the other item's `Checked` property.)

11. [WPF, SimpleEdit] Unlike Windows Forms, WPF's `MenuItem` control doesn't have a `CheckOnClick` property, so the Bullet menu items won't check and uncheck themselves when the user clicks them.

Add code to make those menu items check and uncheck themselves by setting each control's `IsChecked` property equal to the negation of its current value. The `!` character takes the logical negation of a value. In other words, `!true` is `false` and `!false` is `true`. For example, the following code toggles whether the Format menu's Bullet item is checked:

```
formatBulletMenuItem.IsChecked = !formatBulletMenuItem.IsChecked;
```

12. [WPF, SimpleEdit] Repeat Exercise 10 with the WPF application you built for Exercise 11. (Hint: In WPF you need to set the `IsChecked` property instead of the `Checked` property.)

13. [WPF] In WPF, a menu can contain just about anything. Build an application similar to the one shown in Figure 5-10. (Although I'm not saying this is a good idea in an actual program.)

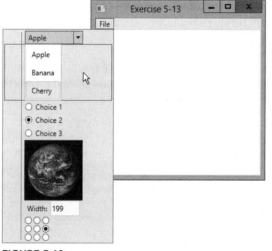

FIGURE 5-10

The program's File menu should contain:

➤ A `ComboBox` with three choices.

➤ A `ListBox` with three choices.

➤ Three `RadioButtons`.

> ➤ An Image.

> ➤ A StackPanel holding a Label and a TextBox.

> ➤ A Grid containing a 3 × 3 arrangement of RadioButtons.

14. Make a Windows Forms program with five levels of nested menus. In other words, make a menu File ➪ Level 1 ➪ Level 2 ➪ Level 3 ➪ Level 4 ➪ Level 5. Make the bottommost menu item display a message box. (Again, I'm not saying this is a good idea in an actual program.)

15. [WPF] Repeat Exercise 14 with a WPF application.

16. A useful user interface technique is to not allow the user to do things that are inappropriate at the time. In a drawing application, for example, if the user isn't editing a drawing, you should disable the drawing tools.

Write a program that has three menus: File, Customers, and Employees. Give them each one menu item: Exit (and give it code), New Customer, and New Employee.

Give the program's form three RadioButtons labeled General, Manage Customers, and Manage Employees. When the user clicks a RadioButton, enable and disable the appropriate menus. (Some applications hide inappropriate menus, but that can be confusing to users who know a menu should exist but can't find it.)

For example, when the user clicks the Manage Customers button, enable the Customers menu and disable the Employees menu. Disable both menus when the user clicks the General button. (Hint: Make sure the program starts with the correct menus enabled.)

17. [WPF] Repeat Exercise 16 with a WPF application.

18. Generally it's better to use as little code as possible so you have less to program, debug, and maintain over time. Copy the application you wrote for Exercise 5-16 and change it so all three RadioButtons share a single event handler.

19. [WPF] Repeat Exercise 18 with the WPF application you wrote for Exercise 17. (Hint: IsChecked.Value tells whether a RadioButton is checked.)

> **NOTE** *Please select the videos for Lesson 5 online at* www.wrox.com/go/
> csharp24hourtrainer2evideos.

6

Making Tool Strips and Status Strips

Not every program needs a tool strip or status strip, but they can make the user's life easier, particularly for complicated programs. This lesson explains how to add tool strips and status strips to your applications.

USING TOOL STRIPS

Usually a tool strip sits below a form's menu bar and displays a series of small buttons that let the user easily perform frequently executed tasks. Usually the buttons duplicate functions that are also available in menus, but placing them on the tool strip makes it easier for the user to find and use them.

Place only the most frequently used commands in the tool strip so it doesn't become cluttered.

Recall from Lesson 5 that you should also give most if not all of your menu items accelerators, and you can give the most important commands shortcuts. That means the user can access the most important and useful commands in at least four ways: mouse menu navigation, accelerators, shortcuts, and tool strip buttons.

To create a single tool strip, simply double-click the Toolbox's ToolStrip tool. By default, the ToolStrip docks to the top of the form so you don't need to position it manually.

> **NOTE** *Recall from Lesson 3 that docked controls are drawn in their stacking order, which by default is the same as their creation order. To avoid confusion, if a form should contain a main menu and a tool strip, create the menu first so the tool strip appears below it and not above it.*

When you select a `ToolStrip`, the Form Designer displays a little icon with a dropdown arrow. Click the arrow to display a list of items that you might want to add to the `ToolStrip`, as shown in Figure 6-1.

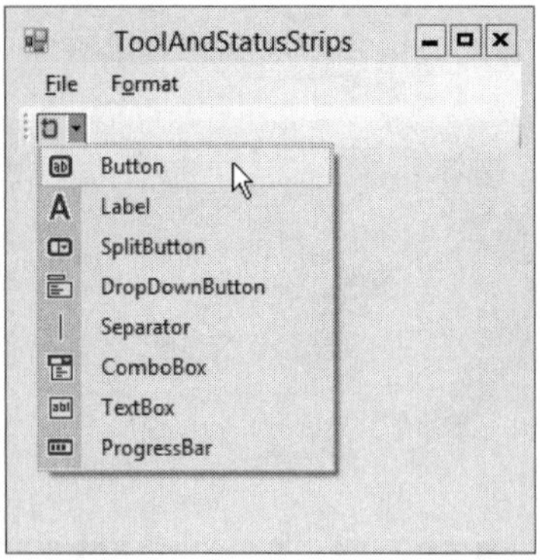

As you can see from Figure 6-1, you can add the following types of objects to a `ToolStrip`:

➤ Button

➤ Label

➤ SplitButton

➤ DropDownButton

➤ Separator

➤ ComboBox

➤ TextBox

➤ ProgressBar

FIGURE 6-1

The `SplitButton` and `DropDownButton` are new controls that you haven't seen before in the Toolbox so they deserve a little explanation.

The `SplitButton` normally displays a button holding an icon and a dropdown arrow. (You can change its `DisplayStyle` property to make it display text instead of an image, both, or neither.) If the user clicks the button, its `Click` event fires. If the user clicks the dropdown arrow, a menu appears. As is the case with all menus, if the user selects an item, that item's `Click` event fires.

One way you might use a `SplitButton` would be to have the menu items perform some action and then change the button's icon to match the action. Clicking the button would perform the action again.

Another way to think of this would be that the button represents a tool and clicking it activates the current tool. Selecting an item from the dropdown menu selects a new tool and activates it.

Like the `SplitButton`, the `DropDownButton` normally displays an icon with a dropdown arrow. (And as is the case with the `SplitButton`, you can use the `DropDownButton`'s `DisplayStyle` property to make it display an image, text, both, or neither.) If the user clicks the dropdown arrow, a menu appears. This control is similar to the `SplitButton` except it doesn't provide a button that the user can click to repeat the previous command.

Although they can contain many different kinds of controls, `ToolStrips` look best when they are not too cluttered and confusing. For example, a `ToolStrip` that contains only `Buttons` and `Separators` is easy to understand and use. `DropDownButtons` and `SplitButtons` are the next easiest controls to understand in a `ToolStrip`, and they don't clutter things up too much so you can add them if necessary.

Avoid using `Labels` in a `ToolStrip` to provide status information. Instead, place status information in a `StatusStrip`.

USING TOOL STRIP CONTAINERS

A `ToolStripContainer` displays areas on a form's top, left, bottom, and right edges that can hold `ToolStrips`. At run time, the user can drag `ToolStrips` back and forth within and among these areas.

The center of the `ToolStripContainer` is a content panel that can hold one or more other controls.

In a typical configuration for these controls, a form optionally contains a `MenuStrip` and `StatusStrip` docked to the form's top and bottom, respectively. A `ToolStripContainer` is docked to fill the rest of the form, and its content panel contains the rest of the program's controls.

Figure 6-2 shows a form that contains a `MenuStrip` at the top, a `StatusStrip` at the bottom, and a `ToolStripContainer` filling the rest of the form. The `ToolStripContainer` contains three `ToolStrips` and a `RichTextBox` docked to fill its content panel.

Figure 6-3 shows this program at run time. Here I have dragged two of the `ToolStrips` to the `ToolStripContainer`'s left and right edges.

Two things in Figure 6-2 are of particular note. First, notice the thin rectangles holding arrows on the middle of the content panel's sides. If you click one of these, the control adds room on that edge so you can insert another `ToolStrip`.

The second thing of note in Figure 6-2 is the smart tag shown as a little square holding an arrow in the control's upper-right corner. If you click the smart tag, the smart tag panel shown in Figure 6-4 appears.

FIGURE 6-2

FIGURE 6-3

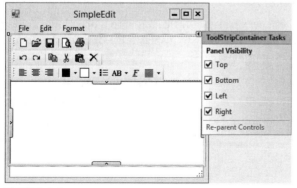

FIGURE 6-4

In general, smart tags provide quick ways to perform common tasks for a control. In this example, the smart tag panel lets you decide which panels the control should allow. If you uncheck one of the panels, the user cannot drag `ToolStrips` to that edge of the `ToolStripContainer` at run time.

> **NOTE** *You can also determine which panels are available by setting the control's* `LeftToolStripPanelVisible`, `RightToolStripPanelVisible`, `TopToolStripPanelVisible`, *and* `BottomToolStripPanelVisible` *properties in the Properties window, but using the smart tag is easier.*

After you build the `ToolStripContainer`, simply place `ToolStrips` on it and build their items as usual.

USING STATUS STRIPS

A status strip is normally docked to a form's bottom and displays labels, status bars, and other controls to give the user a quick summary of the application's status. This area should be reserved for status information and should generally not include buttons and other controls that make the application perform an action. Those commands belong in menus and tool strips.

> **NOTE** *Although the current time is sort of a piece of status information, don't add a clock to the status bar. A user who wants a clock can display one in the system's taskbar. The taskbar clock is more convenient because it provides options (such as display format) that you probably don't want to reproduce in your program, and it also can't be hidden by other programs. If the system provides a convenient tool, there's no need for you to reproduce it in your program.*

To create a status strip, simply double-click the Toolbox's `StatusStrip` tool. By default, the `StatusStrip` docks to the bottom of the form so you don't need to position it manually.

When you select a `StatusStrip`, the Form Designer displays a little icon with a dropdown arrow similar to the one it displays for a `ToolStrip`. Click the arrow to display a list of items that you might want to add to the `StatusStrip`, as shown in Figure 6-5.

As you can see from Figure 6-5, you can add the following types of objects to a `ToolStrip`:

➤ `StatusLabel`

➤ `ProgressBar`

➤ `DropDownButton`

➤ `SplitButton`

The only new control, `StatusLabel`, behaves like a normal `Label`.

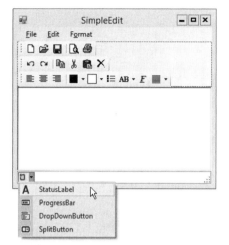

FIGURE 6-5

TRY IT

In this Try It, you create a `MenuStrip` (covered in Lesson 5) and a `ToolStrip`, both containing commands to change a `RichTextBox` control's `ForeColor` and `BackColor` properties. You also create a `StatusStrip` to show the currently selected colors. (Yes, I know this is redundant because the values are shown in the `ToolStrip` and in the text itself.) Figure 6-6 shows the program in action.

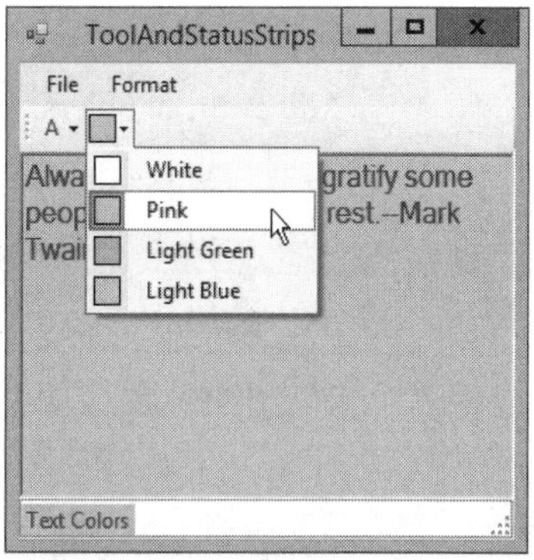

Lesson Requirements

In this lesson, you:

➤ Create the form shown in Figure 6-6.

➤ Create the `MenuStrip`. The menu's hierarchy should be:

File
   Exit
Format
   Text Color
      Black
      Red
      Green
      Blue

FIGURE 6-6

B̲ackground Color

    W̲hite

    P̲ink

    Light G̲reen

    Light B̲lue

➤ Initially check the Text Color menu's Black choice and the Background Color menu's White choice.

➤ Give the Background Color menu items `Images` that display samples of the colors.

➤ Create the `ToolStrip` with buttons that duplicate the menu hierarchy. The `ToolStrip` should hold two `ToolStripDropDownButtons`.

    ➤ Name the first tool **`foreColorButton`** and make it display the text "A." Give it the items B̲lack, R̲ed, G̲reen, and B̲lue. Each item should have the `ForeColor` property set to its color.

    ➤ Name the second tool **`backColorButton`** and make it initially display a white color sample. Give it the items W̲hite, P̲ink, Light G̲reen, and Light B̲lue. Make each of these display an `Image` showing a sample of the color.

➤ Give the `StatusStrip` a `ToolStripStatusLabel` named **`colorLabel`** with Text = **`Text Colors`**.

➤ Add event handlers.

    ➤ Make the F̲ile menu's E̲xit item close the form.

    ➤ Make event handlers for each of the Text Color menu items.

    ➤ Make event handlers for each of the Background Color menu items.

➤ Make the tool strip `Buttons` use the corresponding menu items' event handlers.

DUPLICATE CODE

As you will probably notice, this lesson's Try It includes event handlers that duplicate the same code with minor differences. In general, if large pieces of code do almost the same things with minor changes, then there's probably something wrong with the program's design.

In cases such as this, you should extract the common code into a method. You can use `if`, `switch`, and other C# statements to let the code take different actions for different situations, allowing one method to handle multiple situations.

Unfortunately, you don't know how to do any of that yet, but you will learn. Lesson 18 describes statements such as `if` and `switch`, and Lesson 20 explains how to write methods. Until then, you're stuck with some duplicate code.

After you read Lessons 18 and 20, you can revisit this code to remove the redundant code if you like, making it easier to maintain in the future. (The process of restructuring existing code to make it more reliable, easier to read, easier to maintain, or otherwise better without changing its functionality is called *refactoring*.)

> **NOTE** *You can download the code and resources for this lesson from the website at* www.wrox.com/go/csharp24hourtrainer2e.

Hints

➤ Recall that the E<u>x</u>it menu item can close the program's form by calling `Close()`.

➤ Place the `RichTextBox` inside the `ToolStripContainer`'s content panel.

➤ You may be able to save a lot of typing by making one event handler and then copying and pasting it.

Step-by-Step

➤ Create the form shown in Figure 6-6.

   1. Start a new project.

   2. Add a `MenuStrip` to the form.

   3. Add a `StatusStrip` to the form.

   4. Add a `ToolStripContainer` to the form.

   5. Add a `RichTextBox` named **contentRichTextBox** inside the `ToolStripContainer`'s content panel.

➤ Create the `MenuStrip`.

   1. Add the indicated menu items to the `MenuStrip`. Remember to give them good names and appropriate accelerator keys.

➤ Initially check the Text Color menu's Black choice and the Background Color menu's White choice.

   1. Set the Text Color ⇨ Black menu item's `Checked` property to `True`.

   2. Set the Background Color ⇨ White menu item's `Checked` property to `True`.

➤ Give the Background Color menu items `Images` that display samples of the color.

   1. Set the `Image` properties of these menu items to samples of their colors. (Use Microsoft Paint or some other graphical editor to make small colored images.)

➤ Create the `ToolStrip` with buttons that duplicate the menu hierarchy. The `ToolStrip` should hold two `ToolStripDropDownButtons`.

   ➤ Name the first tool **foreColorButton** and make it display the text "A." Give it the items Black, Red, Green, and Blue. Each item should have `ForeColor` property set to its color.

   1. Create the `ToolStripDropDownButton`.

   2. Below that item, add the items Black, Red, Green, and Blue.

   3. Set the `ForeColor` property for each of these items to show its color. (For example, set the Black item's `ForeColor` property to black.)

   ➤ Name the second tool **backColorButton** and make it initially display a white color sample. Give it the items White, Pink, Light Green, and Light Blue. Make each of these display an `Image` showing a sample of the color.

   1. Create the `ToolStripDropDownButton`.

   2. Below that item, add the items White, Pink, Light Green, and Light Blue.

   3. Set the `Image` property for each of these items to show samples of their colors.

   ➤ Give the `StatusStrip` a `ToolStripStatusLabel` named **colorLabel** with Text = **Text Colors**.

   1. Create the `ToolStripStatusLabel`. Set its `Name` and `Text` properties.

   ➤ Add event handlers.

   ➤ Make the File menu's Exit item close the form.

   1. Type the bold line of code so the event handler looks like this:

```
private void fileExitMenuItem_Click(object sender, EventArgs e)
{
    Close();
}
```

   ➤ Make event handlers for each of the Text Color menu items.

   1. For the Text Color ⇨ Black menu item, type the bold code so the event handler looks like this:

```
private void blackForeColorMenuItem_Click(object sender, EventArgs e)
{
    contentRichTextBox.ForeColor = blackForeColorButton.ForeColor;

    foreColorMenuItem.ForeColor = blackForeColorButton.ForeColor;
    foreColorButton.ForeColor = blackForeColorButton.ForeColor;
    colorLabel.ForeColor = blackForeColorButton.ForeColor;

    blackForeColorMenuItem.Checked = true;
    redForeColorMenuItem.Checked = false;
```

```
        greenForeColorMenuItem.Checked = false;
        blueForeColorMenuItem.Checked = false;

        blackForeColorButton.Checked = true;
        redForeColorButton.Checked = false;
        greenForeColorButton.Checked = false;
        blueForeColorButton.Checked = false;
    }
```

2. Enter similar code for the other Text Color menu items.

➤ Make event handlers for each of the Background Color menu items.

1. For the Background Color ⇨ White menu item, type the bold code so the event handler looks like this:

```
private void whiteBackColorMenuItem_Click(object sender, EventArgs e)
{
    contentRichTextBox.BackColor = Color.White;

    backColorMenuItem.Image = whiteBackColorMenuItem.Image;
    backColorButton.Image = whiteBackColorMenuItem.Image;
    colorLabel.BackColor = Color.White;

    whiteBackColorMenuItem.Checked = true;
    pinkBackColorMenuItem.Checked = false;
    lightGreenBackColorMenuItem.Checked = false;
    lightBlueBackColorMenuItem.Checked = false;

    whiteBackColorButton.Checked = true;
    pinkBackColorButton.Checked = false;
    lightGreenBackColorButton.Checked = false;
    lightBlueBackColorButton.Checked = false;
}
```

2. Enter similar code for the other Background Color menu items.

➤ Make event handlers for each of the Background Color menu items.

1. Repeat the steps you used for the Text Color menu items except use BackColor instead of ForeColor.

➤ Make the tool strip Buttons use the corresponding menu items' event handlers.

1. Click the Properties window's Events button.

2. For each tool strip button:

   a. Click the button in the Form Editor.

   b. On the Properties window, select the Click event. Then click the dropdown arrow to the right.

   c. Select the appropriate menu event handler. For example, for the blackForeColorButton tool strip button, select the blackForeColorMenuItem_Click event handler.

EXERCISES

1. [SimpleEdit] Copy the SimpleEdit program you built in Lesson 5, Exercise 10 (or download Lesson 5's version from the book's website) and add the tool strips, buttons, and separators shown in Figure 6-7. Hints:

   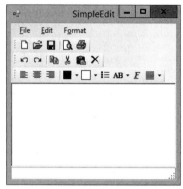

   FIGURE 6-7

   ➤ Delete the `RichTextBox` control, add a `ToolStripContainer`, and then re-add the `RichTextBox` inside the `ToolStripContainer`'s content panel. Then add the `ToolStrips`.

   ➤ The black button (fourth from the left on the third tool strip row) is a `ToolStripSplitButton` that lets the user pick a text color. It contains the choices B̲lack, W̲hite, R̲ed, G̲reen, and B̲lue.

   ➤ The white button next to the text color button is another `ToolStripSplitButton` that lets the user pick a background color. It contains the choices B̲lack, W̲hite, P̲ink, Light G̲reen, Light B̲lue, and Y̲ellow.

   ➤ The button that says "AB" is a `ToolStripDropDownButton` that provides the same options as the Format menu's Offset submenu: N̲ormal, Su̲perscript, and Su̲bscript.

2. [WPF, SimpleEdit] Copy the program you built in Lesson 5, Exercise 12 (or download Lesson 5's version from the book's website) and repeat Exercise 1. Hints:

   ➤ Dock a `ToolBarTray` to the top of the `DockPanel` control below the menus.

   ➤ Add `ToolBars` to the `ToolBarTray`. Set a `ToolBar`'s `Band` property to indicate its row in the `ToolBarTray`. Set its `BandIndex` property to indicate its ordering within the band.

   ➤ Add `Buttons` and `Separators` to the `ToolBars`.

   ➤ For the split buttons, use `ComboBoxes` containing `ComboBoxItems` that hold `Images`. Set one `ComboBoxItem`'s `IsSelected` property to `True` to set a `ComboBox`'s initial selection.

   ➤ Dock a `StatusBar` at the bottom of the `DockPanel`. Give it a `StatusBarItem` containing a `Label`.

3. [SimpleEdit] Copy the SimpleEdit program you built for Exercise 1 and add menu item code to manage the new tool strip buttons. Add code to synchronize corresponding menu, context menu, and tool strip button items. For example, the following shows the new code for the Align Left menu item:

```
private void formatAlignLeftMenuItem_Click(object sender, EventArgs e)
{
    formatAlignLeftMenuItem.Checked = true;
    formatAlignRightMenuItem.Checked = false;
    formatAlignCenterMenuItem.Checked = false;
    alignLeftContextMenuItem.Checked = true;
```

```
        alignRightContextMenuItem.Checked = false;
        alignCenterContextMenuItem.Checked = false;
        alignLeftButton.Checked = true;
        alignRightButton.Checked = false;
        alignCenterButton.Checked = false;
        MessageBox.Show("Align Left");
    }
```

4. [WPF, SimpleEdit] Repeat Exercise 3 with the WPF application you built for Exercise 2. Hints:

   ➤ In WPF `Buttons` don't have `Checked` or `IsChecked` properties, so you can't check and uncheck the alignment toolbar buttons. Instead, make separate images to represent the checked state. Place checked and unchecked images in `Image` controls with the `Visibility` properties set to `Collapsed`. Then use code similar to the following to set a `Button`'s image at run time:

   ```
   alignLeftImage.Source = alignLeftUncheckedImage.Source;
   ```

   ➤ Use a similar trick for the bullet button. Use code similar to the following to set the button's `Image` property. (Sorry but I couldn't think of a way to handle this easily without using `if-else` statements, which you learn about in Lesson 18.)

   ```
   if (formatBulletMenuItem.IsChecked)
       bulletImage.Source = bulletCheckedImage.Source;
   else
       bulletImage.Source = bulletUncheckedImage.Source;
   ```

   ➤ To handle the offset toolbar items, give names to the offset `ComboBoxItems`. Then set the selected item as in the following code. (You don't need to set this to `false` for the items that are not selected.)

   ```
   superscriptOffsetComboBoxItem.IsSelected = true;
   ```

   ➤ Handle the indent toolbar `ComboBox` the same way you handle the offset `ComboBox`.

5. [SimpleEdit] Copy the SimpleEdit program you built for Exercise 3 and attach the tool strip controls to the corresponding event handlers. (Don't worry about the color controls just yet.)

6. [WPF, SimpleEdit] Repeat Exercise 5 with the WPF application you built for Exercise 4. Hints:

   ➤ Handle the `Selected` events for the offset and indentation `ComboBoxItems`.

   ➤ When the window loads, it raises the `Selected` events for the initially selected `ComboBoxItems`. Unfortunately the window hasn't finished loading all of its controls yet, and the program crashes if it tries to set values for controls that aren't yet loaded. To prevent that, begin the event handlers for the initially selected `ComboBoxItems` with the following statement. (The statement basically means, "If the window isn't loaded yet, exit the event handler.")

   ```
   if (!IsLoaded) return;
   ```

   ➤ You may notice that the `ComboBoxItem` event handlers execute twice if you select one of the corresponding menu or context menu items. That's a bit inefficient, but don't worry about it for now. We'll fix it later.

7. [SimpleEdit] Copy the SimpleEdit program you built for Exercise 5 and add code to display the appropriate image in the Text Color and Background tool strip buttons. For example, use code similar to the following for the green text color choice:

    ```
    private void fgGreenButton_Click(object sender, EventArgs e)
    {
        fgButton.Image = fgGreenButton.Image;
        MessageBox.Show("Text Color Green");
    }
    ```

8. [WPF, SimpleEdit] Copy the SimpleEdit program you built for Exercise 6 and add place-holder code to display message boxes when the user selects a Text Color or Background tool strip button. For example, use code similar to the following for the green text color choice:

    ```
    private void greenForeColorComboBoxItem_Selected(object sender,
        RoutedEventArgs e)
    {
        MessageBox.Show("Text Color Green");
    }
    ```

9. [SimpleEdit] Menu items and normal buttons can display text explaining what they do, but toolbar buttons usually display images that may not be intuitively obvious. To help the user understand what toolbar buttons do, you should give them tooltips. Copy the SimpleEdit program you built for Exercise 7. Set each toolbar item's `Text` property to a meaningful name. For example, set the new button's `Text` to "New." That should automatically set each button's tooltip to the same value.

10. [WPF, SimpleEdit] Repeat Exercise 9 with the WPF application you built for Exercise 8. (Hint: Set the `ToolTip` properties for the `Button`, `ComboBox`, and `ComboBoxItem` controls.)

11. [Games] Copy the tic-tac-toe (or naughts-and-crosses) program you built for Exercise 2-3 (or download Lesson 2's version from the book's website). Make these modifications:

    ➤ Add a `StatusStrip` with a `ToolStripStatusLabel` named `turnLabel`. Set its initial `Text` to **Xs Turn**.

    ➤ When the user takes a square for X, hide the little X and O buttons for that square and make the status label say **Os Turn**.

    ➤ When the user takes a square for O, hide the little X and O buttons for that square and make the status label say **Xs Turn**.

    ➤ Add a File menu with two new commands:

      ➤ New resets all of the program's controls to start a new game.

      ➤ Exit closes the program.

12. [WPF, Games] Repeat Exercise 11 with the program you wrote for Exercise 2-4. Hints:

    ➤ To hide a control in WPF, set its `Visibility` property to `Visibility.Hidden`.

    ➤ To change the status label's text, set its `Content` property.

13. [Games] Copy the program you built for Exercise 11 and make the following modifications:

> ➤ Initially disable the little O buttons.

> ➤ When the user clicks an X button, disable all of the X buttons and enable all of the O buttons. (Hint: Write the code for one of the X buttons, make sure it's correct, and then copy and paste that code for the other X buttons. Copying and pasting code like this isn't good programming practice, but we'll fix it in Lesson 20.)

> ➤ When the user clicks an O button, disable all of the O buttons and enable all of the X buttons. (Hint: Use the technique you used for the X buttons.)

14. [WPF, Games] Repeat Exercise 13 with the program you wrote for Exercise 12.

15. [Drawing] Build the Scribbler program shown in Figure 6-8. Give it a `ToolStripContainer` and two `ToolStrips`.

> ➤ Give the first `ToolStrip` buttons representing arrow, line, rectangle, ellipse, curve, and star tools. Make these tools exclusive choices so if the user selects one, the others deselect.

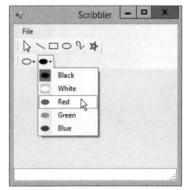

> ➤ Give the second `ToolStrip` two `ToolStripDropDownButtons` to represent foreground and background colors. Make the entries in each dropdown exclusive choices and make the choices display their images on their `ToolStripDropDownButtons`.

16. [WPF, Drawing] Repeat Exercise 15 with a WPF application.

FIGURE 6-8

17. [Drawing] Copy the program you built for Exercise 15 and add tooltips to the toolbar tools.

18. [WPF, Drawing] Repeat Exercise 17 with the program you built for Exercise 17.

> **NOTE** *Please select the videos for Lesson 6 online at* www.wrox.com/go/csharp24hourtrainer2evideos.

7

Using RichTextBoxes

The `TextBox` control lets the user enter text and that's about it. It can display its text in different colors and fonts, but it cannot give different pieces of text different properties. The `TextBox` is intended to let the user enter a simple string, like a name or street address, and very little more.

The `RichTextBox` is a much more powerful control. It can display different pieces of text with different colors, fonts, and styles. It can adjust paragraph indentation and make bulleted lists. It can even include pictures. It's not as powerful as a full-featured word processor, such as Microsoft Word or OpenOffice's Writer, but it can produce a much more sophisticated result than the `TextBox`.

In this lesson you learn about the `RichTextBox` control and how to use it. You have a chance to experiment with the control, and you use it to add enough functionality to the SimpleEdit program to finally make the program useful.

USING RICHTEXTBOX PROPERTIES

To change the appearance of the text inside a `RichTextBox`, you first select the text that you want to change, and then you set one of the control's properties.

To select the text, you use the control's `SelectionStart` and `SelectionLength` properties to indicate where the text begins and how many letters it includes. Note that the letters are numbered starting with 0. (In fact, almost all numbering starts with 0 in C#.) For example, setting `SelectionStart` = 0 and `SelectionLength` = 1 selects the control's first letter.

After you select the text, you set one of the `RichTextBox`'s properties to the value that you want the selected text to have.

For example, the following code makes the `RichTextBox` named `contentRichTextBox` display some text and colors the word "red":

```
contentRichTextBox.Text = "Some red text";
contentRichTextBox.SelectionStart = 5;
contentRichTextBox.SelectionLength = 3;
contentRichTextBox.SelectionColor = Color.Red;
```

Table 7-1 lists properties that you can use to change the text's appearance.

TABLE 7-1

PROPERTY	PURPOSE
SelectionAlignment	Aligns the selection's paragraph on the left, center, or right.
SelectionBackColor	Sets the selection's background color.
SelectionBullet	Determines whether the selection's paragraph is bulleted.
SelectionCharOffset	Determines whether the selection is superscript (offset > 0), subscript (offset < 0), or normal (offset = 0).
SelectionColor	Sets the selection's color.
SelectionFont	Sets the selection's font.
SelectionHangingIndent	The first line in the selection's paragraph is indented normally and then subsequent lines in the paragraph are indented by this amount.
SelectionIndent	All lines are indented by this amount.
SelectionProtected	Marks the selected text as protected so the user cannot modify it.
SelectionRightIndent	All lines are indented on the right by this amount.

The FontFeatures example program shown in Figure 7-1 demonstrates properties that change the appearance of text within a paragraph. These include the `SelectionBackColor`, `SelectionCharOffset`, `SelectionColor`, and `SelectionFont`.

For example, the following code shows how the FontFeatures program sets the background color behind the word "BackColor":

```
contentRichTextBox.SelectionStart = 41;
contentRichTextBox.SelectionLength = 9;
contentRichTextBox.SelectionBackColor = Color.Yellow;
```

FIGURE 7-1

The ParagraphFeatures program shown in Figure 7-2 demonstrates properties that change the way paragraphs are displayed. These include `SelectionIndent`, `SelectionHangingIndent`, `SelectionRightIndent`, `SelectionBullet`, and `SelectionAlignment`.

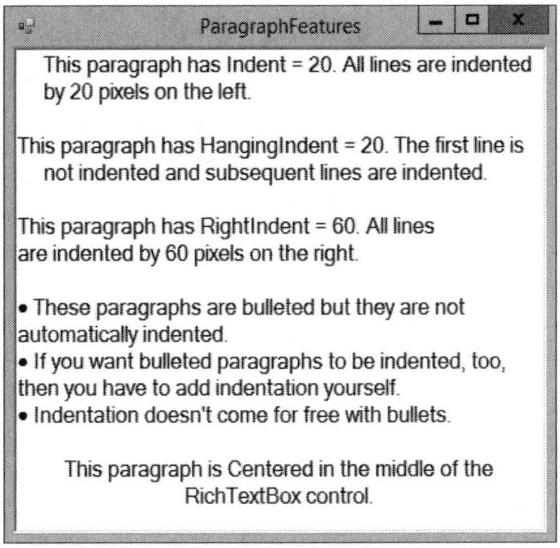

FIGURE 7-2

For example, the following code shows how the ParagraphFeatures program gives the second paragraph a 20 pixel hanging indent:

```
contentRichTextBox.SelectionStart = 82;
contentRichTextBox.SelectionLength = 1;
contentRichTextBox.SelectionHangingIndent = 20;
```

Table 7-2 summarizes four additional properties that change the text displayed by the control that deserve special mention.

TABLE 7-2

PROPERTY	PURPOSE
Text	Gets or sets the control's text without any formatting.
Rtf	Gets or sets the control's Rich Text Format (RTF) contents. This includes the text plus RTF formatting codes that define how the text should be displayed.
SelectedText	Gets or sets the selection's text.
SelectedRtf	Gets or sets the selection's text and RTF codes.

GIVING THE USER CONTROL

Allowing the user to change text settings is easy. When the user selects text in the control, the RichTextBox sets its SelectionStart and SelectionLength properties accordingly. All you need to do is set the appropriate property (for example, SelectionColor) and the selected text is updated.

The SetTextProperties example program shown in Figure 7-3 uses this technique to let the user control text color, character offset, and paragraph alignment. Select some text and then click the tool strip buttons to change the text's properties.

For example, the following code shows how the SetTextProperties program changes the currently selected text to have a black background and white foreground:

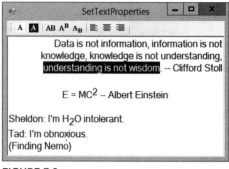

```
private void reverseColorsButton_
Click(object sender, EventArgs e)
{
    contentRichTextBox.SelectionBackColor = Color.Black;
    contentRichTextBox.SelectionColor = Color.White;
}
```

FIGURE 7-3

The program's other buttons work similarly.

USING RICHTEXTBOX METHODS

Lesson 2 briefly described properties, methods, and events. Other lessons have also worked with many properties and events. In fact, most of the event handlers I've discussed in the lessons so far catch an event and change a property in response.

Although you've worked with many properties and events, the only method you've seen is the form's `Close` method, which makes the form go away. For example, the following code closes the form that executes it:

```
Close();
```

The `RichTextBox` provides many new methods that are quite helpful for building a text editing program. Table 7-3 summarizes some of the most useful of those methods.

TABLE 7-3

METHOD	PURPOSE
Clear	Clears all text from the control.
Copy	Copies the current selection into the clipboard.
Cut	Cuts the current selection into the clipboard.
DeselectAll	Deselects all text by setting `SelectionLength = 0`.
LoadFile	Loads the control's text from a file with one of various formats such as RTF or plaintext.
Paste	Pastes whatever is in the clipboard into the current selection. This can be anything that the `RichTextBox` understands such as text, RTF formatted text, or an image.
Redo	Redoes the previously undone command.

METHOD	PURPOSE
SaveFile	Saves the control's text into a file in one of various formats such as RTF or plaintext.
SelectAll	Selects all of the control's text by setting `SelectionStart` = 0 and `SelectionLength` equal to the text's length.
Undo	Undoes the most recent change.

The following code shows how a program can use the `LoadFile` method:

```
contentRichTextBox.LoadFile("Test.rtf", RichTextBoxStreamType.RichText);
```

The first parameter passed into `LoadFile` gives the name of the file, which can be relative to the program's current directory or a full path.

The second parameter gives the type of file. The `RichTextBoxStreamType` enumeration lists file types that you can use. The choices you can use to load files are `PlainText`, `RichText`, and `UnicodePlainText`.

TYPING TIPS

When you type `contentRichTextBox.LoadFile(`, IntelliSense) and displays the popup shown in Figure 7-4 to show the parameters that the `LoadFile` method expects. (Visual Studio adds red squiggly underlines because the statement isn't finished yet. Until I finish typing the statement, Visual Studio flags it as an error.)

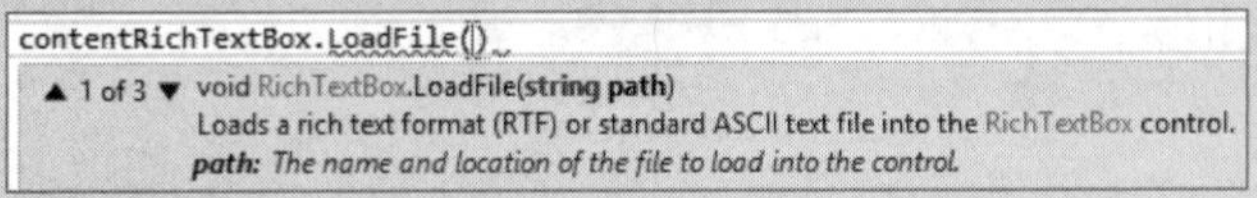

```
contentRichTextBox.LoadFile()
▲ 1 of 3 ▼  void RichTextBox.LoadFile(string path)
            Loads a rich text format (RTF) or standard ASCII text file into the RichTextBox control.
            path: The name and location of the file to load into the control.
```

FIGURE 7-4

You can choose from three different *overloaded* versions of the method, each taking different parameters. Overloaded versions of a method have the same name but take different parameters. You can use the up and down arrow keys to scroll through the method's available versions.

As you enter parameters, IntelliSense updates to describe the next parameter that it expects. Figure 7-5 shows the `LoadFile` method after I entered a filename for the first parameter. IntelliSense shows that the next parameter should be a value of type `RichTextBoxStreamType` named `fileType`. IntelliSense even shows a short description of what the value means at the bottom (although it's not super informative).

```
contentRichTextBox.LoadFile("Test.rtf",)
▲ 2 of 3 ▼  void RichTextBox.LoadFile(string path, RichTextBoxStreamType fileType)
            Loads a specific type of file into the RichTextBox control.
            fileType: One of the RichTextBoxStreamType values.
```

FIGURE 7-5

continues

(continued)

You could type in `RichTextBoxStreamType` followed by a dot to see a list of available choices, but there's an even easier (in other words, better) way to do this: press Ctrl+Space. That makes IntelliSense display a list of things that you might be trying to type. At this point, IntelliSense is smart enough to guess that you want to type `RichTextBoxStreamType` so it initially selects that type and even displays more information about it, as shown in Figure 7-6.

FIGURE 7-6

Now you can press Tab to make IntelliSense fill in the highlighted value `RichTextBoxStreamType` for you.

Next, press the "." key to see the list of choices shown in Figure 7-7, pick one, and press Tab to add it to the code. Finally, add a semicolon at the end of the line and you're done.

FIGURE 7-7

I know this sounds like a big mess, but with a little practice it becomes surprisingly quick and easy. Typing everything by hand, I can enter the previous `LoadFile` statement in about 30 seconds. With IntelliSense's help, I can type the same line in under 10 seconds.

The following code shows how a program can use the `SaveFile` method. As with `LoadFile`, the first parameter gives the file's name and the second gives its type:

```
contentRichTextBox.SaveFile("Test.rtf", RichTextBoxStreamType.RichText);
```

USING WPF COMMANDS

A program can use commands to manipulate the contents of a `RichTextBox`. That control also provides commands that the user can invoke interactively. For example, the user can press Ctrl+E to center paragraphs.

Table 7-4 summarizes the most useful commands. The commands for the Windows Forms and WPF versions of the control differ slightly.

TABLE 7-4

ACTION	WINDOWS FORMS	WPF
Align centered	Ctrl+E	Ctrl+E
Align justified		Ctrl+J
Align left	Ctrl+L	Ctrl+L
Align right	Ctrl+R	Ctrl+R
Bullet	*	Ctrl+Shift+L
Copy	Ctrl+C	Ctrl+C
Cut	Ctrl+X	Ctrl+X
Decrease font size		Ctrl+[
Delete	Delete	Delete
Delete next word	Ctrl+Delete	Ctrl+Delete
Delete previous word	Ctrl+Backspace	Ctrl+Backspace
Increase font size		Ctrl+]
Numbering	*	Ctrl+Shift+N
Paste	Ctrl+V	Ctrl+V
Subscript **	Ctrl++	Ctrl++
Superscript **	Ctrl+Shift++	Ctrl+Shift++
Toggle bold		Ctrl+B
Toggle insert	Insert	Insert
Toggle italic		Ctrl+I
Toggle underline	Ctrl+U	Ctrl+U

* In Windows Forms, Ctrl+Shift+L iterates through the available bullet and numbering styles.

** The subscript and superscript sequences are a bit confusing. For subscript, hold the Ctrl key and press +. For superscript, hold the Ctrl and Shift keys and press +. In WPF, those commands work only for OpenType fonts that come with subscript and superscript variants. Try the Palatino Linotype font. For more information on OpenType fonts, see msdn.microsoft.com/library/ms745109.aspx.

Both controls provide additional navigation commands. For example, Ctrl+Right Arrow moves one word to the right and Ctrl+Down Arrow moves one paragraph downward.

The WPF control also provides a context menu that contains the Copy, Cut, and Paste commands.

For more information on the WPF control's commands, including the navigation commands, see `msdn.microsoft.com/library/system.windows.documents.editingcommands.aspx`.

TRY IT

In this Try It, you add functionality to some of the SimpleEdit program's menu items and tool strip buttons. You use the `RichTextBox` properties and methods to implement the commands in the Edit menu: Undo, Redo, Copy, Cut, Paste, Delete, and Select All. (This also makes the corresponding buttons work at no extra charge.)

Lesson Requirements

In this lesson, you:

➤ Copy the SimpleEdit program you built in Lesson 6, Exercise 9.

➤ Replace the program's `TextBox` with a `RichTextBox` named `contentRichTextBox`.

➤ Add code to handle the Edit menu's commands.

    ➤ Add Undo code.

    ➤ Add Redo code.

    ➤ Add Copy code.

    ➤ Add Cut code.

    ➤ Add Paste code.

    ➤ Add Delete code.

    ➤ Add Select All code.

> **NOTE** *You can download the code and resources for this lesson from the website at* www.wrox.com/go/csharp24hourtrainer2e.

Hints

➤ For the Delete menu item, simply set the control's `SelectedText` property to an empty string: `""`.

Step-by-Step

➤ Copy the SimpleEdit program you built in Lesson 6, Exercise 9 (or download Lesson 6's version from the book's website).

➤ Replace the program's `TextBox` with a `RichTextBox` named `contentRichTextBox`.

➤ Add code to handle the Edit menu's commands.

  1. Open the program's form in the Form Designer. Click the `MenuStrip`, expand the Edit menu, and double-click the Undo menu item.

  2. Replace the placeholder call to `MessageBox.Show` with the following line of code so the event handler looks like this:

```
private void editUndoMenuItem_Click(object sender, EventArgs e)
{
    contentRichTextBox.Undo();
}
```

  3. Repeat the previous two steps for the other Edit menu items. The following code shows the new event handlers:

```
private void editUndoMenuItem_Click(object sender, EventArgs e)
{
    contentRichTextBox.Undo();
}

private void editRedoMenuItem_Click(object sender, EventArgs e)
{
    contentRichTextBox.Redo();
}

private void editCopyMenuItem_Click(object sender, EventArgs e)
{
    contentRichTextBox.Copy();
}

private void editCutMenuItem_Click(object sender, EventArgs e)
{
    contentRichTextBox.Cut();
}

private void editPasteMenuItem_Click(object sender, EventArgs e)
{
    contentRichTextBox.Paste();
}

private void editDeleteMenuItem_Click(object sender, EventArgs e)
{
    contentRichTextBox.SelectedText = "";
}

private void editSelectAllMenuItem_Click(object sender, EventArgs e)
{
    contentRichTextBox.SelectAll();
}
```

When you finish, test the program's new features. One of the `RichTextBox`'s more remarkable features is its ability to paste different kinds of items from the clipboard. For example, copy a picture to the clipboard and then use the program to paste it into the `RichTextBox`.

EXERCISES

1. [WPF, SimpleEdit] Repeat the Try It using the WPF program you built for Lesson 6's Exercise 10. Hint: To delete the current selection, use the statement `contentRichTextBox .Selection.Text = ""`.

2. [SimpleEdit] Copy the program you built for the Try It and add simple code to handle the File menu's New, Open, Save, and Exit commands. For the New command, simply clear the `RichTextBox`. (Hint: Use the `Clear` method.)

    For the Open and Save commands, just load and save the file `Test.rtf`. (The program will create the file the first time you save. If you try to open the file before it exists, the program will crash so don't use Open before you use Save.) Lesson 8 explains how to use file open and save dialogs to let the user pick the file that should be opened or saved.

3. [WPF, SimpleEdit] Repeat Exercise 2 using the program you built for Exercise 1. Hints:

    ➤ One way to clear the control's contents is to use the following code:

    ```
    contentRichTextBox.SelectAll();
    contentRichTextBox.Selection.Text = "";
    ```

    ➤ The preceding code works but is rather slow if the control contains a lot of text. The following code is more complicated but more efficient:

    ```
    TextRange range = new TextRange(
        contentRichTextBox.Document.ContentStart,
        contentRichTextBox.Document.ContentEnd);
    range.Text = "";
    ```

    ➤ To load the saved file, use the following code (sorry, but WPF's version of the `RichTextBox` is a bit more complicated):

    ```
    TextRange range = new TextRange(
        contentRichTextBox.Document.ContentStart,
        contentRichTextBox.Document.ContentEnd);
    using (System.IO.Stream stream =
        new System.IO.FileStream("Test.rtf", System.IO.FileMode.Open))
    {
        range.Load(stream, DataFormats.Rtf);
    }
    ```

    ➤ To save text into a file, use the following code:

    ```
    TextRange range = new TextRange(
        contentRichTextBox.Document.ContentStart,
        contentRichTextBox.Document.ContentEnd);
    using (System.IO.Stream stream =
        new System.IO.FileStream("Test.rtf", System.IO.FileMode.Create))
    {
        range.Save(stream, DataFormats.Rtf);
    }
    ```

4. [SimpleEdit] Copy the SimpleEdit program you built for Exercise 2 and add code to handle the Format menu's commands (except for the Font command and color commands, which are covered in Lesson 8).

Hints:

➤ To turn bullets on and off, use the statement `contentRichTextBox` `.SelectionBullet = formatBulletMenuItem.Checked`.

➤ Make the indentation commands (None, Hanging, Left, Right, and Both) reset any other indentations. For example, the Hanging command should set the `SelectionIndent` and `SelectionRightIndent` properties to 0 as in the following code:

```
contentRichTextBox.SelectionIndent = 0;
contentRichTextBox.SelectionRightIndent = 0;
contentRichTextBox.SelectionHangingIndent = 20;
```

5. [WPF, SimpleEdit] Copy the WPF SimpleEdit program you built for Exercise 3 and add code to handle the Format menu's alignment and bullet commands. Hints:

➤ To turn bullets on and off, use the statement `EditingCommands.ToggleBullets` `.Execute(null, contentRichTextBox)`.

➤ Use similar `EditingCommands` methods for the alignment commands.

6. [SimpleEdit] Copy the SimpleEdit program you built for Exercise 4 and add code to handle the toolbar's color commands.

7. The SimpleEdit program allows only the indentation styles None, Hanging, Left, Right, and Both. It doesn't allow other combinations such as Hanging plus Right. Build a program that uses tool strip buttons to let the user select each of the indentation properties (hanging, left, and right) individually. Provide a fourth button to clear all of the indentation properties.

8. Make a program with two menus and a `RichTextBox`. The File menu should contain the usual Exit command. The Font menu should contain the items Small, Medium, and Large and should use small, medium, and large fonts, respectively. When the user selects one of those items, the program should set the `RichTextBox`'s selected text to use that item's font.

9. [Hard] Make a program with a `RichTextBox` and a toolbar containing Undo and Redo buttons. Initially disable the buttons. Whenever the user changes the `RichTextBox`'s text (catch the `TextChanged` event) or clicks one of the buttons, use the `RichTextBox` control's `CanUndo` and `CanRedo` properties to enable or disable the buttons. Verify that this works as expected when you click the buttons or press Ctrl+Z or Ctrl+Y. Also make sure it works if you press Ctrl+V to paste into the `RichTextBox`.

> **NOTE** *Please select the videos for Lesson 7 online at* www.wrox.com/go/ csharp24hourtrainer2evideos.

Using Standard Dialogs

Many applications need to display dialogs to let the user select certain standard pieces of information. Probably the most common dialogs let the user select a file to open and select a file to save into. Other dialogs let the user select colors, filesystem folders, fonts, and printers for printing.

Closely related to the print dialog are the print preview dialog (which lets the user see a preview of a printout before sending it to the printer, possibly saving paper if the user then cancels the printout) and the page setup dialog (which lets the user select things like margins before printing).

You could build all of these dialogs yourself (or you will be able to once you've finished reading this book), but why should you? If so many programs need the exact same features, why shouldn't someone build standard dialogs that everyone can use?

Happily that's exactly what Microsoft did.

C# comes with the following standard dialogs that handle these common tasks:

- ➤ ColorDialog
- ➤ FolderBrowserDialog
- ➤ FontDialog
- ➤ OpenFileDialog
- ➤ PageSetupDialog
- ➤ PrintDialog
- ➤ PrintPreviewDialog
- ➤ SaveFileDialog

> **NOTE** *You might remember that in Lesson 1, I said, "Normally you don't need to worry about whether a feature is provided by Visual Studio, the C# language, or the .NET Framework." That's true here as well, but it's informative to note that these dialogs are actually provided by the .NET Framework, not C#. That doesn't change the way you use them, but it means they're the same dialogs used by all .NET languages such as Visual Basic, Visual C++, or JScript.*
>
> *By building these standard dialogs into the .NET Framework, Microsoft lets programmers using many languages share the same common features.*

These dialogs provide some fairly sophisticated features for you automatically with no additional code. For example, the OpenFileDialog class lets the user browse through the filesystem to select a file to open. The dialog can automatically verify that the file actually exists so the user cannot type in the name of a non-existent file and click Open.

Similarly, the SaveFileDialog class automatically prompts the user if the selected file *does* exist. For example, if the user selects the existing file Test.txt, the dialog displays the message "Test .txt already exists. Do you want to replace it?" If the user doesn't click Yes, the dialog doesn't close. By the time the dialog closes, the user must have picked a file that doesn't yet exist or signed off on destroying the original file.

In this lesson you learn how to display these standard dialogs. You learn how to initialize them to show the user the program's current settings, how to tell which button the user clicked, and how to use the selections the user made.

> **NOTE** *This lesson actually cheats a bit on the printing dialogs. Although it explains how to display these dialogs, you can't do anything really useful with them until you know how to print, which is a much more complicated topic. Lesson 30 gets into the details of how to print.*

USING DIALOGS IN GENERAL

You can use all of the standard dialogs in more or less the same way. The only differences are in how you initialize the dialogs so they show colors, fonts, files, or whatever and in how you handle the results.

You can use a standard dialog in Windows Forms applications by following these four steps:

1. Add the dialog to the form.
2. Initialize the dialog to show current settings.
3. Display the dialog and check the return result.
4. Process the results.

Adding the Dialog to the Form

You can add a dialog to a form just as you add any other component, such as a `Timer`. Like other components, the dialog appears below the form in the Component Tray.

The control Toolbox has a Dialogs tab that contains most of the standard dialogs so they are easy to find. The printing-related dialogs are contained in the Printing tab so they're also easy to find (if you know to look there). Figure 8-1 shows the Toolbox's Printing and Dialogs tabs.

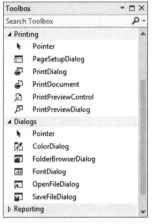

FIGURE 8-1

Initializing the Dialog

Most of the standard dialogs start with some initial selection. The `FontDialog` starts with a font selected, the `ColorDialog` starts with a color selected, and so forth. Normally you should initialize the dialog so it shows the user your program's current settings. For example, a `FontDialog` should show the program's current font.

Usually making these initial selections is easy. Simply set the dialog's key property (`Font`, `Color`, `Filename`) to the value you want to display.

For example, the following code sets a `ColorDialog`'s `Color` property to the form's current `BackColor` value. (Recall that `this` means the form or other object that is currently executing the code.)

```
backgroundColorDialog.Color = this.BackColor;
```

The only real trick here is in knowing what properties to set. Table 8-1 lists the key properties for the different kinds of dialogs.

TABLE 8-1

DIALOG	KEY PROPERTY
ColorDialog	Color
FolderBrowserDialog	SelectedPath
FontDialog	Font
OpenFileDialog	FileName
SaveFileDialog	FileName

The PageSetupDialog, PrintDialog, and PrintPreviewDialog are a bit different from the others so I won't say anything more about them here. Printing is covered in more detail in Lesson 30.

I just said that you should initialize the dialogs to show current values, but the file open and save dialogs have a special feature that might make you decide to skip this step. When you use them, they remember the directories they displayed last. That means if the user opens one of these dialogs again, it starts in the same directory it was in last time. In fact, if the user closes and restarts the program, the dialogs still remember where they were last.

> **NOTE** *If you have several different* OpenFileDialogs *(or* SaveFileDialogs*) in the same program, they all share the same idea of where they were last.*

The only reason you might want to initialize these dialogs is if you want the program to separately track more than one file. For example, you might want different places to save text files, bitmaps, and RTF files.

Also note that the OpenFileDialog and SaveFileDialog remember the same directory, so if you want to be able to load from one directory and save into another, you might want to initialize the dialogs.

Displaying the Dialog and Checking the Return Result

You display all of the standard dialogs by calling their ShowDialog methods. ShowDialog displays the dialog modally and then returns a value to tell the program whether the user clicked OK, Cancel, or some other button.

> **NOTE** *A modal dialog prevents the user from interacting with the program until it is closed. It forces the user to make a choice. In contrast, a modeless dialog would let the user move to the program's other forms without closing the dialog.*

> **NOTE** *Note that the OK buttons on some of the dialogs don't actually say "OK." The* OpenFileDialog's *OK button says "Open," the* SaveFileDialog's *OK button says "Save," and the* PrintDialog's *OK button says "Print." As far as the program is concerned, however, they're all OK buttons, and you test for them all in the same way.*

Your code should test the returned result and, if the user clicked OK, it should do something with the user's selection.

Unfortunately to make that test, you need to use an if statement, and if statements aren't covered until Lesson 18. Luckily this particular use of if statements is quite simple, so I feel only a little guilty about showing it to you now.

The following code shows how a program can display a ColorDialog named backgroundColorDialog:

```
if (backgroundColorDialog.ShowDialog() == DialogResult.OK)
{
    . . .
}
```

The code calls the dialog's ShowDialog method. It then uses the if statement to compare the value that ShowDialog returns to the value DialogResult.OK. If the values are equal (that's what == means in C#), the program does whatever is inside the braces (which I've omitted here).

If the user clicks the Cancel button, ShowDialog returns the value DialogResult.Cancel, so the if test fails and the program skips the code inside the braces.

> **NOTE** *If the user closes the dialog in any way other than clicking the OK button, the* ShowDialog *method returns* DialogResult.Cancel. *For example, if the user presses Alt+F4 or clicks the X button on the dialog's upper-right corner, the dialog considers itself canceled.*

Processing the Results

Finally, if the user clicked OK, the program should do something with whatever the user selected in the dialog. Often this means doing the opposite of the step where you initialized the dialog. For example, suppose a program uses the following code to initialize its ColorDialog:

```
backgroundColorDialog.Color = this.BackColor;
```

Then it would use the following code to set the form's `BackColor` property to the color that the user selected:

```
this.BackColor = backgroundColorDialog.Color;
```

Putting It All Together

The following code shows the whole sequence for a `ColorDialog`. The program initializes the dialog, displays it and checks the return value, and processes the result:

```
backgroundColorDialog.Color = this.BackColor;
if (backgroundColorDialog.ShowDialog() == DialogResult.OK)
{
    this.BackColor = backgroundColorDialog.Color;
}
```

This looks a bit more complicated than code examples in previous lessons, but it's not too bad. The only new part is the `if` test. The other statements simply set the dialog's `Color` property equal to the form's `BackColor` property and vice versa, and you've been setting properties for quite a while now.

USING DIALOG PROPERTIES

Table 8-1 earlier in this lesson listed the dialogs' key properties, but some of the dialogs have other useful properties, too.

For example, the `ColorDialog` has an `AllowFullOpen` property that determines whether the user can click the dialog's Define Custom Colors button to show an area on the right where the user can create new colors. Figure 8-2 shows a `ColorDialog` displaying this area.

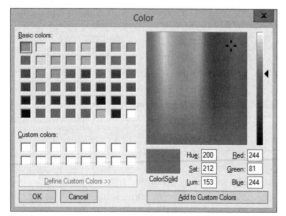

FIGURE 8-2

You can learn more about these extra properties by reading the online help. For example, Microsoft's help page for the `ColorDialog` is msdn.microsoft.com/library/system.windows .forms.colordialog.aspx. You can replace `colordialog` in this URL with the name of another dialog to find its web page.

Table 8-2 summarizes the `ColorDialog`'s most useful properties.

TABLE 8-2

PROPERTY	PURPOSE
AllowFullOpen	Determines whether the user can create custom colors.
Color	The selected color.
FullOpen	Determines whether the custom color area is open when the dialog appears.

Table 8-3 summarizes the `FolderBrowserDialog`'s most useful properties.

TABLE 8-3

PROPERTY	PURPOSE
RootFolder	The root folder where the dialog starts browsing. The Properties window lets you pick from values such as `Desktop`, `Favorites`, `History`, and `MyComputer`.
SelectedPath	The selected folder.

Table 8-4 summarizes the `FontDialog`'s most useful properties.

TABLE 8-4

PROPERTY	PURPOSE
FixedPitchOnly	Determines if the dialog allows the user to select only fixed-width fonts. This is useful, for example, if you are going to use the font to build a report and you need the characters to all have the same width so columns line up properly.
Font	The selected font.
FontMustExist	Determines whether the dialog raises an error if the selected font doesn't exist (for example, if the user types "ExtraBold" for the font style and that style isn't available for the selected font).
MaxSize	The largest allowed size for the font.
ShowColor	Determines whether the dialog lets the user select a font color. If you set this to `True`, use the dialog's `Color` property to see which color was selected.
ShowEffects	Determines whether the dialog lets the user select underline, strikeout, and font color. (To select font color, `ShowColor` and `ShowEffects` must both be `True`.)

Table 8-5 summarizes the `OpenFileDialog`'s most useful properties.

TABLE 8-5

PROPERTY	PURPOSE
AddExtension	If this is `True` and the user selects a filename without an extension, the dialog adds the default extension to the name.
CheckFileExists	If this is `True`, the dialog won't let the user pick a file that doesn't exist.
CheckPathExists	If this is `True`, the dialog won't let the user pick a file path that doesn't exist.
DefaultExt	The default file extension.
FileName	The selected file's name.
Filter	The file selection filter. (See the section "Using File Filters" later in this lesson for details.)
FilterIndex	The index of the currently selected filter. (See the section "Using File Filters" later in this lesson for details.)
InitialDirectory	The directory where the dialog initially starts.
ReadOnlyChecked	Indicates whether the user checked the dialog's Read Only box.
ShowReadOnly	Determines whether the dialog displays its Read Only box.
Title	The text displayed in the dialog's title bar.

The `SaveFileDialog` has many of the same properties as the `OpenFileDialog`. See Table 8-5 for descriptions of the properties `AddExtension`, `CheckFileExists`, `CheckPathExists`, `DefaultExt`, `FileName`, `Filter`, `FilterIndex`, `InitialDirectory`, and `Title`.

Table 8-6 summarizes `SaveFileDialog` properties that are not shared with the `OpenFileDialog`.

TABLE 8-6

PROPERTY	PURPOSE
CreatePrompt	If this is `True`, and the user selects a file that doesn't exist, the dialog asks if the user wants to create the file.
OverwritePrompt	If this is `True` and the user selects a file that already exists, the dialog asks if the user wants to overwrite it.
ValidateNames	Determines whether the dialog verifies that the filename doesn't contain any invalid characters.

Table 8-7 summarizes the `PrintDialog`'s most useful property.

TABLE 8-7

PROPERTY	PURPOSE
Document	You set this property to tell the dialog what document object to print. Lesson 30 has more to say about this.

Table 8-8 summarizes the `PrintPreviewDialog`'s most useful property.

TABLE 8-8

PROPERTY	PURPOSE
Document	You set this property to tell the dialog what document object to preview. Lesson 30 has more to say about this.

USING FILE FILTERS

Most of the dialogs' properties are fairly easy to understand. Two properties that are particularly confusing and important, however, are the `Filter` and `FilterIndex` properties provided by the `OpenFileDialog` and `SaveFileDialog`.

The `Filter` property is a list of text prompts and file-matching patterns separated by the | character. The items alternate between text prompts and the corresponding filter. The dialog provides a dropdown list where the user can select one of the text prompts. When the user selects a prompt, the dialog uses the corresponding filter to decide which files to display.

For example, consider the following value:

```
Bitmap Files|*.bmp|Graphic Files|*.bmp;*.gif;*.png;*.jpg|All Files|*.*
```

This value represents three categories of files:

➤ The text prompt "Bitmap Files" with filter `*.bmp`.

➤ The text prompt "Graphic Files" with filter `*.bmp;*.gif;*.png;*.jpg`. That filter matches files ending with .bmp, .gif, .png, or .jpg.

➤ The text prompt "All Files" with filter `*.*`.

Figure 8-3 shows an `OpenFileDialog`. The filter dropdown (just above the Open and Cancel buttons) has the text prompt "Graphics Files" selected. (The dialog automatically added the filter in parentheses just to confuse the user.) The dialog is listing the files in this directory that match the filter. In this case, the directory contains seven `.png` files.

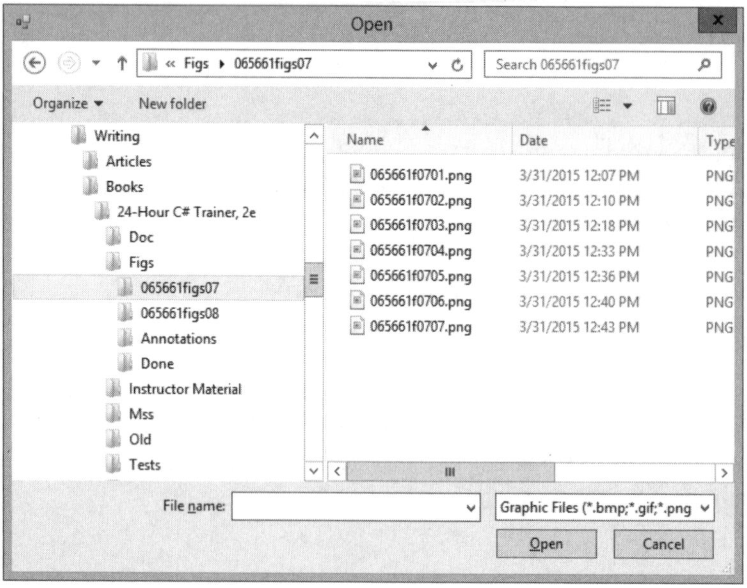

FIGURE 8-3

Once you understand the `Filter` property, the `FilterIndex` property is simple. `FilterIndex` is simply the index of the selected filter, where 1 means the first filter, 2 means the second, and so forth. (Remember in Lesson 7 when I said, "almost all numbering starts with 0 in C#"? This is one of the rare exceptions.) You can use `FilterIndex` to initially select the filter that you think will be most useful to the user.

The `OpenFileDialog` and `SaveFileDialog` both use the same type of `Filter` and `FilterIndex` properties. In fact, usually if a program displays both of these dialogs, they should use the same `Filter` value. If a program can load `.txt` and `.rtf` files, it should probably be able to save `.txt` and `.rtf` files.

> **NOTE** *To carry this idea one step further, you could set the* `SaveFileDialog`'s *`FilterIndex` property to the value selected by the user in the* `OpenFileDialog` *under the assumption that a user who loads a* `.txt` *file is later likely to want to save it as a* `.txt` *file.*

USING DIALOGS IN WPF

Unfortunately, WPF provides only a `PrintDialog` and doesn't include the other standard dialogs.

If you've been paying attention, you're probably saying, "Wait. Earlier in this lesson you said that the standard dialogs were provided by the .NET Framework. Doesn't that mean WPF programs can use them, too?" (If you said this and are reading this book as part of a programming course, tell your instructor that you deserve 5 extra points on the next quiz.)

That's true—WPF programs *can* use the standard dialogs, but not in the same way a Windows Forms application does.

WPF normally doesn't display the common dialogs in the Toolbox, so you can't add them to a window and you can't set their properties in the Properties window at design time. Instead, you need to create, initialize, and display the dialogs with code.

Before you write any code, you need to tell Visual Studio about the part of the .NET Framework that contains the dialogs. To do that, open the Project menu and select Add Reference to open the Reference Manager shown in Figure 8-4.

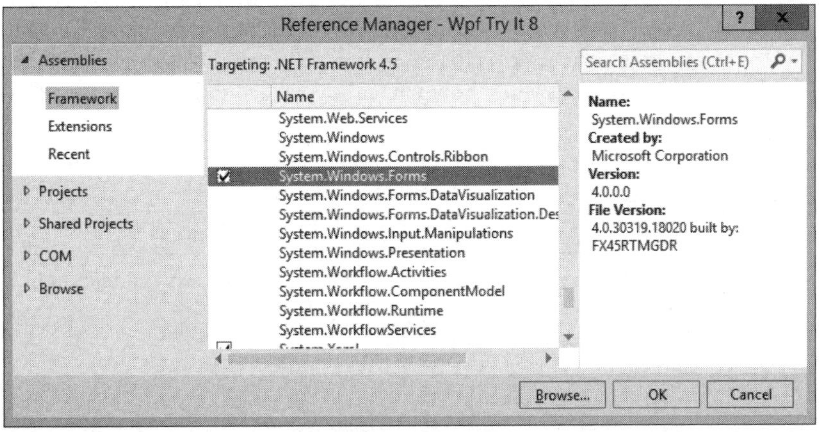

FIGURE 8-4

On this dialog, check the boxes next to System.Windows.Forms and System.Drawing, and click OK. (The first reference tells where the dialogs are defined. The second lets the program understand `Color` and `Font` objects, so you need it if you're working with those two dialogs.)

Now you can use code similar to the following to make a WPF program display an `OpenFileDialog`:

```
// Create the OpenFileDialog.
System.Windows.Forms.OpenFileDialog fileDialog =
    new System.Windows.Forms.OpenFileDialog();

// Set the Filter.
fileDialog.Filter = "Text Files|*.txt|RTF Files|*.rtf|All Files|*.*";

// Display the dialog and check the result.
if (fileDialog.ShowDialog() == System.Windows.Forms.DialogResult.OK)
{
    // Process the selected file.
    MessageBox.Show(fileDialog.FileName);
}
```

The first statement (which spans two lines because it's so long) creates a System.Windows.Forms .OpenFileDialog object. That statement really just creates an OpenFileDialog object. The rest of the declaration tells Visual Studio that this kind of object is located in the System.Windows.Forms part of the .NET Framework.

Next the code initializes the dialog. This example just sets the dialog's Filter property, but you could set other properties, too, such as FilterIndex, CheckFileExists, and ShowReadOnly.

The code then displays the dialog by calling its ShowDialog method as before and compares the returned result with System.Windows.Forms.DialogResult.OK. If the user clicked the OK button, the program processes the result. This example simply displays the selected file's name in a message box, but a real application would do something like open the file.

Unfortunately, the results returned by some of the dialogs aren't directly usable by a WPF program. For example, the ColorDialog lets the user select a Color but WPF programs use Brushes instead of Colors. Similarly, the FontDialog lets the user pick a Font but WPF programs don't use Font objects directly. Some of this lesson's exercises show how you can work around some of those issues.

TRY IT

In this Try It, you get to try out all of the standard dialogs except the PageSetupDialog (which is hard to use until you're doing actual printing). You initialize, display, and process the results of the dialogs (if the user clicks the OK button).

Lesson Requirements

In this lesson, you:

➤ Use Labels, TextBoxes, and Buttons to make a form similar to the one shown in Figure 8-5.

➤ Add ColorDialog, FontDialog, FolderBrowserDialog, OpenFileDialog, SaveFileDialog, PrintDialog, and PrintPreviewDialog components to the form.

➤ When the user clicks the BackColor button, display the ColorDialog but don't allow the user to define custom colors. If the user clicks OK, set the form's BackColor property to the dialog's Color value.

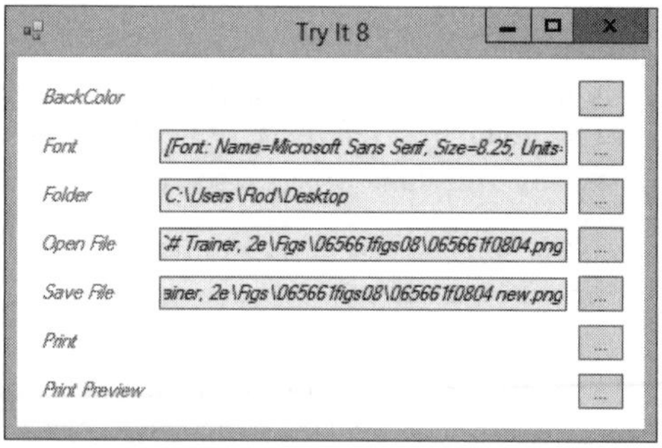

FIGURE 8-5

➤ When the user clicks the Font button, display the FontDialog, allowing the user to select the font's color. If the user clicks OK, set the form's Font property to the dialog's Font value and its ForeColor property to the dialog's Color property.

➤ When the user clicks the Folder button, display the FolderBrowserDialog. Make the dialog start browsing at MyComputer. If the user clicks OK, make the Folder TextBox display the dialog's SelectedPath property.

➤ When the user clicks the Open File button, display the OpenFileDialog. Use a filter that lets the user select text files, RTF files, or all files. If the user clicks Open, make the Open File TextBox display the dialog's FileName property and set the SaveFileDialog's FilterIndex equal to the OpenFileDialog's FilterIndex.

➤ When the user clicks the Save File button, display the SaveFileDialog. Use the same filter used by the OpenFileDialog. If the user clicks Save, make the Save File TextBox display the dialog's FileName property and set the OpenFileDialog's FilterIndex equal to the SaveFileDialog's FilterIndex.

➤ When the user clicks the Print button, display the PrintDialog and ignore the return result.

➤ When the user clicks the Print Preview button, display the PrintPreviewDialog and ignore the return result.

> **NOTE** *You can download the code and resources for this lesson from the web-site at* www.wrox.com/go/csharp24hourtrainer2e.

Hints

➤ Be sure to initialize each of the dialogs before displaying them.

Step-by-Step

➤ Use Labels, TextBoxes, and Buttons to make a form similar to the one shown in Figure 8-5.

1. Add and arrange the controls in whatever manner you find easiest.

2. Set the Buttons' Anchor properties to Top, Right. Set the TextBoxes' Anchor properties to Top, Left, Right.

➤ Add ColorDialog, FontDialog, FolderBrowserDialog, OpenFileDialog, SaveFileDialog, PrintDialog, and PrintPreviewDialog components to the form.

1. Add the dialogs. They appear in the Component Tray, not on the form.

2. Give the dialogs good names.

➤ When the user clicks the BackColor button, display the ColorDialog but don't allow the user to define custom colors. If the user clicks OK, set the form's BackColor property to the dialog's Color value.

1. To prevent the user from defining custom colors, set the ColorDialog's AllowFullOpen property to False.

2. Use code similar to the following:

```
private void backColorButton_Click(object sender, EventArgs e)
{
    backgroundColorDialog.Color = BackColor;
```

```
        if (backgroundColorDialog.ShowDialog() == DialogResult.OK)
        {
            BackColor = backgroundColorDialog.Color;
        }
    }
```

➤ When the user clicks the Font button, display the FontDialog, allowing the user to select the font's color. If the user clicks OK, set the form's Font property to the dialog's Font value and its ForeColor property to the dialog's Color property.

1. To allow the user to select the font's color, set the dialog's ShowColor property to True.

2. Use code similar to the following:

```
private void fontButton_Click(object sender, EventArgs e)
{
    formFontDialog.Font = Font;
    formFontDialog.Color = ForeColor;
    if (formFontDialog.ShowDialog() == DialogResult.OK)
    {
        Font = formFontDialog.Font;
        fontTextBox.Text = formFontDialog.Font.ToString();

        ForeColor = formFontDialog.Color;
    }
}
```

➤ When the user clicks the Folder button, display the FolderBrowserDialog. Make the dialog start browsing at MyComputer. If the user clicks OK, make the Folder TextBox display the dialog's SelectedPath property.

1. To start browsing at MyComputer, use the Properties window to set the dialog's RootFolder property to MyComputer.

2. Use code similar to the following:

```
private void folderButton_Click(object sender, EventArgs e)
{
    if (testFolderBrowserDialog.ShowDialog() == DialogResult.OK)
    {
        folderTextBox.Text = testFolderBrowserDialog.SelectedPath;
    }
}
```

➤ When the user clicks the Open File button, display the OpenFileDialog. Use a filter that lets the user select text files, RTF files, or all files. If the user clicks Open, make the Open File TextBox display the dialog's FileName property and set the SaveFileDialog's FilterIndex equal to the OpenFileDialog's FilterIndex.

1. Use the filter:

   ```
   Text Files|*.txt|RTF Files|*.rtf|All Files|*.*
   ```

2. Use code similar to the following:

   ```csharp
   private void openFileButton_Click(object sender, EventArgs e)
   {
       if (testOpenFileDialog.ShowDialog() == DialogResult.OK)
       {
           openFileTextBox.Text = testOpenFileDialog.FileName;
           testSaveFileDialog.FilterIndex =
               testOpenFileDialog.FilterIndex;
       }
   }
   ```

➤ When the user clicks the Save File button, display the `SaveFileDialog`. Use the same filter used by the `OpenFileDialog`. If the user clicks Save, make the Save File `TextBox` display the dialog's `FileName` property and set the `OpenFileDialog`'s `FilterIndex` equal to the `SaveFileDialog`'s `FilterIndex`.

1. Use the filter:

   ```
   Text Files|*.txt|RTF Files|*.rtf|All Files|*.*
   ```

2. Use code similar to the following:

   ```csharp
   private void saveFileButton_Click(object sender, EventArgs e)
   {
       if (testSaveFileDialog.ShowDialog() == DialogResult.OK)
       {
           saveFileTextBox.Text = testSaveFileDialog.FileName;
           testOpenFileDialog.FilterIndex =
               testSaveFileDialog.FilterIndex;
       }
   }
   ```

➤ When the user clicks the Print button, display the `PrintDialog`. Ignore the return result.

1. Use code similar to the following:

   ```csharp
   private void printButton_Click(object sender, EventArgs e)
   {
       testPrintDialog.ShowDialog();
   }
   ```

➤ When the user clicks the Print Preview button, display the `PrintPreviewDialog`. Ignore the return result.

1. Use code similar to the following:

   ```csharp
   private void printPreviewButton_Click(object sender, EventArgs e)
   {
       testPrintPreviewDialog.ShowDialog();
   }
   ```

EXERCISES

1. [WPF] Repeat the Try It with a WPF program. Because a WPF program can't directly use the values selected by the `ColorDialog` or `FontDialog`, just display the user's selections in `TextBoxes`. For the `ColorDialog`, display the dialog's `Color.ToString()` value. For the `FontDialog`, display the dialog's `Font.ToString()` value. (Hint: Don't worry about setting the dialogs' `FilterIndex` properties.)

2. [WPF] Copy the program you wrote for Exercise 1 and use the color information. Use code similar to the following to set the window's background color:

   ```
   Color backColor = new Color()
   {
       A = 255,
       R = colorDialog.Color.R,
       G = colorDialog.Color.G,
       B = colorDialog.Color.B
   };
   Background = new SolidColorBrush(backColor);
   ```

   For the font color, use a similar technique to set the foreground color of the font `TextBox`. (Setting the foreground color for the entire window is harder.)

3. [WPF] Make a program similar to the one shown in Figure 8-6.

   Hints:

   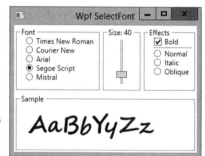

   FIGURE 8-6

   ➤ If any of the event handlers make the program crash when it starts, add the following statement at the beginning of the event handler to prevent the program from trying to use controls before they are created.

   ```
   if (!IsLoaded) return;
   ```

   ➤ For the font `RadioButtons`' `Checked` events, use code similar to the following:

   ```
   sampleLabel.FontFamily = new FontFamily("Arial");
   ```

   ➤ For the `Slider`'s `ValueChanged` event, use code similar to the following:

   ```
   if (!IsLoaded) return;
   sizeGroupBox.Header = "Size: " + sizeSlider.Value.ToString();
   sampleLabel.FontSize = sizeSlider.Value;
   ```

   ➤ Give `Checked` and `Unchecked` event handlers to the Bold `CheckBox`. Make them set `sampleLabel.FontWeight` to `FontWeights.Bold` or `FontWeights.Normal`.

   ➤ Give `Checked` event handlers to the Normal, Italic, and Oblique `RadioButtons`. Make them set `sampleLabel.FontStyle` to `FontStyles.Normal`, `FontStyles.Italic`, and `FontStyles.Oblique`, respectively.

4.   [SimpleEdit] Copy the SimpleEdit program you built in Lesson 7, Exercise 6 (or download Lesson 7's version from the book's website) and add the file open and save dialogs for the File menu's Open and Save As commands. Use `Filter` properties that let the user select RTF files, text files, or all files. Continue using the `RichTextBox`'s `LoadFile` and `SaveFile` methods even though they don't work properly for non-RTF files.

5.   [SimpleEdit] Copy the SimpleEdit program you built for Exercise 4 and add a font selection dialog for the Format menu's Font item, and the font tool strip button. If the user selects a font and clicks OK, make the `RichTextBox`'s selected text use the selected font.

6.   [SimpleEdit] Copy the SimpleEdit program you built for Exercise 5 and modify it so it allows the user to select a color on the font dialog.

7.   [SimpleEdit] Copy the SimpleEdit program you built for Exercise 6 and add color selection dialogs for the Format and context menus' Text Color and Background Color items. (Allow custom colors.)

> **NOTE** *Please select the videos for Lesson 8 online at* www.wrox.com/go/ csharp24hourtrainer2evideos.

9

Creating and Displaying New Forms

Most of this book so far has dealt with building forms. Previous lessons explained how to add, arrange, and handle the events of controls on a form. They explained how to work with specific kinds of controls such as `Buttons`, `MenuStrips`, `ContextMenuStrips`, and `ToolStrips`. Using these techniques, you can build some pretty nice forms that use simple code to manipulate properties. So far, however, you've only learned how to use a single form.

In this lesson you learn how to display multiple forms in a single program. You see how to add new forms to the project and how to display one or more instances of those forms. Once you've mastered these techniques, you can make programs that display any number of forms for all kinds of different purposes.

ADDING NEW FORMS

To add a new form to a project, open the Project menu and select Add Windows Form to see the dialog shown in Figure 9-1.

Leave the Windows Form template selected, enter a good name for the new type of form, and click Add. After you click Add, Visual Studio adds the new form type to the project. Figure 9-2 shows the new form in Solution Explorer.

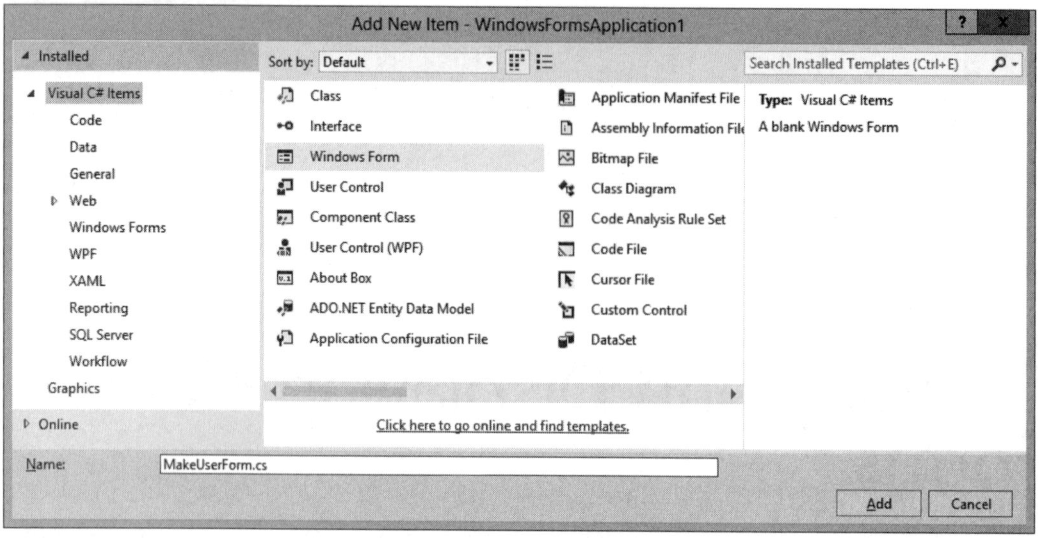

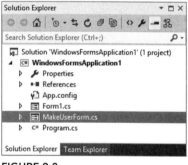

FIGURE 9-1

FIGURE 9-2

Now you can add `Labels`, `TextBoxes`, `Buttons`, `MenuStrips`, and any other controls you like to the new form.

> **NOTE** *Remember, to open a form in the Form Designer, double-click it in Solution Explorer.*

UNDERSTANDING CLASSES AND INSTANCES

When you add a new form to the project, you're really adding a new *type* of form, not a new instance of that type. If you add the `MakeUserForm` type to a project and then run the program, you still only see the original startup form (with the catchy name `Form1`) and `MakeUserForm` is nowhere to be seen.

Form types such as `Form1` and `MakeUserForm` are *classes*. They're like blueprints for making copies of the class, which are called *instances*. These are important and sometimes confusing topics so I'm going to explain them briefly now and explain them again in greater detail later in the book in the lessons in Section IV.

A class defines the characteristics of any objects from that class. Your code can use the `new` keyword to create objects of the class. Once you define the class you can make as many copies (instances) as you like, and every copy is identical in structure to all of the others. Different instances may have different property values but their overall features are the same.

> **NOTE** *You've actually been working with classes and instances for quite a while.* `Form1` *is a class. When you create a new project, Visual Studio adds code to create and display an instance of the* `Form1` *class.*
>
> *Controls are also classes. For example, the* `Label` *class defines the behaviors of labels. When you add* `Labels` *to a form, you're adding instances of the* `Label` *class to the form. Those instances can have different property values such as* `BackColor`, `Enabled`, `Anchor`, *and* `Text`, *but they all follow the rules defined by the* `Label` *class.*

For a form example, suppose you define a `MakeUserForm` that has First Name, Last Name, Street, City, State, and ZIP `Labels` and `TextBoxes`. Now suppose your program displays two instances of this form class. Both of the forms will have the same `Labels` and `TextBoxes`, so they have basically the same structure. However, the user can type different values into the two forms.

Your code can also change different instances in various ways. For example, menu items, buttons, and other controls could invoke event handlers that modify the form: change its colors, move controls around, resize the form, or whatever. Here's one of the more potentially confusing features of classes: the code in the event handlers modify the form that is currently running the code.

For example, suppose you build a form that has three `Buttons` that change the form's `BackColor` property to red, green, and blue, respectively, and then you display three instances of the form. When the user clicks the first form's Red button, the event handler makes the first form red but the other forms are unchanged. The code in the event handler is running in the first form's instance so that's the form it affects.

If you then click the Green button on the second form, the event handler changes that form's background color to green. The first form still has its red background and the third form still has its original background color.

Hopefully by now you think I've beaten this topic into the ground and you understand the difference between the class (`MakeUserForm`) and the instance (a copy of `MakeUserForm` visible on the screen). If so, you're ready to learn how to actually display forms.

DISPLAYING FORMS

The `new` keyword creates a new instance of a form. If you want to do anything useful with the form, your code needs a way to refer to the instance it just created. It can do that with a *variable*. I'm jumping the gun a bit by discussing variables (they're covered in detail in Lesson 11) but, as was the case when I introduced the `if` statement in Lesson 8, this particular use of the concept is very useful and not too confusing, so I feel only a little guilty about discussing it now.

In short, a variable is a named chunk of memory that can hold a piece of data. To declare a variable to refer to a form instance, you enter the form's type followed by whatever name you want to give the variable. For example, the following code declares a variable named `newUserForm` of type `MakeUserForm`:

```
MakeUserForm newUserForm;
```

At this point, the program has a variable that *could* refer to a `MakeUserForm` object but right now it doesn't refer to anything. It's like an empty envelope that could hold a `MakeUserForm` instance. At this point the variable contains the special value `null`, which basically means it doesn't refer to anything.

You can use the `new` keyword to create a new instance of the form class. You can then set the variable equal to the new form instance. For example, the following code creates a new `MakeNewUser` form and makes the `newUserForm` variable point to it:

```
newUserForm = new MakeUserForm();
```

Now the variable refers to the new form. The final step is to display the new form. You can do that by calling the new form's `ShowDialog` or `Show` method.

> **NOTE** *Technically the variable doesn't hold or contain the form. Instead, it contains a reference to the form. The reference is like an address that points to where the form really is in memory. When your code says something like* `newUserForm.Show()`, *the program hunts down the actual form instance and invokes its* `Show` *method.*
>
> *For now the distinction is small and you don't need to worry too much about it, but later it will be useful to know that some variables are value types that actually hold their values (things like* `int`, `long`, `double`) *and some are reference types that hold references to their values (things like controls, forms, and, interestingly,* `string`).
>
> *Lesson 17 says more about this when it discusses structures.*

The `ShowDialog` method displays the form *modally*. That means the form appears on top of the program's other forms and the user cannot interact with the other forms until this form closes.

This is the way dialogs normally work. For example, when you open the Project menu and select Add Windows Form, the Add New Item dialog displays modally so you cannot interact with other parts of the IDE (such as the Properties window, Solution Explorer, or menus) until you close the dialog by clicking Add or Cancel.

The following code displays the form referred to by the variable newUserForm modally:

```
newUserForm.ShowDialog();
```

The Show method displays the form *non-modally*. That means the form appears and the user can interact with it or with the program's other forms.

The following code displays the form referred to by the variable newUserForm non-modally:

```
newUserForm.Show();
```

The UserForms example program shown in Figure 9-3 displays a main form with a New User button. Each time you click the button, the program displays a new MakeUserForm non-modally. Figure 9-3 shows the main form and two MakeUserForms.

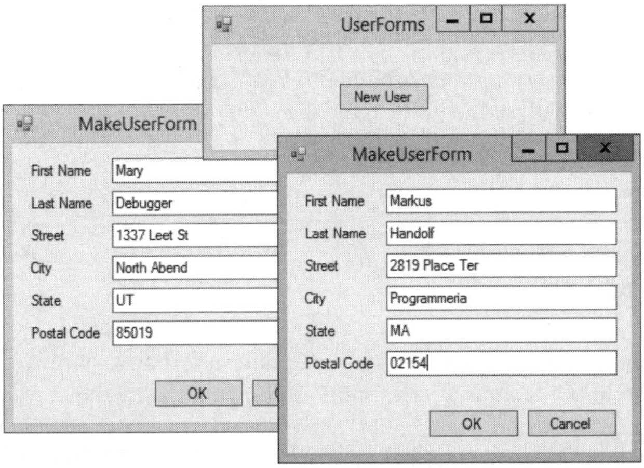

FIGURE 9-3

The following code shows how the UserForms program displays a new MakeUserForm when you click its button:

```
private void newUserButton_Click(object sender, EventArgs e)
{
    MakeUserForm newUserForm;
    newUserForm = new MakeUserForm();
    newUserForm.Show();
}
```

The code declares a variable to refer to the form, creates the new form instance, and displays the instance non-modally.

Each time you click the button, the event handler executes again. Each time it runs, the event handler creates a new version of the variable named newUserForm, makes a new instance of the MakeUserForm, and displays that instance, so each time you click the button, you get a new form.

FLOOD OF FORMS

In Windows Forms applications, the startup form's type `Form1` is just like any other form type, so a program can make new instances of it. That means you can create more forms that look just like the startup form if you want.

Although all forms look about the same to the user, the startup form has a special position in the application. The program keeps running only as long as the startup form exists. If you close that form, all of the others close, too.

To avoid confusion, you should generally make the startup form look different from other forms so the user knows that it's special.

By default, the windows in WPF applications run independently so if you close the main window, the others keep running. If you want all of the windows to close when the main window does, execute the following statement when the program starts, for example, in the main window's `Loaded` event handler:

```
Application.Current.ShutdownMode = ShutdownMode.OnMainWindowClose;
```

CONTROLLING REMOTE FORMS

When you create a new form and make a variable to refer to it, you can later use that variable to manipulate the form. There's just one catch: the techniques described so far don't keep the new form variable around long enough to be useful.

For example, the following code defines the `newUserForm` variable, makes it point to a new form, and displays the form:

```
private void newUserButton_Click(object sender, EventArgs e)
{
    MakeUserForm newUserForm;
    newUserForm = new MakeUserForm();
    newUserForm.Show();
}
```

When the program finishes executing the event handler, the event handler stops running. If the user clicks the button again, the event handler springs back into action.

Unfortunately, when the event handler stops running, it loses its grip on the `newUserForm` variable. The next time the event handler runs, it creates a new variable named `newUserForm` and works with that one.

This is bad for a program that wants to manipulate the new form later. Because the variable is gone, it can't refer to it so it can't manipulate the form.

The good news is that this is fairly easy to fix. If you move the variable's declaration out of the event handler, the variable exists throughout the program's lifetime. The event handler can make the variable point to a new form, and it can then use the variable later to manipulate that form.

The RemoteForm example program shown in Figure 9-4 uses the following main form code to manage a secondary ColorForm:

```
// The remote form we will manipulate.
ColorForm remoteColorForm;

// Create and display the remote form.
private void Form1_Load(object sender,
EventArgs e)
{
    remoteColorForm = new ColorForm();
    remoteColorForm.Show();
}

// Make the color form red.
private void redButton_Click(object sender, EventArgs e)
{
    remoteColorForm.BackColor = Color.Red;
    remoteColorForm.ForeColor = Color.Pink;
}
```

FIGURE 9-4

The code starts by declaring the variable remoteColorForm outside of any event handler.

When the program displays the main form, its Load event handler creates and displays a new ColorForm.

When the user clicks the main form's Red button, its event handler changes the remote form's BackColor and ForeColor properties to red and pink, respectively. The startup form also contains green and blue buttons that have similar event handlers.

The remoteColorForm variable is declared outside of the event handlers, so the event handlers have access to it. The form's Load event handler initializes the variable and displays the remote form. The redButton_Click event handler uses it. Because the variable is declared outside of the event handlers, they can all use it. (Lesson 13 has more to say about when and where variables are available to the code.)

In addition to modifying a remote form's properties, you can change the properties of the controls on that form. You refer to a control by using the form variable, followed by a dot, followed by the control's name.

For example, the bold line in the following code accesses the form referred to by the remote ColorForm variable. It locates that form's messageLabel control and changes its Text property to "I'm red!":

```
private void btnRed_Click(object sender, EventArgs e)
{
    color_form.BackColor = Color.Red;
    color_form.ForeColor = Color.Pink;
    color_form.lblMessage.Text = "I'm red!";
}
```

There's one small catch to this technique: by default the controls on a form are private so the code in other forms can't manipulate at them. You can easily fix this by setting a control's Modifiers property to `Public`, either in the Form Designer or in code. Now other forms can see the control and change its properties.

> **NOTE** *Controls on a form are private to prevent other pieces of code from accidentally messing them up. By making a variable public, you remove this safeguard. In technical terms, you have weakened the form's encapsulation—its ability to hide its internal details from the outside world.*
>
> *In this case, you want to allow access to this label's* Text *property so marking the label as public is reasonable. However, by making the label public you make all of its properties, methods, and events public, not just its* Text *property.*
>
> *A more restrictive approach would be to add a public* SetCaption *method to the* ColorForm. *Then other code would call that method instead of setting the label's text directly. You learn how to build those kinds of methods in Lesson 20.*

TRY IT

In this Try It, you create an application similar to the one shown in Figure 9-5. When the user clicks the main form's buttons, the program displays the other forms non-modally.

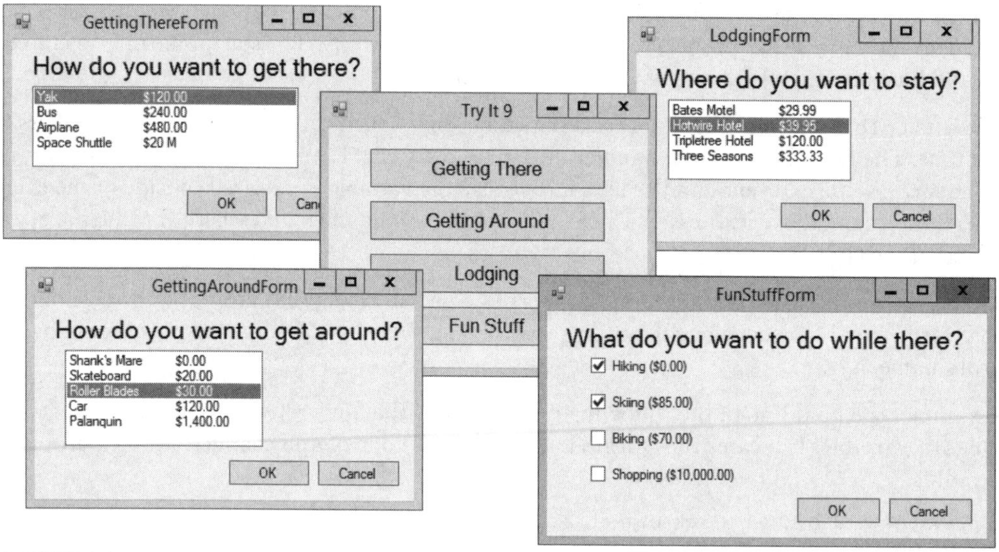

FIGURE 9-5

Lesson Requirements

In this lesson, you:

➤ Create the forms shown in Figure 9-5.

➤ Declare the form variables outside of any event handler.

➤ In the main form's Load event handler, add code to create the form instances but don't display the forms.

➤ Add code to the main form's Button event handlers to display the corresponding secondary forms non-modally.

> **NOTE** *You can download the code and resources for this lesson from the web-site at* www.wrox.com/go/csharp24hourtrainer2e.

Hints

➤ Normally every form appears in the taskbar. To avoid cluttering the taskbar with all of the secondary forms, set their ShowInTaskbar properties to False.

Step-by-Step

➤ Create the forms shown in Figure 9-5.

1. Create the main form.

    a. Start a new project. In the Properties window, expand the main form's Font property and set its Size subproperty to 12.

    b. Add the Buttons. Center them as a group and set their Anchor properties to None.

2. Create the GettingThereForm.

    a. Open the Project menu and select Add Windows Form. Enter the form type name **GettingThereForm** and click Add.

    b. Set the form's ShowInTaskbar property to False.

    c. Add the Label, ListBox, and Buttons. Set the ListBox's Anchor property to Top, Bottom, Left. Set the Buttons' Anchor properties to Bottom, Right.

3. Create the GettingAroundForm.

    a. Repeat step 2 for the GettingAroundForm.

4. Create the LodgingForm.

    a. Repeat step 2 for the LodgingForm.

5. Create the `FunStuffForm`.

    a. Repeat step 2 for the `FunStuffForm`. Leave the `CheckBoxes`' `Anchor` properties with their default values `Top`, `Left`.

➤ Declare the form variables outside of any event handler.

    1. Add the following to the main form's code module outside of any event handlers:

```
// The remote forms.
GettingThereForm gettingThereForm;
GettingAroundForm gettingAroundForm;
LodgingForm lodgingForm;
FunStuffForm funStuffForm;
```

➤ In the main form's `Load` event handler, add code to create the form instances but don't display the forms.

    1. Use code similar to the following:

```
// Initialize the forms but don't display them.
private void Form1_Load(object sender, EventArgs e)
{
    gettingThereForm = new GettingThereForm();
    gettingAroundForm = new GettingAroundForm();
    lodgingForm = new LodgingForm();
    funStuffForm = new FunStuffForm();
}
```

➤ Add code to the main form's `Button` event handlers to display the corresponding secondary forms non-modally.

    1. Create the `Button Click` event handlers and make each call the corresponding form variable's `Show` method:

```
// Display the getting there form.
private void gettingThereButton_Click(object sender, EventArgs e)
{
    gettingThereForm.Show();
}

// Display the getting around form.
private void gettingAroundButton_Click(object sender, EventArgs e)
{
    gettingAroundForm.Show();
}

// Display the lodging form.
private void lodgingButton_Click(object sender, EventArgs e)
{
    lodgingForm.Show();
}

// Display the fun stuff form.
private void funStuffButton_Click(object sender, EventArgs e)
{
    funStuffForm.Show();
}
```

EXERCISES

1. Build the UserForms application shown in Figure 9-3.

2. [WPF] Repeat Exercise 1 with a WPF application. (Hint: Don't forget to make all of the forms close when you close the main window.)

3. Build the RemoteForm application shown in Figure 9-4.

4. [WPF] Repeat Exercise 3 with a WPF application. Hints:

   ➤ In WPF, set colors equal to brushes as in `Brushes.Red`.

   ➤ To set the remote window's background color, set its `Background` property.

   ➤ To set the remote form's text color, set the `Label`'s `Foreground` property.

   ➤ You don't need to set the `Modifiers` property in WPF. (WPF controls don't have that property.)

5. Modify the program you wrote for Exercise 3 so the buttons also change the label on the color form. For example, the Red button should make the label say, "I'm red!" (Hint: Don't forget to set the `Label`'s `Modifiers` property to `Public`.)

6. [WPF] Repeat Exercise 5 with the WPF application you built for Exercise 4.

7. [WPF] Repeat the Try It with a WPF application. (Hint: Don't forget to set the `ShowInTaskbar` property.)

8. Unfortunately the Try It has a major problem. If you close one of the secondary forms and then click the main form's button to redisplay that form, the program crashes.

   When you close the form, it is destroyed. When you click the button again, the program tries to display the destroyed form and that won't work.

   To fix the program, give each of the secondary forms a `FormClosing` event handler similar to the following:

   ```
   private void LodgingForm_FormClosing(object sender,
       FormClosingEventArgs e)
   {
       e.Cancel = true;
       Hide();
   }
   ```

   The first statement cancels the close so the form stays open. The second statement makes the form invisible but keeps it alive.

9. [WPF] Repeat Exercise 8 for the WPF program you built in Exercise 7. (Hint: In WPF you need to use the `Closing` event.)

10. Make a program that displays a `Button` that says "New Form." When the user clicks the `Button`, display a new non-modal instance of the same kind of form. (What happens when you click the new form's button? What happens if you close the new form? What happens if you make several forms and then close the original one?)

11. [WPF] Repeat Exercise 10 with a WPF application. After you experiment a bit, set `Application.Current.ShutdownMode = ShutdownMode.OnMainWindowClose` and test the program again.

12. Copy the program you made for Exercise 10 and add a `TextBox` named `valueTextBox` to the form. Before you display the new form, copy the main form's `TextBox` value into the new form's `TextBox`. (Hint: You don't need to set the `TextBox`'s `Modifiers` property to `Public` because the new form is the same kind as the old one. You need to do this only if a form of one type wants to peek at the controls on a form of a different type.)

13. [WPF] Repeat Exercise 12 with the WPF program you made for Exercise 11.

14. Make a program that displays a `TextBox` and a "New Form" `Button`. When the user clicks the `Button`, display a new form of type `MessageForm` modally.

The `MessageForm` holds two `Label`s. The first `Label` says "You entered." The second is blank. When it displays the `MessageForm`, the main program should copy whatever is in its `TextBox` into the `MessageForm`'s second label. (Hint: Now you need to set the label's `Modifiers` property to `Public`.)

15. [WPF] Repeat Exercise 14 with a WPF application.

16. Build the Pick A Picture program shown in Figure 9-6. When the user clicks one of the thumbnail images on the main form, the program displays a `PictureForm` showing the image at full scale. Use whatever images you like.

FIGURE 9-6

Hints:

➤ Display the thumbnail images in `PictureBoxes` with `ScaleMode` set to `Zoom`.

➤ Place a `PictureBox` with `Location = (0, 0)` on the `PictureForm`. Set its `SizeMode` property to `AutoSize`.

➤ Just before you display the `PictureForm`, use the following code to make it fit the `PictureBox` it contains:

```
newPictureForm.ClientSize = newPictureForm.imagePictureBox.Size
```

17. [WPF] Repeat Exercise 16 with a WPF application. Hints:

➤ On the `PictureWindow`, set the size of the `Image` control to match the size of the pictures.

➤ To make the `PictureWindow` fit the `Image` control, set the window's `SizeToContent` property to `WidthAndHeight`.

18. [Bonus] As I've mentioned before, redundant code is usually a sign that the program's structure can be improved. The Pick A Picture program from Exercise 16 uses four practically identical event handlers. The only difference is the image that they assign to the `PictureForm`'s background.

You can improve this program by making all four `PictureBoxes` use the same event handler and making the event handler figure out which image to use.

The event handler's `sender` parameter is the control that raised the event, in this case, the `PictureBox` that the user clicked. The data type of that parameter is `object`, but it actually holds a `PictureBox`. You can get a variable that refers to that `PictureBox` by using the `as` keyword.

The `as` keyword tells the program to treat some value (in this case the `sender` parameter) as if it were some other type (in this case a `PictureBox`). The following code shows how you can get a variable that treats the `sender` parameter as a `PictureBox`:

```
PictureBox selectedPictureBox;
selectedPictureBox = sender as PictureBox;
```

Copy the program you built for Exercise 16. Modify the first event handler so it uses the `as` keyword to get a reference to the `PictureBox` that the user clicked and then uses that reference to display the correct picture. Then make all of the `PictureBoxes` share that event handler.

19. [Bonus, WPF] Repeat Exercise 18 for the WPF application you build in Exercise 17.

NOTE *Please select the videos for Lesson 9 online at* www.wrox.com/go/csharp24hourtrainer2evideos.

10

Building Custom Dialogs

The standard dialogs described in Lesson 8 make it easy to perform typical chores such as picking files, folders, colors, and fonts. Those dialogs can get you pretty far, but sometimes you may want a dialog that is customized for your application.

For example, you might want to display a dialog where the user can enter a new customer's contact information (name, address, phone number, and hat size). It's unlikely that any predefined standard dialog could ever handle that situation.

Fortunately, it's easy to build custom dialogs. All you need to do is build a new form as described in Lesson 9, add a few buttons, and set a few properties.

In this lesson you learn how to build custom dialogs and make them as easy to use as the standard dialogs that come with C#.

MAKING CUSTOM DIALOGS

Building a custom dialog is pretty easy. Simply add a new form to your project as described in Lesson 9 and give it whatever controls you need.

To allow the user to finish using the dialog, add one or more buttons. Some dialogs have a single OK button. Others have OK and Cancel buttons or some other combination of buttons. Because you're creating the dialog, you can give it whatever buttons you like.

By convention, the buttons should go in the dialog's lower-right corner. Figure 10-1 shows a very simple dialog that contains a single textbox where the user can enter a name.

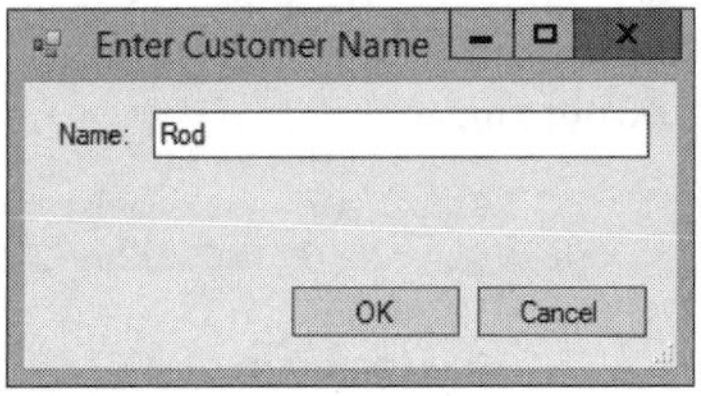

To make using the dialog easier, you can set the form's `AcceptButton` and `CancelButton` properties. These determine which button is triggered if the user presses Enter and Esc, respectively. Typically the `AcceptButton` triggers the dialog's OK or Yes button and the `CancelButton` triggers the Cancel or No button.

FIGURE 10-1

> **NOTE** *Often dialogs set other properties to make them behave more like standard dialogs. Some of these include:*
>
> ➤ *Setting* FormBorderStyle *to* FixedDialog *so the user cannot resize the dialog.*
>
> ➤ *Setting* MinimumSize *and* MaxiumSize *to keep the dialog a reasonable size. (If you give the dialog a resizable border.)*
>
> ➤ *Setting* MinimizeBox *and* MaximizeBox *to* False *so the user cannot minimize or maximize the dialog.*
>
> ➤ *Setting* ShowInTaskbar *to* False *so the dialog doesn't clutter up the taskbar.*

> **NOTE** *You can make the dialog even easier to use if you set the tab order so the focus starts at the top of the form and works its way down. For example, if the dialog contains Name, Street, City, State, and ZIP textboxes, the focus should move through them in that order.*
>
> *The user can press Tab to move between fields and can press Enter or Esc when all of the values are filled in. An experienced user can fill in this kind of dialog very quickly.*

SETTING THE DIALOG RESULT

A program uses the ShowDialog method to display a dialog. This method returns a value that indicates which button the user clicked. As explained in Lesson 8, the program can check that return value to see what it should do with the dialog's results. The examples in Lesson 8 checked that ShowDialog returned the value DialogResult.OK before processing the user's selections.

The dialog form's DialogResult property determines what value the call to ShowDialog returns. For example, you could use the following code to make the dialog's OK Button set the form's DialogResult property to DialogResult.OK to tell the calling program that the user clicked the OK button:

```
// Return OK to ShowDialog.
private void okButton_Click(object sender, EventArgs e)
{
    DialogResult = DialogResult.OK;
}
```

Setting the form's DialogResult property not only determines the return result but also closes the dialog so the call to ShowDialog returns and the calling code can continue.

That means you can set the dialog's return result and close the dialog in a single line of code. Typing one line of code should be no real hardship, but believe it or not, there's an even easier way to close the dialog.

If you set a `Button`'s `DialogResult` property, the `Button` automatically sets the form's `DialogResult` property when it is clicked. For example, suppose you set the `cancelButton`'s `DialogResult` property to `DialogResult.Cancel`. When the user clicks the `Button`, it automatically sets the form's `DialogResult` property to `DialogResult.Cancel` so the form automatically closes. That lets you set the return value and close the form without typing any code at all.

If you think setting one `Button` property is still too much work, you can even avoid that, at least for the Cancel button. When you set a form's `CancelButton` property, C# automatically sets that `Button`'s `DialogResult` property to `DialogResult.Cancel`.

Note that when you set the form's `AcceptButton` property, C# does *not* automatically set the `Button`'s `DialogResult` property. The assumption is that the OK `Button` might need to validate the data the user entered on the form before it decides whether to close the dialog. For example, if the user doesn't fill in all required fields, the OK `Button` might display a message asking the user to fill in the remaining fields instead of closing the dialog.

> **NOTE** *Actually these methods hide the dialog so control returns to the calling code, but they don't call its* `Close` *method. That means the dialog isn't destroyed so the calling code can look at values entered on the dialog by the user.*

If you don't want to perform any validation, you can simply set the OK `Button`'s `DialogResult` property to `DialogResult.OK`.

USING CUSTOM DIALOGS

A program uses a custom dialog in exactly the same way that it uses a standard dialog. It creates, initializes, and displays the dialog. It checks the return result and takes whatever action is appropriate.

There's a slight difference in how the program creates the dialog because you can add standard dialogs to a form at run time and you can't do that with custom dialogs. To use a custom dialog, the code needs to create a new instance of the dialog's form as described in Lesson 9.

The following code shows how a program might display a new customer dialog:

```
// Let the user create a new customer.
private void newCustomerButton_Click(object sender, EventArgs e)
{
    // Create and display a NewCustomerDialog.
    NewCustomerDialog newCustomerDialog;
    newCustomerDialog = new NewCustomerDialog();
    if (newCustomerDialog.ShowDialog() == DialogResult.OK)
```

```
        {
            // ... Create the new customer here ...
        }
    }
```

The code declares a variable to refer to the dialog and makes a new instance of the dialog. It displays the dialog by using its ShowDialog method and checks the return result. If the user clicks OK, the program takes whatever steps are needed to create the new customer, such as adding a record to a database.

TRY IT

In this Try It, you build and use the simple custom dialog shown in Figure 10-2. The dialog lets you enter a name. If you enter a non-blank value and click OK, the main form adds the name you entered to a ListBox.

FIGURE 10-2

This Try It also gives you a little practice using the ListBox control, showing how to add and remove items.

Lesson Requirements

In this lesson, you:

➤ Create the main form shown in the upper left in Figure 10-2. Make the New Comedian Button be the form's AcceptButton and the Delete Comedian Button be the form's CancelButton.

➤ Create the dialog shown in the lower right in Figure 10-2. Set the AcceptButton and CancelButton properties in the obvious way.

➤ Make the New Comedian Button display the dialog. If the dialog returns DialogResult.OK, add the new comedian's name to the ListBox.

➤ Make the Delete Comedian Button remove the currently selected comedian from the ListBox.

➤ When the user clicks the dialog's Cancel `Button`, hide the dialog and return `DialogResult.Cancel`.

➤ When the user clicks the dialog's OK `Button`, check the entered name's length. If the length is 0, display a message asking the user to enter a name. If the length is greater than 0, hide the dialog and return `DialogResult.OK`.

> **NOTE** *You can download the code and resources for this lesson from the website at* www.wrox.com/go/csharp24hourtrainer2e.

Hints

➤ Use the `ListBox`'s `Items.Add` method to add a new item to the `ListBox`.

➤ Use the `ListBox`'s `Items.Remove` method to remove the selected item (which is identified by the `SelectedItem` property).

➤ Check `nameTextBox.Text.Length == 0` to see whether the name entered on the dialog is blank. You can use code similar to the following to take one action if the length is 0 and another if it is not. Notice the new `else` part of the `if` statement. If the condition is true, the statements after the `if` clause are executed. If the condition is false, the statements after the `else` clause are executed. (Lesson 18 covers `if` and `else` in more detail.)

```
if (nameTextBox.Text.Length == 0)
{
    ... Display a message here ...
}
else
{
    ... Return DialogResult.OK here ...
}
```

➤ Don't forget to set the `nameTextBox` control's `Modifiers` property to `Public` so the main form's code can use it.

Step-by-Step

➤ Create the main form shown in the upper left in Figure 10-2. Make the New Comedian `Button` be the form's `AcceptButton` and the Delete Comedian `Button` be the form's `CancelButton`.

1. Start a new project and add a `Label`, `ListBox`, and two `Buttons` roughly as shown in Figure 10-2.

2. Set the `ListBox`'s Anchor property to `Top, Bottom, Left, Right`. Set the `Buttons`' Anchor properties to `Top, Right`.

3. Set the form's `AcceptButton` property to the New Comedian `Button`. Set its `CancelButton` property to the Delete Comedian `Button`.

➤ Create the dialog shown in the lower right in Figure 10-2. Set the `AcceptButton` and `CancelButton` properties in the obvious way.

1. Open the Project menu and select Add Windows Form. Enter the name **NewComedianDialog** and click Add.

2. Add a `Label`, `TextBox`, `PictureBox`, and two `Button`s roughly as shown in Figure 10-2.

3. Set the `TextBox`'s `Anchor` property to `Top, Left, Right`. Set the `Button`s' `Anchor` properties to `Bottom, Right`.

4. Place an image of your choosing in the `PictureBox` and set its `Anchor` property to `Top, Bottom, Left`. Set its `SizeMode` property to `Zoom`.

5. Set the dialog's `AcceptButton` property to the OK `Button`. Set its `CancelButton` property to the Cancel `Button`.

6. Set the dialog's `FormBorderStyle` property to `FixedDialog`, set its `ControlBox` property to `False`, and set its `ShowInTaskbar` property to `False`.

> **NOTE** *Setting the controls'* `Anchor` *properties makes it easier to size the form so you like it. Once you have everything arranged, setting* `FormBorderStyle` *equal to* `FixedDialog` *prevents the user from resizing the form, so the* `Anchor` *properties don't really do anything at run time.*

➤ Make the New Comedian `Button` display the dialog. If the dialog returns `DialogResult.OK`, add the new comedian's name to the `ListBox`.

1. Create an event handler for the New Comedian `Button`. Use code similar to the following:

```
// Create a new comedian entry.
private void newComedianButton_Click(object sender, EventArgs e)
{
    NewComedianDialog newComedianDialog;
    newComedianDialog = new NewComedianDialog();
    if (newComedianDialog.ShowDialog() == DialogResult.OK)
    {
        // Add the new comedian.
        comedianListBox.Items.Add(
            newComedianDialog.nameTextBox.Text);
    }
}
```

➤ Make the Delete Comedian `Button` remove the currently selected comedian from the `ListBox`.

1. Create an event handler for the Delete Comedian `Button`. Use code similar to the following:

```
// Remove the currently selected comedian.
private void deleteComedianButton_Click(object sender, EventArgs e)
{
    comedianListBox.Items.Remove(comedianListBox.SelectedItem);
}
```

This makes the `ListBox` remove the currently selected item. Fortunately if there is no selected item, the `ListBox` does nothing instead of crashes.

➤ When the user clicks the dialog's Cancel `Button`, hide the dialog and return `DialogResult.Cancel`.

   1. You don't need to do anything else to make this work. When you set the dialog's `CancelButton` property to this `Button`, C# sets the `Button`'s `DialogResult` property to `DialogResult.Cancel` so the button automatically sets the return result and closes the dialog.

➤ When the user clicks the dialog's OK `Button`, check the entered name's length. If the length is 0, display a message asking the user to enter a name. If the length is greater than 0, hide the dialog and return `DialogResult.OK`.

   1. Create an event handler for the dialog's OK `Button`. Use code similar to the following:

```
// Make sure the comedian's name isn't blank.
private void okButton_Click(object sender, EventArgs e)
{
    if (nameTextBox.Text.Length == 0)
    {
        MessageBox.Show("Please enter a comedian's name");
    }
    else
    {
        DialogResult = DialogResult.OK;
    }
}
```

EXERCISES

1. [WPF] Repeat the Try It with a WPF application. Hints:

   ➤ To see if the user clicked OK on the dialog, see if the `ShowDialog` method returns `True` as in this code:

   ```
   if (newComedianDialog.ShowDialog().Value)
   {
       ...
   }
   ```

   ➤ To define the Accept `Button`, set the `Button`'s `IsDefault` property to `True`.

   ➤ To define the Cancel `Button`, set the `Button`'s `IsCancel` property to `True`.

   ➤ To close the dialog, the OK `Button`'s code should set `DialogResult = true`.

   ➤ To prevent the user from resizing the dialog, set `ResizeMode` to `NoResize`.

   ➤ To prevent the dialog from appearing in the taskbar, set `ShowInTaskbar` to `False`.

2. It's usually better to prevent the user from performing invalid actions than to allow the user to perform the action and then complain. In the Try It, the user can click the Delete Comedian `Button` even if no comedian is selected. To fix that, copy the program you built for the Try It and add the following event handler to enable or disable the button when the ListBox's selection changes:

```
// Enable the Delete Comedian button if an entry is selected.
private void comedianListBox_SelectedIndexChanged(
    object sender, EventArgs e)
{
    deleteComedianButton.Enabled =
        (comedianListBox.SelectedIndex >= 0);
}
```

Hint: Don't forget to disable the Button initially.

3. [WPF] Repeat Exercise 2 with the WPF program you built for Exercise 1. (Hint: In WPF a Button has an IsEnabled property instead of an Enabled property.)

4. Copy the program you built for Exercise 2. To further help the user avoid making mistakes, modify the dialog so the OK Button is enabled when the text in the TextBox is non-blank. Hints:

   ➤ Use the TextBox's TextChanged event handler.

   ➤ Because the user can't click the OK Button when the text is blank, the OK Button doesn't need a Clicked event handler. Just set its DialogResult property to OK.

5. [WPF] Repeat Exercise 4 with the WPF program you built for Exercise 3. (Hint: In WPF Buttons don't have a DialogResult property. The OK Button still needs a Click event handler, but all it needs to do is set the form's DialogResult property.)

6. Make a program that has First Name, Last Name, Street, City, State, and ZIP Labels as shown on the Contact Information form in Figure 10-3. When the user clicks the Edit Button, the program should display the Edit Contact dialog shown in Figure 10-3 to let the user change the values. If the user clicks OK, the copy the new values back into the main form's Labels.

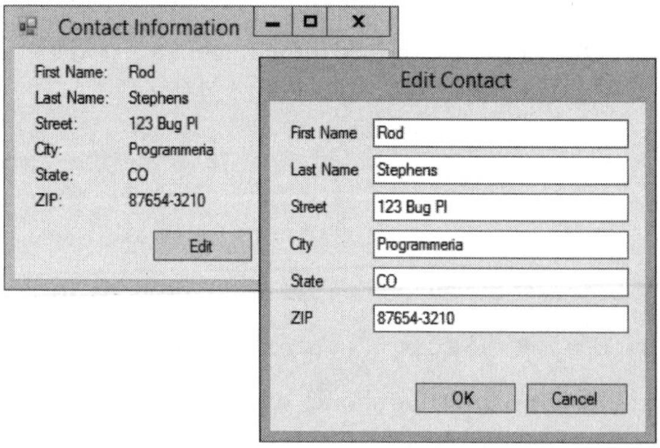

FIGURE 10-3

7. [WPF] Repeat Exercise 6 with a WPF application.

8. Sometimes the standard message box given by MessageBox.Show is almost perfect but you'd like to change the Buttons' text. Create a program that defines the message dialog shown in Figure 10-4.

FIGURE 10-4

The main program should set the Label's text, the dialog's title, and the Buttons' text. Make the Accept Button return DialogResult.OK and make the Decline Button return DialogResult.Cancel. Make the main form display different messages depending on whether the user clicked Accept or Decline.

Hints:

➤ The question mark icon is displayed in a PictureBox.

➤ Set the dialog's properties: FormBorderStyle = FixedDialog, ControlBox = False, and ShowInTaskbar = False.

9. [WPF] Repeat Exercise 8 with a WPF program. Hints:

➤ To set the dialog's title, set its Title property.

➤ The WPF Label control doesn't support word wrapping. To let the dialog wrap text, use a TextBlock with TextWrapping set to Wrap.

10. Create a color selection dialog like the one shown in Figure 10-5. The main program's Buttons should display the same dialog to let the user select foreground and background colors. Only update the main form's colors if the user clicks OK. Don't worry about initializing the dialog to show the current values before displaying it. (Hint: You built a program that lets the user select colors with scrollbars for Lesson 4's Try It.)

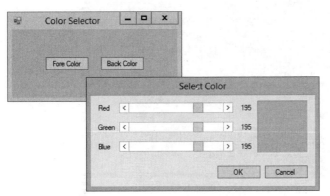

FIGURE 10-5

11. [WPF] Repeat Exercise 10 with a WPF program. Hints:

➤ Display the color sample in a `Border` control.

➤ Make the `ScrollBars` share the following event handler:

```
// Display the color sample.
private void redScrollBar_Scroll(object sender,
    System.Windows.Controls.Primitives.ScrollEventArgs e)
{
    redLabel.Content = redScrollBar.Value.ToString("0");
    greenLabel.Content = greenScrollBar.Value.ToString("0");
    blueLabel.Content = blueScrollBar.Value.ToString("0");

    Color color = Color.FromRgb(
        (byte)redScrollBar.Value,
        (byte)greenScrollBar.Value,
        (byte)blueScrollBar.Value);
    sampleBorder.Background = new SolidColorBrush(color);
}
```

12. Make a background selection dialog like the one shown in Figure 10-6. When the user clicks the main form's Select Background `Button`, the form displays the dialog. When the user clicks one of the thumbnail images, the dialog displays a border around that image's `PictureBox`. If the user clicks OK, the dialog closes and the main form displays the selected image at full scale.

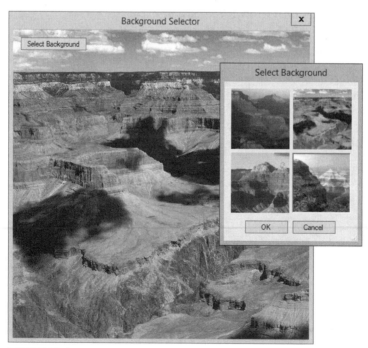

FIGURE 10-6

Hints:

➤ When the user clicks an image, set the BorderStyle property to Fixed3D for that PictureBox and None for the others.

➤ To remember which image was selected, place a hidden PictureBox on the dialog and set its Image property equal to that of the clicked PictureBox.

➤ Use the techniques described for Lesson 9, Exercise 18 to use a single event handler for all four PictureBoxes.

➤ Only allow the user to click the dialog's OK Button if a picture has been selected.

➤ If the user clicks OK, resize the main form to fit its new background image.

➤ Set the Cancel Button's TabStop property to False. (To see why, set it equal to True, run the program, select a picture, and press Enter.)

13. Repeat Exercise 12 with a WPF application. Hints:

➤ Place an Image control on the main window and display the selected picture in it.

➤ Don't worry about sizing the main window to fit the selected picture.

➤ In WPF Image controls don't have a BorderStyle property. Indicate the selected Image control by setting its Opacity property to 1. Set the other Image controls' Opacity properties to 0.5.

> **NOTE** *Please select the videos for Lesson 10 online at* www.wrox.com/go/ csharp24hourtrainer2evideos.

SECTION II
Variables and Calculations

You may have noticed that the lessons up to this point haven't done much with numbers, dates, text (other than to just display it), or any other pieces of data. They've mostly dealt with controls and their properties, methods, and events.

Although you can do some fairly impressive things with controls alone, most programs also need to manipulate data. They need to do things like add purchasing costs, calculate sales tax, sort appointments by time, and search text for keywords.

The lessons in this section explain how to perform these kinds of tasks. They explain the variables that a program uses to represent data in code, and they show how to manipulate variables to calculate new results.

▶ **LESSON 11:** Using Variables and Performing Calculations

▶ **LESSON 12:** Debugging Code

▶ **LESSON 13:** Understanding Scope

▶ **LESSON 14:** Working with Strings

▶ **LESSON 15:** Working with Dates and Times

▶ **LESSON 16:** Using Arrays and Collections

▶ **LESSON 17:** Using Enumerations and Structures

11

Using Variables and Performing Calculations

A *variable* holds a value in memory so a program can manipulate it. Different kinds of variables hold different types of data: numbers, text, LOL cat pictures, Halo scores, even complex groups of data such as employee records.

In this lesson you learn what variables are and how to use them. You learn how to define variables, put data in them, and use them to perform simple calculations.

WHAT ARE VARIABLES?

Technically speaking a variable is a named piece of memory that can hold some data of a specific type. For example, a program might allocate 4 bytes of memory to store an integer. You might name those bytes "payoffs" so you can easily refer to them in the program's code.

Less technically, you can think of a variable as a named place to put a piece of data. The program's code can use the variables to store values and perform calculations. For example, a program might store two values in variables, add the values together, and store the result in a third variable.

DATA TYPES

Every variable has a particular *data type* that determines the kind of data that it can hold. In general, you cannot place data of one type in a variable of another. For example, if price is a variable that can hold a number in dollars and cents, you cannot put the string "Hello" in it.

If you like, you can think of a variable as an envelope (with a name written on the outside) that can hold some data, but each type of data requires a different shaped envelope. Integers need relatively small envelopes, floats (which hold numbers with decimal points) need envelopes that are long and thin, and strings need big fat envelopes.

BITS AND BYTES

A *bit* is a single binary digit of memory that can have the value 0 or 1. (The name "bit" comes from "BInary digiT." Or is it "Binary digIT?") Generally, bits are grouped into bytes and a program doesn't work with bits directly.

A *byte* is a chunk of memory holding 8 bits. If you view the bits as digits in a binary number, then a byte can hold values between 0 (00000000 in binary) and 255 (11111111 in binary). Groups of bytes make up larger data types such as integers and strings.

A *nibble* is half a byte. Way back in the old days when memory was expensive and computers filled warehouses instead of laps, some programs needed to split bytes and consider the nibbles separately to save space. Now that memory is as cheap as day-old lottery tickets, the nibble is a historical curiosity mostly useful for impressing your friends at parties.

Bigger units of memory include kilobyte (KB) = 1,024 bytes, megabyte (MB) = 1,024KB, gigabyte (GB) = 1,024MB, and terabyte (TB) = 1,024GB. These are often used to measure the size of files, computer memory, flash drives, and disk drives. (Although in some contexts people use powers of 1,000 instead of 1,024. For example, most disk drive manufacturers define a gigabyte as 1,000,000,000 bytes, which in a sense shortchanges you out of 70MB.)

Sometimes the line between two data types is a bit fuzzy. For example, if a variable should hold a number, you cannot put in the string "ten." The fact that "ten" is a number is obvious to a human but not to a C# program.

You can't even place a string containing the characters "10" in a variable that holds a number. Though it should be obvious to just about anyone that "10" is a number, C# just knows it's a string containing two characters "1" and "0" and doesn't try to determine that the characters in the string represent a number.

Programs often need to convert a value from one data type to another (particularly switching between strings and numbers), so C# provides an assortment of data-conversion functions to do just that. The section "Type Conversions" later in this lesson describes those functions.

Table 11-1 summarizes C#'s built-in data types. The signed types can store values that are positive or negative, and the unsigned types can hold only positive values.

TABLE 11-1

DATA TYPE	MEANING	RANGE
byte	Byte	0 to 255
sbyte	Signed byte	−128 to 127
short	Small signed integer	−32,768 to 32,767

DATA TYPE	MEANING	RANGE
ushort	Unsigned short integer	0 to 65,535
int	Integer	–2,147,483,648 to 2,147,483,647
uint	Unsigned integer	0 to 4,294,967,295
long	Long integer	–9,223,372,036,854,775,808 to 9,223,372,036,854,775,807
ulong	Unsigned long integer	0 to 18,446,744,073,709,551,615
float	Floating point	Roughly –3.4e38 to 3.4e38
double	Double-precision floating point	Roughly –1.8e308 to 1.8e308
decimal	Higher precision and smaller range than floating-point types	See the following section, "Float, Double, and Decimal Data Types."
char	Character	A single Unicode character. (Unicode characters use 16 bits to hold data for text in scripts such as Arabic, Cyrillic, Greek, and Thai, in addition to the Roman alphabet.)
string	Text	A string of Unicode characters.
bool	Boolean	Can be true or false.
object	An object	Can point to almost anything.

Some of these data types are a bit confusing but the most common data types (int, long, float, double, and string) are fairly straightforward, and they are the focus of most of this lesson. Before moving on to further details, however, it's worth spending a little time comparing the float, double, and decimal data types.

Float, Double, and Decimal Data Types

The computer represents values of every type in binary using bits and bytes, so some values don't fit perfectly in a particular data type. In particular, real numbers such as 1/7 don't have exact binary representations, so the float, double, and decimal data types often introduce slight rounding errors.

For example, a float represents 1/7 as approximately 0.142857149. Usually the fact that this is not exactly 1/7 isn't a problem, but once in a while if you compare two float values to see if they are exactly equal, roundoff errors make them appear different even though they should be the same.

The decimal data type helps reduce this problem for decimal values such as 1.5 (but not non-decimal real values such as 1/7) by storing an exact representation of a decimal value. Instead of storing a value as a binary number the way float and double do, decimal stores the number's digits and its exponent separately as integral data types with no rounding. That lets it hold 28 or 29 significant digits (depending on the exact value) for numbers between roughly –7.9e28 and 7.9e28.

> **NOTE** *The notation 7.9e28 means 7.9 × 10²⁸.*

Note that rounding errors can still occur when you combine decimal values. For example, if you add 1e28 plus 1e–28, the result would have more than the 28 or 29 significant digits that a decimal can provide so it rounds off to 1e28.

The moral of the story is that you should always use the decimal data type for values where you need great accuracy and the values won't get truly enormous. In particular, you should always use decimal for currency values. Unless you're Bill Gates's much richer uncle, you'll never get close to the largest value a decimal can represent, and the extra precision can prevent rounding errors during some fairly complex calculations.

> **NOTE** *Another interesting feature of the decimal type is that, because of the way it stores its significant digits, it remembers zeros on the right. For example, if you add the values 1.35 and 1.65 as floats, you get the value 3. In contrast, if you add the same values as decimals, you get 3.00. The decimal result remembers that you were working with two digits to the right of the decimal point so it stores the result that way, too.*

DECLARING VARIABLES

To declare a variable in C# code, give the data type that you want to use followed by the name that you want to give the variable. For example, the following code creates a variable named numMistakes. The variable's data type is int so it can hold an integer between –2,147,483,648 and 2,147,483,647 (which should be enough for most projects that don't involve the government):

```
int numMistakes;
```

You can use the equals symbol to assign a value to a variable. For example, the following code sets numMistakes to 1337:

```
numMistakes = 1337;
```

As an added convenience, you can declare a variable and give it a value at the same time, as in:

```
int numMistakes = 1337;
```

You can declare several variables of the same type all at once by separating them with commas. You can even initialize them if you like. The following code declares three float variables named x, y, and z and gives them initial values of 1, 2, and –40, respectively:

```
float x = 1, y = 2, z = -40;
```

> **NOTE** *The program must assign a value to a variable before it tries to read its value. For example, C# flags the following code as an error because the second line tries to use x on the right-hand side of the equals sign to calculate y before x has been assigned a value:*
>
> ```
> int x, y;
> y = x + 1;
> ```

LITERAL VALUES

A *literal value* is a piece of data stuck right in the code. For example, in the following statement, numMistakes is a variable and 1337 is a literal integer value:

```
int numMistakes = 1337;
```

Usually C# is pretty smart about using the correct data types for literal values. For example, in the preceding statement C# knows that numMistakes is an integer and 1337 is an integer, so it can safely put the integer value in the integer variable.

Sometimes, however, C# gets confused and assumes a literal value has a data type other than the one you intend. For example, the following code declares a float variable named napHours and tries to assign it the value 6.5. Unfortunately, C# thinks 6.5 is a double and a double won't fit inside a float variable, so it flags this as an error:

```
float napHours = 6.5;
```

In cases such as this one, you can help C# understand what data type a literal has by adding a suffix character. For example, the F character in the following code tells C# that it should treat 6.5 as a float, not a double:

```
float napHours = 6.5F;
```

Table 11-2 lists C#'s data type suffix characters. You can use the suffixes in either lower- or uppercase.

TABLE 11-2

DATA TYPE	SUFFIX
Uint	U
Long	L
Ulong	UL or LU
Float	F
double	D
decimal	M

The int data type doesn't have a literal suffix character. C# assumes a literal that looks like an integer is an int, unless it's too big, in which case it assumes the value is a long. For example, it assumes that 2000000000 is an int because that value will fit in an int. It assumes that 3000000000 is a long because it's too big to fit in an int.

The byte, sbyte, short, and ushort data types also have no literal suffix characters. Fortunately, you can assign an integer value to these types and C# will use the value correctly, as long as it fits.

You can use double quotes to surround strings and single quotes to surround chars as in the following code:

```
string firstName = "William";
string lastName = "Gates";
char middleInitial = 'H';
```

Sometimes you might like to include a special character such as a carriage return or tab character in a string literal. Unfortunately, you can't simply type a carriage return into a string because it would start a new line of code, and that would confuse Visual Studio.

To work around this dilemma, C# provides escape sequences that represent special characters. An *escape sequence* is a sequence of characters that represent a special character such as a carriage return or tab.

Table 11-3 lists C#'s escape sequences.

TABLE 11-3

SEQUENCE	MEANING
\a	Bell
\b	Backspace
\f	Formfeed
\n	Newline
\r	Carriage return
\t	Horizontal tab
\v	Vertical tab
\'	Single quotation mark
\"	Double quotation mark
\\	Backslash
\?	Question mark
\ooo	ASCII character in octal (ooo represents the octal code)
\xhh	ASCII character in hexadecimal (hh represents the hexadecimal code)
\xhhhh	Unicode character in hexadecimal (hhhh represents the hexadecimal code)

For example, the following code makes a variable that refers to a string that contains quotes and a newline character:

```
string txt = "Unknown value \"ten.\"\nPlease enter a number.";
```

When you display this string in a `MessageBox`, the user sees text similar to the following:

```
Unknown value "ten."
Please enter a number.
```

> **NOTE** *When you display text in a* `Label` *(or* `MessageBox`*), you can start a new line by using the newline escape (*\n*). When you display text in a* `TextBox`*, however, you must start a new line by using the carriage return and newline escapes together (*\r\n*). (The* \r\n *sequence also works for* `Labels` *and* `MessageBoxes`*.)*

C# also provides a special *verbatim string literal* that makes using some special characters easier. This kind of value begins with `@"` and ends with a corresponding closing quote (`"`). Between the quotes, the literal doesn't know anything about escape sequences and treats every character literally.

A verbatim string literal cannot contain a double quote because that would end the string. It can't even use an escaped double quote because verbatim string literals don't understand escape sequences.

Verbatim string literals are very useful if you need a string that contains a lot of backslashes such as a Windows directory path (`C:\Tools\Binary\Source\C#\PrintInvoices`) or that needs to describe escape sequences themselves (`"Use \r\n to start a new line"`).

You can even type new lines and tab characters inside a string literal, although those may make your code harder to read.

TYPE CONVERSIONS

C# performs implicit data type conversions where it knows the conversion is safe. For example, the following code declares a `long` variable and sets it equal to the `int` value 6. Because an `int` can always fit in a `long`, C# knows this is safe and doesn't complain:

```
long numBananas = 6;
```

The converse is not always true, however. A `long` value cannot always fit in an `int` variable. Because it cannot know for certain that any given `long` will fit in an `int`, C# won't quietly sit by while your code assigns a `long` value to an `int`.

For example, the following code assigns a value to a `long` variable. It then tries to save that `long` value into an `int` variable. At this point, C# panics and flags the line as an error:

```
long numBananas = 6;
int numFruits = numBananas;
```

In cases such as this, you can use three methods to coerce C# into converting data from one type to another: casting, converting, and parsing.

Casting

To *cast* a value from one data type to another, you put the target data type inside parentheses in front of the value. For example, the following code explicitly converts the variable numBananas into an int:

```
long numBananas = 6;
int numFruits = (int)numBananas;
```

Casting works only between compatible data types. For example, because double and int are both numbers, you can try to cast between them. (When you cast from a double to an int, the cast simply discards any fractional part of the value with no rounding.) In contrast, the string and bool data types are not compatible with the numeric data types or each other, so you cannot cast between them. (What would the statement (int) "platypus" even mean?)

Normally a cast doesn't check whether it can succeed. If you try to convert a long into an int and the long won't fit, C# sweeps its mistake under the rug like a politician in an election year, and the program keeps running. The value that gets shoved into the int may be gibberish, but the program doesn't crash.

If the int now contains garbage, any calculations you perform with it will also be garbage so, in many cases, it's better to let your program throw a tantrum and crash. (Lesson 21 explains how to catch errors such as this so you can do something more constructive than merely crash.)

To make C# flag casting errors, surround the cast in parentheses and add the word checked in front as in the following code:

```
long worldPopulation = 7309000000;
int peopleInWorld = checked((int)worldPopulation);
```

Now when the code executes at run time, the program will fail on the second statement because the value is too big to fit in an int.

> **NOTE** *If you have several statements that you want to check, you can make a checked block. In the following code, both of the statements between the braces are checked:*
>
> ```
> long worldPopulation = 7309000000;
> long asiaPopulation = 4428000000;
> checked
> {
>     int peopleInWorld = (int)worldPopulation;
>     int peopleInAsia = (int)asiaPopulation;
> }
> ```
>
> *The checked keyword also checks integer calculations for overflow. For example, if you multiply two huge int variables together, the result won't fit in an int. Normally the program keeps running without complaint even though the result overflowed, so it isn't what you expect.*
>
> *If you are working with values that might overflow and you want to be sure the results make sense, protect the calculations with checked.*

Converting

Casting only works between compatible types. The `Convert` utility class (which is provided by the .NET Framework) gives you methods that you can use to try to convert values even if the data types are incompatible. These are shared methods provided by the `Convert` class itself, so you don't need to create an instance of the class to use them.

For example, the `bool` and `int` data types are not compatible, so C# doesn't let you cast from one to the other. Occasionally, however, you might want to convert an `int` into a `bool` or vice versa. In that case you can use the `Convert` class's `ToBoolean` and `ToInt32` methods. (You use `ToInt32` because `int`s are 32-bit integers.)

The following code declares two `int` variables and assigns them values. It uses `Convert` to change them into `bool`s and then changes one of them back into an `int`:

```
int trueInt = -1;
int falseInt = 0;
bool trueBool = Convert.ToBoolean(trueInt);
bool falseBool = Convert.ToBoolean(falseInt);
int anotherTrueInt = Convert.ToInt32(trueBool);
```

> **NOTE** *When you treat integer values as booleans, the value 0 is false and all other values are true. If you convert the* `bool` *literal value* true *into an integer value, you get –1.*

In a particularly common scenario, a program must convert text entered by the user into some other data type such as an `int` or `decimal`. The following uses the `Convert.ToInt32` method to convert whatever the user entered in the `ageTextBox` into an `int`:

```
int age = Convert.ToInt32(ageTextBox.Text);
```

This conversion works only if the user enters a value that can be reasonably converted into an `int`. If the user enters 13,914 or –1, the conversion works. If the user enters "seven," the conversion fails.

Converting text into another data type is more properly an example of parsing than of data type conversion, however. So although the `Convert` methods work, your code will be easier to read and understand if you use the parsing methods described in the next section.

Parsing

Trying to find structure and meaning in text is called *parsing*. All of the simple data types (`int`, `double`, `decimal`) provide a method that converts text into that data type. For example, the `int` data type's `Parse` method takes a string as a parameter and returns an `int`. At least it does if the string contains an integer value.

The following code declares a `decimal` variable named `salary`, uses the `decimal` class's `Parse` method to convert the value in the `salaryTextBox` into a `decimal`, and saves the result in the variable:

```
decimal salary = decimal.Parse(salaryTextBox.Text);
```

As is the case with the `Convert` methods, this works only if the text can reasonably be converted into a `decimal`. If the user types "12,345.67," the parsing works. If the user types "ten" or "1.2.3," the parsing fails.

> **NOTE** *Unfortunately, C#'s conversion and parsing methods get confused by some formats that you might expect them to understand. For example, they can't handle currency characters, so they fail on strings like "$12.34" and "€54.32."*
>
> *You can tell the `decimal` class's `Parse` method to allow currency values by passing it a second parameter, as shown in the following code:*
>
> ```
> decimal salary = decimal.Parse(salaryTextBox.Text,
>     System.Globalization.NumberStyles.Any);
> ```

PERFORMING CALCULATIONS

You've already seen several pieces of code that assign a value to a variable. For example, the following code converts the text in the `salaryTextBox` into a `decimal` and saves it in the variable `salary`:

```
decimal salary = decimal.Parse(salaryTextBox.Text);
```

You can also save a value that is the result of a more complex calculation into a variable on the left side of an equals sign. Fortunately, the syntax for these kinds of calculations is usually easy to understand. The following code calculates the value 2736 + 7281 / 3 and saves the result in the variable `result`:

```
double result = 2736 + 7281 / 3;
```

The operands (the values used in the expression on the right) can be literal values, values stored in variables, or the results of methods. For example, the following code calculates the sales tax on a purchase's subtotal. It multiplies the tax rate stored in the `taxRate` variable by the `decimal` value stored in the `subtotalTextBox` and saves the result in the variable `salesTax`:

```
decimal salesTax = taxRate * decimal.Parse(subtotalTextBox.Text);
```

Note that a variable can appear on both sides of the equals sign. In that case, the value on the right is the variable's current value and, after the calculation, the new result is saved back into the same variable.

For example, the following code takes x's current value, doubles it, adds 10, and saves the result back in variable x. If x started with the value 3, then when this statement finishes x holds the value 16:

```
x = 2 * x + 10;
```

A variable may appear more than once on the right side of the equals sign but it can appear only once on the left.

The following sections provide some additional details about performing calculations.

Operands and Operators

One issue that confuses some people is the fact that C# uses the data types of an expression's operands to determine the way the operators work. If an expression contains two `int`s, the operators use integer arithmetic. If an expression contains two `float`s, the operators use floating-point arithmetic.

Sometimes this can lead to confusing results. For example, the following code tries to save the value 1/7 in the `float` variable `ratio`. The values 1 and 7 are integers so this calculation uses integer division, which discards any remainder. Because 1 / 7 = 0 with a remainder of 1, `ratio` is assigned the value 0, which is probably not what you intended:

```
float ratio = 1 / 7;
```

To force C# to using floating-point division, you can convert the numbers into the `float` data type. The following code uses the `F` suffix character to indicate that 1 and 7 should have the `float` data type instead of `int`. Now the program performs floating-point division, so it assigns `ratio` the value 0.142857149 (approximately):

```
float ratio = 1F / 7F;
```

Instead of using data type suffixes, you can also use casting to make the program treat the values as `float`s as in the following code:

```
float ratio = (float)1 / (float)7;
```

Promotion

If an expression uses two different data types, C# *promotes* the one with the more restrictive type. For example, if you try to divide an `int` by a `float`, C# promotes the `int` to a `float` before it performs the division.

The following code divides a `float` by an `int`. Before performing the calculation, C# promotes the value 7 to a `float`. This is sometimes called *implicit casting*. The code then performs the division and saves the result 0.142857149 in the variable `ratio`:

```
float ratio = 1F / 7;
```

Operator Summary

C# has many operators for manipulating variables of different data types. The following sections describe the most commonly used operators grouped by operand type (arithmetic, string, logical, and so forth).

Remember that some operators behave differently depending on the data types of their operands.

Arithmetic Operators

The arithmetic operators perform calculations on numbers. Table 11-4 summarizes the arithmetic operators. The Example column shows sample results. For the final examples, assume that `x` is an `int` that initially has value `10`.

TABLE 11-4

OPERATOR	MEANING	EXAMPLE
+	Addition	3 + 2 is 5
-	Negation	-3 is negative 3
-	Subtraction	3 - 2 is 1
*	Multiplication	3 * 2 is 6
/	Division (integer)	3 / 2 is 1
/	Division (floating point)	3F / 2F is 1.5
%	Modulus	3 % 2 is 1
++	Pre-increment	++x: x is incremented to 11 and then the statement uses the new value 11
++	Post-increment	x++: the statement uses the current value of x, 10, and then x is incremented to 11
--	Pre-decrement	−x: x is decremented to 9 and then the statement uses the new value 9
--	Post-decrement	x−: the statement uses the current value of x, 10, and then x is decremented to 9

Integer division discards any remainder and returns the integer quotient. The modulus operator, which applies only to integer data types, does the opposite: it discards the quotient and returns the remainder. For example, 17 % 5 returns 2 because 17 divided by 5 is 3 with a remainder of 2.

The pre- and post-increment and decrement operators return a value either before or after it is incremented or decremented. For example, the following code sets x equal to 10 + y = 20 and then adds 1 to y. When the code finishes, x = 20 and y = 11:

```
int x, y = 10;
x = 10 + y++;
```

In contrast, the following code increments y first and then uses the new value to calculate x. When this code finishes, x = 21 and y = 11:

```
int x, y = 10;
x = 10 + ++y;
```

The decrement operators work similarly except they subtract 1 instead of add 1.

The increment and decrement operators can be very confusing, particularly when they're in the middle of a complex expression. If you have trouble with them, simply don't use them. For example, the following code gives you the same result as the previous code but without the pre-increment operator:

```
int x, y = 10;
y = y + 1;
x = 10 + y;
```

Logical Operators

The logical operators perform calculations on boolean (`true` or `false`) values. They let you combine logical statements to form new ones.

Lesson 18 explains how to use these values to perform tests that let a program take action only under certain circumstances. For example, a program might pay an employee overtime if the employee is hourly and worked more than 40 hours in the last week.

Table 11-5 summarizes the boolean operators.

TABLE 11-5

OPERATOR	MEANING
&	AND
|	OR
^	XOR
!	NOT
&&	Conditional AND
||	Conditional OR

The `&` operator returns `true` if and only if both of its operands are `true`. For example, you must buy lunch if it's lunchtime *and* you forgot to bring a lunch today:

```
mustBuyLunch = isLunchTime & forgotToBringLunch;
```

The `|` operator returns `true` if either of its operands is `true`. For example, you can afford lunch if either you brought enough money *or* you have a credit card (or both):

```
canAffordLunch = haveEnoughMoney | haveCreditCard;
```

The `^` operator (the *exclusive OR* operator) is the most confusing. It returns `true` if one of its operands is `true` and the other is `false`. For example, you and Ann will get a single lunch check and pay each other back later if either Ann forgot her money and you brought yours *or* Ann remembered her money and you forgot yours. If neither of you forgot your money, you can get separate checks. If you both forgot your money, you're both going hungry today:

```
singleCheck = annForgotMoney ^ youForgotMoney;
```

The ! operator returns true if its single operand is false. For example, if the cafeteria is *not* closed, you can have lunch there:

```
canHaveLunch = !cafeteriaIsClosed;
```

The *conditional operators*, which are also called *short-circuit operators*, work just like the regular ones except they don't evaluate their second operand unless they must. For example, consider the following AND statement:

```
mustBuyLunch = isLunchTime && forgotToBringLunch;
```

Suppose it's only 9:00 a.m. so isLunchTime is false. When the program sees this expression, it evaluates isLunchTime and then encounters the && operator. Because isLunchTime is false, the program already knows that mustBuyLunch must also be false no matter what value follows the && (in this case forgotToBringLunch). In that case, the program doesn't bother to evaluate forgotToBringLunch and that saves a tiny amount of time.

Similarly, consider the following OR statement:

```
canAffordLunch = haveEnoughMoney || haveCreditCard;
```

If you have enough money, haveEnoughMoney is true, so the program doesn't need to evaluate haveCreditCard to know that the result canAffordLunch is also true.

Because the conditional && and || operators are slightly faster, most developers use them whenever they can instead of using & and |.

> **NOTE** *There is one case where the conditional operators may cause problems. If the second operand is not a simple value but the result returned from some sort of method call, then if you use a conditional operator, you cannot always know whether the method was called. This might matter if the method has side effects: consequences that last after the method has finished, like opening a database or creating a file. In that case, you cannot know later whether the database is open or the file is created.*
>
> *This is seldom a problem and you can avoid it completely by avoiding side effects.*

String Operators

The only string operator C# provides is +. This operator concatenates (joins) two strings together. For example, suppose the variable username contains the user's name. Then the following code concatenates the text "Hello " (note the trailing space) with the user's name and displays the result in a message box:

```
MessageBox.Show("Hello " + username);
```

Lesson 14 explains methods that you can use to manipulate strings: find substrings, replace text, check length, and so forth.

> **NOTE** *One very non-obvious fact about string operations is that a string calculation does not really save the results in the same memory used by the variable on the left of an assignment statement. Instead it creates a new string holding the result of the calculation and makes the variable refer to that.*
>
> *For example, consider the following code:*
>
> ```
> string greeting = usernameTextBox.Text;
> greeting = "Hello " + greeting;
> ```
>
> *This code looks like it saves a user's name in the variable* greeting *and then tacks "Hello" onto the front. Actually, the second statement creates a whole new string that holds "Hello" plus the user's name and then makes* greeting *refer to the new string.*
>
> *For many practical applications, the difference is small, and you can ignore it. However, if you're performing a huge number of concatenations (perhaps in one of the loops described in Lesson 19), your program might have performance issues. The* StringBuilder *class can help address this issue, but it's a bit more advanced so I'm not going to cover it here. See* msdn.microsoft.com/library/2839d5h5.aspx *for more information.*

Comparison Operators

The comparison operators compare two values and return true or false depending on the values' relationship. For example, x < y returns true if x is less than y.

Table 11-6 summarizes the comparison operators.

TABLE 11-6

OPERATOR	MEANING	EXAMPLE
==	Equals	2 == 3 is false
!=	Not equals	2 != 3 is true
<	Less than	2 < 3 is true
<=	Less than or equal to	2 <= 3 is true
>	Greater than	2 > 3 is false
>=	Greater than or equal to	2 >= 3 is false

Bitwise Operators

The bitwise operators enable you to manipulate the individual bits in integer values. For example, the bitwise | operator combines the bits in two values so the result has a bit equal to 1 wherever either of the two operands has a bit equal to one.

For example, suppose x and y are the byte values with bits `10000000` and `00000001`. Then x | y has bits `10000001`.

This may be easier to understand if you write y below x as in the following:

```
x:       10000000
y:       00000001
         --------
Result: 10000001
```

Now it's easy to see that the result has a 1 where either x or y had a 1.

The bitwise operators are fairly advanced so I'm not going to do much with them, but Table 11-7 summarizes them. The shift operators are not "bitwise" because they don't compare two operands one bit at a time, but they are bit-manipulation operators so they're included here.

TABLE 11-7

OPERATOR	MEANING	EXAMPLE
&	Bitwise AND	11110000 & 00111100 = 00110000
|	Bitwise OR	11110000 | 00111100 = 11111100
^	Bitwise XOR	11110000 ^ 00111100 = 11001100
~	Bitwise complement	~11110000 = 00001111
<<	Left shift	11100111 << 2 = 10011100
>>	Right shift (for signed types)	11100111 >> 2 = 11111001
>>	Right shift (for unsigned types)	11100111 >> 2 = 00111001

If the operand has a signed type (such as sbyte, int, or long), then >> makes new bits on the left be copies of the value's sign bit (its leftmost bit). If the operand has an unsigned type (byte, uint, ulong), then >> makes the new bits 0.

All of these except ~ also have corresponding compound assignments operators, for example, &= and <<=. Compound assignment operators are described in the next section.

Assignment Operators

The assignment operators set a variable (or property or whatever) equal to something else. The simplest of these is the = operator, which you have seen several times before. This operator simply assigns whatever value is on the right to the variable on the left.

The other assignment operators, which are known as *compound assignment operators*, combine the variable's current value with whatever is on the right in some way. For example, the following code adds 3 to whatever value x currently holds:

```
x += 3;
```

This has the same effect as the following statement that doesn't use the += operator:

```
x = x + 3;
```

Table 11-8 summarizes the assignment operators. For the examples, assume i is an int, x is a float, and a and b are bools.

TABLE 11-8

OPERATOR	MEANING	EXAMPLE	MEANS
=	Assign	x = 10;	x = 10;
+=	Add and assign	x += 10;	x = x + 10;
-=	Subtract and assign	x -= 10;	x = x - 10;
*=	Multiply and assign	x *= 10;	x = x * 10;
/=	Divide and assign	x /= 10;	x = x / 10;
%=	Modulus and assign	x %= 10;	x = x % 10;
&=	Logical AND and assign	a &= b;	a = a & b;
|=	Logical OR and assign	a |= b;	a = a | b;
^=	Logical XOR and assign	a ^= b;	a = a ^ b;
<<=	Left shift and assign	i <<= 3;	i = i << 3;
>>=	Right shift and assign	i >>= 5;	i = i >> 5;

Precedence

Sometimes the order in which you evaluate the operators in an expression changes the result. For example, consider the expression 2 + 3 * 5. If you evaluate the + first, you get 5 * 5, which is 25, but if you evaluate the * first, you get 2 + 15, which is 17.

To prevent any ambiguity, C# defines operator precedence to determine which comes first.

Table 11-9 lists the major operators in order of decreasing precedence. In other words, the operators listed near the beginning of the table are applied before those listed later. Operators listed at the same level have the same precedence and are applied in left-to-right order.

TABLE 11-9

CATEGORY	OPERATORS
Primary	x++, x--
Unary	+, -, !, ++x, --x
Multiplicative	*, /, %
Additive	+, -
Relational	<, <=, >, >=
Equality	==, !=
Logical AND	&
Logical XOR	^
Logical OR	|
Conditional AND	&&
Conditional OR	||

The compound assignment operators (+=, *=, ^=, and so forth) always have lowest precedence. The program evaluates the expression on the right, combines it with the original value of the variable on the left, and then saves the result in that variable.

By carefully using the precedence rules, you can always figure out how a program will evaluate an expression, but sometimes the expression can be confusing enough to make figuring out the result difficult. Trying to figure out precedence in confusing expressions can be a great party game (a programmer's version of "Pictionary"), but it can make understanding and debugging programs hard.

Fortunately you can always use parentheses to change the order of evaluation or to make the default order obvious. For example, consider the following three statements:

```
x = 2 + 3 * 5;
y = 2 + (3 * 5);
z = (2 + 3) * 5;
```

The first statement uses no parentheses so you need to use the precedence table to figure out which operator is applied first. The table shows that * has higher precedence than +, so * is applied first and the result is 2 + 15, which is 17.

The second statement uses parentheses to emphasize the fact that the * operator is evaluated first. The result is unchanged, but the code is easier to read.

The third statement uses parentheses to change the order of evaluation. In this case the + operator is evaluated first, so the result is 5 * 5, which is 25.

> **NOTE** *Parentheses are a useful tool for making your code easier to understand and debug. Unless an expression is so simple that it's obvious how it is evaluated, add parentheses to make the result clear.*

CONSTANTS

A constant is a lot like a variable except you must assign it a value when you declare it and you cannot change the value later.

Syntactically a constant's declaration is similar to a variable except it uses the keyword const.

For example, the bold line in the following code declares a decimal constant named taxRate and assigns it the value 0.09M. The code then uses the constant in a calculation:

```
const decimal taxRate = 0.09M;

decimal subtotal = decimal.Parse(subtotalTextBox.Text);
decimal salesTax = taxRate * subTotal;
decimal grandTotal = subTotal + salesTax;
```

Constants work just like literal values, so you could replace the constant taxRate with the literal value 0.09M in the preceding calculation. Using a constant makes the code easier to read, however. When you see the value 0.09M, you need to remember or guess that this is a tax rate.

Not only can it be hard to remember what this kind of "magic number" means, but it can also make changing the value difficult if it appears in many places throughout the program. Suppose the code uses the value 0.09M in several places. If the sales tax rate went up to 0.10M, you would have to hunt down all of the occurrences of that number and change them. If you miss some of them, you could get very confusing results. Things could be even more confusing if the program also used 0.09M in some places to represent other values. If you changed them to 0.10M, you would break the code that uses those values.

Note that constants can contain calculated values as long as C# can perform the calculation before the program actually runs. For example, the following code declares a constant that defines the number of centimeters per inch. It then uses that value to define the number of centimeters per foot:

```
const double cmPerInch = 2.54;
const double cmPerFoot = cmPerInch * 12;
```

TRY IT

In this Try It you make some simple calculations. You take values entered by the user, convert them into numbers, do some multiplication and addition, and display the results.

Lesson Requirements

In this lesson, you:

➤ Create the form shown in Figure 11-1.

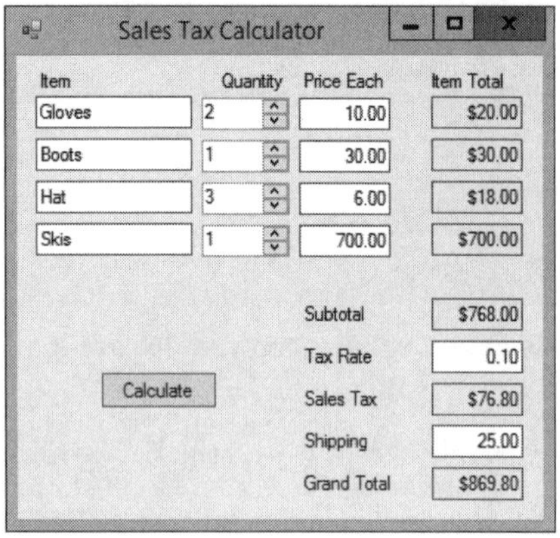

FIGURE 11-1

➤ When the user clicks the Calculate `Button`, make the program:

➤ Multiply each item's Quantity value by its Price Each value and display the result in the corresponding Item Total `TextBox`.

➤ Add up the Item Total values and display the result in the Subtotal `TextBox`.

➤ Multiply the Subtotal value by the entered Tax Rate and display the result in the Sales Tax `TextBox`.

➤ Add the Subtotal, Sales Tax, and Shipping values, and display the result in the Grand Total `TextBox`.

> **NOTE** *You can download the code and resources for this lesson from the website at* www.wrox.com/go/csharp24hourtrainer2e.

Hints

➤ It is often helpful to perform this kind of calculation in three separate phases:

1. Gather input values from the user and store them in variables.

2. Perform calculations.

3. Display results.

➤ Use the `decimal` data type for the variables that represent currency values.

➤ Lesson 14 has more to say about manipulating and formatting strings, but for this Try It it's helpful to know that all data types provide a `ToString` method that converts a value into a string. An optional parameter string indicates the format to use. For this Try It, use the format `"C"` (including the quotes) to indicate a currency format, as in:

```
grandTotalTextBox.Text = grandTotal.ToString("C");
```

➤ If the program tries to perform the calculations and some of the values it needs are missing (for example, if one of the Price Each `TextBox`es is empty), the program will crash. Don't worry about it for now.

Step-by-Step

➤ Create the form shown in Figure 11-1.

1. Create the controls needed for the program shown in Figure 11-1.

   a. The Quantity values are `NumericUpDown` controls.

   b. All of the other box-like controls are `TextBox`es.

   c. The output controls (for the Item Total values, Subtotal, Sales Tax, and Grand Total) are `TextBox`es with `ReadOnly` set to `True`.

   d. Set the form's `AcceptButton` property to the Calculate `Button`.

2. Give names to the controls that the program needs to manipulate. That includes the `NumericUpDown` controls, all of the `TextBox`es, and the `Button`.

➤ When the user clicks the Calculate `Button`, make the program:

   ➤ Multiply each item's Quantity value by its Price Each value and display the result in the corresponding Item Total `TextBox`.

   ➤ Add up the Item Total values and display the result in the Subtotal `TextBox`.

   ➤ Multiply the Subtotal value by the entered Tax Rate and display the result in the Sales Tax `TextBox`.

   ➤ Add the Subtotal, Sales Tax, and Shipping values, and display the result in the Grand Total `TextBox`.

This is easy to do in three steps:

1. Gather input values from the user and store them in variables. Because they are already numeric, the code doesn't need to parse the values that come from the `NumericUpDown` control's `Value` properties. The program *does* need to parse the values in `TextBox`es to convert them into `decimal` values:

```
// Get input values.
decimal quantity1 = qty1NumericUpDown.Value;
decimal quantity2 = qty2NumericUpDown.Value;
decimal quantity3 = qty3NumericUpDown.Value;
decimal quantity4 = qty4NumericUpDown.Value;
```

```
decimal priceEach1 = decimal.Parse(priceEach1TextBox.Text);
decimal priceEach2 = decimal.Parse(priceEach2TextBox.Text);
decimal priceEach3 = decimal.Parse(priceEach3TextBox.Text);
decimal priceEach4 = decimal.Parse(priceEach4TextBox.Text);
decimal taxRate = decimal.Parse(taxRateTextBox.Text);
decimal shipping = decimal.Parse(shippingTextBox.Text);
```

2. Perform calculations. In this Try It, the calculations are pretty simple. To keep the code simple, the program uses a separate variable for each result instead of tries to add them all up at once:

```
// Calculate results.
decimal total1 = quantity1 * priceEach1;
decimal total2 = quantity2 * priceEach2;
decimal total3 = quantity3 * priceEach3;
decimal total4 = quantity4 * priceEach4;
decimal subtotal = total1 + total2 + total3 + total4;
decimal salesTax = subtotal * taxRate;
decimal grandTotal = subtotal + salesTax + shipping;
```

3. Display results. The program uses `ToString("C")` to display values in a currency format:

```
// Display results.
total1TextBox.Text = total1.ToString("C");
total2TextBox.Text = total2.ToString("C");
total3TextBox.Text = total3.ToString("C");
total4TextBox.Text = total4.ToString("C");
subtotalTextBox.Text = subtotal.ToString("C");
salesTaxTextBox.Text = salesTax.ToString("C");
grandTotalTextBox.Text = grandTotal.ToString("C");
```

EXERCISES

1. [WPF] Repeat the Try It with a WPF program.

2. When the user changes a value used in a calculation, it can be confusing if the program displays old calculated values. Copy the program you built for the Try It and make these modifications:

   ➤ Disable the Calculate Button.

   ➤ When the user modifies any value used in the calculations, blank the calculated TextBoxes and enable the Calculate Button.

   ➤ After it displays the calculated values, make the Button's code disable the Button again.

3. [WPF] Repeat Exercise 2 with the program you built for Exercise 1. Hint: When the program first starts, the TextBoxes will fire their TextChanged events, but not all of the TextBoxes will have been built yet, so the program can't clear their text. To avoid crashing, make the event handlers use the following statement to see if the window has finished loading before it starts clearing TextBoxes:

```
if (!IsLoaded) return;
```

4. Copy the program you built for Exercise 2. As it stands, the program crashes if any of the input values it needs are missing. Modify the program to prevent that by enabling the Calculate `Button` only if all of the needed values are present. Hints:

   ➤ In the event handlers, disable the Calculate `Button`. Then use code similar to the following for each of the required values before you re-enable the `Button`:

   ```
   if (priceEach1TextBox.Text.Length == 0) return;
   ```

   ➤ The program will still crash if the user enters a non-numeric value such as "ten." Don't worry about that for now. You'll learn how to fix that in Lesson 21.

5. [WPF] Repeat Exercise 4 with the program you built for Exercise 3.

6. The program you built for Exercise 4 doesn't understand currency values. For example, if you enter $6.00 in a Price Each `TextBox` and click Calculate, the program crashes. Fix that. Hints:

   ➤ Use code similar to the following to allow currency values, thousands separators, parentheses, leading and trailing signs, and other numeric formats:

   ```
   decimal priceEach1 = decimal.Parse(priceEach1TextBox.Text,
       System.Globalization.NumberStyles.Any);
   ```

   ➤ Don't make that change for the quantity values or the tax rate because they're not currency values.

7. [WPF] Repeat Exercise 6 with the program you built for Exercise 5.

8. Make a program similar to the one shown in Figure 11-2. When the user checks or unchecks either of the A or B `CheckBoxes`, the program should check or uncheck the result `CheckBoxes` appropriately. For example, if A and B are both checked, the A && B `CheckBox` should also be checked.

   FIGURE 11-2

   Hints:

   ➤ Set a result `CheckBox`'s `Checked` property equal to a boolean expression. For example:

   ```
   aAndBCheckBox.Checked = aCheckBox.Checked && bCheckBox.Checked;
   ```

   ➤ To make a `CheckBox`'s caption display an ampersand, place two in its `Text` property. To display two ampersands, use four in the `Text` property as in "A &&&& B."

   ➤ The last `CheckBox` is checked at the same time as one of the others. Which one? Does that make sense?

9. A program can get information about the operating system in many ways. Three useful values include:

   ➤ `Environment.UserName`—The current user's name.

   ➤ `DateTime.Now.ToShortTimeString()`—The current time in short format.

   ➤ `DateTime.Now.ToShortDateString()`—The current date in short format.

Make a program that greets the user when it starts by displaying a message box similar to the one shown in Figure 11-3. (Hint: You'll need to concatenate several strings.)

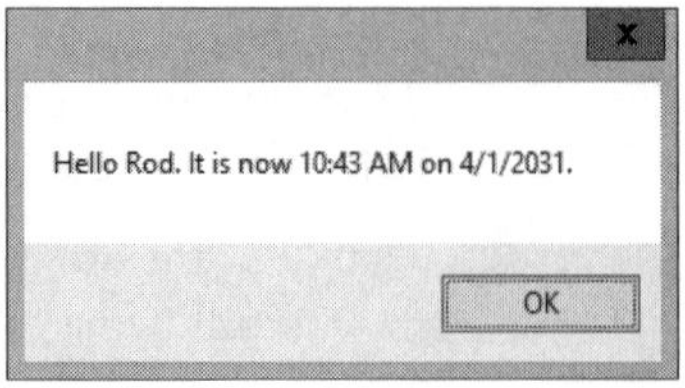

10. Copy the program you wrote for Exercise 9 and make it display its greeting in a `Label` instead of a message box.

FIGURE 11-3

Hello Rod. It is now 10:43 AM on 4/1/2031.

OK

11. Make a program to determine whether 12345 * 54321 > 22222 * 33333. In three `Label`s, display the result of 12345 * 54321, the result of 22222 * 33333, and the boolean value 12345 * 54321 > 22222 * 33333. The final value should be true or false. (Hint: Use `ToString` to convert the boolean result into a string.)

12. Make a program that converts degrees Celsius to degrees Fahrenheit. It should have two `TextBox`es with associated `Button`s. When the user enters a value in the Celsius `TextBox` and clicks its `Button`, the program converts the value into degrees Fahrenheit and displays the result in the other `TextBox`. Make the other `Button` convert from Fahrenheit to Celsius. Hints:

➤ °F = °C * 9 / 5 + 32 and °C = (°F – 32) * 5 / 9.

➤ What's special about the temperature –40° Celsius?

13. Make a currency converter that converts between U.S. dollars, British pounds, Euros, Japanese yen, Indian rupees, and Swiss francs. Make constants for the following conversion factors (or go online and look up the current exchange rates):

```
// Exchange rates in USD.
const decimal eurPerUsd = 0.68M;
const decimal gbpPerUsd = 0.63M;
const decimal jpyPerUsd = 89.16M;
const decimal inrPerUsd = 47.24M;
const decimal chfPerUsd = 1.03M;
```

To make the constants usable by every event handler in the program, place these declarations outside of any event handler. (Right after the end of the `Form1` method would work.)

Make a `TextBox` and `Button` for each currency. When the user clicks the `Button`, the program should:

➤ Get the value in the corresponding `TextBox`.

➤ Convert that value into U.S. dollars.

➤ Use the converted value in U.S. dollars to calculate the other currency values.

➤ Display the results.

14. Make a program similar to the one you made for Exercise 13 but make this one convert between inches, feet, yards, miles, centimeters, meters, and kilometers.

15. [Games] Make a program that contains a `PictureBox` (holding a picture of something that flies) and a `Timer` (with `Interval = 50`).

Inside the code but outside of any event handler, declare two `double` variables named `Theta` and `Dtheta` initialized to `0` and `Math.PI / 30`, respectively. (`System.Math` contains several useful mathematical values and methods including `Sin` and `Cos`, which you'll use in a moment.)

When the user clicks the `PictureBox`, enable or disable the `Timer`.

In the `Timer`'s `Tick` event handler, move the `PictureBox` to the point: `(100 + 100 * Math.Cos(Theta), 100 + 75 * Math.Sin(Theta))` Then add `Dtheta` to `Theta`. (Convert data types if necessary.)

16. [Games] Copy the program you built for Exercise 15 and add an `HScrollBar` with `Minimum = 1`, `Maximum = 10`, and `LargeChange = 1`. In its `Scroll` event handler, display the new value in a read-only `TextBox` and set the `Timer`'s `Interval` property to: `110 - 10 * speedScrollBar.Value`.

17. [Games, Advanced] One way to handle projectile motion is to use variables `Vx` and `Vy` to represent an object's velocities in the X and Y directions, respectively. At every tick of a `Timer`, you add `Vx` and `Vy` to the object's current X and Y coordinates, respectively. For projectile motion, you then add a downward acceleration due to gravity to `Vy`.

For this exercise, build a program similar to the one shown in Figure 11-4 to simulate projectile motion. To keep the program simple for the user, the angle is in degrees, the speed is in feet per second, and the scale is 1 pixel = 1 foot.

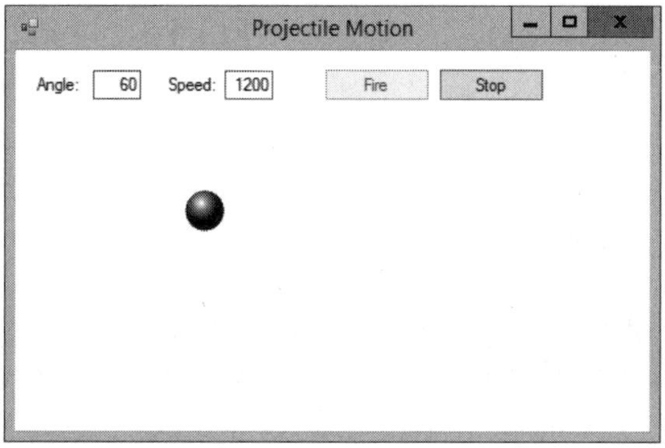

FIGURE 11-4

Hints:

➤ Build the form as shown in Figure 11-4. The cannonball is an image displayed in a `PictureBox`. Also add a `Timer` named `moveTimer` and set its `Interval` property to 50.

➤ Outside of any event handler, create six `float` variables named `TicksPerSecond`, `X`, `Y`, `Vx`, `Vy`, and `Ay`.

➤ When the user clicks the Fire `Button`:

    ➤ Use the form's `ClientSize` and the `PictureBox`'s `Size` to move the `PictureBox` to the form's lower-left corner.

    ➤ Parse the angle and speed entered by the user.

    ➤ Convert the angle from degrees to radians by using the formula: `radians = degrees * Math.PI / 180`.

➤ Calculate the number of `Timer` ticks per second by using the formula: `TicksPerSecond = 1000 / moveTimer.Interval`.

➤ Use the following equations (converting data types as necessary) to calculate the ball's initial velocities `Vx` and `Vy` in feet per tick:

```
Vx = speed * Math.Cos(radians) / TicksPerSecond
Vy = speed * Math.Sin(radians) / TicksPerSecond
```

➤ Use the following equation to calculate the ball's acceleration due to gravity in feet per tick per tick:

```
Ay = 32 / TicksPerSecond / TicksPerSecond
```

➤ Enable the `Timer`.

➤ Disable the Fire `Button`.

➤ Enable the Stop `Button`.

➤ When the user clicks the Stop `Button`:

➤ Disable the `Timer`.

➤ Enable the Fire `Button`.

➤ Disable the Stop `Button`.

➤ When the `Timer`'s `Tick` event fires:

➤ Move the cannonball by adding `Vx` to the `PictureBox`'s `Left` property and subtracting `Vy` from the `PictureBox`'s `Top` property. (You subtract `Vy` because Y coordinates on the form decrease upward.)

➤ Add the downward acceleration due to gravity to `Vy` by subtracting `Ay`

➤ If all goes well, then for a 60° angle and a speed of 120 feet per second, the cannonball should take around 8.5 seconds to drop off the bottom of the form. (It may seem like a long time, but the ball travels more than 400 feet horizontally during that time.)

NOTE *Please select the videos for Lesson 11 online at* www.wrox.com/go/csharp24hourtrainer2evideos.

Debugging Code

A *bug* is a programming error that makes a program fail to produce the correct result. The program might crash, display incorrect data, or do something completely unexpected such as delete the wrong file.

In this lesson you learn how to use the excellent debugging tools provided by Visual Studio's IDE to find bugs in C#. You learn about different kinds of bugs and you get to practice debugging techniques on some buggy examples that you can download from the book's website.

DEFERRED TECHNIQUES

Unfortunately, at this point in the book you don't know enough about writing code to be able to understand and fix certain kinds of bugs. For example, a program crashes if it tries to access an array entry that is outside of the array, but you won't learn about arrays until Lesson 16.

So why does this lesson cover debugging when you don't even know all of the techniques you need to cause and fix certain kinds of bugs? It makes sense for two reasons.

First, the previous lesson was the first part of the book where you were likely to encounter bugs. Whenever I teach beginning programming, students start seeing bugs as soon as they write code that performs calculations like those covered in Lesson 11. These kinds of bugs are easy to fix if you know just a little bit about debugging, but they can be extremely frustrating if you don't.

Second, it turns out that you don't need to know more advanced techniques to learn simple debugging. Once you learn how to track down simple bugs, you can use the same techniques to find more advanced bugs. (If you learn to swim in 3 feet of water, you can later use the same techniques to swim in 10 feet or 100 feet of water.)

Later, when you know more about C# programming and can create more advanced bugs, that same knowledge will help you fix those bugs. When you know enough to have array indexing errors, you'll also know enough to fix them.

DEBUGGING THEN AND NOW

Back in the bad old days, programmers often fixed bugs by staring hard at the code, making a few test changes, and then running the program again to see what happened. This trial-and-error approach could be extremely slow because the programmer didn't really know exactly what was going on inside the code. If the programmer didn't have a good understanding of what was really happening, the test changes often didn't help and may have even made the problem worse.

Visual Studio's IDE provides excellent tools for debugging code. In particular, it lets you stop a program while it's running and see what it's doing. It lets you follow the program as it executes its code one line at a time, look at variable values, and even change those values while the program is still running.

The following sections describe some of Visual Studio's most useful debugging tools.

SETTING BREAKPOINTS

A *breakpoint* stops code execution at a particular statement. To set a breakpoint, open the Code Editor and click the gray margin to the left of the line of code where you want to stop. Alternatively, you can place the cursor on the line and press F9.

The IDE indicates the breakpoint by displaying a red circle in the left margin and highlighting the line of code in red. Figure 12-1 shows a breakpoint set on the following line of code:

```
decimal grandTotal = subtotal + salesTax + shipping;
```

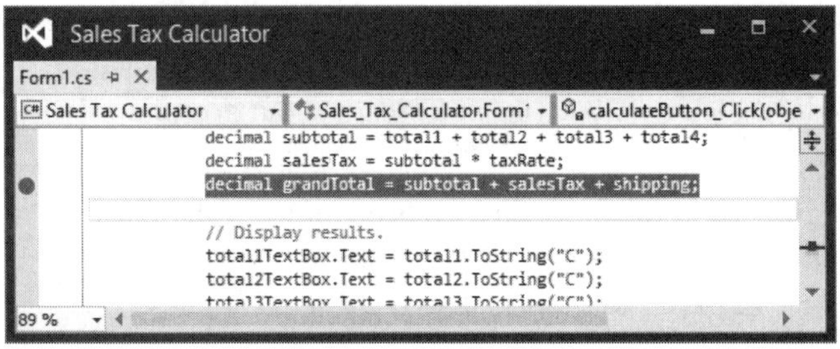

FIGURE 12-1

If you run the program now, execution stops when it reaches that line. You can then study the code to see what it's doing.

The debugger provides an *edit-and-continue* feature that lets you modify a stopped program's code. You can add new statements, remove existing statements, declare new variables, and so forth. Unfortunately, the debugger gets confused if you make certain changes, and you'll have to restart your program. But sometimes you can make small changes without restarting.

To remove a breakpoint, click the red breakpoint circle or click the line and press F9 again.

SPONTANEOUS STOP

If you need to stop a program while it is running and you haven't set any breakpoints, you can select the Debug menu's Break All command or press Ctrl+Alt+Break. The debugger will halt the program in the middle of whatever it is doing and enter break mode.

If the Break All command isn't in the Debug menu (it may not be for some versions of Visual Studio), you can still use the shortcut Ctrl+Alt+Break.

This technique is particularly useful for interrupting long tasks or infinite loops.

READING VARIABLES

It's easy to read a variable's value while execution is stopped. Simply hover the mouse over a variable and its value appears in a popup window.

For example, consider the order summary program shown in Figure 12-2. The program is supposed to add a subtotal, 9% sales tax, and shipping costs to get a grand total. You don't have to be Neil deGrasse Tyson to realize that something's wrong in Figure 12-2. If you're really paying a total of $204.50 for a $19.95 purchase, you need to find a new place to shop.

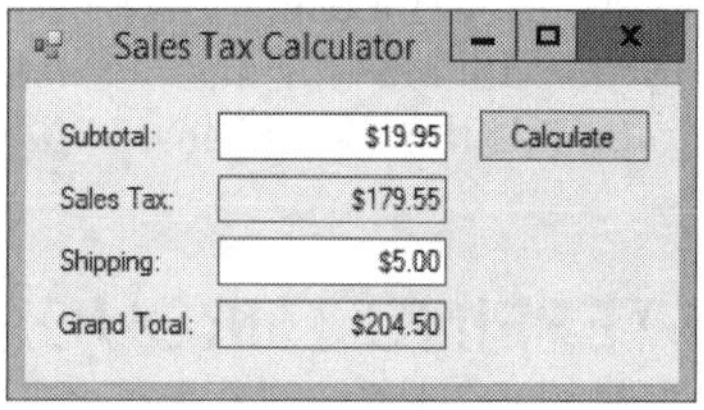

FIGURE 12-2

To debug this program, you could place a breakpoint on a line of code near where you know the bug occurs. For example, the line of code containing the breakpoint in Figure 12-1 calculates the grand total. Because the total displayed in Figure 12-2 is wrong, this seems like a good place to begin the bug hunt. (You can download the Sales Tax Calculator program from the book's website and follow along if you like.)

When the code is stopped, you can hover the mouse over a variable to learn its value. If you hover the mouse over the variables in that line of code, you'll find that subTotal is 19.95 (correct), shipping is 5 (correct), and salesTax is 179.55 (very much incorrect). Figure 12-3 shows the mouse hovering over the salesTax variable to display its value.

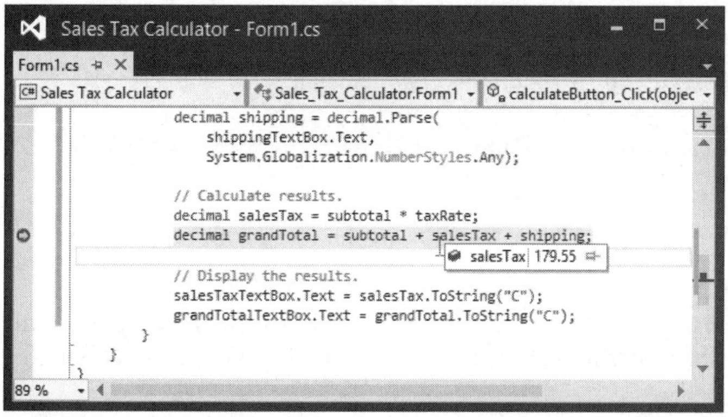

FIGURE 12-3

Now that you know the bug is lurking in the variable `salesTax`, you can hover the mouse over other variables to see how that value was calculated. If you hover the mouse over the variables in the previous line of code, you'll find that `subTotal` is `19.95` (still correct) and `taxRate` is `9`.

You may need to think about that for a bit to realize what's going wrong. To apply a tax rate such as 9%, you divide by 100 and then multiply. In this case, `taxRate` should be 0.09, not 9.

Having figured out the problem, you can stop the program by opening the Debug menu and selecting the Stop Debugging command, by clicking the Stop Debugging button on the toolbar, or by pressing Shift+F5.

Now you can fix the code and run the program again to see if it works. The following line shows the incorrect line of code (I scrolled it out of view in Figure 12-3 so it wouldn't be a complete giveaway):

```
const decimal taxRate = 9M;
```

When you run the program again, you should get the correct sales tax ($1.80) and grand total ($26.75). In a more complicated program, you would need to perform a lot more tests to make sure the program behaved properly for different inputs, including weird ones such as when the user enters "ten dollars" for the subtotal or leaves the shipping cost blank. This example isn't robust enough to handle those problems.

STEPPING THROUGH CODE

Once you've stopped the code at a breakpoint, you can step through the execution one statement at a time to see what happens. The Debug menu provides four commands that control execution:

➤ **Continue (F5)**—Makes the program continue running until it finishes or it reaches another breakpoint. Use this to run the program normally after you're done looking at the code.

➤ **Step Into (F11)**—Makes the program execute the current statement. If that statement calls a method, execution stops inside that method so you can see how it works.

➤ **Step Over (F10)**—Makes the program execute the current statement. If that statement calls another piece of executable code, the program runs that code and returns without stopping inside that code (unless there's a breakpoint somewhere inside that code).

➤ **Step Out (Shift+F11)**—Makes the program run the current routine until it finishes and returns to the calling routine (unless it hits another breakpoint first).

> **NOTE** *When it is stopped, the debugger highlights the next line of code that it will execute in yellow.*

In addition to using the Debug menu or shortcut keys, you can invoke these commands from the toolbar.

Normally the program steps through its statements in order, but there is a way to change the order if you feel the need. Right-click the line that you want the code to execute next and select Set Next

Statement from the context menu. Alternatively, you can place the cursor on the line and press Ctrl+Shift+F10. When you let the program continue, it starts executing from this line.

Setting the next statement to execute is useful for replaying history to see where an error occurred, re-executing a line after you change a variable's value (described in the "Using the Immediate Window" section later in this lesson), or to jump forward to skip some code.

Note that you can jump to only certain lines of code. For example, you can't jump to a comment or other line of code that doesn't actually do anything (you can't set a breakpoint there either), you can't jump to a different method, you can't jump at all if an error has just occurred, you can't jump to a variable declaration unless it also initializes the variable, and so forth. C# does its best, but it has its limits.

USING WATCHES

Sometimes you may want to check a variable's value frequently as you step through the code one line at a time. In that case, pausing between steps to hover over a variable could slow you down, particularly if you have a lot of code to step through.

To make monitoring a variable easier, the debugger provides watches. A *watch* displays a variable's value whenever the program stops.

To create a watch, break execution, right-click a variable, and select Add Watch from the context menu. The bottom of Figure 12-4 shows a watch set on the variable subtotal. Each time the program executes a line of code and stops, the watch updates to display the variable's current value.

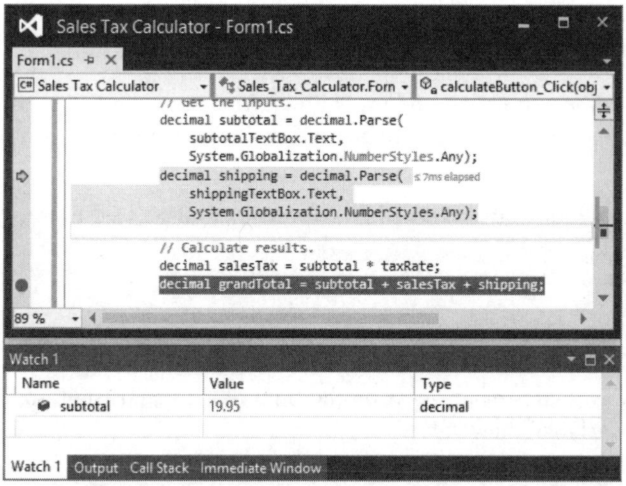

FIGURE 12-4

The Watch window also highlights variables that have just changed in red. If you're tracking a lot of watches, this makes it easy to find the values that have just changed.

> **NOTE** *The Locals window is similar to the Watch window except it shows the values of all of the local variables (and constants). This window is handy if you want to view many of those variables all at once. It also highlights recently changed values in red so you can see what's changing.*

USING THE IMMEDIATE WINDOW

While the program is stopped, the Immediate window lets you execute simple commands. The four most useful commands that this window supports let you view variable values, evaluate expressions, set variable values, and call methods.

> **NOTE** *If you can't find the Immediate window, open the Debug menu, expand the Windows submenu, and select Immediate.*

To view a variable's value, simply type the variable's name and press Enter. (Optionally, you can type a question mark in front if it makes you feel more like you're asking a question.)

The following text shows the Immediate window after I typed in the name of the variable `subtotal` and pressed Enter:

```
subtotal
19.95
```

To evaluate an expression, simply type in the expression and press Enter. You can include literal values, variables, properties, constants, and just about anything else that you can normally include inside an expression in the code.

The following text shows the Immediate window after I typed an expression and pressed Enter:

```
taxRate * subtotal
179.55
```

To set a variable's value, simply type the variable's name, an equals sign, and the value that you want to give it. The new value can be a literal value or it can be the result of an expression. After you press Enter, the Immediate window evaluates whatever is on the right of the equals sign, saves it in the variable, and then displays the variable's new value.

> **NOTE** *The same technique lets you set new values for properties. For example, you can change a control's* `Location`, `Text`, `Visible`, `BackColor`, *and other properties on the fly.*

The following text shows the Immediate window after I typed a statement to give the `grandTotal` variable a new value and pressed Enter:

```
grandTotal = subtotal + salesTax
199.50
```

Finally, to call a method, simply type the method call into the Immediate window and press Enter. Don't forget to add parentheses to the method call even if the method takes no parameters. The Immediate window calls the method and displays any returned result. If the method has no return value, the Immediate window displays "Expression has been evaluated and has no value."

The following text shows the Immediate window after I executed the `grandTotalTextBox`'s `Clear` method:

```
grandTotalTextBox.Clear()
Expression has been evaluated and has no value
```

> **NOTE** *You must type commands in the Immediate window just as you would in the Code Editor. In particular, you must use the correct capitalization or the window will complain.*

TRY IT

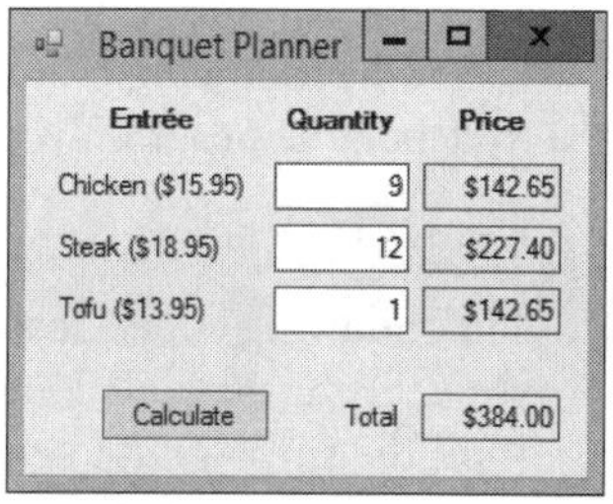

If you look closely at Figure 12-5, you'll see that this program has a serious problem. One tofu dinner at $13.95 each probably shouldn't add up to $142.65. If you look a little more closely, you'll also see that the grand total doesn't add up properly.

In this Try It, you debug this program. You set breakpoints and use the debugger to evaluate variable values to figure out where the code is going wrong.

Banquet Planner		
Entrée	**Quantity**	**Price**
Chicken ($15.95)	9	$142.65
Steak ($18.95)	12	$227.40
Tofu ($13.95)	1	$142.65
Calculate	Total	$384.00

FIGURE 12-5

> **NOTE** *The downloads for this chapter, which are available at* www.wrox.com/ go/csharp24hourtrainer2e, *include buggy and debugged versions of the Try It and exercises. For example, the initial flawed version of the Try It is called "Try It 12" and the fixed version is called "Try It 12 Fixed."*

Lesson Requirements

In this lesson, you:

➤ Use the debugger to fix this program. To follow along in the debugger, download this lesson's material from the book's website and open the "Try It 12" solution.

➤ Run the program and experiment with it for a bit to see what seems to work and what seems to be broken. This should give you an idea of where the problem may lie.

➤ Set a breakpoint in the code near where you think there might be a problem. In this case, the tofu dinner cost calculation is wrong so you might set a breakpoint on this line:

```
decimal priceTofu = tofuCost * numTofu;
```

➤ Run the program so it stops at that breakpoint. Hover the mouse over different variables to see whether their values make sense.

➤ Step through the code, watching each line closely to see what's wrong.

➤ Fix the error.

➤ Run the program again and test it to make sure the change you made works. Try setting two of the quantities to 0 and the third to 1 to see if the program can correctly calculate the non-zero value.

➤ Repeat these steps until you can't find any more problems.

> **NOTE** *You can download the code and resources for this lesson from the website at* `www.wrox.com/go/csharp24hourtrainer2e.`

Step-by-Step

The first two lesson requirements for this Try It are fairly straightforward so they aren't repeated here. The following paragraphs discuss the solution to the mysterious problem, so if you want to try to debug the program yourself, do so before you read any further.

Ready? Let's go.

The following code shows how the program works. The bold line is where I set my breakpoint. If you stare at the code long enough, you'll probably find the bug, so don't look too closely or you'll spoil the surprise. Remember, the point is to practice using the debugger (which will be your only hope in more complicated programs), not to simply fix the program.

```
// Calculate the prices for each entree and the total price.
private void calculateButton_Click(object sender, EventArgs e)
{
    const decimal chickenCost = 15.85M;
    const decimal steakCost = 18.95M;
    const decimal tofuCost = 13.95M;

    // Get inputs.
    int numChicken = int.Parse(chickenQuantityTextBox.Text);
    int numSteak = int.Parse(steakQuantityTextBox.Text);
    int numTofu = int.Parse(tofuQuantityTextBox.Text);

    // Calculate results.
    decimal total = 0;

    decimal priceChicken = chickenCost * numChicken;
    total += priceChicken;
```

```
decimal priceSteak = steakCost * numSteak;
total += priceSteak;

decimal priceTofu = tofuCost * numTofu;
total += priceTofu;

// Display results.
chickenPriceTextBox.Text = priceChicken.ToString("C");
steakPriceTextBox.Text = priceSteak.ToString("C");
tofuPriceTextBox.Text = priceChicken.ToString("C");
totalTextBox.Text = total.ToString("C");
}
```

➤ Run the program so it stops at that breakpoint. Hover the mouse over different variables to see whether they look like they make sense.

1. If you run to the breakpoint and hover the mouse over the variables, you'll find that most of them make sense; the values numChicken = 9, priceChicken = 142.65, and so forth.

➤ Step through the code, watching each line closely to see what's wrong.

1. While the program is stopped on the breakpoint, the variable priceTofu has value 0 because the code hasn't yet executed the line that sets its value. Press F10 to step over that line and you'll see that priceTofu is 13.95 as it should be. So far, you haven't found the bug.

   If you continue stepping through the code, watching each line carefully, you'll eventually see the problem in this line:

   ```
   tofuPriceTextBox.Text = priceChicken.ToString("C");
   ```

   Here the code is making the tofu price TextBox display the value priceChicken!

> **NOTE** *This is a fairly typical copy-and-paste error. The programmer wrote one line of code, copied and pasted it several times to perform similar tasks (displaying the values in the TextBoxes), but then didn't update each pasted line correctly.*

➤ Fix the error.

1. This bug is easy to fix. Simply change the offending line to this:

   ```
   tofuPriceTextBox.Text = priceTofu.ToString("C");
   ```

➤ Run the program again and test it to make sure the change you made works. Try setting two of the quantities to 0 and the third to 1 to see if the program can correctly calculate the non-zero value.

1. If you run the program again, all should initially look fine. If you reproduce some calculations by hand, however, you may find a small discrepancy in the chicken prices.

2.   You can see the problem more easily if you set the quantities of steak and tofu to 0 and the quantity of chicken to 1. Then the program calculates that the price of one chicken dinner (at $15.95 each) is $15.85.

➤   If the program still has problems, run through these steps again.

1.   Having found another bug, run through the debugging process again. Set a breakpoint on the line that calculates priceChicken and hover over the variables to see if their values make sense.

   If you're paying attention, you'll see that the value of the constant costChicken is 15.85, not 15.95 as it should be.

2.   Fix the constant declaration and test the program again.

> **NOTE** *It's extremely common for a program to contain more than one bug. In fact, it's an axiom of software development that any nontrivial program contains at least one bug.*
>
> *A consequence of that axiom is that, even after you fix the program's "last" bug, it still contains another bug. Sometimes fixing the bug introduces a new bug. (That's not as uncommon as you might think in a complex program.) Other times more bugs are hiding; you just haven't found them yet.*
>
> *In complex projects, the goal is still to eradicate every single bug, but the reality is that often the best you can do is fix as many as you can find until the odds of the user finding one in everyday use are extremely small.*

EXERCISES

Putting debugging exercises in a book can be a bit strange. If the book includes the code, you can stare at it until you see the bugs without using the debugger, and that would defeat the purpose.

For that reason, this section only describes the programs containing the bugs and you'll have to download the buggy programs from the book's website at www.wrox.com/go/ csharp24hourtrainer. The corrected versions are named after their exercises, for example, "Exercise 12-1 Fixed." Modified lines are marked with comments.

1.   Debug the Temperature Converter program shown in Figure 12-6. (Hint: 0° Celsius = 32° Fahrenheit and 100° Celsius = 212° Fahrenheit.)

2.   Debug the Distance Converter program shown in Figure 12-7. (After you fix this one, notice that using constants instead of magic numbers would make fixing these bugs easier and might have avoided them from the start. Also note again that duplicated code is a bad thing. You learn how to fix that in Lesson 20.)

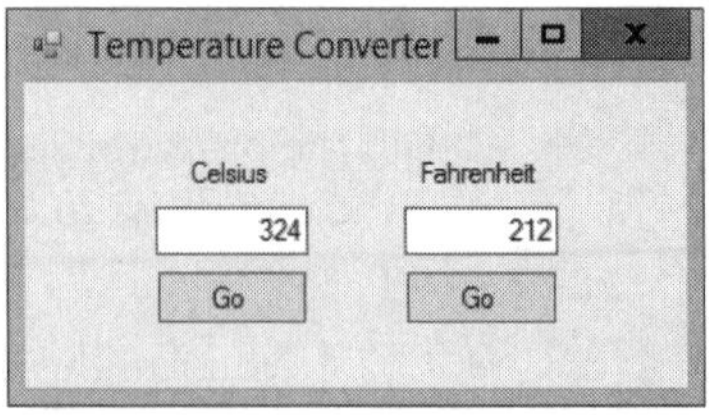

FIGURE 12-6

3. The Picture Resizer program is supposed to zoom in on a picture when you adjust its `TrackBar`. Unfortunately, when you move the `TrackBar`, the picture seems to shrink and move to a new location. Debug the program.

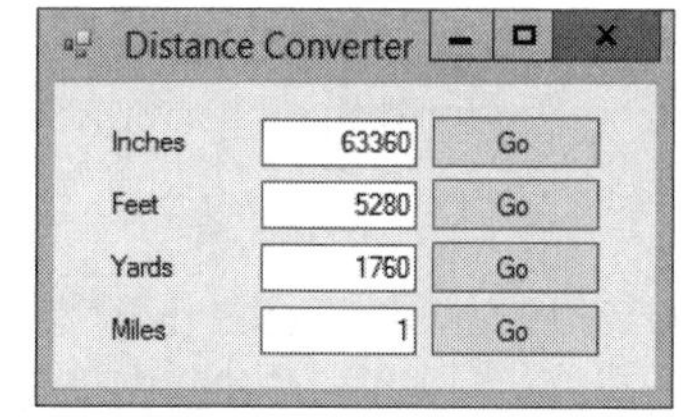

4. Debug the Tax Form program, which performs a fictitious tax calculation based on a real one. It's an ugly little program, but it's probably the most realistic one in this lesson. (Hint: For the program's initial inputs, the tax due should be $290.00.)

FIGURE 12-7

5. The Play Tone program is supposed to let the user play tones between 1000 Hz and 10,000 Hz for durations between 0.1 and 2.0 seconds. Unfortunately, for durations of 1.0 seconds or longer, the program plays a short click, and for durations under 1.0 seconds the program crashes. Download and debug the program.

6. [Games] When you scroll the Orbit program's scrollbar from 0 to 359 degrees, the program moves an image of the Earth around an image of the sun. Unfortunately, the Earth jumps all over the place and it sometimes falls off the bottom and right edges of the form. Download and debug the program.

7. [Games] The Satellite program uses a `Timer` to make a picture of a satellite orbit the Earth. Unfortunately, the satellite sometimes moves off the bottom of the form. Download and debug the program.

8. [Games, WPF] The Rotate Image program lets the user load and rotate an image. (The code shows how to load an image at run time and prevent WPF from resizing it, so it's worth looking at for that alone.) Unfortunately, when the user changes the slider's value from 0 to 359 degrees, the image rotates only a tiny amount. Download and debug the program.

9. [Graphics] The Draw Star program is supposed to draw a five-pointed star. (This book doesn't have enough room to say a lot about drawing graphics, but this example can help you get started.) Unfortunately, the program draws an upside-down pentagon. Download and debug the program.

10. The Equal Shares program takes as inputs a money amount and a number of people. It then calculates the amount of money you should give each person to divide the money evenly. Unfortunately, the program crashes. Download and debug the program so it doesn't crash and so it displays the shares as a currency value.

11. The Interest Calculator program uses the formula $F = P * (1 + R)^N$ to calculate the future value of a savings account where F is the future value, P is the initial principle, R is the annual interest rate, and N is the number of years. Unfortunately, the program has two problems. First, it won't compile because of some data type errors. Second, once you get it to compile, it indicates that a $1,000 investment at 5% interest for 10 years ends with a total value of more than $60 billion. (If you know of an investment that can turn my $1,000 into $60 billion in 10 years, please let me know!) Download and debug the program.

12. In finance, the Rule of 72 lets you approximate the number of years it takes to double an investment at a particular interest rate. If the annual interest rate is R, then the rule says it will take approximately $T = 72 / R$ years to double an investment. (The Rule of 70 and the

Rule of 69.3 are similar except they use values other than 72. Different versions are closest for different interest rates.)

The exact formula for calculating doubling time is $T = Ln(2) / Ln(1 + R)$. The advantage of the Rules is that you can approximate them in your head. (I would have a harder time dividing into 69.3 than 70 or 72, but at least you can divide into 69.3 with a simple accounting calculator that doesn't do logarithms.)

The Doubling Time program takes as input an interest rate and calculates the results of the Rules of 72, 70, and 69.3, plus the exact formula. The results for a 6% interest rate are 12.00, 11.67, 115.50, and 0.36 years, respectively. Download and debug the program.

> **NOTE** *Please select the videos for Lesson 12 online at* www.wrox.com/go/ csharp24hourtrainer2evideos.

13

Understanding Scope

A variable's *scope* is the code that can "see" or access that variable. It determines whether a piece of code can read the variable's value and give it a new value.

In this lesson you learn what scope is. You learn why restricting scope is a good thing and how to determine a variable's scope.

SCOPE WITHIN A CLASS

A C# class (and note that Form types are classes, too) contains three main kinds of scope: class scope, method scope, and block scope. (If you have trouble remembering what a class is, review Lesson 9's section "Understanding Classes and Instances.")

Variables with *class scope* are declared inside the class but outside of any of its methods. These variables are visible to all of the code throughout the instance of the class and are known as *fields*.

Variables with *method scope* are declared within a method. They are usable by all of the code that follows the declaration within that method.

Variables with *block scope* are declared inside a block defined by curly braces {} nested inside a method. The section "Block Scope" later in this lesson says more about this.

For example, consider the following code that defines the form's constructor (Form1), a field, and some variables inside event handlers:

```
namespace VariableScope
{
    public partial class Form1 : Form
    {
        public Form1()
        {
            InitializeComponent();
        }

        // A field.
        int a = 1;
```

```
private void clickMeButton_Click(object sender, EventArgs e)
{
    // A method variable.
    int b = 2;
    MessageBox.Show("a = " + a.ToString() +
        "\nb = " + b.ToString());
}

private void clickMeTooButton_Click(object sender, EventArgs e)
{
    // A method variable.
    int c = 3;
    MessageBox.Show("a = " + a.ToString() +
        "\nc = " + c.ToString());
}
    }
}
```

The field a is declared outside of the three methods (Form1, clickMeButton_Click, and clickMeTooButton_Click) so it has class scope. That means the code in any of the methods can see and use this variable. In this example, the two Click event handlers can each display the value.

The variable b is declared within clickMeButton_Click so it has method scope. Only the code within this method that comes after the declaration can use this variable. In particular, the code in the other methods cannot see it.

Similarly, the code in the clickMeTooButton_Click event handler that comes after the c declaration can see that variable.

Two variables with the same name cannot have the same scope. For example, you cannot create two variables named a at the class level nor can you create two variables named b inside the same method.

Same Named Variables

Although you cannot give two variables the same name within the same scope, you can give them the same name if they are in different methods or one is a field and the other is declared inside a method. For example, the following code defines three variables all named count:

```
// A field.
int count = 0;

private void clickMeButton_Click(object sender, EventArgs e)
{
    // A method variable.
    int count = 1;
    MessageBox.Show(count.ToString());
}

private void clickMeTooButton_Click(object sender, EventArgs e)
```

```
    {
        // A method variable.
        int count = 2;
        MessageBox.Show(count.ToString());
    }
```

In this example, the method-level variable hides the class-level variable with the same name. For example, within the `clickMeButton_Click` event handler, its local version of `count` is visible and has the value 1. The class-level field with value 0 is hidden.

> **NOTE** *You can still get the class-level value if you prefix the variable with the executing object. Recall that the special keyword* `this` *means "the object that is currently executing this code." That means you could access the class-level field while inside the* `clickMeButton_Click` *event handler like this:*
>
> ```
> private void clickMeButton_Click(object sender, EventArgs e)
> {
>     // A method variable.
>     int count = 1;
>     MessageBox.Show(count.ToString());
>     MessageBox.Show(this.count.ToString());
> }
> ```
>
> *Usually it's better to avoid potential confusion by giving the variables different names in the first place.*

Method Variable Lifetime

A variable with method scope is created when its method is executed. Each time the method is called, a new version of the variable is created. When the method exits, the variable is destroyed. If its value is referenced by some other variable, it might still exist, but this variable is no longer available to manipulate it.

One consequence of this is that the variable's value resets each time the method executes. For example, consider the following code:

```
private void clickMeButton_Click(object sender, EventArgs e)
{
    // A method variable.
    int count = 0;
    count++;
    MessageBox.Show(count.ToString());
}
```

Each time this code executes, it creates a variable named `count`, adds 1 to it, and displays its value. The intent may be to have the message box display an incrementing counter but the result is actually the value 1 each time the user clicks the button.

To save a value between method calls, you can change the variable into a field declared outside of any method. The following version of the preceding code displays the values 1, 2, 3, and so on when the user clicks the button multiple times:

```
// A field.
int count = 0;

private void clickMeButton_Click(object sender, EventArgs e)
{
    count++;
    MessageBox.Show(count.ToString());
}
```

Note that a parameter declared in a method's declaration counts as having method scope. For example, the preceding event handler has two parameters named sender and e. That means you cannot declare new variables within the method with those names.

Block Scope

A method can also contain nested blocks of code that define other variables that have scope limited to the nested code. This kind of variable cannot have the same name as a variable declared at a higher level of nesting within the same method.

Later lessons explain some kinds of nesting used to make decisions (Lesson 18), loops (Lesson 19), and error handlers (Lesson 21).

One type of nested block simply uses braces to enclose code. The scope of a variable declared within this kind of block includes only the block, and the variable is usable only later in the block.

For example, consider the following code:

```
private void clickMeTooButton_Click(object sender, EventArgs e)
{
    // A method variable.
    int count = 1;
    MessageBox.Show(count.ToString());

    // A nested block of code.
    {
        int i = 2;
        MessageBox.Show(i.ToString());
    }

    // A second nested block of code.
    {
        int i = 3;
        MessageBox.Show(i.ToString());
    }
}
```

This method declares the variable count at the method level and displays its value.

The code then makes a block of code surrounded by braces. It declares the variable i and displays its value. Note that the code could not create a second variable named count inside this block because the higher-level method code contains a variable with that name.

After the first block ends, the code creates a second block. It makes a new variable i within that block and displays its value. Because the two inner blocks are not nested (neither contains the other), it's okay for both blocks to define variables named i.

ACCESSIBILITY

A field's scope determines what parts of the code can see the variable. So far I've focused on the fact that all of the code in a class can see a field declared at the class level, outside of any methods. In fact, a field may also be visible to code running in other classes depending on its accessibility.

A field's *accessibility* determines which code is allowed to access the field. For example, a class might contain a public field that is visible to the code in any other class. It may also define a private field that is visible only to code within the class that defines it.

Accessibility is not the same as scope, but the two work closely together to determine what code can access a field.

Table 13-1 summarizes the field accessibility values. Later when you learn how to build properties and methods, you'll be able to use the same accessibility values to determine what code can access them.

TABLE 13-1

ACCESSIBILITY VALUE	MEANING
public	Any code can see the variable.
private	Only code in the same class can see the variable.
protected	Only code in the same class or a derived class can see the variable. For example, if the Manager class is derived from the Person class, a Manager object can see a Person object's protected variables. (You learn more about deriving one class from another in Lesson 23.)
internal	Only code in the same assembly can see the variable. For example, if the variable's class is contained in a library (which is its own assembly), a main program that uses the library cannot see the variable.
protected internal	The variable is visible to any code in the same assembly or any derived class in another assembly.

If you omit the accessibility value for a field, it defaults to private. You can still include the private keyword, however, to make the field's accessibility obvious.

> **NOTE** *You may remember from earlier lessons that you needed to set a control's* Modifiers *property to* public *to allow a program's main form to get and set the values of that control's properties. For example, suppose you build a custom dialog with a* TextBox *where the user can enter a name. Now you know why you need to set the* TextBox's Modifiers *property to* public. *If you don't, the main form can't see the* TextBox's Text *property.*

There's one aspect of `private` accessibility that sometimes confuses people. A `private` field is visible to any code in *any instance* of the same class, not just to the *same instance* of the class.

For example, suppose you build a `Person` class with a private field named `Salary`. Not only can all of the code in an instance see its own `Salary` value, but *any* `Person` object can see any other `Person` object's `Salary` value.

> **NOTE** *Note that public fields are considered to be bad programming style. It's better to make a public property instead. Lesson 23 explains why and tells how to make properties. Public fields do work, however, and are good enough for this discussion on accessibility.*

RESTRICTING SCOPE AND ACCESSIBILITY

It's a good programming practice to restrict scope and accessibility as much as possible to limit the code that can access it. For example, if a piece of code has no business using a particular field, there's no reason to give it the opportunity. This not only reduces the chances that you will use the variable incorrectly but also removes the variable from IntelliSense so it's not there to clutter up your choices and confuse things.

If you can use a variable declared locally inside an event handler or other method, do so. In fact, if you can declare a variable within a block of code inside a method, such as in a loop, do so. That gives the variable very limited scope so it won't get in the way when you're working with unrelated code.

If you need multiple methods to share the same value or you need to keep track of a value between method calls, store the value in a private field. Only make a variable public if code in another form (or other class) needs to use it.

TRY IT

In this Try It, you build the program shown in Figure 13-1. You use fields to allow two forms to communicate and to perform simple calculations. You also get to try out a new control: `ListView`.

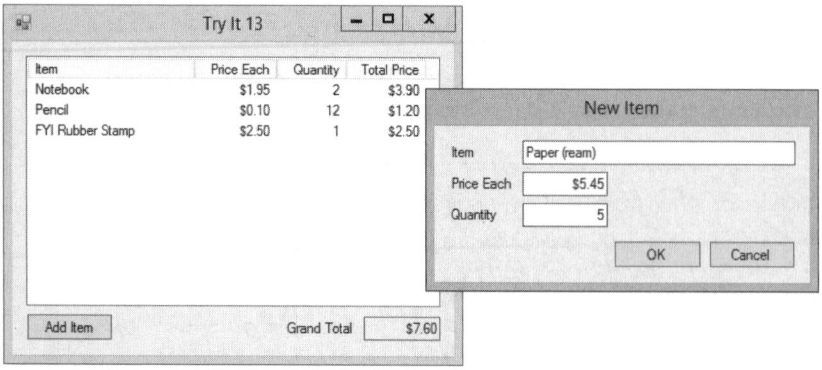

FIGURE 13-1

Lesson Requirements

In this lesson, you:

➤ Create the `NewItemForm` shown on the right in Figure 13-1.

 ➤ Provide public fields to let the main form get the data entered by the user.

 ➤ When the user clicks the OK button, copy the item name, price each, and quantity values into the public fields.

➤ Create the main form shown on the left in Figure 13-1.

➤ When the user clicks the main form's Add Item button, make the program display the `NewItemForm`. If the user enters data and clicks the OK button, display the entered values in the main form's `ListView` control and update the grand total.

> **NOTE** *You can download the code and resources for this lesson from the website at* www.wrox.com/go/csharp24hourtrainer2e.

Hints

➤ Remember to set the `NewItemForm`'s `AcceptButton`, `CancelButton`, `FormBorderStyle`, and `ControlBox` properties appropriately.

➤ Because the main form's grand total must retain its value as the user adds items, it must be a field.

➤ To allow the main form to see the values entered by the user on the `NewItemForm`, use public fields.

Step-by-Step

➤ Create the `NewItemForm` shown on the right in Figure 13-1.

 1. Arrange the controls as shown in Figure 13-1.

 2. Set the form's `AcceptButton` property to the OK button and its `CancelButton` property to the Cancel button. The OK button will always close the form so set its `DialogResult` property to `OK`.

 3. Set the form's `FormBorderStyle` property to `FixedDialog`. Set its `ControlBox` property to `False`.

 ➤ Provide public fields to let the main form get the data entered by the user.

 a. Declare public fields for the program to use in its calculations. Use code similar to the following placed outside of any methods:

```
// Public fields. (They should really be properties.)
public string ItemName;
public decimal PriceEach, Quantity;
```

➤ When the user clicks the OK button, copy the item name, price each, and quantity values into the public fields.

  a. Copy the values entered by the user into the fields you created in the preceding step.

➤ Create the main form shown on the left in Figure 13-1.

  1. Create the `ListView`, `Button`, `Label`, and `TextBox`. Set their `Anchor` properties and make the `TextBox` read-only.

  2. To make the `ListView` display its items in a list as shown:

  a. Set its `View` property to `Details`.

  b. Select its `Columns` property and click the ellipsis to the right to open the ColumnHeader Collection Editor shown in Figure 13-2. Click the Add button four times to make the four columns. Use the property editor on the right to set each column's `Name` and `Text` properties and to set `TextAlign` to `Right` for the numeric columns.

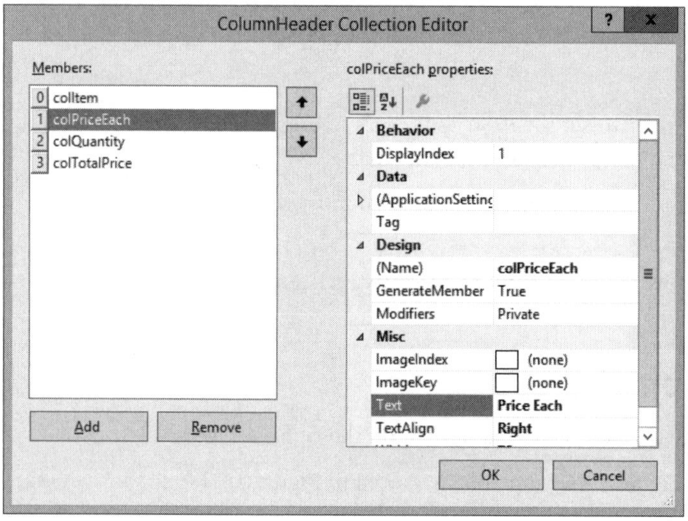

FIGURE 13-2

➤ When the user clicks the main form's Add Item button, make the program display a `NewItemForm`. If the user enters data and clicks OK, display the entered values in the main form's `ListView` control and update the grand total.

  1. The button's `Click` event handler should use code similar to the following:

```
// A private field to keep track of grand total
// across multiple calls to the event handler.
private decimal GrandTotal = 0;
```

```
// Let the user add a new item to the list.
private void addItemButton_Click(object sender, EventArgs e)
{
    NewItemForm frm = new NewItemForm();
    if (frm.ShowDialog() == DialogResult.OK)
    {
        // Get the new values.
        decimal priceEach = frm.PriceEach;
        decimal quantity = frm.Quantity;
        decimal totalPrice = priceEach * quantity;

        // Add the values to the ListView.
        ListViewItem lvi = itemsListView.Items.Add(frm.ItemName);
        lvi.SubItems.Add(priceEach.ToString("C"));
        lvi.SubItems.Add(quantity.ToString());
        lvi.SubItems.Add(totalPrice.ToString("C"));

        // Add to the grand total and display the new result.
        GrandTotal += totalPrice;
        grandTotalTextBox.Text = GrandTotal.ToString("C");
    }
}
```

> **NOTE** *If one form's code tries to directly access a field in another form and do something with the value in the same statement, you may get a design time error. For example, suppose the Try It's main form uses the following code:*
>
> ```
> MessageBox.Show(frm.Quantity.ToString());
> ```
>
> *Here* frm *is the variable referring to an instance of the* NewItemForm *dialog and* Quantity *is a field in the dialog. In that case Visual Studio issues the following warning at design time:*
>
> Accessing a member on 'NewItemForm.Quantity' may cause
> a runtime exception because it is a field of a marshal-by-
> reference class
>
> *The problem here is obscure and happens only if the program is using the dialog across process or machine boundaries, for example, if your program tries to display a dialog defined on another programming thread.*
>
> *This warning may not be as important as a low oil pressure warning in your car, but it's generally not good to ignore warnings. Fortunately it's easy to make this warning go away. Simply copy the returned result into a local variable and then manipulate that variable instead of work with the dialog's field directly. For example, you could use the following code:*
>
> ```
> decimal quantity = frm.Quantity;
> MessageBox.Show(quantity.ToString());
> ```

EXERCISES

1. Copy the program you built for the Try It and modify the New Item form so its OK button is enabled only if its three `TextBoxes` contain non-blank text.

2. [Hard] Copy the program you built for Exercise 1 and add a new Delete Item button to the main form that deletes the currently selected item. Hints:

    ➤ Set the `ListView` control's `MultiSelect` property to `False` and set its `FullRowSelect` property to `True`.

    ➤ Enable the button Only when an item is selected in the `ListView` control.

    ➤ The `ListView` control's `SelectedIndices` property is a collection of the items that are currently selected. Use the collection's `Count` property to determine whether any items are selected.

    ➤ Use the following code to remove the selected item from the `ListView` control:

    ```
    // Delete the selected item.
    private void deleteItemButton_Click(object sender, EventArgs e)
    {
        // Get the selected item.
        ListViewItem item = itemsListView.SelectedItems[0];

        // Get the item's Total Price.
        decimal totalPrice =
            decimal.Parse(item.SubItems[2].Text, NumberStyles.Any);

        // Subtract from the grand total and display the new result.
        GrandTotal -= totalPrice;
        grandTotalTextBox.Text = GrandTotal.ToString("C");

        // Remove the item from the ListView.
        itemsListView.Items.Remove(item);
    }
    ```

3. If you typed the code shown for Exercise 2 correctly, then your program contains a bug. (To see it, add an item and then delete it.) Use the debugger to fix the program.

4. Use a design similar to the one used in Exercise 3 to let the user fill out an appointment calendar. The main form should contain a `ListView` with columns labeled Subject, Date, Time, and Notes. The `NewAppointmentForm` should provide `TextBoxes` for the user to enter these values and should have public fields `AppointmentSubject`, `AppointmentDate`, `AppointmentTime`, and `AppointmentNotes` to let the main form get the entered values. Instead of a grand total, the main form should display the number of appointments. Enable the New Appointment form's OK button Only if the Subject, Date, and Time are non-blank.

5. Build a form that contains a `ListBox`, `TextBox`, and `Button`. When the user clicks the `Button`, display a dialog that lets the user enter a number. Give the dialog a public field to return the value to the main form.

If the user enters a value and clicks OK, the main form should add the number to its `ListBox`. It should then display the average of its numbers. To do that, use a private field containing the numbers' total. Add the new number to the total and divide by the number of values.

6. [WPF] Repeat Exercise 5 with a WPF program.

7. Copy the program you wrote for Exercise 5 and add a Delete Item `Button` to the main form. Enable the button Only when an item is selected in the list. When the user clicks the button, remove the selected item from the list and display the new average.

8. [WPF] Repeat Exercise 7 with the program you built for Exercise 6.

9. [Hard] Build the conference schedule designer shown in Figure 13-3.

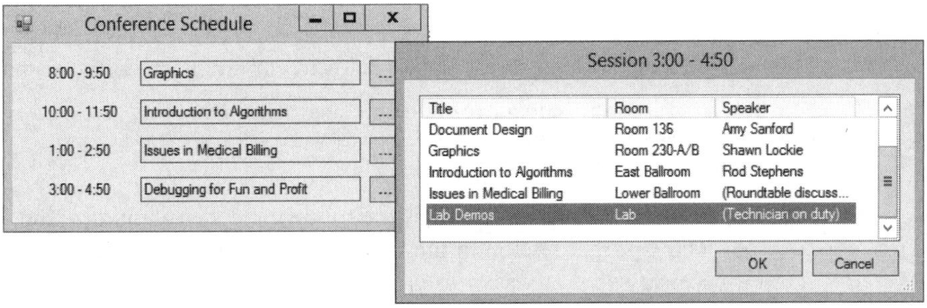

FIGURE 13-3

Give the main form (on the left in Figure 13-3) the following features:

➤ Create private fields named `SessionIndex1`, `SessionIndex2`, and so forth to hold the indexes of the user's choices.

➤ When the user clicks an ellipsis button, display the session selection dialog shown on the right in Figure 13-3.

➤ After creating the dialog but before displaying it, set its `Text` property to indicate the session time as shown in the figure.

➤ Also before displaying the dialog, use code similar to the following to tell the dialog about the user's previous selection for this session. (The `SessionIndex` and `SessionTitle` variables are public fields defined by the dialog and discussed shortly.)

```
frm.SessionIndex = SessionIndex1;
```

➤ If the user clicks OK, use code similar to the following to save the index of the user's choice and to display the session's title:

```
// Save the new selection.
SessionIndex1 = frm.SessionIndex;
choice1TextBox.Text = frm.SessionTitle;
```

Give the dialog the following features:

➤ Set the `ListView`'s `FullRowSelect` property to `True` and set its `MultiSelect` property to `False`.

➤ Use the Properties window to define the `ListView`'s column headers. Select the `ListView`, click its `Columns` property, click the ellipsis to the right, and use the editor to define the headers.

➤ Use the Properties window's editors to define the `ListView`'s items. Select the `ListView`, click its `Items` property, click the ellipsis to the right, and use the editor to define the items. Set the `Text` property to determine an item's text. Click the `SubItems` property and then click the ellipsis to the right to define the sub-items (Room and Speaker).

➤ Use the following code to create public fields to communicate with the main form:

```
// Public fields to communicate with the main form.
public int SessionIndex;
public string SessionTitle;
```

➤ Create a `Load` event handler that uses the following code to initialize the dialog. This code selects the proper session in the `ListView` control and then makes the control scroll if necessary so that session is visible:

```
// Initialize the selection.
private void PickSessionForm_Load(object sender, EventArgs e)
{
    sessionsListView.SelectedIndices.Add(SessionIndex);

    // Ensure that the selection is visible.
    sessionsListView.SelectedItems[0].EnsureVisible();
}
```

➤ In the OK button's `Click` event handler, use the following code to save the selected item's index and title for the main form to use:

```
// Save the user's selection.
private void okButton_Click(object sender, EventArgs e)
{
    SessionIndex = sessionsListView.SelectedIndices[0];
    SessionTitle = sessionsListView.SelectedItems[0].Text;
}
```

10. [WPF, Hard] Repeat Exercise 9 with a WPF application. It's harder to use a `ListView` in WPF than it is in Windows Forms, so for this exercise use a `ListBox` instead.

> **NOTE** *Please select the videos for Lesson 13 online at* www.wrox.com/go/ csharp24hourtrainer2evideos.

Working with Strings

Previous lessons provided a sneak peek at some of the things that a C# program can do with strings. Lesson 11 explained how you can use a data type's `Parse` method to convert a string into a number and how to use the + operator to concatenate two strings. Several lessons show how to use the `ToString` method to convert numeric values into strings that you can then display to the user.

In this lesson, you learn a lot more about strings. You learn about `string` class methods that let you search strings, replace parts of strings, and extract pieces of strings. You also learn new ways to format numeric and other kinds of data to produce strings.

STRING METHODS

The `string` class provides a lot of useful methods for manipulating strings. For example, the `EndsWith` method returns `true` if a string ends with a particular substring. The following code determines whether a string ends with the substring `dog`:

```
string str = "The quick brown fox jumps over the lazy dog";
MessageBox.Show("Ends with \"dog.\": " + str.EndsWith("dog"));
```

Table 14-1 summarizes the `string` class's most useful methods.

TABLE 14-1

METHOD	PURPOSE
Contains	Returns true if the string contains a target string.
EndsWith	Returns true if the string ends with a target string.
IndexOf	Returns the index of a target character or string within the string.
IndexOfAny	Returns the index of the first occurrence of any of a set of characters in the string.
Insert	Inserts text in the middle of the string.
LastIndexOf	Returns the index of the last occurrence of a target character or string within the string.
LastIndexOfAny	Returns the index of the last occurrence of any of a set of characters in the string.
PadLeft	Pads the string to a given length by adding characters on the left if necessary.
PadRight	Pads the string to a given length by adding characters on the right if necessary.
Remove	Removes a piece of the string.
Replace	Replaces occurrences of a string or character with new values within the string.
Split	Splits the string apart at a delimiter (for example, commas) and returns an array containing the pieces.
StartsWith	Returns true if the string starts with a target string.
Substring	Returns a substring.
ToLower	Returns the string converted to lowercase.
ToUpper	Returns the string converted to uppercase.
Trim	Removes leading and trailing characters from the string. The version that takes no parameters removes whitespace characters (space, tab, newline, and so on).
TrimEnd	Removes trailing characters from the string.
TrimStart	Removes leading characters from the string.

> **NOTE** *Remember that string indexing starts with 0 so the first letter has index 0, the second has index 1, and so forth.*

In addition to all of these methods, the string class provides a very useful Length property. As you can probably guess, Length returns the number of characters in the string. (Previous lessons have used Length to determine whether a string is empty.)

The string class also provides the useful static (shared) methods Format and Join. A *static method* is one that is provided by the class itself rather than by an instance of the class. You invoke a static method using the class's name instead of a variable's name.

The Format method formats a series of parameters according to a format string and returns a new string. For example, the following code uses the string class's Format method to display the values in the variables x and y surrounded by parentheses and separated by a comma:

```
int x = 10, y = 20;
string txt = string.Format("({0}, {1})", x, y);
```

The following text shows the result:

```
(10, 20)
```

The next section says more about the Format method.

The Join method does the opposite of the Split method: it joins a series of strings, separating them with a delimiter. Lesson 16 says more about arrays and provides some examples that use Split and Join.

FORMAT AND TOSTRING

The string class's Format method builds a formatted string. Its first parameter is a format string that tells how the method should display its other parameters. The format string can contain literal characters that are displayed as they appear. It can also contain formatting fields.

Each formatting field has the following syntax:

```
{index[,alignment][:formatString]}
```

The curly braces are required. The square brackets indicate optional pieces.

The key pieces of the field are:

➤   index—The zero-based index of the Format method's parameters that should be displayed by this field.

➤   alignment—The minimum number of characters that the field should use. If this is negative, the field is left-justified.

➤   formatString—The format string that indicates how the field's value should be formatted. The following format sections describe some of the many values that you can use here in addition to literal characters.

For example, the following code defines a string and two decimal values. It then uses Console .WriteLine to display a string built by string.Format in the Output window:

```
string itemName = "Fiendishly Difficult Puzzles";
decimal quantity = 2M;
```

```
decimal price_each = 9.99M;

Console.WriteLine(
    string.Format("You just bought {1} {0} at {2:C} each.",
    itemName, quantity, price_each));
```

The format string is `"You just bought {1} {0} at {2:C} each."`

The first field is `{1}`. This displays parameter number 1 (the second parameter—remember they're zero-based).

The second field is `{0}`. This displays the first parameter.

The third field is `{2:C}`. This displays the third parameter with the format string `C`, which formats the value as currency.

The result is:

```
You just bought 2 Fiendishly Difficult Puzzles at $9.99 each.
```

The following code shows an example that uses field widths to make values line up in columns. Before the code executes, assume that `itemName1`, `quantity1`, and the other variables have already been initialized:

```
Console.WriteLine(
    string.Format("{0,-20}{1,5}{2,10}{3,10}",
    "Item", "Qty", "Each", "Total")
);
Console.WriteLine(
    string.Format("{0,-20}{1,5}{2,10:C}{3,10:C}",
    itemName1, quantity1, priceEach1, quantity1 * priceEach1)
);
Console.WriteLine(
    string.Format("{0,-20}{1,5}{2,10:C}{3,10:C}",
    itemName2, quantity2, priceEach2, quantity2 * priceEach2)
);
Console.WriteLine(
    string.Format("{0,-20}{1,5}{2,10:C}{3,10:C}",
    itemName3, quantity3, priceEach3, quantity3 * priceEach3)
);
```

Notice that the code begins with a line that defines the column headers. Its formatting string uses the same indexes and alignment values as the other formatting strings so the headers line up with the values below.

The following text shows the result:

```
Item                  Qty     Each     Total
Pretzels (dozen)        4    $5.95    $23.80
Blue laser pointer      1  $149.99   $149.99
Titanium spork          2    $8.99    $17.98
```

> **NOTE** *Because the format string is just a string, you could define it in a constant or variable and then use that variable as the first argument to the* Format *method. That way you are certain that all of the* Format *statements use the same string. This also makes it easier to change the format later if necessary.*

Every object provides a `ToString` method that converts the object into a string. For simple data types such as numbers and dates, the result is the value in an easy-to-read string.

The `ToString` method for some objects can take a format parameter that tells how you want the item formatted. For example, the following statement displays the variable `cost` formatted as a currency value in the Output window:

```
Console.WriteLine(cost.ToString("C"));
```

The following sections describe standard and custom format strings for numbers, dates, and times. You can use these as arguments to the `ToString` method or as the `formatString` part of the `string.Format` method's format strings.

Standard Numeric Formats

Formatting characters tell `string.Format` and `ToString` how to format a value. For the characters discussed in this section, you can use either an uppercase or a lowercase letter. For example, you can use `C` or `c` for the currency format.

Table 14-2 summarizes the standard numeric formatting characters.

TABLE 14-2

CHARACTER	MEANING	EXAMPLE
C	Currency with a currency symbol, thousands separators, and a decimal point.	$12,345.67
D	Decimal. Integer types only.	12345
E	Scientific notation.	1.234567E+004
F	Fixed-point.	12345.670
G	General. Either fixed-point or scientific notation, whichever is shorter.	12345.67
N	Similar to currency except without the currency symbol.	12,345.67
P	Percent. The number is multiplied by 100 and a percent sign is added appropriately for the computer's locale. Includes thousands separators and a decimal point.	123.45 %
R	Round trip. The number (double or float only) is formatted in a way that guarantees it can be parsed back into its original value.	1234.567
X	Hexadecimal.	3A7

> **NOTE** *In programming, a computer's locale defines the computer's country, language, and formats such as how numbers and currency values should be formatted. For example, the value $1,234.56 in the United States would be written as*
> *1 234,56 € in France and as 1.234,56 € in Germany.*
>
> *Locale codes consist of a language code with an optional country code. For example, en represents English and en-GB represents English as spoken in Great Britain. The capitalization doesn't matter but people often write the country code in all caps. For a list of locale codes, see* `msdn.microsoft.com/library/ ee825488(v=cs.20).aspx`.

You can follow several of these characters with a *precision specifier* that affects how the value is formatted. How this value works depends on the format character that it follows.

For the D and X formats, the result is padded on the left with zeros to have the length given by the precision specifier. For example, the statement `123.ToString("D10")` produces the result `0000000123`. (Yes, C# is smart enough to let you call the `ToString` method for the integer `123`.)

For the C, E, F, N, and P formats, the precision specifier indicates the number of digits after the decimal point. For example, the statement `1.23.ToString("N5")` produces the result `1.23000`. (Yes, C# can handle this one, too.)

> **NOTE** *In general, you should use the standard format specifiers whenever possible so the result makes sense for the computer's locale. For example, suppose you use the following code to display a monetary amount:*
>
> ```
> decimal garageSaleProceeds = 1234.56m;
> MessageBox.Show(string.Format("${0:N}", garageSaleProceeds));
> ```
>
> *If the user's computer is localized for the United States, then the program displays $1,234.56, which is correct. Unfortunately if the user's computer is German, the program displays $1.234,56, which isn't right in either the United States or Germany.*
>
> *The following statement uses the standard currency formatting specifier:*
>
> ```
> MessageBox.Show(string.Format("{0:C}", garageSaleProceeds));
> ```
>
> *In the United States, the computer produces $1,234.56 as before. In Germany, it produces 1.234,56 €, which is what the user expects.*
>
> *If you use standard format specifiers as much as possible, the computer will use its localization settings to display numbers, dates, and times in the appropriate formats.*

Custom Numeric Formats

If the standard numeric formatting characters don't do what you want, you can use a custom numeric format. Table 14-3 summarizes the custom numeric formatting characters.

TABLE 14-3

CHARACTER	MEANING
0	Digit or zero. A digit is displayed here or a zero if there is no corresponding digit in the value being formatted.
#	Digit or nothing. A digit is displayed here or nothing if there is no corresponding digit in the value being formatted.
.	Decimal separator. The decimal separator goes here. Note that the actual separator character may not be a period depending on the computer's locale, although you still use the period in the format string.
,	Thousands separator. The thousands separator goes here. The actual separator character may not be a comma depending on the computer's locale, although you still use the comma in the format string.
%	Percent. The number is multiplied by 100 and the percent sign is added at this point. For example, %0 puts the percent sign before the number and 0% puts it after.
E+0	Scientific notation. The number of 0s indicates the number of digits in the exponent. If + is included, the exponent always includes a + or – sign. If + is omitted, the exponent only includes a sign if the exponent is negative. For example, the statement `1234.56.ToString("#.##E+000")` produces the result `1.23E+003`.
\	Escape character. Whatever follows the \ is displayed without any conversion. For example, the format `0.00\%` would add a percent sign to a number without scaling it by 100 as the format `0.00%` does. Note that you must escape the escape character itself in a normal (non-verbatim) string. For example, a format string might look like `{0:0.00\\%}` in the code.
'ABC'	Literal string. Characters enclosed in single or double quotes are displayed without any conversion.
;	Section separator. See the following text.

You can use a section separator to divide a formatting string into two or three sections. If you use two sections, the first applies to values greater than or equal to zero, and the second section applies to values less than zero. If you use three sections, they apply to values that are greater than, less than, and equal to zero.

For example, Table 14-4 shows the result produced by the three-section custom formatting string
`"{0:$#,##0.00;($#,##0.00);— zero —}"` for different values.

TABLE 14-4

VALUE	FORMATTED RESULT
12345.678	$12,345.68
-12345.678	($12,345.68)
0.000	— zero —

Standard Date and Time Formats

Just as numeric values have standard and custom formatting strings, so too do dates and times.

Table 14-5 summarizes the standard date and time formatting patterns. The examples are those
produced for 1:23:45.678 PM April 5, 2063 on my computer set up for US English. Your results will
depend on your computer's locale. Note that for many of the characters in this table, the uppercase
and lowercase versions have different meanings.

TABLE 14-5

CHARACTER	MEANING	EXAMPLE
d	Short date	4/5/2063
D	Long date	Thursday, April 5, 2063
f	Full date, short time	Thursday, April 5, 2063 1:23 PM
F	Full date, long time	Thursday, April 5, 2063 1:23:45 PM
g	General date/time, short time	4/5/2063 1:23 PM
G	General date/time, long time	4/5/2063 1:23:45 PM
M or m	Month day	April 5
O	Round trip	2063-04-05T13:23:45.6780000
R or r	RFC1123	Thu, 05 Apr 2063 13:23:45 GMT
s	Sortable date/time	2063-04-05T13:23:45
t	Short time	1:23 PM
T	Long time	1:23:45 PM
u	Universal sortable short date/time	2063-04-05 13:23:45Z

CHARACTER	MEANING	EXAMPLE
U	Universal sortable full date/time	Thursday, April 5, 2063 7:23:45 PM
Y or y	Year month	April, 2063

> **NOTE** *The result given by the U format may seem a bit surprising because it gives the time as 7:23:45 PM instead of 1:23:45 PM. The reason is the U specifier automatically converts a local time into Coordinated Universal Time (UTC) before formatting. (UTC is the time at 0° longitude. It's basically the same as Greenwich Mean Time or GMT.) On April 5, 2063, the time 1:23 PM in my time zone will be 7:23 PM in Greenwich.*

The DateTime class also provides several methods that return the date's value as a string formatted in the most common date and time formats. Table 14-6 summarizes the most useful of these methods and shows the results on my computer set up for US English. Your results will depend on how your computer is configured.

TABLE 14-6

METHOD	FORMAT	EXAMPLE
ToLongDateString	Long date (D)	Thursday, April 5, 2063
ToLongTimeString	Long time (T)	1:23:45 PM
ToShortDateString	Short date (d)	4/5/2063
ToShortTimeString	Short time (t)	1:23 PM
ToString	General date and time (G)	4/5/2063 1:23:45 PM

> **NOTE** *As is the case with number formats, you should use the standard specifiers or the standard methods (such as ToLongDateString)whenever possible so your computer can display dates and times in the formats used by the computer's locale.*

Custom Date and Time Formats

If the standard date and time formatting characters don't do the trick, you can use a custom format. Table 14-7 summarizes the custom date and time formatting strings. Note that for many of the characters in this table, the uppercase and lowercase versions have different meanings.

TABLE 14-7

CHARACTER	MEANING
d	Day of month between 1 and 31.
dd	Day of month between 01 and 31.
ddd	Abbreviated day of week (Mon, Tue, and so on).
dddd	Full day of week (Monday, Tuesday, and so on).
f	Digits after the decimal for seconds. For example, ffff means use four digits.
F	Similar to f but trailing zeros are not displayed.
g	Era specifier. For example, A.D.
h	Hours between 1 and 12.
hh	Hours between 01 and 12.
H	Hours between 0 and 23.
HH	Hours between 00 and 23.
m	Minutes between 1 and 59.
mm	Minutes between 01 and 59.
M	Month between 1 and 12.
MM	Month between 01 and 12.
MMM	Month abbreviation (Jan, Feb, and so on).
MMMM	Month name (January, February, and so on).
s	Seconds between 1 and 59.
ss	Seconds between 01 and 59.
t	First character of AM/PM designator.
tt	AM/PM designator.
y	One- or two-digit year. If the year has fewer than two digits, is it not zero padded.
yy	Two-digit year, zero padded if necessary.
yyy	Three-digit year, zero padded if necessary.
yyyy	Four-digit year, zero padded if necessary.
yyyyy	Five-digit year, zero padded if necessary.

CHARACTER	MEANING
z	Signed time zone offset from UTC.
zz	Signed time zone offset from UTC in two digits.
zzz	Signed time zone offset from UTC in hours and minutes.
:	Hours, minutes, and seconds separator.
/	Date separator.
'ABC'	Literal string. Characters enclosed in single or double quotes are displayed without any conversion.

> **NOTE** *The time zone offset values depend on whether daylight savings is in effect. For example, for Pacific Standard Time the* zzz *specifier returns either –08:00 or –07:00 depending on whether daylight savings is in effect on that date.*

> **NOTE** *The date and time formatting methods assume that a single character is a standard format. For example, the* date.ToString("d") *would give you a short date format, not the day of the month.*
>
> *When a single character specifier is inside a longer string, the formatting methods treat it like a custom specifier. For example,* date.ToString("M/d") *gets you the month and day numbers.*
>
> *If you need to use a customer specifier alone, place a* % *symbol in front of it. For example,* date.ToString("%d") *returns the day number by itself.*

Table 14-8 shows some example formats and their results. The date used was 1:23:45.678 PM April 5, 2063 on my computer set up for US English. Your results will depend on how your computer is configured.

TABLE 14-8

FORMAT	RESULT
M/d/yy	4/5/63
d MMM yy	5 Apr 63
HH:mm 'hours'	13:23 hours

continues

TABLE 14-8 *(continued)*

FORMAT	RESULT
h:mm:ss.ff, M/d/y	1:23:45.67, 4/5/63
dddd 'at' h:mmt	Thursday at 1:23P
ddd 'at' h:mmtt	Thu at 1:23PM

TRY IT

In this Try It, you build a program that displays the current date and time in a Label when it starts as shown in Figure 14-1.

FIGURE 14-1

Lesson Requirements

In this lesson, you:

➤ Start a new project and add a Label to its form.

➤ Give the form a Load event handler that sets the Label's text as shown in Figure 14-1.

> **NOTE** *You can download the code and resources for this lesson from the website at* www.wrox.com/go/csharp24hourtrainer2e.

Hints

➤ The DateTime.Now property returns the current date and time.

➤ Either use string.Format or the value's ToString method to format the result.

Step-by-Step

➤ Start a new project and add a Label to its form.

1. Create the new project and its Label.

2. Set the Label's AutoSize property to False and set its font size to 12. Then position and anchor or dock it on the form.

3. Set the Label's TextAlign property to MiddleCenter.

➤ Give the form a Load event handler that sets the Label's text as shown in Figure 14-1.

1. Use code similar to the following:

```
// Display the current date and time.
private void Form1_Load(object sender, EventArgs e)
{
```

```
greetingLabel.Text = DateTime.Now.ToString(
    "'It is' h:mmtt 'on' ddd, MMM dd yyyy");
}
```

EXERCISES

1. Exercise 13-3 reads and displays currency values, but it displays quantities without thousands separators. If you ordered 1,200 pencils, the program would display 1200.

    Copy the corrected version of that program (or download it from the book's website) and modify it so quantities are displayed with thousands separators.

2. Make a program that displays the time every second. Hint: Use a `Timer` control with `Enabled` set to `True`, and `Interval` set to `1000`. Update a `Label`'s `Text` property in the `Timer`'s `Tick` event.

3. Write a program that lets the user enter an integer value. When the user clicks the Format button, parse the value and use a standard format specifier to redisplay it with thousands separators but no digits after the decimal point.

4. Write a program that lets the user enter text in the following format:

    ```
    1200/Gummy slugs/.02/24
    ```

    Use `string` methods to split the string apart, parse the numeric values, and then display a result similar to the following:

    ```
    1,200 Gummy slugs @ $0.02 each = $24.00
    ```

    Remember to allow the input to contain formatted values such as $24.00. Hint: Use `string.Split`, which returns an array of values. We'll talk more about arrays in Lesson 16. For now, just use brackets and an index to get one of the values. For example, the following statement saves the first field in a string:

    ```
    string quantityString = text.Split('/')[0];
    ```

5. [Hard] Write a program that lets the user enter text in the following format:

    ```
    1,200 Gummy slugs @ $0.02 each = $24.00
    ```

    Use the `string` methods `IndexOf`, `LastIndexOf`, `Substring`, and `Trim` to parse the string into item name, quantity, price each, and total price pieces. Convert the numbers into numeric data types and display the results in `TextBoxes`. Hints:

    ➤ Use `IndexOf` to find the position of the first space (which comes after the quantity).

    ➤ Use `LastIndexOf` to find the delimiters "@," "each," and "=" in case the item's name contains those strings.

    ➤ Calculate the length of the pieces of text between the delimiters. For example, the length of the name is [@ location] – [first space location] – 1.

    ➤ Use `Substring` to get the pieces. Trim the name and parse the numeric values.

6. [Hard] Copy the program that you built for Exercise 1 and modify it so the main form displays items in a `ListBox` instead of a `ListView`. Make the program use `string.Format` to add items to the `ListBox` in a format similar to the following:

    ```
    1,200 Gummy slugs at $0.02 each = $24.00
    ```

    Hint: When you remove an item from the list, you need to subtract its total cost from the grand total. Use the item's `ToString` method to convert it into a string. Then use the methods you used for Exercise 5 to parse the string and find the item's total cost.

7. Make a program that replaces all occurrences of the letter E (uppercase and lowercase) in a string entered by the user with the character -.

8. Make a program that lets the user enter an input string, a string to replace, and a replacement string. When the user clicks the Replace button, make the replacement and display the result in the same `TextBox` as the original string so the user can make several replacements easily. To make using the program even easier, also make the button clear the string to replace and the replacement string and set focus to the string to replace.

9. Write a program that lets the user enter a string such as, "The 6th sheik's 6th sheep's sick." When the user clicks the Replace button, replace numerals with their spelled out equivalents as in, "The sixth sheik's sixth sheep's sick." Don't worry about punctuation (like capitalizing if the sentence begins with a numeral), numbers bigger than 9 (so "10" will become "onezero"), or special cases (like converting 3rd into third). (Then try to say "The sixth sheik's sixth sheep's sick" as quickly as you can.)

10. Write a program that lets the user enter a number. When the user clicks the Format button, use a customer format specifier with three sections to format the number. If the number is positive, display it as in +1,234.56 (two digits after the decimal point). If the number is negative, display it as in –1,234.56 (again two digits after the decimal point). If the number is zero, display ZERO.

> **NOTE** *Please select the videos for Lesson 14 online at* www.wrox.com/go/ csharp24hourtrainer2evideos.

15

Working with Dates and Times

One of C#'s more confusing data types is DateTime. A DateTime represents a date, a time, or both. For example, a DateTime variable might represent Thursday April 1, 2020 at 9:15 AM.

In this lesson, you learn how to work with dates and times. You learn how to create DateTime variables, find the current date and time, and calculate elapsed time.

CREATING DATETIME VARIABLES

C# doesn't have DateTime literal values so you can't simply set a DateTime variable equal to a value as you can with some other data types. Instead you can use the new keyword to initialize a new DateTime variable, supplying arguments to define the date and time.

For example, the following code creates a DateTime variable named aprilFools and initializes it to the date April 1, 2020. It then displays the date using the short date format described in Lesson 14 and by calling the variable's ToShortDateString method:

```
DateTime aprilFools = new DateTime(2020, 4, 1);
MessageBox.Show(aprilFools.ToString("d"));
MessageBox.Show(aprilFools.ToShortDateString());
```

The preceding code uses a year, month, and day to initialize its DateTime variable, but the DateTime type lets you use many different kinds of values. The three most useful combinations of arguments specify (all as integers):

➤ Year, month, day

➤ Year, month, day, hour, minute, second

➤ Year, month, day, hour, minute, second, milliseconds

You can also add a `kind` parameter to the end of the second and third of these combinations to indicate whether the value represents local time or UTC time. (Local and UTC times are explained in the next section.) For example, the following code creates a `DateTime` representing 12 noon on March 15, 2020 in the local time zone:

```
DateTime idesOfMarch =
    new DateTime(2020, 3, 15, 12, 0, 0, DateTimeKind.Local);
```

LOCAL AND UTC TIME

Windows has several different notions of dates and times. Two of the most important of these are local time and Coordinated Universal Time (UTC).

Local time is the time on your computer as it is configured for a particular locale. It's what you and a program's user typically think of as time.

UTC time is basically the same as Greenwich Mean Time (GMT), the time at the Royal Academy in Greenwich, London.

For most everyday tasks, local time is fine. If you need to compare data on computers running in different time zones, however, UTC time can make coordination easier. For example, if you want to know whether a customer in New York created an order before another customer created an order in San Salvador, UTC lets you compare the times without worrying about the customers' time zones.

A `DateTime` object has a `Kind` property that indicates whether the object represents local time, UTC time, or an unspecified time. When you create a `DateTime`, you can indicate whether you are creating a local or UTC time. If you do not specify the kind of time, C# assumes you are making an unspecified time.

After you create a `DateTime`, its `ToLocalTime` and `ToUniversalTime` methods convert between local and UTC times.

> **NOTE** *The* `ToLocalTime` *and* `ToUniversalTime` *methods don't affect a* `DateTime` *if it is already in the desired format. For example, if you call* `ToLocalTime` *on a variable that already uses local time, the result is the same as the original variable.*

DATETIME PROPERTIES AND METHODS

The `DateTime` type provides many useful properties and methods for manipulating dates and times. Table 15-1 summarizes some of `DateTime`'s most useful methods. Static methods are indicated with an asterisk. You invoke static methods by using the type name rather than a variable name, as in `DateTime.IsLeapYear(2020)`.

TABLE 15-1

METHOD	PURPOSE
Add	Adds a `TimeSpan` to the `DateTime`. The following section describes `TimeSpan`.
AddDays	Adds a specified number of days to the `DateTime`.
AddHours	Adds a specified number of hours to the `DateTime`.
AddMinutes	Adds a specified number of minutes to the `DateTime`.
AddMonths	Adds a specified number of months to the `DateTime`.
AddSeconds	Adds a specified number of seconds to the `DateTime`.
AddYears	Adds a specified number of years to the `DateTime`.
IsDaylightSavingsTime	Returns `true` if the date and time is within the Daylight Savings Time period for the local time zone.
IsLeapYear*	Returns `true` if the indicated year is a leap year.
Parse*	Parses a string and returns the corresponding `DateTime`.
Subtract	Subtracts another `DateTime` from this one and returns a `TimeSpan`. The following section says more about `TimeSpan`.
ToLocalTime	Converts the `DateTime` to a local value.
ToLongDateString	Returns the `DateTime` in long date format.
ToLongTimeString	Returns the `DateTime` in long time format.
ToShortDateString	Returns the `DateTime` in short date format.
ToShortTimeString	Returns the `DateTime` in short time format.
ToString	Returns the `DateTime` in general format.
ToUniversalTime	Converts the `DateTime` to a UTC value.

Table 15-2 summarizes the `DateTime`'s most useful properties.

TABLE 15-2

PROPERTY	PURPOSE
Date	Gets the `DateTime`'s date without the time.
Day	Gets the `DateTime`'s day of the month between 1 and 31.
DayOfWeek	Gets the `DateTime`'s day of the week, as in Monday.

continues

TABLE 15-2 *(continued)*

PROPERTY	PURPOSE
DayOfYear	Gets the DateTime's day of the year between 1 and 366. (Leap years have 366 days.)
Hour	Gets the DateTime's hour between 0 and 23.
Kind	Returns the DateTime's kind: Local, Utc, or Unspecified.
Millisecond	Gets the DateTime's time's millisecond.
Minute	Gets the DateTime's minute between 0 and 59.
Month	Gets the DateTime's month between 1 and 12.
Now*	Gets the current date and time.
Second	Gets the DateTime's second between 0 and 59.
TimeOfDay	Gets the DateTime's time without the date.
Today*	Gets the current date without a time.
UtcNow*	Gets the current UTC date and time.
Year	Gets the DateTime's year.

TIMESPANS

A DateTime represents a point in time (July 20, 1969 at 20:17:40). A TimeSpan represents an elapsed period of time (1 day, 17 hours, 27 minutes, and 12 seconds).

One of the more useful ways to make a TimeSpan is to subtract one DateTime from another to find the amount of time between them. For example, the following code calculates the time that elapsed between the first and last manned moon landings:

```
DateTime firstLanding = new DateTime(1969, 7, 20, 20, 17, 40);
DateTime lastLanding = new DateTime(1972, 12, 11, 19, 54, 57);
TimeSpan elapsed = lastLanding - firstLanding;
Console.WriteLine(elapsed.ToString());
```

The code creates DateTime values to represent the times of the two landings. It then subtracts the last date from the first to get the elapsed time and uses the resulting TimeSpan's ToString method to display the duration. The following text shows the result in the format days .hours:minutes:seconds:

```
1239.23:37:17
```

Table 15-3 summarizes the TimeSpan's most useful properties and methods.

TABLE 15-3

PROPERTY	MEANING
Days	The number of days.
Hours	The number of hours.
Milliseconds	The number of milliseconds.
Minutes	The number of minutes.
Seconds	The number of seconds.
ToString	Converts the TimeSpan into a string in the format days.hours:minutes:seconds.fractionalSeconds.
TotalDays	The entire TimeSpan represented as days. For a 36-hour duration, this would be 1.5.
TotalHours	The entire TimeSpan represented as hours. For a 45-minute duration, this would be 0.75.
TotalMilliseconds	The entire TimeSpan represented as milliseconds. For a 1-second duration, this would be 1,000.
TotalMinutes	The entire TimeSpan represented as minutes. For a 1-hour duration, this would be 60.
TotalSeconds	The entire TimeSpan represented as seconds. For a 1-minute TimeSpan, this would be 60.

Note that you can use the + and − operators to add and subtract TimeSpans, getting a new TimeSpan as a result. This works in a fairly obvious way. For example, a 90-minute TimeSpan minus a 30-minute TimeSpan gives a 60-minute TimeSpan.

TRY IT

In this Try It, you use DateTime and TimeSpan variables to build the stopwatch application shown in Figure 15-1. When the user clicks the Start Button, the program starts its counter. When the user clicks the Stop Button, the program stops the counter.

FIGURE 15-1

Normally the `TimeSpan`'s `ToString` method displays a value in the format `d.hh:mm:ss.fffffff`. In this example, you use `string.Format` to display the elapsed time in the format `hh:mm:ss.ff`.

Lesson Requirements

In this lesson, you:

➤ Create the form shown in Figure 15-1. In addition to the controls that are visible, give the form a Timer with `Interval` = 10. Initially disable the Stop button.

➤ When the user clicks the Start button, start the `Timer`, disable the Start button, and enable the Stop button.

➤ When the user clicks the Stop button, stop the `Timer`, enable the Start button, and disable the Stop button.

➤ When the `Timer`'s `Tick` event fires, display the elapsed time in the format `hh:mm:ss.ff`.

> **NOTE** *You can download the code and resources for this lesson from the website at* www.wrox.com/go/csharp24hourtrainer2e.

Hints

➤ `TimeSpan` doesn't use the same formatting characters as a `DateTime`, so, for example, you can't simply use a format string such as `hh:mm:ss.ff`. Instead use the `TimeSpan` properties to get the elapsed hours, minutes, seconds, and milliseconds and then format those values.

Step-by-Step

➤ Create the form shown in Figure 15-1. In addition to the controls that are visible, give the form a Timer with `Interval` = 10. Initially disable the Stop button.

   1. Add the Start and Stop buttons and a `Label` to the form as shown in Figure 15-1. Set the Stop button's `Enabled` property to `False`.

   2. Add a `Timer` and set its `Interval` property to 10 milliseconds.

➤ When the user clicks the Start button, start the `Timer`, disable the Start button, and enable the Stop button.

   1. To remember the time when the user clicked the Start button, create a `DateTime` field named `StartTime`:

      ```
      // The time when the user clicked Start.
      private DateTime StartTime;
      ```

   2. Add the following code to the Start button's `Click` event handler:

      ```
      // Start the Timer.
      private void startButton_Click(object sender, EventArgs e)
      {
          StartTime = DateTime.Now;
      ```

```
        startButton.Enabled = false;
        stopButton.Enabled = true;
        updateLabelTimer.Enabled = true;
    }
```

➤ When the user clicks the Stop button, stop the Timer, enable the Start button, and disable the Stop button.

    1. Add the following code to the Stop button's Click event handler:

```
// Stop the Timer.
private void stopButton_Click(object sender, EventArgs e)
{
    startButton.Enabled = true;
    stopButton.Enabled = false;
    updateLabelTimer.Enabled = false;
}
```

➤ When the Timer's Tick event fires, display the elapsed time in the format hh:mm:ss.ff.

    1. Use code similar to the following. Notice that the code divides the number of milliseconds by 10 to convert it into hundredths of seconds:

```
// Display the elapsed time.
private void updateLabelTimer_Tick(object sender, EventArgs e)
{
    // Subtract the start time from the current time
    // to get elapsed time.
    TimeSpan elapsed = DateTime.Now - StartTime;

    // Display the result.
    elapsedTimeLabel.Text = string.Format(
        "{0:00}:{1:00}:{2:00}.{3:00}",
        elapsed.Hours,
        elapsed.Minutes,
        elapsed.Seconds,
        elapsed.Milliseconds / 10);
}
```

EXERCISES

1. The System.Diagnostics.Stopwatch class acts like a stopwatch. It provides methods to start, reset, and stop timing. Copy the program you built for the Try It and modify it so it uses the Stopwatch class instead of a DateTime. Hints:

    ➤ Use the Stopwatch's Elapsed property to see how long it's been since the watch was started.

    ➤ Make the Start button call the watch's Start method.

    ➤ Make the Stop button call the watch's Reset method to stop timing and reset the watch's elapsed time to 0.

2. [Hard] Copy the program you built for Exercise 1 and add a Reset button. The Start button should start the stopwatch, the Stop button should pause it, and the Reset button should reset the stopwatch to 0. Because the purpose of the Stop button has changed, you should change its text to Pause. Change the name of the button and its event handler to match. Only enable the Reset button when the stopwatch is stopped and has non-zero elapsed time. (There's no need to reset it if the elapsed time is already 0.)

3. Make a program with a Birth Date TextBox and a Calculate Button. When the user enters a birth date and clicks the Button, calculate the person's current age and add items to a ListBox that display the age converted into each of days, hours, minutes, and seconds. Format all of the values with thousands separators and two digits after the decimal place.

4. Copy the program you wrote for Exercise 3 and modify it to also display the user's age in years and months. Hint: The DateTime class doesn't have TotalYears or TotalMonths properties (probably because Microsoft didn't want to figure out how to handle leap years). Calculate the number of years by dividing the number of days by 365.2425. Calculate the number of months by multiplying the number of years by 12.

5. Make a program that lets the user enter a birth date, heart rate, and respiration rate. When the user clicks the Calculate button, display the number of heartbeats and breaths since birth. (Typical adult rates range from 12 to 20 breaths per minute and 60 to 100 heartbeats per minute.) Display the results in millions as in "988 million."

6. Make a program that lets you enter a birth date and then displays the date including the weekday for that date and the next nine birthdays.

7. Make a program with two TextBoxes for dates and a Button. When the user clicks the Button, the program should display the time between the dates.

8. Modify the program you built for Exercise 7 to use DateTimePicker controls instead of TextBoxes. To keep things simple, just display the total number of days between the dates using the N0 format specifier. Use the controls' Value properties to get the selected dates. (This control prevents users from entering invalid dates such as April 45.)

9. Write a program that takes the user's birth date as an input and displays the user's age in years on the different planets in our solar system. Hint: The orbital periods for the planets in Earth years are Mercury = 0.24, Venus = 0.62, Earth = 1.00, Mars = 1.88, Jupiter = 11.86, Saturn = 29.46, Uranus = 84.01, Neptune = 164.8, and (if you want to consider Pluto a planet) Pluto = 247.7.

10. Make a countdown timer. When the program starts, it should display a custom dialog where the user can enter a date and time. Then the main program should display the number of days, hours, minutes, and seconds until that time, updated every second.

> **NOTE** *Please select the videos for Lesson 15 online at* www.wrox.com/go/ csharp24hourtrainer2evideos.

16

Using Arrays and Collections

Each of the data types described in previous lessons holds a single piece of data. A variable might hold an integer, string, or point in time.

Sometimes it's convenient to work with a group of related values all at once. For example, suppose you're the CEO of a huge company that just posted huge gains. In that case, you might want to give each hourly employee a certificate of appreciation and give each executive a 15 percent bonus.

In cases like this, it would be handy to be able to store all of the hourly employees' data in one variable so you could easily work with it. Similarly you might like to store the executives' data in a second variable so it's easy to manage.

In this lesson, you learn how to make variables that can hold more than one piece of data. You learn how to make arrays and different kinds of collections such as a `List`, `Dictionary`, `Stack`, and `Queue`.

This lesson explains how to build these objects and add and remove items from them. Lesson 19 explains how to get the full benefit of them by looping through them to perform some action on each of the items they contain.

ARRAYS

An *array* is a group of values that all have the same data type and that all share the same name. To pick a particular item in the array, the program uses an *index*, which is an integer greater than or equal to 0.

An array is similar to the mailboxes in an apartment building. The building has a single bank of mailboxes that all have the same street address (the array's name). You use the apartment numbers to pick a particular cubbyhole in the bank of mailboxes.

Figure 16-1 shows an array graphically. This array is named `values`. It contains eight entries with indexes 0 through 7.

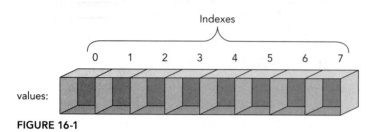

FIGURE 16-1

> **NOTE** *An array's smallest and largest indexes are called its* lower bound *and* upper bound, *respectively. In C#, the lower bound is always 0, and the upper bound is always one less than the length of the array.*

Creating Arrays

The following code shows how you can declare an array of integers. The square brackets indicate an array so the first part of the statement int [] means the variable's data type is an array of integers:

```
int[] values;
```

After you declare an array variable, you can assign it to a new uninitialized array. The following code initializes the variable values to a new integer array that can hold eight elements:

```
values = new int[8];
```

Remember that an array's lower bound is always 0 in C# so this array has indexes 0 through 7.

As is the case with other variables, you can declare and initialize an array in a single step. The following code declares and creates the values array in a single statement:

```
int[] values = new int[8];
```

After you have created an array, you can access its members by using the array's name followed by an index inside square brackets. For example, the following code initializes the values array by setting the Nth entry equal to N^2:

```
values[0] = 0 * 0;
values[1] = 1 * 1;
values[2] = 2 * 2;
values[3] = 3 * 3;
values[4] = 4 * 4;
values[5] = 5 * 5;
values[6] = 6 * 6;
values[7] = 7 * 7;
```

> **NOTE** *Most programmers pronounce* values[5] *as "values of 5," "values sub 5," or "the 5th element of values."*

After you have placed values in an array, you can read the values using the same square bracket syntax. The following code displays a message box that uses one of the array's values:

```
MessageBox.Show("7 * 7 is " + values[7].ToString());
```

To make initializing arrays easier, C# provides an abbreviated syntax that lets you declare an array and set its values all in one statement. Simply set the variable equal to the values you want separated by commas and surrounded by braces as shown in the following code:

```
int[] values = { 0, 1, 1, 2, 3, 5, 8, 13, 21, 34 };
```

When you use this syntax, C# uses the number of values you supply to define the array's size. In the preceding code, C# would give the `values` array 10 entries because that's how many values the code supplies.

A Fibonacci Example

Here's a slightly more interesting example that uses an array. The Fibonacci sequence is defined by the following three rules:

```
Fibonacci[0] = 0
Fibonacci[1] = 1
Fibonacci[n] = Fibonacci[n - 1] + Fibonacci[n - 2]
```

> **NOTE** *The Fibonacci sequence, which was described by the Italian mathematician Fibonacci, is the infinite sequence the numbers 0, 1, 1, 2, 3, 5, 8, 13, 21, ... Each value in the sequence after the first two is the sum of the two previous values. For example, 3 + 5 = 8.*
>
> *The Fibonacci sequence pops up in several strange and interesting mathematical and natural systems. For example, they appear in flower petal arrangements and the number of seeds in a sunflower. You can even use them to convert between miles and kilometers (although that's basically a coincidence). For more information, see* www.mathsisfun.com/numbers/fibonacci-sequence.html, math .stackexchange.com/questions/381/applications-of-the-fibonacci-sequence *or* mathworld.wolfram.com/FibonacciNumber.html.

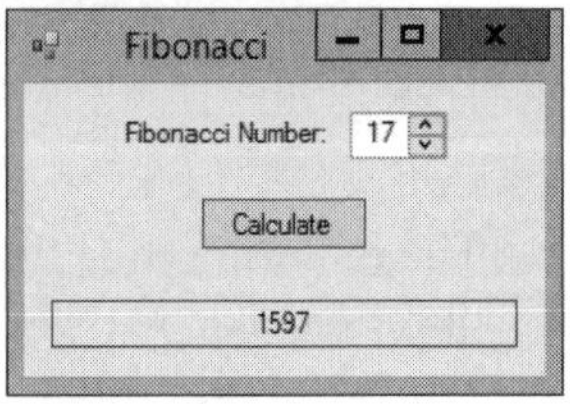

The Fibonacci program shown in Figure 16-2 (and available as part of this lesson's code download) uses an array to display Fibonacci numbers. Use the `NumericUpDown` control to select a number and click Calculate to see the corresponding Fibonacci number.

FIGURE 16-2

When the user clicks Calculate, the program executes the following code:

```
// Calculate and display the desired Fibonacci number.
private void calculateButton_Click(object sender, EventArgs e)
{
    int[] values = new int[21];
    values[0] = 0;
    values[1] = 1;
```

```
        values[2] = values[0] + values[1];
        values[3] = values[1] + values[2];
        values[4] = values[2] + values[3];
        ...
        values[20] = values[18] + values[19];

        int index = (int)numberNumericUpDown.Value;
        resultsTextBox.Text = values[index].ToString();
    }
```

The code starts by initializing the `values` array to hold the first 21 Fibonacci numbers.

After initializing the array, the program gets the value selected by the `NumericUpDown` control and converts it from a `decimal` to an `int`. It then uses that value as an index into the `values` array and displays the result in `resultTextBox`.

Multi-Dimensional Arrays

The arrays described in the previous section hold a single row of items, but C# also lets you define multi-dimensional arrays. You can think of these as higher-dimensional sequences of apartment mailboxes.

Figure 16-3 shows a graphic representation of a two-dimensional array with four rows and eight columns.

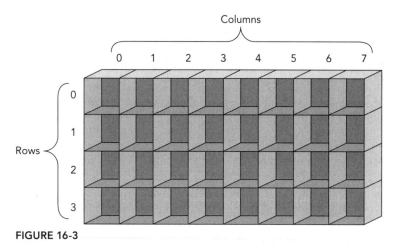

FIGURE 16-3

The following code shows how you could declare, allocate, and initialize this array to hold a multi-plication table with values up to 4 times 7:

```
int[,] values = new int[5, 7];
values[0, 0] = 0 * 0;
values[0, 1] = 0 * 1;
```

```
values[0, 2] = 0 * 2;
...
values[1, 1] = 1 * 1;
values[1, 2] = 1 * 2;
...
values[4, 7] = 4 * 7;
```

The following code shows the C# syntax for quickly defining and initializing a two-dimensional array:

```
int[,] cell =
{
    {0, 1, 2},
    {3, 4, 5},
    {6, 7, 8},
};
```

This syntax basically assigns the array variable equal to an array containing one-dimensional arrays of values.

> **NOTE** *Notice that the definition of the array's final row of data ends with a comma. You don't need this comma because nothing follows this last row, but C# allows you to include it to give the rows a more uniform format. The commas after the other rows are required because more rows follow them.*

You can use similar syntax to make and initialize higher-dimensional arrays, although they're harder to visualize graphically. For example, the following code makes a four-dimensional array of strings:

```
string[, , ,] employeeData = new string[10, 20, 30, 40];
```

Array Properties and Methods

All arrays have a `Length` property that your code can use to determine the number of items in the array. Arrays all have lower bound 0, so for one-dimensional arrays, `Length – 1` gives an array's upper bound.

Arrays also have `GetLowerBound` and `GetUpperBound` methods that return the lower and upper bounds for a particular dimension in an array.

For example, the following code creates a 5-by-10 two-dimensional array. It then displays the lower and upper bounds for the first dimension. (Like an array's indexes, the dimension numbers start at 0.)

```
int[,] x = new int[5, 10];
MessageBox.Show("The first dimension runs from " +
    x.GetLowerBound(0) + " to " + x.GetUpperBound(0));
```

The `Array` class also provides several useful static methods that you can use to manipulate arrays. For example, the following code sorts the array named `salaries`:

```
Array.Sort(salaries);
```

> **NOTE** *To sort an array, the array must contain things that can be compared in a meaningful way. For example,* int *and* string *data have a natural order, so it's easy to say that the string "Jackson" should come before the string "Utah."*
>
> *If an array holds* Employee *objects, however, it's unclear how you would want to compare two items. In fact, it's likely that you couldn't define an order that would always work because sometimes you might want to sort employees by name and other times you might want to sort them by employee ID or salary.*
>
> *You can solve this problem in a couple of ways including the* IComparer *interface (mentioned briefly in Lesson 27's Exercise 2) and making the* Employee *class implement* IComparable *(mentioned in Lesson 28). These are slightly more advanced topics, so they aren't covered in great depth here.*

The Sort method has many overloaded versions that perform different kinds of sorting. For example, instead of passing it a single array you can pass it an array of keys and an array of items. In that case the method sorts the keys, moving the items so they remain matched up with their corresponding keys.

The Table 16-1 summarizes the most useful methods provided by the Array class.

TABLE 16-1

METHOD	PURPOSE
BinarySearch	Uses binary search to find an item in a sorted array.
Clear	Resets a range of items in the array to the default value for the array's data type (0, false, or null).
Copy	Copies a range of items from one array to another.
IndexOf	Returns the index of the first occurrence of a particular item in the array.
LastIndexOf	Returns the index of the last occurrence of a particular item in the array.
Resize	Resizes the array, preserving any items that fit in the new size.
Reverse	Reverses the order of the items in the array.
Sort	Sorts the array's items.

COLLECTION CLASSES

An array holds a group of items and lets you refer to them by index. The .NET Framework used by C# also provides an assortment of *collection classes* that you can use to store and manipulate items in other ways. For example, a Dictionary stores items with keys and lets you very quickly locate an item from its key.

For example, you could use a `Dictionary` to make an employee phone book. It could store phone numbers using names as the keys. Then given someone's name, you could use the dictionary to very quickly look up that person's phone number.

Generic Classes

The following sections describe some particular kinds of classes that come pre-built by the .NET Framework. These are generic classes, so before you learn about them you should know a little about what a generic class is.

A *generic class* is one that is not tied to a particular data type. For example, suppose you build a `StringList` class that can store a list of strings. Now suppose you decide you wanted an `IntegerList` class to store lists of integers. The two classes would be practically identical; they would just work with different data types.

I've mentioned several times that duplicated code is a bad thing. Having two nearly identical classes means debugging and maintaining two different sets of code that are practically the same.

One solution to this situation is to make a more general `AnythingList` class that uses the general `object` data type to store items. An `object` can hold any kind of data, so this class could hold lists of integers, strings, or `Customer` objects. Unfortunately that has two big problems.

First, you would need to do a lot of work converting the items with the general `object` data type stored in the list into the `int`, `string`, or `Customer` type of the items that you put in there. This is annoying because it gives you more work to do and makes your code more complicated and harder to read.

A bigger problem is that a list that can hold anything can hold *anything*. If you make a list to hold customer data, it could still hold `ints`, `strings`, and `PurchaseOrder` objects. Your code would need to do a lot of work to prevent you from accidentally adding the wrong kind of item to the list.

A much better approach is to use generic classes. These classes take data type parameters in their declarations so they know what kind of data they will manipulate. That lets them automatically store and retrieve items using the correct data type. It also lets them perform type checking so you can't accidentally add a `Bicycle` object to a list of `Employees`.

Using this kind of class, you can build a list of integers, strings, or what have you.

`List` is one of the generic collection classes defined by the .NET Framework. The following code declares and initializes a `List`:

```
List<string> names = new List<string>();
```

The `<string>` part of the declaration indicates that the class will work with strings. You can put strings into the list and take strings out of it. You cannot add an integer to the list, just as you can't set a string variable equal to an integer. Visual Studio knows that the list works with strings and won't let you use anything else.

Note that IntelliSense knows about generic classes and provides help. If you begin a declaration with `List`, IntelliSense displays `List<>` to let you know that it is a generic class.

Now if you type the opening pointy bracket, IntelliSense displays a list of the class's type parameters and even describes them as you type. (The List class has only one type parameter but some, such as Dictionary, have more.) After you finish the declaration, the class knows what data types it will manipulate, and it can behave as if it were designed with that data type in mind.

Now, with some understanding of generic classes, you're ready to look at some generic collection classes.

Lists

A List is a simple ordered list of items. You can declare and initialize a List as in the following code:

```
List<string> names = new List<string>();
```

The List class provides several methods for manipulating the items it contains. The three most important are Add, Remove, and RemoveAt:

➤ The Add method adds a new item to the end of the list, automatically resizing the List if necessary. This is easier than adding an item to an array, which requires you to resize the array first.

➤ The Remove method removes a particular item from the list. Note that you pass the target item to Remove, not the index of the item that you want to remove. If you know that the string Zaphod is in the list names, the following code removes the first instance of that name from the list:

```
names.Remove("Zaphod");
```

> **NOTE** *The Remove method removes only the first occurrence of an item from the List.*

➤ The RemoveAt method removes an item from a particular position in the list. It then compacts the list to remove the hole where the item was. This is much easier than removing an item from an array, which requires you to shuffle items from one part of the array to another and then resize the array to reduce its size.

In addition to these methods, you can use square brackets to get and set a List's entries much as you can with an array. For example, the following code sets and then displays the value of the first entry in a list:

```
names[0] = "Mickey";
MessageBox.Show("The first name is " + names[0]);
```

Note that this works only if the index you use exists in the list. If the list holds 10 names and you try to set the 14th, the program crashes.

SortedLists

A SortedList stores a list of key/value pairs, keeping the list sorted by the keys. The types of the keys and values are generic parameters, so, for example, you could make a list that uses numbers (such as employee IDs) for keys and strings (such as names) for values.

Note that the list will not allow you to add two items with the same key. Multiple items can have the same *value*, but if you try to add two with the same *key*, the program crashes.

Table 16-2 summarizes useful methods provided by the SortedList class.

TABLE 16-2

METHOD	PURPOSE
Add	Adds a key and value to the list.
Clear	Empties the list.
Contains	Returns true if the list contains a given value.
ContainsKey	Returns true if the list contains a given key.
ContainsValue	Returns true if the list contains a given value.
GetKeyList	Returns a list holding the keys.
GetValueList	Returns a list holding the values.
Remove	Removes the item with a specific key from the list.

In addition to these methods, you can use square brackets to index into the list, using the items' keys as indexes.

The following code demonstrates a SortedList:

```
SortedList<string, string> addresses =
    new SortedList<string, string>();

addresses.Add("Dan", "4 Deer Dr, Bugville VT, 01929");
addresses.Add("Bob", "8273 Birch Blvd, Bugville VT, 01928");

addresses["Cindy"] = "32878 Carpet Ct, Bugville VT, 01929";
addresses["Alice"] = "162 Ash Ave, Bugville VT, 01928";
addresses["Bob"] = "8273 Bash Blvd, Bugville VT, 01928";

MessageBox.Show("Bob's address is " + addresses["Bob"]);
```

The code starts by declaring and initializing a list to use keys and values that are both strings. It uses the Add method to add some entries and then uses square brackets to add some more.

Next the code uses the square bracket syntax to update Bob's address. Finally the code displays Bob's new address.

You can't see it from this example, but unlike the List class, SortedList actually stores its items ordered by key. For example, you could use the GetKeyList and GetValueList methods to get the list's keys and values in that order.

Dictionaries

The `Dictionary` and `SortedDictionary` classes provide features similar to the `SortedList` class, manipulating key/value pairs. The difference is in the data structures the three classes use to store their items.

Without getting into technical details, the results are that the three classes use different amounts of memory and work at different speeds. In general, `SortedList` is the slowest but takes the least memory. `Dictionary` is the fastest but takes the most memory.

For small programs, the difference is insignificant. For big programs that work with thousands of entries, you might need to be more careful about picking a class. (Personally I like `Dictionary` for most purposes because speed is nice, memory is relatively cheap, and the name is suggestive of the way you use the class: to look up something by key.)

Queues

A `Queue` is a collection that lets you add items at one end and remove them from the other. It's like the line at a bank where you stand at the back of the line and the teller helps the person at the front of the line until eventually it's your turn.

> **NOTE** *Because a queue retrieves items in first-in-first-out order, queues are sometimes called FIFO lists or FIFOs. ("FIFO" is pronounced fife-o.)*

Table 16-3 summarizes the `Queue`'s most important methods.

TABLE 16-3

METHOD	PURPOSE
Clear	Removes all items from the `Queue`.
Dequeue	Returns the item at the front of the `Queue` and removes it.
Enqueue	Adds an item to the back of the `Queue`.
Peek	Returns the item at the front of the `Queue` without removing it.

Stacks

A `Stack` is a collection that lets you add items at one end and remove them from the same end. It's like a stack of books on the floor: you can add a book to the top of the stack and remove a book from the top, but you can't pull one out of the middle or bottom without risking a collapse.

> **NOTE** *Because a stack retrieves items in last-in-first-out order, stacks are some-times called LIFO lists or LIFOs. ("LIFO" is pronounced life-o.)*
>
> *The top of a stack is also sometimes called its head. The bottom is sometimes called its tail.*

Table 16-4 summarizes the `Stack`'s most important methods.

TABLE 16-4

METHOD	PURPOSE
Clear	Removes all items from the `Stack`.
Peek	Returns the item at the top of the `Stack` without removing it.
Pop	Returns the item at the top of the `Stack` and removes it.
Push	Adds an item to the top of the `Stack`.

TRY IT

In this Try It, you use a `Dictionary` to build the order lookup program shown in Figure 16-4. When the user clicks the Add button, the program adds a new item with the given order ID and items. If the user enters an order ID and clicks Find, the program retrieves the corresponding items. If the user enters an order ID and some items and then clicks Update, the program updates the order's items.

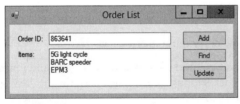

FIGURE 16-4

Lesson Requirements

In this lesson, you:

➤ Create the form shown in Figure 16-4.

➤ Add code that creates a `Dictionary` field named `Orders`. Set its generic type parameters to `int` (for order ID) and `string` (for items).

➤ Add code to the Add button that creates the new entry in the dictionary.

➤ Add code to the Find button that retrieves the appropriate entry from the dictionary.

➤ Add code to the Update button to update the indicated entry.

> **WARNING** *This program will be fairly fragile and will crash if you don't enter an order ID, enter an ID that is not an integer, try to enter the same ID twice, try to find a nonexistent ID, and so on. Don't worry about these problems. You learn how to handle them later, notably in Lessons 18 and 21.*

> **NOTE** *You can download the code and resources for this lesson from the website at* www.wrox.com/go/csharp24hourtrainer2e.

Step-by-Step

➤ Create the form shown in Figure 16-4.

   1. This is relatively straightforward. The only tricks are to set the `Items` TextBox's `MultiLine` and `AcceptsReturn` properties to `true`.

➤ Add code that creates a `Dictionary` named `Orders`. Set its generic type parameters to `int` (for order ID) and `string` (for items).

   1. Use code similar to the following to make the `Orders` field:

   ```
   // The dictionary to hold orders.
   private Dictionary<int, string> Orders =
       new Dictionary<int, string>();
   ```

➤ Add code to the Add button that creates the new entry in the dictionary.

   1. This code should call the `Dictionary`'s `Add` method passing it the order ID and items entered by the user. The `Dictionary`'s order ID must be an integer so use `int.Parse` to convert the value entered by the user into an `int`.

   Optionally you can add code to clear the `TextBox`es to get ready for the next entry.

   The code could be similar to the following:

   ```
   // Add an order.
   private void addButton_Click(object sender, EventArgs e)
   {
       // Add the order data.
       Orders.Add(int.Parse(orderIdTextBox.Text), itemsTextBox.Text);

       // Get ready for the next one.
       orderIdTextBox.Clear();
   ```

```
        itemsTextBox.Clear();
        orderIdTextBox.Focus();
    }
```

➤ Add code to the Find button that retrieves the appropriate entry from the dictionary.

1. Use code similar to the following:

```
// Look up an order.
private void findButton_Click(object sender, EventArgs e)
{
    itemsTextBox.Text = Orders[int.Parse(orderIdTextBox.Text)];
}
```

➤ Add code to the Update button to update the indicated entry.

1. Use code similar to the following:

```
// Update an order.
private void updateButton_Click(object sender, EventArgs e)
{
    Orders[int.Parse(orderIdTextBox.Text)] = itemsTextBox.Text;
}
```

EXERCISES

1. Make a program similar to the Fibonacci program that looks up factorials in an array. When the program starts, make it create the array to hold the first 20 factorials. Use the following definition for the factorial (where N! means the factorial of N):

```
0! = 1
N! = N * (N - 1)!
```

Hint: For testing purposes, make sure the program can calculate 0! and 20! without crashing.

2. Make a program that demonstrates a Stack of Strings. The program should display a TextBox and two Buttons labeled Push and Pop. When the user clicks Push, add the current text to the stack. When the user clicks Pop, remove the next item from the stack and display it in the TextBox.

3. Copy the program you wrote for Exercise 2 and modify it so the Pop button is disabled when the Stack is empty. Hint: Use the Stack's Count property.

4. Copy the program you wrote for Exercise 3 and modify it so it displays the Stack's contents in a ListBox with the most recently added item at the top of the ListBox. Hint: Use the ListBox's Insert and RemoveAt methods to update its contents as you add and remove items from the Stack.

5. Make a program similar to the one you built for Exercise 4 except demonstrating a Queue instead of a Stack. Give the Buttons the captions Enqueue and Dequeue instead of Push and Pop. Make the ListBox display the items with the most recently added item at the bottom.

6. Make a program similar to the one you built for this lesson's Try It except make it store appointment information. The `Dictionary` should use the `DateTime` type for keys and the `string` type for values. Let the user pick dates from a `DateTimePicker`.

   Hint: When the `DateTimePicker` first starts, it defaults to the current time, which may include fractional seconds. After the user changes the control's selection, however, the value no longer includes fractional seconds. That makes it hard to search for the exact same date and time later, at least if the user enters a value before changing the control's initial value.

   To avoid this problem, when the form loads, initialize the `DateTimePicker` to a value that doesn't include fractional seconds. Use the properties provided by `DateTime.Now` to create a new `DateTime` and set the `DateTimePicker`'s `Value` property to that.

7. Make a day planner application. The code should make an array of 31 strings to hold each day's plan. Initialize the array to show fake plans such as "Day 1."

   Use a `ComboBox` to let the user select a day of the month. When the `ComboBox`'s value changes, display the corresponding day's plan in a large `TextBox` on the form.

   Hint: Use the `ComboBox`'s `SelectedIndex` property as an index into the array. Note that this program doesn't let the user enter or modify the plan, it just displays hardcoded values. To let the user modify the plan, you would need Find and Update buttons similar to those used in other exercises.

8. [Games] Copy the program you wrote for Exercise 6-13 (or download the version available on the book's website) and add a two-dimensional array of characters to track the board's position. Initially set the entries to a space character.

   To test the code, set a breakpoint at the beginning of the code that handles the File menu's New command. Run the program and select all of the squares. Then invoke the New menu item and use the debugger to view the array.

   Hint: Use code similar to the following to reset the array when the user starts a new game:

   ```
   Board = new char[,]
   {
       {' ', ' ', ' '},
       {' ', ' ', ' '},
       {' ', ' ', ' '},
   };
   ```

9. [Games, WPF] Repeat Exercise 7 with the program you wrote for Exercise 6-14 (or the version downloaded from the book's website).

10. Use a `Dictionary` to make a simple phone book that lets the user add and look up name and phone number pairs.

11. [Hard] Make an image lookup program similar to the one shown in Figure 16-5. When the user clicks the `PictureBox`, let the user select an image file from an `OpenFileDialog`. Use code similar to the following to display the selected image:

    ```
    imagePictureBox.Image = new Bitmap(imageOpenFileDialog.FileName);
    ```

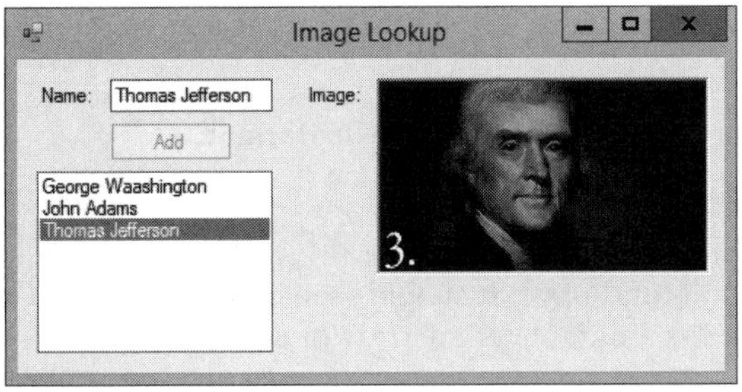

FIGURE 16-5

Enable the Add Button when the TextBox and PictureBox are non-blank. When the user clicks Add, add the PictureBox's image to a Dictionary with the name as its key, add the name to the ListBox, and blank the TextBox and PictureBox. (Blank the PictureBox by setting its Image property to null.)

Finally, when the user clicks a name in the ListBox, display the corresponding name and picture.

12. [Hard] Make a simple bank account register like the one shown in Figure 16-6.

The program should have these features:

➤ Make a Dictionary to hold account balances with integer account numbers as keys.

➤ Enable the Buttons when both TextBoxes contain non-blank text.

➤ When the user clicks Create, add the account number and amount to the dictionary and display the new data in the ListBox.

➤ When the user clicks Credit:

FIGURE 16-6

   ➤ Parse the account number and use the Dictionary to get the account's current balance.

➤ Use the account number and balance to find the index of the account's entry in the ListBox.

➤ Add the new amount to the account's balance in the Dictionary.

➤ Remove the account's entry in the ListBox.

➤ Insert a new entry for the account's new balance in the ListBox at the same position as the old entry.

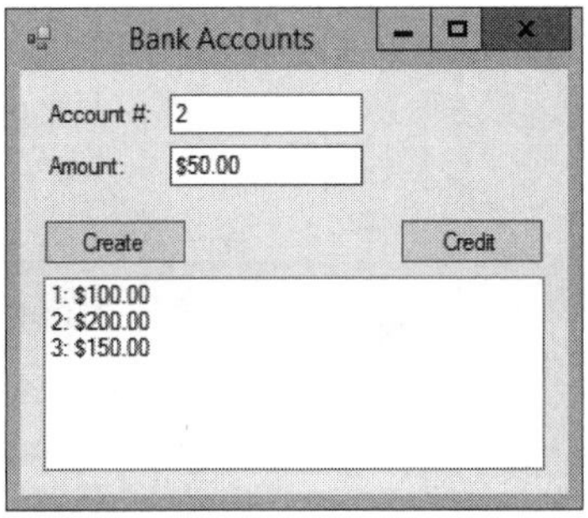

➤ When the user clicks a `ListBox` entry, display the account number and balance in the `TextBox`es.

13. Write a program that lets the user enter text in the following format:

```
1,200 Gummy slugs @ $0.02 = $24.00
```

When the user clicks Parse, the program should use the `string` class's `Split` method to get the item's name, price each, and total price. It should then add the values to a `ListBox`. Hint: The `Split` method can take as a parameter an array of delimiters. (That makes parsing a lot easier.)

14. [Hard] Write a palindrome checker. Whenever the user modifies the text in a `TextBox`, the program should display a `Label` that indicates whether the text is a palindrome. Hints:

➤ Use two `Label`s, one that says "A Palindrome" and one that says "Not A Palindrome." Use a boolean expression to set their `Visible` properties appropriately.

➤ To see if the string is a palindrome:

➤ Remove commas, periods, and spaces.

➤ Then convert the text into lowercase. (I'll call this the processed `string`.)

➤ Use the `string`'s `ToCharArray` method to get an array containing the string's characters.

➤ Use `Array.Reverse` to reverse the array.

➤ Use code similar to the following to convert the reversed characters into a string:

```
string reversed = new string(chars);
```

➤ Compare the processed `string` and the reversed `string`.

➤ Test the program on the two palindromes, "Able was I ere I saw Elba," and "A man, a plan, a canal, Panama."

NOTE *Please select the videos for Lesson 16 online at* www.wrox.com/go/ csharp24hourtrainer2evideos.

17

Using Enumerations and Structures

The data types you've learned about so far hold strings, integers, dates, and other predefined kinds of information, but sometimes it would be nice to define your own data types.

An *enumeration* (or *enumerated type*) lets you define a new data type that can take only one of an allowed list of values. For example, a menu program might define a MealType data type that can hold the values Breakfast, Lunch, and Dinner.

The data types described in previous lessons also can hold only a single piece of data: a name, street address, city, or whatever. Sometimes it would be nice to keep related pieces of data together. Instead of storing a name, address, and city in separate strings, you might like to store them as a single unit.

A *structure* (sometimes called a *struct*) lets you define a group of related pieces of data that should be kept together.

In this lesson, you learn how to define and use enumerations and structures to make your code easier to write, understand, and debug.

ENUMERATIONS

Defining an enumeration is easy. The following code defines a ContactMethod enumeration that can hold the values None, Email, Phone, or SnailMail:

```
// Define possible contact methods.
enum ContactMethod
{
    None = 0,
    Email,
    Phone,
    SnailMail,
}
```

> **NOTE** *The final comma in this example is optional. You don't need it because there is no value after* SnailMail, *but C# allows you to use it if you want to make the lines of code more consistent.*

Internally an enumeration is stored as an integral data type, by default an int. An optional number after a value tells C# explicitly which integer to assign to that value. In the preceding code, None is explicitly assigned the value 0.

If you don't specify a value for an enumeration's item (and often you don't care what these values are), its value is one greater than the previous item's value (the first item gets value 0). In this example, None is 0, Email is 1, Phone is 2, and SnailMail is 3.

You create an instance of an enumerated type just as you make an instance of a primitive type such as int, decimal, or string. The following code declares a variable of type ContactMethod, assigns it the value ContactMethod.Email, and then displays its value in the Output window:

```
ContactMethod contactMethod = ContactMethod.Email;
Console.WriteLine(contactMethod.ToString());
```

An enumeration's ToString method returns the value's name, in this case "Email."

STRUCTURES

Defining a structure is just as easy as defining an enumeration. The following code defines a simple structure named Address that holds name and address information:

```
// Define a structure to hold addresses.
struct Address
{
    public string Name;
    public string Street;
    public string City;
    public string State;
    public string Zip;
    public string Email;
    public string Phone;
    public ContactMethod PreferredMethod;
}
```

Inside the braces, the structure defines the bits of data that it holds together. The public keywords in this example mean that the fields inside the structure (Name, Street, and so on) are visible to any code that can see an Address.

Notice that the structure can use an enumeration. In this example, the Address structure's PreferredMethod field has type ContactMethod.

In many ways structures behave like simple built-in types such as int and float. In particular, when you declare a variable with a structure type, the code not only declares it but also creates it. That means you don't need to use the new keyword to create an instance of a structure.

After defining the variable, you can access its fields using syntax similar to the way you access a control's properties. Start with the variable's name, follow it with a dot, and then add the field's name.

The following code creates and initializes a new `Address` structure named `homeAddress`:

```
Address homeAddress;

homeAddress.Name = nameTextBox.Text;
homeAddress.Street = streetTextBox.Text;
homeAddress.City = cityTextBox.Text;
homeAddress.State = stateTextBox.Text;
homeAddress.Zip = zipTextBox.Text;
homeAddress.Email = emailTextBox.Text;
homeAddress.Phone = phoneTextBox.Text;
homeAddress.PreferredMethod =
    (ContactMethod)preferredMethodComboBox.SelectedIndex;
```

This code fills in the text fields using values entered by the user in `TextBoxes`.

The final field is a `ContactMethod` enumeration. The user selects a value for this field from the `preferredMethodComboBox`. The code takes the index of the `ComboBox`'s selected item, converts it from an integer into a `ContactMethod`, and saves the result in the structure's `PreferredMethod` field.

> **NOTE** *To correctly convert a* `ComboBox` *selection into an enumeration value, the* `ComboBox` *must display the choices in the same order in which they are defined by the enumeration. In this example, the* `ComboBox` *must contain the items None, Email, Phone, and SnailMail in that order to match up with the enumeration's items.*

STRUCTURES VERSUS CLASSES

In many ways structures are very similar to classes. Lesson 23 says a lot more about classes and the sorts of things you can do with them, and many of the same techniques apply to structures.

For example, both can contain properties, methods, and events. Both can also have constructors, special methods that are executed when you use `new` to create a new instance. These are described in greater detail in Lesson 23.

While structures and classes have many things in common, they also have some significant differences. A lot of these differences are outside the scope of this book, so I won't cover them here, but one very important difference that you should understand is that structures are value types while classes are reference types.

Reference Types

A *reference type* doesn't actually hold the data for a class instance. Instead it holds a reference to an instance. The *reference* is like an address that points to where the data is actually stored.

For example, the following code creates a `NewUserForm` and displays it:

```
NewUserForm userForm;
userForm = new NewUserForm();
userForm.ShowDialog();
```

The first statement declares a variable of type `NewUserForm`. Initially that variable doesn't refer to anything so if you tried to display the form at this point, the program would crash.

The second statement creates a new instance of the `NewUserForm` type and saves a reference to the new form in the `userForm` variable.

Now the variable refers to an instance of the `NewUserForm` type, so the third statement can safely display that form.

Value Types

In contrast to reference types, a *value type* actually contains its data instead of refers to it. Many of the primitive data types such as `int`, `double`, and `decimal` are value types.

The following code creates and uses a variable with the `Address` structure type described earlier:

```
Address homeAddress;
homeAddress.Name = "Benjamin";
```

When the code executes the first statement, the program creates the `Address` structure so it's all ready to go, although its fields all contain `null` values. The second statement can immediately set the variable's `Name` value without needing to use the `new` keyword to create a new instance of the structure.

Other Differences

Another important difference between value and reference types involves the way the program assigns values to them.

If a program sets one reference variable equal to another, then they both point to *the same object*. For example, suppose `ann` and `ben` are two variables that hold references to `Student` objects. Then the statement `ben = ann` makes the variable `ben` refer to the same object to which `ann` refers.

Figure 17-1 shows this operation graphically. Initially (the picture on the left) variable `ann` contains a reference to a `Student` object and variable `ben` contains the special value `null` (represented by the box with an X in it) that means it doesn't refer to anything. After executing the statement `ben = ann`, both variables contain references to the same `Student` object (the picture on the right).

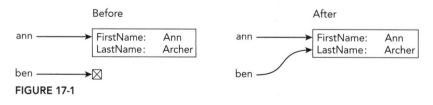

FIGURE 17-1

Because the two reference variables refer to the same object, if you use one variable to change the object, the other variable also sees the change. For example, if you execute the statement ben .FirstName = "Ben", then the value ann.FirstName will also contain the value Ben.

In contrast, if you set a variable with a value type equal to another, the first variable receives a *copy* of the second variable's value. For example, suppose cindy and dan are two variables of the structure type Person. The Person type might be very similar to the Student type, except it's a structure (value type) instead of a class (reference type). In that case, the statement dan = cindy makes the variable dan hold a copy of the values in the structure cindy.

Figure 17-2 shows this operation graphically. Initially (the picture on the left) variables cindy and dan each contain Person data. This time the variables include all of the data inside the rectangles; they're not just references pointing to values stored someplace else. After executing the statement dan = cindy, both variables contain separate copies of the same data.

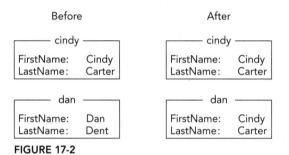

FIGURE 17-2

Because the two value variables refer to different copies of the same data, changing one doesn't change the other. For example, if you execute the statement dan.Name = "Dan", then the value cindy.Name will still be Cindy.

The Structure Versus Class example program, which is available in this lesson's downloads, demonstrates this difference. This issue is quite important, so it will be worth your time to download the example and study it until you're sure you understand it.

So which should you use, a structure or a class? In many programs the difference doesn't matter much. As long as you are aware of the relevant differences, you can often use either.

Microsoft's "Classes and Structs (C# Programming Guide)" web page at msdn.microsoft.com/library/ms173109.aspx gives this advice:

> In general, classes are used to model more complex behavior, or data that is intended to be modified after a class object is created. Structs are best suited for small data structures that contain primarily data that is not intended to be modified after the struct is created.

If you follow that advice, then a more complex piece of data such as a Person or Student should probably be implemented as a class. You may need to update Person or Student information over time, so that also indicates that these should probably be classes.

In contrast, suppose you're writing an oven control program and you want a data type to store temperature data. In that case, you might store data in a Temperature structure.

On some level, it doesn't make sense for a particular *temperature value* to change, although it might make sense for an *oven's temperature* to change. For example, the oven's temperature might start at 75° and warm up to 375°. The temperature 75° hasn't changed; it's the oven's temperature that has changed. Instead of updating the temperature variable, the program would set the variable equal to the new temperature value.

To see the difference, think back to the Student example. If Ann moves, you'll need to change her address (assuming the Student class contains name, address, phone number, and other relevant data). Ann herself hasn't changed, so it doesn't really make sense to set the ann variable equal to a whole new Student object. Instead you can just update the ann.Address value.

If you think I'm just being nit-picky and splitting hairs here, you're right. The difference is there, but for practical purposes it often doesn't make a huge difference whether you use a class or a structure. A lot of C# programmers use classes instead of structures basically all of the time. (Partly I suspect so they don't have to remember the differences between value and reference types.) If you're using classes and structures defined by Microsoft or some other programmer, then the differences matter, but when you're writing your own code, you can pick whichever makes the most sense to you.

WHERE TO PUT STRUCTURES

You can define structures in a couple places.

First, you can define a structure inside a class but outside of any of its methods. For example, you can define a structure inside a form class. Then the structure is visible only inside the class that contains it. If code outside of the class doesn't need to use the structure, this restricts the structure's visibility so it prevents possible confusion in the outside code.

Second, you can define a structure in the file that defines a class but outside of the class's code. For example, you can put it at the bottom of the class just before the final closing brace that ends the namespace statement started at the top of the file. In that case, the structure is visible to all of the code in the project (assuming you give it enough visibility, for example, public).

The second method can be a bit confusing because the same file defines a class and a structure. A third place you can define a structure for use by the whole program is in its own module. The easiest way to do that is to use the Project menu's Add Class command. Give the class the name you want to give the structure and click Add. After Visual Studio creates the class, change the class keyword to struct.

You can define enumerations in the same locations.

TRY IT

In this Try It, you use an enumeration and a structure to make the address book shown in Figure 17-3. When the user clicks the Add button, the program saves the entered address values. If the user enters a name and clicks Find, the program retrieves the corresponding address data.

FIGURE 17-3

Lesson Requirements

In this lesson, you:

➤ Create the form shown in Figure 17-3.

➤ Define the `ContactMethod` enumeration with values `None`, `Email`, `Phone`, and `SnailMail`.

➤ Define an `Address` structure to hold the entered address information.

➤ Create a `Dictionary<string, Address>` field to hold the address data.

➤ Add code to initially select the `ComboBox`'s `None` entry when the form loads (just so something is selected).

➤ Add code to the Add button that creates the new entry in the `Dictionary`.

➤ Add code to the Find button that retrieves the appropriate entry from the `Dictionary` and displays it.

> **NOTE** *You can download the code and resources for this lesson from the website at* www.wrox.com/go/csharp24hourtrainer2e.

Step-by-Step

➤ Create the form shown in Figure 17-3.

1. I'm sure you can do this on your own by now.

➤ Define the `ContactMethod` enumeration with values `None`, `Email`, `Phone`, and `SnailMail`.

1. Use code similar to the following at the form's class level (not inside any event handler):

```
// Define contact methods.
private enum ContactMethod
{
    None,
    Email,
    Phone,
    SnailMail,
}
```

➤ Define an `Address` structure to hold the entered address information.

1. Use code similar to the following at the form's class level (not inside any event handler):

```
// Define the address structure.
private struct Address
{
    public string Name;
    public string Street;
    public string City;
    public string State;
    public string Zip;
    public string Email;
    public string Phone;
    public ContactMethod PreferredMethod;
}
```

➤ Create a `Dictionary<string, Address>` field to hold the address data.

1. Use code similar to the following at the form's class level (not inside any event handler):

```
// Make a Dictionary to hold addresses.
private Dictionary<string, Address> Addresses =
    new Dictionary<string, Address>();
```

➤ Add code to initially select the `ComboBox`'s `None` entry when the form loads.

1. Use code similar to the following:

```
// Make sure the ComboBox starts with an item selected.
private void Form1_Load(object sender, EventArgs e)
{
    preferredMethodComboBox.SelectedIndex = 0;
}
```

➤ Add code to the Add button that creates the new entry in the `Dictionary`.

1. Use code similar to the following. (Using the indexed syntax instead of the `Dictionary`'s `Add` method lets the Add button add or update a record.) Optionally you can clear the `TextBox`es to get ready for the next address.

```
// Add a new address.
private void addButton_Click(object sender, EventArgs e)
{
    // Fill in a new Address structure.
    Address newAddress;
    newAddress.Name = nameTextBox.Text;
```

```
    newAddress.Street = streetTextBox.Text;
    newAddress.City = cityTextBox.Text;
    newAddress.State = stateTextBox.Text;
    newAddress.Zip = zipTextBox.Text;
    newAddress.Email = emailTextBox.Text;
    newAddress.Phone = phoneTextBox.Text;
    newAddress.PreferredMethod =
        (ContactMethod)preferredMethodComboBox.SelectedIndex;

    // Add the name and address to the dictionary.
    Addresses[nameTextBox.Text] = newAddress;

    // Get ready for the next one.
    nameTextBox.Clear();
    streetTextBox.Clear();
    cityTextBox.Clear();
    stateTextBox.Clear();
    zipTextBox.Clear();
    emailTextBox.Clear();
    phoneTextBox.Clear();
    preferredMethodComboBox.SelectedIndex = 0;

    nameTextBox.Focus();
}
```

➤ Add code to the Find button that retrieves the appropriate entry from the Dictionary and displays it.

1. Use code similar to the following:

```
// Look up an address.
private void findButton_Click(object sender, EventArgs e)
{
    // Get the Address.
    Address selectedAddress = Addresses[nameTextBox.Text];

    // Display the Address's values.
    nameTextBox.Text = selectedAddress.Name;
    streetTextBox.Text = selectedAddress.Street;
    cityTextBox.Text = selectedAddress.City;
    stateTextBox.Text = selectedAddress.State;
    zipTextBox.Text = selectedAddress.Zip;
    emailTextBox.Text = selectedAddress.Email;
    phoneTextBox.Text = selectedAddress.Phone;
    preferredMethodComboBox.SelectedIndex =
        (int)selectedAddress.PreferredMethod;
}
```

EXERCISES

1. Copy the program you built for this lesson's Try It. Add a Delete button that removes an item by calling the Dictionary's Remove method.

2. In addition to simple fields, structures can contain arrays. Copy the program you built for Exercise 1 and modify the Address structure so it contains an array holding three phone

numbers: home, work, and cell. (Hint: Before you can store values in the array, you need to allocate it as in `theAddress.Phones = new string[3].`)

3. Exercise 2 uses a structure that contains an array. You can also make an array that contains structures.

   Make a program that creates an array holding five `Address` structures of the kind used by the program you wrote for Exercise 2. When the program starts, initialize the array to literal values hardcoded into the program. Place the structures' names in a `ComboBox`. When the user selects an entry from the `ComboBox`, display the corresponding data.

4. [Games] Make a program that defines an enumeration to represent the pieces on a chess board. Then display each enumeration value as both a `string` and an `int` in a `TextBox`.

5. [Games] Make a program that uses the enumeration you defined for Exercise 4 to create an array that represents a complete board position. When the program loads, initialize the array to represent a new game.

6. [Games] Make a program that defines a structure to represent a chess move. (Hint: Don't record information that you can deduce from the current board position. For example, if a move represents a capture, you don't need to record that fact because you can figure it out.)

7. If you like, you can give multiple enumeration names the same numeric value by setting them equal to that value. You can even use an enumeration name to calculate the value of a later name.

   Suppose you're opening a coffee shop and you want to have the sizes Grande, Enorme, and Demente. Because some customers will be too grouchy to use the fancy names (because they haven't had their coffee yet), those names should be equivalent to the more pedestrian names Big, Huge, and Ginormous. Make a program that creates an enumeration that defines all of those values. Then display each value as both a `string` and an `int` in a `TextBox`.

8. [Games] Suppose you're building a steampunk Wild West fantasy role-playing game. Make a program that defines a structure to represent weapons. It should record the weapon's name, range in feet, and attack value; the number of dice to roll when attacking; and the number of sides on the dice.

9. [Games] To continue building your steampunk Wild West game, make a program that defines a structure to represent a character. It should record the character's name, profession (which can be GunSlinger, Scientist, ConArtist, or Cyborg), primary weapon, and secondary weapon.

10. [Hard] Suppose you're writing a genealogy program. Make a program that defines a structure that can store a person's name and that person's parents (represented by the same structure). When the program starts, initialize a data structure to represent the ancestor tree shown in Figure 17-4. (Hint: Because a structure cannot contain direct instances of itself, you'll need to figure out a way to store the parents in a reference type.)

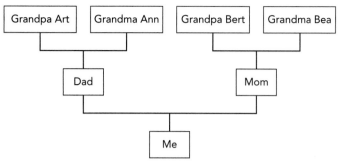

FIGURE 17-4

11. [Hard] Make a program that defines a structure that can store a person's name and that person's children (represented by the same structure). When the program starts, initialize a data structure to represent the descendant tree shown in Figure 17-5.

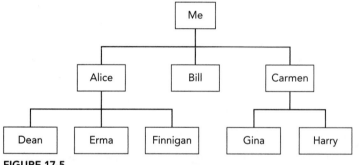

FIGURE 17-5

> **NOTE** *Please select the videos for Lesson 17 online at* www.wrox.com/go/ csharp24hourtrainer2evideos.

SECTION III
Program Statements

The lessons in Section II focused on working with variables. They explained how to declare variables, set their values, and perform calculations.

Those techniques let you do some fairly complex things, but they're still relatively straightforward things that you could do yourself by hand if you really had to. For example, you could easily calculate line item totals, sales tax, shipping, and a grand total for a purchase order.

With what you know so far, you really can't write a program that takes full advantage of the computer's power. You can't make the program add up an unknown number of values stored in a ListBox, perform the same task (such as calculating an account balance) for thousands of customers, or take different actions depending on the user's inputs. You can't even write a program that can tell if the user entered an invalid value such as "seventy-eight" in a TextBox that should contain a number.

The lessons in this section explain how to perform these kinds of tasks. They explain ways you can make a program take different courses of action depending on circumstances, repeat a set of actions many times, break code into manageable pieces to make it easier to write and debug, and handle unexpected errors. After you finish reading these lessons, you'll be able to write applications that are much more powerful than those you can write now.

▶ **LESSON 18:** Making Choices

▶ **LESSON 19:** Repeating Program Steps

▶ **LESSON 20:** Reusing Code with Methods

▶ **LESSON 21:** Handling Errors

▶ **LESSON 22:** Preventing Bugs

Making Choices

All of the code used in the lessons so far has been completely linear. The program follows a series of steps in order with no deviation.

For example, a sales program could multiply a unit price by quantity desired, add several items' values, multiply to get sales tax and shipping costs, and calculate a grand total.

So far there's been no way to perform different steps under different circumstances. For example, the sales program couldn't charge different prices for different quantities purchased or waive shipping charges for orders over $100. It couldn't even check quantities to see if they make sense. So far a clever customer could order –1,000 items to get a huge credit!

In this lesson you learn how a program can make decisions. You learn how the program can take different actions based on user inputs and other circumstances.

DECISION STATEMENTS

Programs often need to decide between two or more courses of action. For example:

➤ If it's before 4:00 p.m., ship today. Otherwise ship tomorrow.

➤ If the order quantity is less than zero, make the user fix it.

➤ If a word processor has unsaved changes, refuse to exit.

➤ Calculate shipping based on order total: $5 if total < $20, $7.50 if total < $50, $10 if total < $75, and free if total ≥ $75.

The basic idea is the same in all of these cases. The program examines a value and takes one of several different actions depending on the value.

The following sections describe the different statements that C# provides for making these kinds of decisions.

IF STATEMENTS

The if statement examines a condition and takes action only if the condition is true. The basic syntax for the if statement is:

```
if (condition) statement;
```

Here `condition` is some boolean expression that evaluates to either true or false, and `statement` is a statement that should be executed if `condition` is true.

For example, suppose you're writing an order entry program and shipping should be $5 for orders under $100 and free for orders of at least $100. Suppose also that the program has already calculated the value `total`. The following code shows how the program might handle this:

```
decimal shipping = 5.00M;           // Default shipping cost.
if (total >= 100) shipping = 0;     // Shipping is free if total >= 100.
```

The code starts by setting the variable `shipping` to $5. Then if the previously calculated value `total` is at least $100, the program sets `shipping` to $0.

If `total` is less than $100, the statement following the if statement is not executed and `shipping` keeps its original value of $5.

If you want to execute more than one statement when `condition` is true, place the statements inside braces as in the following code:

```
decimal shipping = 5.00M;       // Default shipping cost.
if (total >= 100)
{
    shipping = 0;               // Shipping is free if total >= 100.
    giveFreeGift = true;        // Give a free gift if total >= 100.
}
```

You can place as many statements as you like inside the braces, and they are all executed if `condition` is true.

> **NOTE** *To make the code more consistent and easier to read, some programmers always use braces even if the program should execute only one statement. The following code shows an example:*
>
> ```
> if (total >= 100)
> {
>     shipping = 0;
> }
> ```
>
> *Other programmers think that's unnecessarily verbose. You should use the style you find easiest to read.*

IF-ELSE STATEMENTS

The previous example set `shipping` to a default value and then changed it if `total` was at least $100. Another way to think about this problem is to imagine taking one of two actions depending on `total`'s value. If `total` is less than $100, the program should set `shipping` to $5. Otherwise the program should set `shipping` to $0.

The `if-else` construct lets a program follow this approach, taking one of two actions depending on some condition.

The syntax for `if-else` is:

```
if (condition)
    statementsIfTrue;
else
    statementsIfFalse;
```

If `condition` is true, the first block `statementsIfTrue` executes. Otherwise (if `condition` is false) the second block `statementsIfFalse` executes.

Using the `else` keyword, the preceding code could be rewritten like this:

```
decimal shipping;
if (total < 100)
    shipping = 5M;      // Shipping is $5 if total < 100.
else
    shipping = 0M;      // Shipping is free if total >= 100.
```

You can use braces to make either the `if` or `else` part of the `if-else` statement execute more than one command.

CASCADING IF STATEMENTS

The `if-else` construct performs one of two actions depending on whether the condition is true or false. Sometimes a program needs to check several conditions to decide what to do.

For example, suppose an order entry program calculates shipping charges depending on the total purchase amount according to this schedule:

➤ If total < $20, shipping is $5.00.

➤ Otherwise, if total < $50, shipping is $7.50.

➤ Otherwise, if total < $75, shipping is $10.00.

➤ Otherwise, shipping is free.

You can make a program perform each of these tests one after another by making a second if statement be the else part of a first if statement. The following code shows how you can calculate shipping according to the preceding schedule:

```
decimal shipping;
if (total < 20)
{
    shipping = 5M;
}
else if (total < 50)
{
    shipping = 7.5M;
}
else if (total < 75)
{
    shipping = 10M;
}
else
{
    shipping = 0M;
}
```

When the program encounters a cascading series of if statements, it executes each in turn until it finds one with a true condition. It then skips the rest because they are all part of the current if statement's else block.

For example, consider the previous code and suppose total is $60. The code evaluates the first condition and decides that (total < 20) is false, so it does not execute the first code block.

The program skips to the else statement and executes the next if test. The program decides that (total < 50) is also not true, so it skips to this if statement's else block.

The program executes the third if test and finds that (total < 75) is true so it executes the statement shipping = 10M.

Because the program found an if statement with a true condition, it skips the following else statement, so it passes over any if statements that follow without evaluating their conditions.

NESTED IF STATEMENTS

Another common arrangement of if statements nests one within another. The inner if statement is executed only if the first statement's condition allows the program to reach it.

For example, suppose you charge customers 5 percent state sales tax. If a customer lives within your county, you also charge a county transportation tax. Finally, if the customer also lives within city limits, you charge a city sales tax. (Taxes where I live are at least this confusing.)

The following code performs these checks, where the variables inCounty and inCity indicate whether the customer lives within the county and city:

```
if (inCounty)
{
    if (inCity)
    {
```

```
            salesTaxRate = 0.09M;
        }
        else
        {
            salesTaxRate = 0.07M;
        }
    }
    else
    {
        salesTaxRate = 0.05M;
    }
```

You can nest `if` statements as deeply as you like, although at some point the code gets hard to read.

> **NOTE** *There are always ways to rearrange code by using the* `&&` *(logical AND) and* `||` *(logical OR) operators to remove nested* `if` *statements. For example, the following code does the same thing as the previous version without nesting:*
>
> ```
>     if (inCounty && inCity)
>     {
>         salesTaxRate = 0.09M;
>     }
>     else if (inCounty)
>     {
>         salesTaxRate = 0.07M;
>     }
>     else
>     {
>         salesTaxRate = 0.05M;
>     }
> ```
>
> *In fact, if you know that the city lies completely within the county, you could rewrite the first test as* `if (inCity)`.

SWITCH STATEMENTS

The `switch` statement provides an easy-to-read equivalent to a series of cascading `if` statements that compares one value to a series of other values.

The syntax of the `switch` statement is:

```
switch (testValue)
{
    case (value1):
        statements1;
        break;

    case (value2):
        statements2;
        break;
```

```
    . . .
    default:
        statementsDefault;
        break;
}
```

Here *testValue* is the value that you are testing. The values *value1*, *value2*, and so on are the values to which you are comparing *testValue*. The *statements1*, *statements2*, and so on are the blocks of statements that you want to execute for each case. The other pieces (switch, case, break, and default) are keywords that you must type as they appear here.

If you include the optional default section, its statements execute if no other case applies. Actually the case statements are optional, too, although it would be strange to not use any.

Note that a case's code block doesn't need to include any statements other than break. You can use that to make the code take no action when a particular case occurs.

For example, suppose you build a form where the user selects a hotel from a ComboBox. The program uses that selection to initialize an enumerated variable named hotelChoice. The following code sets the lodgingPrice variable depending on which hotel the user selected:

```
decimal lodgingPrice;
switch (hotelChoice)
{
    case HotelChoice.LuxuryLodge:
        lodgingPrice = 45;
        break;

    case HotelChoice.HamiltonArms:
        lodgingPrice = 80;
        break;

    case HotelChoice.InvernessInn:
        lodgingPrice = 165;
        break;

    default:
        MessageBox.Show("Please select a hotel");
        lodgingPrice = 0;
        break;
}
```

The case statements check for the three expected choices and sets lodgingPrice to the appropriate value. If the user doesn't select any hotel, the default section's code displays a message box and sets lodgingPrice to 0 to indicate a problem.

A switch statement is most robust (less prone to bugs and crashes) if its cases can handle every possible comparison value. That makes them work very well with enumerated types because you can list every possible value. In contrast, you can't include a case statement for every possible integer value (unless you include several billion lines of code), so case statements can't check every possible integer value.

Even if the `case` statements check every possible value in an enumeration, it's a good practice to include a `default` section just in case another value sneaks into the code. For example, a bug in the code could convert an integer into an enumeration value that doesn't exist, or you could later add a new value to the enumeration and forget to add a corresponding `case` statement. In those cases, the default statement can catch the bug, take some default action, and possibly warn you that something is wrong.

When you use a `switch` statement with other data types, be sure to consider unexpected values, particularly if the user typed in the value. For example, don't assume the user will always enter a valid string. Allowing the user to select a string from a `ComboBox` is safer, but you should still include a `default` statement.

TRY IT

In this Try It, you build the Order Form program shown in Figure 18-1. The program uses a cascading series of `if` statements to calculate shipping cost based on the subtotal.

Lesson Requirements

In this lesson, you:

➤ Build the form shown in Figure 18-1.

➤ Write the code for the Calculate button so it calculates the subtotal, sales tax, shipping, and grand total. The sales tax should be 7 percent of the subtotal. Shipping should be $5 if subtotal < $20, $7.50 if subtotal < $50, $10 if subtotal < $75, and free if subtotal ≥ $75.

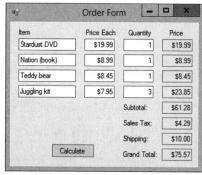

FIGURE 18-1

> **NOTE** *You can download the code and resources for this lesson from the website at* `www.wrox.com/go/csharp24hourtrainer2e`.

Hints

➤ Make the sales tax rate a constant, giving it the most limited scope you can.

Step-by-Step

➤ Build the form shown in Figure 18-1.

1. This is relatively straightforward.

➤ Write the code for the Calculate button so it calculates the subtotal, sales tax, shipping, and grand total. The sales tax should be 7 percent of the subtotal. Shipping should be $5 if subtotal < $20, $7.50 if subtotal < $50, $10 if subtotal < $75, and free if subtotal ≥ $75.

1. Calculate the total costs for each of the four items. Add them together to get the subtotal.

2. Calculate sales tax by multiplying the tax rate by the subtotal.

3. Use a series of cascading `if-else` statements to calculate the shipping cost based on the subtotal as in the following code:

```
// Calculate shipping cost.
decimal shipping;
if (subtotal < 20)
{
    shipping = 5;
}
else if (subtotal < 50)
{
    shipping = 7.5m;
}
else if (subtotal < 75)
{
    shipping = 10;
}
else
{
    shipping = 0;
}
```

4. Add the subtotal, tax, and shipping cost to get the grand total.

5. Display the results.

EXERCISES

1. Build the Conference Coster program shown in Figure 18-2.

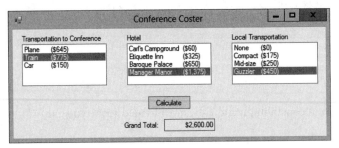

FIGURE 18-2

When the user clicks the Calculate button, first check each `ListBox`'s `SelectedIndex` property. If any `SelectedIndex` is less than zero (indicating the user didn't make a choice), display an error message and use the `return` keyword to stop calculating.

If the user made a choice in all of the ListBoxes, create a variable total to hold the total cost. Use three switch statements to add the appropriate amounts to total and display the result. (Hint: Add a default statement to each switch statement to catch unexpected selections, even though none should occur in this program. Then add a new hotel to the ListBox and see what happens if you select it.)

2. [SimpleEdit, Hard] Copy the SimpleEdit program that you built way back in Exercise 8-7 (or download the version on the book's website) and add code to protect the user from losing unsaved changes.

The basic idea is to check whether the document has been modified before doing anything that will lose the changes, such as starting a new document, opening another file, or exiting the program.

   a. In the File menu's New, Open, and Exit commands, check the RichTextBox's Modified property to see if the document has unsaved changes.

   b. If there are unsaved changes, ask if the user wants to save them. Display a message box with the buttons Yes, No, and Cancel.

   c. If the user clicks Yes, save the changes and continue the operation.

   d. If the user clicks No, don't save the changes (do nothing special) and let the operation continue.

   e. If the user clicks Cancel, don't perform the operation. For example, don't open a new file.

   f. After starting a new document or saving an old one, set the RichTextBox control's Modified property to false to indicate that there are no unsaved changes at that time.

   Hint: Use a local variable named shouldContinue to decide whether the operation should continue.

3. [SimpleEdit] Copy the SimpleEdit program you built for Exercise 2. That program protects against lost changes if the user opens the File menu and selects Exit, but the user can close the program several other ways such as pressing Alt+F4, clicking the "X" button in the program's title bar, and opening the system menu in the form's upper-left corner and selecting Close. Currently the program doesn't protect unsaved changes for any of those.

   To fix this, give the form a FormClosing event handler. When the form is about to close, it raises this event. If you set the event's e.Cancel parameter to true, the form cancels the close and remains open. Add code to this event handler to protect unsaved changes.

   Now that the FormClosing event handler is protecting against lost changes, you don't need to perform the same checks in the Exit menu item's event handler. Make that event handler simply call the Close method and let the FormClosing event handler do the rest.

4. [Games, Hard] Copy the tic-tac-toe program that you built way back in Exercise 16-8 (or download the version on the book's website). That version of the program uses three Labels for each square: two to let the user select the square for X or O, and one to show which player has taken the square.

Modify the program to make the following changes (which should make the program much smaller):

➤ Remove the X and O `Label`s so there's only one `Label` per square.

➤ Set each `Label`'s `Tag` property to indicate its row and column. For example, set the `Tag` property for the upper-left `Label` to "0, 0."

➤ Make a class-level variable to keep track of which player's turn it is.

➤ Use the same `Click` event handler for all of the `Label`s.

➤ When the user clicks a square, convert the event handler's `sender` parameter into the `Label` that raised the `Click` event.

➤ If the square has already been taken, ignore the click.

➤ Otherwise, take the square for the player whose turn it is.

➤ Parse the clicked `Label`'s `Tag` property to see which entry in the `Board` array to set. (Hint: Use `ToString` to convert the `Tag` property into a `string`.)

5. [Games] Copy the program you made for Exercise 4 and modify it so that when the last square is taken, the program says "All squares are taken" in the turn `Label` (instead of saying "O's turn").

6. [Games, Hard] Copy the program you made for Exercise 5 and modify it so it checks for a winner after each square is taken. When the game ends, display the winner (or the fact that it's a tie) in the turn `Label`. After the game is over, ignore any click events until the user starts a new game.

7. [Games, Hard] Make a program that displays a bouncing ball (shown in a `PictureBox`). When the program starts, give the `PictureBox` a random position on the form and random X and Y velocities. When a `Timer` ticks, use the velocities to calculate the `PictureBox`'s new position. If the position makes the `PictureBox` move beyond one of the form's edges, move it back onto the form and reverse the corresponding velocity.

8. [Games, Hard] Copy the program you made for Exercise 7 and add a sound effect by following these steps:

➤ In the Solution Explorer, double-click the Properties item. Select the References tab, open the Add Resource dropdown, and select Add Existing File. Select the sound effect's source file and click Open.

➤ Use class-level code similar to the following to create a sound player associated with the sound resource. (Here "boing" is the name of the resource I used.)

```
// The SoundPlayer.
private System.Media.SoundPlayer BoingSound =
    new System.Media.SoundPlayer(Properties.Resources.boing);
```

➤ Use the statement `BoingSound.Play()` to play the sound when necessary.

9. [Games, Hard] Copy the program you made for Exercise 11-17 (or download the version on the book's website) and make the following changes:

➤ Remove the Stop button.

➤ When the user clicks Fire, play a sound file that sounds like a cannon firing.

➤ Place a new `PictureBox` displaying a picture of a castle or some other target on the form.

➤ If the cannonball hits the target, stop moving it, play an explosion sound file, hide the cannonball, and make the target `PictureBox` display an image of an explosion.

➤ If the cannonball moves off of the form, stop moving it and play a failure sound effect.

10. [Games, Hard] Make a UFO shooting gallery game similar to the one shown in Figure 18-3.

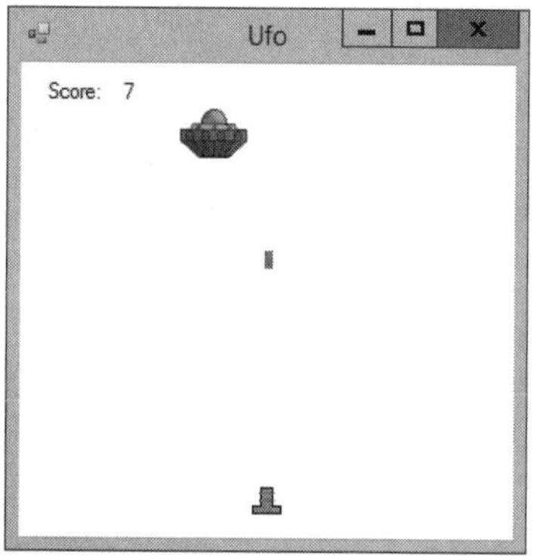

➤ Make the image of a UFO move left-to-right across the top of the form. When the UFO leaves the right side of the form, make it reappear on the left side.

➤ When the user presses Space, fire the red laser bolt (a `PictureBox`) from the laser cannon (an image in another `PictureBox`). (Hint: To know when the user presses Space, catch the form's `KeyDown` event and see if e.`KeyCode` == `Keys.Space`.)

FIGURE 18-3

➤ Don't allow the user to fire a bolt if one is already on the form.

➤ Use variables `UfoX`, `UfoY`, `UfoVx`, and `UfoVy` to track the UFO's position and velocity. Use similar variables for the laser bolt.

➤ When a `Timer` fires, update the positions of the UFO and the bolt.

➤ Use a variable to keep track of hit count.

➤ If the bolt hits the UFO, hide the bolt, increment the hit count, and display the hit count in the score `Label` at the top of the form.

➤ If the bolt leaves the form, hide it.

➤ Play cool sounds when the laser cannon fires and when a bolt hits the UFO.

11. [Games] The program you wrote for Exercise 10 isn't very hard. After a minute or two, you can easily get the timing down and hit the UFO almost every time.

Copy that program and make it more challenging by making these changes.

➤ When you start the UFO at the left edge of the form, give it a random size, speed, and Y coordinate.

➤ When the user hits the UFO, award points that take into account the current size and speed.

12. [Games, Hard] The program you wrote for Exercise 11 is still fairly easy because the user has an unlimited amount of ammunition.

   Copy the program and modify it so the user has only 10 laser bolts. Represent each with a PictureBox visible on the form and keep track of the number of bolts remaining. When the user fires a bolt, use a switch statement to hide the next bolt PictureBox.

   When all of the bolts are used, display a label on top of the game that shows the user's final score and play a triumphant fanfare.

13. [Games] Copy the program you wrote for Exercise 12 and add a File menu with New Game and Exit menu items.

14. [Games, Hard] Copy the program you wrote for Exercise 13 and add high scores to it.

   ➤ Use arrays to keep track of the five highest scores and the names of the players who got those high scores.

   ➤ Give the File menu a new High Scores command that displays the five names and scores in a dialog.

   ➤ When a game ends, compare the player's score to the first item in the high scores array. If the new score is higher:

      ➤ Display a form that lets the user enter a name.

      ➤ Replace the first array entries with the new score and name.

      ➤ Use Array.Sort to sort the arrays.

      ➤ Display the high scores form.

> **NOTE** *Please select the videos for Lesson 18 online at* www.wrox.com/go/
> csharp24hourtrainer2evideos.

19

Repeating Program Steps

One of the computer's greatest strengths is its ability to perform the exact same calculation again and again without getting bored or making careless mistakes. It can calculate the average test scores for a dozen students, print a hundred advertisements, or compute the monthly bills for a million customers with no trouble or complaining.

The lessons you've read so far, however, don't tell you how to do these things. So far every step the computer takes requires a separate line of code. To calculate bills for a million customers, you would need to write at least a million lines of code!

In this lesson you learn how to make the computer execute the same lines of code many times. You learn how to loop through arrays and collections of items to take action or perform calculations on them.

The following sections describe the kinds of loops provided by C#. The final section describes two statements you can use to change the way a loop works: break and continue.

FOR LOOPS

A for loop uses a variable to control the number of times it executes a series of statements. The for loop's syntax is as follows:

```
for (initialization; doneTest; next)
{
    statements...
}
```

Where:

➤ *initialization* gets the loop ready to start. Usually this part declares and initializes the looping variable.

➤ *doneTest* is a boolean expression that determines when the loop stops. The loop continues running as long as this expression is true.

➤ *next* prepares the loop for its next iteration. Usually this increments the looping variable declared in the *initialization*.

➤ *statements* are the statements that you want the loop to execute.

Note that none of the initialization, doneTest, or next statements are required, although they are all used by the simplest kinds of for loops.

For example, the following code displays the numbers 0 through 9 followed by their squares in the Console window:

```
for (int i = 0; i < 10; i++)
{
    int iSquared = i * i;
    Console.WriteLine(string.Format("{0}: {1}", i, iSquared));
}
```

In this code the *initialization* statement declares the variable i and sets it to 0, the *next* statement adds 1 to i, and the *doneTest* keeps the loop running as long as i < 10.

Here's a slightly more complicated example that calculates factorials. The program converts the value selected in the NumericUpDown control named numberNumericUpDown into a long integer and saves it in variable n. It initializes the variable factorial to 1 and then uses a loop to multiply factorial by each of the numbers between 2 and n. The result is 1 * 2 * 3 * ... * n, which is n!:

```
// Get the input value N.
long n = (long)numberNumericUpDown.Value;

// Calculate N!.
long factorial = 1;
for (int i = 2; i <= n; i++)
{
    checked
    {
        factorial *= i;
    }
}

// Display the result.
resultTextBox.Text = factorial.ToString();
```

You may recall that Lesson 16 used code to calculate Fibonacci numbers, and in that lesson's Exercise 1 you calculated factorials. Those programs used 20 lines of code to calculate and store 20 values that the program then used as a kind of lookup table.

The factorial code shown here uses a lot less code. It doesn't require a large array to hold values. It also doesn't require that you know ahead of time how many values you might need to calculate (20 for the earlier programs), although the factorial function grows so quickly that this program can only calculate values up to 20! before the result won't fit in a long.

> **NOTE** *The* for *loop is often the best choice if you know exactly how many times you need the loop to execute.*

FOREACH LOOPS

A `foreach` loop executes a block of code once for each item in an array or list. The syntax of the `foreach` loop is as follows:

```
foreach (variableDeclaration in items)
{
    statements...
}
```

Where:

➤ `variableDeclaration` declares the looping variable. Its type must be the same as the items in the array or list.

➤ `items` is the array or list of items over which you want to loop.

➤ `statements` are the statements that you want the loop to execute.

For example, the following code calculates the average of the test scores stored in the `ListBox` named `scoresListBox`. Note that the `ListBox` must contain integers or something the program can implicitly convert into an integer or else the program will crash:

```
// Add up the values.
int total = 0;
foreach (int value in valuesListBox.Items)
{
    total += value;
}

// Calculate the average.
float average = (float)total / valuesListBox.Items.Count;
```

The code creates a variable named `total` and sets it equal to 0. It then loops through the items in the `ListBox`, adding each value to `total`.

> **WARNING** *This code loops over the items in a* `ListBox`, *treating those items as integers. If the* `ListBox` *contains something other than integers, the program will crash.*

The code finishes by dividing the total by the number of items in the `ListBox`.

> **NOTE** *If you need to perform some operation on all of the items in an array or list, a* `foreach` *loop is often your best choice.*

WHILE LOOPS

A `while` loop executes as long as some condition is true. The syntax for a `while` loop is as follows:

```
while (condition)
{
    statements...
}
```

Where:

➤ `condition` is a boolean expression. The loop executes as long as this expression is true.

➤ `statements` are the statements that you want the loop to execute.

For example, the following code calculates a number's prime factors:

```
// Find the number's prime factors.
private void factorButton_Click(object sender, EventArgs e)
{
    // Get the input number.
    long number = long.Parse(numberTextBox.Text);

    // Find the factors.
    string result = "1";

    // Consider factors between 2 and the number.
    for (long factor = 2; factor <= number; factor++)
    {
        // Pull out as many copies of this factor as possible.
        while (number % factor == 0)
        {
            result += " x " + factor.ToString();
            number = number / factor;
        }
    }

    // Display the result.
    resultTextBox.Text = result;
}
```

The code starts by getting the user's input number. It builds a result string and initializes it to "1."

Next the code uses a `for` loop to consider the numbers between 2 and the user's number as possible factors.

For each of the possible factors, it uses a `while` loop to remove that factor from the number. As long as the factor divides evenly into the remaining number, the program adds the factor to the result and divides the user's number by the factor.

The code finishes by displaying its result.

> **NOTE** *Loops that use incrementing integers to decide when to stop are often easier to write using* for *loops instead of* while *loops. A* while *loop is particularly useful when the stopping condition occurs at a less predictable time, as in the factoring example.*

DO LOOPS

A do loop is similar to a while loop except it checks its stopping condition at the end of the loop instead of at the beginning. The syntax of a do loop is as follows:

```
do
{
    statements...
} while (condition);
```

Where:

➤   statements are the statements that you want the loop to execute.

➤   condition is a boolean expression. The loop continues to execute as long as this expression is true.

The following code uses a do loop to calculate the greatest common divisor (GCD) of two numbers, the largest number that divides them both evenly:

```
// Calculate GCD(A, B).
private void calculateButton_Click(object sender, EventArgs e)
{
    // Get the input values.
    long a = long.Parse(aTextBox.Text);
    long b = long.Parse(bTextBox.Text);

    // Calculate the GCD.
    long remainder;
    do
    {
        remainder = a % b;
        if (remainder != 0)
        {
            a = b;
            b = remainder;
        }
    } while (remainder > 0);

    resultTextBox.Text = b.ToString();
}
```

> **NOTE** *Notice that the variable* `remainder` *used to end the loop is declared outside of the loop even though it doesn't really do anything outside of the loop. Normally to restrict scope as much as possible, you would want to declare this variable inside the loop if you could.*
>
> *However, the end test executes in a scope that lies outside of the loop, so any variables declared inside the loop are hidden from it.*

It's important that any loop eventually ends, and in this code it's not completely obvious why that happens. It turns out that each time through the loop (with the possible exception of the first time), a and b get smaller. If you step through a few examples, you'll be able to convince yourself.

If the loop runs long enough, b eventually reaches 1. At that point b must evenly divide a no matter what a is so the loop ends. If b does reach 1, then 1 is the greatest common divisor of the user's original numbers and those numbers are called *relatively prime*.

EUCLID'S ALGORITHM

This algorithm was described by the Greek mathematician Euclid (circa 300 BC), so it's called the *Euclidean algorithm* or *Euclid's algorithm*. I don't want to explain why the algorithm works because it's complicated and irrelevant to this discussion of loops (you can find a good discussion at `primes.utm.edu/glossary/xpage/EuclideanAlgorithm.html`), but I do want to explain what the code does.

The code starts by storing the user's input numbers in variables a and b. It then declares variable `remainder` and enters a `do` loop.

Inside the loop, the program calculates the remainder when you divide a by b. If that value is not 0 (that is, b does not divide a evenly), then the program sets a = b and b = remainder.

Now the code reaches the end of the loop. The `while` statement makes the loop end if `remainder` is 0. When that happens, b holds the greatest common divisor.

You may want to step through the code in the debugger to see how the values change.

> **NOTE** *A* `do` *loop always executes its code at least once because it doesn't check its condition until the end. Often that feature is why you pick a* `do` *loop over a* `while` *loop. If you might not want the loop to execute even once, use a* `while` *loop. If you need to run the loop once before you can tell whether to stop, use a* `do` *loop.*

BREAK AND CONTINUE

The break and continue statements change the way a loop works.

The break statement makes the code exit the loop immediately without executing any more statements inside the loop.

For example, the following code searches the selected items in a ListBox for the value Carter. If it finds that value, it sets the boolean variable carterSelected to true and breaks out of the loop. If the ListBox has many selected items, breaking out of the loop early may let the program skip many loop iterations and save some time:

```
// See if Carter is one of the selected names.
bool carterSelected = false;
foreach (string name in namesListBox.SelectedItems)
{
    if (name == "Carter")
    {
        carterSelected = true;
        break;
    }
}
MessageBox.Show(carterSelected.ToString());
```

The continue statement makes a loop jump to its looping statement early, skipping any remaining statements inside the loop after the continue statement.

For example, the following code uses a foreach loop to display the square roots of the numbers in an array. The Math.Sqrt function cannot calculate the square root of a negative number so, to avoid trouble, the code checks each value. If it finds a value less than zero, it uses the continue statement to skip the rest of that trip through the loop so it doesn't try to take the number's square root. It then continues with the next number in the array:

```
// Display square roots.
float[] values = { 4, 16, -1, 60, 100 };
foreach (float value in values)
{
    if (value < 0) continue;
    Console.WriteLine(string.Format("The square root of {0} is {1:0.00}",
        value, Math.Sqrt(value)));
}
```

The following text shows this program's results:

```
The square root of 4 is 2.00
The square root of 16 is 4.00
The square root of 60 is 7.75
The square root of 100 is 10.00
```

NOTE *The* break *and* continue *statements make loops work in nonstandard ways and sometimes that can make the code harder to read, debug, and maintain. Use them if it makes the code easier to read, but ask yourself whether there's another simple way to write the loop that avoids these statements. For example, the following code does the same things as the previous square root code but without a* continue *statement:*

```
// Display square roots.
float[] values = { 4, 16, -1, 60, 100 };
foreach (float value in values)
{
    if (value >= 0)
    {
        Console.WriteLine(string.Format("The square root of {0} is
            {1:0.00}",
            value, Math.Sqrt(value)));
    }
}
```

TRY IT

In this Try It, you make the simple login form shown in Figure 19-1. When the program's startup form loads, it enters a loop that makes it display this form until the user enters the correct username and password or clicks Cancel.

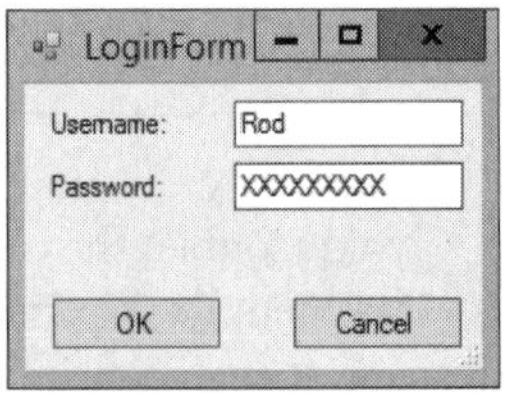

Lesson Requirements

In this lesson, you:

➤ Build a main form that displays a success message.

➤ Build the login dialog shown in Figure 19-1.

➤ In the main form's Load event handler, create an instance of the login dialog. Then enter a while loop that displays the dialog and doesn't stop until the user enters a username and password that match values in the code. If the user clicks Cancel, close the main form.

FIGURE 19-1

NOTE *You can download the code and resources for this lesson from the website at* www.wrox.com/go/csharp24hourtrainer2e.

Hints

➤ Use a boolean variable named tryingToLogin to control the loop. Initialize it to true before the loop and set it to false when the user either cancels or enters the right username and password.

➤ To decide whether the user entered a valid username and password, compare them to the strings "User" and "Secret." (A real application would validate these values with an encrypted database or by using some other authentication method.)

Step-by-Step

➤ Build a main form that displays a success message.

1. Place labels on the form to display the message.

➤ Build the login dialog shown in Figure 19-1.

1. Create the controls shown in Figure 19-1.

2. Set the password TextBox's PasswordChar property to X.

➤ In the main form's Load event handler, create an instance of the login dialog. Then enter a while loop that displays the dialog and doesn't stop until the user enters a username and password that match values in the code. If the user clicks Cancel, close the main form and break out of the loop.

1. The following code shows one possible solution:

```
// Make the user log in.
private void Form1_Load(object sender, EventArgs e)
{
    // Create a LoginForm.
    LoginForm frm = new LoginForm();

    // Repeat until the user successfully logs in.
    bool tryingToLogin = true;
    while (tryingToLogin)
    {
        // Display the login dialog and check the result.
        if (frm.ShowDialog() == DialogResult.Cancel)
        {
            // The user gives up. Close and exit the loop.
            this.Close();
            tryingToLogin = false;
        }
        else
        {
            // See if the user entered valid values.
            if ((frm.usernameTextBox.Text == "User") &&
                (frm.passwordTextBox.Text == "Secret"))
            {
                // Login succeeded. Stop trying to log in.
                tryingToLogin = false;
            }
            else
            {
                // Login failed. Display a message and
                // let the loop continue.
                MessageBox.Show("Invalid username and password.");
            }
```

```
        }
    }

    // If we get here, we're done trying to log in.
}
```

EXERCISES

1. Make a program that calculates the sum 1 + 2 + 3 + ... + N for a number N entered by the user.

2. [Hard] Make a program that calculates the Nth Fibonacci number for a number N entered by the user. The Fibonacci sequence is defined by:

    ```
    Fibonacci(0) = 0
    Fibonacci(1) = 1
    Fibonacci(N) = Fibonacci(N - 1) + Fibonacci(N - 2)
    ```

    Hint: Use a loop. Define variables `fibo1`, `fibo2`, and `fiboN` outside the loop. Inside the loop, make the variables hold `Fibonacci(N - 1)`, `Fibonacci(N - 2)`, and `Fibonacci(N)`. (To test your code, `Fibonacci(10)` = 55 and `Fibonacci(20)` = 6,765.)

3. Make a program that lets the user enter test scores into a `ListBox`. After adding each score, display the minimum, maximum, and average values. (Hint: Before you start the loop, initialize `minimum` and `maximum` variables to the value of the first score. Then loop through the list revising the variables as needed.)

4. Copy the program you wrote for Exercise 14-1 (or download the version on the book's website) and add a List Items button. When the user clicks the button, use the `Console` class to display the items and their values in the Output window as a semicolon-separated list similar to the following:

    ```
    **********
    Pencil;$0.10;12;$1.20;
    Pen;$0.25;12;$3.00;
    Notebook;$1.19;3;$3.57;
    **********
    ```

    Hint: The `ListView` control's `Items` property is a collection of `ListViewItem` objects. Loop through that collection to get information about each row.

    Hint: Each `ListViewItem` has a `SubItems` property that is a collection of `ListViewItem.ListViewSubItem` objects. For each row, loop through the item's subitem collection to get the values for that row. Use `Console.Write` to add data to the Console window without adding a carriage return.

5. Make a program similar to the one shown in Figure 19-2 that generates all possible four-letter words using the letters A, B, C, and D. (Hint: Make an array containing the letters A, B, C, and D. Use a `foreach` loop to loop through the letters. Inside that loop, use another loop

FIGURE 19-2

to loop through the letters again. After four depths of nested loops, concatenate the looping variables to get the word.)

6. [Games] Copy the program you built for Exercise 18-8 (or download the version on the book's website) and modify it so it displays four bouncing balls. Hints:

➤ Use four `PictureBox` controls to hold the ball images.

➤ When the program starts:

    ➤ Create class-level arrays `Vx` and `Vy` to hold the balls' velocities.

    ➤ Create and initialize an array named `Balls` to hold references to the balls' PictureBoxes.

    ➤ Loop through the `Balls` array and give the balls random initial locations and velocities.

➤ In the `Timer`'s `Tick` event handler, loop through the `Balls` array and update the balls' locations and velocities.

➤ Because balls will hit the sides of the form more often than they did in Exercise 18-8, you may want to change the boing sound effect to something shorter like a click.

7. [Graphics, Games] If you look closely at the program you wrote for Exercise 6, you can see the corners of the balls' `PictureBoxes` when they overlap each other. Copy that program and fix it by following these steps:

➤ Remove the ball `PictureBoxes`.

➤ Define class-level constants `NumBalls = 4`, `BallWidth = 40`, and `BallHeight = 40`.

➤ Create `X` and `Y` arrays to hold the balls' locations. When the form loads, initialize those arrays with random positions.

➤ When the `Timer`'s `Tick` event fires, update the balls' locations and velocities as before (except using the `X` and `Y` arrays instead of the `PictureBox` controls' `Left` and `Top` properties).

➤ After you update all of the balls' locations, call the form's `Refresh` method to make it redraw itself.

➤ Give the form the following `Paint` event handler to draw the balls:

```
// Draw the balls.
private void Form1_Paint(object sender, PaintEventArgs e)
{
    e.Graphics.SmoothingMode =
        System.Drawing.Drawing2D.SmoothingMode.AntiAlias;

    for (int ball = 0; ball < NumBalls; ball++)
    {
        e.Graphics.FillEllipse(Brushes.Red,
            X[ball], Y[ball], BallWidth, BallHeight);
        e.Graphics.DrawEllipse(Pens.Black,
```

```
                    X[ball], Y[ball], BallWidth, BallHeight);
            }
        }
```

➤ If you experiment with the program for a while, you'll notice some flickering. To fix that, set the form's `DoubleBuffered` property to `True`.

8. [Graphics, Games] Copy the program you wrote for Exercise 7 and modify it to give the balls random sizes and colors. Hints:

➤ Make an array named `BallBrushes` to hold `Brush` objects.

➤ In the form's `Load` event handler:

➤ Make an array named `brushes` to hold `Brush` objects. Initialize it to a selection of standard brushes such as `Brushes.Pink` and `Brushes.LightGreen`.

➤ Use code similar to the following to give each ball a brush selected randomly from the `brushes` array:

```
BallBrushes[ball] = brushes[rand.Next(0, brushes.Length)];
```

9. [Games, Hard] Copy the program you built for Exercise 18-14 (or download the version on the book's website) and modify it so it displays three UFOs. Hints:

➤ Use techniques similar to those you used in Exercise 6 to manage the UFOs' positions and velocities.

➤ Loop through the UFOs to see if the laser bolt has hit any of them. If it has, remove the bolt so it doesn't pass through a UFO, possibly hitting one higher up on the form.

10. [Graphics, Games] Make a worm program similar to the one shown in Figure 19-3. The program should draw a chain of circles that bounces around the form.

Hints:

➤ Use a `List<Point>` to keep track of the positions of the circles.

➤ When the `Timer` ticks:

➤ Use velocity components to calculate a new position for the first position in the list.

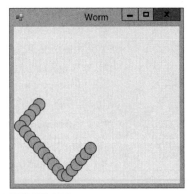

FIGURE 19-3

➤ Use the list's `Insert` method to insert a new `Point` at the beginning of the list for the new position.

➤ Use the list's `RemoveAt` method to remove the last position from the list.

➤ Call the form's `Refresh` method to make it redraw itself.

➤ Make the form's `Paint` event handler loop through the list and draw the worm's circles.

11. [Graphics, Games, Hard] Copy the program you wrote for Exercise 10 and modify it so it displays three worms with different colors. Hints:

   ➤ Store the worms' brushes in an array of Brush objects.

   ➤ Store the lists of worm positions in an array of lists of Point objects (List<Point>[]).

   ➤ Before you use the List<Point>[], you need to initialize it with the new keyword.

   ➤ Before you use a list inside the List<Point>[], you need to initialize it with the new keyword.

12. [Games] Copy the program you built for Exercise 9. The program uses the following code to display the high scores on the HighScoreForm:

```
// Display the high scores.
HighScoresForm highScoresForm = new HighScoresForm();
highScoresForm.nameLabel0.Text = HighScoreNames[0];
highScoresForm.nameLabel1.Text = HighScoreNames[1];
highScoresForm.nameLabel2.Text = HighScoreNames[2];
highScoresForm.nameLabel3.Text = HighScoreNames[3];
highScoresForm.nameLabel4.Text = HighScoreNames[4];

highScoresForm.scoreLabel0.Text = HighScores[0].ToString();
highScoresForm.scoreLabel1.Text = HighScores[1].ToString();
highScoresForm.scoreLabel2.Text = HighScores[2].ToString();
highScoresForm.scoreLabel3.Text = HighScores[3].ToString();
highScoresForm.scoreLabel4.Text = HighScores[4].ToString();
```

Modify the program so it uses two for loops instead. (Hints: Use two arrays holding the form's controls. You'll have to make the change in two places.)

> **NOTE** *Please select the videos for Lesson 19 online at* www.wrox.com/go/ csharp24hourtrainer2evideos.

20

Reusing Code with Methods

Sometimes a program needs to perform the same action in several places. For example, consider the UFO shooting gallery game you wrote for Exercise 19-12 and shown in Figure 20-1.

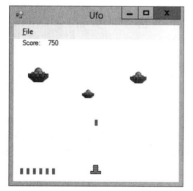

FIGURE 20-1

When a laser bolt hits a UFO, the program takes these steps:

1. Plays the "hit a UFO" sound effect.

2. Increases the player's score and shows it in the score Label.

3. Hides the laser bolt PictureBox.

4. Sets BoltIsAway = false to remember that no laser bolt is currently on the form.

5. If that was the player's last laser bolt:

   a. Plays the "game over" sound effect.

   b. Displays the "game over" label showing the player's final score.

   c. Disables the Timer.

   d. If the player's score is greater than the smallest high score:

   i.   Creates a `NewHighScoreForm`.

   ii.   Places the player's score on the `NewHighScoreForm`.

   iii.   Displays the `NewHighScoreForm`.

   iv.   If the user enters a name and clicks OK:

       1)   Replaces the lowest high score with the player's current score.

       2)   Sorts the high scores.

       3)   Creates a new `HighScoreForm`.

       4)   Places the high scores on the `HighScoreForm`.

       5)   Displays the `HighScoreForm`.

Now suppose a laser bolt moves off the top edge of the form without hitting a UFO. In that case the program must perform the same steps 3 through 5. The way I wrote my program, those steps take 33 lines of code (not counting blank lines and comments). That's a lot of repeated code to write, debug, and maintain.

In fact, the program contains even more repetition. If the user opens the File menu and selects High Scores, the program repeats the last three steps to display a `HighScoresForm`.

Instead of repeating code wherever it was needed, it would be nice if you could centralize the code in a single location and then invoke that code when you need it. In fact, you can do exactly that by using methods.

A *method* is a group of programming statements wrapped in a neat package so you can invoke it as needed. A method can take parameters that the calling code can use to give it extra information. The method can perform some actions and then optionally return a single value to pass information back to the calling code.

> **NOTE** *In programming languages other than C#, methods are sometimes known as routines, subroutines, procedures, subprocedures, subs, or functions (particularly when the method returns a value).*

In this lesson, you learn how to use methods. You learn why they are useful, how to write them, and how to call them from other pieces of code.

METHOD ADVANTAGES

The shooting gallery scenario described in the previous section illustrates one of the key advantages to methods: code reuse. By placing commonly needed code in a single method, you can reuse that code in many places. Clearly that saves you the effort of writing the code several times.

Much more important, it also saves you the trouble of debugging the code several times. Often debugging a piece of complex code takes much longer than typing in the code in the first place, so being able to debug the code in only one place can save you a lot of time and trouble.

Reusing code also greatly simplifies maintenance. If you later find a bug in the code, you only need to fix it in one place. If you had several copies of the code scattered around, you'd need to fix each one individually and make sure all of the fixes were the same. That may sound easy enough, but making synchronized changes is actually pretty hard, particularly in big projects. It's just too easy to miss one change or to make slightly different changes that later cause big problems.

Methods can also sometimes make finding and fixing bugs much easier. For example, suppose you're working on an inventory program that can remove items from inventory for one of many reasons: external sales, internal sales, ownership transfer, spoilage, and so forth. Unfortunately the program occasionally "removes" items that don't exist, leaving you with negative inventory. If the program has code in many places that can remove items from inventory, figuring out which place is causing the problem can be tricky. If all of the code uses the same method to remove items, you can set breakpoints inside that single method to see what's going wrong. When you see the problem occurring, you can trace the program's flow to see where the problem originated.

A final advantage to using methods is that it makes the pieces of the program easier to understand and use. Breaking a complex calculation into a series of simpler method calls can make the code easier to understand. No one can keep all of the details of a large program in mind all at once. Breaking the program into methods makes it possible to understand the pieces separately.

A well-designed method also encapsulates an activity at an abstract level so other developers don't need to know the details. For example, you could write a `FindItemForPurchase` method that searches through a database of vendors to find the best possible deal on a particular item. Now developers writing other parts of the program can call that method without needing to understand exactly how the search works. The method might perform an amazingly complex search to minimize price with sales tax, shipping charges, and long-term expected maintenance costs, but the programmer calling the method doesn't need to know or care how it works.

In summary, some of the key benefits to using methods are:

➤ **Code reuse**—You write the code once and use it many times.

➤ **Centralized debugging**—You only need to debug the shared code once.

➤ **Centralized maintenance**—If you need to fix the code, you only need to do so in the method, not everywhere it is used.

➤ **Problem decomposition**—Methods can break complex problems into simpler pieces.

➤ **Encapsulation**—The method can hide complex details from developers.

METHOD SYNTAX

In C#, all methods must be part of some class. In many simple programs, the main form contains all of the program's code, including all of its methods.

The syntax for defining a method is:

```
accessibility returnType methodName(parameters)
{
    ...statements...
    [return [returnValue];]
}
```

Where:

➤   *accessibility* is an accessibility keyword such as `public` or `private`. This keyword determines what other code in the project can invoke the method.

➤   *returnType* is the data type that the method returns. It can take normal values such as `int`, `bool`, or `string`. It can also take the special value `void` to indicate that the method won't return a result to the calling code.

➤   *methodName* is the name that you want to give the method. You can give the method any valid name. Valid names must start with a letter or underscore and include letters, underscores, and numbers. A valid name also cannot be a keyword such as `if`, `for`, or `while`.

➤   *parameters* is an optional parameter list that you can pass into the method. I'll say more about this shortly.

➤   *statements* are the statements that the method should execute.

➤   *returnValue* is the value returned to the calling code. You can use `return` without a parameter to return from a `void` method. The method also returns if the program executes its last line of code and reaches the closing curly bracket (`}`).

> **NOTE** *You can use the* `return` *statement as many times as you like in a method. For example, some of the branches in an* `if-else` *sequence could lead to* `return` *statements.*
>
> *If the method has a non-*`void` *return type, the C# compiler tries to guarantee that all paths through the code end at a* `return` *statement and will warn you if the code might not return a value.*

The method's parameters allow the calling code to pass information into the method. The parameters in the method's declaration give names to the parameters while they are in use inside the method.

For example, recall the definition of the factorial function. The factorial of a number N is written N! and pronounced *N factorial*. The definition of N! is 1 * 2 * 3 * . . . * N.

The following C# code defines a `Factorial` method:

```
// Return value!
private long Factorial(long value)
{
    long result = 1;
    for (long i = 2; i <= value; i++)
    {
        result *= i;
    }
    return result;
}
```

The method is declared `private` so only code within this class can use it. For simple programs, that's all of the code anyway so this isn't an issue.

The method's data type is `long` so it must return a value of type `long`.

The method's name is `Factorial`. You should try to give each method a name that is simple and that conveys the method's purpose so it's easy to remember what it does.

The method takes a single parameter of type `long` named `value`. Parameters have method scope so `value` is only defined inside the method. In that sense parameters are similar to variables declared inside the method.

The method creates a variable `result` and multiplies it by the values 2, 3, . . . , `value`.

The method finishes by executing the `return` statement, passing it the final value of `result`.

The following code shows how a program might call the `Factorial` method:

```
long number = long.Parse(numberTextBox.Text);
long answer = Factorial(number);
resultTextBox.Text = answer.ToString();
```

This code starts by creating a `long` variable named `number` and initializing it to whatever value is in `numberTextBox`.

The code then calls the `Factorial` method, passing it the value `number` and saving the returned result in the new `long` variable named `answer`.

Notice that the names of the variables in the calling code (`number` and `answer`) have no relation to the names of the parameters and variables used inside the method (`value` and `result`). The method's parameter declaration determines the names the parameters have while inside the method.

The code finishes by displaying the result.

A method's parameter list can include zero, one, or more parameters separated by commas. For example, the following code defines the method `Gcd`, which returns the greatest common divisor (GCD) of two integers. (The GCD of two integers is the largest integer that evenly divides them both.)

```
// Calculate GCD(a, b).
private long Gcd(long a, long b)
{
    long remainder;
    do
    {
        remainder = a % b;
        if (remainder != 0)
        {
            a = b;
            b = remainder;
        }
    } while (remainder > 0);

    return b;
}
```

The following code shows how you might call the `Gcd` method:

```
// Get the input values.
long a = long.Parse(aTextBox.Text);
long b = long.Parse(bTextBox.Text);

// Calculate the GCD.
long result = Gcd(a, b);

// Display the result.
resultTextBox.Text = b.ToString();
```

The code initializes two integers, passes them to the `Gcd` method, and saves the result. It then displays the two integers and their GCD.

USING REF PARAMETERS

Parameter lists have one more feature that's confusing enough to deserve its own section. Parameters can be passed to a method by value or by reference.

When you pass a parameter *by value*, C# makes a *copy* of the value and passes the copy to the method. The method can then mess up its copy without damaging the value used by the calling code.

In contrast, when you pass a value *by reference*, C# passes the *location* of the value's memory into the method. If the method modifies the parameter, the value is changed in the calling code as well.

Normally values are passed by value. That's less confusing because changes that are hidden inside the method cannot mess up the calling code.

Sometimes, however, you may want to pass a parameter by reference. To do that, add the keyword `ref` before the parameter's declaration.

To tell C# that you understand that a parameter is being passed by reference and that it's not just a terrible mistake, you must also add the keyword `ref` before the value you are passing into the method.

For example, suppose you want to write a method named `GetMatchup` that selects two chess players to play against each other. The method should return `true` if it can find a match and `false` if no other matches are possible (because you've played them all). The method can only return one value (`true` or `false`) so it must find some other way to return the two matched players.

The following code shows how the method might be structured:

```
private bool GetMatchup(ref string player1, ref string player2)
{
    // Do complicated stuff to pick an even match.
    ...
    // Somewhere in here the code should set player1 and player2.
    ...

    // We found a match.
    return true;
}
```

The method takes two parameters, `player1` and `player2`, that are `strings` passed by reference. The method performs some complex calculations not shown here to assign values to the variables `player1` and `player2`. It then returns `true` to indicate that it found a match.

The following code shows how a program might call this method:

```
string playerA = null, playerB = null;

if (GetMatchup(ref playerA, ref playerB))
{
    MessageBox.Show(playerA + " versus " + player);
}
else
{
    MessageBox.Show("No match is possible");
}
```

This code declares variables `playerA` and `playerB` to hold the selected players' names. It calls the method, passing it the two player name variables preceded with the `ref` keyword. Depending on whether the method returns `true` or `false`, the program announces the match or says that no match is possible.

USING OUT PARAMETERS

The `out` keyword works similarly to the `ref` keyword except it doesn't require that the input variables be initialized. For example, in the preceding example if you don't initialize `playerA` and `playerB` to some value, Visual Studio will warn you that the variables are not initialized and won't let you run the program. The idea is that the method might need to use the input values of those variables to do its work.

In contrast, if you use the `out` keyword instead of `ref`, the values are assumed to be output-only parameters from the method, and you are not required to initialize them.

If you use the `out` keyword for a parameter, be sure that the method does not try to use the value passed in for that parameter because it may not be initialized. In fact, if the method does try to use the parameter's incoming value, Visual Studio will warn you that it may not be initialized.

> **NOTE** *In general it's considered good practice to avoid returning results through parameters passed by reference because it can be confusing. It's better to use output parameters if possible.*
>
> *An even better approach is to pass the method inputs through parameters and make the method return all of its return values with the* return *statement. For instance, the chess matchup example could return a structure or instance of a class that contains the names of the two players.*

TRY IT

In this Try It, you make a method that calculates the minimum, maximum, and average values for an array of `doubles`. You build the program shown in Figure 20-2 to test the method.

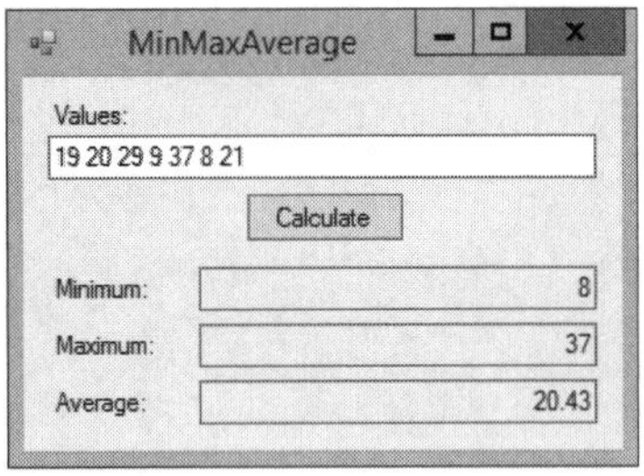

FIGURE 20-2

Lesson Requirements

In this lesson, you:

➤   Build the program shown in Figure 20-2.

➤   Build a method that takes four parameters: an array of `doubles`, and three more return `doubles`. It should loop through the array to find the minimum and maximum and to calculate the average.

➤   Write code to test the method.

> **NOTE** *You can download the code and resources for this lesson from the website at* www.wrox.com/go/csharp24hourtrainer2e.

Hints

➤   Think about how the method needs to use the return parameters. Should they be declared `ref` or `out`?

Step-by-Step

➤   Build the program shown in Figure 20-2.

   1.   This is reasonably straightforward.

➤   Build a method that takes four parameters: an array of `doubles`, and three more return `doubles`. It should loop through the array to find the minimum and maximum and to calculate the average.

   1.   This method calculates its results purely by examining the values in the input array so it doesn't need to use whatever values are passed in through its other parameters. That

means the minimum, maximum, and average parameters should use the out keyword
instead of the ref keyword.

2. Initialize the minimum and maximum variables to the first entry in the array.

3. Initialize a total variable to the first entry in the array.

4. Loop through the rest of the array (skipping the first entry because it has already been
   considered), updating the minimum and maximum variables as needed and adding the
   values in the array to the total.

5. After finishing the loop, divide the total by the number of values to get the average.

The following code shows how you might build this method:

```
// Calculate the minimum, maximum, and average values for the array.
private void FindMinimumMaximumAverage(double[] values,
    out double minimum, out double maximum, out double average)
{
    // Initialize the minimum, maxiumum, and total values.
    minimum = values[0];
    maximum = values[0];
    double total = values[0];

    // Loop through the rest of the array.
    for (int i = 1; i < values.Length; i++)
    {
        if (values[i] < minimum) minimum = values[i];
        if (values[i] > maximum) maximum = values[i];
        total += values[i];
    }

    // Calculate the average.
    average = total / values.Length;
}
```

➤ Write code to test the method.

1. When the user clicks the button, take the TextBox's text and use its Split method to
   break the user's values into an array of strings.

2. Make a double array and use a for loop to parse the text values into it.

3. Call the method to calculate the necessary results.

4. Display the results.

The following code shows how you might build the button's event handler:

```
// Find and display the minimum, maximum, and average of the values.
private void calculateButton_Click(object sender, EventArgs e)
{
    // Get the values.
    string[] textValues = valuesTextBox.Text.Split();
    double[] values = new double[textValues.Length];
    for (int i = 0; i < textValues.Length; i++)
    {
```

```
            values[i] = double.Parse(textValues[i]);
    }

    // Calculate.
    double smallest, largest, average;
    FindMinimumMaximumAverage(values,
        out smallest, out largest, out average);

    // Display the results.
    minimumTextBox.Text = smallest.ToString();
    maximumTextBox.Text = largest.ToString();
    averageTextBox.Text = average.ToString("0.00");
}
```

> **NOTE** *This lesson mentions that returning values through parameters passed by reference isn't a good practice. So how could you modify this example to avoid that?*
>
> *You could break the* `FindMinimumMaximumAverage` *method into three separate methods:* `FindMinimum`, `FindMaximum`, *and* `FindAverage`. *Then each method could return its result via a* `return` *statement. In addition to avoiding parameters passed by reference, that makes each routine perform a single well-focused task so it makes them easier to understand and use. It also makes them easier to use separately in case you only wanted to find the array's minimum and not the maximum or average.*
>
> *(Also note that arrays provide methods that can find these values for you, so you really don't need to write these functions anyway. They're here purely to demonstrate parameters passed by reference.)*

EXERCISES

1. Make a program that calculates the least common multiple (LCM) of two integers. (The LCM of two integers is the smallest integer that the two numbers divide into evenly.) Hints: LCM(a, b) = a * b / GCD(a, b). Also don't write the LCM method from scratch. Instead, make it call the GCD method described earlier in this lesson.

2. A *recursive method* is one that calls itself. Write a recursive factorial method by using the definition:

    ```
    0! = 1
    N! = N * (N-1)!
    ```

    Hint: Be sure to check the stopping condition N = 0 so the method doesn't call itself forever. (Also note that recursive methods can be very confusing to understand and debug so often it's better to write the method without recursion if possible. Some problems have natural recursive definitions, but usually a non-recursive method is better.)

3. Write a program that recursively calculates the Nth Fibonacci number using the definition:

```
Fibonacci(0) = 0
Fibonacci(1) = 1
Fibonacci(N) = Fibonacci(N - 1) + Fibonacci(N - 2)
```

Compare the performance of the recursive factorial and Fibonacci methods when N is around 30 or 40.

4. [SimpleEdit] Copy the SimpleEdit program you built for Exercise 18-3 (or download the version on the book's website) and move the code that checks for unsaved changes into a method named IsDataSafe. The IsDataSafe method should perform the same checks as before and return true if it is safe to continue with whatever operation the user is about to perform (new file, open file, or exit).

Other code that needs to decide whether to continue should call IsDataSafe. For example, the fileNewMenuItem_Click event handler can now look like this:

```
private void fileNewMenuItem_Click(object sender, EventArgs e)
{
    // See if it's safe to continue.
    if (IsDataSafe())
    {
        // Make the new document.
        contentRichTextBox.Clear();

        // There are no unsaved changes now.
        contentRichTextBox.Modified = false;
    }
}
```

5. [Games] Copy the program you wrote for Exercise 19-12 (or download the version on the book's website) and extract the code that moves a UFO into a new method. To do that:

   ➤ Select the code that moves a UFO.

   ➤ Right-click the code and select Quick Actions.

   ➤ Click Extract Method.

   ➤ Change the new method's name to MoveUfo.

6. [Games] Copy the program you wrote for Exercise 5 and extract the code that moves the laser bolt into a new method named MoveLaserBolt.

7. [Games] Copy the program you wrote for Exercise 6 and write a BoltHitUfo method that returns true if the laser bolt hits the UFO with a particular index (passed into the method as a parameter). Use that method in the MoveLaserBolt method.

8. [Games] Copy the program you wrote for Exercise 7. Find the code that removes a laser bolt, determines whether the game is over, and updates the high scores if necessary. Extract that code into a new RemoveLaserBolt method. Modify the program to call RemoveLaserBolt in two places: if the laser bolt hits a UFO and if the laser bolt moves off the top of the form.

9. [Games] Copy the program you wrote for Exercise 8. Find the code that executes when the game is over. (It plays the "game over" sound effect and updates and displays the high scores if necessary.) Extract that code into a new `GameOver` method.

10. [Games] Copy the program you wrote for Exercise 9 and extract the code that displays the high score form into a new `ShowHighScores` method. The program should call this method in two places: once in the `GameOver` method if the user has a new high score and once if the user selects the File menu's High Scores command.

11. [Games] Copy the program you wrote for Exercise 10. Find the code that determines whether the user got a new high score and, if so, updates and displays the high scores. Extract that code into a new `UpdateHighScores` method.

12. [Games] Copy the program you wrote for Exercise 11 and extract the code that randomizes a UFO into a new `RandomizeUfo` method.

Usually it's better to start with a solid design in mind and write methods as you need them rather than refactor an older program as was done in the last several exercises, but at this point the UFO shooting gallery should have no big chunks of duplicated code and no methods that are so long they are hard to understand. It should be much easier to maintain and improve in the future.

Many of the other examples and exercises shown in earlier lessons also contain duplicated code. For further practice, rewrite some of them to move the duplicated code into methods.

NOTE *Please select the videos for Lesson 20 online at* www.wrox.com/go/ csharp24hourtrainer2evideos.

Handling Errors

The best way to avoid user errors is to not give the user the ability to make them in the first place. For example, suppose a program can take purchase orders for between 1 and 100 reams of paper. If the program lets you specify the quantity by using a NumericUpDown control with Minimum = 1 and Maximum = 100, you cannot accidentally enter invalid values like −5 or 10,000.

Sometimes, however, it's hard to build an interface that protects against all possible errors. For example, if the user needs to type in a numeric value, you need to worry about invalid inputs such as 1.2.3 and ten. If you write a program that works with files, you can't always be sure the file will be available when you need it. For example, it might be on a CD that has been removed, or it might be locked by another program.

In this lesson, you learn how to deal with these kinds of unexpected errors. You learn how to protect against invalid values, unavailable files, and other problems that are difficult or impossible to predict and prevent.

ERRORS AND EXCEPTIONS

An *error* is a mistake. It occurs when the program does something incorrect. Sometimes an error is a bug, for example, if the code just doesn't do the right thing.

Sometimes an error is caused by circumstances outside of the program's control. If the program expects the user to enter a numeric value in a textbox but the user types "seven," the program won't be able to continue its work until the user fixes the problem.

Sometimes you can predict when an error may occur. For example, if a program needs to open a file, there's a chance that the file won't exist. In predictable cases such as this one, the program should try to anticipate the error and protect itself. It should check to see if the file exists before it tries to open it. It can then display a message to the user and ask for help.

Other errors are hard or impossible to predict. Even if the file exists, it may be locked by another program. The user entering invalid data is another example. In those cases, the program may need to just try to do its job. If the program tries to do something seriously invalid, it will receive an exception.

An *exception* tells the program that something generally very bad occurred such as trying to divide by zero, trying to access an entry in an array that doesn't exist (for example, setting values[100] = 100 when values only holds 10 items), or trying to convert the text "pickle" into an integer.

In cases like these, the program must *catch* the exception and deal with it. Sometimes it can figure out what went wrong and fix the problem. Other times it might only be able to tell the user about the problem and hope the user can fix it.

> **NOTE** *In C# terms, the code that has the problem* throws *the exception. Code higher up in the chain can catch the exception and try to handle it.*

To catch an exception, a program uses a try-catch block.

TRY-CATCH BLOCKS

In C#, you can use a try-catch block to catch exceptions. One common form of this statement has the following syntax:

```
try
{
    ...codeToProtect...
}
catch (ExceptionType1 ex)
{
    ...exceptionCode1...
}
catch (ExceptionType2 ex)
{
    ...exceptionCode2...
}
finally
{
    ...finallyCode...
}
```

Where:

> ➤ *codeToProtect* is the code that might throw the exception.

> ➤ *ExceptionType1, ExceptionType2* are exception types such as FormatException or DivideByZeroException. If this particular exception type occurs in the *codeToProtect*, the corresponding catch block executes.

> ➤ *ex* is a variable that has the same type as the exception. You pick the name for this variable just as you do when you declare any other variable. If an error occurs, you can use this variable to learn more about what happened.

➤ *exceptionCode* is the code that the program should execute if the corresponding exception occurs.

➤ *finallyCode* is code that always executes whether or not an error occurs.

A `try-catch` block can include any number of `catch` blocks with different exception types. If an error occurs, the program looks through the `catch` blocks in order until it finds one that matches the error. It then executes that block's code and jumps to the `finally` statement if there is one.

If you use a `catch` statement without an exception type and variable, that block catches all exceptions.

NOTE *If you omit the* `catch` *statement's exception type and variable, the code cannot learn anything about the exception that occurred. Sometimes that's okay if you don't really care what went wrong as long as you know that something went wrong.*

An alternative strategy is to catch a generic `Exception` *object, which matches any kind of exception and provides more information. Then you can at least display an error message as shown in the following code, which tries to calculate a student's test score average assuming the variables* `totalScore` *and* `numTests` *are already initialized. If the code throws an exception, the* `catch` *block displays the exception's default description.*

```
try
{
    // Calculate the average.
    int averageScore = totalScore / numTests;

    // Display the student's average score.
    MessageBox.Show("Average Score: " +
        averageScore.ToString("0.00"));
}
catch (Exception ex)
{
    // Display a message describing the exception.
    MessageBox.Show("Error calculating average.\n" + ex.Message);
}
```

In this example the error that this code is most likely to encounter is a `DivideByZeroException` *thrown if* `numTests` *is 0. Because that kind of error is predictable, the code should probably specifically look for* `DivideByZeroException`. *The best strategy is to catch the most specific type of exception possible to get the most information. Then catch more generic exceptions just in case. Better still, it should check* `numTests` *and not perform the calculation if* `numTests` *is 0. Then it can avoid the exception completely.*

A `try-catch` block must include at least one `catch` block or the `finally` block, although none of them needs to contain any code. For example, the following code catches and ignores all exceptions:

```
try
{
    ...codeToProtect...
}
catch
{
}
```

The code in the `finally` block executes whether or not an exception occurs. If an error occurs, the program executes a `catch` block (if one matches the exception) and then executes the `finally` block. If no error occurs, the program executes the `finally` block after it finishes the `codeToProtect` code.

In fact, if the code inside the `try` or `catch` section executes a `return` statement, the `finally` block still executes before the program actually leaves the method! The `finally` block executes no matter how the code leaves the `try-catch` block.

TRYPARSE

One place where problems are likely to occur is when a program parses text entered by the user. Even if users don't enter obviously ridiculous values such a "twelve," they might enter values in a format that you don't expect. For example, you might expect the user to enter an integer dollar amount such as 1200 but the user enters $1,200.00. If you use the `decimal` data type's `Parse` method and don't allow the currency symbol, thousands separator, and decimal point, the `Parse` method will throw an exception.

You can use a `try-catch` block to handle the exception, but it's more efficient to detect the invalid format instead. To do that, you can use the `decimal` data type's `TryParse` method.

A data type's `TryParse` method attempts to parse some text and save the result in a parameter passed with the `out` keyword. The `TryParse` method returns `true` if it successfully parsed the text and `false` if it could not.

For example, the following code tries to parse a value entered by the user:

```
decimal amount;
if (!decimal.TryParse(amountTextBox.Text, out amount))
{
    MessageBox.Show("Invalid format for amount: " +
        amountTextBox.Text +
        "\r\nThe amount should be an integer such as 12.");
    return;
}
```

The code uses `decimal.TryParse` to try to parse the value in `amountTextBox`. If `TryParse` returns `false`, the code displays an error message and then uses a `return` statement to stop processing the value.

The `TryParse` methods can take a `NumberStyles` parameter just as the `Parse` methods can. For example, you can pass `decimal.TryParse` the parameter `NumberStyles.Any` to allow the user to enter values that include currency symbols and thousands separators.

To make things a bit more confusing, the version of `TryParse` that takes a `NumberStyles` parameter also takes a format provider that gives the method information about the culture it should use when parsing the text. If you set that parameter to `null`, the method uses the program's current culture information. For example, the following code is similar to the previous code except it allows thousands separators. The new code is highlighted in bold:

```
decimal amount;
if (!decimal.TryParse(amountTextBox.Text,
    NumberStyles.AllowThousands, null, out amount))
{
    MessageBox.Show("Invalid format for amount: " +
        amountTextBox.Text +
        "\r\nThe amount should be an integer such as 12.");
    return;
}
```

It's generally considered good programming practice to look for the most predictable errors first and only use `try-catch` blocks as a last resort. That usually allows you to give the user the most meaningful error messages.

THROWING EXCEPTIONS

Occasionally it's useful to be able to throw your own exceptions. For example, consider the factorial method you wrote in Lesson 20 and suppose the program invokes the method passing it the value –10 for its parameter. The value –10! is not defined, so what should the method do? It could just declare that –10! is 1 and return that, but that approach could hide a bug in the rest of the program.

A better solution is to throw an exception telling the program what's wrong. The calling code can then use a `try-catch` block to catch the error and tell the user what's wrong.

The following code shows an improved version of the factorial method described in Lesson 20. Before calculating the factorial, the code checks its parameter and, if the parameter is less than zero, it throws a new `ArgumentOutOfRangeException`. The exception's constructor has several overloaded versions. The one used here takes as parameters the name of the parameter that caused the problem and a description of the error:

```
// Return value!
private long Factorial(long value)
{
    // Check the parameter.
    if (value < 0)
    {
        // This is invalid. Throw an exception.
        throw new ArgumentOutOfRangeException(
            "value",
            "value must be at least 0.");
    }
```

```
// Calculate the factorial.
long result = 1;
for (long i = 2; i <= value; i++)
{
    result *= i;
}
return result;
}
```

The following code shows how the program might invoke the new version of the Factorial method. It uses a try-catch block to protect itself in case the Factorial method throws an exception. The block also protects against other errors such as the user entering garbage in the TextBox.

```
// Calculate the factorial.
private void calculateButton_Click(object sender, EventArgs e)
{
    try
    {
        // Get the input value.
        long number = long.Parse(numberTextBox.Text);

        // Calculate the factorial.
        long answer = Factorial(number);

        // Display the factorial.
        resultTextBox.Text = answer.ToString();
    }
    catch (Exception ex)
    {
        // Display an error message.
        MessageBox.Show(ex.Message);
        resultTextBox.Clear();
    }
}
```

> **TIP** *Exceptions take additional overhead and disrupt the natural flow of the code, making it harder to read, so only throw exceptions to signal exceptional conditions.*
>
> *If a method needs to tell the calling code whether it succeeded or failed, that isn't an exceptional condition so use a return value. If a method has an invalid input parameter (such as a 0 in a parameter that cannot be 0), that's an error, so throw an exception.*

TRY IT

In this Try It, you add validation and error handling code to the program you built for Exercise 19-4. When the user clicks the NewItemForm's Calculate and OK buttons, the program should verify that the values make sense and protect itself against garbage such as the user entering the quantity "one," as shown in Figure 21-1.

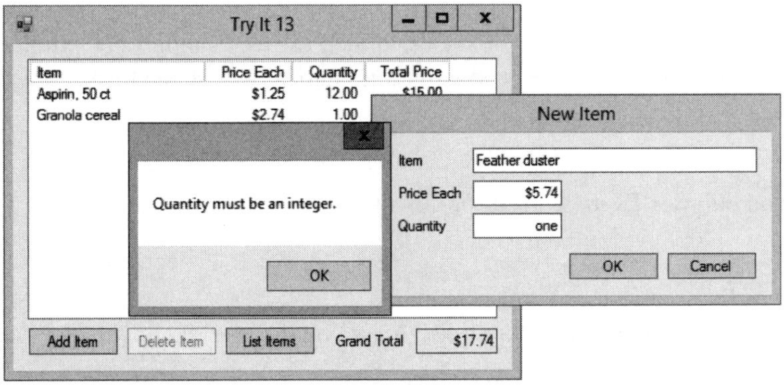

FIGURE 21-1

Lesson Requirements

In this lesson, you:

➤ Copy the program you built for Exercise 19-4 (or download the version on the book's website).

➤ Write a ValuesAreOk method to validate the values entered by the user. It should:

  ➤ Verify that Item, Price Each, and Quantity aren't blank.

  ➤ Use TryParse methods to get the Price Each and Quantity values.

  ➤ Verify that Price Each and Quantity are greater than zero.

  ➤ Calculate the product of Price Each and Quantity to see if the result is too large to fit in a decimal value.

➤ If ValuesAreOk finds a problem, it should:

  ➤ Tell the user.

  ➤ Set focus to the textbox that caused the problem.

  ➤ Return false.

➤ If ValuesAreOk finds that all of the values are okay, it should return true.

> **NOTE** *You can download the code and resources for this lesson from the web-site at* www.wrox.com/go/csharp24hourtrainer2e.

Hints

➤ If the user clicks the OK button, the form should close only if the user's inputs are valid. Be sure the OK button's `DialogResult` property doesn't automatically close the form.

Step-by-Step

➤ Copy the program you built for Exercise 19-4 (or download the version on the book's website).

1. This is straightforward.

➤ Write a `ValuesAreOk` method to validate the values entered by the user. It should:

➤ Verify that Item, Price Each, and Quantity aren't blank.

➤ Use `TryParse` methods to get the Price Each and Quantity values.

➤ Verify that Price Each and Quantity are greater than zero.

➤ Calculate the product of Price Each and Quantity to see if the result is too large to fit in a `decimal` value.

➤ If `ValuesAreOk` finds a problem, it should:

➤ Tell the user.

➤ Set focus to the textbox that caused the problem.

➤ Return `false`.

1. The current program only enables the OK button when the Item, Price Each, and Quantity are all non-blank, so you don't need to add any code to verify that they aren't blank. The user can't click the OK button unless they're non-blank.

2. The following code shows how you might try to parse Price Each:

```
// Try to parse PriceEach.
if (!decimal.TryParse(priceEachTextBox.Text,
    NumberStyles.Any, null, out PriceEach))
{
    MessageBox.Show("Price Each must be a currency value.");
    priceEachTextBox.Focus();
    return false;
}
```

When you parse quantity, you could use `NumberStyles.Integer` to require a plain integer, or you could use `NumberStyles.AllowThousands` to allow thousands separators.

3. The following code shows how you might verify that `PriceEach` is greater than zero:

```
// Verify that PriceEach is greater than zero.
if (PriceEach <= 0)
{
    MessageBox.Show("Price each must be greater than 0.");
    priceEachTextBox.Focus();
    return false;
}
```

4. The following code shows how you might verify that the product of Price Each and Quantity fits in the `decimal` data type:

```
// See if Quantity * PriceEach is too big.
try
{
    decimal total = Quantity * PriceEach;
}
catch (Exception ex)
{
    MessageBox.Show(ex.Message);
    return false;
}
```

You can test that part of the code by setting Price Each to 1e28 and Quantity to 1000.

➤ If `ValuesAreOk` finds that all of the values are okay, it should return `true`.

1. If the method makes it past all of the previous tests, it should use the statement `ItemName = itemTextBox.Text` to save the item name for the main program to read.

2. The method should then end with the statement `return true`.

EXERCISES

1. Copy the program you wrote for the Try It. That program still has one more problem (at least). If the sum of the values of the items is too big to fit in a `decimal`, the main program will crash. You can test this by entering two items with Price Each 1e28 and Quantity 7.

   Use a `try-catch` block to protect the main program from this problem. Enclose the code that displays the `NewItemForm` in a loop that executes as long as the new item's values cause problems.

   (Did you anticipate this problem? How about the problem of a new item having a price of $1e28 and quantity 1000? Anticipating and protecting against these kinds of problems is part of what makes programming challenging.)

2. The limits used by the program you wrote for Exercise 1 are ludicrous. You could use the program to order 1 million pencils or a notepad that cost $1e28. That's more money than there is in the entire world. (Probably more money than exists in the entire universe, depending on the currency exchange rate with the Andromeda galaxy.)

Copy the program you wrote for Exercise 1 and add *sanity checks*. Modify the ValuesAreOk method so it allows up to 100 items and Price Each up to $100.

3. Even if it's unusual for an item to have a price of more than $100 or for someone to order more than 100 of a particular item, it still may be possible. Copy the program you wrote for Exercise 2 and modify the sanity checks. If a value exceeds the normal limits, ask the user if the value is correct and continue if the user says Yes.

4. Copy the LCM program you built for Exercise 20-1 (or download the version on the book's website) and add error handling to it. If a value causes an error, display a message and set focus to its textbox. Hints: Validate both the GCD and LCM methods so they only allow inputs greater than 0. That way they're both covered if a different program uses GCD directly. Also use a try-catch block in the Calculate button's Click event handler to protect against format errors.

5. Copy the Fibonacci program you built for Exercise 19-2 (or download the version on the book's website) and add error handling and validation to it. Protect the program against format errors. Also move the calculation itself into a new method and make it throw an exception if its input is less than 0. (Hint: Test the program with the input 200 and make sure the result makes sense.)

6. [SimpleEdit] Copy the SimpleEdit program you built for Exercise 20-4 (or download the version on the book's website) and add error handling to the places where the program opens and saves files.

    To test the program, run it, type some text, and then close the program. Then:

    ➤   Use Microsoft Word to open the file Test.rtf in the program's executable directory. Then try to use SimpleEdit to open the file.

    ➤   Close Word, open the file in SimpleEdit, and then open the file again in Word. Now make a change in SimpleEdit and try to save the file.

    ➤   With the file still open in Word, start a new file in SimpleEdit, type some text, and use the File menu's Save As command to try to save the new file as Test.rtf.

    In all three tests, Word should have the Test.rtf file locked so SimpleEdit should display an error message.

7. The quadratic equation finds solutions to equations with the form $ax^2 + bx + c = 0$ where a, b, and c are constants. The solutions to this equation (the values of x that make it true) are given by the quadratic formula:

$$x = \frac{-b \pm \sqrt{b^2 - 4ac}}{2a}$$

Build a program similar to the one shown in Figure 21-2 that calculates solutions to quadratic equations. Hints:

    ➤   Use TryParse to protect against format errors.

    ➤   Use Math.Sqrt to take square roots.

➤ The equation has zero, one, or two real solutions depending on whether the *discriminant b2 – 4ac* is less than, equal to, or greater than zero. Use if statements to avoid trying to take the square root of a negative number.

➤ If *a* is 0, then this is a linear equation not a quadratic, and the quadratic formula tries to divide by zero. Unfortunately C# doesn't consider that an error and just sets the result equal to the special value NaN (which stands for "not a number"). After performing the calculation, use double.IsNaN to see if the result is NaN and display "Not a quadratic" if it is.

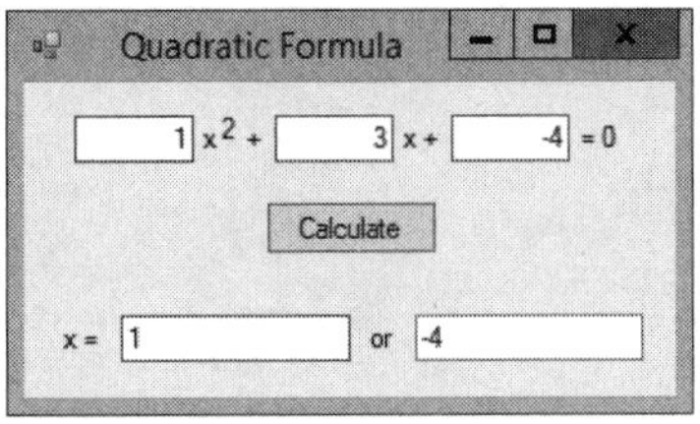

FIGURE 21-2

8. Several of the programs you've built or described in this book so far enable a Button only when a TextBox contains non-blank text. If the user should enter a number, you can improve the program by only enabling the Button if the text has a valid format. Try this out by writing a program that calculates the area of a circle. Hints:

➤ Use TryParse to make the TextBox's TextChanged event handler enable the Calculate Button when the user has entered a valid double and that value is at least zero.

➤ Use the formula *area* = $\pi \times radius^2$.

➤ If the user enters a value that is too large (such as 1e200), display the message, "The radius is too big."

9. Make a program that contains a TextBox for each of the basic data types byte, sbyte, ushort, short, uint, int, ulong, long, float, double, decimal, bool, and char. Use event handlers to set each TextBox's background color to white if the TextBox contains a valid value of the corresponding data type and pink if it does not.

NOTE *Please select the videos for Lesson 21 online at* www.wrox.com/go/ csharp24hourtrainer2evideos.

Preventing Bugs

Many programmers believe that the way to make a program robust is to make it able to continue running even if it encounters errors. For example, consider the following version of the Factorial method:

```
// Recursively calculate n!
private long Factorial(long n)
{
    if (n <= 1) return 1;
    return n * Factorial(n - 1);
}
```

This method is robust in the sense that it can handle nonsensical inputs such as −10. The function cannot calculate −10!, but at least it doesn't crash so you might think this is a safe method.

Unfortunately, although the function doesn't crash on this input, it also doesn't return a correct result because −10! is not defined. That makes the program continue running even though it has produced an incorrect result.

The method also has a problem if its input is greater than 20. In that case, the result is too big to fit in the long data type so the calculations cause an integer overflow. By default, the program silently ignores the error, and the result you get uses whatever bits are left after the overflow. In this case, the result looks like a large negative number. Again the method doesn't crash but it doesn't return a useful result, either.

In general, bugs that cause a program to crash are a lot easier to find and fix than bugs like this one that produce incorrect results but that continue running.

In this lesson, you learn techniques for detecting and correcting bugs. You learn how to make bugs jump out so they're easy to fix instead of remain hidden.

INPUT ASSERTIONS

In C# programming, an *assertion* is a statement that the code claims is true. If the statement is false, the program stops running so you can decide whether a bug occurred.

One way to make an assertion is to evaluate the statement and, if it is false, throw an exception. That guarantees that the program cannot continue running if the assertion is false.

The following code shows a `Factorial` method with assertions. If the method's parameter is less than 0 or greater than 20, the code throws an exception:

```
// Recursively calculate n!
private long Factorial(long n)
{
    // Validate the input.
    if ((n < 0) || (n > 20))
        throw new ArgumentOutOfRangeException(
            "n", "Factorial parameter must be between 0 and 20.");

    if (n <= 1) return 1;
    return n * Factorial(n - 1);
}
```

To make this kind of assertion easier, the .NET Framework provides a `Debug` class. The `Debug` class's static `Assert` method takes as a parameter a boolean value. If the value is `false`, `Assert` displays an error message showing the program's stack dump at the time so you can figure out where the error occurred.

The following code shows a new version of the factorial method that uses `Debug.Assert`. The optional second parameter to `Debug.Assert` gives a message that should be displayed if the assertion fails:

```
// Recursively calculate n!
private long Factorial(long n)
{
    // Validate the input.
    Debug.Assert((n >= 0) && (n <= 20),
        "Factorial parameter must be between 0 and 20.");

    if (n <= 1) return 1;
    return n * Factorial(n - 1);
}
```

> **NOTE** *The* Debug *class is in the* System.Diagnostics *namespace. If you want to use it without including the namespace, as in the preceding code, you should include the following* using *directive at the top of the file:*
>
> ```
> using System.Diagnostics;
> ```

Normally when you develop a program you make debug builds. These include extra debugging symbols so you can step through the code in the debugger. If you switch to a release build, those symbols are omitted, making the compiled program a bit smaller. The `Debug.Assert` method also has no effect in release builds.

The idea is that you can use Debug.Assert to test the program but then skip the assertions after the program is debugged and ready for release to end users. Of course this works only if the code is robust enough to behave correctly even if a bug does slip past the testing process and appears in the release build. In the case of the Factorial method, this code must always protect itself against input errors so it should throw an exception rather than use Debug.Assert.

To switch from a debug to a release build or vice versa, open the Build menu and select the Configuration Manager command to display the dialog shown in Figure 22-1. Select Debug or Release from the dropdown and click Close.

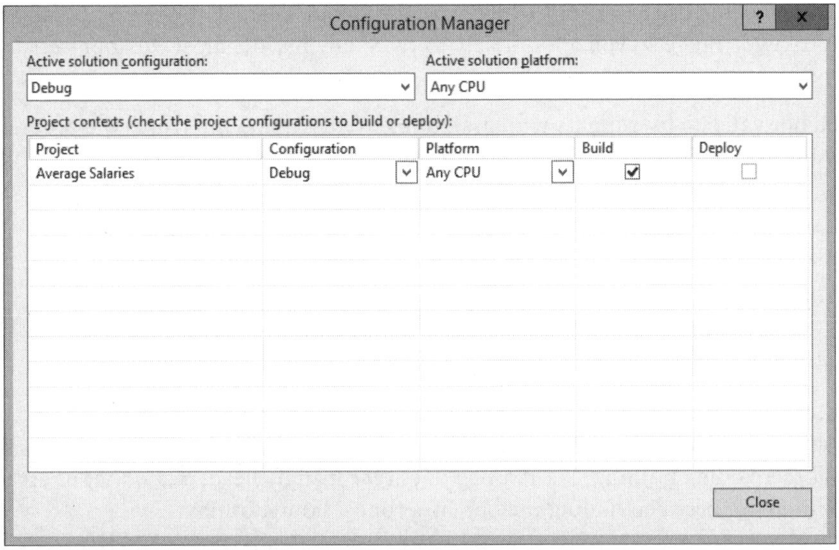

FIGURE 22-1

When you build the program, Visual Studio places the compiled executable in the project's bin\Debug or bin\Release subdirectory. Be sure you use the correct version or you may find Debug.Assert statements displaying errors in what you thought was a release build.

> **NOTE** *The* Debug *class provides some other handy methods in addition to* Assert. *The* WriteLine *method displays a message in the Output window. You can use it to display messages showing you what methods are executing, to display parameter values, and to give you other information that you might otherwise need to learn by stepping through the code in the debugger.*
>
> *The* Debug *class's* Indent *method lets you change the indentation of output produced by* Debug.WriteLine *so, for example, you can indicate nesting of method calls.*
>
> *Like the other* Debug *methods, these do nothing in release builds so the end user never sees these messages.*

OTHER ASSERTIONS

In addition to input assertions, a method can make other assertions as it performs calculations. A method can use assertions to check intermediate results and to validate final results before returning them. A method can even use assertions to validate the value it receives from another method.

Often these assertions cannot be as exact as those you can perform on inputs, but you may still be able to catch some really ludicrous values.

For example, suppose an order-processing form lets the user enter items for purchase and then calculates the total cost. You could use assertions to verify that the total cost is between $0.01 and $1 million. This is a pretty wide range so you are unlikely to catch any but the most egregious errors, but you may catch a few.

Note that you should not validate user inputs with assertions. An assertion interrupts the program so you can try to find a bug. Your code should check for user input errors and handle them without interrupting the program. Instead of using assertions, you should use `TryParse`, `try-catch` blocks, and `if` statements to determine whether the user's input makes sense. Remember, when you make a release build, `Debug.Assert` calls go away so you cannot rely on them to validate the user's values.

One drawback to assertions is that it's hard to make programmers use them. When you're writing code, it's hard to convince yourself that the code could be wrong. After all, if you knew there was a bug in the code, you'd fix it.

Assertions are like seat belts, airbags, and bicycle helmets. You don't use them because you expect to need them today; you use them just on the off chance that you'll need them someday. Usually your assertions will just sit there doing nothing, but if a bug does rear its ugly head, a good set of assertions can make the difference between finding the bug in seconds, hours, or days.

To summarize, you can use assertions to protect a method against invalid inputs and to validate its outputs. If you want an assertion to only occur in debug builds, use `Debug.Assert`. If you want a test to be included in release builds, use your own `if` statement to check the condition and throw an exception if the condition fails. In particular, use `Debug.Assert` to catch unusual but valid values so you can decide whether they are bugs during testing.

TRY IT

In this Try It, you write a method to calculate the average of a set of salaries. Calculating the average is easy. The interesting part is adding assertions to make sure the method is being used correctly.

To test the method, you build the program shown in Figure 22-2.

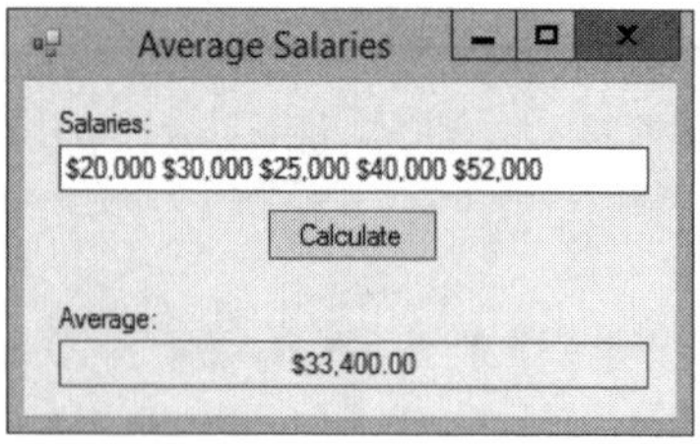

The focus of this Try It is on the method that calculates the average, not on the user interface. The assumption is that some other

FIGURE 22-2

part of a larger program would call this method, so the user interface shown in Figure 22-2 is purely for testing purposes. A real program would not allow the user to enter invalid values. Instead it might take the values from a database. In that case, the method's assertions protect it from invalid data in the database.

Lesson Requirements

In this lesson, you:

➤ Build a program similar to the one shown in Figure 22-2.

➤ When the user clicks Calculate, make the program split the values entered in the TextBox apart, copy them into an array of decimals, pass them to the AverageSalary method, and display the result.

➤ Make the AverageSalary method validate its inputs by asserting that the array has a reasonable number of elements and that the salaries are reasonable. (Assume you're not working on Wall Street so salaries are at least $10,000 and less than $1 million.) Also validate the average.

> **NOTE** *You can download the code and resources for this lesson from the website at* www.wrox.com/go/csharp24hourtrainer2e.

Hints

➤ Think about how the program should react in a final release build for each of the input conditions.

For example, if the values array contains a salary of $1,600, what should the method do? In this case, that value is unusual but it could be valid (perhaps the company hired an intern for a week) so the method can calculate a meaningful (although unusual) result. The method should check this condition with Debug.Assert so it can calculate a result in the release version.

For another example, suppose the values array is empty. In this case the method cannot calculate a meaningful value so it should throw an exception to make the calling code deal with the problem.

Step-by-Step

➤ Build a program similar to the one shown in Figure 22-2.

1. This is reasonably straightforward.

➤ When the user clicks Calculate, make the program split the values entered in the TextBox apart, copy them into an array of decimals, pass them to the AverageSalary method, and display the result.

1. You can use code similar to the following:

```
// Calculate and display the average salary.
private void calculateButton_Click(object sender, EventArgs e)
{
    try
    {
        // Copy the salaries into an array.
        string[] string_salaries = salariesTextBox.Text.Split();
        decimal[] salaries = new decimal[string_salaries.Length];
        for (int i = 0; i < string_salaries.Length; i++)
        {
            salaries[i] =
                decimal.Parse(string_salaries[i], NumberStyles.Any);
        }

        // Calculate the average.
        decimal averageSalary = AverageSalary(salaries);

        // Display the result.
        averageTextBox.Text = averageSalary.ToString("C");
    }
    catch (Exception ex)
    {
        averageTextBox.Clear();
        MessageBox.Show(ex.Message);
    }
}
```

➤ Make the AverageSalary method validate its inputs by asserting that the array has a reasonable number of elements and that the salaries are reasonable. (Assume you're not working on Wall Street so salaries are at least $10,000 and less than $1 million.) Also validate the average.

2. You can use code similar to the following:

```
// Calculate the average of this array of salaries.
private decimal AverageSalary(decimal[] salaries)
{
    // Sanity checks.
    if (salaries.Length < 1)
    {
        throw new ArgumentOutOfRangeException("salaries",
            "AverageSalary method cannot calculate average " +
            "salary for an empty array.");
    }
    Debug.Assert(salaries.Length < 100, "Too many salaries.");
    for (int i = 0; i < salaries.Length; i++)
    {
        Debug.Assert(salaries[i] >= 10000, "Salary is too small.");
        Debug.Assert(salaries[i] < 1000000, "Salary is too big.");
    }

    // Calculate the result.
    decimal total = 0;
```

```
        for (int i = 0; i < salaries.Length; i++)
        {
            total += salaries[i];
        }
        decimal result = total / salaries.Length;

        // Validate the result.
        Debug.Assert(result >= 10000, "Average salary is too small.");
        Debug.Assert(result < 1000000, "Average salary is too big.");

        return result;
    }
```

EXERCISES

1. Suppose you're writing a method to sort orders based on priority. Use the following definition for an Order structure:

    ```
    private struct Order
    {
        public int OrderId;
        public int Priority;
    }
    ```

    Write the SortOrders method, which takes as a parameter an array of Orders and sorts them. Don't actually write the code that sorts the orders, just write assertions to validate the inputs and outputs.

2. Build the program shown in Figure 22-3 to convert temperatures between the Fahrenheit, Celsius, and Kelvin scales.

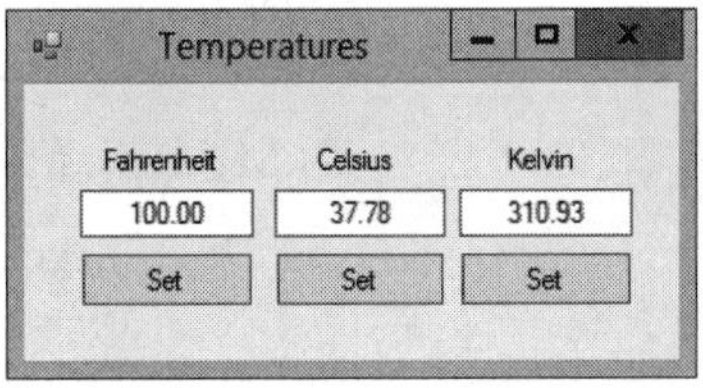

    Write the methods FahrenheitToCelsius, KelvinToCelsius, CelsiusToFahrenheit, and CelsiusToKelvin to perform the conversions using the following formulas:

    FIGURE 22-3

    $$°C = (°F − 32) × 5 / 9$$

    $$°C = °K − 273.15$$

    $$°F = °C × 9 / 5 + 32$$

    $$°K = °C + 273.15$$

    Make the conversion methods use assertions to ensure that Fahrenheit values are between −130 and 140, Celsius values are between −90 and 60, and Kelvin values are between 183 and 333.

3. Make a program that lets the user input miles and gallons of fuel and calculates miles per gallon using a MilesPerGallon method. Make the method protect itself against miles and gallons values that are too big or too small. Make it also validate its result so it doesn't return values that are too large or small.

4. Copy the Fibonacci program you wrote for Exercise 20-3 (or download the version on the book's website). Because of the recursive way the program calculates Fibonacci numbers, it takes a noticeable amount of time to calculate values larger than around the 35th Fibonacci number. It can still calculate larger values, however. Add appropriate input validation to the Fibonacci method.

5. Exercise 12-11 asks you to debug a program that calculates interest. Copy the fixed program (or download the version on the book's website) and add appropriate input validation.

6. Exercise 12-12 asks you to debug a program that uses several methods to calculate the amount of time needed to double an investment at various interest rates. Copy the fixed program (or download the version on the book's website) and add appropriate input validation.

7. [Graphics, Hard] Make a program similar to the one shown in Figure 22-4 to display a histogram showing student test scores.

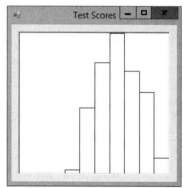

FIGURE 22-4

Hints:

➤ Make a class-level Scores array and initialize it to random values in the form's Load event handler. (Hint: For each score, I used the sum of three random values in the ranges 10–25, 10–25, and 10–50 to get a somewhat curved distribution.)

➤ Place a PictureBox on the form. Make its Resize event handler refresh the PictureBox. Make its Paint event handler call a DrawGraph method.

➤ Make the DrawGraph method do the following:

➤ Take as parameters the available size in which to draw the bar chart, the Graphics object on which to draw, and the test scores.

➤ Make 10 bins to count scores in the ranges 0–19, 20–29, 30–39, ... , 90–100. (Hint: Make the number of bins a constant so you can change it easily.)

➤ Loop through the scores and increment the corresponding bins. (Hint: Be sure to place scores of 100 in the last bin.)

➤ Loop through the bins and find the largest count. Use that value to calculate a scale factor that makes the largest count fill the available height. (Hint: scale = available height / largest count.)

➤ Calculate the bar width. (Hint: width = available width / number of bars.)

➤ Loop through the bins and draw their bars. (Hint: Remember that drawing coordinates start with (0, 0) in the upper-left corner and increase down and to the right.)

8.   [Graphics] Copy the program you wrote for Exercise 7. (Or download the version on the book's website if you didn't do it. I warned you that it was hard.) Add validation code to the DrawGraph method to make sure the available size and test scores are reasonable.

> **NOTE** *Please select the videos for Lesson 22 online at* www.wrox.com/go/ csharp24hourtrainer2evideos.

SECTION IV
Classes

The lessons in Section III focus on C# programming statements. They explain how to make decisions with `if` and `switch` statements, repeat program steps with loops, reuse code with methods, and catch exceptions.

Methods are particularly useful for programming at a higher level because they let you encapsulate complex behaviors in a tightly wrapped package. For example, you might write a `CalculateGrade` method that determines a student's grades. This method can hide all of the details of how grades are calculated. (Are tests graded on a curve? Is the grade a weighted average of tests and homework assignments? How much is attendance worth?) The main program only needs to know how to call the method, not how it works.

Classes provide another even more powerful method for abstracting complex entities into manageable packages. For example, a `Student` class might embody the idea of a student and include basic information (name, address, phone), the courses that the student is taking, grades (test scores, homework grades), and even attendance. It could also include methods such as `CalculateGrade` for manipulating the `Student` data.

The lessons in this section explain classes. They explain how you can build classes, make one class inherit the capabilities of another, and make a class override the features of its parent class.

▶ **LESSON 23:** Defining Classes

▶ **LESSON 24:** Initializing Objects

▶ **LESSON 25:** Fine-Tuning Classes

▶ **LESSON 26:** Overloading Operators

▶ **LESSON 27:** Using Interfaces

▶ **LESSON 28:** Making Generic Classes

Defining Classes

This book hasn't emphasized the fact, but you've been working with classes since the very beginning. The very first program you created in Lesson 1 included several classes such as the program's main form and some behind-the-scenes classes that help get the program running. Since then, you've used all kinds of control classes, the `MessageBox` class, the `Array` class, collection classes, and more. You can even treat primitive data types such as `int` and `string` as classes under some circumstances.

In this lesson you learn how to create your own classes. You learn how to define a class and give it properties, methods, and events to make it useful.

WHAT IS A CLASS?

A *class* defines a type of object. It defines the properties, methods, and events provided by its type of object. After you define a class, you can make as many instances of that class as you like.

For example, the `Button` class defines the properties and behaviors of a button. You can create any number of instances of `Buttons` and place them on your forms.

You can think of a class as a blueprint for making objects. When you create an instance of the class, you use the blueprint to make an object that has the properties and behaviors defined by the class.

You can also think of a class as a cookie cutter. Once you've created the cookie cutter, you can make any number of cookies that all have the same shape.

Classes are very similar to the structures described in Lesson 17, and many of the techniques you learned there apply here as well. For example, you can give a class fields that an instance of the class can use to perform calculations.

Several important differences exist between structures and classes, but one of the most important is that structures are value types while classes are reference types. Perhaps the most confusing consequence of this is that when you assign structure variable A equal to structure variable B, A becomes a copy of B. In contrast, if you assign class variable C equal to class variable D, then variable C now points to the same object that variable D does.

For a more detailed discussion of some of these differences, see the section "Structures Versus Classes" in Lesson 17.

The rest of this lesson focuses on classes and doesn't talk specifically about structures.

> **NOTE** *Note that the same techniques apply to structures and classes. For example, structures have the same benefits as classes described in the following section. Just because I'm describing them here doesn't mean I'm trying to imply that classes are better because they have these advantages and structures don't.*

CLASS BENEFITS

The biggest benefit of classes is encapsulation. A well-designed class hides its internal workings from the rest of the program so the program can use the class without knowing how the class works.

For example, suppose you build a Turtle class to represent a turtle crawling across the screen drawing lines as it moves. The class would need properties such as X, Y, and Direction to define the Turtle's location and direction. It might also provide methods such as Turn to make it change direction and Move to make it move.

The Turtle class needs to know how to draw the Turtle's path as it moves, but the main program doesn't need to know how it works. It doesn't need to know about Graphics objects, Pens, or the trigonometric functions the Turtle uses to figure out where to go. The main program only needs to know how to set the Turtle's properties and call its methods.

Some other benefits of classes (and structures) include:

➤ **Grouping data and code**—The code that makes a Turtle move is right in the same object as the data that determines the Turtle's position and direction.

➤ **Code reuse**—You only need to write the code for the Turtle class once and then all instances of the class get to use it. You get even more code reuse through inheritance, which is described in the section "Inheritance" later in this lesson.

➤ **Polymorphism**—Polymorphism means you can treat an object as if it were from another class as long as it inherits from that class. For example, a Student is a type of Person so you should be able to treat a Student object as if it were either a Student or a Person. The section "Polymorphism" later in this lesson describes this further.

MAKING A CLASS

Now that you know a bit about what classes are good for, it's time to learn how to build one.

Making a class in C# is simple. Open the Project menu and select Add Class. Give the class a good name and click Add.

Initially the class looks something like the following:

```
using System;
using System.Collections.Generic;
using System.Linq;
using System.Text;
using System.Threading.Tasks;

namespace MyProgram
{
    class Employee
    {
    }
}
```

Here `MyProgram` is your program's default namespace, which is normally the same as the program's name. It is used as the namespace for all of the forms and other classes that you add to the program.

`Employee` is the name that I gave the class in this example.

At this point, the class doesn't contain any data or methods so it can't do anything. You can write code to create an instance of the class, but it will just sit there. To make the class useful, you need to add properties, methods, and events:

➤ *Properties* are values associated with a class. For example, an `Employee` class might define `FirstName`, `LastName`, and `EmployeeId` properties.

➤ *Methods* are actions that an object can perform. For example, an `Employee` class might provide a `CalculateBonus` method that calculates the employee's end-of-year bonus based on performance during the year.

➤ *Events* are *raised* by the class to tell the rest of the program that something interesting happened, sort of like raising a flag to draw attention to something. For example, the `Employee` class might raise a `TooManyHours` event if the program tried to assign an employee more than 40 hours of work in a week.

Properties, methods, and events allow a program to control and interact with objects. The following sections explain how you can add properties, methods, and events to your classes.

Properties

If you give a class a public variable, other pieces of code can get and set that variable values. This kind of variable is called a *field*. A field is similar to a property but it has one big disadvantage: it provides unrestricted access to its value. That means other parts of the program could dump any garbage into the field without the class being able to stop them.

In contrast, a class implements a property by using *accessor methods* that can include code to protect the class from garbage values. You learn more about this as you see how to build properties.

The following sections describe the two most common approaches for implementing properties: auto-implemented properties and backing fields.

Auto-Implemented Properties

The easiest way to make a property is to use an auto-implemented property. The syntax for an auto-implemented property is:

```
accessibility dataType Name { get; set; }
```

Here `accessibility` determines what code can use the property. It can be `public`, `private`, and so on. The `dataType` determines the property's data type and `Name` determines its name. The `get` and `set` keywords indicate that other code should be able to get and set the property's value.

> **NOTE** *You can omit the* set *clause to create a read-only property.*

The following code creates a simple property named `FirstName` of type `string`:

```
public string FirstName { get; set; }
```

Backing Fields

When you make an auto-implemented property, C# automatically generates accessors that let you get and set the property's value. You can use those accessors without needing to know the details of how they work.

When you make a property that is not auto-implemented, you need to write the accessors yourself.

The following shows the basic syntax used to define a property that is not auto-implemented:

```
accessibility dataType Name
{
    get
    {
        ...getCode...
    }
    set
    {
        ...setCode...
    }
}
```

Here `accessibility`, `dataType`, and `Name` are the same as before. The `getCode` and `setCode` are the pieces of code that get and set the property's value somehow.

One common way to implement this kind of property is with a backing field. A *backing field* is a field that stores data to represent the property. The `getCode` and `setCode` use the backing field to get and set the property's value.

The following C# code shows a version of the `Direction` property stored in the backing field named `direction`:

```
// The Turtle's direction in degrees.
private int direction = 0;        // Backing field.
public int Direction
{
    get { return direction; }
    set { direction = value; }
}
```

The code starts by defining the field `direction` to hold the property's value. The field is private so only the code inside the class can see it.

The property's `get` accessor simply returns the value of `direction`.

The property's `set` accessor saves a new value in the backing field `direction`. The new value that the calling code is trying to assign to the property is stored in a parameter named `value`. This parameter is a bit odd because it isn't declared anywhere. The `set` accessor implicitly defines `value` and can use it.

The preceding code simply copies values in and out of the backing field, so why didn't you just make the backing field public and not bother with a property? There are several reasons.

First, a property hides its details from the outside world, increasing the class's encapsulation. As far as the outside world is concerned, a description of the `Direction` property tells you *what* is stored (the direction in degrees) but not *how* it is stored (as an integer value in degrees).

This example stores the direction in degrees, but suppose you decided that the class would work better if you stored the direction in radians. If `Direction` is a field, then any code that uses it would now break because it is using degrees. If you use accessors, they can translate between degrees and radians as needed so the code outside the class doesn't need to know that anything has changed.

The following code shows a new version of the `Direction` property that stores the value in radians. As far as the code outside the class is concerned, nothing has changed and that code can still work in degrees.

```
// The Turtle's direction in radians.
private double direction = 0;        // Backing field.
public int Direction
{
    get { return (int)(direction * 180 / Math.PI); }
    set { direction = value * Math.PI / 180; }
}
```

You can also add validation code to property accessors. For example, suppose the `Direction` property represents an angle in degrees and you only want to allow values between 0 and 359. The following code asserts that the new value is between 0 and 359 degrees. The program can continue correctly if the value is outside of this range so the code uses `Debug.Assert` instead of throwing an exception:

```
// The Turtle's direction in degrees.
private int direction = 0;        // Backing field.
public int Direction
```

```
{
    get { return direction; }
    //set { direction = value; }
    set
    {
        Debug.Assert((value >= 0) && (value <= 359),
            "Direction should be between 0 and 359 degrees");
        direction = value;
    }
}
```

Property accessors also give you a place to set breakpoints if something goes wrong. For example, if you know that some part of your program is setting a Turtle's Direction to 45 when it should be setting it to 60 but you don't know where, you could set a breakpoint in the set accessor to see where the change is taking place.

TRY IT

Because classes are important and somewhat confusing, this lesson includes three Try Its. In this first Try It, you create a simple Person class with FirstName, LastName, City, Street, and Zip properties that have some simple validations. You also build a simple test application shown in Figure 23-1.

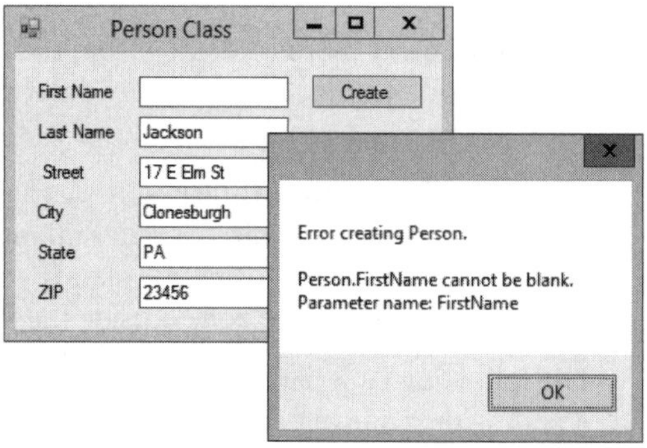

Lesson Requirements

In this lesson, you:

➤ Build the program shown in Figure 23-1.

➤ Create a Person class.

➤ Make auto-implemented properties for Street, City, State, and Zip.

➤ Make FirstName and LastName properties that use backing fields. Add validation code to their set accessors to prevent you from setting FirstName or LastName to a null or blank value.

FIGURE 23-1

Step-by-Step

➤ Build the program shown in Figure 23-1.

   1. This is reasonably straightforward.

➤ Create a Person class.

   1. Use the Project menu's Add Class item. Name the class Person.

➤ Make auto-implemented properties for Street, City, State, and Zip.

   1. You can use code similar to the following:

```
// Auto-implemented properties.
public string Street { get; set; }
```

```
public string City { get; set; }
public string State { get; set; }
public string Zip { get; set; }
```

➤ Make `FirstName` and `LastName` properties that use backing fields. Add validation code to their `set` accessors to prevent you from setting `FirstName` or `LastName` to a null or blank value.

1. The following code shows how you might implement the `FirstName` property. The code for the `LastName` property is similar.

```
// FirstName property.
private string firstName = "";// Backing field.
public string FirstName
{
    get
    {
        return firstName;
    }
    set
    {
        if (value == null)
            throw new ArgumentOutOfRangeException("FirstName",
                "Person.FirstName cannot be null.");
        if (value.Length < 1)
            throw new ArgumentOutOfRangeException("FirstName",
                "Person.FirstName cannot be blank.");
    }
}
```

METHODS

A method is simply a piece of code in the class that other parts of the program can execute. The following method shows how the `Turtle` class might implement its `Move` method:

```
// Make the Turtle move the indicated distance
// in its current direction.
public void Move(int distance)
{
    // Calculate the new position.
    double radians = Direction * Math.PI / 180;
    int newX = (int)(X + Math.Cos(radians) * distance);
    int newY = (int)(Y + Math.Sin(radians) * distance);

    // Draw to the new position.
    using (Graphics gr = Graphics.FromImage(Canvas))
    {
        gr.DrawLine(Pens.Blue, X, Y, newX, newY);
    }

    // Save the new position.
    X = newX;
    Y = newY;
}
```

The method takes as a parameter the distance it should move. It uses the `Turtle`'s current position and direction to figure out where this move will finish. It uses some graphics code to draw a line from the current position to the new one (don't worry about the details) and finishes by saving the new position.

EVENTS

Events let the class tell the rest of the program that something interesting is happening. For example, if a `BankAccount` object's balance falls below 0, it could raise an `AccountOverdrawn` event to notify the main program.

Declaring an event in C# is a bit tricky because you first need to understand delegates.

Delegates

A *delegate* is a data type that can hold a specific kind of *method*. For example, you could make a delegate type that represents methods that take no parameters and return a `double`. You could then declare a variable of that type and save a method in it.

Confusing? You bet!

The key to understanding delegates is to remember that a delegate type is a new data type just like a `string` or `int`. The difference is that a variable with a delegate type holds a method, not a simple value like "Hello" or 27.

The Delegates example program, which is part of this lesson's download on the book's website, provides a simple example. The program uses four steps to demonstrate delegates: declare the delegate type, create variables of that type, initialize the variables, and use the variables' values.

First the program defines a delegate type:

```
// Define a delegate type that takes no parameters and returns nothing.
private delegate void DoSomethingMethod();
```

The declaration begins with the accessibility keyword `private` and then the keyword `delegate` to tell C# that it is defining a delegate type. The rest of the declaration gives the delegate type's name `DoSomethingMethod`. It also indicates that instances of this type must refer to methods that take no parameters and return nothing (`void`).

Now that it has defined the delegate type, the code declares three variables of that type. Each of the variables can hold a reference to a method that takes no parameters and returns nothing:

```
// Declare three DoSomethingMethod variables.
private DoSomethingMethod method1, method2, method3;
```

Next the program defines two methods that match the delegate's definition:

```
// Define some methods that have the delegate's type.
private void SayHi()
{
    MessageBox.Show("Hi");
}
```

```
private void SayClicked()
{
    MessageBox.Show("Clicked");
}
```

When the program starts, the following Load event handler sets the variables method1, method2, and method3 so they point to these two methods. Notice that the code makes method1 and method3 point to the same method, SayHi:

```
// Initialize the delegate variables.
private void Form1_Load(object sender, EventArgs e)
{
    method1 = SayHi;
    method2 = SayClicked;
    method3 = SayHi;
}
```

At this point, the program has defined the delegate type, created three variables of that type, and initialized those variables so they refer to the SayHi and SayClicked methods. Now the program is ready to use the variables.

The program displays three buttons. When you click them, the following event handlers execute. Each button simply invokes the method referred to by one of the delegate variables.

```
// Invoke the method stored in the delegates.
private void method1Button_Click(object sender, EventArgs e)
{
    method1();
}
private void method2Button_Click(object sender, EventArgs e)
{
    method2();
}

private void method3Button_Click(object sender, EventArgs e)
{
    method3();
}
```

When it executes, a Button's event handler doesn't "know" what method is stored in its variable. For example, the last Button invokes method3 without knowing which "real" method will execute.

This isn't an extremely practical program, and it's hard to imagine a situation where you would just want buttons to invoke the methods stored in different delegates. However, this example is much simpler than many programs that use delegates so it's worth studying before you look at more realistic examples.

Event Handler Delegates

Now that you know a bit about delegates, you can learn how to use them to make an event.

First, in the class that will raise the event, declare a delegate type to define the event handler. Usually developers end the delegate's name with EventHandler to make it obvious what the delegate represents.

By convention, event handlers usually take two parameters named `sender` and `e`. The `sender` parameter is an object that contains a reference to whatever `object` is raising the event. The `e` parameter contains data specific to the event. Often you will define a class to provide that information and the parameter `e` will be of that class.

For example, suppose you want the `Turtle` class to raise an `OutOfBounds` event to tell the program that it is trying to move the `Turtle` off the drawing area. You want the parameter `e` to tell the program the X and Y coordinates where the `Turtle` was trying to move.

In that case, you could use the following `TurtleOutOfBoundsEventArgs` class to store the X and Y coordinates:

```
// The TurtleOutOfBoundsEventArgs data type.
public class TurtleOutOfBoundsEventArgs
{
    // Where the Turtle would stop if
    // this were not out of bounds.
    public int X { get; set; }
    public int Y { get; set; }
};
```

The following code shows how the `Turtle` class could declare its `OutOfBoundsEventHandler` delegate:

```
// Declare the OutOfBound event's delegate.
public delegate void OutOfBoundsEventHandler(
    object sender, TurtleOutOfBoundsEventArgs e);
```

Next the class must declare the actual event to tell C# that the class will provide this event. The declaration should begin with an accessibility keyword (`public`, `private`, and so on) followed by the keyword `event`. Next it should give the event handler's delegate type. It finishes with the event's name.

The following code declares the `OutOfBounds` event, which is handled by event handlers of type `OutOfBoundsEventHandler`:

```
// Declare the OutOfBounds event.
public event OutOfBoundsEventHandler OutOfBounds;
```

The final piece of code that you need to add to the class is the code that raises the event. This code simply invokes the event handler, passing it any parameters that it should receive.

Before it raises the event, however, the code should verify that some other piece of code has registered to receive the event. The code does that by checking whether the event is `null`. (This syntax seems a bit strange to me. The code looks like it is checking that an *event* is null when really it's asking whether another piece of code has asked to receive the event. This is just the syntax used by C#.)

The following code raises the `Turtle` class's `OutOfBounds` event:

```
if (OutOfBounds != null)
{
    TurtleOutOfBoundsEventArgs args = new TurtleOutOfBoundsEventArgs();
    args.X = newX;
    args.Y = newY;
    OutOfBounds(this, args);
}
```

If OutOfBounds is not null (in other words, some other code wants to receive the event), the code creates a new TurtleOutOfBoundsEventArgs object, initializes it to indicate the point the Turtle was trying to move to, and then calls OutOfBounds, passing it the object raising the event and the TurtleOutOfBoundsEventArgs object.

A class uses code to decide when to raise the event. The following code shows how the Turtle class raises its event when the Move method tries to move beyond the edge of the Turtle's Bitmap. The bold code determines whether the Turtle is moving out of bounds and raises the event if necessary.

```
// Make the Turtle move the indicated distance
// in its current direction.
public void Move(int distance)
{
    // Calculate the new position.
    double radians = Direction * Math.PI / 180;
    int newX = (int)(X + Math.Cos(radians) * distance);
    int newY = (int)(Y + Math.Sin(radians) * distance);

    // See if the new position is off the Bitmap.
    if ((newX < 0) || (newY < 0) ||
        (newX >= Canvas.Width) || (newY >= Canvas.Height))
    {
        // Raise the OutOfBounds event, passing
        // the event handler the new coordinates.
        if (OutOfBounds != null)
        {
            TurtleOutOfBoundsEventArgs args =
                new TurtleOutOfBoundsEventArgs();
            args.X = newX;
            args.Y = newY;
            OutOfBounds(this, args);
        }
        return;
    }

    // Draw to the new position.
    using (Graphics gr = Graphics.FromImage(Canvas))
    {
        gr.DrawLine(Pens.Blue, X, Y, newX, newY);
    }

    // Save the new position.
    X = newX;
    Y = newY;
}
```

There's still one piece missing to all of this. The main program must register to receive the OutOfBound event or it won't know when the Turtle has raised it.

When the Turtle program starts, its Form_Load event handler executes the following code. This adds the Turtle_OutOfBounds method as an event handler for the MyTurtle object's OutOfBounds event. Now if the MyTurtle object raises its event, the program's Turtle_OutOfBounds event handler executes.

```
// Register to receive the OutOfBounds event.
MyTurtle.OutOfBounds += Turtle_OutOfBounds;
```

> **NOTE** *You can remove an event handler by using code like this:*
>
> ```
> MyTurtle.OutOfBounds -= Turtle_OutOfBounds;
> ```

The following code shows the Turtle program's `Turtle_OutOfBounds` event handler:

```
// Handle the OutOfBounds event.
private void Turtle_OutOfBounds(object sender, Turtle.TurtleOutOfBoundsEventArgs e)
{
    MessageBox.Show(string.Format("Oops! ({0}, {1}) is out of bounds.",
        e.X, e.Y));
}
```

TRY IT

In this second Try It in the lesson, you create a `BankAccount` class. You give it a `Balance` property and two methods, `Credit` and `Debit`. The `Debit` method raises an `Overdrawn` event if a withdrawal would give the account a negative balance.

You also build the test application shown in Figure 23-2.

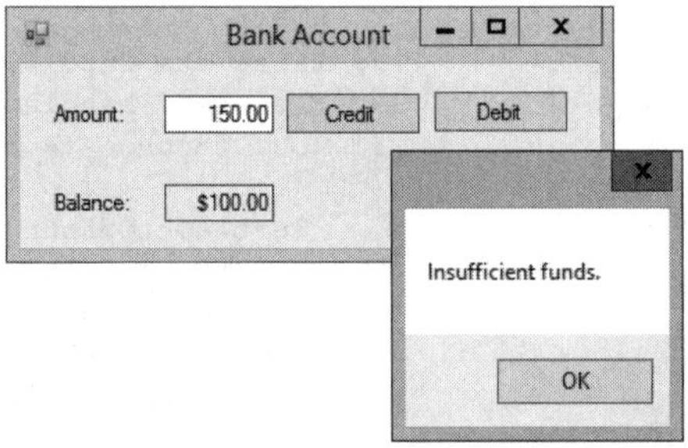

Lesson Requirements

In this lesson, you:

FIGURE 23-2

➤ Build the program shown in Figure 23-2.

➤ Create a `BankAccount` class. Give it a `Balance` property.

➤ Add `Debit` and `Credit` methods to add and remove money from the account.

➤ Define the `AccountOverdrawnArgs` class to pass to event handlers.

➤ Define the `OverdrawnEventHandler` delegate type.

➤ Declare the `Overdrawn` event itself.

➤ Make the `Debit` method raise the event when necessary.

➤ In the main program, register to receive the `Overdrawn` event so it can display a message box.

➤ In the main program, make the Credit and Debit buttons add and remove money from the bank account, respectively.

> **NOTE** *You can download the code and resources for this lesson from the web-site at* `www.wrox.com/go/csharp24hourtrainer2e`.

Hints

➤ This example doesn't do anything special with the `Balance` property so you can make it auto-implemented.

➤ Make the main form create an instance of the `BankAccount` class to manipulate.

Step-by-Step

➤ Build the program shown in Figure 23-2.

1. This is reasonably straightforward.

➤ Create a `BankAccount` class. Give it a `Balance` property.

1. Use code similar to the following:

```
// The account balance.
public decimal Balance { get; set; }
```

➤ Add `Debit` and `Credit` methods to add and remove money from the account.

1. Start with code similar to the following. You'll modify the `Debit` method later to raise the `Overdrawn` event.

```
// Add money to the account.
public void Credit(decimal amount)
{
    Balance += amount;
}

// Remove money from the account.
public void Debit(decimal amount)
{
    Balance -= amount;
}
```

➤ Define the `AccountOverdrawnArgs` class to pass to event handlers.

1. Use code similar to the following:

```
// Define the OverdrawnEventArgs type.
public class OverdrawnEventArgs
{
    public decimal currentBalance, invalidBalance;
}
```

➤ Define the `OverdrawnEventHandler` delegate type.

1. Use code similar to the following:

```
// Define the OverdrawnEventHandler delegate type.
public delegate void OverdrawnEventHandler(
    object sender, OverdrawnEventArgs args);
```

➤ Declare the `Overdrawn` event itself.

1. Use code similar to the following:

```
// Declare the Overdrawn event.
public event OverdrawnEventHandler Overdrawn;
```

➤ Make the `Debit` method raise the event when necessary.

1. Modify the initial version of the method so it raises the event when necessary. Use code similar to the following:

```
// Remove money from the account.
public void Debit(decimal amount)
{
    // See if there is enough money.
    if (Balance < amount)
    {
        // Not enough money. Raise the Overdrawn event.
        if (Overdrawn != null)
        {
            OverdrawnEventArgs args = new OverdrawnEventArgs();
            args.currentBalance = Balance;
            args.invalidBalance = Balance - amount;
            Overdrawn(this, args);
        }
    }
    else
    {
        // There's enough money.
        Balance -= amount;
    }
}
```

➤ In the main program, register to receive the `Overdrawn` event so it can display a message box.

1. Use code similar to the following:

```
// Declare an account.
BankAccount MyAccount;

// Initialize the account.
private void Form1_Load(object sender, EventArgs e)
{
    // Initialize the account.
    MyAccount = new BankAccount();
    MyAccount.Balance = 100M;

    // Register to receive the Overdrawn event.
    MyAccount.Overdrawn += MyAccount_Overdrawn;

    // Display the current balance.
    balanceTextBox.Text = MyAccount.Balance.ToString("C");
}
```

```
    // We're overdrawn.
    private void MyAccount_Overdrawn(object sender,
        BankAccount.OverdrawnEventArgs args)
    {
        MessageBox.Show("Insufficient funds.");
    }
```

➤ In the main program, make the Credit and Debit buttons add and remove money from the bank account, respectively.

1. Use code similar to the following:

```
    // Add money to the account.
    private void creditButton_Click(object sender, EventArgs e)
    {
        // Add the money.
        decimal amount = decimal.Parse(amountTextBox.Text);
        MyAccount.Credit(amount);

        // Display the current balance.
        balanceTextBox.Text = MyAccount.Balance.ToString("C");
    }

    // Remove money from the account.
    private void debitButton_Click(object sender, EventArgs e)
    {
        // Remove the money.
        decimal amount = decimal.Parse(amountTextBox.Text);
        MyAccount.Debit(amount);

        // Display the current balance.
        balanceTextBox.Text = MyAccount.Balance.ToString("C");
    }
```

INHERITANCE

Often when you build one class, you end up building a bunch of other closely related classes. For example, suppose you're building a program that models your company's organization. You might build an `Employee` class to represent employees. After a while, you may realize that there are different kinds of employees: managers, supervisors, project leaders, and so forth.

You could build each of those classes individually but you'd find that these classes have a lot in common. They all probably have `FirstName`, `LastName`, `Address`, `EmployeeId`, and other properties. Depending on the kinds of operations you need the objects to perform, you might also find that they share a lot of methods: `ScheduleVacation`, `PrintTimesheet`, `RecordHours`, and so forth. Although you could build each of these classes individually, you would end up duplicating a lot of code in each class to handle these common features.

Fortunately, C# allows you to make one class *inherit* from another and that lets them share common code. When you make one class inherit from another one, you *derive* the new class from the existing class. In that case, the new class is called the *child class* and the class from which it inherits is called the *parent class*.

In this example, you could build a `Person` class with properties that all people have: `FirstName`, `LastName`, `Street`, `City`, `State`, `Zip`, `Email`, and `Phone`. You could then derive the `Employee` class from `Person` and add the new property `EmployeeId`.

Next you could derive the `Manager` class from `Employee` (because all `Managers` are also `Employees`) and add new manager-related properties such as `DepartmentName` and `DirectReports`.

Syntactically, to make a class that inherits from another you add a colon and the parent class's name after the child class's declaration. For example, the following code defines the `Manager` class, which inherits from `Employee`. In addition to whatever features the `Employee` class provides, `Manager` adds new `DepartmentName` and `DirectReports` properties:

```
class Manager : Employee
{
    public string DepartmentName { get; set; }
    public List<Employee> DirectReports = new List<Employee>();
}
```

> **NOTE** *Note that C# only supports single inheritance. That means a class can inherit from at most one parent class. For example, if you define a* House *class and a* Boat *class, you cannot make a* HouseBoat *class that inherits from both.*

POLYMORPHISM

Polymorphism is a rather confusing concept that basically means a program can treat an object as if it were any class that it inherits. Another way to think of this is that polymorphism lets you treat an object as if it were any of the classes that it *is*. For example, an `Employee` is a kind of `Person` so you should be able to treat an `Employee` as a `Person`.

Note that the reverse is not true. A `Person` is not necessarily an `Employee` (it could be a `Customer` or some other unrelated person), so you can't necessarily treat a `Person` as an `Employee`.

For a more detailed example, suppose you make the `Person`, `Employee`, and `Manager` classes and they inherit from each other in the natural progression: `Employee` inherits from `Person` and `Manager` inherits from `Employee`.

Now suppose you write a `SendEmail` method that takes a `Person` as a parameter and sends a message to the e-mail address stored in the `Person's` `Email` property. `Employee` inherits from `Person` so you should be able to pass an `Employee` into this method and the method should be able to treat it as a `Person`. This makes intuitive sense because an `Employee` *is* a `Person`, just a particular kind of `Person`.

Similarly, `Manager` inherits from `Employee` so a `Manager` is a kind of `Employee`. If an `Employee` is a kind of `Person` and a `Manager` is a kind of `Employee`, then a `Manager` must also be a kind of `Person`, so the same method should be able to take a `Manager` as its parameter.

TRY IT

In the final Try It of this lesson, you get to experiment with classes, inheritance, and polymorphism. You build `Person`, `Employee`, and `Manager` classes. To test the classes, you build a simple program that creates instances of each class and passes them to a method that takes a `Person` as a parameter.

Lesson Requirements

In this lesson, you:

➤ Create a `Person` class with properties `FirstName`, `LastName`, `Street`, `City`, `State`, `Zip`, `Email`, and `Phone`. Give the `Person` class a `GetAddress` method that returns the `Person`'s name and address properties as a string in the format:

Alice Archer

100 Ash Ave

Bugsville   CO   82010

➤ Derive an `Employee` class from `Person`. Add the properties `EmployeeId` and `MailStop`.

➤ Derive a `Manager` class from `Employee`. Add a `DepartmentName` property and a `DirectReports` property of type `List<Employee>`. Make a `GetDirectReportsList` method that returns the names of the `Manager`'s `Employees` separated by newlines.

➤ Make the main program create two `Employees` named Alice and Bob, a `Manager` named Cindy who has Alice and Bob in her department, and a `Person` named Dan.

➤ Make a `ShowAddress` method that takes a `Person` as a parameter and displays the `Person`'s address.

➤ On the main form, make buttons that call `ShowAddress` for each of the people, passing the method the appropriate object.

➤ Make a final button that displays Cindy's list of direct reports.

> **NOTE** *You can download the code and resources for this lesson from the website at* www.wrox.com/go/csharp24hourtrainer2e.

Hints

➤ This example doesn't do anything fancy with the class's properties so you can use auto-implemented properties.

➤ The `ShowAddress` method should take a `Person` parameter even though some of the objects it will be passed are `Employees` or `Managers`.

Step-by-Step

➤ Create a `Person` class with properties `FirstName`, `LastName`, `Street`, `City`, `State`, `Zip`, `Email`, and `Phone`. Give the `Person` class a `GetAddress` method that returns the `Person`'s name and address properties as a string in the format:

Alice Archer

100 Ash Ave

Bugsville   CO   82010

1. Make a new `Person` class with code similar to the following:

```
class Person
{
    public string FirstName { get; set; }
    public string LastName { get; set; }
    public string Street { get; set; }
    public string City { get; set; }
    public string State { get; set; }
    public string Zip { get; set; }

    // Display the person's address.
    // A real application might print this on an envelope.
    public string GetAddress()
    {
        return FirstName + " " + LastName +
            "\n" + Street + "\n" + City +
            "    " + State + "    " + Zip;
    }
}
```

➤ Derive an `Employee` class from `Person`. Add the properties `EmployeeId` and `MailStop`.

1. Make the `Employee` class similar to the following:

```
class Employee : Person
{
    public int EmployeeId { get; set; }
    public string MailStop { get; set; }
}
```

➤ Derive a `Manager` class from `Employee`. Add a `DepartmentName` property and a `DirectReports` property of type `List<Employee>`. Make a `GetDirectReportsList` method that returns the names of the `Manager`'s `Employees` separated by newlines.

1. Make the `Manager` class similar to the following:

```
class Manager : Employee
{
    public string DepartmentName { get; set; }
    public List<Employee> DirectReports = new List<Employee>();

    // Return a list of this manager's direct reports.
    public string GetDirectReportsList()
```

```
        {
            string result = "";
            foreach (Employee emp in DirectReports)
            {
                result += emp.FirstName + " " + emp.LastName + "\n";
            }
            return result;
        }
    }
```

➤ Make the main program create two `Employees` named Alice and Bob, a `Manager` named Cindy who has Alice and Bob in her department, and a `Person` named Dan.

1. Because the program's buttons need to access the objects, these objects should be stored in class-level fields as in the following code:

```
// Define some people of various types.
private Person Dan;
private Employee Alice, Bob;
private Manager Cindy;
```

2. Add code to the main form's `Load` event handler to initialize the objects. The following code shows how the program might create Alice's `Employee` object:

```
// Make an Employee named Alice.
Alice = new Employee();
Alice.FirstName = "Alice";
Alice.LastName = "Archer";
Alice.Street = "100 Ash Ave";
Alice.City = "Bugsville";
Alice.State = "CO";
Alice.Zip = "82010";
Alice.EmployeeId = 1001;
Alice.MailStop = "A-1";
```

3. Creating and initializing the other objects is similar. The only odd case is adding Alice and Bob as Cindy's employees as in the following code:

```
Cindy.DirectReports.Add(Alice);
Cindy.DirectReports.Add(Bob);
```

➤ Make a `ShowAddress` method that takes a `Person` as a parameter and displays the `Person`'s address.

1. Use code similar to the following:

```
// Display this Person's address.
private void ShowAddress(Person person)
{
    MessageBox.Show(person.GetAddress());
}
```

➤ On the main form, make buttons that call `ShowAddress` for each of the people, passing the method the appropriate object.

1. Create the buttons' `Click` event handlers. The following code shows the event handler that displays Cindy's address:

    ```
    private void cindyAddressButton_Click(object sender, EventArgs e)
    {
        ShowAddress(Cindy);
    }
    ```

    Note that the variable `Cindy` is a `Manager` but the `ShowAddress` method treats it as a `Person`. That's okay because `Manager` inherits indirectly from `Person`.

➤ Make a final button that displays Cindy's list of direct reports.

1. This method simply calls the `Cindy` object's `GetDirectReportsList` method and displays the result:

    ```
    // Display Cindy's direct reports.
    private void cindyReportsButton_Click(object sender, EventArgs e)
    {
        MessageBox.Show(Cindy.GetDirectReportsList());
    }
    ```

EXERCISES

1. Write a program similar to the one shown in Figure 23-3 to manipulate complex numbers. When you enter the complex numbers' real and imaginary parts in the textboxes and click Calculate, the program should display the sum, difference, and product of the two complex numbers.

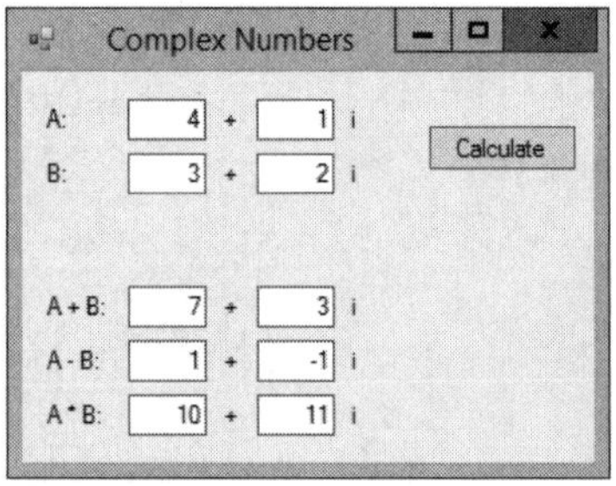

    Make a `ComplexNumber` class with properties `Real` and `Imaginary` to hold a number's real and imaginary parts, respectively. Give the class `AddTo`, `MultiplyBy`, and `SubtractFrom` methods that combine the current `ComplexNumber` with another taken as a parameter and return the result as a new `ComplexNumber`.

    FIGURE 23-3

    Hints: Recall from school these equations for calculating with complex numbers:

    $$(A + Bi) + (C + Di) = (A + C) + (B + D)i$$
    $$(A + Bi) - (C + Di) = (A - C) + (B - D)i$$
    $$(A + Bi) \times (C + Di) = (A \times C - B \times D) + (A \times D + B \times C)i$$

    For more review of complex numbers, see `en.wikipedia.org/wiki/Complex_numbers` or `mathworld.wolfram.com/ComplexNumber.html`.

2. [Games] Suppose you're writing a role-playing game and design classes to represent the player's class choices: fighter, magic-user, and rogue. Hints:

    ➤ Give each class a few representative properties, but you don't need to include everything you would need to actually build the game.

    ➤ Use auto-implemented properties.

➤ Give each class a few methods that might make sense for the class but don't give them any code. (You may need to add a return statement if a method returns a value.)

➤ Make most properties strings instead of objects. For example, you can represent a weapon as a string holding the weapon's name (as in "sword"); you don't need to use some sort of Weapon or Sword class.

➤ Think about what the classes have in common and how you can avoid duplicating code.

3. Build Person and Student classes. Give the Student class (directly or via inheritance) typical name and address properties, plus a list to hold the courses (strings) that the Student is enrolled in. Also give the class an Enroll method that adds a course to the list.

Next make a user interface that lets the user add courses to a Student. After adding a new course, display the Student's courses in a ListBox. (Hint: The word class is a keyword used by C# so it's easier to use the word "course" instead when you're talking about enrollment.)

4. Copy the program you wrote for Exercise 3 and modify the Enroll method so it throws an ArgumentException if the program tries to enroll the student in the same course twice or if the student is already enrolled in six courses.

5. Copy the program you wrote for Exercise 4 and modify the Enroll method so it raises an Overenrolled event instead of throwing an exception if the student tries to enroll in more than six courses.

6. Sometimes you can use an event handler to tell the program about unusual circumstances and let the program decide whether to allow some action. For example, a form's FormClosing event handler can use its e.Cancel parameter to cancel the close and force the form to remain open.

Consider the program you wrote for Exercise 5. Under some circumstances, you may want to allow a student to enroll in more than six courses. (For example, students such as Hermione Granger who have time turners.) Copy that program and add an Allow field to the OverenrolledEventArgs class. Make the Student class initialize Allow to false and then invoke the event handlers.

Make the main program catch the event, display a message box asking the user whether it should allow the student to overenroll, and set Allow accordingly.

After the event handlers return, make the Student class allow the student to overenroll if Allow is true.

7. [Games, Hard] Most games that involve moving objects use sprites to represent those objects. A sprite is simply an instance of a class that represents the game object's position, velocity, colors, and other attributes. The goal is to move as much information about the objects as possible into the sprite class so the main program doesn't need to know about it.

Copy the bouncing ball program you built for Exercise 19-8 (or download the version available on the book's website) and modify it so it uses a Ball class to track balls. Hints:

➤ Add the directive using System.Drawing to the file that defines the Ball class.

➤ Give the Ball class the fields (or properties) X, Y, Vx, Vy, Width, Height, and Brush. Also give it a new ClientSize property of type Size.

➤ Give the `Ball` class an `Initialize` method that randomizes the `Ball`'s properties. Hints:

  ➤ Pass the main form's `ClientSize` into the `Initialize` method. Make the method save it in the `Ball`'s `ClientSize` field.

  ➤ Make a `private static` array called `brushes` that lists the brushes from which to pick randomly. (Making the array `private` means code outside of the `Ball` class cannot see it. Making it `static` means all instances of the `Ball` class share the same array, so they don't waste space by creating a new array for each `Ball` object.)

  ➤ Make a `private static Random` object for the `Ball` instances to share. (This solves a tricky problem. When a program makes a `Random` object, it uses the system time to initialize itself by default. This program makes all of the `Ball`s at the same time. That means if each `Ball` made its own `Random` object, they would all be initialized at almost exactly the same time so the `Random` objects would all produce the same sequence of "random" values. The result would be a bunch of `Ball`s with the same positions, velocities, and colors. Using the `static` keyword makes all of the `Ball`s share the same `Random` object so they get different "random" values. To see the problem, just remove the `static` keyword from the `Random` object's declaration.)

➤ Give the `Ball` class a `Move` method that updates the `Ball`'s position. If the `Ball` hits a wall, raise a `HitWall` event.

➤ Give the `Ball` class a `Draw` method that takes a `Graphics` object as a parameter and draws the ball on it.

➤ Make the form's code use the `Ball` methods to initialize, move, and draw the balls. (This should make the form's code much simpler.)

➤ Make the form's code catch the `Ball`s' `HitWall` events and play the appropriate sound.

NOTE *Please select the videos for Lesson 23 online at* www.wrox.com/go /csharp24hourtrainer2evideos.

Initializing Objects

Most of the time when you create an object, you need to initialize its properties. You generally wouldn't create an Employee object without at least setting its FirstName and LastName properties. The following code shows how you might initialize an Employee object:

```
// Make an Employee named Alice.
Employee alice = new Employee();
alice.FirstName = "Alice";
alice.LastName = "Archer";
alice.Street = "100 Ash Ave";
alice.City = "Bugsville";
alice.State = "CO";
alice.Zip = "82010";
alice.EmployeeId = 1001;
alice.MailStop = "A-1";
```

Though this is relatively straightforward, it is fairly tedious. Creating and initializing a bunch of Employees would take a lot of repetitive code. Fortunately C# provides alternatives that make this task a little easier.

In this lesson you learn how to initialize an object's properties as you create it. You also learn how to define constructors that make initializing objects easier and how to make destructors that clean up after an object.

INITIALIZING OBJECTS

C# provides a simple syntax for initializing an object's properties as you create it. Create the object as usual but follow the new keyword and the class's name with braces. Inside the braces, place comma-separated statements that initialize the object's properties.

For example, the following code creates and initializes an Employee object named alice similar to the one created in the previous code. The statements inside the braces initialize the object's properties.

```
// Make an Employee named Alice.
Employee alice = new Employee()
{
    FirstName = "Alice",
    LastName = "Archer",
    Street = "100 Ash Ave",
    City = "Bugsville",
    State = "CO",
    Zip = "82010",
    EmployeeId = 1001,
    MailStop = "A-1",
};
```

> **NOTE** *Note that an initializer can only initialize properties that the code can access. For example, if a property is private, the initializer cannot set its value.*

This may not seem like much of an improvement because it has just as many lines of code as the previous version. (Two more lines if you count the braces.) It is easier to type, however, partly because you don't need to repeatedly type the name of the object.

IntelliSense also helps. When you open the braces and type F, IntelliSense can figure out that you're trying to initialize the `FirstName` property. At that point, you can press Tab to fill in the rest of the property's name without typing it.

IntelliSense also knows what values you've entered previously and won't show them to you again. For example, if you initialize the `Street` property and then later type `S`, IntelliSense knows that you must be initializing the `State` property.

CONSTRUCTORS

Initializers are handy and easy to use but sometimes you might like some extra control over how an object is created. Constructors give you that extra control.

A *constructor* is a method that is executed when an object is created. The constructor executes before the code that creates the object gets hold of it. The constructor can perform any setup tasks that are necessary to prepare the object for use. It can look up data in databases, prepare data structures, and initialize properties.

To create a constructor, you make a method that has no return type and that is named after the class. Alternatively, you can think of it as a method that returns the class's type and that has no name. You'll see examples shortly.

The next two sections describe two kinds of constructors: parameterless constructors and parameterized constructors. A later section explains how one constructor can invoke another to avoid duplicated code.

Parameterless Constructors

A constructor can take parameters just like any other method to help it in its setup tasks. A *parameterless constructor* (sometimes called an *empty constructor*) takes no parameters, so it's somewhat limited in what it can do.

For example, suppose the Manager class has a DirectReports property, which is a list of Employees that report to a given manager. A parameterless constructor cannot build that list because it doesn't know what employees to put in it. It can, however, initialize the DirectReports property to an empty list, as shown in the following code:

```
class Manager : Employee
{
    public List<Employee> DirectReports;

    // Initialize the Manager.
    public Manager()
    {
        DirectReports = new List<Employee>();
    }
}
```

You implicitly invoke a parameterless constructor any time you create an object without using any parameters. For example, the following code creates a new Person object. When this code executes, control jumps briefly to the parameterless constructor so it can prepare the object for use.

```
Manager fred = new Manager();
```

Note that C# creates a default public parameterless constructor for you if you don't define any constructors explicitly. If you give the class *any* constructors, however, C# doesn't create the default constructor. In that case, if you want a parameterless constructor, you must make it yourself.

Parameterized Constructors

Parameterless constructors are useful but fairly limited because they don't have much information to go by. To give a constructor more information, you can make it take parameters just like you can with any other method.

One simple type of parameterized constructor uses its parameters to initialize properties. For example, you could make a constructor for the Person class that takes the person's first and last names as parameters. The constructor could then set the object's FirstName and LastName properties.

Why would you bother doing this when you could use an initializer? First, the syntax for using a constructor is slightly more concise than initializer syntax. The following code uses a constructor that takes eight parameters to initialize an Employee's properties:

```
Employee alice = new Employee("Alice", "Archer", "100 Ash Ave",
    "Bugsville", "CO", "82010", 1001, "A-1");
```

Compare this code to the earlier snippet that used initializers. This version is more concise, although it's less self-documenting because it doesn't explicitly list the property names.

The second reason you might prefer to use a parameterized constructor instead of an initializer is that a constructor can perform all sorts of checks that an initializer cannot. For example, a constructor can validate its parameters against each other or against a database. An `Employee` class's constructor could take an employee ID as a parameter and use a database to verify that the employee really exists.

A constructor can also require that certain parameters be provided. For example, a `Person` constructor could require that the first and last name parameters be provided. If you rely on initializers, the program could create a `Person` that has no first or last name.

To make a constructor that takes parameters, simply add the parameters as you would for any other method. The following code shows a constructor for the `Person` class that uses its parameters to initialize the new `Person` object's properties:

```
// Initialize all values.
public Person(string firstName, string lastName, string street,
    string city, string state, string zip)
{
    FirstName = firstName;
    LastName = lastName;
    Street = street;
    City = city;
    State = state;
    Zip = zip;
}
```

DESTRUCTORS

Constructors execute when a new object is created to perform initialization chores. Destructors execute when an object is being destroyed to perform cleanup chores. For example, a destructor might disconnect from databases, close files, free memory, and do whatever else is necessary before the object gets carted off to the electronic recycle center.

Destructors are simpler than constructors because:

➤ A class can have only one destructor.

➤ You cannot call a destructor directly; they are only called automatically.

➤ A destructor cannot invoke another destructor.

➤ Destructors cannot take parameters.

➤ Destructors automatically call base class destructors when they are finished.

To make a destructor, you create a method named after the class with a tilde character (~) in front of its name. You cannot include an access specifier (such as `private` or `public`), return type, or parameters. For example, the following code shows a simple destructor for the `Person` class:

```
~Person()
{
    // Perform cleanup chores here...
}
```

Destructors are a fairly specialized topic and you are unlikely to need to build one until you have more programming experience, but I wanted to describe them for an important reason: so you know when destructors execute and you can help them perform well.

You might think that so far destructors are fairly simple and that would be the end of the story except for one remaining question: "When are destructors called?" This turns out to be a trickier question than you might imagine. To understand when a destructor runs, you need to understand the garbage collector.

Normally a C# program runs merrily along, creating variables and objects as needed. Sometimes all of the references to an object disappear so the program no longer has access to the object. In that case, the memory (and any other resources) used by that object are lost to the program. If the program makes a lot of objects and then discards them in this way, the program will eventually use up a lot of memory.

Eventually the program may start to run out of available memory. At that point, the garbage collector springs into action. The *garbage collector* runs when it thinks the program may have used a lot of inaccessible memory such as old, discarded `Employee` objects. When the garbage collector runs, it reclaims the memory lost by objects that are inaccessible and makes that memory available for future objects.

It is only when the garbage collector reclaims an object's memory that the object's destructor executes. So the answer to the question "When are destructors called?" is: "Whenever the garbage collector runs." So when does the garbage collector run? The answer to this new question is: "Whenever it feels like it."

The end result is that you cannot really know when a destructor will run. The fancy name for this is *non-deterministic finalization.* Many programs never run low on memory so the garbage collector doesn't run until the program ends.

The moral of the story is that you can use destructors to clean up after an object but you shouldn't rely on them to handle tasks that must be done in a timely fashion. For example, if a destructor closes a file so other programs can use it, the file may not actually be closed until the program ends.

If you want to perform actions such as this in a timely fashion, give the class a `Dispose` method that the program can call explicitly to clean up after the object.

> **NOTE** *The* `IDisposable` *interface formalizes the notion of providing a* `Dispose` *method that cleans up after an object. It's a fairly advanced topic, however, so it isn't covered here. For more information, see* `msdn.microsoft.com/library /b1yfkh5e.aspx` *and* `msdn.microsoft.com/library/system.idisposable .aspx`.

If an object (whether or not you created its class) provides a `Dispose` method, you should use it when you are done with the object so you can free its resources.

For example, you can use a `Graphics` object to draw on a bitmap. A `Graphics` object uses limited system resources, so it's a good practice to call its `Dispose` method when you're done using it.

Unfortunately, it's easy to forget to call `Dispose`. To help you remember, C# provides the `using` statement. The `using` statement is followed by the object that it manages and, when the `using` block ends, the program automatically calls the object's `Dispose` method.

The usual syntax for a `using` block is:

```
using (variableInitialization)
{
    ... Statements ...
}
```

In this syntax, the `variableInitialization` declares and initializes the variable that the block controls. (You can declare the object outside of the `using` block, but putting it inside the block usually makes it easier to read and restricts its scope to the block.)

For example, the following code creates a `Graphics` object named `gr` associated with the bitmap `bigBitmap`. The `using` block ensures that the program executes the `gr` object's `Dispose` method when it finishes the block.

```
using (Graphics gr = Graphics.FromImage(bigBitmap))
{
    // Draw stuff...
}
```

Note that the object's `Dispose` method is called even if the program exits from the block because of an exception, a `return` statement, or some other method.

INVOKING OTHER CONSTRUCTORS

You can give a class many different constructors as long as they have different parameter lists (so C# can tell them apart). For example, you might give the `Person` class a parameterless constructor, a second constructor that takes first name and last name as parameters, and a third constructor that takes first and last name, street, city, state, and ZIP code as parameters.

Often when you give a class multiple constructors, some of them perform the same actions. In the `Person` example, the constructor that initializes first name, last name, street, city, state, and ZIP code probably does the same things that the second constructor does to initialize just first and last name.

You can also find overlapping constructor functionality when one class inherits from another. For example, suppose the `Person` class has `FirstName` and `LastName` properties. The `Employee` class inherits from `Person` and adds some other properties such as `EmployeeId` and `MailStop`. The `Person` class's constructor initializes the `FirstName` and `LastName` properties, something that the `Employee` class's constructors should also do.

Having several methods perform the same tasks makes debugging and maintaining code harder. Fortunately, C# provides a way you can make one constructor invoke another.

To make one constructor invoke another in the same class, follow the constructor's parameter declarations with a colon and the keyword `this`, passing `this` any parameters that the other constructor should receive. For example, the following code shows three constructors for the `Person` class that invoke each other. The code that invokes other constructors is shown in bold:

```
// Parameterless constructor.
public Person()
{
    // General initialization if needed ...
}

// Initialize first and last name.
public Person(string firstName, string lastName)
    : this()
{
    FirstName = firstName;
    LastName = lastName;
}

// Initialize all values.
public Person(string firstName, string lastName, string street,
    string city, string state, string zip)
    : this(firstName, lastName)
{
    Street = street;
    City = city;
    State = state;
    Zip = zip;
}
```

The first constructor is a parameterless constructor. In this example it doesn't do anything.

The second constructor takes first and last names as parameters. The : this() at the end of the declaration means the constructor should invoke the parameterless constructor when it starts.

The third constructor takes name and address parameters. Its declaration ends with: this(firstName, lastName) to indicate that the constructor should begin by calling the second constructor, passing it the firstName and lastName parameters. (That constructor in turn invokes the parameterless constructor.)

Notice that the third constructor doesn't save the firstName and lastName values. That's handled by the second constructor.

You can use a similar syntax to invoke a parent class constructor by simply replacing the keyword this with the keyword base.

For example, the Employee class inherits from the Person class. The following code shows two of the class's constructors. The code that invokes the Person class constructors is shown in bold:

```
// Parameterless constructor.
public Employee()
    : base()
{
}

// Initialize first and last name.
public Employee(string firstName, string lastName)
    : base(firstName, lastName)
{
}
```

The first constructor is parameterless. It invokes its parent class's parameterless constructor by using : `base()`.

The second constructor takes first and last name parameters and invokes the `Person` class's constructor that takes two strings as parameters.

> **NOTE** *Notice how the constructors invoke other constructors by using the keyword* this *or* base *followed by a parameter list. C# uses the parameter list to decide which constructor to invoke. That's why you cannot have more than one constructor with the same kinds of parameters. For example, if two constructors each took a single* string *as a parameter, how would C# know which one to use?*

TRY IT

In this Try It, you enhance the `Person`, `Employee`, and `Manager` classes you built for the third Try It in Lesson 23. You add constructors to make initializing objects easier and you add destructors so you can trace object destruction when the program ends. You also build the user interface shown in Figure 24-1 to test the classes' constructors and destructors.

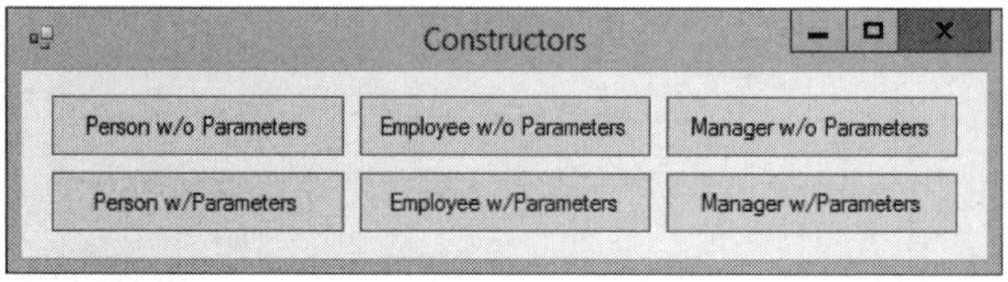

FIGURE 24-1

Lesson Requirements

In this lesson, you:

➤ Copy the `Person`, `Employee`, and `Manager` classes you built for the third Try It in Lesson 23 (or download the version that's available on the book's website).

➤ Give the `Person` class a parameterless constructor. Make it print a message to the Console window indicating that a new `Person` is being created.

➤ Give the `Person` class a constructor that initializes all of the class's properties. Make it invoke the parameterless constructor and also display its own message.

➤ Give the `Person` class a destructor that displays a message in the Console window.

➤ Make similar constructors and destructors for the `Employee` and `Manager` classes.

➤ Build the user interface shown in Figure 24-1. Add code behind the `Buttons` to create `Person`, `Employee`, and `Manager` objects.

➤ Run the program, make some objects, and close the program. Study the Console window messages to see if they make sense.

> **NOTE** *You can download the code and resources for this lesson from the website at* www.wrox.com/go/csharp24hourtrainer2e.

Hints

➤ Make the constructors and destructors invoke each other where possible to avoid duplicate work.

➤ When you use parameterless constructors, use object initialization to set the objects' properties.

Step-by-Step

➤ Copy the Person, Employee, and Manager classes you built for the third Try It in Lesson 23 (or download the version that's available on the book's website).

1. This is relatively straightforward.

➤ Give the Person class a parameterless constructor. Make it print a message to the Console window indicating that a new Person is being created.

1. The Person class's parameterless constructor should look something like this:

```
public Person()
{
    Console.WriteLine("Person()");
}
```

➤ Give the Person class a constructor that initializes all of the class's properties. Make it invoke the parameterless constructor and also display its own message.

1. This constructor should look something like this:

```
public Person(string firstName, string lastName,
    string street, string city, string state, string zip)
    : this()
{
    FirstName = firstName;
    LastName = lastName;
    Street = street;
    City = city;
    State = state;
    Zip = zip;
    Console.WriteLine("Person(parameters)");
}
```

➤ Give the Person class a destructor that displays a message in the Console window.

1. This destructor should look something like this:

```
~Person()
{
    Console.WriteLine("~Person");
}
```

➤ Make similar constructors and destructors for the Employee and Manager classes.

1. The following code shows the Employee class's constructors and destructor:

```
public Employee()
    : base()
{
```

```
        Console.WriteLine("Employee()");
    }

    public Employee(int employeeId, string mailStop,
        string firstName, string lastName, string street,
        string city, string state, string zip)
        : base(firstName, lastName, street, city, state, zip)
    {
        EmployeeId = employeeId;
        MailStop = mailStop;
        Console.WriteLine("Employee(parameters)");
    }

    ~Employee()
    {
        Console.WriteLine("~Employee");
    }
```

2. The following code shows the Manager class's constructors and destructor:

```
    public Manager()
        : base()
    {
        DirectReports = new List<Employee>();
        Console.WriteLine("Manager()");
    }

    public Manager(string departmentName, int employeeId,
        string mailStop, string firstName, string lastName,
        string street, string city, string state, string zip)
        : base(employeeId, mailStop, firstName, lastName, street,
        city, state, zip)
    {
        DepartmentName = departmentName;
        Console.WriteLine("Manager(parameters)");
    }

    ~Manager()
    {
        Console.WriteLine("~Manager");
    }
```

➤ Build the user interface shown in Figure 24-1. Add code behind the Buttons to create Person, Employee, and Manager objects.

1. This is relatively straightforward.

➤ Run the program, make some objects, and close the program. Study the Console window messages to see if they make sense.

1. The following text shows the program's output if you create a Manager with parameters and then close the program. I've removed some messages generated by the program itself showing when various threads exited.

```
Creating a Manager with parameters
Person()
Person(parameters)
Employee(parameters)
Manager(parameters)
~Manager
~Employee
~Person
```

2. When I clicked the Manager w/Parameters `Button`, the program performed the following actions:

   a. The `Button`'s `Click` event handler displayed the message "Creating a Manager with parameters." It then called the `Manager` class's parameterized constructor.

   b. That constructor invoked the parameterized `Employee` constructor.

   c. That constructor invoked the parameterized `Person` constructor.

   d. That constructor invoked the parameterless `Person` constructor.

   e. That constructor displayed the message "Person()" and returned control to the parameterized `Person` constructor that called it.

   f. The parameterized `Person` constructor displayed the message "Person(parameters)" and returned control to the parameterized `Employee` constructor that called it.

   g. The parameterized `Employee` constructor displayed the message "Employee(parameters)" and returned control to the parameterized `Manager` constructor that called it.

   h. The parameterized `Manager` constructor displayed the message "Manager(parameters)" and returned control to the `Button`'s `Click` event handler.

3. When the `Button`'s `Click` event handler ended, the `Manager` object it created went out of scope so it was lost to the program. It wasn't destroyed, however, because the garbage collector didn't think it needed to run. (The program undoubtedly had plenty of memory left over.) It only ran when I closed the program. At that point, the program performed the following actions:

   a. The program was ending, so the garbage collector ran. It called the `Manager` object's destructor.

   b. That destructor displayed a message and then automatically called its base class destructor in the `Employee` class.

   c. That destructor displayed a message and then automatically called its base class destructor in the `Person` class.

   d. That destructor displayed a message.

EXERCISES

1. Copy the program you built for Exercise 23-1 (or download the version that's available on the book's website) and change the main program so it uses initializers to prepare its ComplexNumber objects. Be sure to update new instances created inside the ComplexNumber class.

2. Copy the program you built for Exercise 1 and give the ComplexNumber class a constructor that initializes the new number's real and imaginary parts. Modify the program to use this constructor.

3. Copy the program you built for Lesson 23's second Try It (or download the TryIt23b program from the book's website) and give the BankAccount class a constructor that guarantees that you cannot create an instance with an initial balance under $10. Change the main program so it uses this constructor.

4. Make a MemoryWaster class that has two fields: an integer named Megabytes and an array of bytes named Bytes. Give the class a constructor that takes a number of megabytes as a parameter, saves that value in the Megabytes field, allocates the array to hold that amount of memory, and writes a message in the Console window saying how many megabytes it is allocating. (Don't forget to multiply by 1,024 × 1,024 to convert megabytes to bytes.)

   Also give the class a destructor that writes a message in the Console window saying how many megabytes it is freeing.

   Finally, make a user interface that lets the user enter a number of megabytes and click a Button to create a MemoryWaster. Use the program to allocate memory until the garbage collector runs. For example, on my system I can allocate a 500 MB MemoryWaster, but when I try to allocate a second, the garbage collector reclaims the first one. (Hint: You may want to protect the Button's event handler with a try-catch block. For example, try making a 10,000 MB MemoryWaster.)

5. [Graphics] Create a Shape class that has three properties: a Pen, a Brush, and a Rectangle. (Hint: Include the statement using System.Drawing in the class's file.)

   Give the class two initializing constructors. The first should have the following signature:

   ```
   public Shape(Pen pen, Brush brush, int x, int y, int width, int height)
   ```

   Make the constructor use its parameters to initialize its properties.

   The second constructor should have the following signature:

   ```
   public Shape(Pen pen, Brush brush, Point location, Size size)
   ```

   Make this constructor invoke the first one.

   Also give the class a Draw method that takes a Graphics object as a parameter and uses it to draw the shape's bounding rectangle with the Shape's pen and brush. Make the main program create several Shape objects and draw them in a PictureBox's Paint event handler.

6. [Graphics] Copy the program you wrote for Exercise 5 and add an Ellipse class that inherits from Shape. Give it two constructors that invoke the corresponding base class constructors. Make the main program create a few instances of the new class. (The Ellipse

class inherits the Shape class's Draw method so the Ellipses will be drawn as rectangles on the PictureBox. Don't worry about that. We'll fix that in the next lesson's exercises.)

7. [Graphics, Hard] Copy the program you wrote for Exercise 6 and add a Circle class that inherits from Ellipse. Give the new class a constructor with the following signature:

```
public Circle(Pen pen, Brush brush, Point center, int radius)
```

Make this constructor initialize the object by invoking a parent class constructor.

8. [Graphics] Copy the program you wrote for Exercise 7 and modify it so the Shape class stores two Color properties named Foreground and Background instead of a Pen and a Brush. Also add a new integer Thickness property and corresponding parameters to the class's constructors. (You'll need to make similar changes to the classes that inherit from Shape.)

Modify the Draw method so it fills and draws the Shape with the appropriate colors and line thickness. To fill the Shape, create a new SolidBrush object. To outline the Shape, create a new Pen object. Include using statements to automatically dispose of the brush and pen.

Finally, update the main program to use the new constructors and make some sample shapes with different colors and line thicknesses.

9. [Graphics] Copy the program you wrote for Exercise 8 and modify the Draw method so it uses dashed lines. To do that, set the Pen object's DashStyle property to System.Drawing.Drawing2D.DashStyle.Dash. (This is the only way you can make dashed pens. The stock Pen objects such as Pens.Blue and Pens.Chartreuse are solid and one pixel wide.)

> **NOTE** *Please select the videos for Lesson 24 online at* www.wrox.com/go/csharp24hourtrainer2evideos.

25

Fine-Tuning Classes

In Lesson 24 you learned how to build constructors and destructors, special methods that execute when an object is created or destroyed. In this lesson you learn about other special methods you can give a class. You learn how to overload and override class methods.

OVERLOADING METHODS

Lesson 24 mentioned that you can give a class any number of constructors as long as they have different parameter lists. For example, it's common to give a class a parameterless constructor that takes no parameters and one or more other constructors that take parameters.

Making multiple methods with the same name but different parameter lists is called *overloading*. C# uses the parameter list to decide which version to use when you invoke the method.

For example, suppose you're building a course assignment application and you have built Student, Course, and Instructor classes. You could give the Student class two versions of the Enroll method, one that takes as a parameter the name of a class the student is taking and a second that takes a Course object as a parameter.

You could give the Instructor class similar versions of the Teach method to make the instructor teach a class by name or Course object.

Finally, you could give the Course class different Report methods that:

➤ Display a report in a dialog if there are no parameters.

➤ Append a report to the end of a file if the method receives a FileStream as a parameter.

➤ Save the report into a new file if the method receives a string (the filename) as a parameter.

Making overloaded methods is so easy that there's little else to say. The only catch (and it's a tiny one) is that you need to be sure the parameter lists must differ in number, type, or arrangement. For example, consider the following two method declarations:

```
public void MakeReport(string fileToCreate)
{
    . . .
}

public void MakeReport(string fileToAppend)
{
    . . .
}
```

You might intend the first version to create a report in a file and the second to append a report to the end of a file. As far as C# is concerned, however, they both take a single `string` as a parameter. Even though the parameters have different names, C# wouldn't be able to tell which one to use under different circumstances. For example, which version should the statement `MakeReport("MyReport.txt")` use?

OVERRIDING METHODS

When one class inherits from another, you can add new properties, methods, and events to the new class to give it features that were not provided by the parent class.

Once in a while it's also useful to replace a method provided by the parent class with a new version. This is called *overriding* the parent's method.

Before you can override a method, you should mark the method in the parent class with the `virtual` keyword so it allows itself to be overridden. Next, add the keyword `override` to the derived class's version of the method to indicate that it overrides the parent class's version.

For example, suppose the `Person` class defines the usual assortment of properties: `FirstName`, `LastName`, `Street`, `City`, and so on. Suppose it also provides the following `GetAddress` method that returns the `Person`'s name and address formatted for printing on an envelope:

```
// Return the Person's address.
public virtual string GetAddress()
{
    return FirstName + " " + LastName + "\n" +
        Street + "\n" + City + "    " + State + "    " + Zip;
}
```

Now suppose you derive the `Employee` class from `Person`. An `Employee`'s address looks just like a `Person`'s except it also includes `MailStop`. The `MailStop` property was added by the `Employee` class to indicate where to deliver mail within the company.

The following code shows how the `Employee` class can override the `GetAddress` method to return an `Employee`-style address:

```
// Return the Employee's address.
public override string GetAddress()
{
    return base.GetAddress() + "\n" + MailStop;
}
```

Notice how the method calls the base class's version of `GetAddress` to reuse that version of the method and avoid duplicated code.

> **NOTE** *IntelliSense can help you build overridden methods. For example, when you type* `public override` *and a space in the* `Employee` *class, IntelliSense lists the virtual methods that you might be trying to override. If you select one, IntelliSense fills in a default implementation for the new method. The following text shows the code IntelliSense generated for the* `GetAddress` *method:*
>
> ```
> public override string GetAddress()
> {
>     return base.GetAddress();
> }
> ```

The most miraculous thing about overriding a virtual method is that the object uses the method even if you invoke it from the base class. For example, suppose you have a `Person` variable pointing to an `Employee` object. Remember that an `Employee` is a kind of `Person`, so a `Person` variable can refer to an `Employee` as in the following code:

```
Employee bob = new Employee();
Person bobAsAPerson = bob;
```

Now if the code calls `bobAsAPerson.GetAddress()`, the result is the `Employee` version of `GetAddress`.

> **NOTE** *You can think of the* `virtual` *keyword as making a slot in the base class for the method. When you override the method, the derived class fills this slot with a new version of the method. Now even if you call the method from the base class, it uses whatever is in the slot.*

OVERRIDING TOSTRING

Overriding a class's `ToString` method is particularly useful. All classes inherit a `ToString` method from `System.Object` (the ultimate ancestor of all other classes), but the default implementation of `ToString` isn't always useful. For classes that you define, such as `Person` and `Employee`, the default version of `ToString` simply returns the class's name. For example, in a program named ListPeople, the `Employee` class's `ToString` method would return "ListPeople.Employee."

Although this correctly reports the object's class, it would be more useful if it returned something that contained information about the object's properties. In this example, it might be nice if it returned the Employee object's first and last names.

Fortunately the ToString method is virtual, so you can override it. The following code shows how you can override the ToString method to return an Employee's first and last name:

```
// Return first and last name.
public override string ToString()
{
    return FirstName + " " + LastName;
}
```

This makes a lot more sense. Now your program can use an Employee object's ToString method to learn about the object.

Overriding ToString also has a nice side benefit for Windows Forms development. Certain controls and parts of Visual Studio use an object's ToString method to decide what to display. For example, the ListBox and ComboBox controls display lists of items. If those items are not simple strings, the controls use the items' ToString methods to generate output.

If the list is full of Employee objects and you've overridden the Employee class's ToString method, a ListBox or ComboBox can display the employees' names.

FIGURE 25-1

The ListPeople example program shown in Figure 25-1 (and available as part of this lesson's code download) demonstrates method overriding.

When it starts, the ListPeople program uses the following code to fill its ListBox with two Student objects and two Employee objects. Both of these classes inherit from Person.

```
private void Form1_Load(object sender, EventArgs e)
{
    // Make some people.
    peopleListBox.Items.Add(new Student("Ann", "Archer", "101 Ash Ave",
        "Debugger", "NV", "72837"));
    peopleListBox.Items.Add(new Student("Bob", "Best", "222 Beach Blvd",
        "Debugger", "NV", "72837"));
    peopleListBox.Items.Add(new Employee("Cat", "Carter", "300 Cedar Ct",
        "Debugger", "NV", "72837", "MS-1"));
    peopleListBox.Items.Add(new Employee("Dan", "Dental", "404 Date Dr",
        "Debugger", "NV", "72837", "MS-2"));
}
```

The Employee class overrides its ToString method so you can see the Employees' names in Figure 25-1 instead of their class names. The Student class does not override its ToString method so Figure 25-1 shows class names for the Student objects.

If you select a person in this program and click the Show Address button, the program executes the following code:

```
// Display the selected Person's address.
private void showAddressButton_Click(object sender, EventArgs e)
```

```
    {
        Person person = peopleListBox.SelectedItem as Person;
        MessageBox.Show(person.GetAddress());
    }
```

This code converts the `ListBox`'s selected item into a `Person` object. The item is actually either a `Student` or an `Employee`, but both of those inherit from `Person` (they are kinds of `Person`) so the program can treat them as `Persons`.

The program calls the `Person`'s `GetAddress` method and displays the result. If the object was actually a `Student`, the result is a basic name and address. If the object was actually an `Employee`, the result is a name and address plus mailstop.

In addition to `ListBoxes` and `ComboBoxes`, some parts of Visual Studio use an object's `ToString` method, too. For example, if you stop an executing program and hover the mouse over an object in the debugger, a tooltip appears that displays the result of the object's `ToString` method. Similarly, if you type an object's name in the Immediate window and press Enter, the result is whatever is returned by the object's `ToString` method.

TRY IT

In this Try It, you improve the shape drawing program you built for Exercise 24-9 by overriding the `Shape` class's `Draw` method so `Ellipse` and `Circle` objects can draw themselves appropriately.

Lesson Requirements

In this lesson, you:

➤ Copy the program you wrote for Exercise 24-9 (or download the version that's available on the book's website).

➤ Add the `virtual` keyword to the `Shape` class's `Draw` method.

➤ Override the `Draw` method in the `Ellipse` class so it draws an ellipse instead of a rectangle.

➤ Modify the form's `Paint` event handler to draw smooth shapes.

> **NOTE** *You can download the code and resources for this lesson from the website at* www.wrox.com/go/csharp24hourtrainer2e.

Hints

If `gr` is the `Graphics` object, you can use these techniques:

➤ `gr.SmoothingMode = SmoothingMode.AntiAlias`—Makes the object draw shapes smoothly. (`SmoothingMode` is defined in the `System.Drawing.Drawing2D` namespace.)

➤ `gr.FillEllipse(brush, rect)`—Fills an ellipse defined by the `Rectangle` rect with brush.

➤ `gr.DrawEllipse(pen, rect)`—Outlines an ellipse defined by the `Rectangle` rect with pen.

Step-by-Step

➤ Copy the program you wrote for Exercise 24-9 (or download the version that's available on the book's website).

1. This is straightforward.

➤ Add the `virtual` keyword to the `Shape` class's `Draw` method.

1. Change the `Shape` class's `Draw` method so its declaration looks like this. (The `virtual` keyword is highlighted in bold.)

```
public virtual void Draw(Graphics gr)
```

➤ Override the `Draw` method in the `Ellipse` class so it draws an ellipse instead of a rectangle.

1. Use code similar to the following:

```
// Draw the ellipse.
public override void Draw(Graphics gr)
{
    using (Brush brush = new SolidBrush(Background))
    {
        gr.FillEllipse(brush, Bounds);
    }
    using (Pen pen = new Pen(Foreground, Thickness))
    {
        gr.DrawEllipse(pen, Bounds);
    }
}
```

2. Note that you don't need to override the `Circle` class's `Draw` method. The `Circle` class inherits from `Ellipse`, so it will inherit the version shown here that's defined by the `Ellipse` class. The `Circle` class's constructors ensure that the `Circle`'s width and height are the same, and that makes the ellipse-drawing code produce a circle.

➤ Modify the form's `Paint` event handler to draw smooth shapes.

1. Add the following `using` directive at the top of the form's code file:

```
using System.Drawing.Drawing2D;
```

2. Add the following statement at the beginning of the form's `Paint` event handler:

```
e.Graphics.SmoothingMode = SmoothingMode
.AntiAlias;
```

Figure 25-2 shows the result for the objects I created.

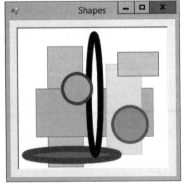

FIGURE 25-2

EXERCISES

1. [Graphics] Copy the program you built for the Try It and override the `Shape` class's `Draw` method to create a new version that takes a `Pen` and `Brush` as parameters and uses them to draw. Then make similar changes to the `Ellipse` and `Circle` classes. Test the new methods by modifying the form's code so it passes `Pens.Red` and `Brushes.Pink` into the objects' `Draw` methods.

2. [Graphics] Copy the program you built for Exercise 1 and add `Rect` and `Square` classes. (I'm calling the first of those classes `Rect` instead of `Rectangle` because .NET already has a `Rectangle` class so that name could cause confusion.) Modify the form's code to create a random `Shape`, `Ellipse`, `Circle`, `Rect`, and `Square`. Hints:

    ➤ Make the `Rect` class analogous to the `Ellipse` class.

    ➤ Make the `Square` class somewhat analogous to the `Circle` class but give its constructor X and Y coordinates and a width instead of a center point and radius.

    ➤ Make a `GetRandomParameters` method to generate random thickness, width, height, and position for a new shape.

    ➤ Remove the code that makes all of the shapes pink so you can see the shapes' colors.

3. [Graphics, Advanced] The `abstract` keyword is somewhat similar to the `virtual` keyword. When you mark a method as `abstract`, you allow it to be overridden in derived classes. In fact, an abstract method has no code so you *must* override it before you can make an instance of the class.

    Because you cannot make an instance of a class that contains an `abstract` method, you must also mark the class as `abstract`.

    Why would you do this? Think about the program you wrote for the Try It. You probably don't really intend the program to make instances of the `Shape` class. It's really just there to be a base class so you can treat other objects such as `Ellipses` and `Circles` as `Shapes`.

    Copy the program you wrote for Exercise 2 and make the `Shape` class's `Draw` methods abstract. Then modify the form's code so it doesn't try to make a `Shape` object. Hints:

    ➤ An abstract method cannot include any code. Just end it with a semicolon after the method's parameter list.

    ➤ Place the `abstract` keyword before the `class` keyword.

    ➤ An abstract class can contain non-abstract properties and methods and they are inherited as usual. In this example, the `Shape` class can still define drawing parameters (`Bounds`, `Foreground`, `Background`, and `Thickness`) and constructors.

4. [Graphics, Hard] Create a new program that displays a `PictureBox` with `Cursor` property set to Cross. Copy the shape classes you build for Exercise 3 into it. To copy a class from one project to another, you can create a class with the same name in the new project and then copy and paste its code into it. Alternatively you can:

   ➤ Copy the class's file into the new project's directory.

   ➤ Use the Project menu's Add Existing Item command to add the class to the project.

   ➤ Edit the class's code and change its `namespace` statement so it uses the same namespace as the rest of the project. (You can look at the top of the main form's code to see what the statement should look like.)

   Next create a class-level `List<Shape>` named `Shapes`.

   Write code to allow the user to select a rectangle on the `PictureBox`.

   ➤ Create two class-level `Point` variables named `StartPoint` and `EndPoint`. Also create a class-level `bool` variable named `Drawing` and initialize it to `false`.

   ➤ In the `PictureBox`'s `MouseDown` event handler, save the mouse's location in `StartPoint` and `EndPoint` and set `Drawing = true`.

   ➤ In the `PictureBox`'s `MouseMove` event handler, if `Drawing` is `false`, return. Otherwise, save the mouse's current position in `EndPoint` and refresh the `PictureBox`.

   ➤ In the `PictureBox`'s `MouseUp` event handler, if `Drawing` is `false`, return. Otherwise, if `StartPoint` and `EndPoint` have different X and Y coordinates, use them to create a new `Rect` and add it to the `Shapes` list.

   ➤ In the `PictureBox`'s `Paint` event handler, loop through the `Shapes` list and make the objects it contains draw themselves. Then if `Drawing` is `true`, draw a red dashed rectangle with corners at `StartPoint` and `EndPoint`. (Hints: The `DrawRectangle` method can't draw rectangles with negative widths or heights so you'll need to figure out where the upper-left corner of the newly selected rectangle is. The `Math.Min` and `Math.Abs` methods may help.)

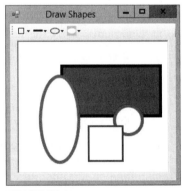

FIGURE 25-3

5. [Graphics, Hard] Copy the program you built for Exercise 4 and add the toolbar holding four dropdown buttons shown in Figure 25-3.

   The dropdown buttons represent the user's selected shape, line thickness, foreground color, and background color. When the user finishes selecting an area on the `PictureBox`, add the appropriate shape to the `Shapes` list. Hints:

   ➤ Use the properties of the menu items to store the selected values.

   ➤ Use the menu items' `Tag` properties to store the line thickness values. (You'll need to parse those values when you need them.)

➤ Use the menu items' `ForeColor` properties to store colors.

➤ Use the menu items' `Text` properties to store shape names.

➤ Use code similar to the following when the user selects an item from the shapes drop-down button:

```
// Save this shape selection.
private void shapeMenuItem_Click(object sender, EventArgs e)
{
    ToolStripMenuItem item = sender as ToolStripMenuItem;
    shapeDropdownItem.Image = item.Image;
    shapeDropdownItem.Tag = item.Text.Replace("&", "").ToLower();
}
```

This code is shared by all of the shape menu items. It converts the `sender` parameter into the `ToolStripMenuItem` that the user selected. It then copies that item's `Image` and `Text` (converted to lowercase and with any ampersands removed) into the dropdown button.

➤ Use similar code for the other dropdown buttons' items. Copy the selected item's `Image` property and the appropriate value (`Tag` or `ForeColor`) into the dropdown button.

6. Copy the complex number program you built for Exercise 24-2 (or download the version that's available on the book's website). Override the class's `ToString` method so it returns the number in a form similar to "2 + 3i." Overload the `ComplexNumber` class's `AddTo`, `MultiplyBy`, and `SubtractFrom` methods so you can pass them a single `double` parameter representing a real number with no imaginary part. Modify the form so you can test the new methods.

7. Copy the bank account program you built for Exercise 24-3 (or download the version that's available on the book's website). Derive a new `OverdraftAccount` class from the `Account` class. Give it a constructor that simply invokes the base class's constructor. Override the `Debit` method to allow the account to have a negative balance and charge a $50 fee if any debit leaves the account with a negative balance. Change the main program so the `Account` variable is still declared to be of type `Account` but initialize it as an `OverdraftAccount`. (Hint: Don't forget to make the `Account` class's version of `Debit` virtual.)

8. Copy Lesson 23's Turtle program. The `Turtle` class has a `Move` method that moves the turtle a specified distance in the object's current direction. Overload this method by making a second version that takes as parameters the X and Y coordinates where the turtle should move. Raise the `OutOfBounds` event if the point is not on the canvas. (Hint: Can you reuse code somehow between the two `Move` methods?)

NOTE *Please select the videos for Lesson 25 online at* www.wrox.com/go/
csharp24hourtrainer2evideos.

Overloading Operators

In Lesson 25 you learned how to overload a class's methods. C# also lets you overload operators such as + and * to give them new meanings when working with the structures and classes that you create. For example, you could overload the + operator so the program would know how to add a `Student` object and a `Course` object. Sometimes that allows you to use a more natural syntax when you're working with objects.

In this lesson, you learn how to overload operators so you can use them to manipulate objects.

> **WARNING** *Before you jump into operator overloading, be warned that just because you* can *overload an operator doesn't mean you* should. *You should only overload operators in intuitive ways.*
>
> *For example, it makes sense to overload the + operator so you can add two* ComplexNumber *objects. It might also make sense to overload + so you can add an item to a purchase order.*
>
> *It probably doesn't make sense to define + between two* Employee *objects to return a list of projects that included both employees. You could do that, but you probably shouldn't because it would be confusing.*

OVERLOADABLE OPERATORS

In C#, you can overload the unary, binary, and comparison operators listed in Table 26-1.

TABLE 26-1

TYPE	OPERATORS
Unary	+, −, !, ~, ++, −−
Binary	+, −, *, /, %, &, |, ^, <<, >>
Comparison	==, !=, <, >, <=, >=

The comparison operators come in pairs. For example, if you overload the < operator, you must also overload the > operator.

The compound assignment operators (+=, −=, *=, /=, %=, &=, |=, ^=, <<=, and >>=) are automatically overloaded when you overload the corresponding binary operator. For example, if you overload *, C# automatically overloads *= for you.

The syntax for overloading operators is easiest to understand by looking at examples. The following sections explain how to overload the different types of operators.

UNARY OPERATORS

The following code shows how you can overload the unary - operator for the `ComplexNumber` class:

```
public static ComplexNumber operator -(ComplexNumber me)
{
    return new ComplexNumber(-me.Real, -me.Imaginary);
}
```

The method begins with `public static` followed by the operator's return type. In this case the operator returns a `ComplexNumber` because the negation of a complex number is another complex number.

Next comes the keyword `operator` and the operator's symbol, in this case -.

The parameter list tells on which class the operator should be defined. Because this code is defining an operator for the `ComplexNumber` class, that's the parameter's data type. I often name this parameter `me` to help me remember that this is the object to which the operator is being applied.

Note that the overload must be declared inside the class used by the parameter. In this case, the parameter is a `ComplexNumber` so this code must be in the `ComplexNumber` class.

The code inside this method simply negates the `ComplexNumber`'s real and imaginary parts and returns a new `ComplexNumber`.

The following code shows how a program might use this operator:

```
ComplexNumber a = new ComplexNumber(1, 2);      //  1 + 2i
ComplexNumber minusA = -a;                       // -1 - 2i
```

BINARY OPERATORS

Overloading binary operators is similar to overloading unary operators except the operator takes a second parameter. The first parameter is still the object to which the operator is being applied.

For example, the following code overloads the binary - operator to subtract two ComplexNumbers:

```
public static ComplexNumber operator -(ComplexNumber me, ComplexNumber other)
{
    return new ComplexNumber(me.Real - other.Real,
        me.Imaginary - other.Imaginary);
}
```

The first parameter gives the object on the left of the - sign and the second parameter gives the object on the right. To help keep them straight, I often name the parameters me and other.

Note that the overload must be declared inside a class or structure used by one of the parameters. In this case, both parameters are ComplexNumbers so this code must be in the ComplexNumber class.

Although this example subtracts two ComplexNumbers, in general the parameters do not need to have the same data types. The following code defines the binary - operator for subtracting a double from a ComplexNumber:

```
public static ComplexNumber operator -(ComplexNumber me, double x)
{
    return new ComplexNumber(me.Real - x, me.Imaginary);
}
```

Note that this is not the same as subtracting a ComplexNumber from a double. If you want to handle that situation as well, you need the following separate overload:

```
public static ComplexNumber operator -(double me, ComplexNumber other)
{
    return new ComplexNumber(me - other.Real, other.Imaginary);
}
```

With these overloads, a program could execute the following code:

```
ComplexNumber a = new ComplexNumber(2, 3);
ComplexNumber b = new ComplexNumber(4, 5);
ComplexNumber c = a - b;              // ComplexNumber - ComplexNumber

ComplexNumber d = a - 10;             // ComplexNumber - double
ComplexNumber e = 10 - a;             // double - ComplexNumber
```

> **NOTE** *The shift operators << and >> are a little different from the other binary operators because the second parameter must always be an integer.*

COMPARISON OPERATORS

The comparison operators are simply binary operators that return a boolean result. The only oddity to these is that they come in pairs. For example, if you define ==, then you must also define !=. The pairs are == and !=, < and >, and <= and >=.

The following code shows how you could overload the < and > operators for the ComplexNumber class:

```
// Return the number's magnitude.
public double Magnitude
{
    get { return Math.Sqrt(Real * Real + Imaginary * Imaginary); }
}

public static bool operator <(ComplexNumber me, ComplexNumber other)
{
    return (me.Magnitude() < other.Magnitude());
}

public static bool operator >(ComplexNumber me, ComplexNumber other)
{
    return (me.Magnitude() > other.Magnitude());
}
```

> **WARNING** *The* Object *class provides* Equals *and* GetHashCode *methods that are tied closely to an object's notion of equality, because* Equals *should return* true *if two objects are equal and* GetHashCode *should return the same value for two objects that are considered equal. To avoid confusion, you should not overload* == *and* != *unless you also override* Equals *and* GetHashCode. *In fact, Visual Studio flags an error if you overload* == *or* != *but not these two methods.*

CONVERSION OPERATORS

C# provides one more kind of operator you can overload: conversion operators. These let a C# program convert one data type to another, either implicitly or explicitly. For example, consider the following code:

```
int i = 10;
double d = i;       // Implicitly convert i into a double.
int j = (int)d;     // Explicitly convert d into an int.
```

The first statement declares and initializes the integer i. The next statement sets the double variable d equal to the variable i. Because any int value can fit in a double variable, this conversion is safe so C# allows you to make it implicitly.

The third statement sets integer variable j equal to the value in the double variable. Not all double values can fit in an int, so C# won't let you make that assignment implicitly. The cast operator (int) explicitly tells C# to make the conversion anyway and you're willing to take the risk that the value may not fit.

You can overload conversion operators to allow your program to convert between types that you define. For example, consider the following code in the ComplexNumber class:

```
// Convert double to ComplexNumber.
public static implicit operator ComplexNumber(double x)
{
    return new ComplexNumber(x, 0);
}

// Convert ComplexNumber to double.
public static explicit operator double (ComplexNumber me)
{
    return me.Magnitude;
}
```

The first method defines a conversion operator that converts a double into a ComplexNumber. You can easily convert any double into a ComplexNumber by simply setting its imaginary part to 0. This conversion never causes a loss of data so it can be made implicitly.

The second method defines a conversion operator that converts a ComplexNumber into a double by returning the number's magnitude. This does cause a loss of data (unless the number's imaginary part happens to be 0) so the conversion is declared explicit. It allows your code to convert from a ComplexNumber to a double, but you need to explicitly use a cast to make it happen.

TRY IT

In this Try It, you extend the ComplexNumber class you built in Exercise 25-6. That version of the class included methods such as AddTo and SubtractFrom to perform simple operations. Now you'll replace those cumbersome methods with overloaded +, -, *, and unary - operators.

Lesson Requirements

In this lesson, you:

➤   Copy the complex number program you built for Exercise 25-6 (or download the version that's available on the book's website). Remove the ComplexNumber class's AddTo, MultiplyBy, and SubtractFrom methods.

➤   Give the class new overloaded operators to handle these cases:

➤   ComplexNumber + ComplexNumber

➤   ComplexNumber + double

> ➤   double + ComplexNumber

> ➤   ComplexNumber * ComplexNumber

> ➤   ComplexNumber * double

> ➤   double * ComplexNumber

> ➤   -ComplexNumber

> ➤   ComplexNumber - ComplexNumber

> ➤   ComplexNumber - double

> ➤   double - ComplexNumber

➤   Revise the main form's code to use the new operators.

> **NOTE** *You can download the code and resources for this lesson from the website at* www.wrox.com/go/csharp24hourtrainer2e.

Hints

➤   You can use operators to define other operators. For example, if you define the unary - operator, the following two operations have the same result:

```
ComplexNumber - ComplexNumber
ComplexNumber + -ComplexNumber
```

Step-by-Step

➤   Copy the complex number program you built for Exercise 25-6 (or download the version that's available on the book's website). Remove the ComplexNumber class's AddTo, MultiplyBy, and SubtractFrom methods.

1.   This is reasonably straightforward.

➤   Give the class new overloaded operators to handle these cases:

> ➤   ComplexNumber + ComplexNumber

> ➤   ComplexNumber + double

> ➤   double + ComplexNumber

> ➤   ComplexNumber * ComplexNumber

> ➤   ComplexNumber * double

> ➤   double * ComplexNumber

> ➤   -ComplexNumber

> ➤   ComplexNumber - ComplexNumber

➤ ComplexNumber - double

➤ double - ComplexNumber

1. You can use code similar to the following:

```
// ComplexNumber + ComplexNumber.
public static ComplexNumber operator +(ComplexNumber me, ComplexNumber other)
{
    return new ComplexNumber(
        me.Real + other.Real,
        me.Imaginary + other.Imaginary);
}

// ComplexNumber + double.
public static ComplexNumber operator +(ComplexNumber me, double x)
{
    return new ComplexNumber(me.Real + x, me.Imaginary);
}

// double + ComplexNumber.
public static ComplexNumber operator +(double x, ComplexNumber other)
{
    return other + x;
}

// ComplexNumber * ComplexNumber.
public static ComplexNumber operator *(ComplexNumber me, ComplexNumber other)
{
    return new ComplexNumber(
        me.Real * other.Real - me.Imaginary * other.Imaginary,
        me.Real * other.Imaginary + me.Imaginary * other.Real);
}

// ComplexNumber * double.
public static ComplexNumber operator *(ComplexNumber me, double x)
{
    return new ComplexNumber(me.Real * x, me.Imaginary * x);
}

// double * ComplexNumber.
public static ComplexNumber operator *(double x, ComplexNumber other)
{
    return other * x;
}

// Unary -.
public static ComplexNumber operator -(ComplexNumber me)
{
    return new ComplexNumber(-me.Real, -me.Imaginary);
}

// ComplexNumber - ComplexNumber.
public static ComplexNumber operator -(ComplexNumber me, ComplexNumber other)
{
    return me + -other;
}
```

```
// ComplexNumber - double.
public static ComplexNumber operator -(ComplexNumber me, double x)
{
    return new ComplexNumber(me.Real - x, me.Imaginary);
}

// double - ComplexNumber.
public static ComplexNumber operator -(double x, ComplexNumber other)
{
    return -other + x;
}
```

➤ Revise the main form's code to use the new operators.

1. You can use code similar to the following:

```
// Perform the calculations between two ComplexNumbers.
private void calculateButton_Click(object sender, EventArgs e)
{
    ComplexNumber a = new ComplexNumber(
        double.Parse(real1TextBox.Text),
        double.Parse(imaginary1TextBox.Text));
    ComplexNumber b = new ComplexNumber(
        double.Parse(real2TextBox.Text),
        double.Parse(imaginary2TextBox.Text));

    ComplexNumber aPlusB = a + b;
    aPlusBTextBox.Text = aPlusB.ToString();

    ComplexNumber aMinusB = a - b;
    aMinusBTextBox.Text = aMinusB.ToString();

    ComplexNumber aTimesB = a * b;
    aTimesBTextBox.Text = aTimesB.ToString();
}

// Perform the calculations with a real number.
private void calculateRealOnlyButton_Click(
    object sender, EventArgs e)
{
    double x = double.Parse(realOnlyTextBox.Text);
    ComplexNumber b = new ComplexNumber(
        double.Parse(real2TextBox.Text),
        double.Parse(imaginary2TextBox.Text));

    ComplexNumber xPlusB = x + b;
    aPlusBTextBox.Text = xPlusB.ToString();

    ComplexNumber xMinusB = x - b;
    aMinusBTextBox.Text = xMinusB.ToString();

    ComplexNumber xTimesB = x * b;
    aTimesBTextBox.Text = xTimesB.ToString();
}
```

EXERCISES

1. Providing methods that combine ComplexNumbers and doubles requires a lot of similar code. For example, to perform addition with ComplexNumbers, you need to overload the + operator three times to handle ComplexNumber + ComplexNumber, ComplexNumber + double, and double + ComplexNumber.

   Fortunately, there's a better approach. Just provide an implicit conversion operator to convert a double into a ComplexNumber. Now if the program needs to perform the operation ComplexNumber + double, it automatically converts the double into a ComplexNumber and can then perform the addition.

   Copy the program you built in this lesson's Try It and remove the code that combines ComplexNumbers with doubles. Then add an implicit conversion operator to convert doubles into ComplexNumbers. Verify that the program still works.

2. Copy the program you built for Exercise 1 and overload the ComplexNumber class's / operator to perform division using this equation:

$$\frac{a + bi}{c + di} = \frac{(ac + bd) + i(bc - ad)}{c^2 + d^2}$$

   Use this operator to define operators for ComplexNumber / double and double / ComplexNumber. (Hint: Don't perform all of the calculations for these. Convert the double into a ComplexNumber and then use the previous definition of /.)

   Change the main program to calculate A / B. Verify these calculations:

   ➤ (10+11i) / (3+2i) = 4 + 1i

   ➤ (15+24i) / 3 = 5 + 8i

   ➤ 4 / (1+1i) = 2 – 2i

3. Build an application with an OrderItem class that has the properties Description, Quantity, and PriceEach. Also make an Order class that has the properties CustomerName and Items, which is a List<OrderItem>. Then overload the Order class's + operator so you can use it to add OrderItems to an Order. Build a simple user interface to test the classes. Hints:

   ➤ Give the form a class-level Order object and then add items to it.

   ➤ Make the + operator return the Order to which it is adding an item.

   ➤ Override the OrderItem class's ToString method so you can easily display items in a ListBox.

4. [Advanced] By default, a class's Equals method tests *reference equality*. That means it considers two variables equal if they refer to the same instance of the class. For example, it would consider two Employee variables different if they refer to separate instances of the class even if they have the same FirstName and LastName property values. Sometimes that makes sense, but other times it's inconvenient.

Make a program that defines an `Employee` class with `FirstName` and `LastName` properties. Override the `ToString` method to return the concatenated names.

Use the following code to override the class's `Equals` method so it returns `true` if two `Employees` have the same `FirstName` and `LastName` values:

```
// Return true if the object is an Employee with
// the same first and last names as this object.
public override bool Equals(object obj)
{
    if (obj == null) return false;
    if (!(obj is Employee)) return false;

    Employee other = obj as Employee;
    return (
        (FirstName == other.FirstName) &&
        (LastName == other.LastName));
}
```

The first line checks that the other object is not `null`. (You already know that the current "this" object isn't `null` or else it couldn't be executing this code.)

The `is` keyword returns `true` if an object can be converted into a specific type, so the second line makes sure that `obj` inherits from the `Employee` type.

The method then converts `obj` into an `Employee` and compares its `FirstName` and `LastName` values to the current object's values.

If you override `Equals`, you should also override `GetHashCode`. This method converts an object into an `int` that acts as a sort of shorthand representation for it. The hash code for two equal objects must be the same. (That's why you need to override `GetHashCode` if you override `Equals`.) Ideally, two different objects should also be unlikely to have the same hash value.

For this exercise, give the `Employee` class the following `GetHashCode` method:

```
// Return a hash code for the object.
public override int GetHashCode()
{
    return FirstName.GetHashCode() ^ LastName.GetHashCode();
}
```

Now that you've defined the `Employee` class, create a `Department` class that has the properties `Name` and `Employees`, which is a `List<Employee>`. Overload its + operator to add an `Employee` to the `Employees` list.

Give the form a class-level `Department` object and initialize it. Then build the user interface shown in Figure 26-1.

When the user clicks Add, create an `Employee` object with the entered names, and use the `Department` object's + operator to add the `Employee` to the `Department`.

When the user clicks Remove, create an `Employee` object with the entered names. Use the `Contains` method of the `Department` object's `Employees` list to see if the `Employee` is in the list. If the `Employee` is present, use the list's `Remove` method to remove it. (The `Contains` and `Remove` methods wouldn't work if you hadn't overridden the `Equals` method. Comment out `Equals` and `GetHashCode` to see what happens.)

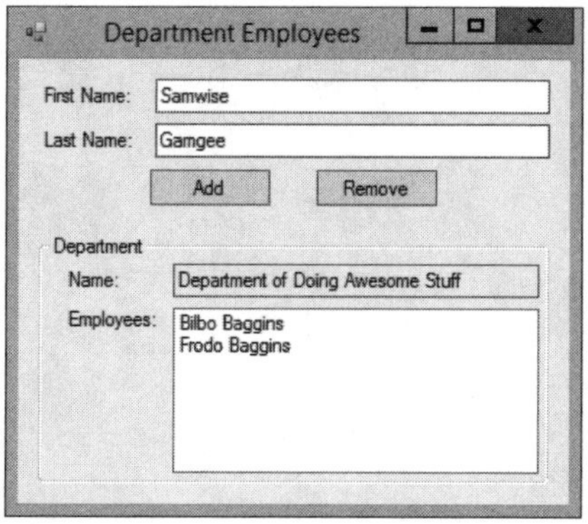

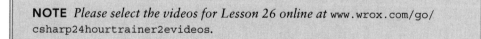

FIGURE 26-1

5. Make a new program and give it a copy of the Employee class you built for Exercise 4. Use the Equals method to overload the == and != operators. Then use an interface similar to the one shown in Figure 26-2 to test the operators.

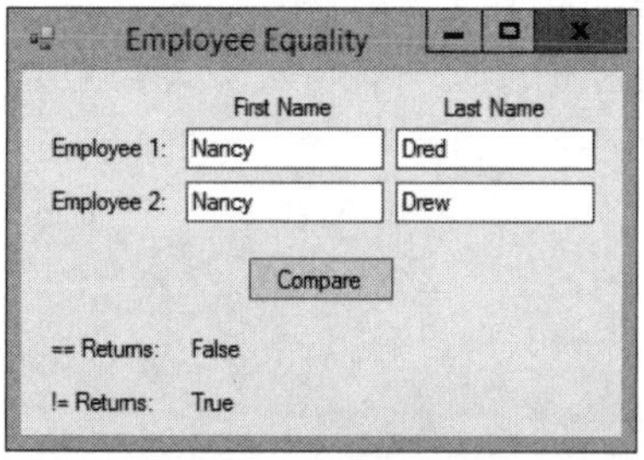

FIGURE 26-2

When the user clicks Compare, the program should create two Employee objects, use == and != to compare them, and display the results, as shown in the figure.

> **NOTE** *Please select the videos for Lesson 26 online at* www.wrox.com/go/ csharp24hourtrainer2evideos.

Using Interfaces

In .NET programming, an *interface* is like a contract. It defines the public properties, methods, and events that a class must provide to satisfy the contract. It doesn't indicate how the class must provide these features, however. That's left up to the class's code. It only defines an interface that the class must show to the rest of the world.

In this lesson, you learn how to implement interfaces that are predefined by the .NET Framework. You also learn how to define your own interfaces to make your code safer and more efficient.

INTERFACE ADVANTAGES

The following sections discuss two of the most important advantages provided by interfaces: multiple inheritance and code generalization.

Multiple Inheritance

Suppose you define a Vehicle class with properties such as NumberOfPassengers, MilesPerGallon, and NumberOfCupHolders. From this class you can derive other classes such as Car, PickupTruck, and Unicycle.

Suppose you also define a Domicile class that has properties such as SquareFeet, NumberOfBedrooms, and HasAnnoyingNeighbor. From this class you can derive Apartment, Condo, and VacationHome.

Next you might like to derive the MotorHome class from both Vehicle and Domicile so it has the properties and methods of both parent classes. Unfortunately you can't do that in C#. In C#, a class can inherit from only a single parent class.

Although a class can have only one parent, it can implement any number of interfaces. For example, if you turn the Domicile class into the IDomicile interface, the MotorHome class can inherit from Vehicle and implement IDomicile. The interface doesn't provide the code needed to implement such features as the HasAnnoyingNeighbor property, but at least it defines that property so code that uses a MotorHome object knows the property is available.

> **NOTE** *To make recognizing interface names easy, you should begin interface names with* I *as in* IDomicile, IComparable, *and* IWhatever.

Defining a property such as SquareFeet but not implementing it may not seem very useful, but it lets your code treat all IDomicile objects in a uniform way. Instead of writing separate methods to work with Duplex, RusticCabin, and HouseBoat objects, you can write a single method that manipulates objects that implement IDomicile.

That brings us to the second big advantage provided by interfaces: code generalization.

Code Generalization

Interfaces can make your code more general while still providing type checking. They let you treat objects that have common features as if they were of the interface type rather than their true individual types.

For example, suppose you write the following method that displays an array of strings in a ListBox:

```
private void DisplayValues(string[] items, ListBox listbox)
{
    listbox.Items.Clear();
    foreach (string value in items)
        listbox.Items.Add(value);
}
```

This method works reasonably well, but suppose you later decide that you need to display the items that are in a List<string> instead of an array. You could write a new version of the method that was nearly identical to this one but that works with a list instead of an array, as in the following code:

```
private void DisplayValues(List<string> items, ListBox listbox)
{
    listbox.Items.Clear();
    foreach (string value in items)
        listbox.Items.Add(value);
}
```

If you compare these two methods, you'll see that they are practically identical, so you must write, debug, and maintain two pieces of code that do almost exactly the same thing.

This is where interfaces can help.

Look again at the two methods. They differ only in their parameter definitions and the rest of their code is the same. The reason is that the methods don't really care that the parameters are arrays or lists. All they really care about is that you can use a foreach loop to iterate through them.

The IEnumerable<> interface requires that a class provide an enumerator that a program can use to loop through the items in the object. In particular, the enumerator supports foreach loops.

This is a generic interface so you must provide a type parameter for it to indicate the type of the items over which the interface can loop.

Both `string[]` and `List<string>` implement `IEnumerable<string>`, so you can combine and generalize the methods by making the `items` parameter have the type `IEnumerable<string>` instead of `string[]` or `List<string>`. The following code shows the new version of the method:

```
private void DisplayValues(IEnumerable<string> items, ListBox listbox)
{
    listbox.Items.Clear();
    foreach (string value in items)
        listbox.Items.Add(value);
}
```

This version can display the items in a `string[]`, `List<string>`, or any other object that implements `IEnumerable<string>` such as `LinkedList<string>`, `Stack<string>`, or `SortedSet<string>`.

IMPLEMENTING INTERFACES

To make a class that implements an interface, add the interface name in the class's declaration as if the class were inheriting from the interface. For example, the following code shows the declaration for a `Person` class that implements `IComparable`:

```
class Person : IComparable
{
    . . .
}
```

You can include a class and multiple interfaces in the inheritance list. For example, the `Manager` class could inherit from `Person` and implement the interfaces `IComparable` and `IDisposable`.

The only other thing you need to do is implement the properties, methods, and events defined by the interface. For example, the `IComparable` interface defines a `CompareTo` method that takes an object as a parameter and returns an integer that is less than, equal to, or greater than zero to indicate whether the object should be considered less than, equal to, or greater than the parameter.

Many interfaces come in generic versions. For example, the `IComparable<Person>` interface requires a class to define a `CompareTo<Person>` method.

For a concrete example, suppose the `Person` class defines `FirstName` and `LastName` properties. The following code implements a version of `CompareTo<Person>` that orders `Person` objects according to their last names first:

```
class Person : IComparable<Person>
{
    . . .
    // Compare this Person to another Person.
    public int CompareTo(Person other)
    {
        // If other is null, it comes first.
        if (other == null) return 1;
```

```
            // If our last name comes first, we come first.
            if (LastName.CompareTo(other.LastName) < 0) return -1;

            // If our last name comes second, we come second.
            if (LastName.CompareTo(other.LastName) > 0) return 1;

            // If our last names are the same, compare first names.
            return FirstName.CompareTo(other.FirstName);
        }
        ...
    }
```

First, if the other `Person` object is `null`, the method returns 1 to indicate that the current `Person` should come after it. (By convention, `null` values come before non-`null` values.)

Next, the method compares the two objects' `LastName` values. If the values are not the same, the code returns –1 or 1 to indicate that the current `Person` comes before or after the `other`.

Finally, if the two `LastName` values are the same, the code uses the `CompareTo` method provided by the `string` class to compare the two `FirstName` values and returns the result.

You can write the code to implement an interface yourself, but it's easier to let Visual Studio build a default implementation for you. Write the class declaration including the interface. Then hover the mouse over the interface's name in the class declaration and look for the change suggestion lightbulb to appear. You can see it under the word "class" in Figure 27-1.

FIGURE 27-1

Click the lightbulb and select the Implement Interface command from the dropdown list, as shown in Figure 27-2.

When you select that command, Visual Studio adds placeholder code to satisfy the interface. The following code shows the placeholder method for the `ICompare<Person>` interface:

```
public int CompareTo(Person other)
{
    throw new NotImplementedException();
}
```

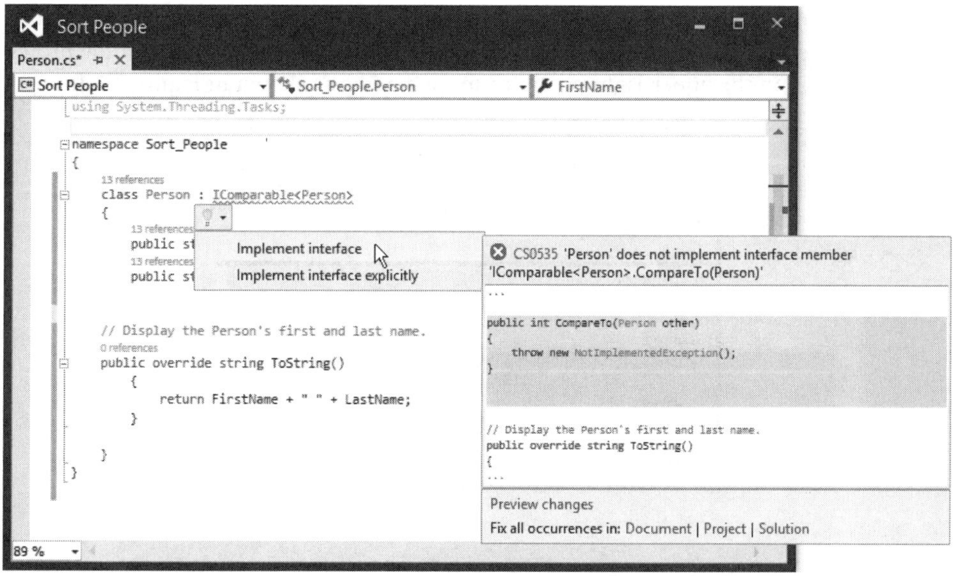

FIGURE 27-2

Now you can fill in the code you want to use.

You can learn more about what an interface is for and what it does in several ways. You can always search the online help. You can also right-click the interface's name and select Go To Definition to see information, as shown in Figure 27-3. Click the plus signs on the left to view detailed comments describing the purposes of the pieces of code.

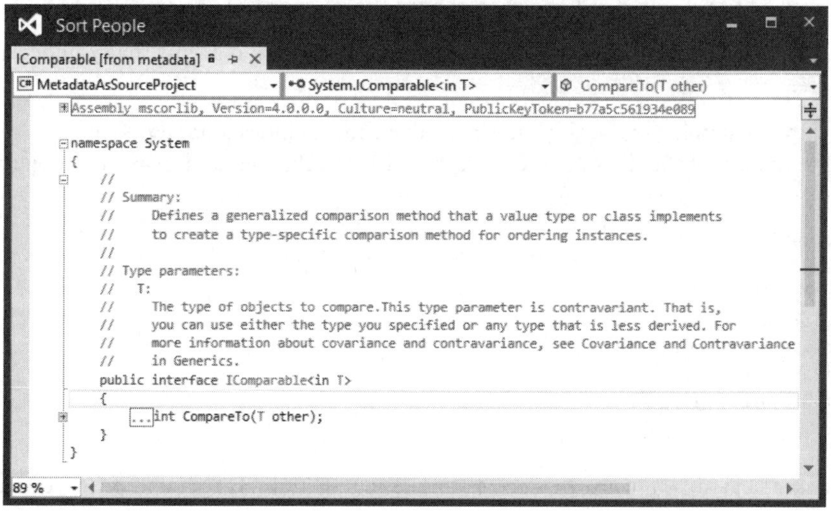

FIGURE 27-3

Finally, you can open the Object Browser (use the View menu's Object Browser command) and search for the interface's name (without the generic parameters). Select the interface in the browser's left panel. Click an item in the upper-right panel for more details, as shown in Figure 27-4.

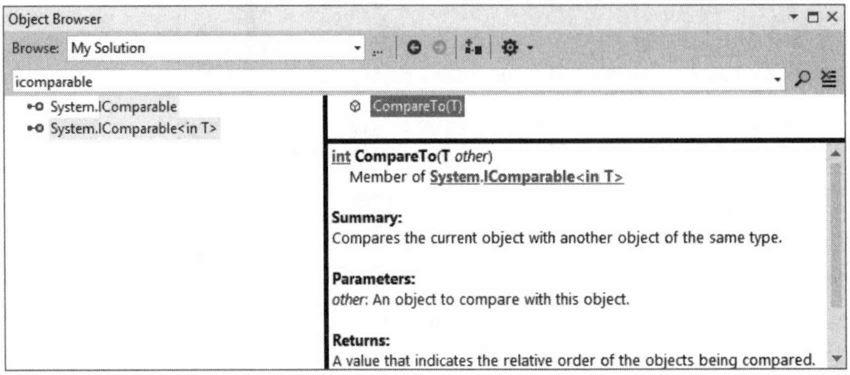

FIGURE 27-4

DEFINING INTERFACES

The preceding sections give examples that implement predefined interfaces. This section explains how you can define your own.

Defining an interface is a lot like defining a class, with two main differences:

➤ First, you use the keyword `interface` instead of `class` in the declaration. (You can use the Project menu's Add Class command and then change the keyword `class` to `interface`.)

➤ Second, you don't provide any code for the properties, methods, and events that you declare in the interface.

The following code shows a simple `IDrawable` interface. The code includes a `using System` `.Graphics` directive at the top of the file to make working with `Brush`, `Pen`, and `Graphics` objects easier.

```
interface IDrawable
{
    int X { get; set; }
    int Y { get; set; }
    Brush Background { get; set; }
    Pen Foreground { get; set; }
    void Draw(Graphics gr);
}
```

A class that implements `IDrawable` must provide `X`, `Y`, `Background`, and `Foreground` properties and a `Draw` method.

You cannot provide an accessibility modifier such as `private` to the items defined by an interface because they are always assumed to be public. That means a class that implements the interface must declare these items as `public`.

The declarations for the properties look like they are providing a default implementation, but they actually only indicate which accessors are required. For example, you could omit the `set` accessor to require a read-only property.

A class that implements `IDrawable` must still provide its own implementations, although you can use auto-implemented properties if you like. For example, the following code shows how the `DrawableCircle` class might implement its X property:

```
public int X { get; set; }
```

> **NOTE** *This example might work better with true inheritance instead of an interface. If you make a* `Drawable` *class that implements the* X, Y, Background, *and* Foreground *properties, other classes such as* DrawableCircle *could inherit them. In this example an interface makes sense only if the classes already inherit from some other class so they cannot also inherit from* Drawable.

TRY IT

In this Try It, you build the `Vehicle` class and the `IDomicile` interface described earlier in this lesson. You then make a `MotorHome` class that inherits from the first and implements the second. Finally, you create an instance of the derived class.

Lesson Requirements

In this lesson, you:

➤ Start a new project. Create a `Vehicle` class with the properties `NumberOfPassengers`, `MilesPerGallon`, and `NumberOfCupHolders`. Give it an initializing constructor and override its `ToString` method so it returns the object's property values separated by the escape sequence \r\n.

➤ Make an `IDomicile` interface that defines the properties `SquareFeet`, `NumberOfBedrooms`, and `NumberOfBathrooms`. Also make it define a `ToString` method that returns a string as usual.

➤ Derive the `MotorHome` class from `Vehicle`, making it implement `IDomicile`. Give it an initializing constructor and override its `ToString` method so it returns all of the object's property values separated by the escape sequence \r\n.

➤ Create an instance of the `MotorHome` class. Then use its `ToString` method to display its properties in a textbox.

> **NOTE** *You can download the code and resources for this lesson from the web-site at* www.wrox.com/go/csharp24hourtrainer2e.

Hints

➤ Don't forget to make the `MotorHome` class's constructor invoke the base class's constructor. If you don't remember how, see the section "Invoking Other Constructors" in Lesson 24.

➤ You can save a little work by making the `MotorHome` class's `ToString` method call the `Vehicle` class's version.

Step-by-Step

➤ Start a new project. Create a `Vehicle` class with the properties `NumberOfPassengers`, `MilesPerGallon`, and `NumberOfCupHolders`. Give it a constructor to make it easy to initialize a new object's properties. Override its `ToString` method so it returns the object's property values separated by the escape sequence `\r\n`.

1. Use code similar to the following:

```
class Vehicle
{
    // Properties.
    public int NumberOfPassengers { get; set; }
    public double MilesPerGallon { get; set; }
    public int NumberOfCupHolders { get; set; }

    // Initializing constructor.
    public Vehicle(int numberOfPassengers, double milesPerGallon,
        int numberOfCupHolders)
    {
        NumberOfPassengers = numberOfPassengers;
        MilesPerGallon = milesPerGallon;
        NumberOfCupHolders = numberOfCupHolders;
    }

    // Return the object's properties.
    public override string ToString()
    {
        return
            "NumberOfPassengers: " + NumberOfPassengers +
            "\r\nMilesPerGallon : " + MilesPerGallon +
            "\r\nNumberOfCupHolders: " + NumberOfCupHolders;
    }
}
```

➤ Make an `IDomicile` interface that defines the properties `SquareFeet`, `NumberOfBedrooms`, and `NumberOfBathrooms`. Also make it define a `ToString` method that returns a string as usual.

1. Use code similar to the following:

```
interface IDomicile
{
    int SquareFeet { get; set; }
    int NumberOfBedrooms { get; set; }
    double NumberOfBathrooms { get; set; }
    string ToString();
}
```

➤ Derive the MotorHome class from Vehicle, making it implement IDomicile. Give it a constructor to make it easy to initialize a new object's properties. Override its ToString method so it returns the object's property values separated by the escape sequence \r\n.

1. Use code similar to the following:

```
class MotorHome : Vehicle, IDomicile
{
    // IDomicile methods.
    public int SquareFeet { get; set; }
    public int NumberOfBedrooms { get; set; }
    public double NumberOfBathrooms { get; set; }

    // Initializing constructor.
    public MotorHome(int numberOfPassengers, double milesPerGallon,
        int numberOfCupHolders, int squareFeet,
        int numberOfBedrooms, double numberOfBathrooms)
        : base(numberOfPassengers, milesPerGallon,
        numberOfCupHolders)
    {
        SquareFeet = squareFeet;
        NumberOfBedrooms = numberOfBedrooms;
        NumberOfBathrooms = numberOfBathrooms;
    }

    // Return the object's properties.
    public override string ToString()
    {
        return base.ToString() +
            "\r\nSquareFeet: " + SquareFeet +
            "\r\nNumberOfBedrooms: " + NumberOfBedrooms +
            "\r\nNumberOfBathrooms: " + NumberOfBathrooms;
    }
}
```

➤ Create an instance of the MotorHome class. Then use its ToString method to display its properties in a textbox.

1. The following code creates an instance of the MotorHome class and displays its properties in resultTextBox:

```
private void Form1_Load(object sender, EventArgs e)
{
    // Make a MotorHome.
    MotorHome motorHome = new MotorHome(6, 8.25, 32, 150, 3, 0.5);
```

```
        // Display its properties.
        resultTextBox.Text = motorHome.ToString();
    }
```

EXERCISES

1. Build a program that defines the `IDrawable` interface described earlier in this lesson. Make the `DrawableCircle` and `DrawableRectangle` classes implement the interface. Hints: Give `DrawableCircle` an additional `Radius` property and give `DrawableRectangle` additional `Width` and `Height` properties. Use code similar to the following to draw the circle centered at the point (X, Y):

   ```
   // Draw the circle centered at (X, Y).
   public void Draw(Graphics gr)
   {
       gr.FillEllipse(Background, X - Radius, Y - Radius,
           2 * Radius, 2 * Radius);
       gr.DrawEllipse(Foreground, X - Radius, Y - Radius,
           2 * Radius, 2 * Radius);
   }
   ```

   Use code similar to the following to draw the rectangle with upper-left corner (X, Y):

   ```
   // Draw the rectangle.
   public void Draw(Graphics gr)
   {
       gr.FillRectangle(Background, X, Y, Width, Height);
       gr.DrawRectangle(Foreground, X, Y, Width, Height);
   }
   ```

   (For bonus points, make a `DrawableStar` class that has a `NumberOfPoints` property and draws a star with that number of points.)

2. [Hard] An array's `Sort` method can take as a parameter an object that implements the generic `IComparer` interface. Because this interface is generic, you can tell it what kinds of objects the class can compare. For example, `IComparer<Car>` means the class can compare `Car` objects.

   Build a `Car` class with the properties `Name`, `MaxSpeed`, `Horsepower`, and `Price`. Override the `ToString` method to display the object's properties formatted with fixed column widths so the values for different `Cars` in a `ListBox` will line up nicely, as shown in Figure 27-5. (The `ListBox` uses the fixed-width font Courier New so all of the letters have the same width.)

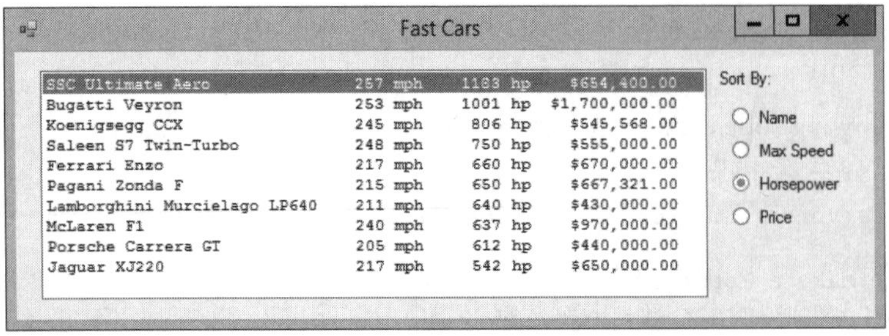

FIGURE 27-5

Build a `CarComparer` class that implements `IComparer<Car>`. Give it the following `SortType` enumeration:

```
// Different kinds of sorts.
public enum SortType
{
    ByName,
    ByMaxSpeed,
    ByHorsepower,
    ByPrice,
}
```

Next give `CarComparer` a `Sort` property that has type `SortType`.

Finally, give the `CarComparer` a `Compare` method to satisfy the `IComparer<Car>` interface. Use a `switch` statement to make the method return a value that depends on the `Sort` value. For example, if `Sort` is `ByPrice`, then compare the two `Cars'` prices. Make the method sort the `MaxSpeed`, `Horsepower`, and `Price` values in decreasing order.

Now create and initialize a class-level list of `Car` objects. When the user clicks a `RadioButton`, follow these steps:

➤   Set the `ListBox` control's `DataSource` property to `null`.

➤   Create a `CarComparer` with the appropriate `SortType`.

➤   Call the `Car` list's `Sort` method, passing it the comparer.

➤   Set the `ListBox` control's `DataSource` property to the `Car` list.

> **NOTE** *Note that you have many ways to do this sort of thing. For example, Lesson 36 explains how you can use LINQ to sort items. As with all of the examples and exercises in this book, these examples are primarily designed to demonstrate particular topics, in this case interfaces, rather than to provide the perfect solution.*

3.   [Hard] If you set a `ListView` control's `ListViewItemSorter` property equal to an object that implements the `System.Collections.IComparer` interface, then the `ListView` uses that object to sort its rows. To sort the rows, the control calls the object's `Compare` method, passing it two `ListViewItem` objects. (Unfortunately the `ListView` control's `ListViewItemSorter` property is a non-generic `IComparer`, so it works with non-specific objects instead of something more concrete like `ListViewItems`.)

For this exercise, make a program with a `ListView` control similar to the one shown in Figure 27-6. At design time, edit the `ListView`'s `Columns` collection to define the columns. Edit its `Items` collection to define the data and set the control's `View` property to `Details`.

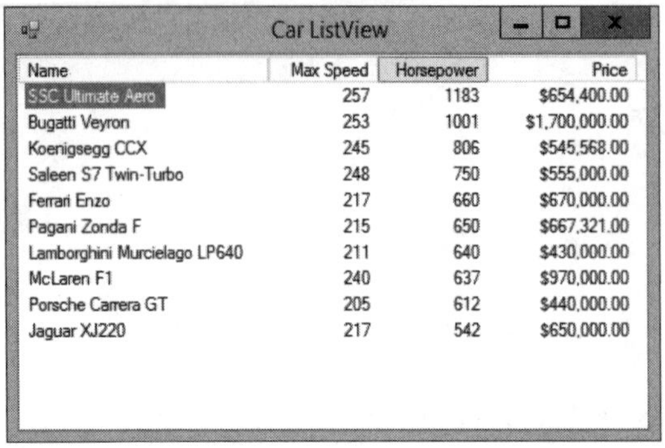

FIGURE 27-6

Next, make a ListViewComparer class that implements System.Collections.IComparer. Give it a ColumnNumber property that indicates the number of the column in the ListView that the object should use when sorting.

Finally, give the ListView a ColumnClick event handler. The event handler should create a new ListViewComparer object to sort on the clicked column and then set the ListView control's ListViewItemSorter property to that object.

4. The IEquatable interface requires a class to provide an Equals method that returns true if two objects should be regarded as equal. Some classes, such as List, can use that interface. For example, if you fill a List with objects that implement IEquatable, then the list's Contains method can tell if the list contains an object that is equivalent to another object.

Make a Person class that has the properties FirstName and LastName and that implements IEquatable<Person>. Then build a program similar to the one shown in Figure 27-7 to let the user add and remove Person objects in a list. If the user tries to add a duplicate Person or tries to remove a Person that isn't in the list, display an error message.

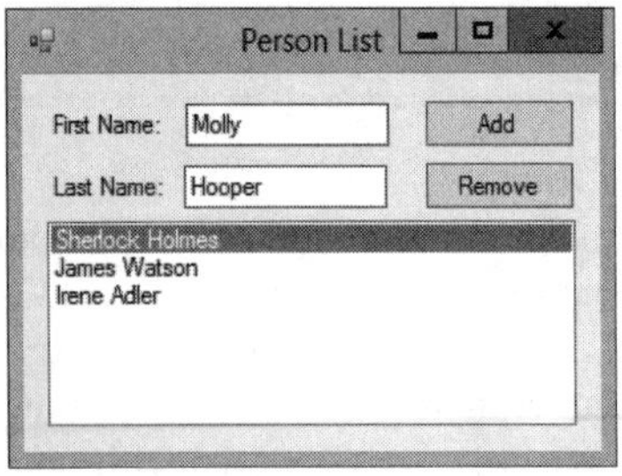

FIGURE 27-7

Hints

➤ Store the Person objects in a List<Person> named People. (Unfortunately, the ListBox control's Items collection doesn't assume its contents implement IEquatable so you can't just store the Person objects there.)

➤ After modifying the list, make the ListBox display the list of people by setting the ListBox's DataSource property to null and then setting it equal to People.

5. It's always better to prevent the user from making a mistake than it is to display an error message. Copy the program you wrote for Exercise 4 and make the following changes:

➤ Remove the previous error messages.

➤ Enable the Add button only if both TextBoxes have non-blank text and the list doesn't already contain a person with those first and last names.

➤ Enable the Remove button only if both TextBoxes have non-blank text and the list contains a person with those first and last names.

6. Make a program that defines the following classes and interfaces:

➤ An IWolf interface with PackName and Rank properties, and a WolfInfo method that returns a string. (In classes that implement IWolf, make this method return the person's name and pack name.)

➤ A Person class with FirstName and LastName properties and an overridden ToString method.

➤ An Employee class that inherits from Person, adds a new EmployeeId property, and makes ToString include EmployeeId.

➤ A Werewolf class derived from Person and IWolf.

➤ A WereEmployee class derived from Employee and IWolf.

Create instances of the Person, Employee, Werewolf, and WereEmployee classes. Place them all in a List<Person> and place those that you can in a List<IWolf>. Loop through the lists and display the objects' information in two ListBoxes.

7. Copy the program you built for Exercise 6 and modify it so WereEmployee inherits from Werewolf. What are the advantages and disadvantages to this approach? Which approach seems better? (Look at the comments in the WereEmployee class in the download to see my thoughts.)

NOTE *Please select the videos for Lesson 27 online at* www.wrox.com/go/
csharp24hourtrainer2evideos.

Making Generic Classes

The section "Generic Classes" in Lesson 16 explained how to use generic collection classes. For example, the following code defines a list that holds `Employee` objects:

```
public List<Employee> Employees = new List<Employee>();
```

This list can only hold `Employee` objects, and when you get an object out of the list, it has the `Employee` type instead of the less-specific `object` type.

Lesson 16 also described the main advantages of generic classes: code reuse and specific type checking. You can use the same generic `List<>` class to hold a list of `strings`, `doubles`, or `Person` objects. By requiring a specific data type, the class prevents you from accidentally adding an `Employee` object to a list of `Order` objects, and when you get an object from the list you know it is an `Order`.

In this lesson, you learn how to build your own generic classes so you can raise code reuse to a whole new level.

> **NOTE** *Many other things can be generic. You can probably guess that you can build generic structures because structures are so similar to classes. You can also create generic methods (in either generic or non-generic classes), generic interfaces, generic delegate types, and so on. This lesson focuses on generic classes.*

DEFINING GENERIC CLASSES

A generic class declaration looks a lot like a normal class declaration with one or more generic type variables added in angled brackets. For example, the following code shows the basic declaration for a generic `TreeNode` class:

```
class TreeNode<T>
{
    ...
}
```

The `<T>` means the class takes one type parameter, `T`. Within the class's code, the type `T` means whatever type the program used when creating the instance of the class. For example, the following code declares a variable named `rootNode` that is a `TreeNode` that handles `strings`:

```
TreeNode<string> rootNode = new TreeNode<string>();
```

If you want the class to use multiple type parameters, separate them with commas. For example, suppose you want to make a `Matcher` class that takes two kinds of objects and matches objects in the two kinds. It might match `Employee` objects with `Job` objects to assign employees to jobs. The following code shows how you might declare the `Matcher` class:

```
public class Matcher<T1, T2>
{
    . . .
}
```

The following code shows how you might create an instance of the class to match `Employees` with `Jobs`:

```
Matcher<Employee, Job> jobAssigner = new Matcher<Employee, Job>();
```

> **NOTE** *Many developers use* `T` *for the name of the type in generic classes that take only one type.*
>
> *If the class takes more than one type, you should use more descriptive names so it's easy to tell the types apart. For example, the generic* `Dictionary` *class has two type variables named* `TKey` *and* `TValue` *that represent the types of the keys and values that the* `Dictionary` *will hold.*

Inside the class's code, you can use the types freely. For example, the following code shows more of the `TreeNode` class's code. A `TreeNode` object represents a node in a tree, with an associated piece of data attached to it. The places where the class uses the data type `T` are highlighted in bold.

```
class TreeNode<T>
{
    // This node's data.
    public T Data { get; set; }

    // This node's children.
    private List<TreeNode<T>> children = new List<TreeNode<T>>();

    // Constructor.
    public TreeNode(T data)
    {
        Data = data;
    }

    // Override ToString to display the data.
    public override string ToString()
    {
```

```
            if (Data == null) return "";
            return Data.ToString();
        }

        ...

    }
```

Notice how the class uses the type T throughout its code. The class starts by defining a Data field of type T. This is the data (of whatever data type) associated with the node.

Each node also has a list of child nodes. To hold the right kind of TreeNode objects, the children variable is a generic List<TreeNode<T>>, meaning it can hold only TreeNode<T> objects.

The class's constructor takes a parameter of type T and saves it in the object's Data property.

To make displaying a TreeNode easier, the class overrides its ToString method so it calls the ToString method provided by the Data object. For example, if the object is a TreeNode<string>, this simply returns the string's value.

USING GENERIC CONSTRAINTS

The previous example overrides the TreeNode class's ToString method to make it call the Data object's ToString method. Fortunately, all objects have a ToString method so you know this is possible, but what if you want to call some other method provided by the object?

For example, suppose you want to create a new instance of type T. How do you know that type T provides a constructor that takes no parameters? What if you want to compare two objects of type T to see which is greater? Or what if you want to compare two type T objects to see if they are the same (an important test for the Dictionary class)? How do you know whether two type T objects are comparable?

You can use *generic constraints* to require that the types used by the program meet certain criteria such as comparability or providing a parameterless constructor.

To use a generic constraint, follow the normal class declaration with the keyword where, the name of the type parameter that you want to constrain, a colon, and the constraint. Some typical constraints include:

➤ A class from which the type must inherit

➤ An interface (or interfaces) that the type must implement

➤ new() to indicate that the type must provide a parameterless constructor

➤ struct to indicate that the type must be a value type such as the built-in value types (int, bool) or a structure

➤ class to indicate that the type must be a reference type

Separate multiple constraints for the same type parameter with commas. If you want to constrain more than one type parameter, use a new where clause.

For example, the following code defines the generic `Matcher` class, which takes two generic type parameters `T1` and `T2`. (Note that this code skips important error handling such as checking for `null` values to keep things simple.)

```
public class Matcher<T1, T2>
    where T1 : IComparable<T2>, new()
    where T2 : new()
{
    private void test()
    {
        T1 t1 = new T1();
        T2 t2 = new T2();
        ...

        if (t1.CompareTo(t2) < 0)
        {
            // t1 is "less than" t2.
            ...
        }
    }
    ...
}
```

The first constraint requires that type parameter `T1` implement the `IComparable` interface for the type `T2` so the code can compare `T1` objects to `T2` objects. The next constraint requires that the `T1` type also provide a parameterless constructor. You can see that the code creates a new `T1` object and uses its `CompareTo` method (which is defined by `IComparable`).

The second `where` clause requires that the type `T2` also provide a parameterless constructor. The code needs that because it also creates a new `T2` instance.

In general, you should use as few constraints as possible because that makes your generic code usable in as many circumstances as possible. If your code won't need to create new instances of a data type, don't use the `new` constraint. If your code won't need to compare objects, don't use the `IComparable` constraint.

MAKING GENERIC METHODS

In addition to building generic classes, you can also build generic methods inside either a generic class or a regular non-generic class.

For example, suppose you want to rearrange the items in a list so the new order alternately picks items from each end of the list. If the list originally contains the numbers 1, 2, 3, 4, 5, 6, then the alternated list contains 1, 6, 2, 5, 3, 4.

The following code shows how a program could declare an `Alternate` method to return an alternated list. The part of the code that defines the generic parameter `T` is shown in bold.

```
public List<T> Alternate<T>(List<T> list)
{
    // Make a new list to hold the results.
    List<T> newList = new List<T>();
```

```
   . . .
   return newList;
}
```

The `Alternate` method takes a generic type parameter `T`. It takes as a regular parameter a `List` that holds items of type `T` and it returns a new `List` containing items of type `T`.

The code creates a new `List<T>` to hold the results. (Note that it does not need to require the type `T` to have a default constructor because the code is creating a new `List`, not a new `T`.) The code then builds the new list (not shown here) and returns it.

The following code shows how a program might use this method:

```
List<string> strings = new List<string>(stringsTextBox.Text.Split(' '));
List<string> alternatedStrings = Alternate<string>(strings);
alternatedStringsTextBox.Text = string.Join(" ", alternatedStrings);
```

The first statement defines a `List<string>` and initializes it with the space-separated values in the `TextBox` named `stringsTextBox`.

The second statement calls `Alternate<string>` to create an alternated `List<string>`. Notice how the code uses `<string>` to indicate the data type that `Alternate` will manipulate. (This is actually optional and the program will figure out which version of `Alternate` to use if you omit it. However, this makes the code more explicit and may catch a bug if you try to alternate a list containing something unexpected such as `Person` objects.)

The third statement joins the values in the new list, separating them with spaces, and displays the result.

Generic methods can be quite useful for the same reasons that generic classes are. They allow code reuse without the extra hassle of converting values to and from the non-specific `object` class. They also perform type checking, so in this example, the program cannot try to alternate a `List<int>` by calling `Alternate<string>`.

TRY IT

In this Try It, you build a generic `Randomize` method that randomizes an array of objects of any type. To make it easy to add the method to any project, you add the method to an `ArrayMethods` class. To make the method easy to use, you make it `static`, so the main program doesn't need to instantiate the class to use it.

Lesson Requirements

In this lesson, you:

➤   Start a new project and give it an `ArrayMethods` class.

➤   Create a generic `Randomize` method with one generic type parameter `T`. The method should take as a parameter an array of `T` and randomize the items it contains.

➤   Make the main program test the method.

> **NOTE** *You can download the code and resources for this lesson from the website at* www.wrox.com/go/csharp24hourtrainer2e.

Hints

➤ Try to figure out the `Randomize` method's declaration yourself before you read the step-by-step instructions that follow.

Step-by-Step

➤ Start a new project and give it an `ArrayMethods` class.

  1. This is reasonably straightforward. You don't need to make the `ArrayMethods` class generic.

➤ Create a generic `Randomize` method with one generic type parameter `T`. The method should take as a parameter an array of `T` and randomize the items it contains.

  1. The following code shows how you can implement this method:

```
class ArrayMethods
{
    // Make a Random object to use to pick random items.
    private static Random Rand = new Random();

    // Randomize the items in an array.
    public static void Randomize<T>(T[] items)
    {
        // For each spot in the array, pick
        // a random item to swap into that spot.
        for (int i = 0; i < items.Length - 1; i++)
        {
            // Pick a random item j between i and the last item.
            int j = Rand.Next(i, items.Length);

            // Swap item j into position i.
            T temp = items[i];
            items[i] = items[j];
            items[j] = temp;
        }
    }
}
```

➤ Make the main program test the method.

  1. The program I wrote uses two `TextBoxes`, one to hold the original items and one to display the randomized items. When you click the Randomize button, the following code executes:

```
// Randomize the items and display the results.
private void randomizeButton_Click(object sender, EventArgs e)
{
    // Get the items as an array of strings.
```

```
                    string[] items = itemsTextBox.Lines;

                    // Randomize the array.
                    ArrayMethods.Randomize<string>(items);

                    // Display the result.
                    randomizedTextBox.Lines = items;
                }
```

Notice that the code uses the TextBox's Lines property to get the entered values. That property returns the lines in a multi-line TextBox as an array of strings.

Also notice that the code doesn't need to make an instance of the ArrayMethods class. That's the advantage of making the Randomize method static.

EXERCISES

1. [Hard] The Randomize method in the Try It doesn't actually need to work with an array. What it really needs is to access items by index. The IList interface requires that a class provide a Count property and indexes.

   Write a new version of the generic Randomize method that takes as a parameter an IList. (Hint: You'll also need a type parameter for the items inside the list.) Update the program to test both versions of the method. Note that C# cannot infer which version to use if you don't include type parameters when the main program invokes the method.

2. Finish building the generic Alternate method described earlier in this lesson. Add the code needed to make the alternating version of the list. To make using the method easy, make it static in the ArrayMethods class. Make the main program test the method with lists containing odd and even numbers of items.

3. [Hard] The solution to Exercise 1 rearranges the items in an IList randomly. The same approach would be tricky for the Alternate method in Exercise 2 because it's not obvious how you would shuffle the items around in the same array without losing track of where they all belong. (At least I couldn't think of a good way to do it.)

   However, you can use a slightly different approach. Add an Alternate method to the ArrayMethods class that uses an intermediate array to arrange the items in an IList.

4. [Hard] Make the TreeNode class to represent a tree node associated with a piece of data of some generic type. In addition to the code shown earlier in this lesson, give the class:

   ➤ An AddChild method that adds a new child node to the node for which the method is invoked. Have the method take a piece of data of the class's generic type as a parameter and return a new TreeNode representing that piece of data.

   ➤ A private AddToListPreorder method that adds a node's subtree to a list in preorder format. The preorder format lists the node's data first and then recursively calls the method to add the data for the node's children. You can use code similar to the following:

   ```
   // Recursively add our subtree to an existing list in preorder.
   private void AddToListPreorder(List<TreeNode<T>> list)
   {
   ```

```
            // Add this node.
            list.Add(this);

            // Add the children.
            foreach (TreeNode<T> child in Children)
                child.AddToListPreorder(list);
        }
```

➤ A public `Preorder` method that returns the node's subtree items in a list in preorder format. The method should call `AddToListPreorder` to do all of the work. You can use code similar to the following:

```
// Return a list containing our subtree in preorder.
public List<TreeNode<T>> Preorder()
{
    List<TreeNode<T>> list = new List<TreeNode<T>>();
    AddToListPreorder(list);
    return list;
}
```

➤ For extra credit, add similar methods to build lists in postorder and inorder. In postorder, a node recursively adds its children to the list and then adds its own data. In inorder, a node recursively adds the first half of its children to the list, then itself, and then the rest of its children.

Make the main program build the tree shown in Figure 28-1, although it doesn't need to display it graphically as in the figure. Make the program display the tree's preorder, postorder, and inorder representations, as shown in Figure 28-2.

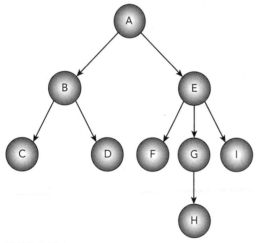

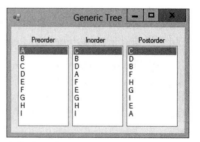

FIGURE 28-2

FIGURE 28-1

5. Make a generic `PriorityQueue` class. The class is basically a list holding generic items where each item has an associated priority. Give the class a nested `ItemData` structure similar to the following to hold an item:

```
// A structure to hold items.
private struct ItemData
{
```

```
        public int Priority { get; set; }
        public T Data { get; set; }
    }
```

This structure is defined inside the `PriorityQueue` class and won't be used outside of the class, so it can be `private`. Note that this structure uses the class's generic type parameter `T` for the data it holds.

The class should store its `ItemData` objects in a generic `List`.

Give the `PriorityQueue` class a public `Count` property that returns the number of items in the list.

Give the class an `AddItem` method that takes as parameters a piece of data and a priority. It should make a new `ItemData` object to hold these values and add it to the list.

Finally, give the class a `GetItem` method that searches the list for the item with the smallest priority number (priority 1 means top priority), removes that item from the list, and returns the item and its priority via parameters passed for output. (If there's a tie for lowest priority number, return the first item you find with that priority.)

6. Make a generic `Sack` class that holds items with weights. Give the class the following features:

   ➤ A constructor that takes as a parameter the `Sack`'s total capacity.

   ➤ An `Add` method that takes as parameters a data item and a weight. If the total weight in the `Sack` exceeds the `Sack`'s capacity, the method should throw an `ArgumentException`.

   ➤ An `Items` method that returns a `List` holding the items in the `Sack`.

   ➤ A `Weights` method that returns a `List` holding the weights of the items in the `Sack`.

   Build a user interface that lets the user add items with weights to a `Sack` with a capacity of 100. Use two `ListBoxes` to display the items in the `Sack` and their weights after each addition.

7. Make a program similar to the one you built for Exercise 6 except using a `Box` class. A `Box` should be similar to a `Sack` class except it should have a maximum total volume in addition to a maximum total weight.

8. Make a generic method that swaps its two parameters' values.

9. [Advanced] The `Math.Min` and `Math.Max` methods are very useful, but they have two big drawbacks. First, they take only two parameters. That means if you want to find the largest and smallest of more than two values, you need to use them repeatedly. (Other available methods, notably LINQ, are described in Lesson 36.)

   The second drawback is that they only work with `double` parameters. If you pass `ints` or `floats` into the methods, the values are promoted to the `double` data type so the methods still work, but their results are `doubles` so you'll need to convert them if you want the results to have the original data types.

   For this exercise, write generic `Min` and `Max` methods that can take any number of parameters and that return a value in the parameters' data type. Hints:

➤ To allow a method to take any number of parameters, you can use a *parameter array*. A parameter array should begin with the `params` keyword, should be an array, and must come last in the method's parameter list. For example, `DoSomething(params string[] values)`.

➤ Obviously you'll need to be able to compare the parameters to each other.

> **NOTE** *Please select the videos for Lesson 28 online at* `www.wrox.com/go/` `csharp24hourtrainer2evideos.`

SECTION V
System Interactions

The lessons up to this point have explained how you can do some pretty remarkable things. Using their techniques you can read inputs entered by the user, perform intricate calculations, repeat a sequence of commands a huge number of times, and even build your own classes to model complex situations.

All of the programs that you've written so far, however, are self-contained. They get input from the user, but otherwise they don't interact with the computer.

The lessons in this section explain some of the ways a program can interact with the system. They explain how to read and write files, explore the filesystem, and print.

▶ **LESSON 29:** Using Files

▶ **LESSON 30:** Printing

> **NOTE** *A program can interact with the computer in lots of other ways. It can interact with hardware through serial ports and special devices and connect to websites or other programs over a network. It can use copy-and-paste and the clipboard to interact with other programs. It even has many different ways to interact with the same part of the system. For example, a program has many ways to manipulate files, read and modify the Windows registry, and save and restore program parameters. The lessons in this part of the book describe some of the ways a program can interact with the wider system, but these are by no means the only ways.*

Using Files

Files play an extremely important role on a computer. They hold text, pictures, Microsoft Word documents, spreadsheets, and all sorts of other data. They also hold executable programs including programs that you write, programs provided by Microsoft and other software vendors, and even the programs that make up the operating system itself.

In this lesson you learn how to explore the filesystem. You also learn some basic techniques for reading and writing files. Using some fairly simple techniques, you can use text files to store and retrieve data used by a program.

> **NOTE** *This is one of those topics where there are many ways to perform the same tasks. There are lots of approaches to searching the filesystem and manipulating files. This lesson describes only a few.*

FILESYSTEM CLASSES

Before you can manipulate a file, you need to be able to find it. This section describes .NET Framework classes that let you search the computer's filesystem.

> **NOTE** *These classes are in the* `System.IO` *namespace so you can make using them easier by including the directive:*
>
>   using System.IO;

DriveInfo

The `DriveInfo` class provides information about the system's drives. Its static `GetDrives` function returns an array of `DriveInfo` objects describing all of the system's drives. Table 29-1 summarizes the `DriveInfo` class's most useful properties.

TABLE 29-1

PROPERTY	PURPOSE
AvailableFreeSpace	The total number of bytes available.
DriveFormat	The drive format, as in NTFS or FAT32.
DriveType	The drive type, as in Fixed or CDRom.
IsReady	Returns true if the drive is ready. A drive must be ready before you can use the AvailableFreeSpace, DriveFormat, TotalSize, or VolumeLabel properties.
Name	The drive's name, as in C:\.
RootDirectory	A DirectoryInfo object representing the drive's root directory.
TotalFreeSpace	The number of bytes available, taking quotas into account.
TotalSize	The drive's total size in bytes.
VolumeLabel	The drive's label.

The List Drives example program, which is in this lesson's code download and shown in Figure 29-1, uses `DriveInfo` properties and methods to show information about the computer's drives. For details about how the program works, download it from the book's website

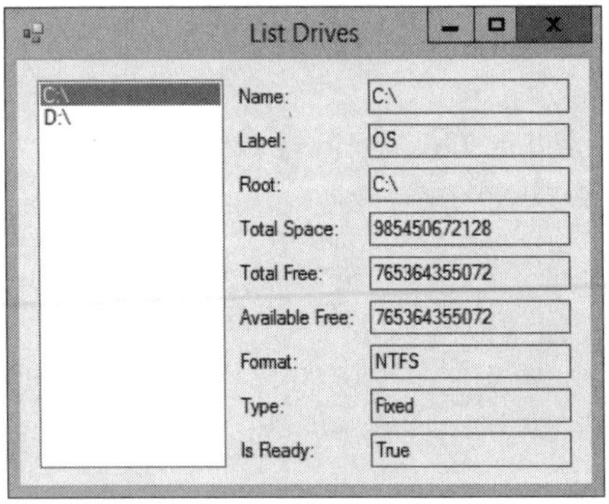

FIGURE 29-1

DirectoryInfo

The `DirectoryInfo` class provides information about directories. Table 29-2 summarizes useful `DirectoryInfo` methods for manipulating directories.

TABLE 29-2

METHOD	PURPOSE
Create	Creates a new directory. To use this, make a `DirectoryInfo` object, passing its constructor the name of the directory to create. Then call the `Create` method.
CreateSubdirectory	Creates a subdirectory inside this directory.
Delete	Deletes the directory. If you pass no parameters to this method, it deletes the directory only if it's empty. You can also pass it a boolean parameter indicating whether you want to delete all of the directory's files and subdirectories.
GetDirectories	Returns the directory's immediate subdirectories. Optionally you can include a search string to select particular subdirectories.
GetFiles	Returns the directory's files. Optionally you can include a search string to select particular files.
MoveTo	Moves the directory to a new path.

The `DirectoryInfo` class also provides a few useful properties, which are summarized in Table 29-3.

TABLE 29-3

PROPERTY	PURPOSE
Attributes	The directory's attributes, such as `Compressed`, `Hidden`, or `System`.
CreationTime	The time at which the directory was created.
Exists	Returns `true` if the directory actually exists.
FullName	Gives the directory's fully qualified path.
LastAccessTime	The time at which the directory was last accessed.
LastWriteTime	The time at which the directory was last written.
Name	The directory's name without the path.
Parent	A `DirectoryInfo` object representing this directory's parent directory.
Root	The directory's filesystem root.

Example program Use DirectoryInfo (found in this lesson's code download) uses a `DirectoryInfo` object to display information about directories.

Directory

The `Directory` class provides static methods for manipulating directories. Table 29-4 lists the most used methods. For simple tasks these are sometimes easier to use than the comparable `DirectoryInfo` class methods because you don't need to create a `DirectoryInfo` object to use them.

TABLE 29-4

METHOD	PURPOSE
CreateDirectory	Creates the directory and any missing directories in its path up to the root.
Delete	Deletes a directory.
Exists	Returns `true` if the directory exists.
GetCreationTime	Returns the time at which the directory was created.
GetDirectories	Returns a directory's subdirectories.
GetDirectoryRoot	Returns the directory's root.
GetFiles	Returns a directory's files, optionally looking for files matching a pattern.
GetLastAccessTime	Returns the time at which a directory was last accessed.
GetLastWriteTime	Returns the time at which a directory was last written.
GetParent	Returns a `DirectoryInfo` object representing a directory's parent directory.
Move	Moves a file or directory to a new location.
SetCreationTime	Sets the directory's creation time.
SetLastAccessTime	Sets the directory's last access time.
SetLastWriteTime	Sets the directory's last write time.

FileInfo

The `FileInfo` class, as you can probably guess at this point, provides information about files. Table 29-5 summarizes useful `FileInfo` methods for manipulating files.

TABLE 29-5

METHOD	PURPOSE
CopyTo	Copies the file to a new location.
Decrypt	Decrypts a file that was encrypted by the `Encrypt` method.
Delete	Deletes the file.

METHOD	PURPOSE
Encrypt	Encrypts the file so it can only be read by the account used to encrypt it.
MoveTo	Moves the file to a new location.

The `FileInfo` class also provides some useful properties, summarized in Table 29-6.

TABLE 29-6

PROPERTY	PURPOSE
Attributes	The file's attributes, such as `Compressed`, `Hidden`, or `System`.
CreationTime	The time at which the file was created.
Directory	A `DirectoryInfo` object for the directory containing the file.
Exists	Returns `true` if the file exists.
Extension	Returns the file's extension.
FullName	Gives the file's fully qualified path.
IsReadOnly	Returns `true` if the file is marked read-only.
LastAccessTime	The time at which the file was last accessed.
LastWriteTime	The time at which the file was last written.
Length	The file's size in bytes.
Name	The file's name without the path.

Example program Use FileInfo (which is in this lesson's code download) uses a `FileInfo` object to display information about files.

File

The `File` class provides static methods for manipulating files (see Table 29-7). For simple tasks these are sometimes easier to use than the comparable `FileInfo` class methods because you don't need to create a `FileInfo` object to use them.

The `AppendAllText`, `ReadAllLines`, `ReadAllText`, `WriteAllLines`, and `WriteAllText` methods are particularly useful for reading and writing text files all at once, although you may still want to use the `StreamReader` and `StreamWriter` classes described later in this lesson if you need to manipulate files one line at a time.

TABLE 29-7

METHOD	PURPOSE
AppendAllText	Appends a string to the end of a file.
Copy	Copies a file to a new file.
Create	Creates a file.
Decrypt	Decrypts a file that was encrypted by the Encrypt method.
Delete	Deletes a file.
Encrypt	Encrypts the file so it can only be read by the account used to encrypt it.
Exists	Returns true if a file exists.
GetAttributes	Returns a file's attributes, such as ReadOnly, System, or Hidden.
GetCreationTime	Returns the time at which the file was created.
GetLastAccessTime	Returns the time at which a file was last accessed.
GetLastWriteTime	Returns the time at which a file was last written.
Move	Moves a file to a new location.
ReadAllBytes	Returns a file's contents in an array of bytes.
ReadAllLines	Returns the lines in a text file as an array of strings.
ReadAllText	Returns a text file's contents in a string.
SetAttributes	Sets a file's attributes.
SetCreationTime	Sets a file's creation time.
SetLastAccessTime	Sets a file's last access time.
SetLastWriteTime	Sets a file's last write time.
WriteAllBytes	Writes a file's contents from an array of bytes.
WriteAllLines	Writes a text file's contents from an array of strings.
WriteAllText	Writes a text file's contents from a string.

PATH

The Path class provides static methods that perform string operations on file paths. For example, you can use the ChangeExtension method to change the extension part of a file's name. Table 29-8 summarizes the Path class's most useful methods.

TABLE 29-8

METHOD	PURPOSE
ChangeExtension	Changes a filename's extension.
Combine	Combines two path strings, adding a backslash between them if needed.
GetDirectoryName	Returns the directory name part of a path.
GetExtension	Returns the extension part of a filename.
GetFileName	Returns the filename part of a file's path.
GetFileNameWithoutExtension	Returns the filename part of a file's path without the extension.
GetTempFileName	Returns a name for a temporary file.
GetTempPath	Returns the path to the system's temporary folder.

STREAMS

A computer can contain many kinds of files: web pages, video, audio, executable, and lots of others. At some level, however, files are all the same. They're just a series of bytes stored on a filesystem somewhere.

Thinking about files at this very low level lets you treat them uniformly. It lets you define common classes and methods that you can use to manipulate any kind of file.

Many programming languages, including C#, make working with files at a low level easier by defining the concept of a stream. A *stream* is simply an ordered series of bytes.

> **NOTE** *Streams can also represent things other than files. For example, a stream could represent data being sent from one program to another, a series of bytes being downloaded from a website, or the flow of data as it moves through some complex process such as encryption or compression. This section focuses on file streams.*

Stream objects provide methods for manipulating data at a low level. For example, the Stream class provides Read and Write methods that move bytes of data between the stream and an array of bytes in your program.

Working with streams at this low level is convenient for some programs, but it makes day-to-day file handling difficult. You probably don't want to read the bytes from a text file and then reassemble them into characters.

The `StreamReader` and `StreamWriter` classes make reading and writing text streams much easier. As you can probably guess from their names, `StreamReader` lets you read text from a stream and `StreamWriter` lets you write text into a stream. If that stream happens to represent a file, then you're reading and writing files.

> **NOTE** *The* `StreamReader` *and* `StreamWriter` *classes are in the* `System.IO` *namespace. To make it easier to use these classes, you can add the following* `using` *directive to your code:*
>
>   using System.IO;

Writing Files

The `StreamWriter` class provides several constructors to build a `StreamWriter` associated with different kinds of streams. One of the simplest constructors takes a filename as a parameter. It opens the file for writing and associates the new `StreamWriter` with it.

> **NOTE** *Note that* `StreamWriter` *implements* `IDisposable`, *so you should use it inside a* `using` *block to call its* `Dispose` *method automatically.*

The following code shows how a program can open the file `Memo.txt` for writing. If the file already exists, it is overwritten.

```
// Write into the file, overwriting it if it exists.
using (StreamWriter memoWriter = new StreamWriter("Memo.txt"))
{
    // Write into the file.
    ...
}
```

> **NOTE** *If you pass the constructor a filename without a path such as* `Memo.txt`, *the program creates the file in its current directory. You can use a fully qualified filename such as* `C:\Temp\Memo.txt` *to create the file in a particular directory.*

Another version of the class's constructor takes a second `bool` parameter that indicates whether you want to open the file for appending. If you set this parameter to `true`, the `StreamWriter` opens the existing file and prepares to add text to the end. If the file doesn't exit, the object silently creates a new file and gets ready to append.

The StreamWriter class provides a Write method to add text to the file. The WriteLine method adds text followed by a new line. Both Write and WriteLine have overloaded versions that write various data types into the file: bool, char, string, int, decimal, and so on. They also provide versions that take a format string and parameters much as the string.Format method does.

The StreamWriter provides one other very important method that I want to cover here: Close. The Close method closes the StreamWriter and its associated file. When you use the Write and WriteLine methods, the StreamWriter may actually buffer its output in memory and only write to the file when it has enough data stored up. The Close method forces the StreamWriter to flush its buffer into the file, and until you call Close the data may not actually be in the file. If your program crashes or ends without calling Close, there's a very good chance that some or all of your text will be lost.

The following code shows how a program could save the contents of a TextBox in a file:

```
// Write the file, overwriting it if it exists.
using (StreamWriter memoWriter = new StreamWriter("Memo.txt"))
{
    // Write the file.
    memoWriter.Write(memoTextBox.Text);
    memoWriter.Close();
}
```

Reading Files

The StreamReader class lets you easily read text from a file. Like the StreamWriter class, StreamReader provides a constructor that takes a parameter giving the name of the file to open.

The StreamReader constructor throws an exception if the file doesn't exist, so your program should verify that the file is there before you try to open it. For example, you can use the File class's static Exists method to see if the file exists.

The StreamReader class provides a Read method that lets you read from the file one or more bytes at a time, but usually you'll want to use its ReadLine and ReadToEnd methods.

As you may be able to guess, ReadLine reads the next line from the file and returns it as a string. ReadToEnd reads the rest of the file from the current position onward and returns it as a string.

The following code reads the file Memo.txt and displays its contents in a TextBox:

```
// Read the file.
using (StreamReader memoReader = new StreamReader("Memo.txt"))
{
    memoTextBox.Text = memoReader.ReadToEnd();
    memoReader.Close();
}
```

The StreamReader's EndOfStream property returns true if the reader is at the end of the stream. This is particularly useful when you're reading a stream of unknown length. For example, the program can enter a while loop that uses ReadLine to read lines and continue as long as EndOfStream is false.

TRY IT

In this Try It, you build the program shown in Figure 29-2 to let the user search for files that match a pattern and that contain a target string. Enter a directory at which to start the search, select or enter a file pattern in the Pattern combo box, and enter a target string in the Search For textbox. When you click Search, the program searches for files matching the pattern and containing the target string.

FIGURE 29-2

Lesson Requirements

In this lesson, you:

➤ Start a new project and arrange its form, as shown in Figure 29-2. Give the combo box the choices *.cs, *.txt, *.*, and any other patterns that you think would be useful.

➤ Give the form a Load event handler that places the application's startup path in the Directory textbox (just to have somewhere to start).

➤ Give the Search button a Click event handler that searches for the desired files.

> **NOTE** *You can download the code and resources for this lesson from the website at* www.wrox.com/go/csharp24hourtrainer2e.

Hints

➤ Use the DirectoryInfo class's GetFiles method to search for files matching the pattern.

➤ Use the FileInfo class's ReadAllText method to get the file's contents. Then use string methods to see if the text contains the target string.

➤ To ignore case, convert the target string and the files' contents to lowercase.

Step-by-Step

➤ Start a new project and arrange its form, as shown in Figure 29-2. Give the combo box the choices *.cs, *.txt, *.*, and any other patterns that you think would be useful.

1. This is reasonably straightforward.

➤ Give the form a Load event handler that places the application's startup path in the Directory textbox (just to have somewhere to start).

1. Use code similar to the following:

```
// Start at the startup directory.
private void Form1_Load(object sender, EventArgs e)
{
```

```
        directoryTextBox.Text = Application.StartupPath;
    }
```

➤ Give the Search button a `Click` event handler that searches for the desired files.

1. Use code similar to the following:

```
// Search for files matching the pattern
// and containing the target string.
private void searchButton_Click(object sender, EventArgs e)
{
    // Get the file pattern and target string.
    string pattern = patternComboBox.Text;
    string target = targetTextBox.Text.ToLower();

    // Clear the result list.
    fileListBox.Items.Clear();

    // Search for files.
    DirectoryInfo dirinfo =
        new DirectoryInfo(directoryTextBox.Text);
    foreach (FileInfo fileinfo in
        dirinfo.GetFiles(pattern, SearchOption.AllDirectories))
    {
        // See if we need to look for target text.
        if (target.Length > 0)
        {
            // If this file contains the target string,
            // add it to the list.
            string content =
                File.ReadAllText(fileinfo.FullName).ToLower();
            if (content.Contains(target))
                fileListBox.Items.Add(fileinfo);
        }
        else
        {
            // Just add this file to the list.
            fileListBox.Items.Add(fileinfo);
        }
    }
}
```

EXERCISES

1. Write a program that sorts a text file. (Hint: Load the file's lines of text into an array and use `Array.Sort` to do the actual sorting.) Test the program on the file `Names.txt` included in this lesson's download.

2. Write a program that removes duplicate entries from a text file. (Hint: Copy the program you built for Exercise 1. After you sort the array, run through the entries, copying them into a new list. If you see a duplicate entry, skip it and write it to the Console window.) Test the program on the file `Names.txt` included in this lesson's download.

3. Make a program that has Labels and TextBoxes for first name, last name, street, city, state, and ZIP code. When the form closes, save the values in the TextBoxes in a text file. When the program loads, reload the values. (Hint: Write each TextBox's value on a separate line in the text file.)

4. Build a Memo program that saves and loads a single memo saved in the file in a multi-line TextBox. (This is so easy I wouldn't even bother using it as an exercise except it's actually useful. You can use it to record notes during the day and easily read them the next day.)

5. Make a program that lets the user select a number from a NumericUpDown control and then generates a text file containing a multiplication table that goes up to that number times itself. Use formatting to make the numbers line up in columns.

6. Build a program with a TextBox, a ListBox, an Add button, and a Save button. When the user enters a value in the TextBox and clicks Add, add the value to the ListBox. When the user clicks Save, write the values from the ListBox into a file and then clear the ListBox. When the form loads, make it read the values back into the ListBox.

7. Build a simple text editor. Give it a TextBox and a File menu with Open, New, and Save As commands. Use an OpenFileDialog and a SaveFileDialog to let the user select the file to open and save. (Don't worry about any of the other things a real editor would need to handle, such as locked files and ensuring that the user doesn't close the program with unsaved changes.)

NOTE *Please select the videos for Lesson 29 online at* www.wrox.com/go/ csharp24hourtrainer2evideos.

30

Printing

Most of the programs described in earlier lessons display output on the computer's screen. Lesson 29 explained how to save output in files.

This lesson explains a third method for producing output: printing. Using the techniques described in this lesson, you can print text, shapes, images—just about anything you want.

> **WARNING** *Before you start a printing project, however, be warned that printing in C# isn't trivial. It's easy enough to display some text or a few lines in a printout, but producing a complex formatted document can be a lot of work.*
>
> *If you need to produce a nicely formatted résumé, graph, or grid of values, you should ask yourself whether there's an easier way. For example, Microsoft Word and Google Docs are great at producing nicely formatted text documents. Similarly, Microsoft Excel does a wonderful job of making charts and graphs. You can certainly generate these sorts of printouts using C#, but it may be a lot faster and easier if you use another tool.*

WINDOWS FORMS PRINTING

Windows Forms and WPF applications handle printing in very different ways. A Windows Forms application responds to events and makes method calls to draw text, shapes, and images on the printed page. In contrast, a WPF application uses objects such as the Label and TextBox controls to represent text, shapes, and images that you can print.

The following sections explain how a Windows Forms application prints. The sections after those explain how a WPF application prints.

Getting Started

The PrintDocument component sits at the center of the Windows Forms printing process. To print, a program creates an instance of this class either at design time or at run time. It adds event handlers to catch the object's events and then lets the object do its thing. As the object generates pieces of the printout, it raises events to let the program supply graphics for it to print.

The PrintDocument object raises four key events:

➤   BeginPrint—Raised when the object is about to start printing to let the program do whatever it must to get ready to print.

➤   QueryPageSettings—Raised when the object is about to start printing a page to let the program modify the upcoming page's settings. For example, it might adjust the margins so odd pages have bigger margins on the left and even pages have bigger margins on the right to allow room for a staple in a double-sided document.

➤   PrintPage—Raised when the object needs to generate contents for a page. This is where the program does its drawing. The event handler should set the its e.HasMorePages value to false after it draws its last page.

➤   EndPrint—Raised after the object has finished printing to let the program clean up if necessary.

The BeginPrint, QueryPageSettings, and EndPrint event handlers are optional. For simple printouts, you often only need the PrintPage event handler.

The PrintPage event handler gives you a parameter named e of type PrintPageEventArgs. This object contains:

➤   The HasMorePages parameter that you use to tell the PrintDocument whether this is the last page

➤   A PageBounds property that tells you how big the page is

➤   A MarginBounds property that tells you where the page's margins are

➤   A Graphics object that you use to draw the page's contents

The following section explains how a program starts the printing process. The sections after that give simple examples that show how to draw shapes and text.

Starting a Printout

The easiest way to generate a printout using the PrintDocument object is to place the object on a form at design time and give the object a PrintPage event handler to generate the pages. When you're ready to print, simply call the PrintDocument object's Print method. The object raises its PrintPage event, the event handler generates graphics, and the object sends the results to the default printer.

> **TIP** *The Form Designer's Toolbox has a Printing section that makes it easy to find the printing-related components.*

Once you've built a `PrintPage` event handler, it's practically trivial to add a print preview capability to the program. Add a `PrintPreviewDialog` object to the form and set its `Document` property to the `PrintDocument` object that you already created. To display a print preview, simply call the dialog's `ShowDialog` method. When you do, the dialog uses the associated `PrintDocument` object to generate the necessary preview and displays the result.

> **TIP** *The* `PrintPreviewDialog` *contains a print button, so for simple programs you may not really need a print command. The program can display a preview and the user can click the button to print.*

Drawing Shapes

You've seen in previous lessons how to use a `Graphics` object's methods to draw. To draw shapes on a printout, you use the same methods with the `PrintPage` event handler's `e.Graphics` parameter.

Figure 30-1 shows the Print Shapes example program displaying a preview that contains a rectangle and an ellipse.

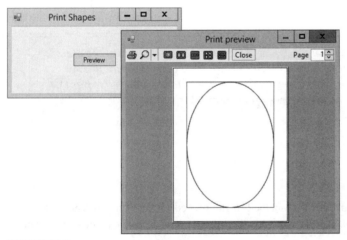

FIGURE 30-1

The following code shows the program's `PrintPage` event handler:

```
// Draw some shapes.
private void shapesPrintDocument_PrintPage(object sender,
    System.Drawing.Printing.PrintPageEventArgs e)
{
    e.Graphics.SmoothingMode = SmoothingMode.AntiAlias;

    // Draw a rectangle around the page margin.
    e.Graphics.DrawRectangle(Pens.Red, e.MarginBounds);
```

```
        // Draw an ellipse inside the page margin.
        e.Graphics.DrawEllipse(Pens.Blue, e.MarginBounds);

        // There are no more pages.
        e.HasMorePages = false;
    }
```

This code sets the `Graphics` object's `SmoothingMode` property. It then draws a rectangle and an ellipse around the page's margins. It finishes by setting `HasMorePages` to `false` to tell the `PrintDocument` object to not raise its `PrintPage` event again.

The following code shows how the program displays print previews and generates printouts:

```
// Print immediately.
private void printButton_Click(object sender, EventArgs e)
{
    shapesPrintDocument.Print();
}

// Display a print preview.
private void previewButton_Click(object sender, EventArgs e)
{
    shapesPrintPreviewDialog.ShowDialog();
}
```

> **NOTE** *Unfortunately, there isn't room in this lesson to really get into the drawing routines that you use to generate fancier printouts. For a more complete introduction to graphics programming in C#, see my PDF-format Wrox Blox C#* Graphics Programming *available at* www.wrox.com/WileyCDA/WroxTitle/productCd-0470343494.html.

Drawing Text

To draw shapes, the Print Shapes program described in the preceding section calls the `e.Graphics` object's `DrawRectangle` and `DrawEllipse` methods. Printing text is similar except you use the `DrawString` method.

Example program Print Text uses the following code to print the page number centered on four pages:

```
// Print immediately.
private void printButton_Click(object sender, EventArgs e)
{
    PageNumber = 1;
    shapesPrintDocument.Print();
}

// Display a print preview.
private void previewButton_Click(object sender, EventArgs e)
{
    PageNumber = 1;
    shapesPrintPreviewDialog.ShowDialog();
```

```
    }

    // The page number.
    private int PageNumber;

    // Draw some shapes.
    private void shapesPrintDocument_PrintPage(object sender,
        System.Drawing.Printing.PrintPageEventArgs e)
    {
        e.Graphics.SmoothingMode = SmoothingMode.AntiAlias;

        // Draw the page number centered on the form.
        using (Font font = new Font("Helvitca", 400))
        {
            using (StringFormat format = new StringFormat())
            {
                format.Alignment = StringAlignment.Center;
                format.LineAlignment = StringAlignment.Center;
                int x = e.MarginBounds.Left + e.MarginBounds.Width / 2;
                int y = e.MarginBounds.Top + e.MarginBounds.Height / 2;
                e.Graphics.DrawString(PageNumber.ToString(),
                    font, Brushes.Blue, x, y, format);
            }
        }

        // If this is page 4, we're done.
        e.HasMorePages = (++PageNumber <= 4);
    }
```

The Print and Print Preview buttons' event handlers first set the class-level variable `PageNumber` to 1 to indicate that the next page to print is page 1. The button event handlers then start the printing or preview process.

The `PrintPage` event handler sets the `Graphics` object's `SmoothingMode` property and creates a really big font. It then creates a `StringFormat` object, which it can use to arrange text. In this example, it sets the object's `Alignment` and `LineAlignment` properties to center the text vertically and horizontally.

The code then finds the center of the printed page and calls `DrawString` to draw the page number. The code finishes by incrementing `PageNumber` and setting `HasMorePages` to `true` if the new value of `PageNumber` is less than or equal to 4. Figure 30-2 shows the program's preview displaying four pages at a time.

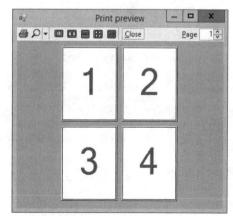

FIGURE 30-2

WPF PRINTING

To print in a Windows Forms application, a program catches a `PrintDocument` object's `Print Page` event handler and uses its `e.Graphics` parameter to generate graphics for each page of the printout. WPF uses a different printing model that many programmers find more intuitive. Instead of responding to `PrintPage` events, a WPF program's code can directly print visual objects that it draws using WPF controls such as `Label` and `TextBox`. You create some sort of container; place `Label`, `TextBox`, and other controls on it; and then print the container.

In addition to being easier to understand, this approach has a couple of other benefits. For example, it lets the program use the same kind of code to display and print data. In Windows Forms, a program uses controls such as `TextBox` and `Label` to display text on the screen but it uses a `Graphics` object's `DrawString` method to draw text on a printout. WPF uses the same kinds of `TextBox` and `Label` objects for both display and printing.

WPF also allows you to zoom in as much as you like without creating a pixelated result. That means, for example, you can enlarge a window as much as you like for a printout and you'll still see a smooth result.

The following sections give more details explaining how to print in WPF applications.

PRINTING VISUALS

In WPF, a `PrintDialog` object starts the printing process. This object can display a printer selection dialog and provides a `PrintVisual` method that prints visual objects.

Although your code can simply call `PrintVisual` to send output to the default printer immediately, most programs first display the dialog so the user can select a printer. To do that, the program creates a `PrintDialog` object and calls its `ShowDialog` method. If the user selects a printer and clicks Print, `ShowDialog` returns `true` and the program can then call the dialog's `PrintVisual` method, passing it the visual object to print.

For example, the Print Window program shown in Figure 30-3 uses the following code to print an image of its main window:

```
// Print the window.
private void printButton_Click(object
sender, RoutedEventArgs e)
{
    // Display the print dialog and
    check the result.
    PrintDialog printDialog =
        new PrintDialog();
    if (printDialog.ShowDialog() == true)
    {
        // Print.
        printDialog.PrintVisual(this, "Print Window Image");
    }
}
```

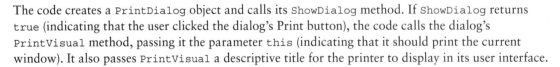

FIGURE 30-3

The code creates a `PrintDialog` object and calls its `ShowDialog` method. If `ShowDialog` returns `true` (indicating that the user clicked the dialog's Print button), the code calls the dialog's `PrintVisual` method, passing it the parameter `this` (indicating that it should print the current window). It also passes `PrintVisual` a descriptive title for the printer to display in its user interface.

This code is simple and produces a high-resolution result, but it has a big drawback: the result appears in the page's upper-left corner. It might be nice to center the image and possibly scale it to use more of the paper.

The simplicity of the previous code may make it seem like fixing these problems would be hard. Where in that code is there room for these sorts of changes?

Fortunately, WPF provides two features that make this problem much easier to solve than you might think:

➤ First, it provides transformations that let you scale, rotate, and translate images easily.

➤ Second, it lets you easily place most graphical objects inside other graphical objects.

Instead of trying to modify the window's image, you can place the image inside other controls such as a `Grid` or `Viewbox`. Then you can transform those controls to fit properly on the printed page.

Example program Print Window Centered uses the following code to print an image of the window centered on the page. Admittedly this code is a lot longer than the previous version, but it's not as complicated as it seems at first glance.

```
// Print an image of the window centered.
private void printButton_Click(object sender, RoutedEventArgs e)
{
    PrintDialog printDialog = new PrintDialog();
    if (printDialog.ShowDialog() == true)
    {
        PrintWindowCentered(printDialog, this, "New Customer", null);
    }
}

// Print a Window centered on the printer.
private void PrintWindowCentered(PrintDialog printDialog, Window win,
    String title, Thickness? margin)
{
    // Make a Grid to hold the contents.
    Grid drawingGrid = new Grid();
    drawingGrid.Width = printDialog.PrintableAreaWidth;
    drawingGrid.Height = printDialog.PrintableAreaHeight;

    // Make a Viewbox to stretch the result if necessary.
    Viewbox viewbox = new Viewbox();
    drawingGrid.Children.Add(viewbox);
    viewbox.HorizontalAlignment = HorizontalAlignment.Center;
    viewbox.VerticalAlignment = VerticalAlignment.Center;

    if (margin == null)
    {
        // Center without resizing.
        viewbox.Stretch = Stretch.None;
    }
    else
    {
        // Resize to fit the margin.
        viewbox.Margin = margin.Value;
```

```
            viewbox.Stretch = Stretch.Uniform;
    }

    // Make a VisualBrush holding an image of the Window's contents.
    VisualBrush br = new VisualBrush(win);

    // Make a Rectangle the size of the Window.
    Rectangle windowRect = new Rectangle();
    viewbox.Child = windowRect;
    windowRect.Width = win.Width;
    windowRect.Height = win.Height;
    windowRect.Fill = br;
    windowRect.Stroke = Brushes.Black;
    windowRect.Effect = new DropShadowEffect();

    // Arrange to produce output.
    Rect rect = new Rect(0, 0,
        printDialog.PrintableAreaWidth, printDialog.PrintableAreaHeight);
    drawingGrid.Arrange(rect);

    // Print it.
    printDialog.PrintVisual(drawingGrid, title);
}
```

> **NOTE** *This code adds a* DropShadowEffect *behind the grid. That class is defined in the* System.Windows.Media.Effects *namespace, so to make using it easier, the program includes the following* using *directive:*
>
> using System.Windows.Media.Effects;

When you click the Print button, the program displays a PrintDialog as before. If you select a printer and click Print, the program calls the PrintWindowCentered method, passing it the PrintDialog object and the Window to print. It also passes the method a title to use for the printout and a margin (which can be null).

The PrintWindowCentered method makes a Grid that fills the printer's printable area. Inside the Grid it places a Viewbox named viewbox. A Viewbox displays a single object that it can optionally stretch in various ways.

If the method receives a margin parameter, the program sets the Viewbox's margin appropriately and makes the control stretch its contents so they are as large as possible without changing shape. If the margin parameter is null, the code makes the Viewbox not stretch its contents.

Next the code makes a VisualBrush from the Window. A VisualBrush fills an area with the image of some visual object such as a control or, in this case, the program's main Window. The code creates a Rectangle, places it inside the Viewbox, and fills it with the brush.

At this point, all of the objects needed to display the Window appropriately sized and centered on the printed page are in place. The code only needs to perform two more steps.

First, it calls the Grid's Arrange method to make its children arrange themselves. Second, the code calls the PrintDialog's PrintVisual method to print the Grid.

Figure 30-4 shows a preview of the result. To make this figure, I printed the `Window` into an XML Paper Specification (XPS) file by selecting the Microsoft XPS Document Writer from the `PrintDialog`. I then double-clicked the XPS file to display it in the XPS Viewer shown in Figure 30-4. You can see in the figure that the `Window`'s image is centered.

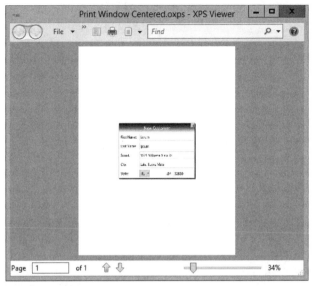

FIGURE 30-4

In Figure 30-4 the image of the window looks a bit grainy and pixelated, but that's caused by the way the XPS Viewer displays the document. The document itself was generated at a very high resolution. In Figure 30-5 the viewer has enlarged the document by 265 percent, so you can see that the result is actually very smooth and the final printout can take advantage of the printer's relatively high resolution.

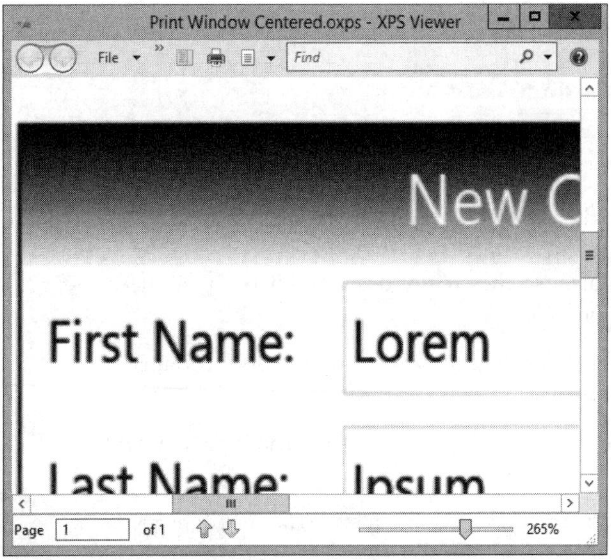

FIGURE 30-5

The Print Window Enlarged example program is similar to the Print Window Centered program except it uses the following code to pass a `Thickness` object to the `PrintWindowCentered` method to use as a margin. That makes the method stretch the `Window`'s image to fill the printable area minus a 50-pixel margin.

```
// Print an image of the window centered and stretched to fill the page.
private void printButton_Click(object sender, RoutedEventArgs e)
{
    PrintDialog printDialog = new PrintDialog();
    if (printDialog.ShowDialog() == true)
    {
        PrintWindowCentered(printDialog, this, "New Customer",
            new Thickness(50));
    }
}
```

Figure 30-6 shows the result. Notice that the `Window`'s image is centered and enlarged to fill most of the printable area.

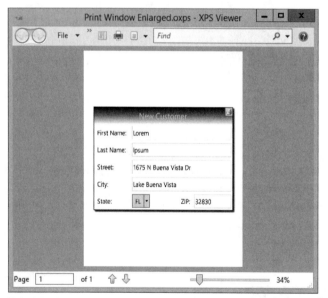

FIGURE 30-6

In addition to the `PrintVisual` method, the `PrintDialog` class provides a `PrintDocument` method that prints multipage output or document objects such as `FlowDocuments` or `FixedDocuments`. Unfortunately these topics are fairly complex, so they're not described here. If you need those capabilities, you can find more information online at:

➤ PrintDocument—msdn.microsoft.com/library/system.windows.controls
.printdialog.printdocument.aspx

➤ FixedDocument—msdn.microsoft.com/library/system.windows.documents
.fixeddocument.aspx

➤ FlowDocument—msdn.microsoft.com/library/system.windows.documents
.flowdocument.aspx

TRY IT

In this Try It, you build a program that prints and displays a preview of the table shown in Figure 30-7. You build an array of Student objects and then loop through them, displaying their values as shown in the figure.

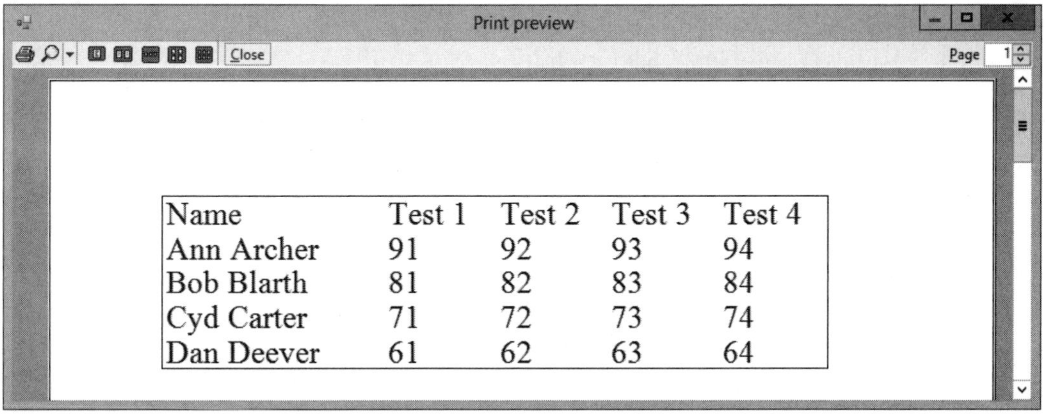

Name	Test 1	Test 2	Test 3	Test 4
Ann Archer	91	92	93	94
Bob Blarth	81	82	83	84
Cyd Carter	71	72	73	74
Dan Deever	61	62	63	64

FIGURE 30-7

Lesson Requirements

In this lesson, you:

➤ Start a new Windows Forms project and create the program's main form. Add PrintDocument and PrintPreviewDialog components to do the printing and previewing.

➤ Add Print and Preview buttons with appropriate event handlers.

➤ Add a Student class with FirstName and LastName properties. Also give it a TestScores property that is an array of integers.

➤ Create the PrintPage event handler.

   ➤ Create an array of Student objects. Initialize them using array and object initializers.

   ➤ Loop through the Student objects, printing them.

   ➤ Draw a rectangle around the table.

> **NOTE** *You can download the code and resources for this lesson from the website at* www.wrox.com/go/csharp24hourtrainer2e.

Hints

➤ Don't forget to set the PrintPreviewDialog's Document property, to the PrintDocument component.

➤ This example doesn't do anything fancy with Student properties, so they can be auto-implemented.

➤ It might help to define variables x0, x1, and so on to keep track of where each column should begin.

Step-by-Step

➤ Start a new Windows Forms project and create the program's main form. Add PrintDocument and PrintPreviewDialog components to do the printing and previewing.

1. This is reasonably straightforward.

➤ Add Print and Preview buttons with appropriate event handlers.

1. Use code similar to the following:

```
// Display a print preview.
private void previewButton_Click(object sender, EventArgs e)
{
    textPrintPreviewDialog.ShowDialog();
}

// Print.
private void printButton_Click(object sender, EventArgs e)
{
    textPrintDocument.Print();
}
```

➤ Add a Student class with FirstName and LastName properties. Also give it a TestScores property that is an array of integers.

1. Use code similar to the following:

```
class Student
{
    public string FirstName { get; set; }
    public string LastName { get; set; }
    public int[] TestScores { get; set; }
}
```

➤ Create the PrintPage event handler.

➤ Create an array of Student objects. Initialize them using array and object initializers.

➤ Loop through the Student objects, printing them.

➤ Draw a rectangle around the table.

1. Use code similar to the following:

```
// Print the table.
private void textPrintDocument_PrintPage(object sender,
    System.Drawing.Printing.PrintPageEventArgs e)
{
    // Make some data.
    Student[] students =
    {
        new Student() {FirstName="Ann", LastName="Archer",
            TestScores=new int[] {91, 92, 93, 94}},
        new Student() {FirstName="Bob", LastName="Blarth",
```

```
            TestScores=new int[] {81, 82, 83, 84}},
        new Student() {FirstName="Cyd", LastName="Carter",
            TestScores=new int[] {71, 72, 73, 74}},
        new Student() {FirstName="Dan", LastName="Deever",
            TestScores=new int[] {61, 62, 63, 64}},
    };

    // Set the coordinates for the first row and the columns.
    int y = e.MarginBounds.Top;
    int x0 = e.MarginBounds.Left;
    int x1 = x0 + 200;
    int x2 = x1 + 100;
    int x3 = x2 + 100;
    int x4 = x3 + 100;

    // Make a font to use.
    using (Font font = new Font("Times New Roman", 20))
    {
        // Draw column headers.
        e.Graphics.DrawString("Name", font, Brushes.Black, x0, y);
        e.Graphics.DrawString("Test 1", font, Brushes.Black, x1, y);
        e.Graphics.DrawString("Test 2", font, Brushes.Black, x2, y);
        e.Graphics.DrawString("Test 3", font, Brushes.Black, x3, y);
        e.Graphics.DrawString("Test 4", font, Brushes.Black, x4, y);
        // Move Y down for the first row.
        y += 30;

        // Loop through the Students displaying their data.
        foreach (Student student in students)
        {
            // Display the Student's values.
            e.Graphics.DrawString(student.FirstName + " " +
                student.LastName, font, Brushes.Black, x0, y);
            e.Graphics.DrawString(student.TestScores[0].ToString(),
                font, Brushes.Black, x1, y);
            e.Graphics.DrawString(student.TestScores[1].ToString(),
                font, Brushes.Black, x2, y);
            e.Graphics.DrawString(student.TestScores[2].ToString(),
                font, Brushes.Black, x3, y);
            e.Graphics.DrawString(student.TestScores[3].ToString(),
                font, Brushes.Black, x4, y);

            // Move Y down for the next row.
            y += 30;
        }
    }

    // Draw a box around it all.
    e.Graphics.DrawRectangle(Pens.Black,
        x0, e.MarginBounds.Top,
        x4 - x0 + 100,
        y - e.MarginBounds.Top);

    // We're only printing one page.
    e.HasMorePages = false;
}
```

EXERCISES

1. Copy the program you built in this lesson's Try It and add lines between the rows and columns.

2. Make a program that prints a bar chart similar to the one shown in Figure 30-8. (Hint: Pick some "random" values for the bars.)

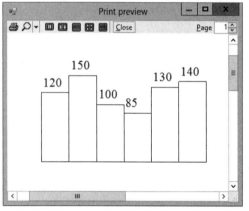

FIGURE 30-8

3. Copy the program you built for Exercise 2 and modify it so the textual values are centered over their bars. (Hint: Use a `StringFormat` object.)

4. Build a program that contains a `DataGridView` control with the columns Item, Quantity, Unit price, and Total. Make Print and Preview menu items that display the data in the grid.

   Add `PrintDocument` and `PrintPreviewDialog` controls as usual. The `PrintPage` event handler should:

   a. Call the grid's `EndEdit` method to commit the current edit (if there is one).

   b. Loop through the grid's `Columns` collection, displaying the column headers. Add each column's `Width` value to the X coordinate for the next column.

   c. Loop through the grid's `Rows` collection. For each row, loop through the row's `Cells` collection, displaying the cells' `FormattedValue` property.

5. Copy the program you built for Exercise 4, add lines between the rows and columns, and draw a box around the table.

6. Copy the Print Window Enlarged program described in this lesson (and available in this lesson's downloads). Modify it so it prints the `Window` sideways to fill more of the printed page.

   Hints: This is a *lot* easier than it sounds. Modify the `PrintWindowCentered` method so it uses the page's printable width and height for the drawing grid's height and width, respectively. Then set the grid's `LayoutTransform` property to a `RotateTransform` object that rotates it by 90°. The code that creates the grid should look like this:

```
Grid drawingGrid = new Grid();
drawingGrid.Width = printDialog.PrintableAreaHeight;
drawingGrid.Height = printDialog.PrintableAreaWidth;
drawingGrid.LayoutTransform = new RotateTransform(90);
```

7. [WPF] The WPF examples described in this lesson print images of a `Window`, but similar techniques work with any visual object such as a `Grid`, `StackPanel`, or `TextBox`.

   For this exercise, build a WPF program that contains a `TabControl`. Give that control three `TabItem` children. Set each `TabItem`'s `Header` property and place a `Grid` inside it. Place some `Labels`, `TextBoxes`, and other controls inside the `Grids`. Finally, give each tab a Print button. (If you don't want to build the controls yourself, download the Exercise 30-7a program available in this lesson's downloads as a starting point. That project defines the user interface but none of the code.)

   To print, use the `PrintWindowCentered` method used by the earlier example programs with a few changes:

   ➤ Change the method's name to `PrintGridCentered`.

   ➤ Make the method take a `Grid` as a parameter instead of a `Window`.

   ➤ The `Grid` control doesn't have a set width or height, so its `Width` and `Height` properties don't return meaningful values. Use the `ActualWidth` and `ActualHeight` properties instead.

   ➤ To avoid repeating code, write a `PrintGrid` method that takes as parameters a `Grid`, title string, and `Thickness`. It should display a `PrintDialog` and, if the user clicks Print, it should call `PrintGridCentered` to do the actual printing.

8. Make a Windows Forms program that previews and prints four pages containing the following shapes outlined in 10-pixel wide lines:

   ➤ Red rectangle

   ➤ Green ellipse

   ➤ Blue triangle

   ➤ Purple diamond

   Make the shapes as large as possible inside the page's margins and outline the page's margins with a dashed black line.

   Hints: To draw the triangle and diamond, use the `DrawPolygon` method with an array of `Point`. You can use a single `Pen` for all of the drawing by changing its `Color` and `DashStyle` properties as needed.

9. [Hard] Suppose you're making a booklet and you want to indent odd numbered pages on the left and even pages on the right to make room for the stapled binding. (That extra alternating indentation is called a "gutter.") Make a Windows Forms program that prints or previews

10 pages with a 100-unit gutter. Draw boxes around the pages' margins and display the page number just inside the margins in the upper corner on the side opposite the gutter. Hints:

➤ Use the `PrintDocument`'s `QueryPageSettings` event to set the margins. It should handle three cases:

 ➤ For the first page, add 100 to `e.PageSettings.Margins.Left`.

 ➤ For subsequent odd pages, add 100 to the left margin and subtract 100 from the right margin.

 ➤ For even pages, subtract 100 from the left margin and add 100 to the right margin.

➤ Use a `StringFormat` object's `Alignment` and `LineAlignment` properties to position the page numbers.

Keep in mind that `QueryPageSettings` works with margins, not bounds. For example, adding 100 to the right margin moves the right edge of the margin bounds 100 units farther from the edge of the page. (Yes, this can be confusing.)

> **NOTE** *Please select the videos for Lesson 30 online at* www.wrox.com/go/ csharp24hourtrainer2evideos.

SECTION VI
Windows Apps

The lessons in the first part of this book focused on Windows desktop applications because they're easy to get up and running. You don't need to take any special steps to register a desktop application, upload it to the Windows Store, or have it tested for safe use on a phone. By working with Windows Forms applications, you used those lessons to focus on using controls and writing C# code.

The lessons in this part of the book explain how you can use what you've learned to build Windows Store apps and Windows Phone apps. You build those kinds of applications using WPF windows and controls similar to those that you learned about in the first part of the book. You can edit them using the Window Designer and modify their XAML code. You can even place C# behind the controls much as you do in a WPF desktop application.

It would be nice if that were all there was to building these kinds of applications, but you have several other to handle overcome before you can publish the next paradigm-shifting mobile app. These lessons focus on those hurdles so you can get to the point where you can use the knowledge you already have about controls and C# code.

These are relatively new technologies so, unlike most of C#, they do change occasionally as Microsoft tweaks things such as Visual Studio, the Windows Store, the Windows Phone operating system, and the Windows operating system. That means some of the techniques described in these lessons may not work with every combination of those tools.

For example, you can't build Windows Phone 8 apps on Windows 7. For this book, I used Windows 8.1 and Visual Studio 2015. Other combinations may work but there may be some differences. (Fortunately most of the rest of the book doesn't depend on your version of Windows or Visual Studio. Most of the examples should work in Visual Studio 2008 if you type in the code.)

Building Windows Store and Phone apps is also a fairly involved topic so the few lessons included here can't cover every possible scenario. Taking full advantage of the special data, filesystem, and device capabilities provided by tablets and phones is fairly complicated so it's not covered here. These lessons do, however, provide enough information to get you started. They also explain where you can go online to find further information.

▶ **LESSON 31:** Windows Store Apps

▶ **LESSON 32:** Windows Phone Apps

31

Windows Store Apps

This lesson explains how you can build Windows Store–style applications. Note that you don't actually need to upload these applications to the Windows Store. You can build and run them locally on your computer if you like. Here "Windows Store apps" simply means they have a style similar to those available in the Windows Store.

NAVIGATION STYLE

Windows Store and Phone apps differ from desktop applications in several ways. One big difference is the way they handle device real estate. Desktop applications typically share the desktop with other applications that you can minimize, maximize, resize, rearrange, and close. Store and Phone apps typically cover the entire device. You can switch between different apps, but you can't resize and rearrange the apps to view more than one on the screen at the same time.

Because Store and Phone apps don't display multiple windows at the same time, they typically use a different navigation model than the one used by desktop applications. A desktop application might display several dialogs and other windows that you can navigate between as needed.

In contrast, Store and Phone apps display a single window. To display other information, the app replaces that window with a new one. Often you can tap a back button to move to the previous window, much as a web browser lets you navigate back through your browsing history.

> **NOTE** *Windows Store and Phone apps are targeted at tablets and phones. Those devices have touch-sensitive screens, so the user taps the screen instead of clicking a mouse. The code handles taps with* Click *and* Tapped *events that are similar to the* Click *events you've seen before.*
>
> *Those devices also support more complicated gestures such as flick, pan, pinch, and stretch. Those are outside the scope of this book so they're not covered here.*

Many of these apps also don't provide buttons or menu items that let the user close them. Instead the user simply opens or navigates to another app and leaves yours sitting the background. Later the device closes your app if it needs to free up memory.

> **NOTE** *Although many apps don't provide a way to close them, you can close an app by making the code call* `Application.Current.Exit()`.

Because these apps cover the entire device, you must arrange the controls to take best advantage of whatever space is available. You don't have control over how large the user's screen is, so you should use container controls such as `Grid` and `StackPanel` to get the most out of the space you have.

APP STYLES

Visual Studio includes templates for building several different styles of Windows Store apps. The following list summarizes the most common kinds of Windows Store templates:

➤ **Blank**—This kind of app displays a single window with no navigation to other windows. It's similar to a one-window desktop application without dialogs.

➤ **Hub**—This kind of app uses a `Hub` control. The main `Hub` control displays a horizontally scrolling window divided into sections holding different kinds of information. You can tap a section heading to open a new page that provides details about that section.

➤ **Grid**—This kind of app displays sections in a grid. You can tap a section to open a list of items in that section. If you then tap an item in the list, the app opens a full page about that item.

➤ **Split**—This kind of app displays a list and a detail area. You can tap an item in the list to see its details.

➤ **Pivot**—This kind of app displays a collection of list categories. When a category is selected, you see its list of items below it. You can scroll horizontally through the different categories. This template is useful for displaying different views of data. For example, my phone displays Outlook mail in a pivot view with categories All, Unread, and Urgent.

If you use one of these templates to create a new project, the app comes pre-loaded with sample data so you can see what the finished app will look like. (In fact, you'll probably get a better sense of how the different templates work if you just create some sample projects and run them rather than staring at the previous descriptions.)

APP IMAGES

Windows and the Windows Store can represent your app in many ways using images with different sizes. For example, the Windows Start screen can displays your app's tile in Small, Medium, Wide, and Large sizes.

The kinds of images are grouped into categories, each of which includes several versions at different sizes. If you include one image in a category and omit the others, that image is scaled if necessary to use when the others are needed.

For example, suppose for the Square 150×150 logo category you provide an image that's 150 pixels wide and 150 pixels tall. Then Windows automatically scales that image if it needs images with sizes 270×270, 210×210, or 120×120 pixels.

Automatic scaling is better than nothing, but sometimes it can produce poor results. For example, if you provide a relatively large image that contains text, when it's scaled down to a small size the text may turn into a fuzzy blur. Enlarged images also tend to have fuzzy edges. To provide the best results, you should create separate images at several different scales.

The images you include in a project must match the required dimensions exactly. For example, you can't use a 100×100 pixel image in place of a 120×120 pixel image.

Table 31-1 lists the kinds of images you can include in a Windows Store app. The bold entries in the Sizes column indicate required images.

TABLE 31-1

CATEGORY	PURPOSE	SIZES
Store Logo	Used by the Windows Store's details section in app listings.	**50×50** 70×70 90×90
Square 30×30 Logo	Used by Windows in several places such as when the user lists all installed apps. (Tap the down arrow button on the Start screen to see the list.)	24×24 **30×30** 42×42 54×54
Square 70×70 Logo	Used for the Small tile on the Windows Start screen.	56×56 70×70 98×98 126×126
Square 150×150 Logo	Used for the Medium tile on the Windows Start screen.	120×120 **150×150** 210×210 270×270
Wide 310×150 Logo	Used for the Wide tile on the Windows Start screen.	248×120 310×150 434×210 558×270

continues

TABLE 31-1 *(continued)*

CATEGORY	PURPOSE	SIZES
Square 310×310 Logo	Used for the Large tile on the Windows Start screen.	248×248 310×310 434×434 558×558
Splash Screen Logo	This image is displayed briefly when the app loads. You also specify a background color to display behind the splash screen.	**620×300** 868×420 1116×540

The purposes of the images depend on the category that contains them, not on their sizes. For example, the Square 70×70 Logo and Store Logo categories both contain 70×70 images but they are not interchangeable. If you specify a 70×70 image in one category and not in the other, Windows won't use the one you specify for both purposes.

If you don't specify images for the Wide 310×150 Logo or Square 310×310 Logo categories, the user cannot use the Wide or Large tiles. To allow the user to arrange tiles flexibly, I highly recommend that you include these images.

If you don't specify an image in the Square 70×70 Logo category, Windows provides a small tile by scaling an image from the Square 150×150 Logo category. (For best results, include at least one image in each category.)

> **NOTE** *To change an app's tile size in Windows with a mouse, go to the Start screen, right-click the tile, select the Resize context menu item, and pick Small, Medium, Wide, or Large.*
>
> *On a touchscreen, go to the Start screen and press and hold on the tile to make a taskbar appear at the bottom of the screen. Click the Resize tool and then pick the Large, Wide, Medium, or Small option.*

When you create your images, give them suggestive names such as MyApp56x56.png so you can tell what they are for.

After you've created the images, you need to attach them to the project. To do that, open Solution Explorer and double-click `Package.appxmanifest` to open the Manifest Editor shown in Figure 31-1. Click the Visual Assets tab to set the app's various images and image-related options.

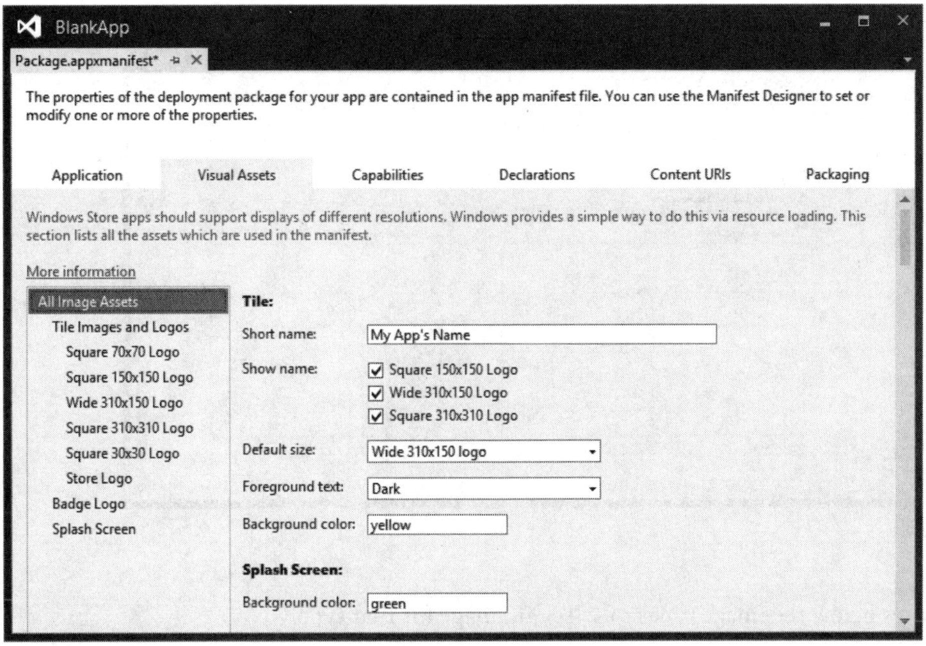

FIGURE 31-1

The following list describes the items shown in Figure 31-1:

➤ **Short name**—This is a name that may be displayed directly on top of the app's tile.

➤ **Show name**—Check the boxes next to the tile sizes that should display the short name. For example, you could have the short name appear on top of the Wide and Large tiles.

➤ **Default size**—Select the size that the app's tile should be by default. This can be Square 150×150 logo, Wide 310×150 logo, or (not set).

➤ **Foreground text**—Select Light or Dark to indicate whether the name displayed on top of the tile should be dark or light. For example, if the tile has a light background, use dark text so it's visible.

➤ **Background color**—This is the tile's background color. Parts of a tile image that are transparent appear in this color. Some displays also outline tiles with this color. If you don't want the outline to be visible, make this color match the colors on the edges of the tiles.

➤ **Splash screen background color**—This is the background color shown behind the splash screen image.

In the category list on the left, you can click All Image Assets to see a list of everything, or you can click a category to see only the images in that category. For example, Figure 31-2 shows an app's Square 150×150 Logo category.

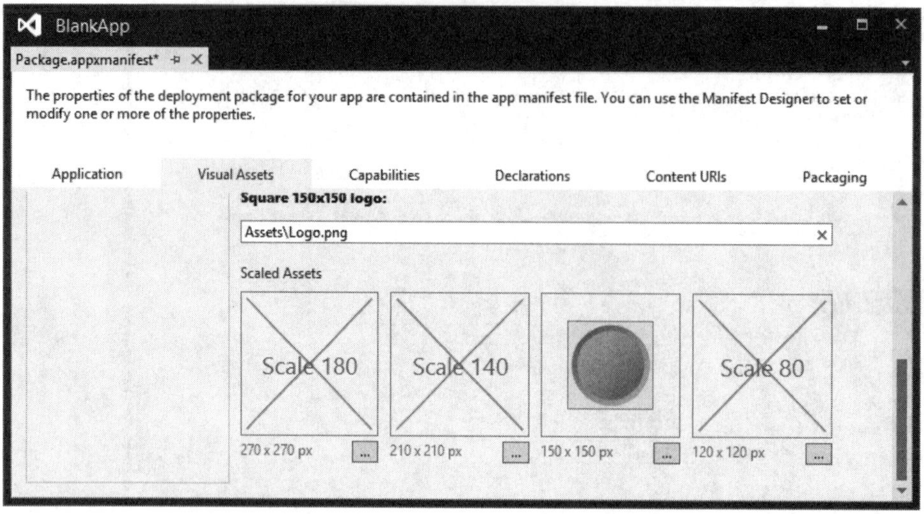

BlankApp

Package.appxmanifest*

The properties of the deployment package for your app are contained in the app manifest file. You can use the Manifest Designer to set or modify one or more of the properties.

| Application | Visual Assets | Capabilities | Declarations | Content URIs | Packaging |

Square 150x150 logo:

Assets\Logo.png

Scaled Assets

Scale 180
Scale 140

Scale 80

270 x 270 px   210 x 210 px   150 x 150 px   120 x 120 px

FIGURE 31-2

Use the ellipses below the image types to select an image for that type.

DEPLOYMENT

You can deploy Windows Store apps in two main ways. First, you can deploy the app on a local or remote computer so you can test it. Second, you can submit the app to the Windows Store so others can download and install it. These approaches are described in the following sections.

Deploying Locally

When you build an app in Visual Studio, it is automatically deployed on your computer. If you use the system's Search tool, you can find the app. You can then click the app to run it. You can also right-click it and select Pin to Start, Pin to Taskbar, or Uninstall.

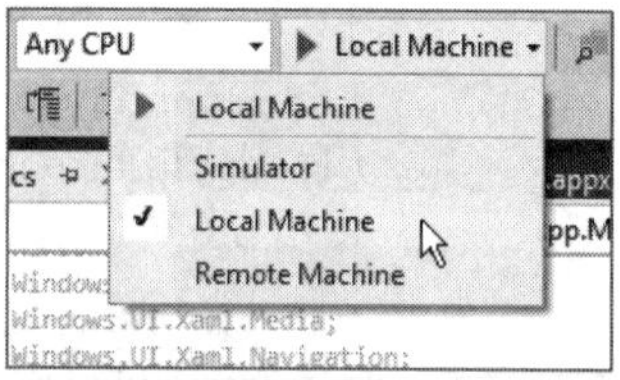

Any CPU		Local Machine
	Local Machine	
	Simulator	
✓	Local Machine	
	Remote Machine	

FIGURE 31-3

You can also manually deploy an app locally or on a remote computer. To do that, open the target dropdown on the Standard toolbar shown in Figure 31-3 and select Simulator, Local Machine, or Remote Machine. If you select Remote Machine, a dialog appears that lets you select the machine where you want to deploy the app.

> **NOTE** *To deploy to a remote machine, that machine must have a developer's license, have Visual Studio Remote Tools installed, and have Remote Debugging Monitor running.*

After you select the deployment target, open the Build menu and select Deploy.

If you deployed to the Simulator target, you can use the Debug menu's Start Debugging command to run the application in the simulator. If you deployed to a local or remote machine, you should be able to find and run the app there.

Deploying to the Windows Store

After you have tested your app and want to make it available to others, you can submit it to the Windows Store.

Before you can submit apps to the Windows Store (or the Windows Phone Store), you need to register for a couple of accounts.

First register for a Microsoft account at `signup.live.com/signup.aspx?lic=1`.

Next, register for a Windows Dev Center developer account at `dev.windows.com/join`. Unfortunately this registration isn't free. It currently costs roughly $19 for individuals and $99 for companies (depending on your location and taxes).

Microsoft charges the fee to cover the cost of inspecting the apps that are submitted to the store. When you submit an app, Microsoft verifies that it meets some standard criteria to make apps more uniform. For example, you must include a description, an app tile icon, and a screen shot. Microsoft also inspects the app to ensure that it doesn't contain a virus or other malware.

After you have the Microsoft and Dev Center accounts, you can build and test your app. When you're finished, you use the unified Windows Dev Center dashboard to submit the app.

If your app fails certification, you can fix it and try again until everything is perfect. Then you can publish the app for the world to use.

Rather than including a lot of extra details (which would probably change before you read this anyway), this section ends with a list of links you can use to get more information:

➤ Sign up for a Microsoft account at `signup.live.com/signup.aspx?lic=1`.

➤ Register for a Windows Dev Center developer account at `dev.windows.com/join`.

➤ Learn about the unified Windows Dev Center dashboard at `msdn.microsoft.com/library/windows/apps/mt169843.aspx`.

➤ Learn more about the submission process at `msdn.microsoft.com/library/windows/apps/hh694062.aspx`.

➤ Learn more about the app certification process at `msdn.microsoft.com/library/windows/apps/mt148554.aspx`.

➤ Read introductory articles at `dev.windows.com/windows-apps`.

➤ Find a list of How-To articles for C# and XAML programming at `msdn.microsoft.com/library/windows/apps/xaml/br229566.aspx`.

➤ Visit the Windows Store at `www.microsoft.com/windows`.

➤ Visit the Apps and Games section of the Windows Store at `www.microsoft.com/en-us/windows/apps-and-games`.

➤ Read Microsoft's article "App features, start to finish (XAML)" at `msdn.microsoft.com/library/windows/apps/xaml/dn632431.aspx`.

➤ Read Microsoft's article "Create your first Windows Store app using C# or Visual Basic" at `msdn.microsoft.com/library/windows/apps/dn631757.aspx`.

> **NOTE** *Windows Store and Windows Phone development are relatively new so the details change occasionally. That means I can't guarantee that Microsoft won't change the fees, URLs, and other details shown here. Hopefully the basic processes won't change too much and you can figure out the details by searching online.*
>
> *A good place to look for basic information and to use as a starting point for searches is* `dev.windows.com/getstarted`.

WPF TECHNIQUES

Before you get to the Try It, I want to briefly describe two more useful WPF techniques that you'll use in the Try It and the Exercises. Those techniques are using styles and setting dependency properties.

> **NOTE** *In addition to Windows Store apps, styles and dependency properties are available to WPF desktop applications. I just didn't have room to cover them in earlier lessons.*

Using Styles

Imagine you have an app that uses several dozen `TextBlocks`. Now suppose you decide that you want to change the font size, color, or some other property for all of those `TextBlocks`. Editing the XAML code to make the change would be straightforward but time-consuming.

XAML makes this easier by allowing you to define styles. A *style* defines some of the properties for a particular type of control in some part of the window's hierarchy. You define styles inside a *resource dictionary* attached to some XAML object.

For example, you could give a resource dictionary to the main `Grid` control that contains the other controls on the window. Next you could create a style for the `TextBlock` class inside that resource dictionary. After you create the style, any `TextBlock` inside that `Grid` will use the style.

The following code shows how you might create a style to set the font size for `TextBlock` controls:

```
<Grid>
    <Grid.Resources>
        <Style TargetType="TextBlock">
            <Setter Property="FontSize" Value="20"/>
        </Style>
    </Grid.Resources>
    ...
    <TextBlock Text="First Name:"/>
    <TextBlock Text="Last Name:"/>
    ...
</Grid>
```

The `Grid` contains a `Resources` section that defines the resource dictionary. That section contains a `Style` object. The `TargetType` property (in this case set to `TextBlock`) indicates the type of object to which the style can apply.

Inside the style, a `Setter` object defines a property that it can set for the target type. In this example, the `Setter` sets the object's `FontSize` property to the value 20.

Now any `TextBlock` objects that come later in the `Grid` automatically use this style. If you later decide to change the size for the `TextBlocks`, you only need to change it in the style.

> **NOTE** *If a* `TextBlock` *explicitly sets its* `FontSize`, *that value overrides the value set by the style.*

There's one other way you can use styles. If you give a style a name, then other controls can explicitly use that style. For example, the following code defines a named style:

```
<Grid>
    <Grid.Resources>
        <Style x:Key="BigStyle" TargetType="TextBlock">
            <Setter Property="FontSize" Value="50"/>
        </Style>
    </Grid.Resources>
    ...
    <TextBlock Text="First Name:" Style="{StaticResource BigStyle}"/>
    <TextBlock Text="Last Name:"/>
    ...
</Grid>
```

This `Grid`'s resource dictionary defines a style named `BigStyle`. Later a `TextBlock` uses that style by explicitly setting its `Style` property to `{StaticResource BigStyle}`. (The keyword `StaticResource` tells the program to look in the resource dictionary for a resource that doesn't change after it is defined.)

Any other `TextBlocks` that don't explicitly set their `Style` properties use default styles or an unnamed style if one is defined.

Setting Dependency Properties

A *dependency property* is a property that is defined for one object by a different object. For example, if you place a `TextBox` inside a `Grid` control, then you can set the `TextBox`'s `Grid.Row` and `Grid.Column` properties. Those properties are defined by the `Grid` class for any controls that are contained inside a `Grid`.

In XAML code at design time, you can simply set dependency properties to a value. For example, the following statement sets the `TextBox`'s `Grid.Row` and `Grid.Column` properties:

```
<TextBox Grid.Row="2" Grid.Column="5" Name="annualRateTextBox"/>
```

However, `Row` and `Column` are not truly properties of the `TextBox` class, so you can't set them directly in C# code. Instead you can use static methods provided by the `Grid` class, passing those methods the object for which you want to set the property (in this example the `TextBox`) and the value you want to set. For example, the following code sets the `Grid.Row` and `Grid.Column` properties for the `TextBox` named `annualRateTextBox`:

```
Grid.SetRow(annualRateTextBox, 2);
Grid.SetColumn(annualRateTextBox, 5);
```

If you need to retrieve the value of a dependency property, use the corresponding `Get` method as in `int row = Grid.GetRow(annualRateTextBox)`.

TRY IT

In this Try It, you build a program that makes colorful balls bounce across the screen and make clicking noises when they hit the screen's edges.

Lesson Requirements

In this lesson, you:

➤ Start a new Windows project by selecting the Blank App. Replace the main window's `Grid` control with a `Canvas` control named `mainCanvas`.

➤ Add a `MediaElement` to the main window's XAML code to play the click sound.

➤ Create a `Ball` sprite class to manage balls. Give it properties and methods to create a random ball, track the ball's position and velocity, and move the ball.

➤ When the window loads, create a `DispatcherTimer` and give it an event handler that moves the balls.

➤ Test the program with both dark and light themes.

> **NOTE** *You can download the code and resources for this lesson from the website at* www.wrox.com/go/csharp24hourtrainer2e.

Hints

➤ Make the `Ball` class use an `Ellipse` object to display itself.

➤ Give the `Ball` class the following `using` directives:

```
using Windows.UI.Xaml.Shapes;
using Windows.UI.Xaml.Controls;
using Windows.UI.Xaml.Media;
```

➤ Give the `Ball` class a randomizing constructor, a `RandomBrush` method, and a `Move` method.

Step-by-Step

➤ Start a new Windows project by selecting the Blank App. Replace the main window's `Grid` control with a `Canvas` control named `mainCanvas`.

1. In Visual Studio 2015's New Project dialog, you can find this template under Templates > Visual C# > Windows > Windows 8 > Windows.

2. Give the `Canvas` the same `Background` property that the initial `Grid` had. It should look like this:

```
Background="{ThemeResource ApplicationPageBackgroundThemeBrush}"
```

This makes the `Canvas` determine its background color at run time by looking at the theme. (In case the user sets the theme to light or dark.)

➤ Add a `MediaElement` to the main window's XAML code to play the click sound.

1. Use the Project menu's Add Existing Item command to add a click sound file to the project.

2. Add a `MediaElement` to the main window's XAML code. Set its `x:Name` property to `clickSound` and set its `Source` property to the sound effect file you added.

➤ Create a `Ball` sprite class to manage balls. Give it properties and methods to create a random ball, track the ball's position and velocity, and move the ball.

1. Use code similar to the following.

```
class Ball
{
    // Used to generate random values.
    static private Random Rand = new Random();

    // All balls have black outlines.
    static private Brush BlackBrush =
        new SolidColorBrush(Windows.UI.Colors.Black);

    public Ellipse MyEllipse;
    public Canvas Parent;
    public double X, Y, Diameter, Vx, Vy;

    // Initialize a random Ball.
    public Ball(Canvas parent)
    {
```

```csharp
            // Save the parent.
            Parent = parent;

            // Create the Ball's geometry.
            const int maxSpeed = 15;
            Vx = Rand.Next(-maxSpeed, maxSpeed + 1);
            Vy = Rand.Next(-maxSpeed, maxSpeed + 1);
            Diameter = Rand.Next(50, 200);
            X = Rand.Next(0, (int)(Parent.ActualWidth - Diameter));
            Y = Rand.Next(0, (int)(Parent.ActualHeight - Diameter));

            // Create the Ellipse.
            MyEllipse = new Ellipse();
            MyEllipse.Width = Diameter;
            MyEllipse.Height = Diameter;
            MyEllipse.Fill = RandomBrush();
            MyEllipse.Stroke = BlackBrush;

            Canvas.SetLeft(MyEllipse, X);
            Canvas.SetTop(MyEllipse, Y);

            // Add the new ball to the parent.
            Parent.Children.Add(MyEllipse);
        }

        // Return a random brush.
        static private Brush RandomBrush()
        {
            Brush[] brushes =
            {
                new SolidColorBrush(Windows.UI.Colors.Red),
                new SolidColorBrush(Windows.UI.Colors.Orange),
                new SolidColorBrush(Windows.UI.Colors.Yellow),
                new SolidColorBrush(Windows.UI.Colors.Lime),
                new SolidColorBrush(Windows.UI.Colors.Blue),
                new SolidColorBrush(Windows.UI.Colors.Indigo),
                new SolidColorBrush(Windows.UI.Colors.Violet),
            };
            return brushes[Rand.Next(0, brushes.Length)];
        }

        // Move the Ball. Return true if the Ball bounces.
        public bool Move()
        {
            // Remember if the ball bounces.
            bool bounced = false;

            // Update the ball's position.
            X += Vx;
            if (X < 0)
            {
                // Hit the left edge.
                X = -X;
                Vx = -Vx;
```

```
            bounced = true;
        }
        else if (X + Diameter > Parent.ActualWidth)
        {
            // Hit the right edge.
            double overshoot = (X + Diameter) - Parent.ActualWidth;
            X = Parent.ActualWidth - overshoot - Diameter;
            Vx = -Vx;
            bounced = true;
        }

        Y += Vy;
        if (Y < 0)
        {
            // Hit the left edge.
            Y = -Y;
            Vy = -Vy;
            bounced = true;
        }
        else if (Y + Diameter > Parent.ActualHeight)
        {
            // Hit the right edge.
            double overshoot = (Y + Diameter) - Parent.ActualHeight;
            Y = Parent.ActualHeight - overshoot - Diameter;
            Vy = -Vy;
            bounced = true;
        }

        // Update the Ellipse's position.
        Canvas.SetLeft(MyEllipse, X);
        Canvas.SetTop(MyEllipse, Y);

        return bounced;
    }
}
```

➤   When the window loads, create a `DispatcherTimer` and give it an event handler that moves the balls.

1.   Add the XAML code `Loaded="Page_Loaded"` to the main window's definition.

2.   Use the following code to prepare the program when the window is loaded:

```
// The movement timer.
private DispatcherTimer MoveTimer;

// Balls.
private const int NumBalls = 10;
private Ball[] Balls = new Ball[NumBalls];

// Used to generate random numbers.
private Random Rand = new Random();

// Create balls and start them moving.
private void Page_Loaded(object sender, RoutedEventArgs e)
{
```

```
        // Create the balls.
        for (int i = 0; i < NumBalls; i++)
            Balls[i] = new Ball(mainCanvas);

        // Create the timer.
        MoveTimer = new DispatcherTimer();
        MoveTimer.Interval = new TimeSpan(0, 0, 0, 0, 20);
        MoveTimer.Tick += MoveTimer_Tick;
        MoveTimer.Start();
    }
```

3.   Use the following code to move the balls when the timer's `Tick` event fires:

```
    // Move the balls.
    private void MoveTimer_Tick(object sender, object e)
    {
        // Remember if a ball bounces.
        bool bounced = false;
        foreach (Ball ball in Balls) if (ball.Move()) bounced = true;

        if (bounced) clickSound.Play();
    }
```

➤   Test the program with both dark and light themes.

1.   Open the `App.xaml` file and add the code `RequestedTheme="Light"` to the `Application` object's definition. Test the program.

2.   Change the `RequestedTheme` to `"Dark"` and test the program again.

3.   After testing, remove the `RequestedTheme` property so the app uses the theme selected on the user's device.

EXERCISES

1.   Make an interest calculator similar to the one shown in Figure 31-4 (shown in the `Light` theme). When the user enters values and clicks Calculate, the program should enter a loop that runs over a sequence of months. Each month it should calculate the payment and the amount of interest for that month and update the user's balance. The loop should run until the balance is zero. (Hint: Give any `Grid` rows and columns relative sizes such as `*` or `1.5*` so they will resize if you change the top-level `Grid`'s size.)

Initial Balance:	$5,000.00		Month	Payment	Interest	Balance
			129	$15.00	$2.08	$118.92
Annual Rate:	18.90%		130	$15.00	$1.87	$105.79
			131	$15.00	$1.67	$92.46
			132	$15.00	$1.46	$78.91
			133	$15.00	$1.24	$65.15
Payment %:	4.00%		134	$15.00	$1.03	$51.18
			135	$15.00	$0.81	$36.99
			136	$15.00	$0.58	$22.57
Min Payment:	$15.00		137	$15.00	$0.36	$7.92
			138	$8.05	$0.12	$0.00

Calculate   Total Payments: $8,109.24

FIGURE 31-4

2. Copy the program you wrote for Exercise 1 and use `Style` objects to set the `FontSize` values to 20 for the app's `TextBlock`, `TextBox`, and `Button` controls. (Resize the app's top-level `Grid` if necessary.)

3. [Hard] There's probably a bug in the program you wrote for Exercise 2. If you enter a payment percentage of 0% and a minimum payment of $15, then the monthly interest will be greater than the monthly payments so the balance will increase over time. That means the program's loop will never end.

To fix that, copy the program you wrote for Exercise 2. Inside the loop, compare the payment and the interest. If the interest is greater, display an error message and break out of the loop.

Unfortunately Windows Store apps can't use `MessageBox.Show`. Instead you can use the `Windows.UI.Popups.MessageDialog` class. Create a dialog, passing its constructor an error message and a title string. Use the object's `Show` method to display the dialog.

The dialog's `Show` method is asynchronous, which means it returns immediately to the calling code and then continues running in the background. That doesn't really hurt the application, but it does make Visual Studio issue a warning. To get rid of the warning, place the `await` keyword before the call to `Show`. That makes the code pause and wait for the call to `Show` to complete before continuing. You can only use `await` in a method that is also asynchronous, so you also need to mark the event handler with the `async` keyword.

4. [Hard] Copy the program you wrote for Exercise 3 and modify it so it displays its own message instead of using the `MessageDialog` class. To do that, add a `Grid` (or some other container) holding the message and an "X" `Button`. Set the `Grid`'s `Visibility` property to `Collapsed`.

Make a `ShowMessage` method that displays the message by doing the following:

➤ Disable the window's `TextBoxes` and the Calculate `Button`.

➤ Set the main `Grid` control's `Opacity` property to `0.5`.

➤ Set the message `Grid`'s `Visibility` property to `Visible`.

Make a `HideMessage` method that reverses the actions performed by `ShowMessage`.

(Bonus: To make the message stand out, make the message `Grid` use the background color given by `ApplicationForegroundThemeBrush` and make the controls it contains use the foreground color given by `ApplicationPageBackgroundThemeBrush`. Be sure to test in the `Dark` and `Light` themes.)

5. When you create a Windows Store app, Visual Studio creates blank PNG files for the required images. Copy the program you wrote for Exercise 4. Make the program use your images and remove the default images. Pin the program to the Windows Start screen and experiment with resizing the app's tile. Notice that the app displays the splash screen image when it starts.

6. Copy the program you wrote for Exercise 5 and add the Wide 310×150 and Square 310×310 images. Verify that you can now change the app's tile to be wide or large on the Windows Start screen.

7. Copy the program you built for the Try It and add the required Wide 310×150, and Square 310×310 images to it.

> **NOTE** *Please select the videos for Lesson 31 online at* www.wrox.com/go/ csharp24hourtrainer2evideos.

Windows Phone Apps

This lesson explains how you can build Windows Phone applications. Note that you don't actually need to upload these applications to the Windows Store. You can build and run them locally on your phone if you like.

BUILDING APPS

Windows Phone apps are similar to Windows Store apps in several ways. Both use XAML to define their user interfaces. Both can use C# code behind the user interface to do whatever it is that makes the app useful. Both also require that you define images of various sizes to represent the app. (More on that later.)

In addition to installing Visual Studio, you need to take a few other steps before you can start building phone apps. First download the Windows Software Development Kit (SDK) for your version of Windows. The Windows 8.1 version is available at msdn.microsoft.com/windows /desktop/bg162891.aspx. The Windows 10 version is at dev.windows.com/downloads /windows-10-sdk.

This SDK contains tools you can use to build phone and Windows Store apps. It's a big download, ranging in size from around 10MB to 1GB depending on your configuration, so be sure you have a high-speed Internet connection.

As is the case with Windows Store development, you'll need a Microsoft account (signup .live.com/signup.aspx) and a Windows Dev Center developer account (dev.windows.com /join).

After you install the SDK and sign up for Microsoft and Dev Center accounts, you can create new phone apps by opening Visual Studio's File menu, selecting New ➪ Project, and using the New Project dialog shown in Figure 32-1. Select the Windows Phone Apps category on the left to see the phone templates.

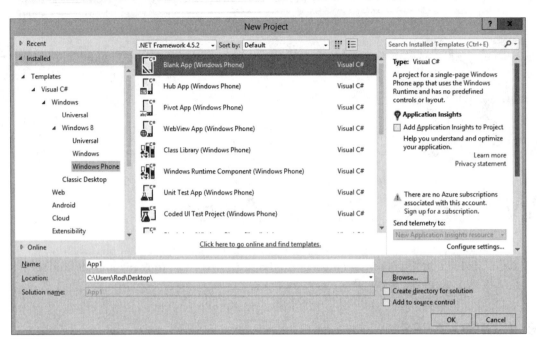

FIGURE 32-1

At this point you can build an app. At some point you'll want to test your app on your phone, so you may as well set up your phone so you can use it for testing now while you're preparing your development environment.

Normally you install apps from the Windows Store. An app in the store has been examined by Microsoft so it shouldn't contain viruses and other malware. To prevent people from easily installing viruses on other people's phones, you cannot simply download an app directly to a phone. First you need to unlock the phone for development.

To do that, connect your phone to your development computer with the USB cable that came with your phone. Turn the phone on and unlock its screen (if you have password protection on the phone).

Next use your computer's search tool to find the app called Windows Phone Developer Registration. (From the desktop, move the mouse to the lower-right corner, move the mouse up, and click the Search tool.)

In the dialog that appears, click the Register button. The dialog will ask you to log in to your Microsoft account and verify that it's associated with your developer account. When you're finished, you should be able to download apps to your phone. (For more details about registering your phone, including troubleshooting information, see `msdn.microsoft.com/library/windows/apps/ff769508`.)

At this point you can add XAML code and C# code behind it as usual. Writing a Windows Phone app is very similar to writing a Windows Store app, although a phone can do things that a computer can't so some differences exist. For example, phones may have cameras, orientation sensors, multi-touch capable screens, location services, near-field communication (NFC), Bluetooth, and more. Using those capabilities is a fairly advanced topic so I won't say any more about them in this book.

After you create your app, you have two options for testing it: running in an emulator and running on your phone. To select an option, open the Run dropdown in the Standard toolbar shown in Figure 32-2. Select one of the emulators or select Device to run on a phone.

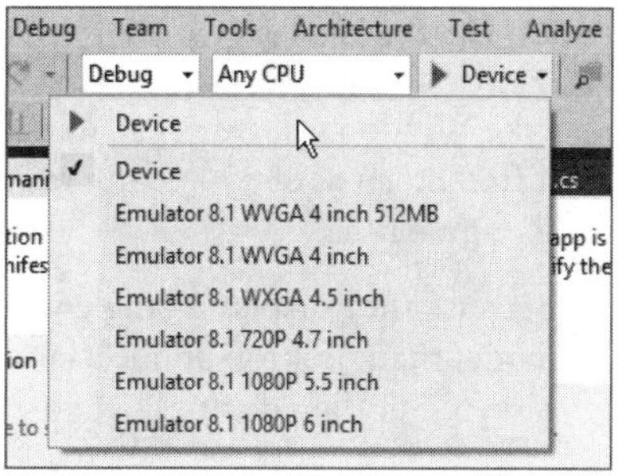

FIGURE 32-2

To run in an emulator, select an emulator from the dropdown shown in Figure 32-2 and press F5 to run the program as usual. For the emulator to work, your computer needs to be running Hyper-V, a tool that allows your computer to run virtual machines.

Unfortunately Hyper-V requires you to have Windows Professional installed. If you don't have Windows Professional installed, you can still run your app on your phone. Select Device from the dropdown, use a USB cable to plug your phone into the computer, turn the phone on and unlock its screen, and press F5 to run the app. Visual Studio will download the app to your phone and run it.

When you're done testing, use the Debug menu's Stop Debugging command or click the Stop Debugging button on the Debug toolbar.

After you run an app on your phone, it will remain installed on the phone so you can use it later even if the phone is disconnected from the computer. You can find the app in the phone's list of installed apps. Press and hold the app to pin it to the Start screen or to uninstall it.

If you pin the app to the Start screen, you can press and hold its tile to change the tile size or unpin it.

Here's a summary of the steps you use to build and test an app:

➤ (Optional) Install Hyper-V if you are using Windows Professional or Enterprise edition and you want to run Windows Phone apps in the device emulator. For instructions, search the Internet or see www.howtogeek.com/196158/how-to-create-and-run-virtual-machines-with-hyper-v/.

➤ Install the Windows Software Development Kit (SDK) for Windows 8.1.

➤ Register for a Microsoft account.

➤ Register for a Dev Center account.

➤ Unlock your phone for development.

➤ Write the app.

➤ To test in an emulator, select an emulator from the dropdown and run the app.

➤ To test on a phone, connect the phone, turn the phone on, unlock the phone's screen, and run the app.

The following sections provide some more details about the kinds of apps you can build and the images you need to set to make them appear properly.

NAVIGATION STYLE

Like Windows Store apps, Windows Phone apps cover the entire device. You can switch between different apps, but you can't resize and rearrange the apps to view more than one on the screen at the same time.

Because they display a single window at a time, phone apps typically use a simpler navigational model than desktop applications. Some apps allow you to use a back button to move to an earlier screen, but they don't allow you to easily jump from screen to screen.

Phone apps also typically don't provide buttons or menu items that let the user close them. Instead the user opens or navigates to another app and leaves yours sitting in the background. Later the device closes your app if it needs to free up memory.

> **NOTE** *Although many apps don't provide a way to close them, you can close an app by making the code call* `Application.Current.Exit()`.

Because these apps cover the entire device, you must arrange the controls to take best advantage of whatever space is available. You don't have control over how large the user's screen is, so you should use container controls such as `Grid` and `StackPanel` to get the most out of the space you have.

APP STYLES

Visual Studio includes templates for building several different styles of Windows Phone apps. The following list summarizes the most common kinds of templates:

> **Blank**—This kind of app displays a single window with no navigation to other windows. It's similar to a one-window desktop application without dialogs.
>
> **Hub**—This kind of app uses a `Hub` control. The main `Hub` control displays a horizontally scrolling window divided into sections holding different kinds of information. You can tap a section heading to open a new page that provides details about that section.
>
> **Pivot**—This kind of app displays a collection of list categories. When a category is selected, you see its list of items below it. You can scroll horizontally through the different categories. This template is useful for displaying different views of data. For example, my phone displays Outlook mail in a pivot view with categories All, Unread, and Urgent.
>
> **WebView**—This kind of app uses the `WebView` control. That control lets an app display a piece of web content, although Microsoft makes it clear that this is not a full-featured web browser. For example, you can use a `WebView` control to display frequently updated information rather than make new builds to update the app's data.

If you use one of these templates to create a new project, the app comes pre-loaded with sample data so you can see what the finished app will look like. (In fact, you'll probably get a better sense of how the different templates work if you just create some sample projects and run them rather than staring at the previous descriptions.)

APP IMAGES

Like Windows Store apps, Windows Phone apps may be represented by images in many different sizes. For example, the phone's Start screen can display your app's tile in Small, Wide, and Large sizes.

The kinds of images are grouped into categories, each of which includes several versions at different sizes. If you include one image in a category and omit the others, then that image is scaled if necessary to provide the others.

As is the case with Windows Phone apps, automatic scaling is better than nothing, but sometimes it can produce poor results. For example, if you provide a relatively large image that contains text, when it's scaled down to a small size the text may turn into a fuzzy blur. To provide the best results, you should create separate images at several different scales.

The images you include in a project must match the required dimensions exactly. For example, you can't use a 100×100 pixel image in place of a 99×99 pixel image.

Table 32-1 lists the kinds of images you can include in a Windows Phone app. The bold entries in the Sizes column indicate required images.

TABLE 32-1

CATEGORY	SIZES
Square 44×44 Logo	**106 × 106** 62 × 62 44 × 44
Square 71×71 Logo	**170 × 170** 99 × 99 71 × 71
Square 150×150 Logo	**360 × 360** 210 × 210 150 × 150
Wide 310×150 Logo	**744 × 360** 434 × 210 310 × 150
Store Logo	**120 × 120** 70 × 70 50 × 50
Splash Screen	**1152 × 1920** 672 × 1120 480 × 800

When you create your images, give them suggestive names such as MyApp106×106.png so you can tell what they are for.

> **NOTE** *To change an app's tile size on your phone, press and hold the tile. Tap the arrows that appear to cycle between the Small, Wide, and Large tile sizes. When you've selected the desired size, tap the tile to get out of resizing mode.*

After you've created the images, you need to attach them to the project. To do that, open Solution Explorer and double click `Package.appxmanifest` to open the Manifest Editor shown in Figure 32-3. This editor lets you select the orientations that your app allows. For example, if you only want your app to be available when the user is holding the phone in the portrait orientation, check the Portrait box.

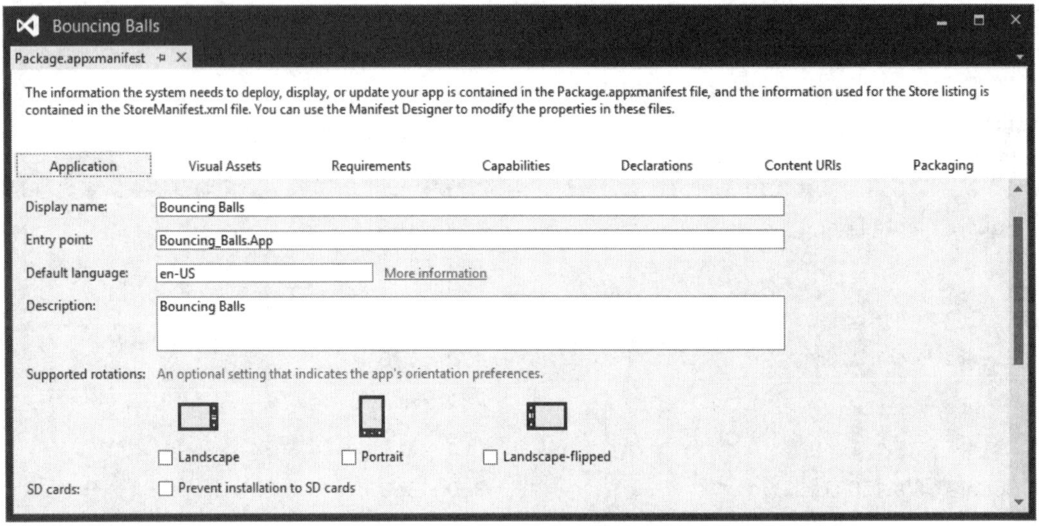

FIGURE 32-3

To set the app's images, click the Visual Assets tab to see the display shown in Figure 32-4. In the category list on the left, you can click All Image Assets to see a list of everything, or you can click a category to see only the images in that category. For example, Figure 32-4 shows an app's Square 71×71 Logo category.

Use the ellipses below the image types to select an image for that type.

Options above the images let you decide whether the phone should display the app's name on top of the large or wide tile.

A third option lets you set the tile's background color. If you set this color to transparent and the image you use for the tile has a transparent background, then the phone's Start screen image will display behind the tile.

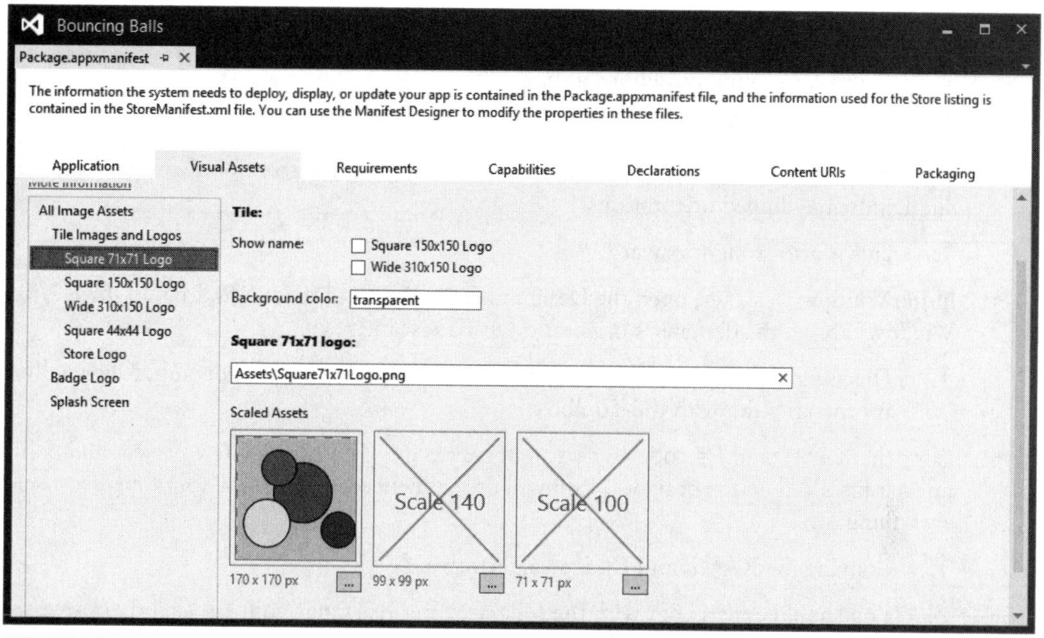

FIGURE 32-4

TRY IT

In this Try It, you build a Windows Phone interest calculator similar to the app you built for Exercise 31-3.

Lesson Requirements

In this lesson, you:

➤ Start a new blank Windows Phone app.

➤ Open the Package.appxmanifest file and allow the program to run only in the Landscape and Landscape-flipped orientations.

➤ In the Window Designer, open the Design menu and select Device Window. In the Device Window tab, set the designer's orientation to Landscape.

➤ Copy the XAML and C# code you wrote for Exercise 31-3 into the new project and fix it up so it fits nicely in the designer. You will probably need to make the fonts smaller to make everything fit.

➤ Test the app in an emulator or on a phone.

> **NOTE** *You can download the code and resources for this lesson from the website at* www.wrox.com/go/csharp24hourtrainer2e.

Step-by-Step

➤ Start a new blank Windows Phone app.

1. This is straightforward.

➤ Open the `Package.appxmanifest` file and allow the program to run only in the Landscape and Landscape-flipped orientations.

1. This is also straightforward.

➤ In the Window Designer, open the Design menu and select Device Window. In the Device Window tab, set the designer's orientation to Landscape.

1. This is straightforward assuming you can find the Device Window tab. It normally appears as a tab with the Toolbox.

➤ Copy the XAML and C# code you wrote for Exercise 31-3 into the new project and fix it up so it fits nicely in the designer. You will probably need to make the fonts smaller to make everything fit.

1. Copying the XAML and C# is straightforward.

2. You should experiment with the font sizes and rearrange controls slightly if necessary to make everything fit on the designer. I set the `TextBlock`, `TextBox`, and `Button` `FontSize` properties to 12. (This is a situation where XAML `Style` objects come in handy.)

➤ Test the app in an emulator or on a phone.

1. This is straightforward.

EXERCISES

1. Apps that look good on a tablet or desktop system don't always look good on a phone. On my phone, the text displayed by the Try It is so small I can barely read it.

   Copy the app you wrote for the Try It and modify it to make it easier to read. Move the `TextBlocks` (used as labels) so they sit above their corresponding `TextBoxes`. Then make the `TextBox` and `ListBox` fonts bigger so they are easier to read. (Hint: You can give the results `StackPanel` a `Resources` section that defines a `Style` to set the `FontSize` property for the result `TextBlocks`.)

2. [Hard] Copy the app you wrote for Exercise 1 and modify it so it displays its warning message in a separate `Grid` control as described in Exercise 31-4.

3. Copy the app you wrote for Exercise 2, add appropriate images to it, and make it display its name on its wide and large tiles.

4. Make a bouncing ball app similar to the Windows Store app you built for the Try It in Lesson 31.

5. Run the app you wrote for Exercise 4 and see what happens if you change the phone's orientation while it's running. The result is distracting and doesn't make the app more useful (not that it's particularly useful to begin with), so copy the project and modify it so it only allows the Portrait orientation.

6. [Games] Copy the app you wrote for Exercise 5 and modify it so when the user taps a ball, that ball disappears with a popping sound. When the user taps the last ball, make the app close. Hints:

   ➤ Catch the main Canvas's Tapped event and use e.GetPosition to get the tap's position. Then loop through the balls and determine whether the user tapped one.

   ➤ To make removing balls easy, store them in a List<Ball>.

   ➤ Check the balls in top-to-bottom order so the app removes the topmost ball that was clicked.

   ➤ Feel free to add other sounds if you like such as a "tap misses" sound and a "game over" sound.

7. [Hard] Make a tip calculator similar to the one shown in Figure 32-5. (This is a screen shot of the designer not the app running in the emulator because my system doesn't have Windows Professional installed and therefore can't run Hyper-V.)

   When the user taps a button or adjusts the percentage Slider, the app should display the corresponding tip amount in the TextBlock above the Slider. (Normally I would place the output TextBlock below all of the other controls, but during testing I found that my finger obscured the result when I adjusted the percentage so this layout worked much better.) Hints:

   ➤ Only allow the Portrait orientation.

   ➤ Use a TotalCost variable to track the value entered by the user.

   ➤ When the user taps a digit button, multiply TotalCost by 10 and add the new digit's value divided by 100. Then display TotalCost and the calculated tip amount.

FIGURE 32-5

   ➤ When the user clicks the X button, reset TotalCost to 0.

   ➤ When the user adjusts the percentage Slider, recalculate and display the new tip amount.

   ➤ Protect the app from the user entering very large values such as $1 billion. (I don't think people tip when they buy soccer stadiums or nuclear submarines anyway.)

8. Copy the app you built for Exercise 7, add appropriate images to it, and make it display its name on its wide and large tiles.

9. Make a simple score-keeping application like the one shown in Figure 32-6. The user should be able to enter team names in the TextBoxes at the top and use the arrow buttons to

increase or decrease the scores. If the user taps the 0-0 button, reset both scores to 0. (Hint: Only allow the Landscape and Landscape-flipped orientations.)

FIGURE 32-6

10.   Copy the app you built for Exercise 9, add appropriate images to it, and make it display its name on its wide and large tiles. Use images of volleyballs, flaming soccer balls, racing ducks, or whatever else is appropriate for your favorite sport.

> **NOTE** *Please select the videos for Lesson 32 online at* www.wrox.com/go/ csharp24hourtrainer2evideos.

SECTION VII
Specialized Topics

Most of the lessons so far have dealt with general programming topics. For example, every desktop application needs to use controls and most also need to use variables, classes, and files.

The lessons in this section explain more specialized topics. They describe ideas and techniques that you won't need for every program you write, although you will still find them useful under many circumstances.

Localizing Programs

Many programmers write applications that are used only in their countries. It's easy enough to find plenty of customers for a small application without looking for customers long distance.

However, the world has grown smaller in the past few decades, and it's not too hard to provide programs for people all over the world. Customers can download your software over the Internet and pay for it using online payment systems in a matter of minutes. Web applications that run in a browser are even more likely to be used by people all over the world.

With such a potentially enormous market, it makes sense in some cases to make programs accessible to people in different countries, particularly since C# and Visual Studio make it relatively easy.

In this lesson, you learn how to make a program accessible to customers in other countries with different cultures. You learn how to make multiple interfaces for a program so users can work in their own languages. You also learn how to work with values such as currencies and dates that have different formats in different locales.

> **WARNING** *Localization is a huge topic so there isn't room to cover everything there is to know about it here. In particular, you should always get a native of a particular locale to help in localizing your application whenever possible. Unless you are extremely well versed in a locale's language, customs, and idioms, it's very easy to make sometimes embarrassing mistakes. (For examples, search the Internet for "funny translation mistakes" to see hundreds if not thousands of cases where someone thought they didn't need help from a native speaker. One of my favorites is, "Do not disturb. Tiny grass is dreaming.")*
>
> *Note that I am not fluent in all of the locales that this lesson uses. I used the Babel Fish automatic translation tool at* www.babelfish.com *to make the simple translations shown here. You can use Babel Fish or a similar tool for practice and for this lesson's exercises, but you should get human help before releasing a program to users.*

UNDERSTANDING LOCALIZATION

A computer's *locale* is a setting that defines the user's language, country, and cultural settings that determine such things as how dates and monetary values are formatted. For example, the Format Values example program shown in Figure 33-1 (and available in this lesson's downloads) displays the same values in American, British, German, and French locales.

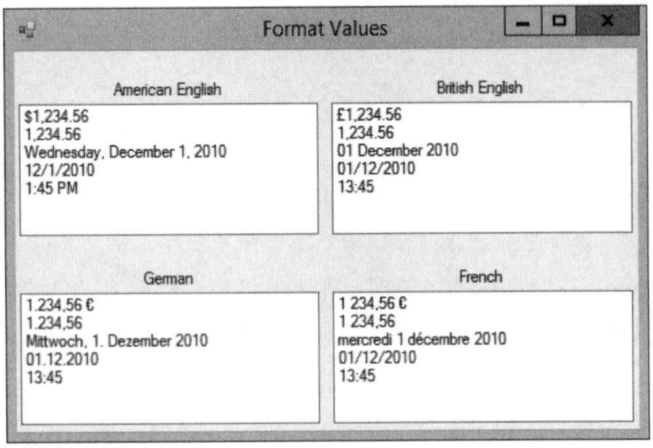

FIGURE 33-1

If you look closely at Figure 33-1, you can see that the same values produce very different results in the different locales. For example, the value 1234.56 displayed as currency appears variously as:

➤ $1,234.56

➤ £1,234.56

➤ 1.234,56 €

➤ 1 234,56 €

Not only do these results use different currency symbols, but they even use different decimal and thousands separators.

> **NOTE** *Globalization is the process of building an application that can be used by users from different cultures.*
>
> *Localization is the process of customizing a globalized application for a specific culture.*

Localizing an application involves two main steps: building a localized user interface and processing locale-specific values.

BUILDING LOCALIZED INTERFACES

At first this may seem like a daunting task. How do you build completely separate interfaces for multiple locales? Fortunately this is one thing that C# and Visual Studio do really well (at least for Windows Forms applications).

To build a globalized program, start by creating the form as usual. Add controls and set their properties as you want them to appear by default.

After you've defined the program's default appearance, you can localize it for other locales. To do that, set the form's `Localizable` property to `true`. Then select a new locale from the dropdown list provided by the form's `Language` property. Now modify the form to handle the new locale. You can change control properties such as the text they display. You can also move controls around and change their sizes, which is particularly important because the same text may take up a different amount of room in different languages.

At run time, the program automatically checks the computer's locale settings and picks the program's localization that gives the closest match.

Note that many languages have several sub-locales. For example, English comes in the varieties used in India, Ireland, New Zealand, and more than a dozen other locales.

There's also locale listed simply as "English." If the user's computer is set up for one of the English locales that the program doesn't support, the program falls back to the generic English locale. If the program can't support that locale either, it uses the default locale that you used when you initially created the form.

The Localized Weekdays example program (available in this lesson's code download) is localized for English (the form's default) and German. Figure 33-2 shows the form's English interface and Figure 33-3 shows its German interface.

FIGURE 33-2

TESTING LOCALIZATIONS

Having the program check the computer's locale automatically at run time is convenient for the user but it makes testing different locales tricky.

One way to force the program to pick a particular locale so you can test it is to select the locale in code. You must do this before the form is initial-

FIGURE 33-3

ized because after that point the form's text and other properties are already filled in and setting the locale won't reload the form.

When you create a form, Visual Studio automatically creates a constructor for it that calls the `InitializeComponent` function. Place your code before the call to `InitializeComponent`.

The following code shows how the Localized Weekdays program explicitly selects either the English or the German locale:

```
using System.Threading;
using System.Globalization;
...

public Form1()
{
    // English.
    //Thread.CurrentThread.CurrentCulture =
    //    new CultureInfo("en-US", false);
    //Thread.CurrentThread.CurrentUICulture =
    //    new CultureInfo("en-US", false);

    // German.
    Thread.CurrentThread.CurrentCulture =
        new CultureInfo("de-DE", false);
    Thread.CurrentThread.CurrentUICulture =
        new CultureInfo("de-DE", false);

    InitializeComponent();
}
```

This code contains statements that set the locale to English or German. Simply comment out the one that you don't want to use for a given test.

> **NOTE** *For a list of more than 100 culture values that you can use in code, such as en-US and de-DE, see* msdn.microsoft.com/library/ee825488.aspx.

Setting the CurrentCulture makes the program use locale-specific methods when processing dates, currency, numbers, and other values in the code. Setting the CurrentUICulture makes the program load the appropriate user interface elements for the form.

> **NOTE** *After you finish testing a form's localized version, be sure to remove the code that selects the culture so the program can use the system's settings. Otherwise you may end up with some very confused users.*

PROCESSING LOCALE-SPECIFIC VALUES

Inside C# code, variables are stored in American English formats. To avoid confusion, Microsoft decided to pick one locale for code values and stick with it.

When you move data in and out of the program, however, you need to be aware of the computer's locale. For example, suppose the program uses the following code to display an order's due date:

```
dueDateTextBox.Text = dueDate.ToString("MM/dd/yy")
```

If the date is November 20, 2010, this produces the result "11/20/10," which makes sense in the United States but should be "20/11/10" in France and "20.11.10" in Germany.

The problem is that the program uses a custom date format that is hard-coded to use an American-style date format. To produce a format appropriate for the user's system, you should use standard date, time, and other formats whenever possible. The following code uses the standard short date format:

```
dueDateTextBox.Text = dueDate.ToString("d")
```

This produces "11/20/2010" on an American system and "20/11/2010" on a French system.

You can run into the same problem if you assume the user will enter values in a particular format. For example, suppose you want to get the whole number part of the value 1,234.56 entered by the user. If you assume the decimal separator is a period and just use whatever comes before it as the integer part, then you'll get the answer 1 when a German user enters "1.234,56" and the program will crash when a French user enters the value "1 234.56."

To avoid this problem, use locale-aware functions such as the numeric classes' `Parse` methods to read values entered by the user. In this example, a good solution is to use `float.Parse` to read the value and then truncate it as shown in the following code:

```
value = (int)float.Parse(valueTextBox.Text);
```

For a list of standard numeric formats, see `msdn.microsoft.com/library/dwhawy9k.aspx`.

For a list of standard date and time formats, see `msdn.microsoft.com/library/az4se3k1.aspx`.

For more information on parsing strings, see `msdn.microsoft.com/library/b4w53z0y.aspx`.

> **NOTE** *Previous lessons have shown how to use* `Parse` *methods to parse currency values. For example, the following statement parses a currency value entered by the user:*
>
> ```
> value = decimal.Parse(valueLabel.Text, NumberStyles.Any);
> ```
>
> *This isn't completely foolproof. If the user has a German system but types a value in a French format, the program will crash, but it seems reasonable to ask a German user to enter German values.*
>
> *The Localized Parsing example program shown in Figure 33-4 (and available in this lesson's code download) parses currency values displayed in labels in different languages, doubles the parsed decimal values, and displays the results. For each language, it selects the appropriate culture so it can parse and display the correct formats.*

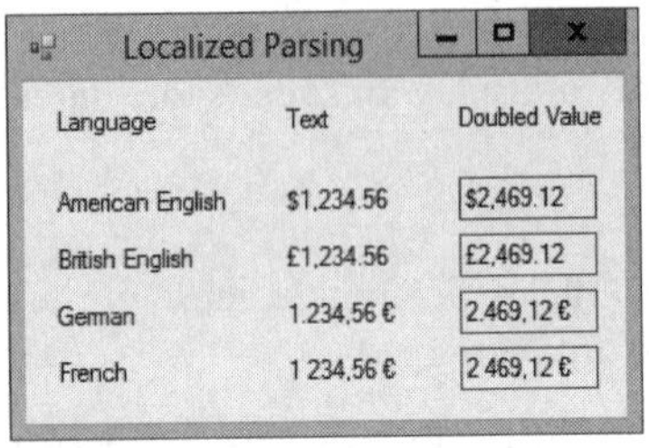

Language	Text	Doubled Value
American English	$1,234.56	$2,469.12
British English	£1,234.56	£2,469.12
German	1.234,56 €	2.469,12 €
French	1 234,56 €	2 469,12 €

FIGURE 33-4

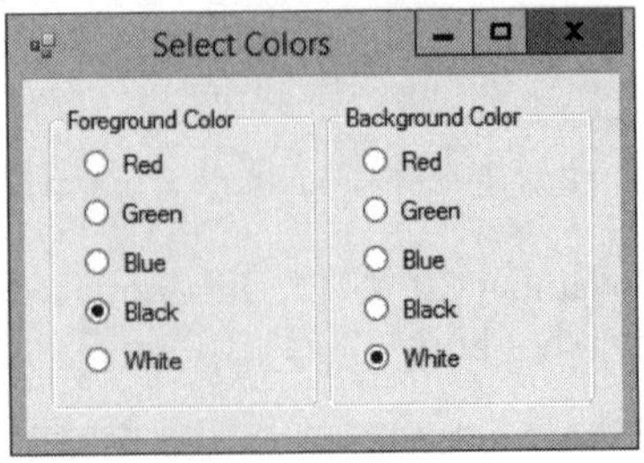

Select Colors

Foreground Color	Background Color
○ Red	○ Red
○ Green	○ Green
○ Blue	○ Blue
◉ Black	○ Black
○ White	◉ White

FIGURE 33-5

TRY IT

In this Try It, you write the program shown in Figures 33-5 and 33-6, which lets you select foreground and background colors in American English and Mexican Spanish.

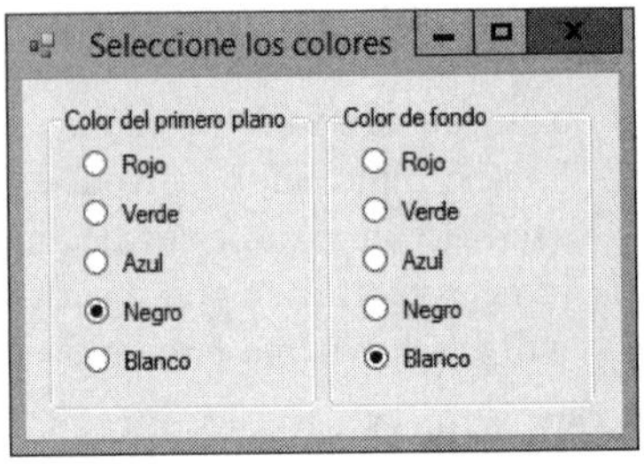

Seleccione los colores

Color del primero plano	Color de fondo
○ Rojo	○ Rojo
○ Verde	○ Verde
○ Azul	○ Azul
◉ Negro	○ Negro
○ Blanco	◉ Blanco

FIGURE 33-6

Lesson Requirements

In this lesson, you:

➤ Build the default interface.

➤ Add code to handle the `RadioButtons`' `Click` events.

➤ Localize the application for Mexican Spanish.

➤ Add code to let you test the form for either locale.

> **NOTE** *You can download the code and resources for this lesson from the website at* `www.wrox.com/go/csharp24hourtrainer2e`.

Hints

➤ There's no need to build a separate event handler for each `RadioButton`. Use one event handler for all of the foreground buttons and one for all of the background buttons.

➤ These event handlers must figure out which button was clicked, but they cannot use the buttons' text because that will change depending on which locale is selected. They could use the buttons' names because they don't change, but it's even easier to store the corresponding colors' names in their `Tag` properties and then use the `Color` class's `FromName` method to get the appropriate `Color`.

Step-by-Step

➤ Build the default interface.

1. Build a form that looks like the one shown in Figure 33-5.

2. Store the color names (red, green, blue, and so forth) in the RadioButtons' Tag properties.

➤ Add code to handle the RadioButtons' Click events.

1. Write an event handler similar to the following:

```
// Set the foreground color.
private void Foreground_Click(object sender, EventArgs e)
{
    // Get the sender as a RadioButton.
    RadioButton rad = sender as RadioButton;

    // Use the color.
    Color clr = Color.FromName(rad.Tag.ToString());
    this.ForeColor = clr;
    fgGroupBox.ForeColor = clr;
    bgGroupBox.ForeColor = clr;
}
```

This code converts the sender object into a RadioButton and uses its Tag property to get the corresponding color. It then applies that color to the form and the two GroupBoxes.

2. Connect the foreground RadioButtons to this event handler.

3. Repeat these steps for the background RadioButtons.

➤ Localize the application for Mexican Spanish.

1. Set the form's Localizable property to true. Click the Language property, click the dropdown arrow to the right, and select "Spanish (Mexico)."

2. Change the controls' Text properties so they have the values shown in Figure 33-6.

➤ Add code to let you test the form for either locale.

1. Use code similar to the following in the form's constructor:

```
// Select a locale for testing.
public Form1()
{
    // English.
    //Thread.CurrentThread.CurrentCulture =
    //    new CultureInfo("en-US", false);
    //Thread.CurrentThread.CurrentUICulture =
    //    new CultureInfo("en-US", false);

    // Spanish.
    Thread.CurrentThread.CurrentCulture =
        new CultureInfo("es-MX", false);
    Thread.CurrentThread.CurrentUICulture =
        new CultureInfo("es-MX", false);

    InitializeComponent();
}
```

EXERCISES

1. Copy this lesson's Try It and add support for Italian (it-IT) as shown in Figure 33-7. Don't forget to add code to let you test it.

2. When a program reads data from a file, it must use the correct locale. Download the files `Dutch.txt`, `German.txt`, and `English.txt` from the book's website and make a program that can read them. The

FIGURE 33-7

program should let the user select a file, check the filename to see which locale it should use, and select the correct locale. It should read and parse the values into appropriate data types and then display the values in a `DataGridView` control. Hints:

➤ Use locale names en-US for English, de-DE for German, and nl-NL for Dutch. Use code similar to the following to select the proper locale before you parse the values:

```
Thread.CurrentThread.CurrentCulture =
    new CultureInfo("en-US", false);
```

➤ The values within a line in the file are separated by tabs, so use `File.ReadAllLines` to get the lines and `Split` to break each line into fields.

The following text shows the values in the file `Dutch.txt`:

```
Potlood    € 0,10        12    € 1,20
Blocnote   € 1,10        10    € 11,00
Laptop     € 1.239,99     1    € 1.239,99
```

3. [Hard] Actually you can change a form's localization after it is loaded: it's just somewhat complicated. The following method sets the locale for a form and makes its controls reload their localizable properties:

```
// Set the form's culture.
private void SetFormCulture(Form form, string culture)
{
    // Make the CultureInfo.
    CultureInfo cultureInfo = new CultureInfo(culture);

    // Make a ComponentResourceManager.
    ComponentResourceManager resourceManager =
        new ComponentResourceManager(form.GetType());

    // Apply resources to the form.
    resourceManager.ApplyResources(form, "$this", cultureInfo);

    // Apply resources to the form and its controls.
    SetControlCulture(form, cultureInfo, resourceManager);
}
```

The `SetFormCulture` method creates a `CultureInfo` object to represent the desired culture. It then creates a `ComponentResourceManager` for the form and uses it to load the form's localized resources. Resources for use by the form are identified by the special name `$this`.

The method then calls the following SetControlCulture method for the form:

```
// Set the control's culture using the indicated
// CultureInfo and ComponentResourceManager.
private void SetControlCulture(Control control,
    CultureInfo cultureInfo,
    ComponentResourceManager resourceManager)
{
    // Apply resources to the control.
    resourceManager.ApplyResources(
        control, control.Name, cultureInfo);

    // Apply resources to the control's children.
    foreach (Control child in control.Controls)
        SetControlCulture(child, cultureInfo, resourceManager);
}
```

The SetControlCulture method uses the resource manager to load culture-specific resources for the control. The method uses the control's name to identify the resource values to use. (When SetFormCulture calls this method, it first sets properties for the form. However, the form's resources are stored with the special name $this, so that first call to ApplyResources doesn't do anything.)

After making the control reload its resources, the code loops through the control's children and calls SetControlCulture to reload their resources. This is necessary to handle controls inside containers such as GroupBoxes or TabControls.

Copy the program you wrote for Exercise 1, remove the testing code that selects a locale, and add English, Español, and Italiano RadioButtons to the top of the form. When the user selects one of them, use the SetFormCulture and SetControlCulture methods to make the form use the appropriate localization. (Hint: Store the locale name in the RadioButtons' Tag properties.)

4. Unfortunately some properties are not localizable. For example, you can't localize a PictureBox's Image property. (I asked people at Microsoft about this and they said, "Gee, we never thought anyone would want to localize that.")

Copy the program you wrote for Exercise 3 and add a PictureBox to display an image of the selected country's flag. Add code to the RadioButtons' Clicked event handler to display the correct flag. (Hint: Add the flag images to the project's resources by selecting Project ➪ Properties, clicking the Resources tab, opening the Add Resource dropdown, and selecting Add Existing File. Then make the code set the PictureBox's Image property to a value such as Properties.Resources.MexicanFlag.)

5. [WPF, Hard] To localize a WPF application, follow these steps:

   a. Create a new application. In Solution Explorer, expand the Properties entry and double-click Resources.resx.

   b. In the resources editor shown in Figure 33-8, create the resources that you want to localize. For example in Figure 33-8, I created a string resource named LeftHeader and set its value to "Foreground Color."

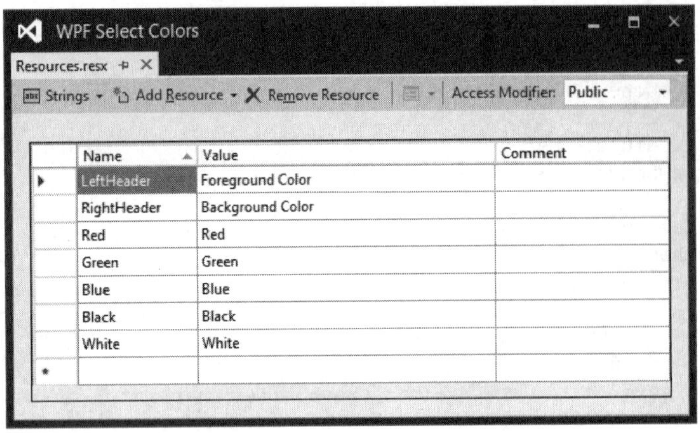

FIGURE 33-8

    c. Set the resource file's Access Modifier (in the upper-right corner in Figure 33-8) to `Public`.

    d. Build the program's XAML code as usual, but use the resources for the values that you want to localize. To make that easier:

        i. Add the following statement with the other namespace statements at the top of the XAML code:

```
xmlns:res="clr-namespace:WPF_Select_Colors.Properties"
```

        This statement lets you use the name `res` to represent the application's properties. (In this example, the application's root namespace is `WPF_Select_Colors`.)

        ii. Use code similar to the following to use a resource. The code in bold makes this `GroupBox` use the value of the `LeftHeader` resource:

```
<GroupBox Grid.Row="0" Grid.Column="0"
    Header="{x:Static res:Resources.LeftHeader}">
```

    e. To make a resource file for another locale, follow these steps:

        i. In Solution Explorer, use Ctrl+C and Ctrl+V to copy and paste the `Resources.resx` file. Rename it to include the locale identifier as in `Resources.es-MX.resx`.

        ii. Place the localized values in the new resource file.

When the program runs, it will select the appropriate resource file. You can test the program by setting its `CurrentCulture` and `CurrentUICulture` in the main window's constructor just as you would for a Windows Forms application.

For this exercise, create a WPF program similar to the program you built for Exercise 1. Hints:

    ➤ Use code similar to the following to convert a color name into a brush:

```
Color clr = (Color)ColorConverter.ConvertFromString("Red");
Brush brush = new SolidColorBrush(clr);
```

➤ To set the foreground color, you only need to set the window's `Background` property.

➤ To set the background color, set the `GroupBoxes`' `Background` properties. Then loop through `Children` collections of the controls (probably `StackPanels`) that hold the `RadioButtons` and set the children's `Background` properties.

6. [WPF, Hard] I have not found a good way to reload a WPF project's resources at run time, but there is a straightforward albeit verbose way. Simply set the application's `CurrentCulture` and `CurrentUICulture` as usual. Then use code similar to the following to reload all of the localized properties:

```
fgGroupBox.Header = Properties.Resources.LeftHeader;
redFgButton.Content = Properties.Resources.Red;
greenFgButton.Content = Properties.Resources.Green;
...
```

You can place all of those statements in a method to make them easier to call.

Copy the program you wrote for Exercise 5 and modify it so it allows the user to change locales at run time (much as you did for Exercise 3).

7. [WPF] Loading images from resources into WPF controls at run time is relatively difficult, but there's an easy way to localize images. Create multiple `Image` controls holding the pictures you want to display and then change their `Visibility` properties at run time. Copy the program you wrote for Exercise 6 and modify it so it displays appropriate flag images when the user changes locales (much as you did for Exercise 4).

> **NOTE** *Please select the videos for Lesson 33 online at* www.wrox.com/go/csharp24hourtrainer2evideos.

34

Programming Databases, Part 1

Database programming is another truly enormous topic, so there isn't room to cover it all here. However, Visual Studio provides tools that make some simple kinds of database programs so easy to write that your education won't be complete until you've written a few.

In this lesson, you learn how to make a simple database application. You learn how to connect to a database, load data, let the user navigate through records, and save any changes.

CONNECTING TO A DATABASE

The first step in building a database program is giving it a connection to the data. You can easily do this interactively at design time, although it requires quite a few steps:

> **NOTE** *If you want to following along with these instructions, you may want to download the database file Contacts.mdb, which is available in this lesson's downloads.*

1. First open the Project menu and select Add New Data Source to display the dialog shown in Figure 34-1. As you can see in the figure, you might want the program to get data from several different places. The data source used in this example is a database, so select Database and click Next.

2. The dialog's next screen lets you decide whether you want to use a data set or an entity data model for your data. (The entity data model option won't be there if you don't have the entity framework tools installed. You won't be using an entity data model in this lesson, so if that option doesn't appear, don't worry about it.) For

this example, pick Dataset and click Next to make the dialog display the screen shown in Figure 34-2.

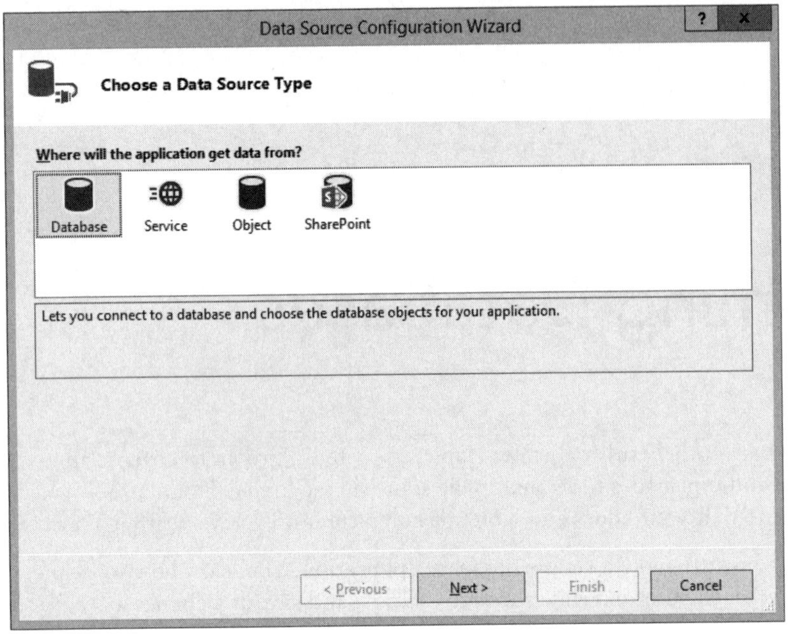

FIGURE 34-1

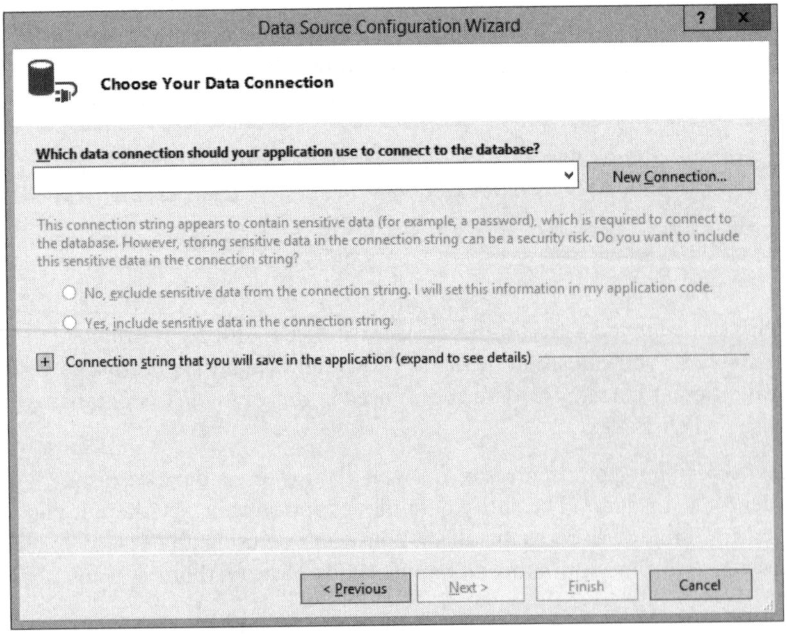

FIGURE 34-2

> **NOTE** *A data set is an in-memory representation of a data source. A data set can include multiple tables that are related with complex database relationships, although this example's database contains only a single table.*

3. If you have previously built data connections, you can pick one from the dropdown list. Otherwise, click the New Connection button to display the dialog shown in Figure 34-3.

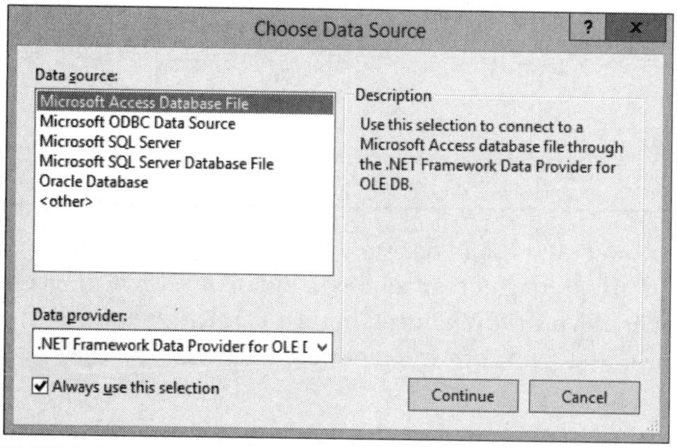

FIGURE 34-3

For this example, select Microsoft Access Database File and click Continue to see the dialog shown in Figure 34-4.

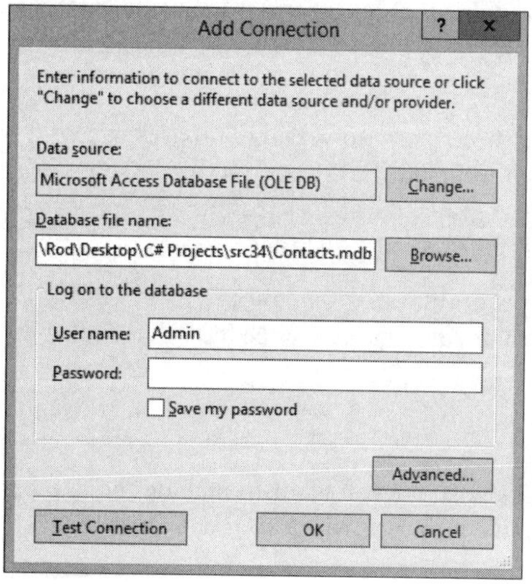

FIGURE 34-4

Enter the name of the database in the textbox or click the Browse button and select it. When you're finished, if you like, you can click Test Connection to see if Visual Studio can connect to the database.

Click OK to create the new connection and return to the dialog shown in Figure 34-2.

> **TIP** *If you click the plus sign at the bottom of the dialog shown in Figure 34-2, you can see the connection string Visual Studio built to connect to the database. You won't need that string now, but you may want it later if you use code to connect to a database.*

PICKING A DATABASE

Picking the right database product is a tough decision. Microsoft Access databases have the advantage that a C# program can read and manipulate one even if Access isn't installed on the computer. That means you can build a database on one computer that has Access installed and then copy it to another computer that doesn't have Access and use it there.

SQL Server, Oracle, MySQL, and similar database products tend to provide more database features than Access. For example, they support bigger databases, triggers, views, and other features that Access doesn't provide.

A common choice is to start development with SQL Server Express Edition, a free version of SQL Server that has some size restrictions. Later if you decide you need the extra space provided by the full version of SQL Server, you can upgrade relatively easily. You can learn more about SQL Server Express and download it at www.microsoft.com/express/Database.

Unfortunately a C# program cannot use these more powerful databases unless you have them installed, an assumption I don't want to make, so this lesson works with Access databases. You can get the necessary databases from the lesson's code download and use them even if you don't have Access installed.

If you're planning to do more database programming, I encourage you to install one of the more powerful database products, particularly since SQL Server Express and MySQL are free.

4. When you click Next, Visual Studio asks whether you want to include the database in the project. Click Yes to copy the database file into the project so it can easily be distributed with the program.

5. The dialog's next page asks whether you want to include the database connection string in the program's configuration file so the program can use that string to connect to the database

at run time. This is often convenient because it lets you change the connection string without rebuilding the application. Note, however, that you shouldn't store database passwords in the configuration file, so if the database requires a password, you may want to leave the connection string out of the configuration file.

When you click Next again, you see the page shown in Figure 34-5.

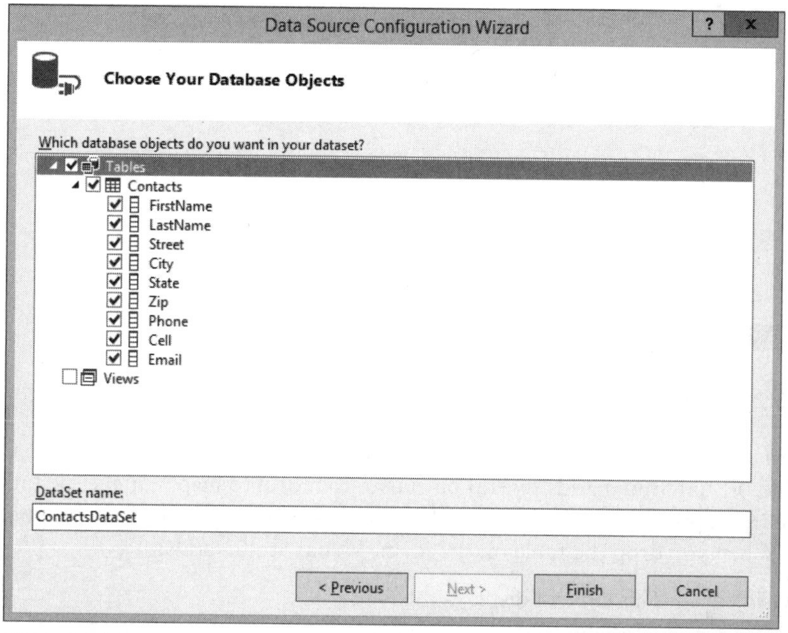

FIGURE 34-5

6. Expand the database object treeview and select the tables and fields that you want the program to use. In this example, the database contains only one table. In Figure 34-5 I selected the Tables entry and that selected the database's single table and all of its fields.

7. When you click Finish, Visual Studio defines a data set that can hold the data in the database. It also adds some code to make working with the data set easier.

Now that you've added a data source to the project, Visual Studio provides easy ways to make two simple kinds of database programs: one that displays data in a grid and one that displays data one record at a time.

DISPLAYING DATA IN A GRID

To display data in a grid, first open the Data Sources window. If you can't find it, use the View ⇨ Other Windows ⇨ Data Sources command to find it. Figure 34-6 shows the Data Sources window after I connected to a Microsoft Access database named Contacts.mdb.

> **TIP** *Often developers make the Data Sources window a tab in the same window as the Toolbox.*

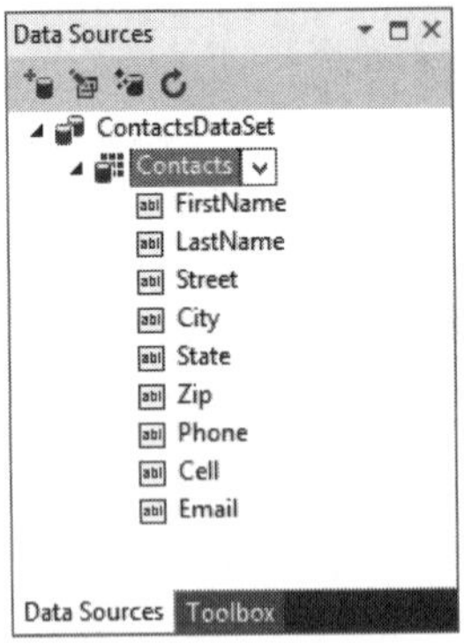

FIGURE 34-6

To display data in a grid, click a table in the Data Sources window and drag it onto the form. When you drop the table, Visual Studio adds several objects to the form to help manage the table's data. A few of these objects appear on the form itself, but most of them appear in the Component Tray below the form. When you drop the table on the form, Visual Studio adds:

➤ **A DataGridView**—This control displays the data.

➤ **A data set**—This data set can hold the table's data at run time.

➤ **A BindingSource**—This object encapsulates the data source. It provides a link between the form's controls and the data source.

➤ **A data adapter**—This object provides methods to move data between the database and the data set.

➤ **A table adapter manager**—This object helps coordinate movement of data by the data adapter.

➤ **Binding navigator**—This object provides navigation services for the controls on the form. For example, buttons that move to the next or previous record use these navigation services.

This seems like a confusing assortment of objects. Fortunately you don't need to do much with them for the simple database applications described in this lesson.

Figure 34-7 shows the program created by Visual Studio at run time. The only changes I made were to resize the form and dock the `DataGridView` control to make it fill the form.

The `DataGridView` and the `BindingNavigator` (which provides the buttons at the top) automatically let the user perform a lot of simple database tasks, including:

➤ Clicking a cell and typing to change its value

➤ Selecting a row and pressing Delete to delete the corresponding record

➤ Clicking and dragging on the left of the data to select multiple rows, which the user can then delete all at once

➤ Using the navigation buttons to move through the records

➤ Entering values in the last row to create a new record

➤ Resizing rows and columns

➤ Clicking the floppy disk button to save changes to the data

➤ Clicking a column header to sort the records using that column

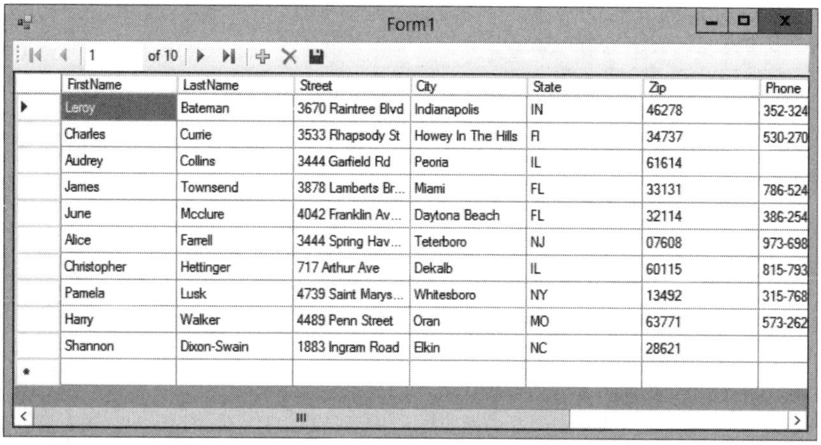

FirstName	LastName	Street	City	State	Zip	Phone
Leroy	Bateman	3670 Raintree Blvd	Indianapolis	IN	46278	352-324
Charles	Currie	3533 Rhapsody St	Howey In The Hills	Fl	34737	530-270
Audrey	Collins	3444 Garfield Rd	Peoria	IL	61614	
James	Townsend	3878 Lamberts Br...	Miami	FL	33131	786-524
June	Mcclure	4042 Franklin Av...	Daytona Beach	FL	32114	386-254
Alice	Farrell	3444 Spring Hav...	Teterboro	NJ	07608	973-698
Christopher	Hettinger	717 Arthur Ave	Dekalb	IL	60115	815-793
Pamela	Lusk	4739 Saint Marys...	Whitesboro	NY	13492	315-768
Harry	Walker	4489 Penn Street	Oran	MO	63771	573-262
Shannon	Dixon-Swain	1883 Ingram Road	Elkin	NC	28621	

FIGURE 34-7

NOTE *In this kind of program, changes are made locally to the data set and are not copied to the database until the user clicks the Save button.*

NOTE *If you build a program as described so far, make a change, and click the* BindingNavigator's *Save button, you may be surprised to find that the changes don't seem to be saved. They actually are saved, but by default the project copies the database into the executable directory every time it runs, and the new copy of the database overwrites the saved data so it looks like the changes weren't saved.*

One way to fix this is to not include the database in the project or to use Solution Explorer to set its Copy to Output Directory *property to* Do not copy *or* Copy if newer.

You should add a few things that this automatically generated program doesn't do to this simple example. The most important of these is to check for unsaved changes before allowing the form to close.

The following `FormClosing` event handler prevents the user from accidentally closing the form with unsaved changes:

```
// Check for unsaved changes.
private void Form1_FormClosing(object sender, FormClosingEventArgs e)
{
    // See if there are unsaved changes.
    if (this.contactsDataSet.HasChanges())
    {
        // Make the user confirm.
        DialogResult result = MessageBox.Show(
            "Do you want to save changes before closing?",
            "Save Changes?",
            MessageBoxButtons.YesNoCancel,
            MessageBoxIcon.Question);
        if (result == DialogResult.Cancel)
        {
            // Cancel the close.
            e.Cancel = true;
        }
        else if (result == DialogResult.Yes)
        {
            // Save the changes.
            contactsTableAdapter.Update(contactsDataSet);

            // Make sure the save worked.
            // If we still have unsaved changes, cancel.
            e.Cancel = (this.contactsDataSet.HasChanges());
        }

        // Else the user doesn't want to save
        // the changes so just keep going.
    }
}
```

If the data set has unsaved changes, the code asks the user whether it should save the changes. If the user clicks Cancel, the code sets `e.Cancel` to `true` so the program doesn't close the form.

If the user clicks Yes, the code calls the table adapter's `Update` method to save the data set's changes back to the database.

If the user clicks No, the code just continues and lets the form close without saving the changes.

DISPLAYING DATA ONE RECORD AT A TIME

Instead of displaying a table's records in a grid, you can display the data one record at a time, as shown in Figure 34-8.

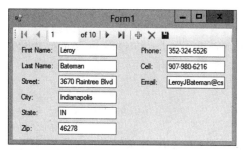

FIGURE 34-8

With this kind of interface, you can click the navigation buttons on the `BindingNavigator` to move through the records. You can use the display controls (`TextBoxes` in Figure 34-8) to change a record's values.

To build this interface, first create a data source as before. Then, instead of dragging a table from the Data Sources window onto the form, drag individual fields onto the form. For each field, Visual Studio adds a `Label` and an appropriate display control (such as a `TextBox`) to the form.

This version of the interface does most of the things the grid-based version does but in different ways. For example, to create a new record you can't simply type values into a new row in a grid. Instead you need to click the `BindingNavigator`'s Add New button (which appropriately looks like a plus sign).

As in the grid-style example, the code created by Visual Studio doesn't check for unsaved changes before the form closes. You can solve this problem by adding a `FormClosing` event handler to check for unsaved changes as before.

This version of the program works a little differently than the previous grid-style version, however. The `DataGridView` control used by the previous program automatically marks the data as modified when the user starts changing a value. In contrast, the new program marks the data as modified only when the user changes a value *and then moves to a new record*. That means if the user changes a value and then tries to close the form without moving to a new record, the program doesn't know there is an unsaved change and closes.

To prevent that, you can add the following two lines to the beginning of the `FormClosing` event handler:

```
this.Validate();
this.contactsBindingSource.EndEdit();
```

These lines make the program officially finish editing any fields that the user is modifying so the data set knows that it has a pending change. After that, the `FormClosing` event handler works exactly as before.

TRY IT

In this Try It, you have a chance to practice the techniques described in this lesson. You create an application that displays contact information in a grid.

Lesson Requirements

In this lesson, you:

➤ Start a new project. Download the `Contacts.mdb` database from the book's website and place it in the project directory.

➤ Add a new data source for this database.

➤ Open the Data Sources window and drag the Contacts table onto the form.

➤ Add code to the `FormClosing` event handler to check for unsaved changes.

> **NOTE** *You can download the code and resources for this lesson from the website at* www.wrox.com/go/csharp24hourtrainer2e.

Hints

➤ Dock the `DataGridView` control so it fills the form.

➤ Resize the form so all fields are visible. Add a little extra width for a vertical scrollbar on the right.

➤ Don't forget to set the database file's `Copy to Output Directory` property to `Copy if newer`.

Step-by-Step

➤ Start a new project. Download the `Contacts.mdb` database from the book's website and place it in the project directory.

1. This is straightforward.

➤ Add a new data source for this database.

1. Follow the steps described earlier in this lesson.

➤ Open the Data Sources window and drag the Contacts table onto the form.

1. This is straightforward.

➤ Add code to the `FormClosing` event handler to check for unsaved changes.

1. Use the code shown earlier in this lesson.

EXERCISES

1. Make a program similar to the one you built for the Try It except make it display one record at a time instead of use a grid. Anchor the TextBoxes so they widen if the form widens. Don't forget to add the FormClosing event handler.

2. Copy the program you built for this lesson's Try It. That program's grid lets the user navigate through the records, add records, and delete records, so you don't really need all of those buttons on the BindingNavigator. Select the BindingNavigator. In the Properties window, click the Items property and click the ellipsis to the right. Set the Visible property to false for every item except the Position, Count, and Save items.

3. Copy the program you built for Exercise 1. Add a MenuStrip with a Data menu that has items First, Previous, Next, Last, Add New, Delete, and Save. Set the Visible property on the corresponding BindingNavigator buttons to false.

   To make the menu items work, use the BindingSource's CurrencyManager. That object's properties and methods let you manipulate the current record (hence the name CurrencyManager). For example, the following code sets the current position to the first record:

   ```
   this.contactsBindingSource.CurrencyManager.Position = 0;
   ```

   Add or subtract one from Position to move to the next or previous record. Set Position to the CurrencyManager's List.Count - 1 value to move to the end of the list.

   Use the RemoveAt method to delete the current record.

   Finally, enter the necessary code for the Save menu item.

4. [WPF] You can use the techniques described in this lesson to make simple database applications in WPF, too. The results are similar, but some differences exist. In particular Visual Studio doesn't place a BindingNavigator on the WPF Window. The program also includes data set and table adapter objects, but they're hidden inside the code.

   For this exercise, repeat the Try It with a WPF application. After you create the database connection, run the program to let it build some data structures that it needs. Then drag the Contacts table onto the Window and arrange it as before.

   Because Visual Studio doesn't create a BindingNavigator, add a File menu with a Save item that uses the following code to save changes to the data:

   ```
   private void saveMenuItem_Click(object sender, RoutedEventArgs e)
   {
       // Save the changes.
       ContactsDataSet contactsDataSet =
           (ContactsDataSet)this.FindResource("contactsDataSet");
       ContactsDataSetTableAdapters.ContactsTableAdapter
           contactsDataSetContactsTableAdapter =
           new ContactsDataSetTableAdapters.ContactsTableAdapter();
       contactsDataSetContactsTableAdapter.Update(contactsDataSet);
   }
   ```

Use the following `Window Closing` event handler to protect the user from losing changes when the program closes:

```
private void Window_Closing(object sender,
    System.ComponentModel.CancelEventArgs e)
{
    ContactsDataSet contactsDataSet =
        (ContactsDataSet)this.FindResource("contactsDataSet");

    // See if there are unsaved changes.
    if (contactsDataSet.HasChanges())
    {
        // Make the user confirm.
        MessageBoxResult result = MessageBox.Show(
            "Do you want to save changes before closing?",
            "Save Changes?", MessageBoxButton.YesNoCancel,
            MessageBoxImage.Question);
        if (result == MessageBoxResult.Cancel)
        {
            // Cancel the close.
            e.Cancel = true;
        }
        else if (result == MessageBoxResult.Yes)
        {
            // Save the changes.
            ContactsDataSetTableAdapters.ContactsTableAdapter
                contactsDataSetContactsTableAdapter =
                new ContactsDataSetTableAdapters.ContactsTableAdapter();
            contactsDataSetContactsTableAdapter.Update(contactsDataSet);

            // Make sure the save worked.
            // If we still have unsaved changes, cancel.
            e.Cancel = (contactsDataSet.HasChanges());
        }

        // Else the user doesn't want to save
        // the changes so just keep going.
    }
}
```

This code is similar to the version used by the Windows Forms application except it's more work getting the data set and table adapter.

5. [WPF] Repeat Exercise 1 for a WPF application. As in Exercise 4, after you create the database connection, run the program to let it build some data structures that it needs. Then drag the Contacts table fields onto the `Window` and align the `Label`s and `TextBox`es.

    Add the `Window`'s `Closing` event handler as in Exercise 4 but don't worry about adding Previous, Next, Save, and other commands. You'll do that in later exercises.

    Run the program and verify that you can see the first record in the data set and that you can save changes to it. (Hint: Don't forget to set the database's `Copy to Output Directory` property.)

6. [WPF, Hard] In Exercise 5, Visual Studio put the `Label` and `TextBox` for each database field inside a separate `Grid` control. Those `Grid`s sit inside the main `Grid` control. That works, but

it makes it hard to rearrange the controls. For example, each `TextBox`'s width is explicitly set to 120.

To make the program more flexible, copy the program you built for Exercise 5 and give the main `Grid` control nine rows with heights `Auto` and two columns with widths `Auto` and `*`. Add the following property to the `Grid`:

```
DataContext="{StaticResource contactsViewSource}"
```

The `DataContext` property tells the controls inside the `Grid` where they should look for data.

Next give the main `Grid` a resource dictionary containing two `Styles` that set the properties for `Labels` and `TextBoxes`. Make the `Styles` set all of the property values shared by the automatically created controls except set the `TextBox` `HorizontalAlignment` property to `Stretch` and omit the `TextBox` `Width` property.

Now when you run the program, the `TextBoxes` should resize to use the available width.

7. [WPF, Hard] Copy the program you wrote for Exercise 6 and add navigation buttons. To do that, make the `Window`'s main control be a `DockPanel`. Dock a `ToolBar` to the top and dock the previous `Grid` control below that.

Give the `ToolBar` the buttons First, Previous, Next, Last, Add, Delete, and Save.

To make managing the data easier, use the following code to make class-level variables to hold the data set, the table adapter, and the view source:

```
private ContactsDataSet DataSet;
private ContactsDataSetTableAdapters.ContactsTableAdapter TableAdapter;
private CollectionViewSource ViewSource;
```

Modify the `Window_Loaded` event handler so it initializes and uses the class-level variables. Also modify the `Window_Closing` event handler so it uses the variables.

Next give the buttons the following code:

```
private void firstButton_Click(object sender, RoutedEventArgs e)
{
    ViewSource.View.MoveCurrentToFirst();
}

private void previousButton_Click(object sender, RoutedEventArgs e)
{
    ViewSource.View.MoveCurrentToPrevious();
}

private void nextButton_Click(object sender, RoutedEventArgs e)
{
    ViewSource.View.MoveCurrentToNext();
}

private void lastButton_Click(object sender, RoutedEventArgs e)
{
    ViewSource.View.MoveCurrentToLast();
}

private void addButton_Click(object sender, RoutedEventArgs e)
```

```
    {
        ContactsDataSet.ContactsRow row =
            DataSet.Contacts.NewContactsRow();
        row.FirstName = "<missing>";
        row.LastName = "<missing>";
        DataSet.Contacts.AddContactsRow(row);
        ViewSource.View.MoveCurrentToLast();
    }

    private void deleteButton_Click(object sender, RoutedEventArgs e)
    {
        int rownum = ViewSource.View.CurrentPosition;
        DataSet.Contacts.Rows[rownum].Delete();
    }

    private void saveButton_Click(object sender, RoutedEventArgs e)
    {
        TableAdapter.Update(DataSet);
    }
```

8. [WPF] Copy the program you wrote for Exercise 7 and add a `Label` at the bottom of the form that displays the current record's number as in "Record 7 of 12." Update the position when the program starts and when the `ViewSource.View` object receives a `CurrentChanged` event.

9. [WPF] The `MoveCurrentToPrevious` and `MoveCurrentToNext` methods can move the current record beyond the beginning or end of the data set. In that case, the bound `TextBoxes` are blank and the user is probably confused. Fortunately those methods return `true` if they successfully move to a new record and `false` if they fall off the data set.

    Copy the program you wrote for Exercise 8 and modify the code to check the values returned by `MoveCurrentToPrevious` and `MoveCurrentToNext`. If they return `false`, move to the first or last record.

10. [WPF] Copy the program you wrote for Exercise 9 and make the `ToolBar` `Buttons` display appropriate images.

11. [WPF] Copy the program you wrote for Exercise 10 and enable and disable the `ToolBar` `Buttons` when appropriate. Hints:

    ➤ To enable a `Button`, set `IsEnabled = true` and `Opacity = 1`.

    ➤ To disable a `Button`, set `IsEnabled = false` and `Opacity = 0.5`.

    ➤ Make the existing `CurrentChanged` event handler enable and disable the movement `Buttons` as appropriate.

    ➤ Catch the `DataSet.Contacts.RowChanged` event and enable the Save `Button` when a record is modified by the user.

> **NOTE** *Please select the videos for Lesson 34 online at* www.wrox.com/go/csharp24hourtrainer2evideos.

35

Programming Databases, Part 2

The simple programs described in the previous lesson are hardly commercial-caliber database applications, but they do let you perform basic database operations with amazingly little code.

In this lesson, you learn how to add a few new features to the programs described in Lesson 34. You learn how to add searching, filtering, and sorting to the programs to make finding data easier.

SEARCHING

In a large database, it can be hard to locate a particular value. A program can make finding records easier by using the `BindingContext`'s `Find` method. This method takes as parameters the name of a field to search and the value that it should find. It returns the index of the first record that has the desired value.

For example, the following code searches the data in the `BindingSource` named `contactsBindingSource` for a record with `FirstName` value equal to Kim:

```
int recordNumber = contactsBindingSource.Find("FirstName", "Kim");
```

Having found the index of the target record, you can then highlight it in some way for the user to see. For example, recall that a `BindingSource`'s `CurrencyManager` controls the current position within the data. The following code makes the current record be the record found by `Find` so any controls displaying the data will show this record:

```
contactsBindingSource.CurrencyManager.Position = recordNumber;
```

> **WARNING** Find *returns* –1 *if it cannot find the target string. Be careful not to try to do anything explicitly with record number* –1 *or your program may crash. That means the previous line of code should really be*
>
> ```
> if (recordNumber != -1)
>     contactsBindingSource.CurrencyManager.Position = recordNumber;
> ```

If the program is displaying data in a grid, focus moves to the found record's row. If the program is displaying data in field controls, those controls now show the found record's data.

FILTERING

The `Find` method is somewhat restrictive. It only searches for exact matches in a single field and only returns the index of the first record that matches. Often you might prefer more flexibility such as searches that can check conditions (`Age > = 21`), look for partial matches (`LastName` begins with S), and combine multiple tests (`State` is VA or DC). It might also be nice to see all of the records that meet a condition instead of just the first record.

Filters let you perform these kinds of searches. A *filter* tests each record in a `BindingSource`'s data and selects those that satisfy the test. Any display controls attached to the `BindingSource` show only the selected records.

To use a filter, set the `BindingSource`'s `Filter` property to a string describing the records that you want to select. The filter compares each record's fields to values and selects the records that match. For example, the clause `State='FL'` selects records where the `State` field has the value FL.

String values should be delimited with single or double quotes. (Single quotes are generally easier to type into a string that is itself delimited by double quotes.) Numeric values should not have delimiters.

Table 35-1 lists the operators that you can use to compare fields to values.

TABLE 35-1

OPERATOR	PURPOSE
=	Equal to
<>	Not equal to
<	Less than
>	Greater than
<=	Less than or equal to
>=	Greater than or equal to
LIKE	Matches a pattern
IN	Is in a list of values

The `LIKE` operator performs pattern matching. Use `*` or `%` as a wildcard that matches zero or more characters.

You can use the `AND`, `OR`, and `NOT` logical operators to combine the results of multiple comparisons. Use parentheses to determine the evaluation order if necessary.

Table 35-2 lists some example filters.

TABLE 35-2

FILTER	SELECTS
`LastName = 'Johnson'`	Records where `LastName` is Johnson
`FirstName = 'Ann' OR FirstName = 'Anne'`	Records where `FirstName` is Ann or Anne
`FirstName LIKE 'Pam%'`	Records where `FirstName` begins with Pam
`State IN('NY','NC','NJ')`	Records where `State` is NY, NC, or NJ
`(Balance < -50) OR ((Balance < 0) AND (DaysOverdue > 30))`	Records where the account is overdrawn by more than $50 or where the account has been overdrawn by any amount for more than 30 days

You can use the `BindingSource`'s `RemoveFilter` method to remove the filter and display all of the records again.

SORTING

If you display data in a `DataGridView`, you can click a column's header to sort the records based on the values in that column. Clicking again reverses the sort order. Sorting doesn't get much easier than that.

If you're displaying the data in fields rather than a grid, however, you don't get automatic sorting. Fortunately, you can make a `BindingSource` sort simply by setting its `Sort` property to the name of the field on which you want to sort. Use its `RemoveSort` method to cancel the sort and display the records in their original order.

TRY IT

In this Try It, you add filtering to a program that displays records in a grid. You let the user enter a filter and you make the program display only records that match the filter.

Lesson Requirements

In this lesson, you:

➤ Copy the program you built for the Try It in Lesson 34 (or download Lesson 34's version from the book's website).

➤ Add a `ToolStrip` containing a `TextBox` and a `Button`.

➤ When the user clicks the `Button`, apply the filter entered in the `TextBox`.

> **NOTE** *You can download the code and resources for this lesson from the website at* www.wrox.com/go/csharp24hourtrainer2e.

Hints

➤ Be sure to protect the program in case the user enters an invalid filter.

Step-by-Step

➤ Copy the program you built for the Try It in Lesson 34 (or download Lesson 34's version from the book's website).

1. This is straightforward.

➤ Add a ToolStrip containing a TextBox and a Button.

1. This is straightforward.

➤ When the user clicks the Button, apply the filter entered in the TextBox.

1. Use code similar to the following:

```
// Apply the filter.
private void filterButton_Click(object sender, EventArgs e)
{
    string filter = filterTextBox.Text.Trim();
    if (filter.Length == 0)
    {
        // No filter.
        contactsBindingSource.RemoveFilter();
    }
    else
    {
        // Add the filter.
        try
        {
            contactsBindingSource.Filter = filter;
        }
        catch (Exception ex)
        {
            MessageBox.Show(ex.Message);
        }
    }
}
```

EXERCISES

1. Copy the program you built for the Try It and replace the ToolBar's TextBox and Button with a "State:" Label and a ComboBox. Make the ComboBox list the state abbreviations present in the database (just hard-code them) plus a blank choice. When the user selects a value, use the selected state to filter the data.

2. Copy the program you built for Exercise 34-1 and add `RadioButtons` to the right of the `TextBoxes`, as shown in Figure 35-1. When the user clicks a `RadioButton`, make the program sort its data using the corresponding field. (Hint: Set each `RadioButton`'s `Tag` property to the name of the field it represents.)

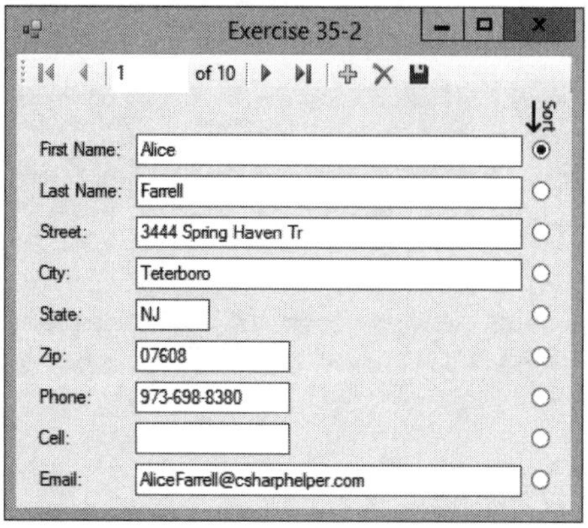

FIGURE 35-1

3. Copy the program you built for Exercise 1. Add a "First Name:" `Label` and a `TextBox` to the `ToolBar`. When the user enters a name, find and highlight the first record with that `FirstName` value. (Hint: If the user selects a new `State` filter, the program must find the name again.)

4. [Hard] Copy the program you built for Exercise 3 and make the program load the `States` `ComboBox`'s items from the database when it starts. Hints:

➤ Set the `ComboBox`'s `Sorted` property to `true`.

➤ Create a class-level variable `List<string>` named `States` to keep track of the states in the database.

➤ Use the following code to initialize the list and make the `ComboBox` use it:

```
// See what State values are in the data.
States = new List<string>();
States.Add("");
foreach (DataRow row in contactsDataSet.Contacts.Rows)
{
    string state = row.Field<string>("State");
    if (!States.Contains(state)) States.Add(state);
}

// Load the stateComboBox's items.
stateComboBox.ComboBox.DataSource = States;
```

5. Copy the program you built for Exercise 2 and add a Filter feature similar to the one you added for this lesson's Try It.

6. Copy the program you built for Exercise 2 and add a Filter by State feature similar to the one you added for Exercise 1.

7. [WPF, Hard] Naturally filtering records is more difficult in WPF than it is in Windows Forms. Copy the program you wrote for Exercise 34-4 and add a ToolBar, "State:" Label, and ComboBox much as you did for Exercise 1. (You may want to rearrange the program's controls to use a DockPanel.) Use the following code to filter the data:

```
// Filter with the selected state.
private void stateComboBox_SelectionChanged(object sender,
    SelectionChangedEventArgs e)
{
    // Get the dataset.
    ContactsDataSet contactsDataSet =
        (ContactsDataSet)this.FindResource("contactsDataSet");

    // Get the selected state.
    ComboBoxItem item = stateComboBox.SelectedItem as ComboBoxItem;
    string state = item.Content.ToString();
    Console.WriteLine("Filtering by state " + state);

    // Set the filter.
    CollectionViewSource contactsViewSource =
        (CollectionViewSource)FindResource("contactsViewSource");
    BindingListCollectionView view =
        (BindingListCollectionView)contactsViewSource.View;

    if (state.Length == 0) view.CustomFilter = "";
    else view.CustomFilter = "State = '" + state + "'";
}
```

8. [WPF, Hard] Copy the program you built for Exercise 34-11 and add a "State:" Label and a ComboBox as you did in Exercise 7. You'll also need to make two additional changes.

First, after you change the filter, you need to update the position label.

Second, you need to change the way you display the current record's position so it uses the selected records and not the entire data table. Modify the ShowPosition method so it uses the following code to determine the number of records selected:

```
// Get the number of records selected.
CollectionViewSource contactsViewSource =
    (CollectionViewSource)FindResource("contactsViewSource");
BindingListCollectionView view =
    (BindingListCollectionView)contactsViewSource.View;
int numselected = view.Count;
```

> **NOTE** *Please select the videos for Lesson 35 online at* www.wrox.com/go/ csharp24hourtrainer2evideos.

36

LINQ to Objects

Lessons 34 and 35 explain how you can use Visual Studio's wizards to build simple database programs. They show one of many ways to connect a program to a data source.

Language-Integrated Query (LINQ) provides another method for bridging the gap between a program and data. Instead of simply providing another way to access data in a database, however, LINQ can help a program access data stored in many places. LINQ lets a program use the same techniques to access data stored in databases, arrays, collections, or files.

LINQ provides four basic technologies that give you access to data stored in various places:

- ➤ **LINQ to SQL**—Data stored in SQL Server databases
- ➤ **LINQ to Dataset**—Data stored in other databases
- ➤ **LINQ to XML**—Data stored in XML (eXtensible Markup Language) files
- ➤ **LINQ to Objects**—Data stored in collections, lists, arrays, strings, files, and so forth

In this lesson you learn how to use LINQ to Objects. You learn how to extract data from lists, collections, and arrays and how to process the results.

LINQ BASICS

Using LINQ to process data takes three steps:

1. Create a data source.
2. Build a LINQ query to select data from the data source.
3. Execute the query and process the result.

You might expect the third step to be two separate steps, "Execute the query" and "Process the result." In practice, however, LINQ doesn't actually execute the query until it must—when the program tries to access the results. This is called *deferred execution*.

For example, the following code displays the even numbers between 0 and 99:

```
// Display the even numbers between 0 and 99.
private void Form1_Load(object sender, EventArgs e)
{
    // 1. Create the data source.
    int[] numbers = new int[100];
    for (int i = 0; i < 100; i++) numbers[i] = i;

    // 2. Build a query to select data from the data source.
    var evenQuery =
        from int num in numbers
        where (num % 2 == 0)
        select num;

    // 3. Execute the query and process the result.
    foreach (int num in evenQuery) Console.WriteLine(num.ToString());
}
```

The program starts by creating the data source: an array containing the numbers 0 through 99. In this example the data source is quite simple, but in other programs it could be much more complex. Instead of an array of numbers, it could be a list of Customer objects or an array of Order objects that contain lists of OrderItem objects.

Next the program builds a query to select the even numbers from the list. I explain queries in more detail later, but the following list describes the key pieces of this query:

➤ var—This is the data type of whatever is returned by the query. In this example the result will be an IEnumerable<int> but in general the results of LINQ queries can have some very strange data types. Rather than trying to figure out what a query will return, most developers use the implicit data type var. The var keyword tells the C# compiler to figure out what the data type is and use that so you don't need to use a specific data type.

➤ evenQuery—This is the name the code is giving to the query. You can think of it as a variable that represents the *result* that LINQ will later produce.

➤ from int num in numbers—This means the query will select data from the numbers array. It will use the int variable num to range over the values in the array. Because num ranges over the values, it is called the query's *range variable*. (If you omit the int data type, the compiler will implicitly figure out its data type.)

➤ where (num % 2 == 0)—This is the query's *where clause*. It determines which items are selected from the array. This example selects the even numbers (where num mod 2 is 0).

➤ select num—This tells the query what to return. In this case the query returns whatever is in the range variable num for the values that are selected. Often you will want to return the value of the range variable but you could return something else such as 2 * num or a new object created with a constructor that takes num as a parameter.

> **NOTE** *I don't recommend using* var *for variables in general if you can figure out a more specific data type. When you use* var, *you can't be sure what data type the compiler will use. That can lead to confusion if the compiler picks different data types for variables that must later work together.*
>
> *For example, in the following code the third statement is allowed because you can store an* int *value in a* double *but the fourth statement is not allowed because a* double *may not fit in an* int:
>
> ```
> var x = 1.2;    // double.
> var y = 1;      // int.
> x = y;          // Allowed.
> y = x;          // Not allowed.
> ```
>
> *If you do know the data type, just use that instead of* var.

In the final step to performing the query, the code loops through the result produced by LINQ. The code displays each int value in the Console window. It's only when the program tries to iterate over the results of the query that the query is actually executed.

The following sections provide more detailed descriptions of some of the key pieces of a LINQ query: where clauses, order by clauses, and select clauses.

WHERE CLAUSES

Probably the most common reason to use LINQ is to filter the data with a *where clause*. The where clause can include normal boolean expressions that use &&, ||, >, and other boolean operators. It can use the range variable and any properties or methods that it provides (if it's an object). It can even perform calculations and invoke functions.

> **NOTE** *The* where *clause is optional. If you omit it, the query selects all of the items in its range.*

For example, the following query is similar to the earlier one that selects even numbers, except this one's where clause uses the IsPrime method to select only prime numbers. (How the IsPrime function works isn't important to this discussion, so it isn't shown here. You can see it in the Find Primes program in this lesson's download.)

```
var primeQuery =
    from int num in numbers
    where (IsPrime(num))
    select num;
```

The Find Customers example program shown in Figure 36-1 (and available in this lesson's code download on the website) demonstrates several `where` clauses.

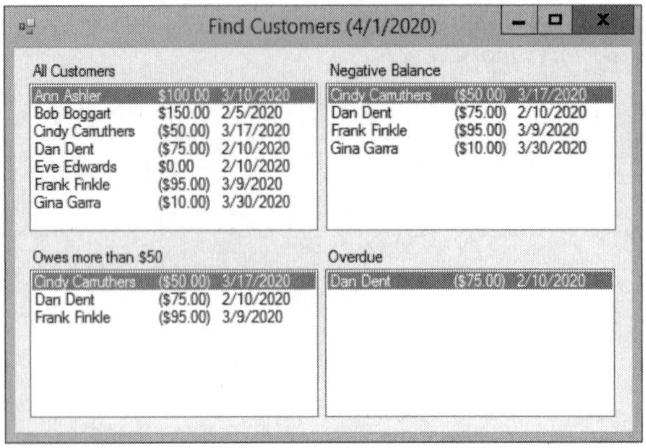

FIGURE 36-1

The following code shows the `Customer` class used by the Find Customers program. It includes some auto-implemented properties and an overridden `ToString` method that displays the `Customer`'s values:

```
class Customer
{
    public string FirstName { get; set; }
    public string LastName { get; set; }
    public decimal Balance { get; set; }
    public DateTime DueDate { get; set; }

    public override string ToString()
    {
        return FirstName + " " + LastName + "\t" +
            Balance.ToString("C") + "\t" + DueDate.ToString("d");
    }
}
```

The following code shows how the Find Customers program displays the same customer data selected with different `where` clauses:

```
// Display customers selected in various ways.
private void Form1_Load(object sender, EventArgs e)
{
    DateTime today = new DateTime(2020, 4, 1);
    //DateTime today = DateTime.Today;
    this.Text = "Find Customers (" + today.ToString("d") + ")";

    // Make the customers.
    Customer[] customers =
    {
        new Customer() { FirstName="Ann", LastName="Ashler",
            Balance = 100, DueDate = new DateTime(2020, 3, 10)},
```

```
            new Customer() { FirstName="Bob", LastName="Boggart",
                Balance = 150, DueDate = new DateTime(2020, 2, 5)},
            // ... Other Customers omitted ...
        };

        // Display all customers.
        allListBox.DataSource = customers;

        // Display customers with negative balances.
        var negativeQuery =
            from Customer cust in customers
            where cust.Balance < 0
            select cust;
        negativeListBox.DataSource = negativeQuery.ToArray();

        // Display customers who owe at least $50.
        var owes50Query =
            from Customer cust in customers
            where cust.Balance <= -50
            select cust;
        owes50listBox.DataSource = owes50Query.ToArray();

        // Display customers who owe at least $50
        // and are overdue at least 30 days.
        var overdueQuery =
            from Customer cust in customers
            where (cust.Balance <= -50) &&
                (DateTime.Now.Subtract(cust.DueDate).TotalDays > 30)
            select cust;
        overdueListBox.DataSource = overdueQuery.ToArray();
    }
```

The program starts by creating a `DateTime` named `today` and setting it equal to April 1, 2020. In a real application you would probably use the current date (commented out), but this program uses that specific date so it works well with the sample data. The program then displays the date in its title bar (so you can compare it to the `Customers`' due dates) and creates an array of `Customer` objects.

Next the code sets the `allListBox` control's `DataSource` property to the array so that `ListBox` displays all of the `Customer` objects. The `Customer` class's overridden `ToString` method makes it display each `Customer`'s name, balance, and due date.

The program then executes the following LINQ query:

```
// Display customers with negative balances.
var negativeQuery =
    from Customer cust in customers
    where cust.Balance < 0
    select cust;
negativeListBox.DataSource = negativeQuery.ToArray();
```

This query's `where` clause selects `Customers` with `Balance` properties less than 0. The query returns an `IEnumerable`, but a `ListBox`'s `DataSource` property requires an `IList` or `IListSource` and

IEnumerable doesn't satisfy either of those interfaces. To handle that problem, the program calls the result's ToArray method to convert it into an array that the DataSource property can handle.

After displaying this result, the program executes two other LINQ queries and displays their results similarly. The first query selects Customers who owe at least $50. The final query selects Customers who owe at least $50 and who have a DueDate more than 30 days in the past.

ORDER BY CLAUSES

Often the result of a query is easier to read if you sort the selected values. You can do this by inserting an *order by clause* between the where clause and the select clause.

The order by clause begins with the keyword orderby followed by one or more values separated by commas that determine how the results are ordered.

Optionally you can follow a value by the keyword ascending (the default) or descending to determine whether the results are ordered in ascending (1-2-3 or A-B-C) or descending (3-2-1 or C-B-A) order.

For example, the following query selects Customers with negative balances and orders them so those with the smallest (most negative) values come first:

```
var negativeQuery =
    from Customer cust in customers
    where cust.Balance < 0
    orderby cust.Balance ascending
    select cust;
```

The following version orders the results first by balance and then, if two customers have the same balance, by last name:

```
var negativeQuery =
    from Customer cust in customers
    where cust.Balance < 0
    orderby cust.Balance, cust.LastName
    select cust;
```

SELECT CLAUSES

The select clause determines what data is pulled from the data source and stored in the result. All of the previous examples select the data over which they are ranging. For example, the Find Customers example program ranges over an array of Customer objects and selects certain Customer objects.

Instead of selecting the objects in the query's range, a program can select only some properties of those objects, a result calculated from those properties, or even completely new objects. Selecting a new kind of data from the existing data is called *transforming* or *projecting* the data.

The Find Students example program shown in Figure 36-2 (and available in this lesson's code download on the website) uses the following simple Student class:

```
class Student
{
    public string FirstName { get; set; }
    public string LastName { get; set; }
    public List<int> TestScores { get; set; }
}
```

The program uses the following query to select all of the students' names and test averages ordered by name:

```
// Select all students and their test averages ordered by name.
var allStudents =
    from Student student in students
    orderby student.LastName, student.FirstName
    select String.Format("{0} {1}\t{2:0.00}",
        student.FirstName, student.LastName,
        student.TestScores.Average());
allListBox.DataSource = allStudents.ToArray();
```

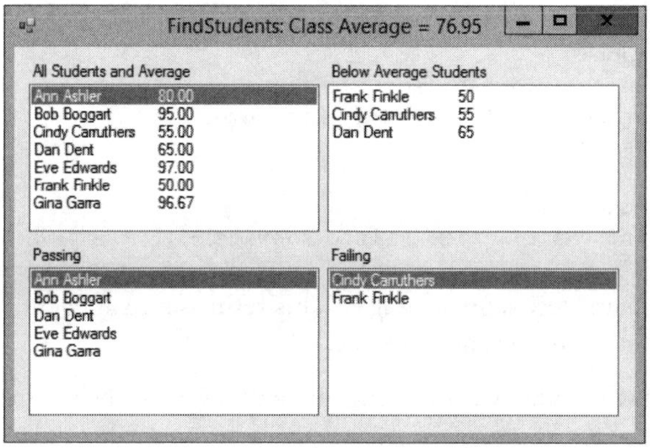

FIGURE 36-2

This query's select clause does not select the range variable student. Instead it selects a string that holds the student's first and last names and the student's test score average. (Notice how the code calls the TestScore list's Average method to get the average of the test scores.) The result of the query is a List<string> instead of a List<Student>.

The program next uses the following code to list the students who have averages of at least 60, giving them passing grades:

```
// Select passing students ordered by name.
var passingStudents =
```

```
        from Student student in students
        orderby student.LastName, student.FirstName
        where student.TestScores.Average() >= 60
        select student.FirstName + " " + student.LastName;
    passingListBox.DataSource = passingStudents.ToArray();
```

This code again selects a `string` instead of a `Customer` object. The code that selects failing students is similar, so it isn't shown here.

The program uses the following code to select students with averages below the class average:

```
    // Select all scores and compute a class average.
    var allAverages =
        from Student student in students
        select student.TestScores.Average();
    double classAverage = allAverages.Average();

    // Display the average.
    this.Text = "FindStudents: Class Average = " +
        classAverage.ToString("0.00");

    // Select students with average below the class average ordered by average.
    var belowAverageStudents =
        from Student student in students
        orderby student.TestScores.Average()
        where student.TestScores.Average() < classAverage
        select new {Name = student.FirstName + " " + student.LastName,
            Average = student.TestScores.Average()};

    foreach (var info in belowAverageStudents)
        belowAverageListBox.Items.Add(info.Name + "\t" + info.Average);
```

This snippet starts by selecting all of the students' test score averages. This returns a `List<double>`. The program calls that list's `Average` function to get the class average.

Next the code queries the student data again, this time selecting students with averages below the class average.

This query demonstrates a new kind of `select` clause that creates a list of objects. The new objects have two properties, `Name` and `Average`, that are given values by the `select` clause. The data type of these new objects is created automatically and isn't given an explicit name so this is known as an *anonymous type*.

After creating the query, the code loops through its results, using each object's `Name` and `Average` property to display the below average students in a `ListBox`. Notice that the code gives the looping variable `info` the implicit data type `var` so it doesn't need to figure out what data type it really has.

> **NOTE** *Objects with anonymous data types actually have a true data type, just not one that you want to have to figure out. For example, you can add the following statement inside the previous code's* foreach *loop to see what data type the objects actually have:*
>
> ```
> Console.WriteLine(info.GetType().ToString());
> ```
>
> *If you look in the Output window, you'll see that these objects have the ungainly data type:*
>
> ```
> <>f__AnonymousType0`2[System.String,System.Double]
> ```
>
> *Although you can sort of see what's going on here (the object contains a* string *and a* double*), you probably wouldn't want to type this mess into your code even if you could. In this case, the* var *type is a lot easier to read.*

LINQ provides plenty of other features that won't fit in this lesson. It lets you:

➤ Group results to produce lists that contain other lists

➤ Take only a certain number of results or take results while a certain condition is true

➤ Skip a certain number of results or skip results while a certain condition is true

➤ Join results selected from multiple data sources

➤ Use aggregate functions such as Average (which you've already seen), Count, Min, Max, and Sum

Microsoft's "Language-Integrated Query (LINQ)" page at msdn.microsoft.com/library/bb397926.aspx provides a good starting point for learning more about LINQ.

TRY IT

In Lesson 29's Try It, you built a program that used the DirectoryInfo class's GetFiles method to search for files matching a pattern and containing a target string. For example, the program could search the directory hierarchy starting at C:\C#Projects to find files with the .cs extension and containing the string "DirectoryInfo."

In this Try It, you modify that program to perform the same search with LINQ. Instead of writing code to loop through the files returned by GetFiles and examining each, you make LINQ examine the files for you.

Lesson Requirements

In this lesson, you:

➤ Copy the program you built for Lesson 29's Try It (or download Lesson 29's version from the book's website) and modify the code to use LINQ to search for files.

> **NOTE** *You can download the code and resources for this lesson from the web-site at* www.wrox.com/go/csharp24hourtrainer2e.

Hints

➤ Use the DirectoryInfo object's GetFiles method in the query's from clause.

➤ In the query's where clause, use the File class's ReadAllText method to get the file's contents. Convert it to lowercase and use Contains to see if the file holds the target string.

Step-by-Step

➤ Copy the program you built for Lesson 29's Try It (or download Lesson 29's version from the book's website) and modify the code to use LINQ to search for files.

1. Copying the program is reasonably straightforward.

2. To use LINQ to search for files, modify the Search button's Click event handler so it looks like the following. The lines in bold show the modified code:

```
// Search for files matching the pattern
// and containing the target string.
private void searchButton_Click(object sender, EventArgs e)
{
    // Get the file pattern and target string.
    string pattern = patternComboBox.Text;
    string target = targetTextBox.Text.ToLower();

    // Search for the files.
    DirectoryInfo dirinfo =
        new DirectoryInfo(directoryTextBox.Text);
    var fileQuery =
        from FileInfo fileinfo
            in dirinfo.GetFiles(pattern,
                SearchOption.AllDirectories)
        where
File.ReadAllText(fileinfo.FullName).ToLower().Contains(target)
        select fileinfo.FullName;
```

```
                    // Display the result.
                    fileListBox.DataSource = fileQuery.ToArray();
            }
```

If you compare this code to the version used by the Try It in Lesson 29, you'll see that this version is much shorter.

EXERCISES

1. Build a program that lists the names of the files in a directory together with their sizes, ordered with the biggest files first.

2. Copy the program you built for Exercise 1 and modify it so it searches for files in the directory hierarchy starting at the specified directory.

3. Make a program that lists the perfect squares between 0 and 999. (Hint: Use the Enumerable class's Range method to initialize the source data.)

For Exercises 4 through 8 download the Customer Orders program. This program defines the following classes:

```
class Person
{
    public string Name { get; set; }
}

class OrderItem
{
    public string Description { get; set; }
    public int Quantity { get; set; }
    public decimal UnitPrice { get; set; }
}

class Order
{
    public int OrderId { get; set; }
    public Person Customer { get; set; }
    public List<OrderItem> OrderItems { get; set; }
}
```

The program's Form_Load event handler creates an array of Order objects. The program's buttons, which are shown in Figure 36-3, let the user display the data in various ways although initially they don't contain any code. In Exercises 4 through 8, you add that code to give the program its features.

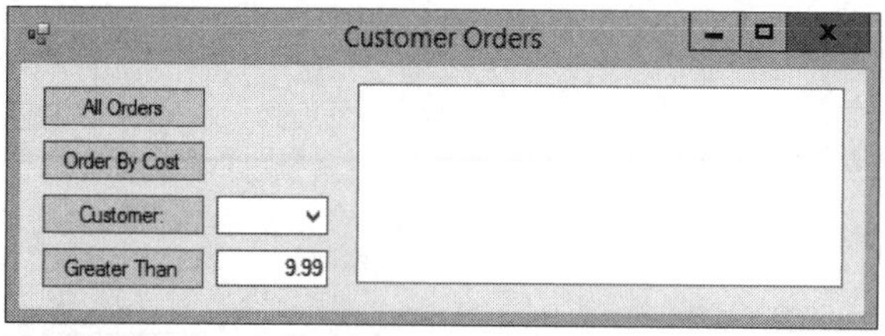

FIGURE 36-3

4.   The Customer Orders program creates several `Order` objects, but it doesn't fill in those objects' `TotalCost` properties. Use LINQ to do that. (Hints: Use a `foreach` loop to loop through the objects. For each object, use a LINQ query to go through the order's `OrderItems` list and select each `OrderItem`'s `UnitPrice` times its `Quantity`. After you define the query, call its `Sum` function to get the total cost for the order.)

5.   Copy the program you built for Exercise 4 and add code behind the All Orders button. That code should use a LINQ query to select the orders' ID, customer name, and total costs. Display the results in the `resultListBox` by setting that control's `DataSource` property to the query.

6.   Copy the program you built for Exercise 5 and add code behind the Order By Cost button. That code should use a query similar to the one used by Exercise 5, but it should order the results by cost so the orders with the largest costs are listed first.

7.   Copy the program you built for Exercise 6 and add code behind the Customer button. That code should use a LINQ query to list orders placed by the customer selected in the `ComboBox`. (If no name is selected, don't do anything.)

8.   Copy the program you built for Exercise 7 and add code behind the Greater Than button. That code should use a LINQ query to list orders with total costs greater than the value entered in the `TextBox`.

> **NOTE** *Please select the videos for Lesson 36 online at* www.wrox.com/go/
> csharp24hourtrainer2evideos.

LINQ to SQL

Lesson 36 provided an introduction to LINQ to Objects. This lesson gives a brief introduction to another of the LINQ family of technologies: LINQ to SQL.

LINQ to SQL lets you use queries similar to those provided by LINQ to Objects to manipulate SQL Server databases. It uses a set of classes to represent database objects such as tables and records. The classes provide intuitive methods for adding, modifying, deleting, and otherwise manipulating the records.

In this lesson you learn the basics of LINQ to SQL. You learn how to make LINQ objects representing a SQL Server database and how to add records to the database. You also learn how to perform queries similar to those described in Lesson 36 to filter and sort data taken from the database.

Note that the programs and techniques described in this lesson demonstrate only very simple uses of LINQ to SQL. For more information, search the web. Microsoft's "LINQ to SQL" page at `msdn.microsoft.com/library/bb386976.aspx` provides a good starting point for learning more about LINQ to SQL.

CONNECTING TO THE DATABASE

The first step in creating a LINQ to SQL program is connecting to the database. Create a Windows Forms application as usual. Then open the Server Explorer shown in Figure 37-1. (Use the View menu's Server Explorer command if you can't find it.)

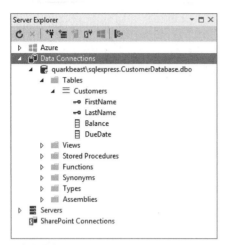

FIGURE 37-1

> **NOTE** *To run most of the programs described in this lesson, you need to have SQL Server installed on your computer. The Visual Studio installation software comes with SQL Server (at least the versions I've seen) or you can download the free SQL Server Express edition at* www.microsoft.com/express/Database. *It's a fairly busy page so the download link can be difficult to see. You can find it by searching for "Express."*

> **NOTE** *Unfortunately there isn't room in this book to say too much about SQL Server and how to use it. You'll have to rely on the web or get a book about SQL Server to do much with it.*
>
> *To make using the examples described in this lesson a bit easier, this lesson's download includes a program named Build Customer Database. This program connects to your SQL Server instance, deletes the database named* CustomerDatabase *if it exists, and creates a new* CustomerDatabase *containing a few records for the examples described in this lesson to use.*
>
> *Obviously don't run this program if you already have a database named* CustomerDatabase *that you want to preserve because that database will be destroyed!*

Click the Connect to Database button (third from the left at the top in Figure 37-1) to display the Add Connection dialog shown in Figure 37-2.

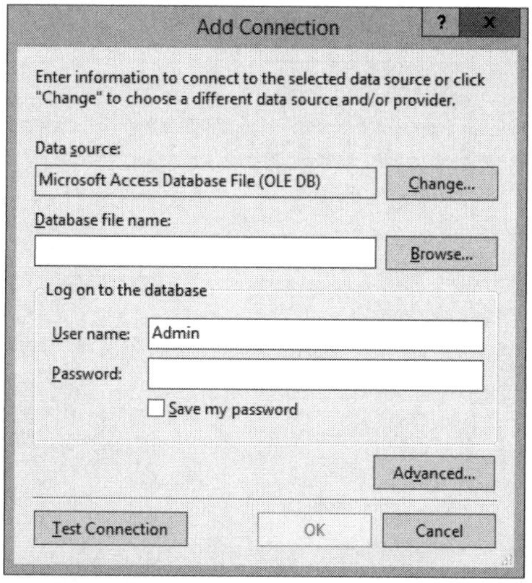

FIGURE 37-2

Initially the Add Connection dialog may have some type of database other than SQL Server selected. The dialog shown in Figure 37-2 is ready to connect to a Microsoft Access database. To switch to SQL Server, click the Change button to display the dialog shown in Figure 37-3.

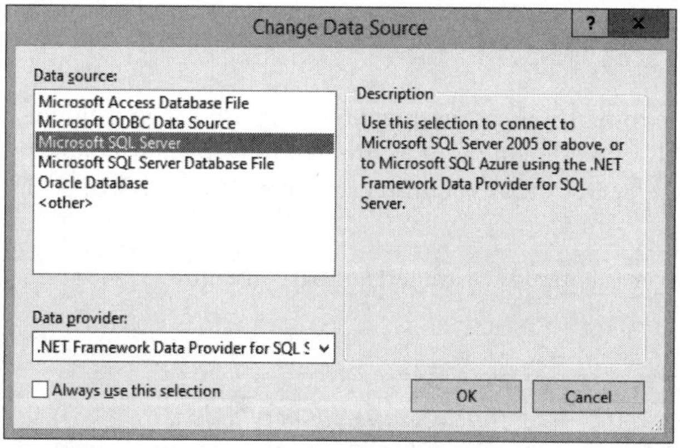

FIGURE 37-3

Select the Microsoft SQL Server entry and click OK. When you return to the Add Connection dialog, it should look like Figure 37-4.

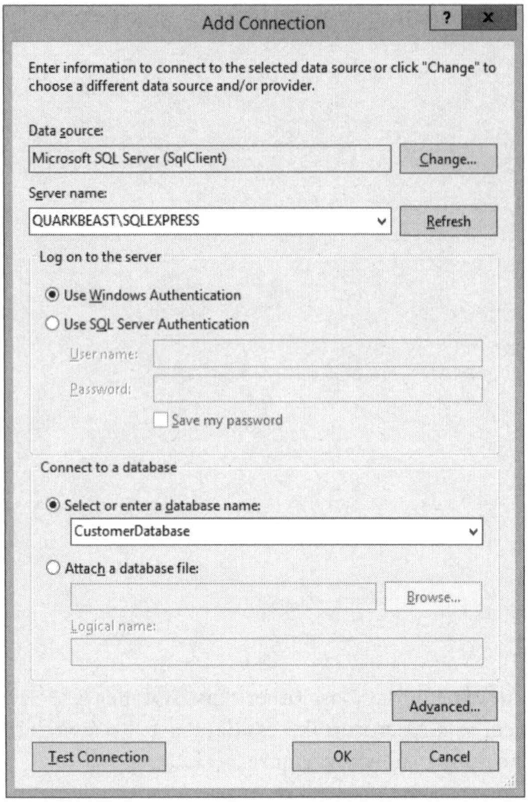

FIGURE 37-4

Enter your server name in the indicated textbox. If you're running SQL Server Express Edition, follow the server's name with \SQLEXPRESS, as shown in the figure. For example, my computer is named Quarkbeast and I'm running SQL Server Express Edition so I entered QUARKBEAST\ SQLEXPRESS in Figure 37-4.

Enter the name of the database on the server (I entered CustomerDatabase in Figure 37-4) and click OK.

> **NOTE** *In the dialog shown in Figure 37-4, if you enter the name of a database that doesn't exist on the server, Visual Studio tells you that the database doesn't exist and asks if you want to create it. If you click Yes, you can use the Server Explorer to build the database. The Server Explorer doesn't provide as many features as a database management tool such as SQL Server Management Studio, but it's handy if you don't have easy access to those tools.*

If you go back to Figure 37-1, you can see the Server Explorer with the quarkbeast\sqlexpress server's `CustomerDatabase` expanded to show its single table, Customers, and its columns.

> **NOTE** *You can use similar steps to connect to other kinds of databases such as Oracle, MySQL, or Microsoft Access databases. Only the details needed to connect to the database in the Add Connection dialog are different. For example, Figure 37-2 shows the details needed for a Microsoft Access database, and Figure 37-4 shows the details needed for a SQL Server database.*
>
> *Note that LINQ to SQL is intended to work with SQL Server and making it work with other types of databases takes some extra work. The section "Using LINQ to SQL with Access" later in this lesson explains how to use LINQ to SQL classes with Access databases, but there's no guarantee that the same techniques will work with every kind of database or that those techniques will keep working in later versions of Visual Studio.*

MAKING LINQ TO SQL CLASSES

After you make a database connection, you're ready to build LINQ to SQL classes that you can use to manipulate the database.

Open the Project menu and select Add New Item. In the Add New Item dialog, select the LINQ to SQL Classes template. If you have trouble finding it, you can narrow your search by looking in the Data template category on the left. Enter a descriptive name for the new file such as `CustomerClasses` and click Add.

At this point Visual Studio creates a `.dbml` file to manage the new LINQ to SQL classes. It opens that file in the Object Relational Designer shown in Figure 37-5, although initially the designer is blank.

In Server Explorer, expand your database until you find its tables and drag the tables that you want to manage onto the designer surface. In Figure 37-5, I dragged the Customers table onto the surface so the designer created a class to represent the table. Each instance of the class will represent a row in the table.

The designer represents the table's fields as properties. If you look closely at Figure 37-5, you can see that the table's primary key fields `FirstName` and `LastName` have little key symbols on the left.

If you click a field in the designer, the Properties window shows the field's properties. Figure 37-6 shows the properties for the table's `FirstName` field.

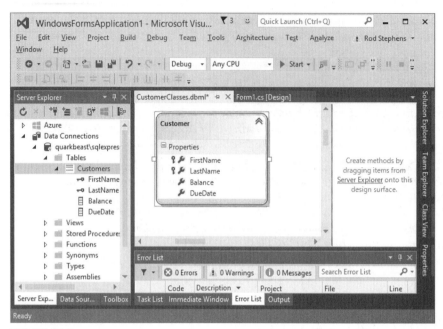

FIGURE 37-5

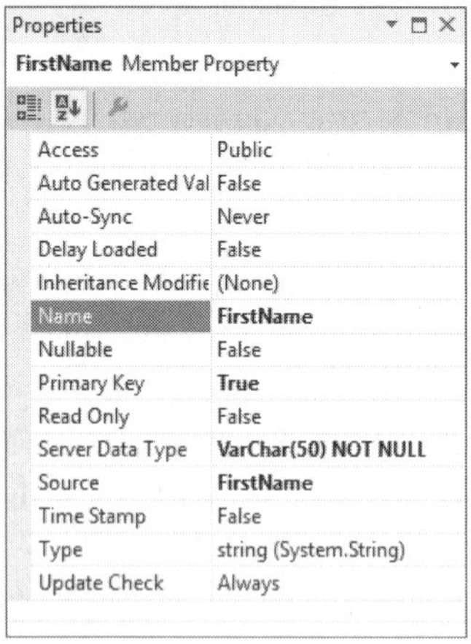

FIGURE 37-6

A few important properties include:

> ➤   `Name`—The name of the field in the class

> ➤   `Nullable`—Indicates whether the field can hold `null` values

> ➤   `Server Data Type`—The data type of the field in the database

> ➤   `Source`—The name of the field in the database

If you make changes and save them, Visual Studio automatically generates a `CustomerClassesDataContext` class to represent the database. (`CustomerClasses` is the name I gave the new LINQ to SQL file.) This object has a `Customers` property that represents the database's Customers table.

Visual Studio also creates a `Customer` class to represent the records in the table.

You can look at these classes (although don't modify them) in the file `CustomerClasses.designer.cs` by double-clicking the `CustomerClassesDataContext` entry in Solution Explorer.

> **NOTE** *Note that this is an extremely simple example. Most real databases contain multiple tables. In that case, you can use the entity-relationship designer to model the relationships between the tables.*
>
> *To add a relationship, right-click the designer's surface, open the Add menu, and select Association. Select the parent and child classes from the dropdown lists and then select the fields that match up in the two classes.*
>
> *For example, an Orders table might hold an `OrderId` field that you can use to find corresponding `OrderItems` records that make up the order. In that case, the parent class would be `Orders`, the child class would be `OrderItems`, and the fields that match up would be the `OrderId` fields in both classes.*
>
> *After you build the association, the designer displays an arrow to represent the one-to-many relationship between the two classes (one `Order` may hold many `OrderItems`).*

WRITING CODE

Now that you've built the LINQ to SQL classes, you can use them to manipulate the database. For example, the Make Customer Data example program shown in Figure 37-7 (and available as part of this lesson's code download) uses LINQ to SQL classes to add new records to a database.

The following code shows how the Make Customer Data example program adds a new record to the database:

FIGURE 37-7

```
// Add a new Customers record.
private void addButton_Click(object sender, EventArgs e)
{
    // Get the database.
    using (CustomerClassesDataContext db =
        new CustomerClassesDataContext())
    {
        // Make a new Customer object.
        Customer cust = new Customer();
```

```
        cust.FirstName = firstNameTextBox.Text;
        cust.LastName = lastNameTextBox.Text;
        cust.Balance = decimal.Parse(balanceTextBox.Text);
        cust.DueDate = DateTime.Parse(dueDateTextBox.Text);

        // Add it to the table.
        db.Customers.InsertOnSubmit(cust);

        // Submit the changes.
        db.SubmitChanges();
    }

    // Prepare to add the next customer.
    firstNameTextBox.Clear();
    lastNameTextBox.Clear();
    balanceTextBox.Clear();
    dueDateTextBox.Clear();
    firstNameTextBox.Focus();
}
```

The code starts with what is probably its least obvious step: creating a new instance of the CustomerClassesDataContext. This object represents the database and provides access to its tables. It provides a Dispose method so the program creates it in a using block to call Dispose automatically.

Next the code creates a new Customer object to represent a new row in the Customers table. The code initializes this object's properties.

The program then calls the Customers table's InsertOnSubmit method, passing it the new Customer object. The following statement calls the database object's SubmitChanges method to send any pending changes (in this case, the new Customer) to the database.

The code finishes by clearing its TextBoxes so the form is ready for you to enter another customer's data.

USING LINQ QUERIES

The Make Customer Data program described in the previous section uses LINQ to SQL classes to manage the database but it doesn't actually use LINQ queries.

You can use LINQ queries with these classes much as you can use them with lists, arrays, and classes that you build yourself in code. For example, you can use a query to select particular records from a table.

The following code shows how the Find Customers program described in Lesson 36 displayed customers with negative account balances:

```
// Display customers with negative balances.
var negativeQuery =
```

```
            from Customer cust in customers
            where cust.Balance < 0
            //orderby cust.Balance ascending, cust.FirstName
            select cust;
        negativeListBox.DataSource = negativeQuery.ToArray();
```

The following code shows how the Find Customers program available in this lesson displays the same customers from the Customers table:

```
        // Display customers with negative balances.
        var negativeQuery =
            from Customer cust in db.Customers
            where cust.Balance < 0
            //orderby cust.Balance ascending, cust.FirstName
            select String.Format("{0} {1}\t{2:C}\t{3:d}",
                cust.FirstName, cust.LastName,
                cust.Balance, cust.DueDate);
        negativeListBox.DataSource = negativeQuery.ToArray();
```

These two queries differ in two ways. First, the second query ranges over items in the db.Customers LINQ to SQL object instead of a customers array created by the program's code.

The second difference is that the new version's select clause doesn't select Customer objects. Instead it concatenates certain fields taken from those objects. I made this change because the Customer class generated by LINQ to SQL doesn't override its ToString method to display a nice representation of the object as the earlier version of the class did in Lesson 36. The new version builds strings that the ListBox can display directly.

UNDERSTANDING NULLABLE FIELDS

Although LINQ to Objects and LINQ to SQL queries work mostly in the same way, some important differences exist behind the scenes.

One difference that you are likely to run into immediately is that values provided by LINQ to SQL classes are often nullable. A *nullable type* is a data type that can hold the special value null in addition to whatever other values it normally holds. The value null represents "no value."

For example, a nullable int can hold an integer or it can hold the special value null, which means it doesn't contain any real integer value.

> **NOTE** *Only value types (such as structures, enumerated types,* ints, *and* doubles) *can be nullable because reference types can already hold the value* null. *The only surprising case is* string, *which looks a lot like a value type but is really a reference type.*

> **NOTE** *You can declare your own nullable variables by following their data types with a question mark. For example, the following code declares a nullable integer variable named* numCourses *and assigns it the initial value* null*:*
>
> ```
> int? numCourses = null;
> ```

Databases often have fields that are allowed to have no value and the LINQ to SQL classes represent them as nullable properties. In the database's Customers table, the `Balance` and `DueDate` fields are not required so the `Customer` LINQ to SQL class makes its `Balance` and `DueDate` fields nullable. That means when the program's C# code looks at those fields, they may not contain any value.

To decide whether a field contains a value, you can compare it to `null` or use its `HasValue` property. Once you know that the value exists, you can use its `Value` property to get the value.

For example, the following code checks whether a `Customer`'s `Balance` field is `null` and, if the value exists, displays it:

```
if (cust.Balance != null)
{
    // There is a Balance. Display it.
    MessageBox.Show("Balance: " + cust.Balance.Value.ToString());
}
```

UNDERSTANDING QUERY EXECUTION

Although LINQ to SQL looks a lot like LINQ to Objects in your C# code, behind the scenes there is a huge difference in the way the two kinds of queries are executed.

The C# compiler converts a LINQ to Objects query into a series of method calls to do all of the work. The code does nothing that you couldn't do yourself in C# code, so it works more or less the way you would expect C# code to work.

In contrast, the compiler converts a LINQ to SQL query into code that can execute within the database. Instead of executing code within your program, it sends commands to the database to make it do all of the work. With a bit of effort, you could come up with similar database commands yourself and make your program execute them on the database, but LINQ to SQL does that for you.

Why should LINQ to SQL handle this differently?

Suppose you want to find a customer with a particular name in a `customers` array that holds 100,000 objects. LINQ to Objects can zip through the array fairly quickly and find the right customer with little problem.

Now suppose you want to find the same customer in a database containing 100,000 records. To perform that search in C# code, the program would need to fetch 100,000 records from the database. Moving that much data from the database into the program would take quite a bit of time and memory. In contrast, the database itself has great tools for finding specific records, particularly if the table uses the `Name` field as an index. In that case, the database may need to perform only a few disk accesses to search through its index structure for the right customer, a much more efficient operation than moving 100,000 records into the program and then searching them sequentially.

For many reasonably simple queries, the translation from LINQ query syntax into something the database can understand works and there's no problem. Sometimes, however, your query code doesn't translate easily into database-speak and the database can't execute it.

For example, the following code shows how the Find Customer program described in Lesson 36 displayed customers who owe more than $50 and who are more than 30 days overdue. (In this code the variable `today` holds the current date and is used to simplify the code.)

```
// Display customers who owe at least $50
// and are overdue at least 30 days.
var overdueQuery =
    from Customer cust in customers
    where (cust.Balance <= -50) &&
          (today.Subtract(cust.DueDate).TotalDays > 30)
    select cust;
overdueListBox.DataSource = overdueQuery.ToList<Customer>();
```

Unfortunately, SQL Server doesn't have a function that subtracts one date from another, so this query doesn't translate perfectly into database commands and at run time the program throws the following exception:

```
Method 'System.TimeSpan Subtract(System.DateTime)' has no supported
translation to SQL.
```

One solution is to rewrite the query in terms that the database can understand. The following code shows a query that LINQ to SQL can translate successfully:

```
// Display customers who owe at least $50
// and are overdue at least 30 days.
var overdueQuery =
    from Customer cust in db.Customers
    where (cust.Balance == null || cust.Balance.Value < -50) &&
          (cust.DueDate == null || today > cust.DueDate.Value.AddDays(30))
    //orderby cust.Balance ascending, cust.FirstName
    select String.Format("{0} {1}\t{2:C}\t{3:d}",
        cust.FirstName, cust.LastName,
        cust.Balance, cust.DueDate);
overdueListBox.DataSource = overdueQuery.ToArray();
```

Although the translation to database code doesn't know how to subtract dates, it does know how to add days to a date so this query uses that capability. It selects records where the customer:

➤ Has no balance or has a balance less than $50, and

➤ Has no due date or today's date is greater than the due date plus 30 days

USING LINQ TO SQL WITH ACCESS

LINQ to SQL is intended to let you use objects to manage SQL Server databases, but with a little extra work you can also use it to manage other kinds of databases.

> **NOTE** *Why would you want to use LINQ to SQL to manage other kinds of databases? One reason is that the LINQ to SQL classes are convenient. They allow you to use fairly intuitive objects to manipulate the data.*
>
> *Another reason for using LINQ to SQL classes with other databases is that it lets me give you examples in Microsoft Access databases. Though SQL Server is generally more powerful, you cannot use it without installing SQL Server (at least the Express Edition). The .NET Framework includes all of the classes you need to interact with an Access database so you can connect to one and use it without installing anything else.*

To get started, create a normal Windows Forms project, open the Project menu, and select Add New Item. Select the LINQ to SQL Classes template as before, give the file a good name, and click Add.

If you were working with SQL Server, you would then drag tables from the Server Explorer onto the design surface to define the classes. Visual Studio won't let you drag tables from other kinds of databases onto the entity-relationship designer, but you can build the classes manually.

Click the Toolbox link on the Object Relational Designer to open the Toolbox shown in Figure 37-8 and use the tools it holds to build the classes.

To get the model to work, you need to set a few properties correctly. For a table class, set the `Source` property to the name of the table in the database. For example, if you want to represent the Customers table's records with `Customer` objects, then create a `Customer` class and set its `Source` property to `Customers`.

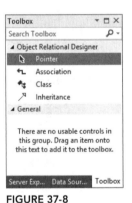

FIGURE 37-8

After you create a class, right-click it and select Add ➪ Property to give the class properties. For each property, set:

➤ `Primary Key`—True if the field is part of the table's primary key

➤ `Nullable`—True if the database field allows nulls

➤ `Server Data Type`—The field's data type in the database (for example, `VARCHAR(50) NOT NULL`)

➤ `Source`—The name of the field in the database (probably the same as the property's name in the class)

➤ `Type`—The property's type in the class (for example, `string`)

After you build the model, Visual Studio generates the classes you need. Now you just need to add code to use them.

If you are using a Microsoft Access database, start by adding the following `using` directive at the top of the file:

```
using System.Data.OleDb;
```

The connection object that you need to open the database is defined in this namespace. (For other kinds of databases, you may need to use different database objects in other namespaces.)

Next build a database connection. The Linq To Access example program that is available in this lesson's download uses the following code to build its connection:

```
// Get the database's location.
string filename = Path.GetFullPath(
    Application.StartupPath + @"\..\..\CustomerData.mdb");

// Connect to the database.
using (OleDbConnection conn = new OleDbConnection(
    "Provider=Microsoft.Jet.OLEDB.4.0;" +
    "Data Source=" + filename))
{
```

This program assumes the `CustomerData.mdb` database is located two directory levels above where the program is executing. This is true if the program is running from its `bin\Debug` directory and the database is stored with the code.

The program gets the location of the database file. It creates a new `OleDbConnection` object, passing its constructor a connect string that includes the location of the database file. (Connect strings for different kinds of databases hold different fields. If you're using some other kind of database, you'll need to build an appropriate connect string.)

Having connected to the database, the program should create an instance of the LINQ to SQL database class, passing its constructor the database connection. The Linq To Access example program uses the following code:

```
// Get the database.
using (CustomerClassesDataContext db =
    new CustomerClassesDataContext(conn))
{
```

From this point on, the code is the same as it is for working with SQL Server. The only complication is that not all databases are created equal. Different databases may provide different features and the automatically generated database code may not work properly for all databases.

The Linq To Access example program executes the same queries as the Find Customers example and has no trouble until the final query, which adds 30 days to the customer's due date. Access cannot understand the automatically generated code for that query and throws an exception.

In this case, you can fix the query by subtracting 30 days from the current date and seeing if the result is after the customer's due date, as shown in the following code:

```
DateTime todayMinus30 = today.Subtract(new TimeSpan(30, 0, 0, 0));
var overdueQuery =
    from Customer cust in db.Customers
    where (cust.Balance == null || cust.Balance.Value < -50) &&
          (cust.DueDate == null || todayMinus30 > cust.DueDate.Value)
    //orderby cust.Balance ascending, cust.FirstName
    select String.Format("{0} {1}\t{2:C}\t{3:d}",
        cust.FirstName, cust.LastName,
        cust.Balance, cust.DueDate);
overdueListBox.DataSource = overdueQuery.ToArray();
```

TRY IT

In this Try It, you extend the Find Customers program to find customers that are missing data. You add a new `ListBox` to display customers that are missing first name, last name, balance, or due date values.

Lesson Requirements

In this lesson, you:

➤ Copy the Find Customers program available in this lesson's download. Add a new `ListBox` to hold customers with missing data.

➤ Use a LINQ to SQL query to display customers that have missing values.

> **NOTE** *You can download the code and resources for this lesson from the website at* www.wrox.com/go/csharp24hourtrainer2e.

Hints

➤ Remember that a blank string (a string with no characters) is not the same as a `null` value. You don't need to check the `FirstName` and `LastName` fields for `null` values, but you should check them for blank values.

Step-by-Step

➤ Copy the Find Customers program available in this lesson's download. Add a new `ListBox` to hold customers with missing data.

1. This is straightforward.

➤ Use a LINQ to SQL query to display customers that have missing values.

1. You can use code similar to the following:

```
// List customers with missing data.
var missingDataQuery =
    from Customer cust in db.Customers
    where (cust.FirstName == "" ||
           cust.LastName == "" ||
           cust.Balance == null ||
           cust.DueDate == null)
    select String.Format("{0} {1}\t{2:C}\t{3:d}",
        cust.FirstName, cust.LastName,
        cust.Balance, cust.DueDate);
missingDataListBox.DataSource = missingDataQuery.ToArray();
```

EXERCISES

For these exercises, use the customer database built by the Build Customer Database program. (If you don't want to install SQL Server, you can use the Access database `CustomerData.mdb` included in the Linq To Access example program in this lesson's download.)

1. Build the user interface shown in Figure 37-9. Make the First and Last Name `TextBoxes` read-only. (Don't worry about the data yet. Just build the user interface.)

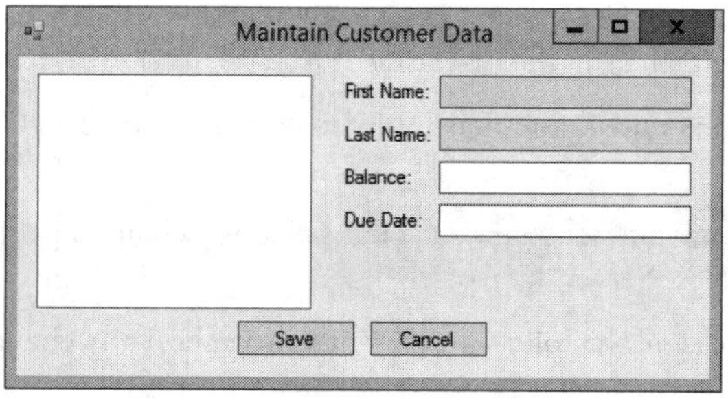

FIGURE 37-9

2. Copy the program you built for Exercise 1 and make it display the list of customers. To do that:

    a. Add LINQ to SQL classes to the program.

    b. Override the `Customer` class's `ToString` method so it displays the customer's name. Instead of modifying the automatically generated `Customer` class, however, add a new class named `Customer`. Modify the class definition as follows:

```
// Add a ToString override to Customer.
public partial class Customer
{
    public override string ToString()
    {
        return FirstName + " " + LastName;
    }
}
```

The partial keyword indicates that this class is part of a class that may have pieces elsewhere. In this case, it means the ToString method should be added to the Customer class built by LINQ to SQL so you don't need to modify the automatically generated code.

c. Declare a field named Db with your DataContext class's type.

d. Write a LoadData method that queries the database and sets the ListBox's DataSource property to the result.

e. In the form's Load event handler, initialize the Db variable and call LoadData.

3. Copy the program you built for Exercise 2 and make it display the currently selected customer's properties. To do that:

a. Write a ShowSelectedCustomer method. It should get the ListBox's SelectedItem property as a Customer object. It should then display the object's properties in the TextBoxes.

b. In the ListBox's SelectedIndexChanged event handler, call ShowSelectedCustomer.

4. Copy the program you built for Exercise 3 and make it update the Customer objects when the user modifies the balance or due date. To do that, give the TextBoxes TextChanged event handlers. They should get the current Customer object, parse the value in the TextBox, and save the value in the Customer object. Use a try catch statement to protect against invalid data and, if a value is invalid, store null in the object.

5. Copy the program you built for Exercise 4 and finish it by making the Save and Cancel buttons work. To do that:

a. Make the Save button call Db.SubmitChanges. That saves any changes pending in the DataContext back to the SQL Server database.

b. Make the Cancel button execute the following statement to cancel any changes pending in the DataContext:

```
Db.Refresh(System.Data.Linq.RefreshMode.OverwriteCurrentValues,
    customerListBox.Items);
```

Then make the button's event handler call ShowSelectedCustomer to redisplay the currently selected customer.

> **NOTE** *Please select the videos for Lesson 37 online at* www.wrox.com/go/ csharp24hourtrainer2evideos.

AFTERWORD

What's Next?

This book provides an introduction to C# but it's far from all-inclusive. This book is intended for beginners and many topics are too advanced to fit in here because they are hard to understand (so would take too long to explain), require knowledge of matters outside the scope of this book (such as how the operating system works), or are just too specialized to be interesting to everyone (or in some cases, anyone).

Hopefully you followed along through all of the lessons, worked through the Try Its and exercises, and feel comfortable with the material presented in this book. In that case, you're ready to move on to more advanced general C# texts such as:

➤ *Professional C# 5.0 and .NET 4.5.1* (Christian Nagel and Jay Glynn, Wrox, 2014)

➤ *C# 5.0 Programmer's Reference* (Rod Stephens, Wrox, 2014)

➤ *MCSD Certification Toolkit (Exam 70-483): Programming in C#* (Tiberiu Covaci et al., Wrox, 2013)

You're also ready to branch out into new uses for C#. Most of this book focuses on the C# language itself and uses Windows Forms programs but some other important uses of C# include:

➤ **WPF**—Many of the lessons introduced you to XAML and WPF programming, but there's a *lot* more to learn. Many books (including my book *WPF Programmer's Reference*, Stephens, Wrox, 2010) provide much more thorough coverage of WPF.

➤ **ASP.NET**—ASP.NET is a web programming framework that lets you build pages, sites, and applications that run on the web. C# (or Visual Basic) code can sit behind the interface presented in the browser much as code-behind sits behind Windows Forms and WPF user interfaces. For more information, see an ASP.NET book such as *Beginning ASP.NET 4.5.1 in C# and VB* (Imar Spaanjaars, Wrox, 2014) or *Professional ASP.NET 4.5 in C# and VB* (Jason N. Gaylord and Christian Wenz, Wrox, 2013).

Finally, you're ready to look at more specialized uses for C#:

➤ **Console applications**—These programs do not have window-based user interfaces. Instead they display textual output in a console window. See `msdn.microsoft.com/0wc2kk78` `.aspx`.

➤ **Class libraries**—A class library holds compiled classes that you can use in other applications. If several applications need to use the same kinds of classes (`Customer`, `Employee`, `Order`), then it makes sense to let them share a common library.

➤ **Control libraries**—A control library is a class library that holds new controls. You can build your own controls that are composed of existing controls, that are derived from existing controls, or that you build completely from scratch.

➤ **Office applications**—You can build C# programs that interact with Microsoft Office applications such as Word or Excel.

➤ **Cryptography**—The .NET Framework includes an extensive set of cryptographic tools for encrypting, decrypting, and signing documents. See `msdn.microsoft.com/92f9ye3s.aspx`.

➤ **Parallel programming**—The .NET Framework also includes classes that let you take advantage of the multiple cores that are available on many new computers. See `msdn.microsoft` `.com/dd460717%28VS.100%29.aspx`.

➤ **Game programming**—Microsoft's game development tools let you build games that run on the desktop, in the browser, on mobile devices, and even on the Xbox game console. See `msdn.microsoft.com/games-development-msdn`.

➤ **Database programming**—A large majority of commercial applications have a significant database component. For information on general database programming, see a book such as *Practical Database Programming with Visual C#.NET* (Ying Bai, Wiley, 2010). For information on designing databases, see a book such as *Beginning Database Design Solutions* (Rod Stephens, Wrox, 2008).

Now that you've finished this book, you're ready to move on to more complicated and interesting topics. As you learn more about C# development, you'll discover more and more fields of programming that you never knew existed.

INDEX

G